Exploring Artificial Intelligence:

Survey Talks
from the National Conferences
on Artificial Intelligence

Exploring Artificial Intelligence:
Survey Talks
from the National Conferences
on Artificial Intelligence

Contributors

David Barstow
Woody Bledsoe
Daniel G. Bobrow
Randall Davis
Gerald DeJong
Kenneth D. Forbus
Nita Goyal
Michael P. Georgeff
Barbara J. Grosz
Walter Hamscher

Richard Hodges
Richard E. Korf
Wendy G. Lehnert
Ramesh S. Patil
Judea Pearl
C. Raymond Perrault
Raymond Reiter
Yoav Shoham
Howard E. Shrobe
Beverly Woolf

Edited by

Howard E. Shrobe and the
American Association for Artificial Intelligence

Morgan Kaufmann Publishers, Inc.
San Mateo, California

Editor and President *Michael B. Morgan*
Production Manager *Shirley Jowell*
Text Design *Michael Rogondino*
Cover Design *Michael Hamilton*
Cover Mechanical *Irene Imfeld*
Copy and Technical Editor *Lee Ballentine*
Composition *Ocean View Technical Publications*
Text Programming *Bruce Boston*
Index *Frances Bowles*
Proofreading *Patricia Feuerstein*

Figure credits can be found on page 671.

Library of Congress Cataloging-in-Publication Data

```
Exploring artificial intelligence
    Papers from the 6th and 7th National Conferences
on Artificial Intelligence, held 1986 in Philadelphia
and 1987 in Seattle.
    Bibliography: p.
    Includes index.
    1. Artificial intelligence--Congresses.  2.Reason-
ing--Congresses.  I. Shrobe, Howard.  II. American
Association for Artificial Intelligence.  III. National
Conference on Artificial Intelligence (6th : 1986 :
Philadelphia, Pa.)  IV. National Conference on
Artificial Intelligence (7th : 1987 : Seattle, Wash.)
Q334.E98  1988          006.3             88-13041
ISBN    0-934613-69-9
        0-934613-67-2 (pbk)
```

Grateful acknowledgment is made to the following for permission to reprint previously published material.

Annual Reviews: Perrault, C. Raymond and Barbara Grosz (1986) Natural Language Interfaces, *Annual Review of Computer Science*, 1:47–82; and Reiter, Raymond (1987) Nonmonotonic Reasoning, *Annual Review of Computer Science*, 2:147–186. Reproduced with permission from the Annual Review of Computer Science © 1986 and 1987 by Annual Reviews Incorporated.

Cover design with the kind permission of Michael Hamilton based on his original concept for the cover of *AI Magazine,* Vol. 6 No. 2.

Morgan Kaufmann Publishers, Inc.
2929 Campus Drive, Suite 260, San Mateo, CA 94403
Order Fulfullment: PO Box 50490, Palo Alto CA 94303

93 92 91 90 89 5 4 3 2 1

Contents

Preface

Howard E. Shrobe

Symbolics Incorporated
Cambridge, Massachusetts

This book is a collection of sixteen papers based on talks presented at the 1986 and 1987 national conferences of the American Association for Artificial Intelligence (AAAI). The original talks were presented as surveys of the scientific state of the art in distinct subareas of artificial intelligence (AI) research. They reflect the depth and breadth of a field that has experienced enormous growth and maturation during the last decade. AI is now a major technical discipline with both a commercial and a scientific component.

As a commercial venture, AI has created a major market for a revolutionary style of computing. There are now hundreds of AI products which solve previously inaccessible problems. These commercial efforts have moved past the application of routinely used research techniques, creating new intellectual challenges even for the purely academic researcher.

As a scientific discipline, AI has undergone major structural changes during the last decade. In 1973 (when I entered the M.I.T. Artificial Intelligence Laboratory as a first-year graduate student), virtually everyone was a generalist. There was an intellectual core to the field shared by researchers in all subareas. While researchers in natural language understanding (for example) might have to master a few techniques (such as parsing) that were particular to their specific discipline, they were likely to speak a technical language accessible to researchers working in other subareas of AI, such as expert systems or intelligent tutoring. Virtually everyone in the field saw knowledge representation, inference, and search as the core concerns of all AI efforts.

But as AI has matured, the subareas of research began to develop into distinct intellectual disciplines, each with its own particular techniques and intellectual framework. Specialization has created so many subareas of research that no longer can any individual stay abreast of the whole of AI literature.

Also, as AI developed into an applied commercial practice, many new researchers and developers entered the field. Based in industry, many of the new practitioners did not share the culture of those who had learned their AI by apprenticeship training in a university research lab.

This led the AAAI program committee to establish a forum in which the AI community as a whole could be brought up-to-date with the state of the art in each of the subareas: A series of invited survey talks was presented at the AAAI national conferences in 1986 and 1987. The 1987 conference (which I co-chaired with Ken Forbus) included an entire track of invited survey talks presented by recognized intellectual leaders in the field.

The reaction to the survey talks was so favorable that we felt they should be made broadly available. The survey talk speakers were invited to revise and update the tape transcriptions of their talks. This book is the result of that process. Regrettably, not every survey talk presented could be included here. In a few cases, the speakers were simply too overloaded with other obligations to undertake the task of revising their talks for publication.

We have grouped the talks into several sections:

- Teaching and Learning
- Interacting through Language
- Planning and Search
- Reasoning about Mechanisms and Causality
- Theoretical Underpinnings
- Architecture and Systems

These cover a broad spectrum of current AI concerns; although it is noticeable and unfortunate that this collection lacks any papers in computer vision or robotics.

The first section, **Teaching and Learning**, includes two papers. The first, by Beverly Woolf, addresses intelligent tutoring systems; the second, by Gerald DeJong, is concerned with explanation-based learning. Learning is a major concern of artificial intelligence; and one which has experienced a resurgence of intellectual effort during the last few years.

DeJong's paper discusses one of the new machine learning techniques. In contrast with many of the classic AI learning programs, explanation-based learning does not induce general rules by finding common patterns in many examples. Instead, it works by using a theory of the domain to generate an *explanation* of how the concept to be learned follows from the givens. The explanation (which may be thought of as a network of deductive links) is then generalized to form a new concept which is added to the program's body of knowledge.

Intelligent tutoring systems, the subject of Beverly Woolf's chapter, is concerned with how to guide a student to learn new concepts. Building an intelligent tutoring system is one of the most difficult tasks in AI because it involves mastering virtually all areas of the field. A tutoring system must understand how a student learns, it must understand the material it is trying to teach, and it must be capable of planning how to instruct the student. Ideally, it should also be capable of using natural language and other advanced modes of interaction. Of course, no system exists today that meets all of those needs. Woolf's paper surveys the progress that has been made in individual systems that successfully attack one or a few of the needs.

The second section of the book, **Interacting through Language**, links closely with at least one of the concerns of intelligent tutoring systems, namely how to interact through the use of natural language. This section also includes two papers, "Knowledge-based Natural Language Understanding" by Wendy Lehnert and "Natural-Language Interfaces" by Ray Perrault and Barbara Grosz.

The latter paper is concerned with natural language interfaces, particularly with natural language interfaces to databases. Perrault and Grosz start with the observation that a natural language query such as, "Who owns the fastest car?" translates into more than 20 lines of code in a formal database query language. Thus, a working natural language interface provides conciseness and naturalness not otherwise available. However, providing this convenience requires solving many technical problems. The syntactic structure of the query must be determined, even though it is often ambiguous. Referents for determiners such as "the," "each," etc. must be discovered. Often this can only be done by understanding the discourse structure of the ongoing dialog between the user and the system. Perrault and Grosz survey the various systems and techniques that have been used in building such interfaces.

Wendy Lehnert's paper is concerned with a different aspect of natural language understanding, namely the part that is "knowledge-based." As Lehnert so gracefully puts it, "this (designation) mercifully allowed me to ignore a large body of work that focuses exclusively on the syntactic structures of natural language." Indeed, much of what is discussed in this survey might be characterized as "story understanding." A story understanding system is typically presented with a brief fragment of a story about which it is expected to be able to answer questions. However, the answer to the question is not always explicitly present in the story, but rather refers to background knowledge that the program is presumed to possess. For example, a program might be told, "When the balloon touched the light bulb, it broke. This caused the baby to cry. Mary gave John a dirty look and picked up the baby." It is reasonable to expect an intelligent agent (person or program) to understand why the balloon broke and why the baby cried. Most of us can guess why Mary gave John the dirty look. Obviously, we are drawing on a huge reserve of commonsense knowledge. But what is this knowledge, and how is it to be organized to facilitate understanding even brief story fragments like this? Lehnert's chapter presents a historical survey of various attempts to solve these problems.

The third section of the book, **Planning and Search**, is concerned with how computer programs can create plans to satisfy goals. Planning and search have always been closely related disciplines in AI, since planning programs inherently engage in a search through a space of actions, looking for a sequence of actions that achieve a desired goal.

Michael Georgeff's chapter, "Reasoning about Plans and Actions," surveys the work that has been done in building AI planning systems. Much of this work is derived from the early STRIPS programs which established a framework for representing actions and their effects. One major concern in this research has been the problem of interactions between substeps of a plan for a conjunctive goal; often a step of a plan, which achieves one part of the conjunctive goal, may undo the prerequisite condition for another plan. Another problem in planning deals with the representation of time. The STRIPS model assumes that actions are atomic and may be described completely by their pre- and post-conditions. However, in many planning contexts of current interest, this representation is inadequate since multiple agents may be cooperating on a task and the actions of these agents may have substantial time durations. Georgeff's chapter discusses several approaches to these problems.

Richard Korf's chapter, "Search in Artificial Intelligence," surveys the huge body of work that tries to formally characterize heuristic search programs. Search is the oldest area of AI research (some of this research on search pre-dates the creation of a distinct field called "artificial intelligence"). Korf reviews the various styles of search problems, such as planning problems and two-player game problems, and presents the various techniques (such as A*, minimax, Alpha-Beta, etc.) that have been developed to increase the efficiency of search programs.

Korf begins by presenting the basic brute-force techniques such as breadth-first and depth-first search. He continues by showing the various ways in which more knowledge can be brought to bear to increase the performance of the search program. The earliest techniques involve using a heuristic evaluation function to guide the search. Increasingly sophisticated versions of this idea lead to A* and iterative deepening A* search. More knowledge can be brought to bear, particularly in the context of planning, by using abstraction and macro-operators—techniques developed originally as part of the STRIPS planning system. This chapter also looks at the areas of open research such as how to exploit parallelism in search and how to learn heuristic evaluation functions.

The fourth section of this book, **Reasoning about Mechanisms and Causality**, includes three chapters. All of these deal with how to represent and reason about mechanisms such as electronic devices, steam power plants, or the human body.

The first of these papers, by Ken Forbus, is concerned with qualitative physics, which is the attempt to capture the informal and imprecise reasoning about mechanisms that engineers use in much of their reasoning about engineered artifacts. Qualitative physics is also an attempt to capture the naive reasoning of ordinary individuals in reasoning about the physical world around them. A typical qualitative physics program might be able to explain why water will flow between two tanks of water that are connected when one is filled higher than the other. It also tries to produce an explanation that is causal and mechanistic; for example, that the higher tank exerts greater pressure which causes the water to flow.

In contrast to classical physics, qualitative physics works with abstract quantities rather than with precise numbers; one major area of concern in this field is how to abstract quantities. Forbus discusses various alternatives: In one, quantities are abstracted into three values—positive, negative, and zero. In other approaches, the abstraction includes a set of inequalities. These abstractions allow a program to work in conditions where precise information is unavailable, but they also introduce ambiguity. The survey also discusses the problems of qualitative reasoning about spatial relationships.

Randall Davis and Walter Hamscher discuss model-based troubleshooting, the attempt to use knowledge of the structure and function of a device and its components to troubleshoot and repair malfunctions. Like Forbus's work on qualitative physics, this work is very much concerned with understanding how a mechanism works and how causality flows within it. In model-based troubleshooting, a model of the device is used to predict how it should respond to its inputs. This prediction is compared with the actual observed behavior; the places where the two differ are symptoms of the underlying malfunction of the device. Model-based troubleshooters typically record the causal flow discovered while simulating the device's expected behavior. This representation can then guide the search for a set of components whose malfunctioning can explain the observed symptoms.

Model-based troubleshooting differs from classical AI diagnostic programs such as Mycin in important ways. The basic framework is applicable to virtually any artifact. In principle, a single program can be given a schematic or a blueprint for a variety of artifacts and be capable of diagnosing all of them. Mycin-style programs, in contrast, are hand-engineering one for each new artifact. Mycin-like programs reason through associations between symptoms underlying causes using probabilistic techniques; model-based systems reason about the causal flows using exact techniques.

Of course, not all diagnostic tasks are subject to model-based techniques. Often we don't have a complete description of the artifact. Frequently, even if we do have the complete description, it's too complicated to be used directly without imposing simplifying abstractions. The cutting edge of research in this field is the search for ways to abstract problems to ease the diagnostic task.

Ramesh Patil's chapter discusses one important diagnostic task where these problems are pressing, namely medical diagnosis. Obviously, our understanding of the human body is more limited than our understanding of the digital components that make up a computer. The body is also a more complex system. Patil discusses several medical diagnosis programs, such as Mycin, Internist, MDX, and PIP, which have attacked a variety of medical diagnostic tasks. He also discusses programs, such as his ABEL, which combine qualitative reasoning, such as Forbus's, with mechanistic reasoning, such as in the model-based troubleshooting programs.

The next section, **Theoretical Underpinnings**, presents four more formal accounts of techniques used throughout AI. The first of these is a survey by Judea Pearl of the techniques used to reason about uncertainty, including the calculus used in Mycin as well as Bayesian calculus. Pearl draws attention to a trade-off between precision and tractability. Many of the techniques in this field have well-understood formal properties, but in practice are computationally very expensive. Other techniques have some rough edges but are quite cheap to apply. Pearl also presents work of his own that attempts to identify conditions under which one can have both nice computational properties and semantic clarity.

Yoav Shoham's chapter, coauthored by Nita Goyal, discusses temporal reasoning, i.e., attempts to model and reason about time. This is of great concern for planning programs that attempt to piece together strings of action which achieve some goal over time. This problem is deceptively simple. When one attempts to capture temporal reasoning in a formal system that can reason about change, several unexpected problems emerge. The *frame* problem is probably the most significant of these: this is the problem of compactly representing how actions affect what's true. In many representational systems, one is forced to say what facts each action *doesn't* affect. This is an unbounded problem. Shoham and Goyal discuss the different representational systems used to attack this problem and the reasoning tasks that result from using them.

One particular system that arises in temporal reasoning is *nonmonotonic* logic, the topic of Ray Reiter's chapter. Nonmonotonic logics are formal systems concerned with reasoning about exceptions and defaults; such as in the statements, "The cup stays put, unless something moves it," or "Normally birds fly." What all such systems have in common is a formal property that, as axioms are added, the set of derivable conclusions may, in fact, decrease (hence the name, since the size of the set of derivable facts is not a monotonic function of the size of the set of axioms). Nonmonotonic reasoning is ubiquitous in commonsense tasks. Most people will believe that Tweety can fly when told that Tweety is a bird; upon learning that Tweety is an ostrich, most people immediately revise that belief. Building formal systems that account for such reasoning is surprisingly difficult. Reiter's survey discusses the various approaches to this task that have been developed.

Woody Bledsoe's survey, coauthored by Richard Hodges, on automated deduction tries to summarize what we know about how to make programs perform deductions, particularly (but by no means exclusively) those deductions that are required in formal contexts such as proving mathematical theorems. This is a herculean task, because this is one of the oldest and most studied parts of AI. Bledso and Hodges trace the development of automated deduction from the discovery of the resoluton principle in the mid-1960s up to the development of some very powerful theorem-proving programs that have produced formal proofs of results that are difficult for mathematicians.

Much of this chapter discusses the development of formal techniques with mathematically guaranteed correctness. However, there is another running theme, which is the search for ways to achieve the efficiency of a professional mathematician who reasons at a very abstract level making large jumps in the proof. This search for strategic efficiency in theorem proving draws upon many ideas from other areas of AI such as planning and knowledge representation. Expert mathematicians know a lot of mathematics and a lot of theorem-proving techniques; they are not mechanical proof generators who proceed a step at a time. Bledsoe and Hodges see the attempt to capture this expertise of the professional mathematician as the key to future progress in the field, and he points to several preliminary results in this direction.

The final section of this book, **Architecture and Systems**, is concerned with computational facilities that support artificial intelligence research.

My own paper on symbolic computing architectures is the first of the three in this group. This paper traces the development of computer architectures motivated by the needs of the AI computing community. The first section tries to show what features are present in modern LISP- and PROLOG-oriented architectures and how these are likely to continue evolving. I pay a lot of attention to machines in whose design I participated (such as the Symbolics 3600 and the new Ivory chip) not only because I know the most about them, but also because these machines contain many leading-edge features. The second half of the paper discusses how parallelism may impact AI computing. I review a large number of attempts to build parallel AI-oriented machines. Not too many of these have been successful, but I believe the failures highlight certain design principles that are crucial.

Daniel Bobrow discusses a newly standardized programming language system called Common LISP Object Standard (or CLOS, usually pronounced "C-

Loss"). This is an object-oriented extension of Common LISP which provides a unifying framework for much of symbolic computing. This dovetails nicely with my survey on computing architectures which emphasizes the object-oriented viewpoint as a key feature.

David Barstow surveys what artificial intelligence can offer to software engineering. AI has long tried to apply its techniques to various programming tasks such as code synthesis, debugging or code understanding. Barstow surveys the work in all these areas. He particularly tries to identify what makes these tasks so difficult and why so little benefit has yet resulted.

Acknowledgments

Before concluding this Preface, I would like to thank many people for their unrewarded contributions to this effort. Each of the authors spent an enormous amount of time converting transcripts of their talks into intelligible text. This is not easy, as I've learned. A number of people were involved in providing the logistical support for these survey talks, particularly Claudia Mazzetti, executive director of AAAI, whose organizational skills are truly remarkable; and Steve Taglio of the AAAI office, who manages the logistics for the AAAI conferences. Several of my colleagues contributed time to reviewing the papers, proofreading, and indexing: Bob Cassels, John Hotchkins, Steve Rowley, John Aspinal, Steve Anthony, and John Watkins. Finally, I'd like to extend a special thanks to Ken Forbus who was co-chair with me of the AAAI-87 program committee. Ken did more than half the work of identifying topics and soliciting just the right people to present the survey talks.

I hope that this collection of papers will prove to be a useful base of information about AI for experts, serious students, and new practitioners in the field. These talks represent a serious attempt by the intellectual leaders of many of the subdisciplines of AI to analyze what their work is about and present it in a way that is accessible to the newcomer while still being informative to the neophyte. The reaction to the talks at the conference was enthusiastic; we hope that the quality of this collection merits the same enthusiasm.

Howard E. Shrobe
Chairman, AAAI Conference Committee

I

TEACHING AND LEARNING

1

Intelligent Tutoring Systems: A Survey

Beverly Woolf

Department of Computer and Information Science

University of Massachusetts

Amherst, Massachusetts

Introduction

This paper surveys the field of intelligent tutoring systems.[1] It focuses on the breakthroughs and barriers in the field, describing how we got where we are today, where we think we're going, and what is needed to accomplish the journey. The survey does not provide implementation details nor does it enumerate advantages or disadvantages of various languages.

Before describing the computer science products that have been built, I'd like to set the stage for this discussion by talking about the state of education today. For those who don't yet know, education is in trouble. Recent studies confirm this view. For example, an NSF study says, "Most Americans are moving toward virtual scientific and technological illiteracy" [National Science Foundation, 1983]. Naisbitt says, "The generation graduating from high school today is the first generation in American history to graduate less skilled than its

1 This work was supported in part by National Science Foundation grant MDR-8751362, Air Force Systems Command, Rome Air Development Center, Griffiss AFB, New York, 13441 and the Air Force Office of Scientific Research, Bolling AFB, DC 20332 under contract #F30602-85-C-0008. This contract supports the Northeast Artificial Intelligence Consortium (NAIC). Partial support also was provided by ONR University Research Initiative Contract #N00014-86-K-0764.

parents..."[Naisbitt, 1984]. R. Buckminister Fuller says, "Classrooms are desensitizing, stultifying and boring" [Fuller, 1962].

Another study found that the average Japanese student scores 100% better in mathematics than the average American student [Walberg, 1982–3]. Andrew Molnar from NSF says that only 75% of the teachers in America are qualified to teach the courses they are teaching [Molnar, 1986]. For example, people trained in *physical education* often end up teaching *physics* because both words have the same root. In addition, America will be short one million teachers within four years. Currently, one-fourth of all college freshmen take remedial mathematics, and there has been a 63% increase in college remedial courses, such as writing, reading, and mathematics. With a 63% increase in college remedial courses, the question is "What kind of learning goes on in high schools?" People graduate without the basic skills necessary to function at the college level.

The problems are great, and I certainly don't suggest that intelligent tutoring systems will solve all the problems in education. But there are some fascinating opportunities provided by these new machines and we shall look into them as we survey what these systems can do.

Building Effective Teaching Systems

A study by Bloom [1984] shows that conventional teaching, which means a teacher presenting material in front of 20–200 people, provides one of the least effective methods for educational delivery. The larger curve in Figure 1 shows the results achieved through conventional teaching—the typical bell curve with a median range of 50 to 60, as you'd expect. The mastery curve in Figure 1 shows the performance results when a teacher not only gives a lecture, but also uses diagnostic tests to determine where the students have problems and misconceptions, and then adjusts his/her lectures accordingly. If mastery teaching takes place, then the mean test results seem to be around 84%.

However, and here is the important part of this study, students involved in one-to-one tutoring seem to perform around the 98th percentile as compared with traditionally trained students. These results were reproduced four times with three different age groups on two different subjects. This study provides evidence that tutoring is one of the most effective educational delivery methods. If we plan to build new tools for education we should not replicate methods that have already failed, such as lecture style teaching. Rather, we should focus on one-to-one tutoring methods and thus, we need to begin by understanding the tutoring process.

Developing one-to-one machine tutors is not a straightforward process. For instance, let's say a student and teacher had the conversation shown in Figure 2. After the student's initial expression of lack of understanding of how rain is made, the tutor might think about what the student doesn't know. It might rea-

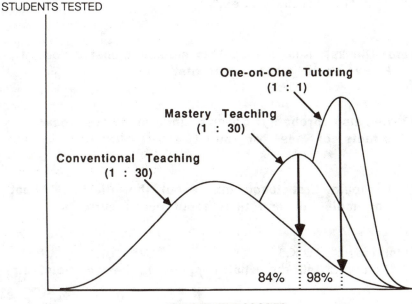

STUDENTS TESTED

One-on-One Tutoring
(1 : 1)

Mastery Teaching
(1 : 30)

Conventional Teaching
(1 : 30)

84%   98%

ACHIEVEMENT SCORES
(PERFORMANCE)

Figure 1 Advantages of One-to-One Tutoring (Adapted from Bloom [1984])

son about the student's knowledge and causal modeling in the domain and his/her ability to make inferences. The tutor might ask diagnostic questions to figure out what the student doesn't know and might then do some planning and choose, as in the figure, to first teach about the effects of heat on moist air, and then to teach about ocean currents, saying "Can you tell me what happens to heated moist air?"

However, to generate this final response on a computer requires reasoning about natural language processing, knowledge representation, diagnosis, and causal modeling (see Figure 3). For example, to reason about "the effect of heat on moist air," the tutor must understand the causal effects of heat on air and moisture, and must comprehend how such components interact in the domain. The tutor must perform qualitative processing, that is, envision the factors that contribute to the production of rain and be able to identify steps within the evaporation/condensation cycle. The tutor must perform planning and plan recognition and should recognize the student's intentions, the pedagogical constraints in effect, and finally, the linguistic and pragmatic considerations that need to be handled. For example, in the figure the tutor chooses to

Student: " I don't see why there is so much
    rain in warm places."

Tutor (thinks): Aha, ha. . . This student probably doesn't
    know about ocean currents.

He also probably doesn't understand the causal
effects of heat on moist air.

I should first teach him about the effects of heat
on moist air and then about ocean currents.

Tutor (says:): "O.K."
    "Can you tell me what happens to heated moist air?"

Adapted from David Littman, 1987

Figure 2 Proposed Tutoring Conversation

say "OK." Why should it say "OK" at this time? Linguistic and natural language considerations, in addition to all of the above processes, are required in order to engage in a tutorial discourse.

Therefore, building an intelligent tutor requires performing most of the other activities of AI researchers (see Figure 4). This field is not an application area of AI in which we can take off-the-shelf material developed by other AI researchers and use it to build our systems. In fact, we have to complement all the work done by researchers in AI, particularly in planning, knowledge acquisition, and discourse management. We must use and augment what AI researchers have been doing for years.

In addition, researchers in our field have several research efforts that go beyond work in AI. For example, we are concerned with visualizing problem solving, as discussed in connection with William Clancey's work (Section 3). Our systems do more than explain how problem solving and diagnosis are done; they need to *show* the student how to construct the knowledge for him/herself and improve his/her ability to understand the material. We study novice/expert research because we need to present materials in a way that enables a novice to understand the domain; in addition, we need to perform error diagnosis on the student's performance.

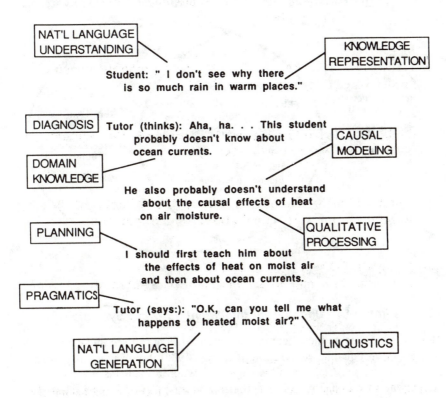

Figure 3 Models of Reasoning in the Proposed Tutoring Conversation

On the other hand, researchers in artificial intelligence are concerned with issues that we don't currently focus on, such as natural language processing and machine learning. We may wrestle with these topics soon. I don't mean to imply that there is an exclusive relationship between AI and work done on intelligent tutoring systems. We obviously need to work together with AI researchers and to use the materials now emerging through expert systems technology. On the other hand, we expect that technology which we produce will ultimately be found useful by other members of the AI community.

The bottom line is that intelligent tutoring systems are AI complete, that is, solving intelligent tutoring problems requires solution of nearly all the problems of artificial intelligence.

So, we take advantage of technology that is just now emerging. Such innovations as high resolution graphics, expert system shells, and qualitative modeling are applications that can now be made available to education.

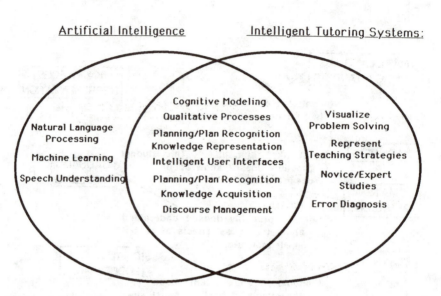

Figure 4 Active Research Areas

Factors in the Development of Intelligent Tutoring Systems

How do we define an intelligent tutoring system? First, we see intelligence as a way to perform qualitative modeling [Clancey, 1986]. Soloway in his programming research, and Clancey in his diagnostic work in medicine, have both described their work as a modeling process [Soloway, 1986]. Soloway described programming as a process whereby a student has a plan of a program and then executes it. Ken Forbus [1986] and Ben Kuipers look at physics problem solving as modeling processes. By this reasoning, intelligent tutoring systems are systems that model teaching, learning, communication, and domain knowledge (Figure 5). They model and reason about an expert's knowledge of a domain and a student's understanding of that domain.

For example, if a system teaches about physics, it should model and reason about physics problems. At some level this is already being done by people who build shells for expert systems. Since expert systems are linked to commercial possibilities, I think such reasoning systems will continue to expand and we can take advantage of them.

We also take advantage of communication models to illustrate the scientific method as well as human problem solving methods. For example, if a system teaches optics, we would expect that it would show a screen with several lenses. It would allow the student to test many lenses on the screen and to send rays through each, measuring the exit angle. Builders of our systems need to take full advantage of the available communication resources, such as simulations and animations, rich icons, pop-up windows, and pop-down menus.

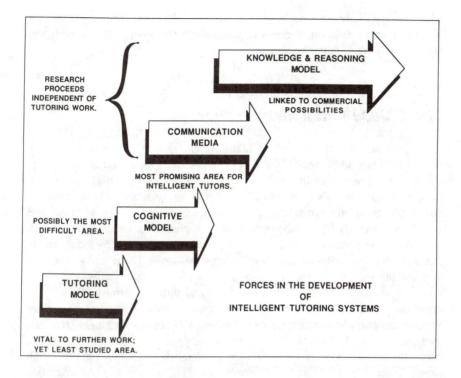

Figure 5 Factors in the Development of Tutoring Systems

Modeling domain and communications knowledge are now being accomplished, since both communications and domain knowledge are being developed independent of our community researchers. Our workers need to focus on models of cognitive processes and tutoring.

By cognitive process modeling, I mean those factors necessary for a person to learn a domain or for a teacher to teach in that same domain. Included in this model is whether or not the student is motivated or has a clear mental model of this domain. We need to determine whether the student's domain model is integrated or fragmented, whether it's compiled, and whether it's interpretable. We also need to look at whether the student (1) knows what he/she is talking about, (2) needs to be interrupted, or (3) might be insecure about the answers. This kind of research takes a long time and requires help from cognitive scientists, instructional designers, psychologists, and expert teachers. We are now learning about cognitive principles and it's possibly the most difficult material in our systems. As shown in Figure 5, we have not yet made great progress in this area.

The fourth and last factor needed is the tutoring model. Tutoring involves knowing how to remediate the student, when to interrupt, what examples to try, what analogy to present, and how to respond to the idiosyncrasies of a student. Without this information, there is nothing about the system that would keep him/her working with the system.

Three Case Examples

I now present a few of the systems that have emerged in this field. I'll look at some key issues addressed by these systems and then later look at many more systems. The purpose of this survey is not to include all existing systems, just those that represent advances in each of the areas mentioned above. Figure 6 shows the envisioning machine by Jeremy Roschelle at Xerox [Roschelle, 1987]. I particularly like this system because it presents a visualization of concepts that have been very difficult to learn in the past. The screen shows an object being thrown in the air and then falling down again. Large arrows are used to show the velocity of the object as it rises and a smaller arrow is used to show the acceleration. If you take an object and throw it upward, the velocity starts off positive and high and then it decreases until it reaches zero at the apex of the curve; as the object comes down, the velocity begins at zero and then increases until it lands. Though the velocity reaches zero at the top of the curve, the acceleration does not, because acceleration is always constant, originating from a gravitational pull downward. The direction of acceleration changes as the ball rises; its direction also changes as the ball descends. Figure 7 shows the original graphic placed beside a picture of the Observable World. In the Newtonian world on the left, the student sees the object moving accompanied by the illustrative arrows, and on the right is a picture of the same movement without the arrows.

In the past, acceleration and velocity have been difficult to demonstrate, in part, because they have been illustrated solely through still-picture problems at the back of the book. Traditional drills with formulas don't allow students to see velocity or acceleration in a way that compares with the rich modeling capability of the computer.

The goal here has been to help the student acquire a mental model of force and acceleration in a way that can be taken back to the observable world. The student can directly manipulate the interface, can move an object in any direction, add two or three balls, and use his/her observations to adjust possible misconceptions. This system contributes in the areas of modeling communications and the domain. In addition, it helps model cognitive processes and represents a student's understanding of physics. The author has also made a judgment about whether the field is coherent or interpretable to the student. Roschelle bases his work on *P-prims*, a system of physics primitives that offers a theoretical basis to the explanation of physics phenomena.

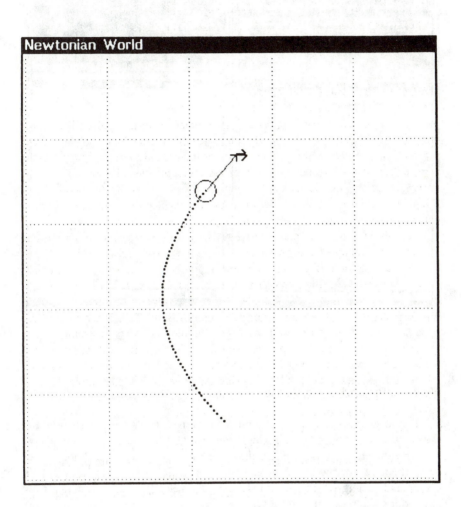

Figure 6 The Envisioning Machine [Roschelle, 1987]

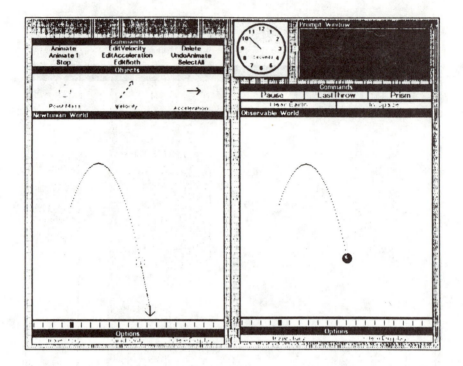

Figure 7 The Envisioning Machine, Part 2: Roschelle

Figure 8 shows a second system from Xerox, the Alternate Reality Kit (ARK) system by Smith [1987], which demonstrates objects in a bubble chamber. The student uses switches, such as the one for "gravity" or "motion," to turn off gravity or motion. You can imagine using objects from Roschelle's system and turning off gravity and watching the velocity and acceleration. New objects or switches can be created by the student.

Figure 9 shows the screen of an older system that remains one of the best in terms of its ability to model tutoring discourse [Brown and Bell, 1982]. This system is from the mid-1970s and was published in 1982. SOPHIE, as it is called, provides a simulation of an electronics circuit and helps a student debug a failure in the system (Figure 9). The student is told that there is a failure and tries to diagnose the bug. SOPHIE has a hypothesis generator that simulates solutions offered by the student, testing whether they are correct. It also has a semantic parser that parses the student's typewritten words, not by using a grammar, but rather by using a semantic representation of possible phrases for each word that might be used in this domain.

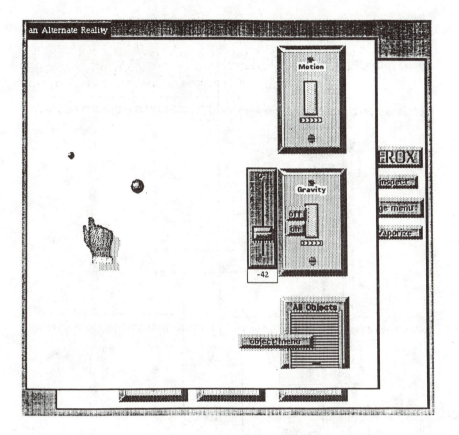

Figure 8 Alternative Reality Kit [Smith et al., 1987]

Figure 10 shows a typical conversation with SOPHIE, although the output is pretty ugly on the screen. The student can say, "What is the output?" and the machine says, "The output voltage is (whatever it is)." The student can say, "What is it in a working instrument?" Using a model of dialogue for reasoning about indefinite pronouns, the machine understands that by saying "it" the student meant the voltage in the previous sentence. And the machine answers. Referring to locations on the circuit, the student can say, "What is the voltage between R8 and Q1?" The machine says the voltage is so-and-so. The student can also say, "I have a hypothesis. Is this the problem?" and suggests that Q6 may be open. The machine actually takes that hypothesis, evaluates it in the simulator, and determines whether the student has solved the problem.

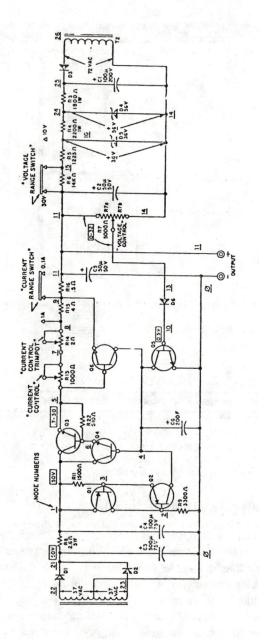

Figure 9 A Regulated Power Supply, from SOPHIE [Brown and Burton, 1982]

Welcome to SOPHIE, a reactive learning environment

The instrument has a fault and its present control settings are:

CC = 1, CR = HIGH, LOAD = 20, VC = 1, VR = HIGH *← Front panel settings*

>>What is the output?
The output voltage is 11.7 volts.

— uses model of dialog for reasoning pronouns

>>What is it in a working instrument?
In a working circuit the output voltage is 19.9 volts.

>>What is the voltage between R8 and Q1?
The voltage at N1 is 47.6 volts.

>>What is the base emitter voltage of the voltage limiting transitor?
= transistor
The base emitter voltage of Q5 is -.037 millivolts.

— hypothesis evaluation

>>Is it possible that Q6 is open?
Is the complete fault mode EB/EC/BC = OP/OK/OP what you intended?
>>Sure

Constructs counter-example

When the settings were:
CC-1.0, CR = HIGH, LOAD = 20, VC = 1.0, VR = HIGH
That fault conflicts with the following measurement. You observed that the
output voltage was 11.7 volts. If Q6 had fault mode EB/EC/BC = OP/OK/OP it
would be 23.9 volts. In a working circuit it is 19.9 volts.

That fault does not explain any of the symptoms you observed but it is
consistent with the values for the base emitter voltage of Q5 and the voltage at
N1.

but also determines what is "good" with the hypothesis.

Figure 10 A Conversation with SOPHIE [Brown and Burton, 1982]

Interestingly, in this case the system finds the student's hypothesis inconsistent with facts already received. This is pointed out to the student. First the system clarifies the student's hypothesis, "Is this what you mean?" (the student says "Sure"). Then the machine says, "The fault that you've suggested conflicts with the following measurements. You observed that the output voltage was 11.7. If this really had a fault mode, it would be 23 volts, and a working circuit is 19.9." It constructs the counter example and says that the fault does not explain any of the symptoms observed, but is consistent with the values of *such-and-such*. In this way, the system determines appropriate portions of the student's hypothesis and inconsistent portions.

This dialogue is quite friendly; it succeeds in modeling tutoring discourse and in some sense, in understanding the student. The researchers stopped work on this project, interestingly enough, because they could not represent in-depth student's reasoning about electronic circuits. They found that their existing quantitative approach enabled success in analysis and diagnosis. Yet the system could not help the student with deep misunderstandings because it didn't understand the student's cognitive models of circuits, which are assumed to be, in part, qualitative. So, the researchers moved on to work in qualitative process models. Subsequent work from this group has led to a new body of research in qualitative process models [deKleer and Brown, 1986; Forbus, 1986]. Also, a nice body of work has been produced by White and Fredricksen [1986] which does represent a student's first-order qualitative mental models about electronic circuits. In this system, multiple models of a circuit are encoded in the system and a student's progression to a more advanced model is prohibited until evidence is provided that he/she has mastered earlier models.

Figure 11 shows a system I've been working on, which been reported in AAAI-86 [Woolf et al., 1986], so I'll review it quickly. This figure shows the screen of the Recovery Boiler Tutor, RBT. The system was built in response to the excessive number of accidents and explosions caused by human error in recovery boilers located at papermills across the United States. The insurance companies threatened to cancel the insurance for the industry if the papermill companies did not learn how to better train their staff in use of the boiler. The system was built by Jansen Engineers, Inc. in Woodenville, Washington, and has been placed in about 60 papermill sites around the country. In light of the usefulness of this system, the insurance companies have offered discounts on the premiums for any company that uses the tutor.

An actual recovery boiler is a difficult mechanism to operate. It is 14 stories high and costs about $90 million to build. It acts like a time bomb in the sense that potential inorganic explosions are always threatening. Explosions, accidents, and inefficient operations are frequent occurrences. Typically an operator has only a high-school education, yet must understand complex physical, chemical, and thermo-dynamic processes to run the boiler. The tutor simulates 100 parameters that participate in the process and it provides students with about 40 problems or critical events to work on. Figure 12 shows a focused display of the boiler and Figure 13 shows the control panel. The tutor encourages the student to abstract his/her information about the process in at least three ways. The first way is to engage in an on-line dialogue with the machine. The second is to use trend lines that show how various variables are measured against each other (Figure 14). The third is to use the meters shown on the left-hand side of Figures 11 through 13. These meters abstract seven or eight parameters that reflect measurements of safety, emission, efficiency, or reliability of the boiler at every moment. These are abstractions that would probably never be calculated by the operator because they are too complicated. Yet they need to be understood in order to operate the boiler.

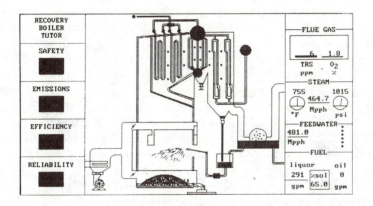

Figure 11 The Recovery Boiler Tutor [Woolf et al., 1986]

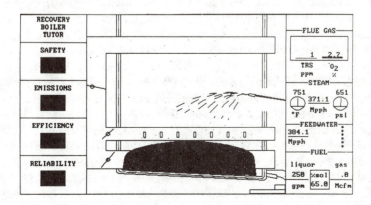

Figure 12 Focus on the Fire Bed

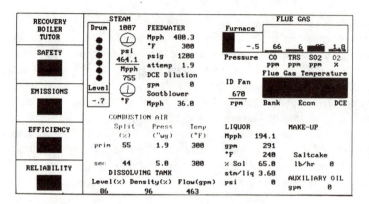

Figure 13 The Control Panel

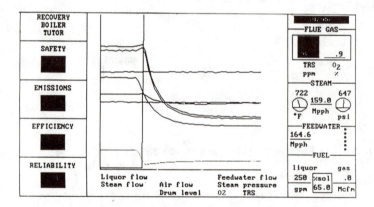

Figure 14 Trends in the Recovery Boiler Tutor

The dialogue shown in Figure 15 is produced by cutting and pasting text loaded with each problem. The dialogue shown here comes directly off the screen. The student says, "Will I check smelt spout cooling water?" The tutor says, "It looks as though the liquor isn't burning." The tutor's response implies that the student wasn't focused on the correct parameters. The system then directs him/her to what should be investigated. The student says, "Help, what is going on here?" He/she can stop at any time and say, "How did I get here?" "How do I get out of this?" "How can I avoid this?" The tutor responds with, "A partial blackout is occurring, etc. and I think part of the bed is not burning." And the student says, "Rod the primary air ports." The system then says,

"Your action is correct, however, at this time, rodding alone is not effective." In other words, if the student had performed this action earlier, it would have worked, but he/she waited so long that now a more serious action must be taken. Finally, after a little bit, the student gets the right answer, and the tutor says, "That solves the problem all right, good thinking."

The third way this system helps a student abstract knowledge is through trending (Figure 14). The student can look at feedwater flow, and can begin to associate it, for instance, with steamwater flow. He/she should identify those parameters unaffected by the problem, and those which have been affected, such as TRS, sulphur, and O_2. The student ought to see which parameters are linked together and which are not.

We try to provide the student with tools that help him/her reason about the problem. Actually, people who work in the mills say that some of these tools would be helpful if put on the actual control panel. This is being considered.

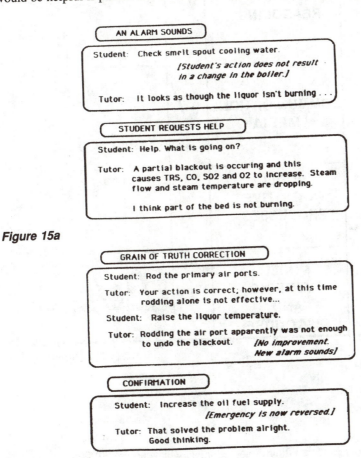

Figure 15a

Figure 15b A Dialogue with RBT

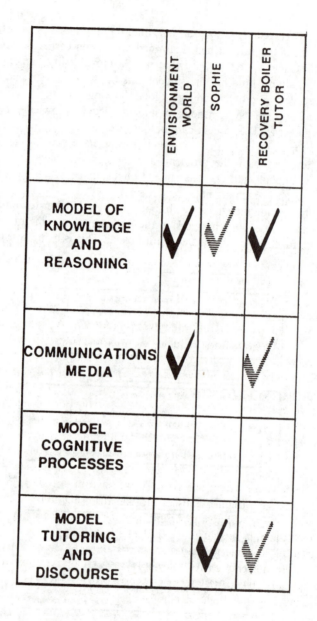

	ENVISIONMENT WORLD	SOPHIE	RECOVERY BOILER TUTOR
MODEL OF KNOWLEDGE AND REASONING	✓	✓	✓
COMMUNICATIONS MEDIA	✓		✓
MODEL COGNITIVE PROCESSES			
MODEL TUTORING AND DISCOURSE		✓	✓

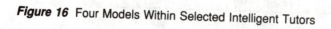

Figure 16 Four Models Within Selected Intelligent Tutors

Accomplishments Thus Far

I stop now after this brief introduction and ask: Where is the intelligence in these three systems? We have moved ahead in some of the areas mentioned in Section 1.2. In others, we're moving ahead less rapidly. Figure 16 gives a preliminary evaluation in terms of modeling accomplished within these four systems. The first system, the Envisionment World, enables a student to visualize and make predictions about physics concepts. I give it good marks in modeling knowledge and communication, and less good marks in modeling cognitive processes and tutoring. SOPHIE, the system about debugging electronic circuits, makes some contribution to knowledge representation, but it has a weak cognitive model because it provides a quantitative, not qualitative model. However, it receives high marks in tutoring. The Recovery Boiler Tutor represents knowledge but its model of the student is weak. Its communication model does not take advantage of icons, windows, and simulation or animation capabilities of computers.

In assessing what we have accomplished thus far, we need to focus on the issues, not just on the machinery built. Thus I look at the relationship between these systems and AI programs in general (Figure 17). As mentioned earlier, there is no need to compete with other AI workers, yet it is valuable to note how our respective jobs differ. We need to recognize that AI systems, often abbreviated to only expert systems, serve a very different purpose than do intelligent tutoring systems. Expert systems are intended to solve a problem. Our systems solve problems yet they also construct a model of the human problem solver. For instance, a system that can solve the electronics problem is not relevant as a tutor if it does not also comprehend how the human solves the same problem. Expert systems can use any problem solving method, such as predicate calculus, semantic networks, PROLOG, or whatever language suits the programmer. Somewhere within our systems, we have to encode human problem solving methods. We might represent the domain using some declarative language, but ultimately we must represent how the human solves the problem in order for the system to recognize the student's reasoning.

Explanations and interpretations are important in expert systems. However, explanations are not enough for tutoring systems. Our systems must actively and systematically engage the user in a dialogue.

A tutoring dialogue might be compared with a police chase of a bank robber; neither can be planned ahead of time. One does not plan, say, four months before the robber comes to town, which streets and buildings to search for the robber. In fact, the police must respond and react to every action taken by the robber. The same principle works in computer tutoring. As programmers, we can't decide what's going to happen after we ask the student a question. The system must plan what will happen in an opportunistic and dynamic way—and must systematically engage a student based on his/her own actions.

An expert system should also justify its reasoning and explain how it made its decisions. In our systems we have to justify and explain our reasoning so that the knowledge and problem solving process is remembered and mimicked by the student. A system might say, "This is how we solve the problem," but that won't help the student. Students should become so enamored of our methods, or at least they should understand them so well that they will mimic that problem solving process.

Expert System ⟹   Intelligent Tutoring
                                        System

Solves a problem. ⟹   Solves a problem and constructs
                                        a model of the human problem
                                        solver

Uses any problem ⟹   Uses human problem solving
solving method.   methods

Responds to the ⟹   Actively and systematically
user.   engages in a dialogue
                                             with the user

Justifies its ⟹   Justifies and explains its reasoning
reasoning.   so that the knowledge and problem
                                            solving process is remembered and
                                            mimicked

Figure 17 Expert System vs. Intelligent Tutors

Figure 18 MYCIN Assists a Doctor

As an example of the difference between expert systems and tutoring systems, I describe one of the most famous tutoring systems derived from an expert system. This is the GUIDON system built from MYCIN, a medical diagnostic system that contains over a thousand rules and provides a diagnosis of an internal disease along with an appropriate therapy (Figure 18) [Clancey, 1979a; Shortliffe, 1976]. While diagnosing a disease, the expert system can provide the user with an explanation of its reasoning and its active rules. The physician dealing with MYCIN can ask, "Why is it important to determine whether or not the patient acquired an infection while hospitalized?" (Figure 19). The answer is, "It has already been established that the morphology of organism-one is rod, the gram stain of organism-one is gram neg, the aerobicity of organism-one is facul; therefore, if the infection with organism-one was acquired while the patient was hospitalized, then there's weakly suggestive evidence (.2) that the identity of the organism is pseudomonas." The system can also show the specific rule, in this case rule 50, that was used.

Why is it important to determine whether or not the patient acquired an infection while hospitalized?

It has already been established that:

    the morphology of ORGANISM-1 is rod
    the gram stain of ORGANISM-1 is gramneg
    the aerobicity of ORGANISM-1 is facul

Therefore, if

    the infection with ORGANISM-1 was acquired while the patient was hospitalized

Then
    there is weakly suggestive evidence (.2) that the identity of ORGANISM-1 is pseudomonas [rule 050].

Figure 19 Conversation with MYCIN [Clancy, 1985]

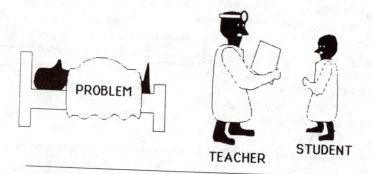

Figure 20 The Doctor as Teacher

Student: The patient has seizures.

Guidon: Seizures may indicate meningitis.

However if you can also show intracranial pressure, then several more consistent interpretations are available to you.

For example, you might explore the possibility of an intracranial mass lesion, a subarachnoid hemorrage, or a brain aneurysm.

Figure 21 Rephrased Conversation with GUIDON (Adapted from Richer and Clancey [1985])

Consider what a teacher might need to *teach* that same material (Figure 20). A system that teaches diagnosis might prefer to show a student its thousand rules. Much of the work that Clancey has done with GUIDON at Stanford is to recognize how medical knowledge is acquired and how medical students analyze data [Clancey, 1984]. Clancey has developed a system that demonstrates how and when a student should ask for new data, which hypotheses to expand, which hypotheses are still viable, and how to refine current hypotheses [Richer and Clancey, 1985].

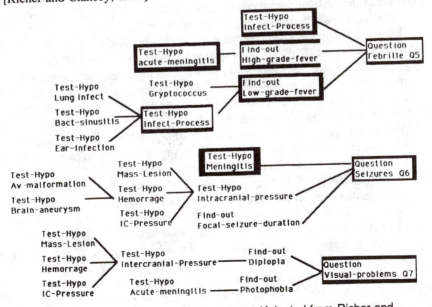

Figure 22 Graphic Conversation with GUIDON (Adapted from Richer and Clancey [1985])

GUIDON demonstrates this knowledge graphically, not in natural language (Figure 22). I've rephrased the conversation into text (Figure 21) for explanation purposes. For example, while examining a patient, the student might say, "The patient has seizures." GUIDON comes back and says, "Seizures may indicate meningitis. However, if you can also show intracranial pressure, then several more consistent interpretations are available to you. For example, you might explore the possibility of an intracranial mass lesion or a subarachnoid hemorrhage or a brain aneurism." The system tells the student how he/she should make hypotheses and which data he/she should collect. GUIDON does not presently use natural language to carry on the conversation. GUIDON uses graphics to explain that "If you have asked about seizures, then you ought to test the hypothesis of meningitis. However, if you want to test the hypothesis of intracranial pressure, then some other hypotheses are available to you. If the pressure hypotheses work, then these other hypotheses are also available to you." For every piece of reasoning that the system performs, it explains the kind of hypotheses the student might consider and the kinds of data to collect.

More Case Examples

I have addressed some of the issues of building intelligent tutoring systems and have looked at a few start-up examples. Now I will examine more cases and evaluate all the systems presented. In the conclusion, I will discuss controversies, bottlenecks, and barriers facing further research.

Figure 23 shows a geometry tutor developed by Anderson at Carnegie-Mellon [Anderson et al., 1985]. This system provides a new form of visual reasoning for the student. Backward and forward chaining of geometry proof steps are made visable. In the top of the top figure, the student is asked to prove that M is the mid-point of EF. In the botton of that same figure, the student is given that M is already a mid-point of AB and CD.

Every time the student suggests a step of the proof, the machine not only writes down the step, but also annotates the triangles with the known relationships. The machine shows the relation of each step and how it lies or does not lie on a path of the proof. If steps performed don't contribute to the proof, they are shown on the trace as disjointed from the path. If the student can't go any further in the forward direction, he/she can always start at the top of the graphic and go backward, adding proof steps in reverse. This system makes a contribution to cognitive modeling and to the communication of tutoring. It provides a structure for problem solving that was not previously available.

Figure 24 shows Anderson's other tutor for teaching LISP [Anderson and Reiser, 1986]. One good feature of Anderson's work is the use of his cognitive model of learning, the ACT theory, to build systems in geometry, algebra, and LISP. The systems are used to test his model. If they don't work well, Anderson can go back to refine his cognitive model. This methodology, the scientific method, involves a hypothesize-test-evaluate cycle and is used too rarely in artificial intelligence. Anderson has demonstrated that he can improve on both his cognitive model and the building of intelligent tutors.

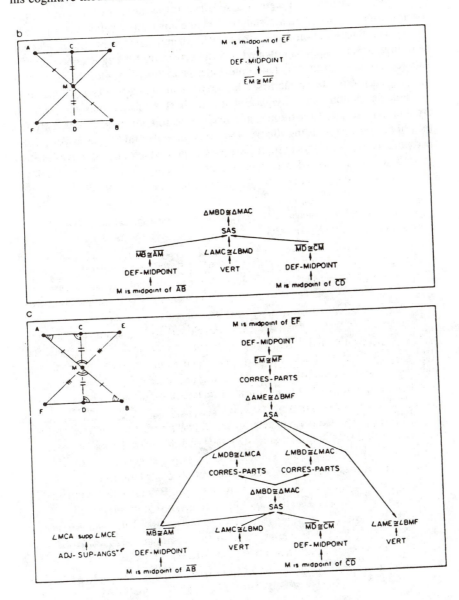

Figure 23 Geometry Tutor [Anderson et al., 1985]

Returning now to the LISP Tutor (Figure 24), the student is asked to produce code for the function Factorial. He/she produces code and the machine comes back with a response every time a new line is entered. In the second line the student tried to test if a number argument was equal to zero. The machine said, "I assume you were trying to test if the number argument is equal to the number zero. There's a special function for testing equivalence to zero. Try to use that function instead of equal." The system uses 325 production rules to represent LISP concepts and 475 rules to represent buggy concepts.

Anderson has accumulated some impressive results with this tutor. This system was used to teach the first six lessons of LISP in a typical college course at Carnegie-Mellon. Anderson says that it takes about forty hours with lecture-style presentations to get through the first six lessons of LISP. It took only fifteen hours for people using this system. He found also that those students who had both lectures and this system produced grades which were 43% better than those of students who had only attended the lectures.

A Student-Tutor Dialogue for Coding a Recursive Function to Calculate Factorial

Define the function fact. It takes a number argument n and computes the factorial of n, which is the result of multiplying n × n − 1 × n − 2 × ··· × 1. For instance, (fact 3) = 3 × 2 × 1 = 6. By definition, the factorial of 0 is 1.

1. (defun <NAME> <PARAMETERS> <BODY>)

2. (defun fact (n)
        (cond ((equal) <ACTION>)
              <RECURSIVE-CASE>))

I assume that you are trying to test if the number argument is equal to the number zero. There is a special function for testing equivalence to zero. Try to use that function instead of EQUAL.

What code can you write to test if the condition for terminating case is true? Try writing a predicate.

3. (defun fact (n)
        (cond ((zero <ACTION>)
              <RECURSIVE-CASE>))

Did you mean zerop (y or n)? y

4. (defun fact (n)
        (cond ((zerop n) 1)
              <RECURSIVE-CASE>))

Is the value of fact in the recursive cases calculated by:
PRESS: IF YOU WANT TO:
 1   Calling fact recursively with n.
 2   Multiplying n by fact of n minus 1.
 3   Getting 1 2 ... n and then
     multiplying the results.
 4   Have the tutor choose.
Menu choice: 3

That is a reasonable way to think of doing factorials, but it is not a plan for a recursive function. Since you seem to be having trouble with the recursive cases, let us work through some examples and figure out the conditions and actions for each of these cases.

The recursive relationship is the relationship between fact called with n and fact called with:
PRESS: IF YOU WANT TO:
 1   n minus 1.
 2   n equal to 0.
 3   n plus 1.
 4   Have the tutor choose.
Menu choice: 1

We will consider some concrete examples. We will characterize the recursive relationship between fact called with 1 and fact called with 0.

What is the value of (fact 1)?
Answer: 1

What is the value of (fact 0)?
Answer: 1

          EXAMPLES
     fact (n)   fact (n − 1)
A.   (fact 1) = 1   (fact 0) = 1

We will consider some more concrete examples. We will characterize the recursive relationship between fact called with 3 and fact called with 2.

What is the value of (fact 3)?
Answer: 6

Figure 24 LISP Tutor [Anderson and Reiser, 1986)]

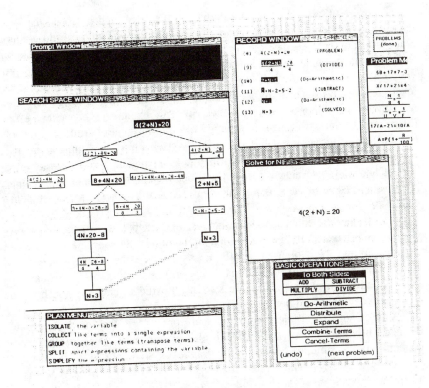

Figure 25 Algebraland [Foss et al., 1987]

Another intelligent tutor teaches algebra (Figure 25) [Foss et al., 1987]. This system provides the student with a problem, such as $4(2 + N) = 20$, and asks the student to solve for N. As the student performs each operation the system allows him/her to plan the solution. The student can say, "I want to collect all like terms," "I want to transpose terms," or "I want to split apart expressions containing like variables." For every plan the student suggests, the system provides the basic operations. The student can perform the operation or ask the system to do it. He/she can expand expressions, add to both sides, subtract from both sides, or divide by both sides simply by asking the machine. Every action is seen in a trace window.

As shown in the figure, both sides of the equation are divided by 4, further steps will be placed on the right side of the trace until the N = 3 value is reached. On the other hand, if dividing by 4 is not the first step, and instead multiplying through by 4 is the next step, then the steps will be shown on the left-hand branch of the trace. The student would arrive at the same answer for either path, as shown at the bottom of the trace.

This system begins to act as a partner in the sense that it can do the steps anytime the student asks for assistance. Certainly the machine can do algebra, that's not the problem. The question is, can it also provide a view of algebra that is intuitive, motivational, and helpful for the student? It does that by providing a trace, a record of all the steps performed, and by providing a higher-level view of algebra operations. It acts as a partner in that if the student cannot solve the problem or cannot do the arithmetic expansion, he/she can effectively say, "I don't want to fool around with this lower-level stuff, I want you to do it" and the machine will do it. Several systems have been implemented in this way. They act as mentors in that they tell the student what is correct or incorrect and they also act as partners and actually perform the required steps. Anderson's LISP tutor acts as a partner in this way by executing the student's code.

The system called STEAMER is famous, in part, because of the icons provided, which the student "inserts" into a simulation of the working steam boiler (Figures 26 and 27 [Hollan et al., 1984]. As a result, the student can see and measure the effects of his/her actions on a working simulation of the steam engine. By adding a pump or a toggle switch, the student can envision how the real steam engine would perform under the same changes.

A tutor with the same methodological approach is the Intelligent Maintenance Tutoring System (IMTS), which also allows the student to place components into a simulated working hydraulics system (Figures 28 and 29) [Towne et al., 1987]. This system trains students to fold helicopter wings. It determines which problem the student should solve next, keeps track of how much time it took to solve the problem, and maintains a model of the student's presumed learning.

One difficulty with the technology of the systems previously discussed is that there's little transference experience for the author building new systems. There's currently no way to implement a new system using technology from an earlier system. The next three systems represent an exception to this rule (Figures 30–32). These systems are built with bite-sized architecture, a representation in which knowledge is bundled in bite-sized units and accessed by several modules of the system [Bonar et al., 1986]. The bites communicate with each other to exchange information about the next curriculum topic, or to evaluate and respond to the student's input.

The economics tutor, built on this architecture, allows a student to adjust parameters in a simulated society, such as the size of the population, the number of stores, and the number of suppliers, etc. (Figure 30). The student's task is to deduce economic principles. For instance, he/she can see how much non-dairy creamer, coffee, and tea have been sold; can change variables such as price, distribution, or size of competition to deduce the rules in place; and then can observe some relations between supply and demand. For each modification made by the student, a record is kept noting how many parameters were changed and what increments were used. When the student has a hypothesis, he/she writes the observed relationships down and the tutor evaluates them. The tutor monitors the student's actions and judges whether he/she is changing the correct parameters and making appropriate changes in those parameters.

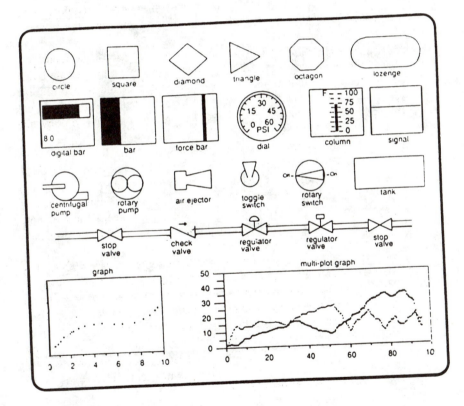

Figure 26 STEAMER Icons [Hollan et al., 1984]

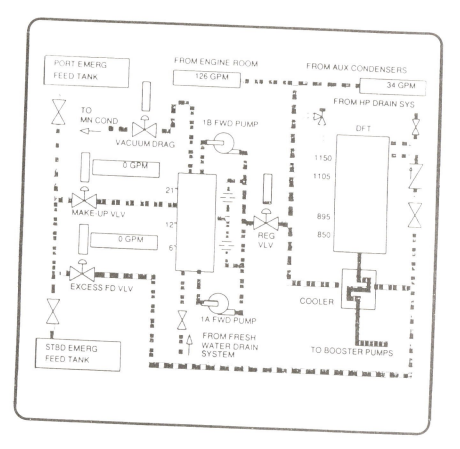

Figure 27 STEAMER [Hollan et al., 1984]

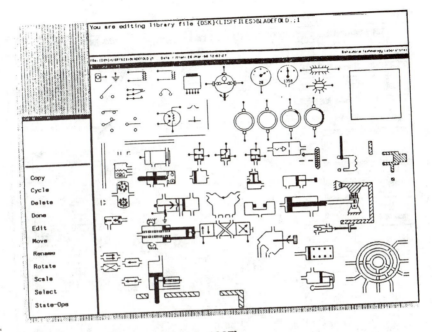

Figure 28 IMTS Icons [Towne et al., 1987]

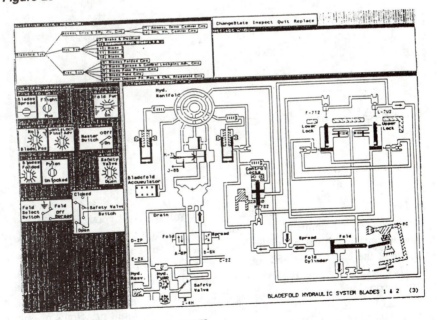

Figure 29 IMTS [Towne et al., 1987]

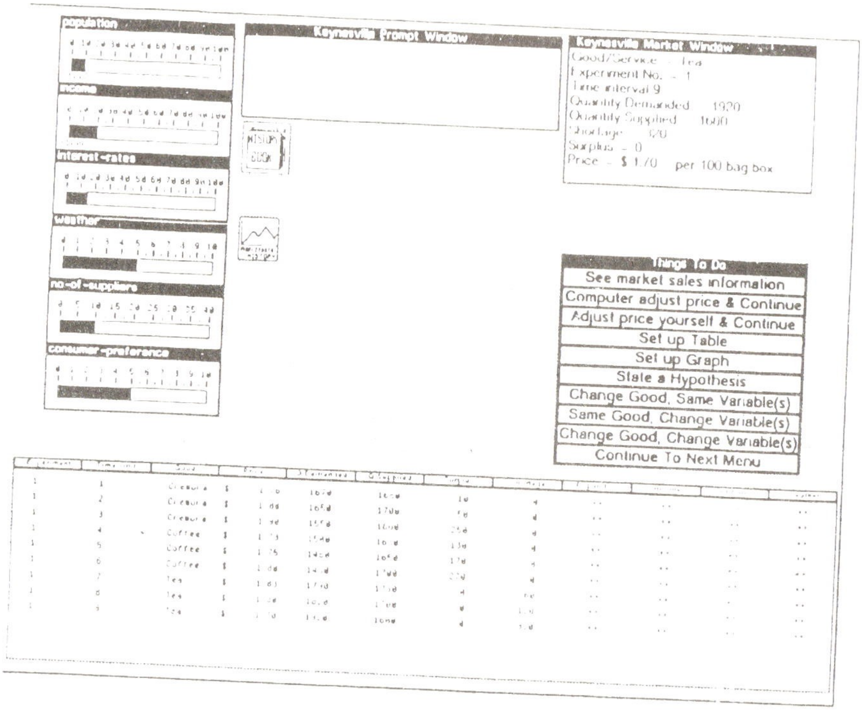

Figure 30 Economics Tutor [Boner, 1986]

Two other tutors in this series also allow for student hypotheses within a rich simulation environment. The OPTICS tutor allows a student to move lenses over a screen; it sends a ray of light through each lens, and allows the student to measure the entry angle and the exit angle for each of these lenses (Figure 31). This system is similar to the economics tutor in that the student creates original experiments and matches his/her hypotheses against the actual performance of the lenses. In this way, the student starts to intuit principles of optics. Similarly, an electronics tutor demonstrates principles of electronics (Figure 32).

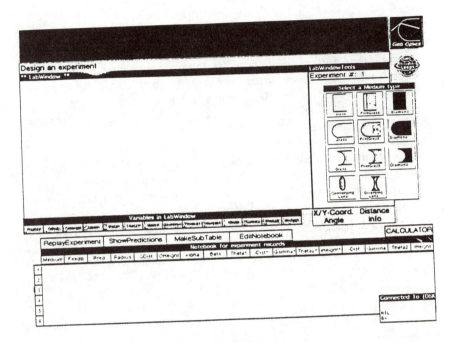

Figure 31 OPTICS Tutor [Boner et al., 1986]

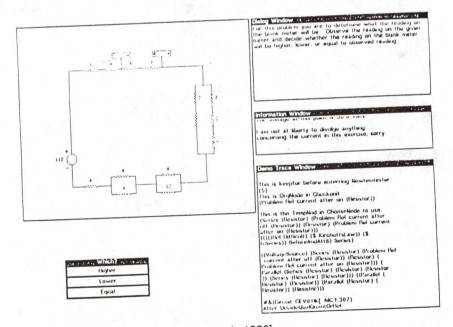

Figure 32 Electronics Tutor [Boner et al., 1986]

Evaluating Tutoring Systems

We have looked at more than a dozen systems and we can now ask: What has been achieved? Do these systems demonstrate completeness and reliability within the four models: knowledge and reasoning, communication, cognitive processing, and tutoring? The answer is no. Yet each system does demonstrate varying amounts of completeness for each model (Figure 33). (Completeness and reliability in a system indicate that it can be used effectively in training or classroom situations.) In the right-hand column, under Advanced Results, I identify those systems that can be used reliably by students and can provide some coverage of a topic, albeit for a limited domain. Such systems can be used generally by many students. Systems listed in the center column have, by and large, demonstrated only knowledge engineering capability for one of the four models. These systems demonstrate the prototypical behavior for an expert in that model; yet that model is not complete and reliable.

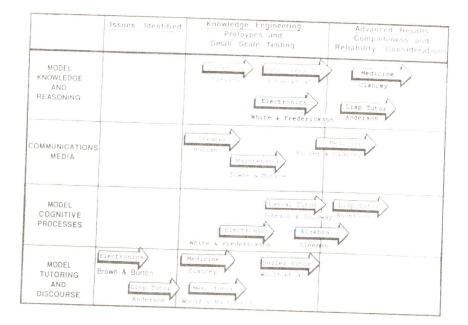

Figure 33 Completeness and Reliability in Tutoring Systems

As you saw, the LISP tutor by Anderson has been placed in schools and has achieved completeness and reliability within its knowledge representation and reasoning model. Its cognitive model is also very good. The medical education tutor by Clancey has also been used by students and seems able to represent complex data in a visual and intuitive way.

The majority of systems discussed lie in the middle column; they reflect good knowledge engineering yet are not fully reliable in the classroom. We've learned to build good prototypes and to perform small-scale testing on these systems.

For some modeling tasks, notably that of representing tutoring primitives, we've only just identified the issues. Development of tutoring models lags behind development of knowledge and reasoning models. We've done some production work in representing knowledge and communications, and are not doing production work in representing cognitive processes or tutoring strategies.

Figures 34 and 35 show how each system might be rated in terms of its ability to implement each of the four models.

	ENVISIONMENT WORLD	SOPHIE	RECOVERY BOILER TUTOR	MAINTENANCE TUTOR	STEAMER	BYTE SIZED TUTOR
MODEL OF KNOWLEDGE AND REASONING	✔ FACT	✔ SYSTEM	✔ SYSTEM	✔ SYSTEM	✔ SYSTEM	✔ SYSTEM
COMMUNICATIONS MEDIA	✔		✔	✔	✔	✔
MODEL COGNITIVE PROCESSES						
MODEL TUTORING AND DISCOURSE		✔ Mentor	✔ Mentor			

Figure 34 Qualitative Models, Part 1

	ELECTRONICS TUTOR	MEDICINE	LISP TUTOR	ALGEBRA-LAND	GEOMETRY TUTOR	BRIDGE TUTOR
MODEL OF KNOWLEDGE AND REASONING	✓ SYSTEM	✓ META KNOWLEDGE	✓ FORMAL	✓ FORMAL	✓ FORMAL	✓ FORMAL
COMMUNICATIONS MEDIA	✓	✓		✓	✓	✓
MODEL COGNITIVE PROCESSES	✓		✓		✓	✓
MODEL TUTORING AND DISCOURSE			✓ PARTNER	✓ PARTNER		

Figure 35 Qualitative Models, Part 2

Figures 34 and 35 also indicate the variety of knowledge we teach and the variety of ways in which we teach it. For example, we are able to teach facts, e.g., velocity and acceleration, as well as whole systems, e.g., electronic systems, boiler system, and maintenance system. We have also begun to teach meta-knowledge, or the knowledge needed to reason about and make inferences in a domain, e.g., the medical education tutor shows how to organize and focus data. Several other systems teach formal logic and formal knowledge, e.g., Algebraland and the geometry tutor.

We have also developed new ways of teaching. Figure 34 indicates that we use a mentor method in the SOPHIE and Recovery Boiler Tutor System, where the system oversees the student's actions and doesn't necessarily comment, or at least might reserve comment, while continuing to model the student's actions.

We have systems that act as partners, e.g., the LISP tutor or Algebraland, which allow the student to ask for help or which themselves execute the next step (Figure 35).

What have we really achieved? Clancey has put it succinctly: "Education has not been turned upside down." Clearly we have not placed a lot of systems in educational institutions. Neither have we performed extensive evaluation on these systems. We require around two years to build each system. Thus, in a few more years we will have more systems in educational institutions, yet even these systems will not be ready for evaluation. Classroom tests do not provide a measure of success for these systems because they have not been integrated into the curriculum. Soon however, we need thorough evaluations of these systems.

As shown in Figure 36, systems have been placed in grade schools, industrial sites, military training sites, and universities. In the grade schools, the geometry and algebra tutors have been tested by Anderson. In industry, 60 or so copies of the Recovery Boiler Tutor have been used at various papermill sites. In military training, the original electronics tutor was used briefly and the equipment maintenance tutor is about to be used. More progress has been made in university training, perhaps because computer science researchers are often found at universities. Thus, the Johnson and Soloway Pascal tutor [Johnson and Soloway, 1984], the Anderson LISP tutor, a second Pascal tutor, called the Bridge tutor [Bonar and Weil, 1985] and the medical education tutor have all been used with university students and in some cases have undergone detailed testing.

Figure 37 provides a rough estimate of the number of units used, where units is taken to mean copies of software, rather than separate pieces of hardware. Obviously the field is still new. As we begin to move into production with these systems and produce hundreds of these units as in the case of the Recovery Boiler, and the geometry, and STEAMER projects, we will be able to more properly evaluate the effectiveness of these systems. Ten units might mean that 10–30 students have used the system, and as we begin to actually use systems for a semester or so, as was done with the Pascal or LISP tutor, we will have hundreds of units available and can begin performing summative evaluation on student performance.

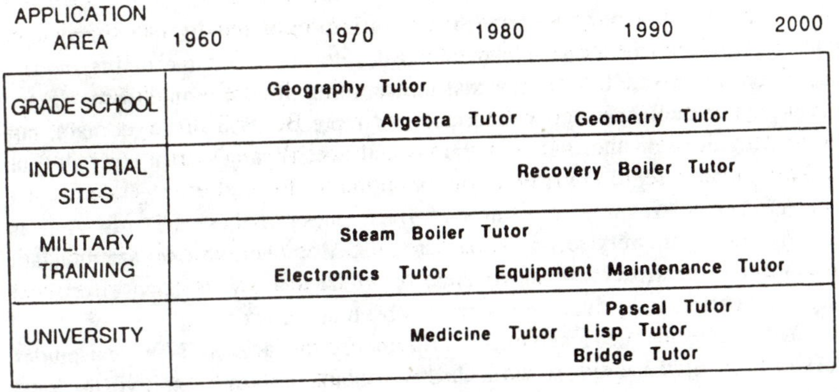

APPLICATION AREA	1960	1970	1980	1990	2000
GRADE SCHOOL		Geography Tutor	Algebra Tutor	Geometry Tutor	
INDUSTRIAL SITES				Recovery Boiler Tutor	
MILITARY TRAINING		Steam Boiler Tutor	Electronics Tutor	Equipment Maintenance Tutor	
UNIVERSITY			Medicine Tutor	Pascal Tutor / Lisp Tutor / Bridge Tutor	

Figure 36 Intelligent Tutors in the Classrom and Training Sites

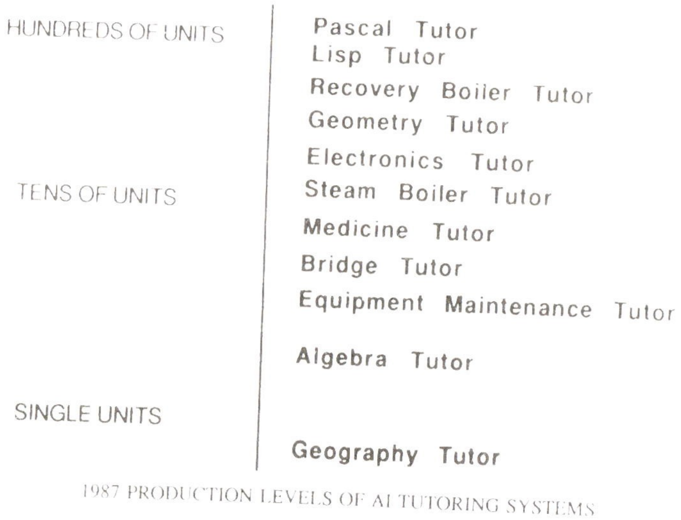

HUNDREDS OF UNITS	Pascal Tutor
	Lisp Tutor
	Recovery Boiler Tutor
	Geometry Tutor
	Electronics Tutor
TENS OF UNITS	Steam Boiler Tutor
	Medicine Tutor
	Bridge Tutor
	Equipment Maintenance Tutor
	Algebra Tutor
SINGLE UNITS	
	Geography Tutor

1987 PRODUCTION LEVELS OF AI TUTORING SYSTEMS

Figure 37 Number of Units

Controversies

Several controversies surround this work. As discussed above, a major problem is that we have not yet evaluated these systems. For example, if a system succeeds, which models should be assigned the credit? How can the various models be fine-tuned to improve the next generation of systems? Such evaluation studies are beginning. Anderson [1988] and Soloway have made detailed studies of the effects of their systems on learning and performance in the classroom.

A second issue of controversy is the definition of intelligent tutoring systems. Frequently, researchers in the field develop two or three of the models suggested in Section 1.2 and say that the resulting system is intelligent. If, for instance, a system has a good interface and representation of the domain, but lacks a cognitive or tutoring model, is it intelligent? I suggest that until all four models are achieved the system is not intelligent.

Another controversy concerns the effectiveness of these systems. And as I've said, there are very few systems out there. Moreover, funders are reluctant to pay for evaluation of these systems. Apart from a few isolated efforts, no large scale effort to evaluate this work has been undertaken.

Yet another controversy concerns the theory, or lack of same, that guides development of these systems. Ideally, we should look at cognitive theories, model them in the design of a new system, and use the systems to test the theory. The crucial step is the iteration, which enables results from one step to inform development of the next: A working tutor should enable refinement and evaluation of a cognitive principle and vice versa. Results from a working tutor should, in theory define a new cognitive model. Currently, precious little theory guides development of these systems. Not enough has been learned from cognitive processes results or from instructional design literature. There is nothing so practical as a good theory.

Another issue is use of the scientific method. Do we hypothesize, test, and evaluate rules and processes? Most of us do not. We need to clarify how hypotheses are generated in this field, how experiments help test those hypotheses, and then how results are to be evaluated.

We have been unclear about the intersection of our field with other applications of computers for education, such as simulations and microworlds. Do they work? For the most part, they do not. There is some evidence that simulations alone do not work, that microworlds are effective in getting the student to manipulate specific parameters. But there is little evidence of transference from either system to other domains. In both cases the missing element is a tutor that guides the interaction. Without some reasoning about the student's intentions and some appropriate remediation, effective teaching does not take place.

Bottlenecks, Barriers, and Breakthroughs

Many bottlenecks stand in the way of full realization of these systems. A primary one is the acquisition of sufficient person-power to build these models. How can researchers in psychology, education, and instructional design participate in this effort? A great deal of education and networking is required. Computer scientists need to work with instructional designers and educators who need to work with psychologists. We all need to benefit from prior work in the other fields. Currently, there is minimal communication between participants. Computer scientists, psychologists, domain experts, and teachers each publish in distinct journals using non-intersecting vocabularies. Results from empiricists are often not precise enough to enable production of knowledge and control structures.

Another barrier concerns the intensive amount of work necessary to build each tutor. Without the aid of shells and authoring systems this task is overwhelming. Even with software tools, each new domain requires indentification of topics and prerequisite topics, causal and temporal reasoning between topics, and the relative difficulty for learning topic. Cognitive modeling requires identification of meta-cognitive skills and an index to how a person might organize knowledge in the new domain, as well as identification of human strengths and weaknesses. Building a communications model requires visualization of the reasoning process, such as Clancey has done with the medical tutor or as Bonar has done with the OPTICS tutor. It also requires taking advantage of high resolution graphics, windows, menus, icons, and other available graphics tools. Building a tutoring model requires specification of the relative difficulty of each topic, as well as strategies and tactics for tailoring instruction to an individual student, and corpus analogies, examples, and error diagnosis techniques for teaching each topic. Thus, each new tutor requires exensive programming and empirical results.

Some breakthroughs however, facilitate future development of these systems. Powerful and inexpensive small computers have become availabe for education. For example, the Recovery Boiler Tutor was built on an IBM AT. It might have had more powerful communication capabilities if it had been developed on an AI-workstation, and we are beginning to scale down such systems to run on microcomputers. Funding for this research has recently become available at different levels through industry, government, and military sources. For example, Xerox PARC has established an Institute for Research on Learning, the purpose of which is to research new ways of teaching adults, using a computer. The founding of this Institute was motivated by the urgent need for adult education, particularly in industry. Xerox contributes a solution to this problem by funding researchers at Palo Alto to look at the cognitive process of learning and applying this knowledge to the building of intelligent tutors. The National Science Foundation and the Office of Naval Research have funded this type of work for a long time.

Existing software facilitates development of these systems. Expert systems, particularly the advent of expert systems shells, enable us to use existing systems, especially those in qualitative process modeling, and to base our tutors on the expert knowledge contained therein. This is not a simple, direct process, as Clancey has shown, but it does provide a starting point. Recent advances in cognitive modeling have also helped. Studies in learning, inferencing, and modeling processes are available. We are beginning to know more about what we're teaching and how to model the individual student as he/she learns. Currently we need more information about activities that engage particular students and that distinguish novice from expert behavior [Larkin et al., 1980; Chi et al., 1981], and about how to respond to the individual student.

Conclusions

In sum, I want to be very clear that we do not offer a panacea for the problems discussed at the beginning of this talk. Even if we build systems as powerful as suggested here, these systems will not fix all the educational deficiencies listed earlier. But they do provide some exciting possibilities, one of the most exciting is the possibility of building enticing learning environments that appear more effective than any existing forms of teaching. They also provide experiments for simplifying complex learning: For example, the Recovery Boiler Tutor and the maintenance tutor attempted to reify complex situations and make numerous components and parameters easy to manipulate.

One potentially significant impact of these machines is to transform education from a *push* to a *pull*, whereby people eagerly *choose* to work using these systems. Operators who have the Recovery Boiler Tutor report working on it up to 76 hours in the first three months. We don't ask the operators to work that many hours, they just enjoy playing with the system. Teaching systems that attract people have a significant advantage over non-attracting forms of teaching media.

As shown above, intelligent tutoring systems research is not an application area of AI. We cannot take off-the-shelf products from AI and use them to build our systems. This means that we are required to do a lot of work and to be more eclectic and persistent in modeling cognitive, tutoring, domain, and communication knowledge. However, the possibility is there for us to create world-class teaching systems that will change the current education delivery system.

References

Anderson, J., C. Boyle, and G. Yost, 1985. The Geometry Tutor. *Proceedings of the International Joint Conference on Artificial Intelligence*. Los Angeles, CA.

Anderson, J., and B. Reiser, 1986. The LISP Tutor. *Byte* **10**(4):159–175.

Anderson, J., 1988. Unpublished talk at NSF MDR Principal Investigator's Meeting, Phoenix, AZ.

Bloom, B. S., 1984. The 2-Sigma Problem: The Search for Methods of Group Instruction as Effective as One-to-One Tutoring, *Educational Researcher* **13**:4–16.

Bonar, J., R. Cunningham, and J. Schultz, 1986. An Object-Oriented Architecture for Intelligent Tutoring. *Proceedings of the ACM Conference on Object-Oriented Programming Systems, Language and Applications*. ACM, New York.

Bonar, J. G., and W. Weil, 1985. An Informed Programming Language. Paper presented at the meeting *Expert Systems in Government*. Washington, D.C.

Brown, J. S., and A. Bell, 1982. SOPHIE: A Sophisticated Instructional Environment for Teaching Electronic Troubleshooting (An Example of A.I. in C.A.I.). In Sleeman, D. and J. S. Brown, ed. *Intelligent Tutoring Systems*. Academic Press, Cambridge, MA.

Chi, M., P. Feltovich, and R. Glaser, 1981. Categorization and Representations of Physics Problems by Experts and Novices. *Cognitive Science* **5**:121–152.

Clancey, W., 1979a. *Transfer of Rule-Based Expertise Through Tutorial Dialogue*. Ph.D. Dissertation, Department of Computer Science, Stanford University.

Clancey, W., 1979b. Case Management for Rule-Based Tutorials. In *Proceedings of the International Joint Conference on Artificial Intelligence*.

Clancey, W., 1979. Tutoring Rules for Guiding a Case Method Dialogue. *International Journal of Man-Machine Studies* **11**. Also in D. Sleeman and J. S. Brown, ed., *Intelligent Tutoring Systems*. Academic Press, Cambridge, MA, 1982.

Clancey, W., 1984. Classification Problem Solving. *Proceedings of the National Conference on Artificial Intelligence*.

Clancey, W., 1986. Qualitative Student Models. In Traub, J. F., ed., *Annual Reviews, Inc.* Palo Alto, CA.

Clement, J., and D. Brown, 1984. *Using Analogical Reasoning to Deal with Deep Misconceptions in Physics*. Cognitive Processes Research Group, Physics Department, University of Massachusetts, Amherst.

deKleer, J., and J. S. Brown, 1986. A Qualitative Physics Based on Confluence. In Bobrov, D. C., ed., *Qualitative Reasoning about Physical Systems*. MIT Press, Cambridge, MA.

Forbus, K., 1986. Qualitative Process Theory. *Artificial Intelligence* **24**:85–168. Reprinted in Bobrow, D. C., ed., *Qualitative Reasoning about Physical Systems*. MIT Press, Cambridge, MA.

Forbus, K., and A. Stevens, 1981. Using Qualitative Simulation to Generate Explanations, Report #4480, Bolt, Beranek and Newman, Inc.

Fuller, R. B., 1962. *Education Automation: Freeing the Scholar to Return to his Studies*. Southern Illinois University Press, Carbondale, Il.

Hollan, J., Hutchins, E., and L. Weitzman, 1984. STEAMER: An Interactive Inspectable Simulation-Based Training System. *AI Magazine*. Summer.

Johnson, L., and E. M. Soloway, 1984. Intention-based Diagnosis of Programming Errors. *Proceedings of the National Conference on Artificial Intelligence*. pp. 369–380. Austin, TX.

Larkin, J., McDermott, J., Simon, D., and H. Simon, 1980. Expert and Novice Performance in Solving Physics Problems. In *Science* **208**:1335–1342.

Molnar, A., 1986. An unpublished talk presented on the panel "AI in Education," E. Soloway, Chair, National Meeting of the American Association on Artificial Intelligence, Philadelphia, PA.

Naisbitt, J., 1984. *Megatrends: Ten New Directions Transforming our Lives*. Warner Books: New York, NY.

National Science Foundation, 1983. *Educating America for the 21st Century*. Washington, DC.

Richer, M., and Clancey, W., 1985. GUIDON-WATCH: A Graphic Interface for Viewing a Knowledge-Based System. *IEEE Computer Graphics and Applications* **5**(11):51–64.

Roschelle, 1987. Unpublished paper title presented at The Third International Conference on Artificial Intelligence and Education, Pittsburgh, PA.

Shortliffe, E., 1976. *Computer-based Medical Consultations: MYCIN*. American Elsevier Publishers, New York, NY.

Sleeman, D., and J. S. Brown, ed., 1982. *Intelligent Tutoring Systems*. Academic Press, Cambridge, MA.

Smith, 1987. ARK. Unpublished Paper presented at The Third International Conference on Artificial Intelligence and Education.

Soloway, E., 1986. Learning to Program vs. Learning to Construct Mechanisms and Explanations. *CACM*. **29**(9):850–858.

Stevens, A., Collins, A., and S. Goldin, 1978. *Diagnosing Student's Misconceptions in Causal Models* Technical Report 3786, Bolt, Beranek and Newman, Cambridge, MA, also in *International Journal of Man-Machines Studies* **11** and in Sleeman, D. and J. S. Brown, ed., *Intelligent Tutoring Systems*. Academic Press: Cambridge, MA, 1982.

Towne, D., A. Munroe, Q. Pizzini, and D. Surmon, 1987. Simulation Composition Tools with Integrated Semantics. *Abstracts of the Third International Conference on Artificial Intelligence and Education*. p. 54. Learning Research and Development Center, University of Pittsburgh, PA.

U.S. Department of Education, 1982. *Computers in Education: Realizing the Potential*.

U.S. Department of Education, 1983. *Proceedings of the Office of Education Research and Improvement*.

White, B. and J. Frederiksen, 1986. Intelligent Tutoring Systems Based upon Qualitative Model Evolutions. *Proceedings of the National Conference on Artificial Intelligence*.

Woolf, B., D. Blegen, J. Jansen, and A. Verloop, 1986. *Teaching a Complex Industrial Process*. National Association of Artificial Intelligence, Philadelphia, PA.

Woolf, B., and D. McDonald, 1984. Context-Dependent Transitions in Tutoring Discourse, National Association of Artificial Intelligence, Austin, TX.

Woolf, B., and D. McDonald, 1984. Design Issues in Building a Computer Tutor. *IEEE Computer* September. Special issue on Artificial Intelligence for Human-Machine Interaction.

Woolf, B., and D. McDonald, 1984. Representing Discourse Conventions in Tutoring. In *Expert Systems for Government Symposium*. IEEE and MITRE Corp., McLean, VA.

Walberg, H., 1982–3. A Series of Reports (1982–3) Concerning Computational Studies of Mathematics Skills Scores between U.S. and Japanese Students.

2

An Introduction to Explanation-based Learning

Gerald DeJong
Coordinated Science Laboratory
University of Illinois

Introduction

What is explanation-based learning? That is the central question we will examine. Unfortunately, there is yet no satisfactory answer to this question. Nor is there universal agreement among researchers on what phenomena should and should not be included under the rubric of explanation-based learning (EBL). Such an admission may first seem rather unsettling to a scientist. Is it impossible to scientifically study a topic whose very boundaries have not been clearly delineated? Is EBL a paradigmatic conundrum? My answer (not surprisingly) is "No!" The difficulties are real but quite natural. They are a reflection in part of EBL's immaturity—it is young even by AI standards, and in part of similar problems with the broader field of AI.

What would it mean to have a satisfactory answer to our central question? We would need a complete and precise characterization of EBL. The conjunction of these two attributes is the problem; it is too early to be complete *and* precise. We can offer imprecise and *ad hoc* characterizations that capture many of our intuitions about EBL, or we can give precise characterizations which are stultifying and shallow.

While we may accept this description of EBL's current state as accurate, we cannot be content with it. It is the presence of these difficulties that makes EBL worthy of scientific study, and it is the struggle of scientific study by which we can eliminate them.

There are two approaches to EBL research. We will call them the "formalist" approach and the "implementationalist" approach. Each has its advocates. The formalist takes small, certain steps, building on a firm foundation. The implementationalist throws caution to the wind, programming large systems with impressive input/output behavior. An ideal researcher must be a bit of both. The proper task of a formalist, aside from formalizing, is to broaden the scope of his research. The proper task of an implementationalist, aside from implementing, is to distill a little true progress from the overabundance of implementational details.

An honest formalist, when asked "How can you be sure what you're studying is important?" must reply "I cannot"; an honest implementationalist, when asked "How can you be sure your work represents a scientific advance?" must give the same response. Both researchers rely ultimately on their own intuition—their own gut feeling for what is an exciting research direction. So it is with explanation-based learning. Each component brings its own brand of progress, and it is only through their nexus that EBL can arrive at the scientific Nirvana of completed research.

In this paper we begin by building an intuitive appreciation for EBL. Next, we will briefly compare EBL with similarity-based learning (SBL). Then we will list and discuss the various types of EBL generalization and present several formalisms that have been advanced to handle some small fraction of them. After discussing why these formalisms fall short of capturing EBL, a brief historical account of EBL development will be given followed by a discussion of a few of the important outstanding research issues.

An Intuitive Specification of EBL

Explanation-based learning is best viewed as a kind of learning from observation [Mitchell, Mahadevan and Steinberg, 1985; DeJong and Mooney, 1986a]. It allows a system to acquire general knowledge through an analysis of a few specific episodes. Background knowledge plays a crucial role in the analysis process. In large part, the background knowledge substitutes for the massive training sets needed in traditional machine learning. It is convenient, though not necessary, to view EBL in the context of problem solving, or more precisely, learning about problem solving. We will primarily explore EBL in this context.

It is important to realize that the determining feature of an EBL system is not the presence of something called an *explanation*. Many systems construct explanations or proofs but are not EBL systems (e.g., [Fikes and Nilsson, 1971; Charniak, 1977; Wilensky, 1978; Schank, 1986]). Rather, it is how the explanation is used that qualifies a system as taking an EBL approach. Each EBL system uses the explanation of a very few examples (usually just one) to define the boundaries of a concept. The concept's definition is determined by a domain-theory-guided inspection of why an example worked, not by similarities and differences between this example (or example's explanation) and previous instances.

"Hey! Look what Zog do!"

Figure 1 Early explanation-based learning. "The FAR SIDE cartoon by Gary Larson is reprinted by the permission of Chronicle Features, San Francisco, California."

Figure 1 is a reproduction of a "Far Side" cartoon which shows an example of early explanation-based learning. A group on the left are Neanderthals. They are familiar with fire but have not yet discovered the concept of a cooking skewer. Zog, the Cro-Magnon with glasses on the right, has invented the world's first skewer and is happily broiling his pterodactyl drumstick over his own fire. Zog is creative and intelligent, the Einstein of the late Pleistocene age. It would be nice to develop a computer model that captures Zog's creative problem solving ability. Sadly, that task is far beyond current AI technology. However, there is another interesting individual in the picture. The smartest of the three Neanderthals has noticed Zog's invention. He realizes that Zog is not scorching his hand in the traditional way and yet Zog is just as successfully cooking his food. Our Neanderthal friend has done much more than rote learning. He has appreciated something of the generality of Zog's cleverness. For example, he probably knows that the cooking technique would work for him as well as for Zog, also that it is not specific to Zog's drumstick but would work equally for his friend's lizard or tomorrow's yet-uncaught wild rabbit. He perhaps realizes some of the parametric constraints on the concept. The skewer concept could be applied to his own fire, though since the fire is larger and hotter than Zog's, a slightly longer stick would be propitious. He probably also understands some of the limitations of the concept: It would not work well when applied to giant turtle eggs or a whole woolly mammoth—the turtle eggs would shatter and the woolly mammoth could not be lifted with the stick. Our Neanderthal has done much more than simply store away a single uninterpreted episode. He has, in fact, acquired a new general concept.

In spite of the fact that our Neanderthal is not as intelligent (or at least not as creative) as the Cro-Magnon Zog, he now has a skewer concept that is quite possibly as effective as Zog's own. Furthermore, he did not have to waste the time or effort that Zog spent—the sleepless nights agonizing over his creation, the endless and tedious trial-and-error experiments. How did our Neanderthal friend learn this useful new concept? There are three steps. First, he *noticed* Zog had a better way of doing things. Second, he *explained* to himself why Zog's method works using his knowledge about the world—knowledge about fire, sharp sticks, flesh, food, and so on. Third, he *generalized* the explanation of the single observed instance into a useful, broadly-applicable problem solving concept.

The Neanderthal's acquisition of the skewer concept illustrates what we term *explanation-based learning* (EBL). Our ultimate goal is to formalize this process. It is a much more modest AI goal than to build an implementable model for Zog's creativity. Much of AI seeks to do the latter, to automatically construct clever original solutions of difficult real-world problems. AI planning systems do everything from scratch. The fourth time through "monkeys and bananas" is no easier than the first time. Planning from scratch is, in general, very difficult [Chapman, 1987] and has not met with much success. Instead, we will be content for our EBL system to gracefully acquire new concepts by observing others who are more intelligent than the system is. We will not insist that the system produce a maximally general concept, just a useful concept. If our Neanderthal friend falsely believes that a skewer can only be used to roast pterodactyl parts, the concept is still worth knowing. He should, of course, always be open to the possibility of later concept refinement. We will insist, however, that the general concept be tractable to learn and efficient to access and use.

Is this too modest a goal? Are we over-simplifying to insure success? Will we be left with anything worthwhile? Consider what the EBL approach does not cover. Since EBL requires a substantial amount of world knowledge both to construct and also to generalize the explanations, acquisition of initial world knowledge is beyond its scope. Also, invention, Zog's process of creative concept formation, is out of its scope. EBL will not result in computer programs that can invent the phonograph or electric light as Thomas Edison did. While such creative insights are essential for our culture's technological advancement, they are very rare. Indeed the number of truly creative advances made by any individual over his lifetime probably averages to less than one. There are a few Thomas Edisons who make perhaps three or four creative advances, but most of us are just plain folk who can appreciate and use inventions but do no significant inventing of our own. The task *is* modest, but its modesty is derived from not trying to surpass average human abilities. This seems to be an entirely reasonable sort of modesty.

Much of adult learning seems to have characteristics that make it susceptible to an explanation-based learning approach. Apprenticeship learning is ubiquitous in human training. After a modicum of classroom-style learning, doctors, plumbers, carpenters, graduate students, farmers, and so on, all finish their training with an extended period of close observation of an established master. This is clearly a very large, interesting, and useful class of learning. We are not claiming that humans *must* be employing EBL in these apprenticeship domains. In this paper we are not even claiming that humans *do* learn this way although there are some recent experimental evidence for the psychological plausibility of the approach [Ahn, Mooney, Brewer and DeJong, 1987]. We only claim that the approach is an interesting one that may prove to be an important component in an over-all model of learning, and that it merits further study.

Informally, then, this is the kind of learning that we term *explanation-based*. It involves determining that an example is worthy of learning, constructing an *explanation* for the example (or examples), and generalizing the explanation into a new concept. It is my own opinion that EBL systems are used to the best advantage when the explanation is constructed from the observation of the behavior of an expert. However, some EBL researchers prefer systems that generalize their own successful problem solving actions. Others have no preference as to where the explanations come from. But learning from observing others has an advantage. More complex and interesting concepts can be acquired by relying on the intelligence and creative abilities of others. This is because the computational complexity of understanding is less than that of creative problem solving [Dejong, 1986b].

Explanation-based and Similarity-based Learning

Next, we wish to briefly compare explanation-based learning with similarity-based learning. The term *similarity-based* is originally due to Michael Lebowitz and has been popularized by Ryszard Michalski and others, but has not been adopted by all researchers. Pat Langley, whose research is also in this vein [Langley et al, 1981a; Rose and P. Langley, 1986], prefers the term *empirical learning* indicating that learning is driven primarily by experience rather than an preexisting theory. Similarity-based learning (SBL), or empirical learning, is the dominant model of learning in both AI and psychology [Winston, 1975; Quinlan, 1986; Michalski, Mozetic, Hong and Lavrac, 1986a; Rendell, 1983; Stepp and Michalski, 1986; Schank, 1982; Kolodner, 1987; Medin, Wattenmaker and Michalski, 1987]. It has to do with discovering a combination of features that best classifies the regularities in a set of examples. The resulting generalization over the examples is the new concept. The hallmarks of SBL are (1) the use of many examples and (2) the need for very little domain knowledge. It is, in these ways, the antithesis of EBL. In SBL, concepts emerge from the consideration of many positive (and often also negative) instances of the concept. The classification is often, but not always, provided by a teacher. The quality of the resulting concept is dependent on the number of examples and also on how representative the training examples are of the concept's actual space.

To illustrate the differences between EBL and SBL we will consider acquiring the concept in Figure 2.

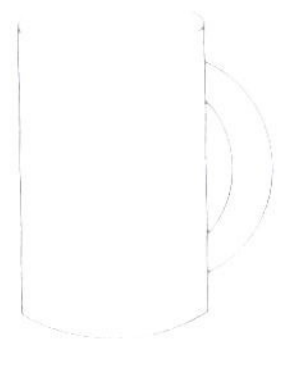

Figure 2 A cup.

What is the object in Figure 2? It is a cup. But suppose we are not familiar with cups. A similarity-based method of acquiring the concept would be to look at a number of examples of a cup, trying to formulate what it is that they have in common. A teacher, or some other mechanism, must be used to classify world objects into *cups* and *non-cups*. Suppose our teacher has produced the labeled objects of Figure 3. The ones on the left are classified as cups and the ones on the right are not cups. The objects (both positive and negative examples) are presented to the SBL system as a conjunction of features. The first positive example is cylindrical and red, has a round handle and a flat bottom; it weighs 5 ounces, and belongs to Herman. The second one is conical and brown, has a fashionable art-deco handle and a flat bottom; it weighs 6.3 ounces and is the property of Mary. The third one is shown in Figure 3.

An SBL system, after examining many positive and negative examples, will construct a general description which ideally is satisfied by all of the positive examples and none of the negative examples. Often, many different descriptions will be consistent with the known examples. Figure 4 shows two different concept descriptions represented as areas in a two-dimensional feature space. Each accounts equally well for the example instances. Positive examples are represented by '+'; negative examples are represented by '−'. Each object

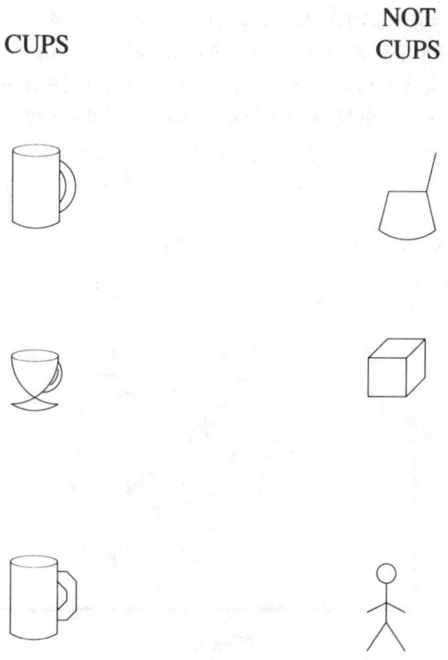

CUPS

NOT CUPS

Figure 3 Positive and negative examples.

is represented as the conjunction of just two feature values. Feature A may be the object's color, and feature B its weight. This is, of course, a trivial representation scheme; in it a brick and a golden retriever puppy are identical objects. In actuality, there would be many, many features and the space would have as many dimensions. Six dimensions were used in the discussion of coffee cups above (shape of body, shape of handle, shape of bottom, weight, and owner). This is also too few. A feature space must be rich enough to support the distinctions necessary for the concept.

A concept description specifies an area in the feature space. Three concept descriptions are shown in Figure 4, each of which successfully includes all of the positive examples and excludes the negative examples. The areas are represented by the contours of their boundaries.

Notice that we are allowing disjunctive concepts—concept 1 is composed of two disjoint areas. Many other concept descriptors can be formed that successfully separate the '+'s from '−'s. Once a concept description is selected, previously unclassified objects are classified by whether or not they fall inside the concept's area. Obviously, an SBL concept description may be wrong. The next negative example supplied by the teacher may not fall within the descriptor's area, or the next positive example may not be included in the area. Either way, the very next instance supplied by the teacher may require adjustment of the concept descriptor.

With enough training instances, an SBL system may come to believe that the shape of the handle is not so important, but all the things that are cups must have handles. The color and owner are completely irrelevant. However, all cups are light weight (say less than 10 ounces), and all must have flat bottoms.

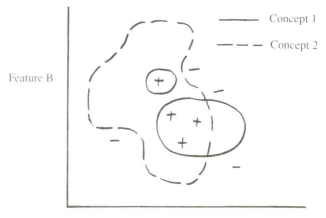

Figure 4 Two alternative concept boundaries.

There are many different SBL algorithms, each with its own strengths and weaknesses. Some perform *incremental* learning in which an existing concept may be adjusted to account for a few new examples without reviewing all of the past positive and negative examples. In others, new examples must be added to the original set of positive and negative examples after which the learning algorithm is again run on the augmented training set. Some systems eliminate the need for a teacher by looking for "well formed" clusters of object instances. "Well formed" means that each instance is more similar (using some metric) to instances in its own cluster than it is to any instance in different clusters. Another variation is whether or not the learning system can tolerate noise. Suppose a teacher occasionally misclassifies objects, or that the representation of an object may be incorrect (e.g., an object which is actually blue is represented as having "red" as the value of the color feature). In the presence of noise, the best concept description may not be one that correctly classifies all of the positive and negative examples. Rather, it may be the description that maximizes the distance (in some metric) between *most* of the positive examples and *most* of the negative examples.

One should not minimize the importance of these variations. When compared with an EBL system, the differences between SBL systems may appear small. But, it is a mistake to lump them together. Research careers are built upon these differences. Having said that, we will now lump all of the SBL systems together, noting that they (1) rely on many examples and (2) make minimal use of background knowledge. Notice that having a large number of examples improves the confidence we may have in the system's concept description, provided, of course, that the examples are more or less evenly distributed throughout the feature space (no large areas are devoid of classified objects). If the feature space were totally labeled, that is, if the teacher exhaustively classified every possible object, then there would be a uniquely correct concept area, and all acceptable concept descriptions would be notational variants of each other. Notice also that no semantic properties of the features need be used to construct the concept description. The adjustments to the concept's description, when presented with a newly classified example, can be specified entirely in terms of changing the area covered. It matters little what the new area corresponds to in the real world. Parenthetically we should note that many researchers in SBL are incorporating more background knowledge into their systems [Stepp and Michalski, 1986]. However, the amount of background knowledge is relatively small and always optional; the lack of background knowledge does not preclude the formation of concept description.

A major advantage of SBL is that it can be done in almost any domain, even one in which there is little or no understood domain theory. A disadvantage is that the system must be given many, many examples, and even then generalizations formed may reflect coincidences in the examples rather than systematic truths. For example, one system (IPP [Lebowitz, 1980]) advanced the generalization that terrorist bombings in El Salvador do not kill people.

How is explanation-based learning different? Consider the same problem of learning a cup. This is an example that is based on an example of Mitchell's [Mitchell, Keller and Kedar-Cabelli, 1986], which he based on an example from Winston [Winston et al., 1983].

First, we need a domain theory from which explanations can be built. This is shown in Figure 5a. We have chosen first order predicate calculus as a formalism for the domain theory. This is not required; other representation systems would work as well.

Second, EBL requires a functional specification of the desired concept, shown in Figure 5b. This has been called a non-operational goal definition [Mitchell, Keller and Kedar-Cabelli, 1986]. However, it should not be viewed as giving the learning system a definition of the goal concept (which sounds suspiciously like cheating). Rather it is better to think of it as an effective procedure with which to recognize when an object has the desired functionality. For example, we may specify to the system the goal of designing a *Star Trek* transporter mechanism. We may have no idea of how to build one ourselves and, indeed, the mechanism may be impossible. Nonetheless, we may functionally specify its attributes: A transporter is a device that makes people disappear from one location and appear somewhere else. Such a specification is surely not cheating and yet provides a success criterion. In our "cup" example, we define a cup to be anything one can drink from. This is too broad (it includes the concept of a "glass"), but it will suffice for pedagogical purposes.

Thus, in EBL, concepts are individuated by their functionalities. Any object with the specified functionality is necessarily an instance of the concept. Incidentally, *functionality* is not to be interpreted in any kind of "action-like" way. This notion of functionality has only to do with the role played in the domain. The implications of individuating concepts in this way is can be sur-

```
1) ∀x [(Liftable(x) & Open(x) & Stable(x) & Liquid-container(x))
      => Drinkable-from(x)]

2) ∀x ∃y [(Weight(x,LIGHT) & Has-part(x,y) & Isa(y,HANDLE))
      => Liftable(x)]

3) ∀x ∃y [(Has-part(x,y) & Isa(y,CONCAVITY)) => Open(x)]

4) ∀x ∃y [(Has-part(x,y) & Isa(y,CONCAVITY) & Orientation(y,UPWARD))
      => Liquid-container(x)]

5) ∀x ∃y [(Has-part(x,y) & Isa(y,FLAT-BOTTOM)) => Stable(x)]
      Figure 5A The Domain Theory


   Cup(x) <=> Drinkable-from(x)
   Figure 5B The Functional Specification
```

Figure 5 The functional specification.

prisingly subtle. It enforces a kind of abstract homogeneity among instances of a concept for which there is no obvious analog in SBL.

Third, the EBL system must observe an instance of the desired concept, in this case, OBJ1 whose semantic network representation is shown in Figure 6. In fact, OBJ1 is just the name given to this collection of properties. OBJ1 has a concavity (CON12), it's a red color, Herman is its owner, it has a handle (HAN31), etc.

It is the case that OBJ1 is a cup. This can be proved using our domain theory. The proof is given in Figure 7. Such a proof is called an *explanation*. It is a kind of data dependency support graph of the "cupness" of OBJ1. EBL does not require that the explanation be constructed in any specific way. It may be done by a resolution theorem prover internal to the learning system, by some backward-chaining natural deduction mechanism, or the explanation itself may simply be input to the system.

The explanation, once constructed, can itself drive the generalization process. Not all of the attributes of OBJ1 are used in the explanation. These features, such as "color" and "owner," could have other values without compromising the veracity of the explanation. The explanation makes explicit which features of OBJ1 are necessary for its "cupness" and which are irrelevant. The remaining features directly contribute to the cupness of OBJ1. However, such features of a training example, while sufficient to satisfy the functional goal, may not be necessary. Some may represent particular points along a continuum of satisfactory values. Others represent a particular resolution of a set of mutual constraints. But, perhaps, other resolutions are also possible. By examining the explanation structure of the particular training example in the light of the system's domain knowledge, some of the variability may be discovered. The result can be a new concept that is much more general than the observed instance.

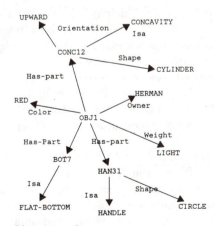

Figure 6 OBJ1, a positive example.

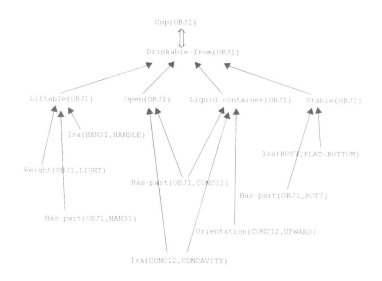

Figure 7 Proof that OBJ1 is a cup.

Types of Generalization

Before examining the types of generalization that we will expect from explanation-based learning systems, it is important to clarify what is meant by the term "generalization." In EBL we will use the term in a slightly different fashion than it is used in similarity-based learning. The difference is subtle, but it has caused past communication problems. Being precise will help shed light on the issues of over-generalization and learning at the knowledge level [Dietterich, 1986] which will be discussed briefly in the conclusion. It is important to make the difference in terminology explicit.

In SBL, one concept specification is a generalization of an instance if the instance is contained in the extension of the concept. The Venn diagram in Figure 8a shows an instance (represented as a '+') along with several generalizations.

SBL generalization is a purely syntactic notion. It is best viewed as a *candidate* specification for the concept. Michalski [1983] has provided a taxonomy of syntactic generalizations. There is no guarantee that such a generalization will be useful or even semantically well-formed when interpreted in the real world. Rather, desired properties such as expected utility and semantic well-formedness are dependent on features of the training set as a whole (e.g., how representative it is of the actual concept). Since generalizing a particular instance is performed without regard to semantic considerations, the resulting generalization may be an over-generalization of the desired concept. By contrast, the generalization process in EBL has semantic as well as syntactic components. Figure 8b shows the relationships involved in an EBL generalization. A qualitatively new sort of boundary is present: the solid line represents the extent, in feature space, of the functional goal concept as supported by the domain theory. This concept boundary may be defined by goal regression [Waldinger, 1977; Nilsson, 1980]. Its shape can be very complex, even encompassing several disjoint areas. Its determination is intractable in all but the simplest of domains. Instead, EBL relies on efficient generalization techniques which may undergeneralize but which do not cross the true boundary. In Figure 8b the instance point is generalized via EBL to the area enclosed by the dashed triangular boundary. Two sides and a portion of the third side of the EBL boundary (represented by coincident dashed and solid lines) are shared with the true concept boundary. This reflects concept limits that the functional goal specification imposes on the explanation. Another portion, represented as a single dashed line, reflects limits imposed by the explanation's structure. Thus, in EBL, the generalization process itself guarantees that the generalization specifies a (possibly improper) subset of the concept's feature-space area. It is less susceptible to over-generalization. Over-generalization is unavoidable only when the domain theory itself results in fuzzy concept boundaries. SBL does not make this commitment in the generalization process, and over-generalization is much more common, even desirable. However, it requires a large training set of examples to justify the semantic correctness of the ultimate generalization.

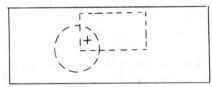

Figure 8a Two syntactic generalizations of an instance.

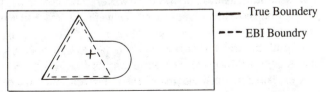

Figure 8b The true boundary of the concept illustrated by the instance and an EBL-generated boundary.

It might have been desirable to use the term consistently, especially since it is so central to learning. But perhaps not. The meaning of the term "generalization" has already evolved; Soloway used it in a rather different SBL fashion ten years ago [Soloway, 1978]. Most SBL researchers have not so much *excluded* a semantic facet of the term as simply never *included* one, and, when discussing a concept's limits in transformed spaces (as in constructive induction [Rendell, 1985]), "generalization" is used freely to refer to volumes in more abstract spaces.

In EBL circles, attributing a semantic facet to the term "generalization" was consummated by Mitchell, Keller and Kedar-Cabelli [1986]. This should not be thought of as a redefinition, but rather a natural evolution in the term to reflect simultaneous changes in syntactic feature space *and* in the semantic functional space. In any case, we will use the term "generalization" in this sense. If the reader objects he should do an internal RPLACA throughout the paper of "generalization" with "valid generalization" or "useful generalization."

Irrelevant Feature Elimination

The features that are not used to support the conclusion of *cupness* for OBJ1 (e.g., "color" and "owner") can be removed. The result is a generalization of the specific training example. We will call this kind of generalization *irrelevant feature elimination*. In the cup domain, the amount of generalization provided to OBJ1 is rather modest. In rich domains, this is a powerful method that, in large part, solves the feature selection problem faced by similarity-based and empirical learning methods. Furthermore, in problem solving domains, it results in the elimination of unnecessary operators, which means that the learning system can itself perform a measure of optimization, as well as generalization, of the observed training example.

Identity Elimination

The second generalization type, *identity elimination*, removes unnecessary dependence on particular objects. OBJ1 has a handle, HAN31. We can see by the explanation that without a handle this particular proof of OBJ1's cupness would not be valid. It is not important, however, that OBJ1 must have handle HAN31. Any particular handle would work as well; if OBJ1 had handle HAN32 instead, it would be just as liftable and just as much of a cup. Thus, we can parameterize specific components occurring in the explanation. OBJ1 will become ?X and HAN31 will become ?Y. But this goes too far. The relations that appear in the explanation must be maintained. For example, Handle(?Y) and Haspart(?X, ?Y) must be true. With our particular training instance, this relationship is enforced by reality. OBJ1 in fact does have handle HAN31 as a part.

Once the particular objects are replaced with variables, the EBL system must insure that only mutually consistent objects be allowed to bind to the variables. It can do this by simply asserting, as constraint requirements among the variables, those relations that appear in the explanation. This kind of generalization is called identity elimination since it is not the identity of the particular real world item HAN31 that is important for "cupness" but only HAN31's property by virtue of the fact that it is a handle and is attached to the object of interest.

Identity elimination works because of generalities already built into the domain theory. These preexisting generalities are exploited to the advantage of acquiring new concepts. Such preexisting generalities are essential for EBL. This is not a requirement about theoretical functionality or the adequacy with which our domain theory captures the world, but rather about how the domain theory is written. A different domain theory might support all of the same conclusions as the domain theory in Figure 5, but prohibit an EBL acquisition of a broad "cup" concept. Consider the domain theory like the one in Figure 5 but with rule 2 replaced with the rules given in Figure 9.

Using this domain theory OBJ1 is still liftable but not by virtue of the fact that it has a handle that incidentally happens to be HAN31 but rather directly because HAN31 is part of OBJ1. Explanation-based generalization about the handles of cups is very limited in this domain theory, even though the theory adequately supports a proof of the training instance: the cupness of OBJ1. Clearly, we would prefer to avoid domain theories such as this. Ideally the role that an object may play in the domain theory is entirely determined by its properties—never by its identity. Philosophically this has some interesting ramifications, but it is uncontroversial, at least so far, in AI. It may be termed the principle of no "function in form" [Anderson and Thompson, 1987a] and is often implicitly followed by AI researchers. Adherence to this principle helps to improve the generative power of the domain theory as well as allowing EBL; a domain theory designed with this principle can often support the same set of inferences using fewer rules. The principle is also very important for the next type of generalization, operationality pruning.

```
2A) ∀x ∃y [(Weight(x,LIGHT) & Has-part(x,HAN31)) => Liftable(x)]

2B) ∀x ∃y [(Weight(x,LIGHT) & Has-part(x,HAN32)) => Liftable(x)]

2C) ∀x ∃y [(Weight(x,LIGHT) & Has-part(x,HAN33)) => Liftable(x)]

2D) ∀x ∃y [(Weight(x,LIGHT) & Has-part(x,HAN34)) => Liftable(x)]
                              •
                              •
                              •
```

Figure 9 Alternative domain rules for liftability.

Operationality Pruning

The third component of generalization based on explanations we will term *operationality pruning*. It eliminates easily reconstructable sub-explanation from the explanation. We will call any constituent of the explanation *operational* (after Mostow [1983]) if its truth can easily be verified. Parenthetically, we should note that this is a rather informal definition and that "operationality" can be a slippery issue, but for now we will pretend that it is well defined. The leaves of a well-formed explanation must all be operational, but some internal constituents may be operational as well. The particular sub-explanation supporting an operational internal constituent should be dropped from the concept definition. Such sub-explanations can be filled in as needed. This can lead to greater generality because the particular sub-explanation used in the training instance may be arbitrary: A number of satisfactory alternative sub-explanations might also have been used. Once the specific constituent's support is pruned, the concept is no longer constrained to the specific sub-explanation.

To illustrate this, consider a slight modification of the "cup" example. Suppose it were the case that the predicate "liftable" were operational. This does not necessarily mean that liftable is a feature that can be immediately observed (like "color"), but only that the truth value of "liftable" can be easily determined for most objects of interest. In the case of OBJ1, "liftable" is true because OBJ1 has a handle. Suppose there are a few (say half a dozen) very easy ways to prove "liftable." Further, suppose that there are a relatively few and easy ways to prove "not liftable." It might be that if an object does not satisfy one of the half-dozen easy proofs, it is certainly not liftable. Then the predicate "liftable" itself is operational. There is no reason to keep a trace of the particular proof, liftable-via-a-handle, as part of the concept definition for "cup." To determine the "cupness" of something, it is almost as easy for the system to remanufacture the liftable-via-a-handle proof as to verify an already-expanded version. Greater concept generality is achieved by means of a handle.

Structural Generalization

The fourth type of generalization we will call *structural generalization*. By this we mean a generalization that alters the internal structure of the explanation itself. This is the most difficult and the most interesting of the generalization types, and merits a sub-taxonomy. The previous three generalization types, irrelevant feature elimination, identity elimination, and operationality pruning, do not alter the structure of the explanation for the training example, except perhaps to remove nodes. Structural generalization includes rearranging, transforming, and adding components to the explanation. We will briefly discuss three important sub-types of structural generalization: *disjunctive augmentation*, *temporal generalization*, and *number generalization*.

Figure 10 Alternative method for achieving stability. Zarf with round bottomed cup.

Disjunctive Augmentation *Disjunctive augmentation* involves adding alternative options to an explanation constituent. If, as part of the domain theory, the system knows a different but acceptable method of supporting a constituent, that alternative is specified along with the method used in the example. For example, consider the "cup" domain theory with the additional concept of a "zarf," which is a chalice-like holder for small round-bottomed objects (see Figure 10).

The domain theory includes a different method for achieving stability. The example cup, OBJ1, is stable because it has a flat bottom, but stability might have been achieved in another way. If the domain theory included the possibility of employing a "zarf" to achieve stability, then the generalized operational concept should include a disjunct at the stability constituent. Note that this is very different from operationality pruning. Stable(?X) itself is not operational, but Isa(?X,FLATBOTTOM) and Isa(?X,ZARF) are. Of course, if the original constituent support is a specialization of one of the alternative methods, then the original constituent may be dropped altogether without loss of generality.

It may seem that allowing disjunctive augmentation opens a rather nasty can of worms. It is possible, indeed likely, that in any interesting explanation there are augmentations possible which are fraught with many subtle constraints and result in only minor improvements in the concept's generality. Discovering them and processing them is expensive, and their benefit is small. Indeed this is true of most forms of structural generalization. Does this call into question the validity or the desirability of performing such generalizations? Not at all. An important point to remember for structural generalization, which applies to all of EBL, is that the resulting concept need not be fully general to be useful. *Any* generalization is better than none. There is a truism called the 80/20 rule: one gets 80% of the work done with 20% of the effort, and the remaining 20% of the work requires 80% of the effort. The rule is usually cited as a caution against extrapolating the performance characteristics of prototype systems. However, in EBL it works to our advantage. Getting 80% of the generalization with 20% of the work is a great bargain. We can afford to be content with less-than-totally-general concepts; there is nothing magical about generalizing any particular concept to its utmost limits. A problem solving area not covered by one concept will likely be covered by another, and if not, the system's overall performance is still improved due to efficiency gains in the problem solving areas that *are* covered.

Temporal Generalization *Temporal generalization* applies particularly to planning. A plan is a sequence of operators that achieve a goal. The training example demonstrates how a goal is achieved by a particular sequence of operators. It is possible that a different sequence of the same operators would work as well. The example's explanation explicitly specifies required dependency orderings among states and operators. The timing of some operators may be arbitrary; other operator sub-sequences may require a particular ordering but allow other sub-sequences to be interleaved, and so on. The general problem solving concept should allow for variations in operator orderings.

Mooney [1988] has specified an algorithm to perform temporal generalization for STRIPS-type operators. This can be quite an involved and expensive process. Things get much worse when considering a more general specification of operators. Non-instantaneous processes allow simultaneous and overlapping changes in the world (as is common in qualitative reasoning [Forbus, 1984; de Kleer, 1979; Kuipers, 1984]). Full temporal generalization under such real-world conditions is not completely understood. One possibility might be to deny the apparently special status of "time." Time might be represented explicitly as one more aspect of the domain model (e.g., [Allen, 1983; Dean, 1983]). Then temporal generalization might be adequately subsumed by the other EBL generalization types.

As with disjunctive augmentation, discovering all possible temporal orderings is not necessary. Any temporal variability aids in the generality of the
concept.

Number Generalization *Number generalization* refers to the recognition
that a particular sub-explanation can be replicated. For example, suppose we
wish to teach a system, which knows about immediate support and stability,
how to build a tower of blocks. A training example is given in which three red
blocks are stacked. With the generalization types described so far, the resulting
concept will be limited to building three-block towers. The system will recognize that the particular blocks used in the example are not required, that the
blocks need not be the same color, etc. The system will realize the requirement
that the lower blocks be flat on top, that they be relatively incompressible, and
so on, as dictated by the domain knowledge and explanation. However, the
new concept will not apply to building towers with four blocks. Another training example of stacking four blocks will be required, and yet another for five
blocks, and so on. Clearly, this is inadequate. The system should itself realize
that the particular techniques for building three-block towers also apply to
stacking four or more blocks.

Number generalization is difficult because the parameter being generalized
(in our example, the number of blocks) is not explicitly represented anywhere
in the explanation. Rather the "threeness" of the tower is implicitly coded in
the topology of the explanation itself. There are three sub-explanations proving
the resulting stability after a block is grasped and moved. The three sub-explanations are not identical; the blocks are different, their initial and final locations are different, etc. Number generalization crucially involves a representation transformation of the explanation into a form in which "sets" or
"loops" are included in the theory's ontology. Several systems [Prieditis, 1986;
Shavlik, 1988; Cohen, 1987] have advanced directions to investigate number
generalization.

It is interesting to note that not all cases in which number generalization is
theoretically supportable should result in number-generalized concepts. Consider rotating the tires on an automobile. Even though the procedure readily
generalizes to automobiles with 5, 6, or 7 tires (and such automobiles are logically possible), there is no particular advantage in complicating the ROTATE-
TIRE problem solving concept to include them.

Formalisms for Explanation-based Learning

The first attempt at formalizing EBL is due to O'Rorke [1987]. He formalized
EBL as the posting and propagating of constraints through a network. The system that was implemented to demonstrate the formalism's feasibility, named

MA, required the assertion of retractable equality relations. This was performed by a McAllester-style TMS [McAllester, 1982]. Only a limited form of structural generalization was performed. While theoretically pleasing, the formalism proved too unwieldy to directly support implementations.

More recently there have been two major formalizations of the EBL generalization process. These are the *EBG* algorithm of Mitchell, Keller and Kedar-Cabelli [1986] and the *EGGS* algorithm of Mooney and Bennett [1986]. Both advance a domain-independent generalization process. They produce similar (perhaps identical) generalizations of an explanation. However, neither is a full solution to the problem of formalizing explanation-based learning.

We will first consider the EBG algorithm. Generalization is performed by *regressing* the goal concept through the example's explanation structure. Goal regression [Waldinger, 1977] of a formula through a rule computes the necessary and sufficient conditions under which the rule can be used to infer the formula. That is, for a given rule and a desired formula it yields the weakest constraints that must be met by the antecedents of the rule to insure that the consequent unifies with the desired formula. The goal regression of EBG is similar to the goal regression algorithm of Waldinger except for two important differences. First, the algorithm is expanded to regress a formula through explanations (proof structures) instead of single rules. Second, disjunctive possibilities are ignored; this is equivalent to representing only a sufficient condition for inferring the formula rather than necessary and sufficient conditions. In particular, the sufficient conditions chosen correspond to the example's explanation structure.

Extending goal regression to an explanation structure complicates the standard goal-regression algorithm. The simplest use of goal regression would be to start at the final consequent of the explanation. Since the explanation succeeded, this formula, which is the final consequent, must be an instance of the goal concept. Instead of the final consequent, the general (functional and non-operational) goal concept itself might be used as the formula to regress across the last inference rule. The resulting formula can then be regressed across the penultimate inference rule(s), and so on until the leaves of the explanation are reached.

There are two problems with the simple algorithm. First, once a rule is selected for a goal regression step, only the portion of the goal concept supported by the rest of the explanation should be regressed through the rule. Since the example's explanation itself may not support the full generality of the goal concept, regressing the general goal concept via strict back-propagation may result in weakest preconditions which are in fact too general. A second complication is due to the fact that explanations are tree structured. Tree structured explanations result from implication rules with conjunctive antecedents. An example of a conjunctive rule is the rule for inferring "liftable" in the cup domain theory of Figure 5. Goal regression is a local algorithm. The problem with tree structures is that mutually inconsistent constraints may be imposed on a variable by different sub-explanation branches.

The EBG solution is a two-stage propagation algorithm. First, forward propagation is done from the leaves up to the final consequent. This results in a general formula that is fully supported by the particular explanation structure. The resulting formula (which may be more specific than the original goal concept) is then back-propagated through the explanation structure to produce the weakest operational preconditions.

The other formalism for generalization is called EGGS (for Explanation Generalization using Global Substitutions). It requires that an explanation be made up of constituents (called *units*) and that units are connected by unifications. A domain theory of implication rules and propositions (as in Figure 5), fits this requirement: A unit is a proposition or implication that is connected into an explanation structure by unifying propositions and consequents with antecedents.

Some of the unifications in the explanation are specific to the example; others are required by the interaction of domain theory units. EGGS maintains separate *specific* and *general* unification binding lists. The specific list records all unifications in the explanation. The general list records only those unifications that are imposed among the domain theory units; no unifications to attributes of the particular example are made. Thus, the general list reflects the most general version of the explanation proof. Applying the general substitution list to the input goal concept yields the functional specification of the achievable goal concept—which, as discussed earlier, may be a specialization of the input goal concept. Applying the general substitution to the leaves of the explanation (excluding formulas representing features of the training instance), produces the weakest operational features required of an object to be an instance of the new concept.

In EGGS the order of unification is unimportant since the unification algorithm itself correctly propagates global effects of each unification. Furthermore, the general unification substitution list may be constructed simultaneously with the specific list while the explanation is constructed. Thus, the general concept may be available immediately upon explanation. This means that within-trial learning is possible; a new concept may be acquired as the result of the construction of a sub-explanation that may be useful in constructing another sub-explanation.

There are many similarities between the two algorithms. Both are reasonably efficient; both rely heavily on unification. Provided the domain model is cast in terms of first order predicate calculus implication rules so that goal regression is well defined, they appear to compute identical solutions. It has not yet been proved, but is strongly suspected, that the algorithms are, in a sense, notational variants. The difficulty in proving this is due to the very different way unification is used. EBG asserts more unifications than EGGS, but the EGGS unifications tend to be more complex. Order of unification is important for EBG but not for EGGS.

What the Formalisms Miss

Formalizing EBL is one of the great challenges for researchers in machine learning. The two formalisms of EBG and EGGS are excellent first steps, but they are only first steps; neither is close to a full answer. Both perform irrelevant feature elimination and identity elimination well, but their approaches to operationality pruning are unsatisfactory. Furthermore, neither even attempts disjunctive augmentation, temporal generalization, or number generalization.

To perform operationality pruning, both build on an incomplete characterization of *operationality*. Informally, a constituent of an explanation is operational if its achievability is easily judged. If it is easy to achieve, the precise method of achievement need not be selected until the time of achievement. No prior problem solving effort need be spent on its achievement. This is an appealing concept, but like so many other appealing concepts, it is not rigorously defined. While both formalisms drop the explanation's support of "operational" constituents, their methods for determining operationality are too narrow.

In EBG, operationality is determined by an *a priori* classification of *predicates*. EGGS does not commit itself to any particular method of judging operationality, but in practice, EGGS systems assign operationality on the basis of an *a priori* classification of *units*. In both cases, operationality is treated as a context-free notion; operationality is assigned to a unit without consideration for the relation of the unit to other units in the explanation, or to a predicate without consideration for its arguments. This works well for directly observable or static properties. Consider the predicates `Color` and `Isa` in a simple system. These can be classified as operational because the truth value of `Color(?X,?Y)` and `Isa(?X,?Y)` are always easy to determine regardless of what `?X` or `?Y` are bound to. For `Color`, the system looks at the object; for `Isa` it looks up the object in its memory. Unfortunately, most important predicates/units are not operational by this definition. Consider the predicate `Possess`. It is operational, in the informal sense, for some of its arguments but not all. The expected ease of determining the truth value depends crucially on what is being possessed and by whom. The possession of a driver's license may well be considered operational for adults and for grade school children; almost all adults have one and almost no grade school children have one. The formalisms of EBG and EGGS cannot take advantage of this very compelling generality. `Possess` is operational when the object is a driver's license, but only when person is not in the ambiguous high school years. As another example, consider the problem of determining the operationality of `Provable`. In particular, compare `Provable("2+2=4")` and `Provable("Fermat's last theorem")`. Suppose the first expression arises in a concept that somehow needs the number '4', which is achieved in the training instance as the sum of 2 and 2. Even though the proof is trivial, given a few easy axioms about addition, it cannot be judged as *operational* by EBG or EGGS because with another argument (Fermat's last theorem) its truth value is not easy to determine. It does not help that we are guaranteed that such difficult arguments will not show up when attempting to additively produce 4 from two integers. The expanded proof must remain as part of the concept definition, explicitly deriving 4 from 2+2 and not from 3+1 or –6+10, etc.

Neither EGGS nor EBG attempts to formalize any form of structural generalization (disjunctive augmentation, temporal generalization, or number generalization).

The History of EBL

The roots of EBL can be traced back a long way, at least long as judged by AI standards. There is some question whether Waterman's poker player system [Waterman, 1970] should be included. It had three learning methods. One, which he called *analytic* can be viewed as explanation-based. Unfortunately, it was the least successful of the three, and probably cost more than it benefited the system.

The first truly explanation-based research is the MACROPS learning work done in the STRIPS system [Fikes and Nilsson, 1971]. It worked in a simple robot world and stored generalized versions of successful plans. The resulting general problem solving concept was stored in an interesting data structure called a Triangle Table. The Triangle Table specified all of the preconditions that needed to be tested in the current world state to insure that an entire sequence of actions would succeed.

In an historical context, it was a very impressive system. It included a notion of *operationality* by transforming all the preconditions of a plan's component operators into a form directly testable in one of a set of possible initial states. It also introduced as a central concept the notion of *chunked knowledge structures.* This notion was to be reinvented several years later as *frames, scripts,* and *schemata* [Chafe, 1975; Minsky, 1975, Schank and Abelson, 1977]. Automatic acquisition of chunked knowledge structures would not re-emerge for even longer [Rosenbloom, 1983; DeJong, 1981; Mitchell, Keller and Kedar-Cabelli, 1986].

Lest we find ourselves too enraptured we should examine a few shortcomings of the research. While clearly ahead of its time, it also had many faults. It only performed identity elimination generalization; it did no operationality pruning or structural generalization. The overall system behaved as if it could perform irrelevant feature elimination, but this generalization was not reflected in the Triangle Table data structure. Rather, a clever indexing hack (of questionable efficiency) allowed the system to skip over irrelevant operators at execution time. Additionally, the domain was so simple as to preclude addressing many important issues. Only a handful of simple operators were allowed. Finally, the research was never formalized. It is important to realize that to formalize research one need not adopt any particular language or representation scheme. Indeed, STRIPS and MACROPS were deeply and effectively committed to predicate calculus. But this is not enough. To formalize research means to separate the science of the model from the implementation of the system. Theoretical claims must be clear and explicit and not tied up with irrelevant programming details. This was never achieved or, indeed, attempted for MACROPS.

The next system of interest is Sussman's HACKER [Sussman, 1973]. HACKER learned to improve its planning skills in a simple blocks world domain. One of its forms of learning was explanation-based in nature and called the *subroutinization process*. It relied on a trace of the execution of the patched program kept by a simulator. The trace served the role of an explanation during generalization. Generalization consisted of variablizing constants while taking any dependencies into account.

Eliot Soloway's baseball system [Soloway, 1978] induced many of the rules of baseball from conceptual representations of players' action. The system was primarily similarity-based but had a strong explanation-based component. The program was given initial background knowledge about competition and games in general. This formed the system's domain theory. Input game sequences were embellished and interpreted using the background knowledge. The result was then generalized, also using the background knowledge, to form hypotheses for the underlying rules of the game. Other game sequences were then examined to confirm the generalizations.

Mostow devised a model which also made use of background knowledge [Mostow, 1981]. The system worked in the domain of the card game "hearts." Not one for half-way measures, Jack did away with the training examples altogether. The system operationalized advice without necessarily seeing any instances of the concept. A teacher provided good but non-operational advice such as "avoid taking points." The system then "operationalized" this advice into usable rules like "don't lead with high cards."

Finally, there were the first EBL systems of the modern era: Mitchell's LEX2 [Mitchell, Utgoff and Banerji, 1983b], Bernard Silver's LP [Silver, 1984], and my own work in acquiring schemata for natural language processing [Dejong, 1981]. Independently, all three researchers hit upon the idea of substituting a knowledge-based examination of a single instance for the large or carefully tailored training sets needed by other machine learning systems (e.g., [Michalski, Mozetic, Hong and Lavrac, 1986a; Quinlan, 1986; Mitchell, Utgoff and Banerji, 1983b; Winston, 1975]. The exciting discovery of each other's work occurred at the 1983 International Machine Learning Workshop. These three systems were only tentative first steps. My work was ad hoc. In LEX2 Mitchell did not realize the advantage of forming or generalizing new knowledge-chunked concepts, and Silver's LP often queried the user to input the correct generalization directly. But basically, we were on the right track.

Since then there has been an explosion of explanation-based learning research. As can be seen in Figure 11, there are significantly more EBL systems every year.

WHEN	WHAT	WHO	WHERE
1970	POKER	Waterman	Stanford
1972	STRIPS/ MACROPS	Fikes et al	SRI
1973	HACKER	Sussman	MIT
1978	BASEBALL*	Soloway	University of Massachusetts/ Amherst
1981	KIDNAP*	DeJong	University of Illinois/Urbana
1982	CRITTER	Kelly & Steinberg	Rutgers
	LEX2	Mitchell	Rutgers
1983	ANALOGY	Winston	MIT
	CLAUDAGGY*	O'Rorke	University of Illinois/Urbana
	HANDICAPPER	Salzberg	Yale
	LP	Silver	University of Edinburgh
1984	GAMES*	Minton	Carnegie Mellon University
	MA	O'Rorke	University of Illinois/Urbana
	PET	Porter & Kibler	University of California/ Irvine
1985	ADEPT	Rajamoney	University of Illinois/Urbana
	ARMS	Segre	University of Illinois/Urbana
	CHEF	Hammond	Yale
	GENESIS	Mooney	University of Illinois/Urbana
	LEAP	Mitchell et al	Rutgers
	OCCAM	Pazzani	University of California/ Los Angles
	PDA	Kedar-Cabelli	Rutgers
	PHYSICS-101	Shavlik	University of Illinois/Urbana
	SHIFT*	Ellman	Columbia
1986	ACES	Pazzani	The Aerospace Corporation
	CONSTELLATION	Lathrop & Kirk	MIT/Gould
	EBG	Mitchell et al	Rutgers
	EBL-LT*	O'Rorke	University of Illinois/Urbana
	EBL-SOAR	Rosenbloom & Laird	Xerox PARC/Stanford
	EGGS	Mooney & Bennett	University of Illinois/Urbana
	FERMI	Cheng & Carbonell	Carnegie Mellon University
	MORRIS	Minton	Carnegie Mellon University
	RE-ANALYZE*	Hall	MIT
	REFINE*	Doyle	MIT
	UNIMEM	Lebowitz	Columbia
	WYL	Flann & Dietterich	Oregon State University

* Denotes invented names for un-named systems. For hybrid systms, year indicates when an EBL component was first reported.

Figure 11 Explanation-based learning systems.

Continuing Research Issues

There are some important areas for future EBL research. In this section we list and briefly discuss a few.

The whole notion of operationality is a cloudy one. It is clearly a central concept for EBL but, in general, operationality judgements would seem to be context sensitive. A particular generalized structure (say a plan) may be operational in one state of the world but not in another. This is a strong statement that is possibly surprising and probably unfortunate. Note that "operationality" is quite different than "applicability." Obviously, a plan may be applicable in some world states but not others. Operationality is a bit more abstract. A concept is operational if, given a world state, the applicability judgment of that concept is easy. If we persist in our current notion of operationality (which is unquestionably sensitive to the state of the world), and if EBL continues to define the border of a new concept based on operationality, then it follows that the concept's definition changes in different world states. This is odd, at best.

Formalization is another area in need of work. There is an interesting obstacle to formalizing structural generalization. To formalize a model means to separate the theoretical claims from its incidental details. Ideally, we want a "structural generalization" module into which we may plug domain theories. Then to implement an EBL system in a new domain, we need only supply the domain. The rest of the system remains unchanged. The easy road to formalization is to provide a domain-free specification. Sadly, this is not possible for structural generalization. Structural generalization depends on aspects of the domain itself. This is not to say that a domain-*independent* specification is impossible, however. It only means that the generalization algorithm must know crucial characteristics of the domain, and that the domain implementation must follow this discipline so that relevant domain characteristics are coded explicitly. Part of the formalization of structural generalization is to provide a taxonomy of domain characteristics upon which generalizations depend. Thus, formalizing structural generalization requires a fair amount of progress in knowledge representation.

EBL does not pretend to be a complete answer to the problem of machine learning. Much work remains to be done on combining EBL ideas with ideas from other learning paradigms such as similarity-based learning [Quinlan, 1986; Stepp and Michalski, 1986], empirical learning [Langley, Bradshaw and Simon, 1981a; Rose and Langley, 1986], analogy [Falkenhainer, Forbus and Gentner, 1986; Gentner, 1983; Anderson and Thompson, 1987a; Carbonell, 1985], and connectionism [Rumelhart, Hinton and Williams, 1986; Hinton and Sejnowski, 1986; Anderson, 1987b]. Hybrid systems can range from applying EBL ideas in other areas (e.g., Kedar-Cabelli's work on EBL and analogy [Kedar-Cabelli, 1985]), to constructing unified learning systems composed of identifiable modules (e.g., Kodratoff's DISCIPLE system [Kodratoff and Tecuci, 1987]).

Of particular importance is combining EBL and SBL. There has been some work in this area already [Pazzani, 1985; Pazzani, Dyer and Flowers, 1987; Lebowitz, 1986; Flann and Dietterich, 1986; Danyluk, 1987]. There are two obvious combinations. EBL can be done first, followed by SBL, or they can be reversed. Interestingly, they both make sense. Using EBL first allows it to perform the task of feature selection. Feature selection is a notoriously difficult problem for SBL. Another way of looking at the arrangement with EBL first is that SBL then performs its induction in a kind of "explanation" space instead of the original feature space. Using SBL first can greatly focus the job of constructing an explanation. It is useful in domains where the domain theory is uncertain, where explanations are difficult to construct, or where many spurious EBL concepts may be constructed. SBL first detects significant patterns in the examples; EBL is then only run on these SBL-filtered candidates. Other more integrated approaches may be even more productive.

Are there other less obvious future directions for EBL research? Yes, of course. My favorite way to find them is to pick a real-world domain and pose the question: "Why won't current EBL solutions work here?" Most often, EBL will not work, and analyzing why yields large inadequacies in the current research.

Consider again our prehistoric friend acquiring the skewer concept. He could not have constructed an air-tight proof of why Zog's skewer worked. To begin with, he has only a mediocre theory for combustion and radiant energy. The caloric theory of heat, so central to explaining why cooking works, will not surface for thousands of years. His "explanation" is very different from a logical proof. His first attempt at building his own skewer may well fail. The stick may be too short or too dry. Does this mean he should give up, that Zog's solution is somehow unavailable to him? Certainly not. He must be able to analyze the failure and refine his skewer concept accordingly. The notion of concept refinement must play a large part in almost all real-world domains. It is unrealistic to expect a computer system to get things right the first time, since people seldom do. Such behavior is beyond any formalization of EBL, although there has been some initial work in this direction [Hammond, 1987; Chien, 1987; Bennett, 1987].

This is just one view of the *ugly domain* problem: Domains are characterized by theories that are necessarily incomplete, incorrect, or inconsistent. Most real-world domains cannot be captured by clean, first-order rules. Furthermore, humans work incredibly well with incomplete, incorrect, and inconsistent views of the world. This is probably a strength and not a failing. A quantum physicist does not consider the Schrödinger wave of his cup when pouring coffee. Even though he has a more accurate formalism than the rest of us, he chooses (correctly) not to use it. Furthermore, most interesting domains that support clean formalizations (like chess, go, or robotics kinematics and dynamics) are intractable. In principle everything can be solved in these domains, but in reality anything worth doing is too complex to achieve. Humans often deal with such complexity by introducing fuzzy terms like "weak queen side" and "exposed king," thus transforming an intractable domain into an incomplete or inconsistent one.

The notion of an *explanation* must be broadened to include much more than just proofs in first order predicate calculus. Almost all real-world problems involve gradual changes that persist over time. Furthermore, it is seldom possible to specify all of an operator's preconditions or effects. Operators are never instantaneous. World situations are never fully known. Actions may overlap. A single agent assumption is seldom tenable, and even simple objects defy definition. Philosophers have long wrestled with the problem of defining everyday concepts such as "chair" and "game."

Richer formalisms (such as those offered by qualitative reasoning [Forbus, 1984; de Kleer, 1979; Kuipers, 1984], must be examined. Formalizing EBL in these contexts will be far more difficult than in the idealized paradigms of situational calculus or STRIPS-type operators.

Extending the domain theory is another important avenue of future research. This is another facet of the incomplete/incorrect theory problem. EBL is very sensitive to the particular domain rules used in an explanation. The initial implementer of an EBL system cannot correctly anticipate all of the concepts that the system will learn. Yet without this knowledge, he cannot be certain that his domain theory will adequately support the acquisition of all the desired concepts. The system must itself detect and remedy inadequacies in its domain theory. There has been some important initial EBL work on this topic [Rajamoney, 1986]. Additionally, a unified system might be able to apply some of the current SBL, empirical, or discovery (e.g., [Lenat, 1983]) techniques to the problem of refining its domain theory.

More work must be done on determining when an EBL generalization should be made. The current formalisms begin to address "how" a generalization can be performed, but have nothing to say about whether overall system performance will improve or degenerate from the learning experience. Minton [1985] has pointed out the problem of unconstrained acquisition of concepts. System performance can be degraded by spending inordinate amounts of time evaluating complex applicability tests of irrelevant concepts. The obvious solutions are to be selective in learning concepts and to simplify the applicability tests. Segre [1987] has proposed that concepts only be retained if they satisfy a learning criterion. In particular, his system generalizes and retains only that portion of a new experience that includes the explanation of subgoals interacting in a novel way. One of the interesting methods of simplifying applicability tests for new concepts has been proposed by Keller [1987]. He suggests retaining a set of test problems for each concept. The test problems are best if they are representative of the problems the system will face. Applicability conditions (and concepts themselves) are syntactically simplified while monitoring performance on the test sets. Simplification is performed until a concept satisfies some externally imposed criteria of speed and accuracy on its test set.

Finally, there is work to be done on a cognitive science front. The classical approach to concept acquisition in psychology involves only artificial concepts. For example, cards, each with two or three geometrical objects of different colors, are presented to the subject. A concept is fabricated by the experimenter to describe some but not all cards. For example, "a star or a circle of any color along with any other blue shape." The subject has "learned" the concept when he can classify the cards correctly. Isolating the study of concept formation from any intrusion of a subject's background knowledge was originally seen as an advantage. However, in recent years psychologists have questioned these semantic-free paradigms as ecologically unsound [Murphy and Medin, 1985]. There is some evidence that EBL is psychologically valid [Ahn, Mooney, Brewer and DeJong, 1987]. Furthermore, the SOAR system [Laird, Rosenbloom and Newell, 1986], which has a strong EBL flavor, is primarily motivated by psychological considerations.

Conclusions

Where might EBL systems be used? The one obvious and compelling application is in "expert" systems. A major obstacle in the road to more competent expert systems is the problem faced by the knowledge engineer of extracting information from the task expert. The expert is quite capable of superior performance of the task but cannot accurately introspect on his own algorithmic rules. This has been termed the knowledge-acquisition bottleneck, and it causes endless trouble and expense to the knowledge engineer. EBL might be used to observe the experts problem solving thus eliminating the need for the expert's inaccurate introspections. Interestingly, EBL does not require any special behavior of the expert. To return to the prehistoric skewer for a moment, the EBL Neanderthal acquires the new concept through non-intrusive observation of the Cro-Magnon expert. Zog is not required to verbalize about his invention or help the Neanderthal's explanation process or even provide any hints about the representational features for the new concept. He simply carries on with his own unimpeded problem solving behavior while the Neanderthal watches. EBL, therefore, may offer a solution to the knowledge-acquisition bottleneck faced by expert systems.

Since EBL involves reasoning from the specific to the general it is a form of induction, but it also has a strong deductive flavor. The deductive component is from the application of a system's background knowledge or domain theory. Creating explanations can be viewed as problem solving or theorem proving.

Reliance on background knowledge restricts the EBL approach to domains in which such knowledge exists. Without a theory of the domain, explanations are not possible, nor is explanation-based generalization.

EBL is not an alternative to SBL. Rather the two are complementary, each possessing strengths and weaknesses. SBL approaches can learn in areas where EBL cannot (e.g., where little background knowledge exists). Conversely, EBL is not hamstrung by the feature selection problem in rich spaces that forces SBL systems to adopt strong learning biases [Utgoff, 1986].

Initially, EBL may appear not to support knowledge-level learning. *Knowledge level* is a term coined by Newell [1981] and formalized by Dietterich [1986] referring to the deductive closure of the knowledge in an AI system. Since explanations are constructed from the system's original domain theory and since the generalization process is guided by the domain theory, it would seem that any EBL-acquired concept must already be implicitly contained in the domain theory, albeit in an intractable and unusable form. Thus, there is no change at the knowledge level, and hence no learning at the knowledge level. This is true if applied to the narrow EBL formulations of EGGS and EBG. However, it does not apply to broader formulations. In particular, the ADEPT system of Rajamoney [1986] is designed to alter the components of its domain theory. The work on approximations [Bennett, 1987] also yields a system that changes at the knowledge level. Finally, Dietterich's system defines the knowledge level in terms of first-order inference closure on monotonic theories. It is not clear what the knowledge-level learning claims have to say about non-monotonic systems (e.g., [Chien, 1987; Hirsch, 1987]).

EBL is a burgeoning research area. Every new AI conference brings exciting advances. EBL has attracted some of the very finest young AI Ph.Ds, but it cries out for more. Research to date has only scratched the surface, and in this limited space we have only sampled the surface scratches of existing research. Explanation-based learning is an exciting, fresh, and promising new approach in machine learning. I believe it will play an increasingly important role both in AI research and in AI applications systems. Of course, my own view is somewhat biased, but I hope that some of my excitement has been captured here.

Acknowledgments

I wish to thank the members of the Illinois Explanation-based Learning Group and the Office of Naval Research for support under grant N-00014-86-K0309.

References

Ahn, W., R. J. Mooney, W. F. Brewer and G. F. DeJong. 1987. Schema Acquisition from One Example: Psychological Evidence for Explanation-based Learning. *Proceedings of the Ninth Annual Conference of the Cognitive Science Society*. Seattle, WA. pp. 50–57. Also appears as Technical Report UILU-ENG-87-2231, Coordinated Science Laboratory, University of Illinois at Urbana-Champaign.

Allen, J. F. 1983. Maintaining Knowledge about Temporal Intervals. *Communications of the Association for Computing Machinery* **26**(11):832–843.

Anderson J. R. and R. Thompson. 1987a. Use of Analogy in a Production System Architecture. In *Similarity and Analogical Reasoning* S. Vosniadou and A. Ortony, ed. Cambridge University Press, Cambridge, England.

Anderson, C. W. 1987b. Strategy Learning with Multilayer Connectionist Representations. *Proceedings of the 1987 International Machine Learning Workshop*, Irvine, CA. pp. 103–114.

Bennett, S. W. 1987. Approximation in Mathematical Domains. *Proceedings of the Tenth International Joint Conference on Artificial Intelligence*. Milan, Italy, pp. 239–241. Also appears as Technical Report UILU-ENG-87-2238, AI Research Group, Coordinated Science Laboratory, University of Illinois at Urbana-Champaign.

Carbonell, J. G. 1985. Derivational Analogy: A Theory of Reconstructive Problem Solving and Expertise Acquisition. Submitted paper. Department of Computer Science, Carnegie-Mellon University, Pittsburgh, PA.

Chafe, W. 1975. Some Thoughts on Schemata. *Theoretical Issues in Natural Language Processing* **1**:89–91.

Chapman, D. 1987. Planning for Conjunctive Goals. *Artificial Intelligence* **32**(3):333–378.

Charniak, E. 1977. MS. MALAPROP, A Language Comprehension System. *Proceedings of the Fifth International Joint Conference on Artificial Intelligence*. Cambridge, MA.

Chien, S. A. 1987. *Simplifications in Temporal Persistence: An Approach to the Intractable Domain Theory Problem in Explanation-based Learning*. M.S. Thesis, Department of Computer Science, University of Illinois, Urbana, IL. Also appears as UILU-ENG-87-2255. AI Research Group, Coordinated Science Laboratory, University of Illinois at Urbana-Champaign.

Cohen, W. W. 1987. *A Technique for Generalizing Number in Explanation-based Learning*. ML-TR-19, Department of Computer Science, Rutgers University, New Brunswick, NJ.

Danyluk, A. P. 1987. The Use of Explanations for Similarity-based Learning. *Proceedings of the Tenth International Joint Conference on Artificial Intelligence*. Milan, Italy. pp. 274–276.

DeJong, G. F. 1981. Generalizations Based on Explanations. *Proceedings of the Seventh International Joint Conference on Artificial Intelligence.* Vancouver, B.C., Canada. pp. 67–70. Also appears as Working Paper 30, AI Research Group, Coordinated Science Laboratory, University of Illinois at Urbana-Champaign.

DeJong, G. F. and R. J. Mooney. 1986a. Explanation-based Learning: An Alternative View. *Machine Learning* 1(2):145–176. Also appears as Technical Report UILU-ENG-86-2208. AI Research Group, Coordinated Science Laboratory, University of Illinois at Urbana-Champaign.

DeJong, G. 1986b. An Approach to Learning from Observation. In *Machine Learning: An Artificial Intelligence Approach, Vol. II.* R. S. Michalski, J. G. Carbonell and T. M. Mitchell, ed. Morgan Kaufmann, San Mateo, CA. pp. 571–590.

de Kleer, J. 1979. *Causal and Teleological Reasoning in Circuit Recognition* Technical Report 529, Ph.D. Thesis, MIT AI Lab, Cambridge, MA.

Dean, T. 1983. *Time Map Maintenance.* Technical Report 289, Yale University, New Haven, CT.

Dietterich, T. G. 1986. Learning at the Knowledge Level. *Machine Learning* 1(3):287–316.

Falkenhainer, B., K. Forbus and D. Gentner. 1986. The Structure-Mapping Engine. *Proceedings of the National Conference on Artificial Intelligence.* Philadelphia, PA pp. 272–277.

Fikes, R. E. and N. J. Nilsson. 1971. STRIPS: A New Approach to the Application of Theorem Proving to Problem Solving. *Artificial Intelligence* 2(3/4):189–208.

Fikes, R. E., P. E. Hart and N. J. Nilsson. 1972. Learning and Executing Generalized Robot Plans. *Artificial Intelligence* 3(4):251–288.

Flann, N. S. and T. G. Dietterich. 1986. Selecting Appropriate Representations for Learning from Examples. *Proceedings of the National Conference on Artificial Intelligence.* Philadelphia. PA. pp. 460–466.

Forbus, K. D. 1984. Qualitative Process Theory. *Artificial Intelligence* 24:85–168.

Gentner, D. 1983. Structure-Mapping: A Theoretical Framework for Analogy. *Cognitive Science* 7:155–170.

Hammond, K. J. 1987. Learning and Reusing Explanations. *Proceedings of the 1987 International Machine Learning Workshop.* Irvine, CA. pp. 141–147.

Hinton, G. E. and T. J. Sejnowski. 1986. Learning and Relearning in Boltzmann Machines. In *Parallel Distributed Processing. Vol. I* D. E. Rumelhart and J. L. McClelland, ed. MIT Press, Cambridge, MA. pp. 282–317.

Hirsch, H. 1987. Explanation-based Generalization in a Logic-Programming Environment. *Proceedings of the Tenth International Joint Conference on Artificial Intelligence.* Milan, Italy. pp. 221–227.

Kedar-Cabelli, S. 1985. Purpose-Directed Analogy. *Proceedings of the Seventh Annual Conference of the Cognitive Science Society.* Irvine, CA. pp. 150–159.

Keller, R. M. 1987. *The Role of Explicit Contextual Knowledge in Learning Concepts to Improve Performance.* Ph.D. Thesis. Department of Computer Science, Rutgers University, New Brunswick. Also appears as Machine Learning Technical Report #7, Laboratory for Computer Science Research, Rutgers University.

Kodratoff, Y. and G. Tecuci. 1987. Disciple-1: Interactive Apprentice System in Weak Theory Fields. *Proceedings of the Tenth International Joint Conference on Artificial Intelligence.* Milan, Italy. pp. 271–273.

Kolodner, J. L. 1987. Extending Problem Solver Capabilities Through Case-based Inference. *Proceedings of the 1987 International Machine Learning Workshop.* Irvine, CA. pp. 167–178.

Kuipers, B. 1984. Commonsense Reasoning About Causality: Deriving Behavior from Structure. *Artificial Intelligence* **24**:169–204.

Laird, J., P. Rosenbloom and A. Newell. 1986. Chunking in Soar: The Anatomy of a General Learning Mechanism. *Machine Learning* **1**(1):11–46.

Langley, P., G. L. Bradshaw and H. A. Simon. 1981a. BACON.5: The Discovery of Conservation Laws. *Proceedings of the Seventh International Joint Conference on Artificial Intelligence.* Vancouver, B.C., Canada. pp. 121–126.

Langley, P. 1981b. Data-Driven Discovery of Physical Laws. *Cognitive Science* **5**(1):31–54.

Lebowitz, M. 1980. *Generalization and Memory in an Integrated Understanding System.* Technical Report 186, Ph.D Thesis. Department of Computer Science, Yale University, New Haven, CT.

Lebowitz, M. 1986. Integrated Learning: Controlling Explanation. *Cognitive Science* **10**(2):219–240.

Lenat, D. B. 1983. The Role of Heuristics in Learning by Discovery: Three Case Studies. In *Machine Learning: An Artificial Intelligence Approach.* R. S. Michalski, J. G. Carbonell and T. M. Mitchell ed. Morgan Kaufmann Publishers. San Mateo, CA. pp. 243–306.

McAllester, D. A. 1982. *Reasoning Utility Package User's Manual, Version One, Memo 667.* MIT AI Lab, Cambridge, MA.

Medin, D. L., W. D. Wattenmaker and R. S. Michalski. 1987. Constraints and Preferences in Inductive Learning: An Experimental Study of Human and Machine Performance. *Cognitive Science* **11**(3):299–239.

Michalski, R. S. 1983. A Theory and Methodology of Inductive Learning. In *Machine Learning: An Artificial Intelligence Approach.* R. S. Michalski, J. G. Carbonell, T. M. Mitchell ed. Morgan Kaufmann Publishers. San Mateo, CA. pp. 83–134.

Michalski, R. S., I. Mozetic, J. Hong and N. Lavrac. 1986a. The Multi-Purpose Incremental Learning System AQ15 and its Testing Application in Three Medical Domains. *Proceedings of the National Conference on Artificial Intelligence*. Philadelphia, PA. pp. 1041–1047.

Michalski. R. S., I. Mozetic, J. Hong and N. Lavrac. 1986b. The AQ15 Inductive Learning System: An Overview and Experiments. *Proceedings of the International Meeting on Advances in Learning*. Les Arcs, Switzerland

Minsky, M. L. 1975. A Framework for Representing Knowledge. In *The Psychology of Computer Vision*. P. H. Winston ed. McGraw-Hill, New York, NY. pp. 211–277.

Minton, S. N. 1985. Selectively Generalizing Plans for Problem-Solving. *Proceedings of the Ninth International Joint Conference on Artificial Intelligence*. Los Angeles, CA. pp. 596–599.

Mitchell, T. 1983a. Learning and Problem Solving. *Proceedings of the Eighth International Joint Conference on Artificial Intelligence*. Karlsruhe, West Germany. pp. 1139–1151.

Mitchell, T. M., P. E. Utgoff and R. Banerji. 1983b. Learning by Experimentation: Acquiring and Refining Problem-solving Heuristics. In *Machine Learning: An Artificial Intelligence Approach*. R. S. Michalski, J. G. Carbonell, T. M. Mitchell, ed. Morgan Kaufmann Publishers. San Mateo, CA. pp. 163–190.

Mitchell, T. M., S. Mahadevan and L. I. Steinberg. 1985. LEAP: A Learning Apprentice for VLSI Design. *Proceedings of the Ninth International Joint Conference on Artificial Intelligence*. Los Angeles, CA. pp. 573–580.

Mitchell, T. M., R. Keller and S. Kedar-Cabelli. 1986. Explanation-based Generalization: A Unifying View. *Machine Learning* 1(1):47–80.

Mooney, R. J. and S. W. Bennett. 1986. A Domain Independent Explanation-based Generalizer. *Proceedings of the National Conference on Artificial Intelligence*. Philadelphia, PA. pp. 551–555. Also appears as Technical Report UILU-ENG-86-2216, AI Research Group. Coordinated Science Laboratory, University of Illinois at Urbana-Champaign.

Mooney, R. J. 1988. *A General Explanation-based Learning Mechanism and its Application to Narrative Understanding*. Ph.D. Thesis, Department of Computer Science, University of Illinois. Urbana, IL. Also appears as UILU-ENG-87-2269, AI Research Group, Coordinated Science Laboratory, University of Illinois at Urbana-Champaign.

Mostow, J. 1981. *Mechanical Transformation of Task Heuristics into Operational Procedures*. Ph.D. Thesis, Department of Computer Science, Carnegie-Mellon University, Pittsburgh, PA.

Mostow, D. J. 1983. Machine Transformation of Advice into a Heuristic Search Procedure. In *Machine Learning: An Artificial Intelligence Approach*. R. S. Michalski, J. G. Carbonell, T. M. Mitchell, ed., Morgan Kaufmann Publishers. San Mateo, CA. pp. 367–404.

Murphy, G. L. and D. L. Medin. 1985. The Role of Theories in Conceptual Coherence. *Psychological Review* **92**(3):289–316.

Newell, A. 1981. The Knowledge Level. *Artificial Intelligence Magazine* **2**:1–20.

Nilsson, N. J. 1980. *Principles of Artificial Intelligence.* Morgan Kaufmann Publishers. San Mateo, CA.

O'Rorke, P. V. 1987. *Explanation-based Learning Via Constraint Posting and Propagation.* Ph.D. Thesis, Department of Computer Science, University of Illinois, Urbana, IL. Also appears as UILU-ENG-87-2239, AI Research Group, Coordinated Science Laboratory, University of Illinois at Urbana-Champaign.

Pazzani, M. J. 1985. Explanation and Generalization Based Memory. *Proceedings of the Seventh Annual Conference of the Cognitive Science Society.* Irvine, CA. pp. 323–328.

Pazzani, M., M. Dyer and M. Flowers. 1987. Using Prior Learning to Facilitate the Learning of New Causal Theories. *Proceedings of the Tenth International Joint Conference on Artificial Intelligence.* Milan, Italy. pp. 277–279.

Prieditis, A. E. 1986. Discovery of Algorithms from Weak Methods. *Proceedings of the International Meeting on Advances in Learning.* Les Arcs, Switzerland. pp. 37–52.

Quinlan, J. R. 1986. Induction of Decision Trees. *Machine Learning* **1**(1):81–106.

Rajamoney, S. A. 1986. *Automated Design of Experiments for Refining Theories.* M.S. Thesis, Department of Computer Science. University of Illinois, Urbana, IL. Also appears as Technical Report UILU-ENG-86-2213, AI Research Group, Coordinated Science Laboratory. University of Illinois at Urbana-Champaign.

Rendell, L. 1983. A New Basis for State-Space Learning Systems and a Successful Implementation. *Artificial Intelligence* **20**(4):203–226.

Rendell, L. 1985. Substantial Constructive Induction using Layered Information Compression: Tractable Feature Formation in Search. *Proceedings of the Ninth International Joint Conference on Artificial Intelligence.* Los Angeles, CA. pp. 650–658.

Rose, D. and P. Langley. 1986. STAHL: Belief Revision in Scientific Discovery. *Proceedings of the National Conference on Artificial Intelligence,* Philadelphia, PA. pp. 528–532.

Rosenbloom, P. S. 1983. *The Chunking of Goal Hierarchies: A Model of Practice and Stimulus-Response Compatibility.* Ph.D. Thesis, Department of Computer Science, Carnegie-Mellon University, Pittsburgh, PA.

Rumelhart, D. E., G. E. Hinton and J. R. Williams. 1986. Learning Internal Representations by Error Propagation. In *Parallel Distributed Processing.*

Vol. 1. D. E. Rumelhart and J. L. McClelland, ed. MIT Press, Cambridge, MA. pp. 318–362.

Schank, R. C. and R. P. Abelson. 1977. *Scripts, Plans, Goals and Understanding: An Inquiry into Human Knowledge Structures.* Lawrence Erlbaum and Associates, Hillsdale, NJ.

Schank, R. C. 1982. *Dynamic Memory.* Cambridge University Press, Cambridge, England.

Schank, R. C. 1986. *Explanation Patterns: Understanding Mechanically and Creatively.* Lawrence Erlbaum and Associates, Hillsdale, NJ.

Segre, A. M. 1987. *Explanation-based Learning of Generalized Robot Assembly Tasks.* Ph.D. Thesis, Department of Electrical and Computer Engineering, University of Illinois, Urbana, IL. Also appears as UILU-ENG-87-2208, AI Research Group, Coordinated Science Laboratory, University of Illinois at Urbana-Champaign.

Shavlik, J. W. 1988. *Generalizing the Structure of Explanations in Explanation-based Learning.* Ph.D. Thesis, Department of Computer Science, University of Illinois, Urbana, IL. Also appears as UILU-ENG-87-2276, AI Research Group, Coordinated Science Laboratory, University of Illinois at Urbana-Champaign.

Silver, B. 1984. *Using Meta-level Inference to Constrain Search and to Learn Strategies in Equation Solving.* Ph.D. Thesis. Department of Artificial Intelligence, University of Edinburgh.

Soloway, E. 1978. *Learning = Interpretation + Generalization: A Case Study in Knowledge-Directed Learning.* Ph.D. Thesis, University of Massachusetts, Amherst, MA. Also appears as COINS Technical Report 78–13.

Stepp, R. E. and R. S. Michalski. 1986. Conceptual Clustering: Inventing Goal-Oriented Classifications of Structured Objects. In *Machine Learning: An Artificial Intelligence Approach, Vol. II.* R. S. Michalski, J. G. Carbonell and T. M. Mitchell, ed. Morgan Kaufmann, San Mateo, CA. pp. 471–498.

Sussman, G. J. 1973. *A Computational Model of Skill Acquisition.* Technical Report 297, MIT AI Lab, Cambridge, MA.

Utgoff, P. E. 1986. Shift of Bias for Inductive Concept Learning. In *Machine Learning: An Artificial Intelligence Approach, Vol. II.* R. S. Michalski, J. G. Carbonell and T. M. Mitchell, ed. Morgan Kaufmann, San Mateo, CA. pp. 107–148.

Waldinger, R. 1977. Achieving Several Goals Simultaneously. In *Machine Intelligence 8.* E. Elcock and D. Michie, ed. Ellis Horwood Limited, London.

Waterman, D. A. 1970. Generalization Learning Techniques for Automating the Learning of Heuristics. *Artificial Intelligence* 1(2):121–170.

Wilensky, R. W. 1978. *Understanding Goal-based Stories.* Technical Report 140, Ph.D. Thesis, Department of Computer Science, Yale University, New Haven, CT.

Winston, P. H. 1975. Learning Structural Descriptions from Examples. In *The Psychology of Computer Vision*. P. H. Winston, ed. McGraw-Hill, New York, NY. pp. 157–210.

Winston, P. H., T. O. Binford, B. Katz and M. Lowry. 1983. Learning Physical Descriptions from Functional Definitions, Examples, and Precedents. *Proceedings of the National Conference on Artificial Intelligence*. Washington, D.C. pp. 433–439.

II

INTERACTING THROUGH LANGUAGE

3

Knowledge-based Natural Language Understanding

Wendy G. Lehnert

Department of Computer and Information Science
University of Massachusetts
Amherst, Massachusetts

1 *Introduction*

This overview is organized within an historical framework, although time limitations have forced me to invent a version of history that is necessarily incomplete. The title of the talk was given to me by the AAAI Program Committee, which wisely restricted the scope of my task by including the descriptor "knowledge-based." This mercifully allowed me to ignore a large body of work that focuses exclusively on the syntactic structures of natural language. Even so, the body of work that can accurately be described as "knowledge-based natural language understanding" is large, and difficult to cover in the space available. To maintain continuity, I have utilized the recurring theme of weak methods vs. strong methods. This foundational theme helped me pare down my view of history and serves as my only defense against otherwise unforgivable omissions in the overview. Even so, it was difficult to pick and choose from the corpus of potentially relevant research, and the usual disclaimers about intelligible brevity at the cost of comprehensive coverage must be piously invoked to ward off inevitable accusations of ignorance, prejudice, and other sins associated with warped thinking.

I'm going to use a lot of examples to illustrate key concepts, interleaving the examples with a chronological survey of the literature. We'll periodically try to rise above the trees to see the forest, and search for threads of strong methods and weak methods throughout. We'll see how strong methods came to dominate the field for a period of time, only to be followed by the pendulum's swing toward weak methods, where we seem to be today.

If we go back to the beginning of time, we go back about 15 years. I would date 1972 as a convenient starting point for knowledge-based natural language processing. There were two very important pieces of work that surfaced around 1972. First, Terry Winograd published his Ph.D. dissertation under the title *Understanding Natural Language* [Winograd, 1972]. At the same time, Eugene Charniak completed his Ph.D. dissertation on a model of children's story comprehension [Charniak, 1972]. Both of these theses came out of MIT—in fact, Charniak and Winograd were office-mates at MIT.

Despite the physical proximity of the authors at the time, these two views of natural language processing couldn't be more different. Let me read you an excerpt from a recently published retrospective by Terry Winograd. In his own words, he sums it up as follows:

> Fifteen years ago, a program named SHRDLU demonstrated that a computer could carry on a simple conversation about a blocks world in written English. Its success led to claims that the natural language problem had been solved and predictions that within a short time conversations with computers would be just like those with people.

> ... With years of hindsight and experience, we now understand better why the early optimism was unrealistic. Language, like many human capabilities, is far more intricate and subtle than it appears on first inspection [Winograd, 1987].

That's Terry Winograd speaking in 1987. To understand the significance of his cautionary hindsight, we must first understand that there was tremendous excitement over SHRDLU when it was initially publicized in the early 70s. There was much less excitement over Charniak's relatively unknown thesis, although we do find people referencing it even now. Philosopher Hubert Dreyfus, a well-known critic of AI, says the following about Charniak:

> ... by 1970, AI had turned into a flourishing research program, thanks to a series of microworld successes, such as Winograd's SHRDLU, Evan's Analogy Problem Program and Winston's program which learned concepts from examples.

> ... Then rather suddenly, the field ran into unexpected trouble. It started, as far as I can tell, with the failure of Charniak's attempts to program chil-

dren's story understanding. It turned out to be a much harder problem than one expected to formulate a theory of common sense. It was not, as Minksy had hoped, just a question of cataloging a few hundred thousand facts [Dreyfus, 1987].

To sum up, Winograd was dealing with a view of language that was very optimistic and designed to convince the world that natural language processing was a viable research problem. Charniak was taking a somewhat more unpopular but realistic stand in looking at the really hard problems we would eventually have to tackle if we were to deal with language in any truly general sense. To digress for a moment, I would like to mention something ironic about Winograd and Charniak. While Charniak was clearly the pessimistic foil to Winograd's optimist, it is amusing to note that Charniak remains extremely active and productive in the field of natural language processing, whereas Winograd has ceased to make contributions to AI, opting instead to investigate the philosophical implications of hermeneutics [Winograd and Flores, 1986].

We will look at Charniak's thesis just long enough to note the general emphasis in that research. Here's a quotation from the dissertation abstract:

> An earlier version of the model described in this thesis was computer implemented and handled two story fragments, about a hundred sentences. The problems involved in going from natural language to internal representation were not considered, so the program does not accept English, but an input language similar to the internal representation is used [Charniak, 1972].

To be blunt, Charniak's program never analyzed sentences. In some sense, Charniak's thesis was not a thesis about language analysis at all, although I view it as a milestone thesis for knowledge-based language understanding. Charniak was looking at a set of problems that are not specific to sentence analysis *per se*, but which nevertheless are key to understanding natural language. Charniak was concerned with the problem of inference. That concern evolved into a driving motivation for much of the research on knowledge-based natural language processing we've seen over the last 15 years.

It is useful to contrast the two veins of research that were more or less initiated by Charniak and Winograd. There is *problem-driven* research and there is *technology-driven* research. I'll characterize problem-driven research as basic research designed for the long haul: Given the difficulties inherent in understanding language, what techniques might be of use to us in surmounting these difficulties? Technology-driven research is the research of near-term applications: Given the current state-of-the-art, what applications are appropriate for the existing technologies?

SHRDLU was a wonderful example of technology-driven research. The blocks world lent itself to techniques that were available at the time. But

SHRDLU was just a prototype designed to inspire further work. The contemporary offspring of that inspiration are found today in database query interfaces. We have a technology-driven research program on natural language interfaces that works (more or less), but is successful primarily because it does not need to deal with natural language in its full generality.

To appreciate the problems of natural language in general, we have to understand what is meant by the inference problem in natural language—the problem that made Charniak such a pessimist about life outside the blocks world. Let's take an example of a short narrative to illustrate the problem:

> When the balloon touched the light bulb, it broke. This caused the baby to cry. Mary gave John a dirty look and picked up the baby. John shrugged and picked up the balloon.

This is a typical example of narrative text. We can analyze it in terms of its information content by distinguishing explicit information from implicit information. We are explicitly told about seven events in this story and one explicit causal relationship signaled by the verb "caused." But implicitly, there's more information. There are at least six implicit events and states that are present in the paragraph, eight implicit causal relationships, and six implicit goal states or emotional states (see Figure 1).

For example, probably the balloon was inflated. Probably the balloon exploded when it broke. There is an ambiguity associated with the pronoun when we are told "it broke." Was it the balloon that broke or the light bulb that broke? Most readers have no trouble understanding that the balloon broke. Furthermore, we might conjecture that the light bulb was on and it was the heat from the light bulb that broke the balloon. These are all plausible commonsense inferences people are able to make—but they are only assumptions, and assumptions that could be wrong. We will define an inference to be an assumption that could be wrong. Technically speaking, this type of inference is known as *defeasible inference*, but for the remainder of this talk we'll just call them inferences.

Charniak's interest in children's stories was centered on the problem of inference generation. Children are capable of highly sophisticated inferences, a fact which makes children's stories extremely complicated for computers. Although the language in children's stories may be relatively simple in terms of syntax and vocabulary, the underlying processes of inference required to understand a typical children's story are not so easy to characterize. The basic problem has to do with knowledge about the world. Children have a great deal of knowledge, although the magnitude of this underlying knowledge base is largely unappreciated by people who have never tried to get a computer to operate with comparable facility.

The balloon was originally inflated.
The balloon broke (not the light bulb)
The light bulb was hot.
The light bulb was on.
* The heat caused the balloon the break.
* The balloon exploded.
* The explosion made a loud noise.
⊘ The baby was scared.
* The loud noise scared the baby.
* The baby cried because it was scared.
⊘ Mary is mad at John.
Mary communicated her anger to John.
⊘ Mary picked up the baby to comfort it.
⊘ John is not overly concerned
⊘ John will throw the balloon away.
* John was responsible for the balloon breaking.
* John was responsible for the baby crying.
* Mary is mad at John for making the baby cry.

* causal connections
⊘ goal states/emotional states

Figure 1 Inferences from the Balloon Story

The general problem of inference generation inspired a lot of work in the mid-to-late 70s devoted to identifying knowledge structures that could spawn inferences. During this period, we saw progress that I would characterize as work in strong methods for natural language processing. By this I mean to say that there was a strong preoccupation with specific knowledge structures and knowledge-specific mechanisms of inference generation. I will briefly outline the major contributions of that period since the work was highly influential, not only within the AI community, but within cognitive psychology as well. Eventually, we will get around to looking at problems of sentence analysis *per se*.

2 *Knowledge Structures*

The first knowledge structure that was proposed as a powerful device for inference generation was the script [Schank and Abelson, 1977]. Scripts have trickled down into the introductory textbooks on AI, but for those who are not familiar with the concept, I'll run through it very briefly.

Scripts are designed to encode stereotypic event sequences. This is mundane knowledge about some standard scenario for which a common linguistic community shares knowledge. So, for example, we all have knowledge about going to the movies. And if I say to you, "I went to a movie last night," you are capable of generating a lot of inferences about what I did last night that go far beyond the explicit information content of that sentence. You understand that I must have had money to buy a ticket and the ticket was purchased at the theatre. I may have had to wait in line for a bit before I could go into the theatre, but once inside I could have bought popcorn, candy, or ice cream. I exchanged the ticket with an usher who gave me a stub back ... .

You have all these little facts about going to the movies. These are all assumptions that could be wrong. But for the most part, these are the assumptions you have to make. And if we want to create computers that can understand language, we have to worry about creating systems that generate these inferences as well. This is the implicit information content underlying language.

A system called SAM was first implemented in 1975, which was given simple narratives and then tried to generate inferences appropriate for those stories on the basis of scripts [Cullingford, 1978]. SAM stood for "Script Applier Mechanism." The architecture of SAM was fairly simple. There was a parser that mapped sentences into an internal memory representation, in this case, *Conceptual Dependency* [Schank, 1975]. Then the actual script applier mechanism accessed the appropriate scriptal knowledge structure and tried to fill in any missing implicit events in a causal chain representation. "I went to a movie last night" would be expanded into a very long causal chain representation containing all the implicit events associated with knowledge about movies.

SAM was a prototype program designed to demonstrate the utility of one particular knowledge structure. That knowledge structure became somewhat controversial in terms of its generality. Where do scripts work? Where don't they work? Are they appropriate for generating all the inferences we need?

If we go back to our balloon story, we could, for example, hypothesize the existence of a balloon script. Here is our stereotypic event knowledge about balloons: They start out in an uninflated state. They get inflated in one of two stereotypic manners, they get tied, and then they die a natural death in one of three ways (see Figure 2).

THE BALLOON SCRIPT

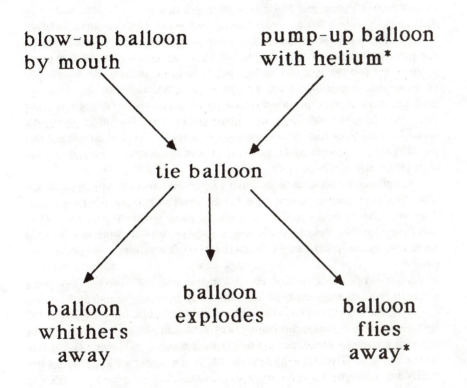

blow-up balloon
by mouth

pump-up balloon
with helium*

tie balloon

balloon
whithers
away

balloon
explodes

balloon
flies
away*

Figure 2 The Balloon Script

This is event-oriented knowledge about balloons. If we wanted to understand our little story about the light bulb and the balloon using 1975 technology, we would simply match the explicit input against the events described in the balloon script, and infer that the balloon was inflated and tied before it broke. While these are undeniably nice inferences to have, we wouldn't know anything about why the balloon broke or why it was reasonable for it to break. Indeed, if our "light bulb script" included breakage as one of the stereotypic ways that light bulbs come to an end, there would be no way of knowing which referent (for "it") was broken on the basis of these scripts alone.

At the time that scripts were being proposed by Roger Schank at Yale, Schank also understood that scripts were not the solution to all of the problems of knowledge-based inference generation. He proposed other knowledge structures as well. For example, there was knowledge about plans and goals.

If I told you I hired someone to clean my house, you could make a number of inferences about exactly what that entailed. I had to find someone who would be willing to clean the house, I had to approach this person, ask them to clean my house, there was probably some negotiation over payment, and so on and so forth. All of these inferences are very general in the sense that they would apply to anyone I might hire to do a periodic task for me, such as mow my grass or do my shopping for me. Any number of tasks that keep popping up over and over again could be handled in the same manner. So these inferences appear to originate from a more general understanding of plans and goals. In this case, we have a problem of goal subsumption (finding a solution to a recurring goal), and a solution in terms of agency (locating an agent who will do the work for me). So plans and goals involve a level of abstraction that goes beyond scripts, but which still allows us to characterize stereotypic situations [Wilensky, 1978].

A well-known book came out in 1977 that put down in writing all of the ideas that were floating around Yale at that time [Schank and Abelson, 1977]. This was a book about knowledge structures, more specifically, scripts, plans, and goals, among other things. It was a seminal piece of work insofar as it generated, by my count, ten Ph.D. theses in AI (there were probably a comparable number of Ph.D.s in psychology as well). So there was a tremendous amount of work along these lines in the mid and late 70s, and that work created a foundation for the more recent research to which we now turn.

First, we'll look at two different directions that took off after that initial foundation in knowledge structuring was first laid. In so doing, we'll see different knowledge structures: (1) plot units [Lehnert, 1981], and (2) thematic abstraction units [Dyer, 1983b], both of which were designed to produce summaries for narratives.

In both systems, we assume that multiple levels of memory representation are being generated in response to the input text. Sentences are translated into Conceptual Dependency, and inferences are generated via script application and the analysis of plans and goals. In the case of plot units, additional levels of abstraction are required to produce an affect state map, and finally a plot unit graph. The plot unit graph rests on top of all these "lower" levels of memory representation, which act, in turn, as conceptual scaffolding for the narrative summarization task.

In the tradition initiated by Charniak's thesis, most experiments run on plot units require hand-coded memory representations at the lower levels in order to see anything of interest at the level of a plot unit graph. Granting that, there is a program called PUGG (the Plot Unit Graph Generator) that generates memory representations of the sort found in Figure 3.

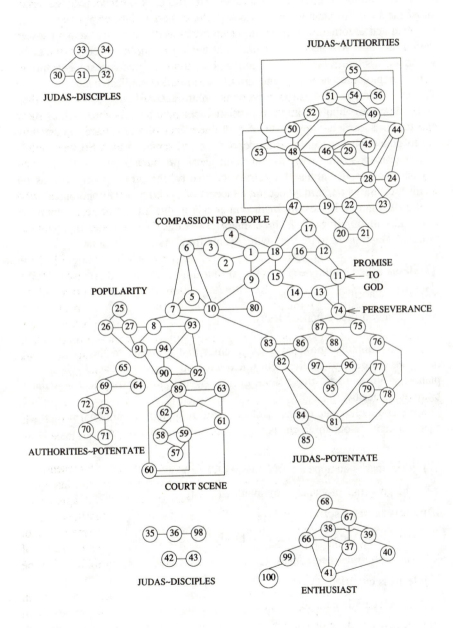

Figure 3 The New Testament in a Plot Unit Graph

This is a plot unit graph generated in response to Arnold Toynbee's synopsis of the New Testament [Alker et al., 1985]. Note that this graph could never be generated automatically from the source text of the New Testament, given the current state of the art. Just the hand coding of the knowledge structures would necessitate sacrificing an entire generation of graduate students in an orgy of exploitation normally unheard of outside the biological sciences.

Each node in this graph represents an instantiated plot unit where plot units describe things like competition between two characters, or one character's successful resolution of a problem situation. Arcs are created between nodes when two plot units depend on a shared component from the affect state map. In this way, the plot unit graph provides a picture of the conceptual connectivity across the narrative. Ideally, this graph will allow us to identify the salient and most central concepts by looking at the topological features of the graph. For example, the cut points in this graph are very important plot units for our story. The three major cut points for the main body of this plot unit graph point to the following events from the New Testament:

(7)   Jesus called on the people to support him.

(47)   The authorities arrested Jesus.

(89)   The authorities crucified Jesus.

If we wanted to produce a truly minimalist synopsis of the New Testament, we are perhaps on the right track here, although we do not have the explanatory power to tie these three events together into a truly self-contained blurb about Jesus.

We could elaborate on this skeleton a bit by invoking a minimal path algorithm to connect our three cut points. These produce the following event-summary:

(7)   Jesus makes an appeal to the masses for support.

(9)   The government wants to maintain authority over the masses.

(10)   Jesus causes a scandal.

(18)   Jesus takes the law into his own hands to avenge God.

(47)   The authorities arrest Jesus.

(89)   Jesus is crucified.

(92)   Jesus' death is a triumph.

(93)   Jesus is worshipped.

I am told that this is, in fact, a Marxist interpretation of the New Testament.

Let us now return to the other line of work on narrative summarization that relied on scripts, plans, and goals. As we saw with plot units, it is possible to produce narrative summaries based on event descriptions alone, as long as you can identify the central events of the story. But there are other kinds of summaries that operate on a more abstract level of understanding. Fables are famous for the adages associated with them, and the ability to associate an appropriate adage with a novel narrative is considered a hallmark of mature intelligence (understanding the meaning of proverbs is a task used by the Stanford Binet IQ test as a standard for measuring adult intelligence).

Research on thematic abstraction units addressed this aspect of narrative summarization [Dyer, 1983a]. Dyer claimed that adages are properly associated with abstractions at the level of plans and goals. Each thematic abstraction unit describes a pattern of plan-oriented behavior, and if all the required components of the pattern are met, the specific adage associated with that thematic abstraction unit will apply.

So, for example, a close call, which would perhaps be described by the adage, "A miss by an inch is as good as a mile," could be recognized via the following thematic abstraction unit:

(1)   X experiences a major preservation goal, G.

(2)   G was created in response to an event not intended by X.

(3)   G is a fleeting goal so no recovery plan is required.

Note that a close call can be easily transformed into a regrettable mistake (don't cry over spilt milk) if G is not characterized as a fleeting goal and a recovery plan therefore becomes appropriate.

It is interesting to note that a plot unit analysis can be performed without the benefit of thematic abstraction units, and thematic abstraction units can be recognized without any of the effort associated with affect state maps and plot unit graphs. These two approaches to narrative summarization are fully independent of one another and simply reflect different types of summarization tasks. As far as the computational models are concerned, skills with one task do not predict seemingly associated skills in the other.

Plot units and thematic abstraction units both emerged from a large research effort centered around a system named BORIS [Lehnert et al., 1983]. BORIS attempted to integrate a large number of knowledge structures in a single system, addressing the architectural problems posed by multiple knowledge structures. The BORIS system, completed in 1982, marks the end of the knowledge structuring era. For the most part, people stopped proposing new knowledge structures at about that time, and interests shifted into other areas.

To understand why, we need only look at the diagram in Figure 4 (taken from [Dyer, 1983a]).

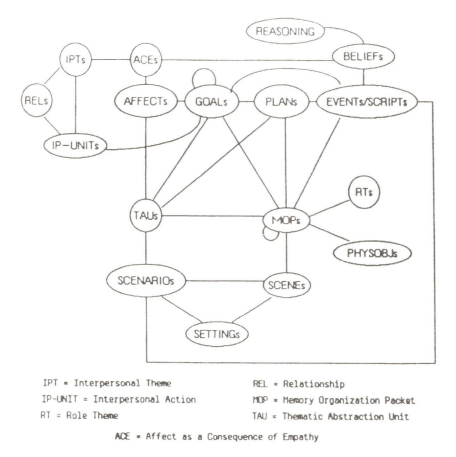

IPT = Interpersonal Theme   REL = Relationship
IP-UNIT = Interpersonal Action   MOP = Memory Organization Packet
RT = Role Theme   TAU = Thematic Abstraction Unit

ACE = Affect as a Consequence of Empathy

Figure 4 The Knowledge Dependency Graph for BORIS

BORIS attempted to integrate no less than 22 different knowledge structures, each responsible for generating its own class of inferences encoded with
structurally-specific knowledge representations, and using its own structure-
specific inference mechanism. Figure 4 tells us what lines of communication
were open between the various knowledge structures. Each node of the graph
represents a generic knowledge structure, and each arc tells us when one
knowledge structure was allowed to talk to another one. Rather than having all
possible pairwise channels of communication open, we limit communication

between knowledge structures and impose some order on the potential chaos that would otherwise break loose.

Unfortunately, the rich diversity of the knowledge structures requires unique forms of communication between sanctioned pairs of knowledge structures. No two arcs in this diagram are quite the same in terms of the type of information being requested or the methods of computation required to produce a response. Not only are there inference processes specific to each knowledge structure, but the communications between pairs of knowledge structures are pairwise specific.

However impressive BORIS may have been as a tour de force in knowledge-based natural language understanding, the word "elegant" has never graced any noun phrase describing the flow of control in BORIS. "Ad hoc" was rather closer to the truth, and the difficulties of continuing on in this vein were apparent to all. Suffice it to say, no one ever attempted to re-implement the BORIS system after Dyer completed his noteworthy thesis based on the system, and no one associated with the original BORIS system went on to produce a son of BORIS. The complexity of the architecture, the fragile scaffolding needed to make it all hang together, and the methodologically difficult business of engineering mundane knowledge for natural language were all overwhelming. Although Dyer has never been accused of being a pessimist, his thesis, published 10 years after Charniak's, was another milestone destined to send the faint-hearted elsewhere in search of smoother sailing.

I think a lot of people realized the implications of BORIS in 1982. Although there was no way to walk away from the need for knowledge, the growing commitment to knowledge-based natural language processing gradually shifted into a wistful longing for processes operating over uniform knowledge representations, inference mechanisms that transcend individual knowledge structures, and elegant control mechanisms that can be explained within the confines of a single page. Of course, there were always people in the field who felt compelled by these aesthetic criteria: Winograd was involved in the development of KRL [Bobrow and Winograd, 1977], and even Charniak once described himself as a methodological "scruffy" with a "neat" struggling to get out.[1]

---

1 See [Abelson, 1981] for the official explanation of "scruffy" and "neat" as technical terms referring to methodological styles.

3 *Marker Passing*

The excitement associated with PROLOG in the early 1980s, and the more recent fever surrounding connectionism, have both exerted a predictable pull over researchers in knowledge-based natural language processing who felt a need to swing the pendulum back a bit from the strong methods associated with wildly propagating knowledge structures. At this time we seem to be swinging back in the direction of weak methods, with a clear question to be answered: Does the commitment to knowledge-based techniques necessarily force us into a technology dominated by strong methods? Ten years ago the answer was maybe. Today we seem to be saying maybe not.

In keeping with this general trend, we are seeing new work on homogeneous inference generation. The roots for this do go back, so we should take a little time to give credit where credit is due. Probably the earliest reference is Quillian, who first promoted the idea of intersection search in a computational framework. This was followed up by Rieger's thesis work, for which Rieger was honored by being asked to give the Computers and Thought Lecture at the 1975 IJCAI. Let me talk a little bit about all of that so we can appreciate the significance of more contemporary contributions to homogeneous inference.

The idea of an intersection search is fairly simple. Quillian is generally credited with the earliest description of an intersection search algorithm [Quillian, 1968], but we'll introduce the idea in the context of Rieger's thesis because Rieger's work is more on-target with respect to inference generation [Rieger, 1974].

Suppose we have a meaning representation for sentence S1, and a meaning representation for a second sentence, S2. These two representations serve as input to Rieger's program, MEMORY. Each meaning representation then generates a first generation of immediate inferences, which will each recursively spawn a second generation of inferences, then a third generation, "and so forth and upward and onward" (gee whizz! [Geisel, 1950]). In theory, we can produce inferences arbitrarily far away from the original input sentences.

In an intersection search, this recursive generation of inferences halts when we find a path of inferences connecting the two input generators. If MEMORY can find a path of inferences that starts at S1 and concludes at S2, then we have a good candidate for a causal chain between the two sentences. That is, we have a string of causally connected events and states that take us from one sentence to the next. So we might understand, for example, if the balloon touches the lightbulb (S1) and the balloon subsequently breaks (S7), then there is a causal chain going from (S1) the balloon coming into contact with the lightbulb, to (S2) the balloon coming into contact with a light bulb that is turned on, to (S3) the balloon coming into contact with a light bulb that is turned on and hot, to (S4) the balloon coming into contact with a hot object, to (S5) the balloon being in contact with a hot object, to (S6) the balloon exploding as a result of contact with a hot object, to (S7) the balloon breaking. Note that S2 and S3 would each be generated from S1, while S4, S5, and S6 would be generated from S7. If an intersection can be established between S3 and S4, we will have a causal chain analysis of the two sentences.[2]

When Rieger employed intersection search for inference generation back in the early 70s, he was not working in a knowledge-based framework. Consequently, there was no knowledge in MEMORY—certainly nothing we would recognize today as a declarative knowledge structure. Rather, Rieger had 16 inference "molecules" that were responsible for the propagation of inferences underlying the intersection search. If there was any knowledge in MEMORY at all, it had to be buried inside the lisp code that realized these 16 inference classes. But in fact, most of the inferences that MEMORY generated were based on simple manipulations of Conceptual Dependency event and state descriptions, and none of those manipulations were dependent on structures outside of the search space being generated during the intersection search. Despite its name, MEMORY had no long-term memory, and the expanding circles of inference it generated were essentially pulled out of thin air (or at least 16 thin inference molecules).

If Rieger's thesis looks weak from the perspective of knowledge-based systems, we must remember that he intended to make a contribution regarding search. Indeed, he had an elegant idea concerning the relationship between inference generation and causal chain construction: The construction of a causal chain was a search problem and the undirected generation of inferences created the search space in which to operate. Both components were nicely addressed within the simple framework of an intersection search. This emphasis on the algorithm for search created a model about control, and the beauty of MEMORY's control was its simplicity and homogeneous generality.

Rieger's work is important for us because it illustrates a weak method for inference generation based on a simple mechanism of great generality. We should also note that Roger Schank was Rieger's thesis advisor, and Schank has said that his work on scripts was strongly motivated by what he perceived to be the fatal flaw in Rieger's MEMORY: a lack of knowledge. In Schank's view, the real problems were inside those inference molecules (or whatever mechanisms were needed to generate inferences). The key problem must be to understand the organization of knowledge needed to create inferences. MEMORY was appealing, but sadly predicated on the wrong framework for the problem of inference generation. If inference generation is essentially a problem of search, then MEMORY should give us some answers worth

---

2 In fact, Rieger's meaning representation language (Conceptual Dependency) was not well suited for this particular example, and MEMORY probably couldn't have found this causal chain, but we're just trying to illustrate the general idea.

pondering. But if inference generation is better characterized as a problem of knowledge application, then MEMORY must fall very short of the mark. If Rieger made a mistake, it was in asking the wrong question more than in finding the wrong answer.

Now we can move the clock up to 1987 and look at a program called FAUSTUS, which identifies seven classes of inference and activates selected concepts throughout a potentially large search space in an effort to identify useful inferences [Norvig, 1987]. At first glance, this may look like a reincarnation of Rieger, but we need to look a little closer. First we note that the simple intersection search has been replaced by a more sophisticated marker passing algorithm. The new algorithm looks like a step in the right direction (it narrows the potential search space), yet we still have homogeneous control for inference generation. How is this possible?

It seems that FAUSTUS benefited from all the work that followed and superseded Rieger without sacrificing the weak method of homogeneous control. FAUSTUS utilizes extensive amounts of knowledge, yet the intelligent manipulation of that knowledge is handled by a marker passing algorithm that can be described in terms of a simple grammar. FAUSTUS has a fixed memory which is rich in knowledge, but it is structured very carefully using a knowledge representation language called KODIAK [Wilensky 1986]. When activation passes from one concept to another, it must conform to a legal path "shape" specified by the grammar in the marker passing algorithm. When independent markers collide at a shared node, the resulting path of activated nodes provides useful inferences about the original input items. The idea of the intersection search is still there—it's just harder to generate false positives (bogus intersections).

The best way I can give you a feel for FAUSTUS is by looking at an example. The following example was manufactured for this talk and is undoubtedly all wrong as far as the details of KODIAK and Norvig's actual algorithm are concerned, but we'll settle for ballpark accuracy to get the main idea across.

Let's go back to our overworked text about the balloon and the light bulb. The first sentence was, "When the balloon touched the light bulb, it broke." We have a reference to a light bulb, a reference to a balloon, and physical contact between the two of them. That's explicit in the sentence. We also know something broke, but the pronoun leaves us up in the air as to exactly what broke. It could have been the light bulb or it could have been the balloon. We would like to be able to disambiguate the pronoun and infer a plausible causal relationship between the two events described. Figure 5 shows us what a meaning representation for the input sentence might look like before any inferences are made.

INPUT:

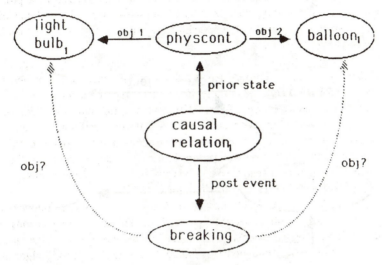

Figure 5 When the Balloon Touched the Light Bulb, it Broke

Now let's look at some knowledge we should have available to us. We have knowledge about breaking that tells us all the different ways things can break. For example, we can understand that one way things break is by exploding. An exploding event is a further specification or "concretion" of a breaking event, and this further specification is only valid under certain circumstances. Using KODIAK, we can create inheritance hierarchies that encode structured inheritance via role-play links. As we will see, this notion of structured inheritance will help us make some important inferences about what broke and exactly what the breaking event describes.

We have a hierarchy of entailed event concepts going from breaking down to exploding, with role-play links telling us how these structures are inherited. These hierarchies bottom out with very specific event descriptions: specific, for example, at the level of a balloon exploding (see Figure 6). And we understand that there's a constraint on the balloon exploding event that the object of any such event must be a balloon. This is not a constraint available to us at the higher levels, where we may only be constrained by the specification of an inflatable object, or even more generally, a physical object.

A hierarchy with these richly constrained specifications allows us to generate concretion inferences that help us see beyond the explicit meanings available to us from the source text. For example, if we are told that a balloon broke, we should be able to infer the constraints operating at low levels of greater specificity in order to understand that if the object of a breaking event was a balloon, then it may be safe to assume that the balloon exploded.

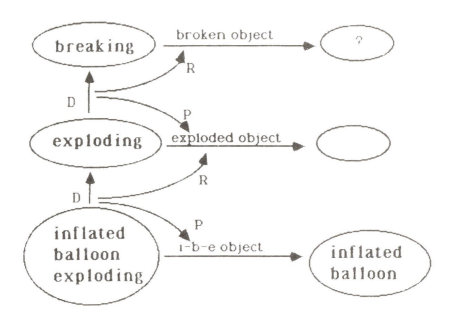

Figure 6 Inheritances for Exploding Balloons

Concretion inferences are one of the inference types handled by FAUS-TUS, but the simple inheritance mechanism described above cannot resolve complicated ambiguities of the type present when we have to understand what it was that broke in the first place. In our original text, we have to decide between a balloon breaking or a light bulb breaking. It is nice to know that the balloon would break by exploding, whereas the light bulb would break by shattering (see Figure 7), but we still have to decide which object we think we're dealing with.

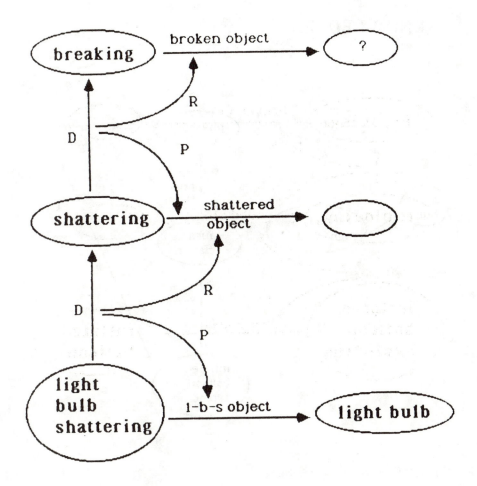

Figure 7 Inheritances for Shattering Light Bulbs

If we really want to resolve the reference, we have to drag in more knowledge. So let's assume we have knowledge about balloons (see Figure 8).

This is somewhat reminiscent of the balloon script we discussed earlier. We understand that one of the things that can happen to an inflated balloon is that it might come into contact with a hot object, in which case we can make a pretty fair prediction about a causal relationship with a balloon exploding event. The preconditions for this balloon exploding event can be obtained from the light bulb if we understand that a light bulb can be a hot light bulb, and that hot light bulbs are further specifications under turned-on light bulbs. With

KNOWLEDGE:

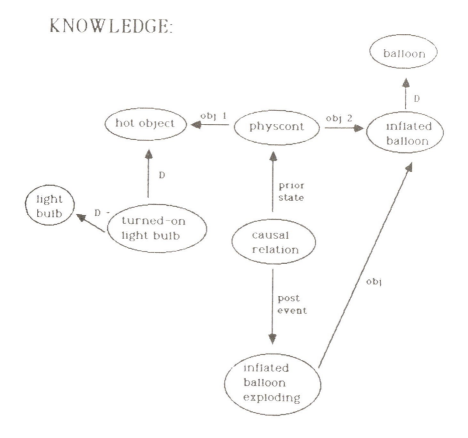

Figure 8 Knowledge About Balloons

appropriate inheritance inferences (including the fact that a touching event is a further specification for physical contact, and the fact that an inflated balloon is a further specification for a balloon), we might manage to fill out a causal chain if all the pieces are available to us in memory and the paths of relevant inference are recognized by the marker passing grammar.

As this example shows, FAUSTUS attempts to marry extensive knowledge access to a homogeneous control structure realized in terms of marker passing. The approach represents an appealing synthesis of two seemingly contradictory directions: the weak methods of homogeneous control and the strong methods associated with large amounts of knowledge. However, it is difficult to say what happened to the strong methods associated with traditional knowledge structures when we encoded our knowledge base in KODIAK. Can a marker passing algorithm achieve the computational power of a script applier mechanism? Can generic concepts be instantiated and utilized by multiple referents without getting confused? What if our story references two balloons and we have to keep distinct concretions straight? These are questions about the possible limits of marker passing algorithms. The homogeneous control is great, but is it powerful enough for our needs? These are questions we need to answer about marker passing as a weak method for inference generation.

4 *Syntax and Semantics*

We've been talking a lot about inference generation, but it would be a mistake to assume that's all there is to knowledge-based natural language processing. In fact, homogeneous control for inferences really goes hand in hand with homogeneous control for other problems. For example, we are also seeing a trend toward homogeneous control for the integration of syntax and semantics, a problem that is very important for models of sentence analysis. Let's see how some people have worked to bring homogeneous control back down to the level of sentence analysis.

What do you usually see when you look at a textbook on AI with a section devoted to natural language processing? There's a good chance you'll see a flow-of-control diagram that looks something like tho one shown in Figure 9.

Here we see that the problem of sentence analysis has been divided into specific modules. We have syntactic knowledge—knowledge about grammar—that is important in analyzing the structure of a sentence. We also have semantic knowledge, which is where concept frames are defined and various constraints operate to control the slot fillers for those frames. And we often see a reference to pragmatic knowledge, which is where all the common sense reasoning needed for inference generation resides. Pragmatics is also where knowledge about discourse is stored. Generally speaking, pragmatic knowledge is defined to be anything we need which wasn't already covered by syntax and semantics.

The flow of control that we see here is serial control. This is a nice modular idea about language analysis that lays out the pieces clearly and simply. Unfortunately, systems built along these lines just don't work very well. Serial control is used for some database interfaces, but it doesn't work for continuous narrative text at all.

To see why not, let's look at a couple of sentences (see Figure 10). The sentences I'm interested in are, "John took her flowers" and "A stranger took her money." These two sentences are syntactically identical, and they are syntactically ambiguous as well. "Her flowers" could be a single noun phrase, or it could be an indirect object followed by a direct object. Similarly, "her money" could be a single noun phrase, or it could be an indirect object followed by a direct object.

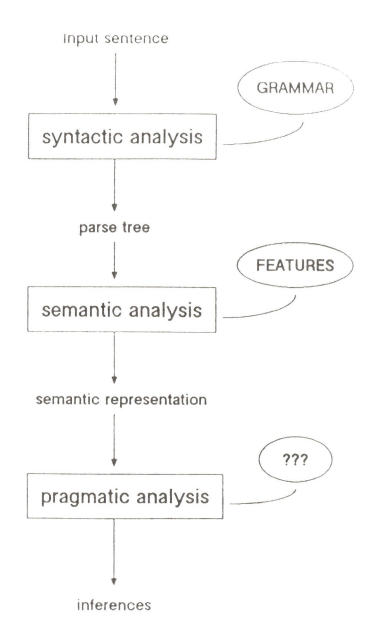

Figure 9 Serial Flow of Control

Mary was in the hospital.

John took her flowers.

(John took flowers to Mary)

Mary was walking through Central Park.

A stranger took her money.

(A stranger took money from Mary)

Figure 10 Context Effects for Sentence Analysis

When Mary is in the hospital, we understand, without effort or conscious thought, that John brought flowers to Mary. The sentence contains an indirect object and a direct object. But when Mary is in Central Park, we see a single noun phrase operating as a direct object. Somehow we fail to consider the absurd possibilities of John taking flowers away from Mary in the hospital, or even sillier, the possibility that a stranger could walk up to Mary in Central Park and hand her money.

Apart from the syntactic ambiguities confronting us, we also have a lexical ambiguity associated with the verb "to take." In the hospital this verb means "to bring," while in Central Park we understand it to mean "to take away." This is a strictly semantic ambiguity that forces us to choose between competing word senses.

So we have two interesting ambiguities operating here. We have a syntactic ambiguity that needs to be resolved, and the semantic ambiguity associated with multiple word senses. Both ambiguities must be resolved in order to arrive at appropriate interpretations for the sentences.

How do we do it? Well, first we note that there are useful relationships between syntax and semantics. When "take" is used to mean "bring," it predicts a different set of syntactic constituents than when "take" is used to mean "take away." When you take something away from someone, you can't have an indirect object. This means that a resolution of the semantic ambiguity will automatically take care of the syntactic ambiguity as a natural side effect. Once we know what the verb means, we'll know how to parse the sentence syntactically. We'll return to the problem of knowing what the verb means in a minute.

In the meantime, notice that we're already in trouble using our serial architecture. This architecture assumes that all the syntactic decisions are made before we even look at the semantics of the sentence. The dependency is running the wrong way. If we stick with this architecture, we'll have to allow the syntax module to operate nondeterministically, handing multiple parse trees over to semantics in the hope that semantics can decide which one is appropriate.

This is, in fact, exactly what a lot of language processing systems do. In the "syntax-first" tradition, whole sentences are analyzed syntactically, and multiple parse trees are passed on for further analysis, making the job of semantic analysis a job of sorting through all the parse trees. When sentences contain prepositional phrases, reduced relative clauses, and other sources of rich syntactic ambiguity, the number of syntactic parse trees available to us can easily run into the hundreds.

Most researchers in knowledge-based natural language processing reject the syntax-first approach to sentence analysis and strive to integrate syntax and semantics in a more natural and effective manner. But once we open the door to integrated models of sentence analysis, we must necessarily ask whether the problem is restricted only to syntax and semantics. After all, just how do we decide what word sense for "took" is the appropriate one?

It seems that the answer to this question must be obtained by using a lot of knowledge about the world. Although you may not have thought about it, you make an inference when you hear "Mary was in the hospital." Probably, Mary was a patient in the hospital (note that this could be wrong). It follows that Mary was probably sick or injured. And there's a tradition in our culture about people who are sick or injured. Friends and relatives usually send something to cheer up the invalid: Cards and flowers are traditional items. All of this is useful in disambiguating the proper word sense in "John took her flowers." Given the strong context surrounding the sentence, we might reasonably expect to be dealing with a bringing event as soon as we hear "John took ... ."

On the other hand, we also have knowledge about Central Park. We all have a strong association between Central Park and muggers, we know what a mugging is, what the goals of a mugger are, and we know that pedestrians in

Central Park are at risk. All of this is available to most adult Americans because it's a part of our shared culture. And this is the knowledge that helps us to understand the appropriate word sense for the verb when we hear "A stranger took ..." in the context of pedestrians and Central Park.

If we define pragmatic knowledge to be the basis for inference generation, then we have to integrate not just semantics with syntax, but semantics and pragmatics with syntax as well. For this reason, many people believe that the line between semantics and pragmatics is not well-motivated: There is no good basis for distinguishing semantic knowledge from pragmatic knowledge if you are going to work within an integrated framework for sentence analysis.

People who are interested in this integration problem are interested in ideas for control. How are we going to integrate the top-down processes, which are knowledge-based, with low-level bottom-up processes, which are not knowledge-based? Although there are many answers to this question based on co-routines and message passing, it has been difficult to find solutions that are truly elegant and readily adaptable if your grammar changes or your theory of semantics begins to shift.

However, two interesting approaches to this problem have surfaced very recently, and I'd like to give you a rough feeling for those solutions. I am not convinced that anyone has a good solution to the pragmatic context effects we've been looking at in Figure 10, but we can at least see progress at the level of syntax and semantics with hopeful hand waving aimed at pragmatic interactions.

In the first case, structured inheritance is being pushed as a key mechanism for integrated sentence analysis. This approach argues that the key to the problem lies in the correct design and organization of our knowledge base. For example, a selling event can be characterized in terms of two transfer events, where the object of one transfer is money and the object of the other transfer is merchandise. The sources and recipients for these two transfer events constrain one another by exchanging roles, and at a very high level of abstraction, each of these transfer events are instances of some very vague event which corresponds to the primitive ATRANS in Conceptual Dependency. Figure 11 shows how all of this knowledge about selling might be represented using KODIAK.

In KODIAK diagrams we use a bit of shorthand that is important to understand. Whenever you see a named link like the actor link in Figure 12, that's actually a shorthand notation for structured inheritance via a role-play link. It's very cumbersome to work with the fully expanded notation all the time, so the shorthand notation is useful, but we must remember that this shorthand implies a structured inheritance that is not explicit in the diagram.

What we're trying to do here is create a very systematic and highly constrained style of knowledge representation through which we inherit a lot of implicit structure as needed. Let's try to look at some examples of this in action.

Structured Inheritance

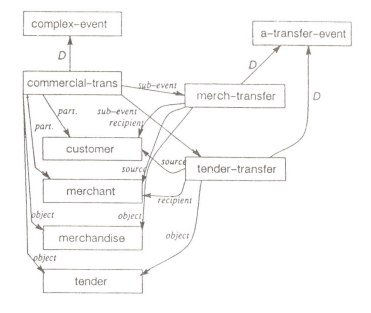

Figure 11 Representing the Verb "To Sell"

Selling is interesting because it's two transactions, and both of those transactions are transfers. We have some very high level of generality, a transfer of an object from one person to another, or from one entity to another. And in one case, the transfer is a merchandise transfer, so we have an object of barter being moved from one person to another. In the other case, moving in the opposite direction is a transfer of tender: Money is changing hands. If we're very careful with our representation, we can understand how these two transfers relate to one another. They are not isolated transfers. Rather, they are connected through a series of links that identify specific roles, such as customer, merchant, merchandise, tender. Whenever there's a selling event, we implicitly know that four roles must be present, whether we can instantiate them with referents or not.

Structured Inheritance

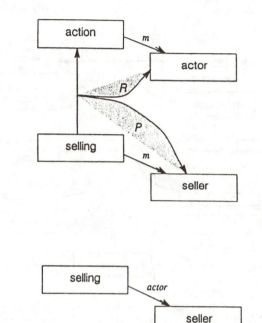

OR

Figure 12 Implicit Roll-Play Links

While this network is designed to represent semantic information, the idea of structured inheritance networks has been applied to traditionally linguistic (syntactic) knowledge as well [Jacobs, 1987a]. It is possible to take knowledge about grammar, the rules for recognizing legitimate sentence structure, and encode that knowledge in a KODIAK network utilizing structured inheritance. Once this is done, we have our linguistic knowledge together with the semantic knowledge within a single representational framework (see Figure 13).

Concretion mechanisms (or any other marker passing algorithm) that worked for inference generation can now be applied to syntactic structures as well since the underlying data structures are indistinguishable. Whether all such mechanisms generalize to useful applications is another question, but at least we are now in a position to ask.

Putting it Together

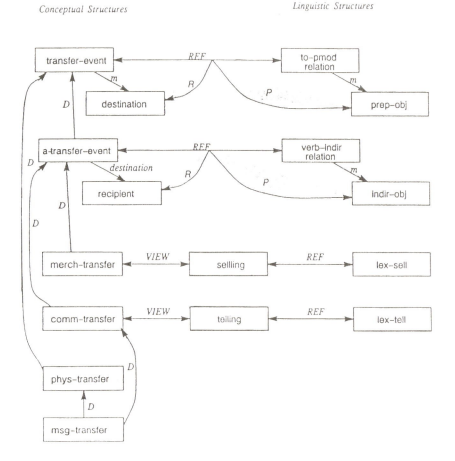

Conceptual Structures

Linguistic Structures

Figure 13 Integrating Syntax and Semantics

Although we are concentrating here on techniques for sentence analysis, it is interesting to note that the integrated KODIAK structures we've been discussing are used for both sentence analysis and sentence generation [Jacobs, 1987b].

Although Jacobs is probably the first researcher to investigate highly integrated methods for syntactic/semantic processing from the two perspectives of analysis and generation, he was not the first to work with a uniform representational framework for sentence analysis. The earlier Word Expert Parsing effort [Small, 1980] deserves to be mentioned along with related work on lexical access [Cottrell and Small, 1983] which focused on the problem of word sense ambiguity.

A very different approach to the problem of integrating syntax and semantics can be found in an effort that was strongly influenced by Cottrell and Small's earlier work. Waltz and Pollack [1985] picked up where Cottrell and Small left off, and tried to generalize connectionist techniques into higher levels of sentence analysis. While we have seen a lot of exciting work by connectionists on sentence analysis within the last year or two (see for example, [McClelland and Kawamoto, 1986]), I've chosen to talk about Waltz and Pollack because the techniques they use are much more accessible to an AI audience without an introductory tutorial on connectionism.

Waltz and Pollack work with large, knowledge-rich networks in their system, but these networks are not as carefully structured as the KODIAK networks we saw before. Indeed, one of the weaknesses of this system is its lack of inheritance in any form. There are no theoretical claims about knowledge representation here either: One could invent a node for any sort of frame with additional nodes for any kind of role or slot constraint imaginable.

The key idea here is spreading activation and network relaxation. But now the activation is analog activation, which means that nodes are given numerical values to indicate how much activation is present at any given time. Relaxation is the process of systematically adjusting activation levels within the network until the network assumes a stable state. A stronger connectionist flavor is obtained by the use of lateral inhibition to expedite the stabilization of competing nodes where activation levels are expected to be mutually exclusive. If we appear to have walked off some sort of cliff in terms of your familiarity with these terms, that's probably because this is a numerical algorithm and not the sort of thing we normally associate with "mainstream" symbolic AI.

Consider, for example, an eating node, which has arcs leading out to role nodes that represent things like agents and objects (see Figure 14). When we understand the sentence "Mary ate spaghetti with Sue," we want to see the network stabilize with a high level of activation on this eating node as well as the appropriate slot-filling nodes. It is important to settle on a high level of activation for the co-agent node lest we interpret Sue to be a co-object (like meatballs) or instrument (like fork) for the eating event. If all goes well, semantic constraints within the network will push the relaxation process in the right direction, and inappropriate pathways in the network will die off for lack of sufficient activation.

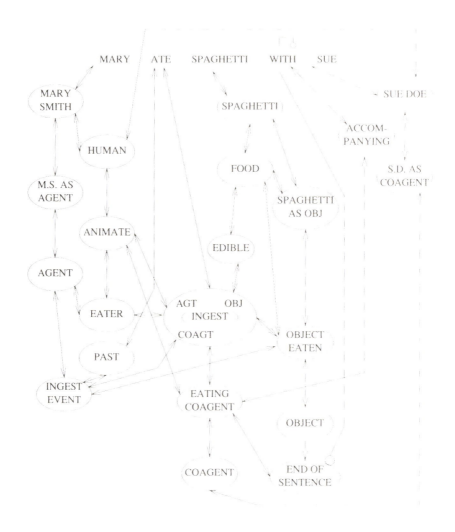

Figure 14 Eating Spaghetti with Massive Parallelism

If ever there was an algorithm to illustrate homogeneous control, numerical relaxation must be it. This idea can be applied to networks of nodes representing anything you want. We can have different nodes for different word senses, other nodes for semantic features, and even nodes for traditional syntactic constituents. Plug in a grammar by wiring the nodes correctly, and you can produce syntactic parse trees as a side effect of network relaxation (see Figure 15).

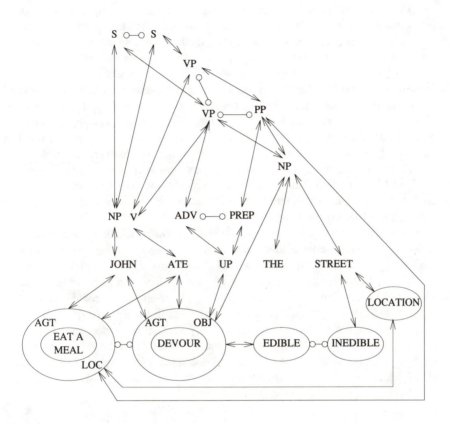

Figure 15 Adding Syntactic Constraints

Within this framework we integrate semantic constraints and syntactic constraints in a massively parallel architecture that can readily compute a global assessment of the situation after each word of the sentence is received. Preferred word senses and syntactic preferences may shift around as we move through the sentence, making it possible to run interesting experiments by taking "snapshots" of the network as we move through a sentence. Activation levels from a syntactic constituent may inhibit or support a specific semantic interpretation, and semantic preferences can flow back toward the nodes deciding about syntax.

This provides us with a very nice framework for investigating a lot of problems, and in particular, garden path processing phenomena are especially well suited for analog spreading activation models. Of course, all of the problems we have with marker passing algorithms apply here as well: E.g., what happens if two different referents activate the same sections of the network? In fact, the interference effects associated with analog activation are even worse than with marker passing algorithms because we have to make sure that nodes "die out" within a reasonable period of time by tweaking the numeric algorithm. In a marker passing framework, a node can be told to die after a fixed number of words have been parsed or after a specific marker like a clause boundary is encountered. In the symbolic paradigm it is at least easier to understand why a node is turned on or off. In the analog paradigm, the status of each node is dependent on the status of every other node in the network, making the whole business rather inscrutable.

Now that we've seen how syntax and semantics might be intertwined under homogeneous control, let's return to the issue of pragmatics and how processes of inference might be interleaved with processes of sentence analysis. As I said earlier, I don't think a lot of progress has been made in this area. Waltz and Pollack have designated a subset of their nodes as "context nodes," but it is difficult to evaluate the utility of that idea in the absence of a systematic methodology for building large, massively parallel networks. Probably the best I can do is show you some more places where "high-level" knowledge must be allowed to influence "low-level" decisions about syntax. One of the places where this appears to happen involves analogies and the role of analogical thinking in natural language.

5 *Analogical Reasoning and Language*

Her hair was like lamb's wool, her teeth were like pearls.

We're supposed to understand from this that her hair was soft and her teeth were white. We're not supposed to conclude that her hair was white and her teeth were hard. One discovers that the mapping of a sentence onto appropriate analogical features is not such a simple business. Perhaps her hair was smelly and her teeth were very round?

Analogical reasoning is a major problem in natural language communication, and we don't have to reach for poetry to find instances of it. In fact, it's much more common than you might imagine. Sometimes we see it explicitly, in the example above. The word "like" warns us that we may be talking about an analogy and we'd better get the mapping right. But analogies can also operate more subtly.

For example, idioms often rely on analogies of one sort or another. I can pick up an article in the newspaper and read about a conflict in the Middle East: "Despite the fact that the two factions had been fighting for 20 years, they finally agreed to bury the hatchet." This is a standard idiom. Everyone understands what is meant by it. Or we can go back to Mary in the hospital. Maybe after John took her flowers, she took a turn for the worse and kicked the bucket. Another idiom. In fact, there were two idioms in there. Nobody I know can take a turn for the inferior.

For a long time, no one in AI had much to say about idioms. They were just conventionalized and fossilized expressions in the language—a part of the phrasal lexicon that had to be learned case by case. But if you look at it with analogy in mind, there are some very interesting phenomena associated with idioms. To be precise, there appear to be some rules that govern the syntactic flexibility of idioms, and those rules are based on analogical reasoning processes.

First, we must understand that some idioms are more fossilized than others. The burying of the hatchet can be passivized: "After the peace talks, the hatchet was buried." The kicking of the bucket cannot be passivized: "After a long illness, the bucket was kicked by Mary." That's just not an option. One of these idioms can tolerate a syntactic transformation while the other can't.

In a recent Ph.D. thesis we find a claim about this [Zernik, 1987]. The key question is whether or not a given idiom can be explained via analogical reasoning. If an idiom can be explained, then it will be syntactically flexible. If it can't be explained, then it will be brittle. Let's look at this in a little more detail.

In the case of the hatchet, we have associations and we have knowledge. You always have to have knowledge in order to have an analogy. And the knowledge that's relevant here is knowledge about war. One can imagine a war script, where we have stereotypic events. You have some initial conflict, you gather your troops, you attack, you defend, you win, lose, draw, you establish an agreement, and you bring your troops home. Somehow, we have to get from burying the hatchet, which is a very specific literal event, to the withdrawal of armed troops. If we can make that connection, then the hatchet operates as an instrument of aggression (just as the armed troops are a symbol of aggression), and burying the hatchet translates into a deliberate disarmament, a halt to aggression.

How do you make those connections? This is a very difficult problem for knowledge representation and memory organization. We could call it a concretion problem, but that doesn't solve anything. Is there an abstract event that dominates both troop withdrawals and hatchet burials in some massive inheritance hierarchy? If we go up the abstraction hierarchy too far, all events will map to all other events (because they're all dominated by some very general event node way up at the top).

Concretion by itself is probably too powerful a mechanism in the sense that it could be used to make sense out of idioms no one ever heard of. If burying a hatchet is a further specification of weapon burial, then burying a rifle should be recognized just as easily as burying the hatchet. Somehow we lost track of the fact that one of these is an idiom and the other is not. What distinguishes the one from the other is an instance (real or plausibly constructable) where someone actually buried a hatchet following a conflict. Perhaps we all remember a story about the pilgrims and the Indians from our 4th grade history lessons. It's at least conceivable that an Indian might have buried a hatchet in a war ritual. To bury a rifle is to impose an event from a ritually rich culture on an object from a culture largely lacking in symbolic rituals. The mismatch arouses cognitive inconsistency and seems disturbing.

Ignoring the very difficult problems associated with analogical reasoning, we can hypothesize that some such processes take place. Or at least they take place for the idioms that can be explained. If we had to explain "burying the hatchet" to a child, we would probably describe a scenario where a hatchet got buried to symbolize the end of physical aggressions. But what would you do if someone asked you to explain "kicking the bucket?" Most people explain this one by saying *it's just an expression* (don't bother me kid). There is no analogical mapping that gives us a plausible explanation for why death is associated with kicking a bucket. Most of us do not know of any such explanations and can't construct a plausible one even if we try.

So why should any of this matter to a syntactic transformation? The fact that some idioms are syntactically flexible while others are not suggests that the processes associated with the two types of idioms are very different. An explainable idiom is understood at a deep conceptual level... the idiom maps into a conceptual structure retrieved by analogical reasoning. An inexplicable idiom is understood (she kicked the bucket ⇒ she died) but not explained by analogical mappings.

When an explanation is available, all of the language processing power available for the targeted conceptual structures can be applied. The explanatory concept underneath the idiom can be expressed using a variety of syntactic structures, and this makes the idiom receptive to syntactic transformations. When no explanation is available, there is no underlying concept associated with the idiom, and so there is no language processing capability that applies. Brittle idioms lack the conceptual scaffolding required to loosen them up.

Before we leave the topic of analogical reasoning, I want to give you some more examples of its utility for natural language. One way that analogical reasoning creeps in is via metaphor. Metaphors are abundant in natural language, and so pervasive we don't even notice them most of the time. For example, it is common to assume that technical literature is characterized by very dry and literal language. If there is one place where metaphors might not intrude, it must be when people discuss technical or scientific concepts.

Surprisingly, technical descriptions are often very rich in metaphors. Consider, for example, the language we commonly use when talking about computers:

> You can *get into* the editor by...
>
> I *ran* it *through* spell to...
>
> The editor *died* when...

If you have a language processing system that assumes only living things can die, you're going to have a lot of trouble with a sentence like "The editor died on me" [Wilensky, Arens and Chin, 1984].

Oliver North has given us a beautiful example of how intimately interdependent language and analogical reasoning can be. If you were listening to the Congressional hearings, you heard Col. North explain a misunderstanding he had about the term "delete" in the context of electronic mail. He thought that when you pushed the delete button, the mail really went away.

I suspect that this faulty interpretation of deletion was the direct result of an analogical mapping to a bad analogy. Given the rest of his testimony before the Congressional hearing, it seems quite likely that Col. North mapped the delete command in his mail system to the on button of a paper shredding machine. When you turn on the shredding machine, things really do go away. Unfortunately, shredding machines are not very good models for what happens to electronic mail. If Col. North had ever worked with icon-infested software of the sort found on personal computers, he might have mapped the delete command to a wastepaper basket, and been more concerned about the security of his deleted documents for the same reason that one should worry about wastepaper baskets.

I do not mean to disparage Col. North or his memory organization. This kind of misunderstanding happens to all of us and it's especially dangerous when a word appears to be so simple. How do people usually explain something like a delete command? When you say delete, the message will go away. When you delete a message you throw it out. Deleting a message destroys the message. None of these explanations are quite correct but how many of us really want technically correct explanations? Natural language communications are generally very effective in trading off accuracy for brevity. But every so often the trade-off slips up and mistakes result. What's amazing is how we all get by as well as we do.

6 *Episodic and Semantic Memory*

Let me close on a topic that is in keeping with our theme of homogeneity. In addition to homogeneous control, we can talk about homogeneous memory. There's some very interesting work that I think is just beginning to get off the ground. The one example that I'll draw from in order to illustrate what I'm talking about is some recent work done at Yale [Riesbeck and Martin, 1986].

Traditionally, people who talk about memory make a distinction between semantic memory and episodic memory. To understand this distinction, let's think about how we might go about answering a simple question. Suppose I ask you, "Does a penguin have skin?" If you have a semantic memory available to you that involves penguins, you will understand that a penguin is a type of bird, and as a bird, it has specific features, one of which is skin. If you have any kind of retrieval algorithm available for answering questions, you will traverse links of this sort in order to confirm that penguins do indeed have skin.

Now suppose I ask a very similar question. What about a chicken? "Does a chicken have skin?" Now, if you have semantic memory, you're going to answer the question much the same way you answered it for penguins. You won't have associations available to you about Antarctica, but you'll find chickens, you'll find birds, you'll find features for birds, and you'll find skin. Just like before. This is the semantic view of memory.

However, a number of people believe something else goes on, that perhaps semantic memory can sometimes be short-circuited by something much scruffier called episodic memory. Episodic memory has to do with personal first-hand experience with the world. For example, dinner last night is a good example of episodic knowledge. If dinner last night happened to be fried chicken and you really like the skin on fried chicken, you might have a much faster path for answering the question about chicken skin than the one available through semantic memory (see Figure 16).

Traditionally, semantic knowledge and episodic knowledge have always been thought to be in competition with one another: These are two distinct views of memory and there really isn't room in this world for both of them to coexist peaceably [Tulving, 1972].

But very recently we've begun to see some work that seems to blur the semantic/episodic barrier and cross lines between the two without any trouble at all. We've already seen some of this with FAUSTUS. What sort of a node is the node that represents balloons exploding? An exploding balloon sounds pretty episodic. Yet two steps up the hierarchy we'll see general nodes for explosions and breaking events. Nodes like that are commonly found in semantic networks. If we examine the memory structures engineered for FAUSTUS, it seems that the task of inference generation needs both types of memory and would be badly impaired if forced to function without one or the other.

Semantic Memory vs. Episodic Memory

Does a penguin have skin?

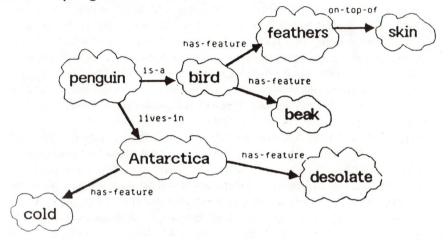

Does a chicken have skin?

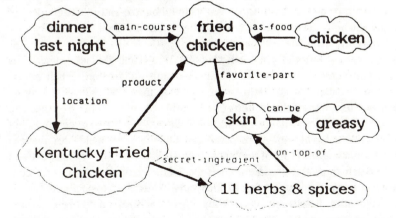

Figure 16 Semantic Memory vs. Episodic Memory

Now let's get back to Riesbeck and Martin to see how the semantic/episodic issue relates to sentence analysis. Before describing their system, DMAP (Direct Memory Access Parsing), Riesbeck makes an interesting claim about language analysis at the level of sentence comprehension. He points out that there are really two distinct views about what it means to analyze a sentence. In one perspective, we think of a sentence as mapping into existing concepts in memory. That is, you really only understand this sentence because you have knowledge in memory that allowed you to make sense out of it. Then when you understand the sentence, the very act of understanding the sentence operates to reinforce or modify existing structures in memory. This view of sentence analysis might not sound terribly controversial, until you realize that virtually every sentence analyzer ever implemented operates under different premises.

In most models of sentence analysis, sentences do not map directly into memory. They create meaning representations, and these meaning representations may be influenced by some form of memory, but the act of sentence analysis rarely has any side effects that alter memory as the target meaning representation is being produced. The processes that analyze a sentence are normally segregated from the processes that alter memory (if indeed, any process is capable of altering memory).

Riesbeck characterizes the traditional framework as the "build-and-store" approach to sentence analysis. He calls the non-traditional framework the "recognize-and-record" style of sentence analysis. He then goes on to argue that it would be much to our advantage to investigate recognize-and-record models of parsing as a wholly new style of parsing that lends itself more naturally to a truly memory-intensive view of language.

In fairness, we should point out that the Waltz and Pollack parser falls somewhere in between build-and-store and recognize-and-record. Their analyzer produces a pattern of activation over its entire memory. Indeed, it may be very difficult to interpret this pattern of activation should anyone ever need to know what a particular sentence means. So Pollack and Waltz are certainly not consistent with the build-and-store paradigm. On the other hand, the changes made to memory as a result of sentence analysis are completely transient and wiped out each time a new sentence is processed. So this is not exactly consistent with the recognize-and-record idea either. Yet the connectionist enterprise in general is clearly operating within the recognize-and-record paradigm if we look at the learning algorithms that adjust weights and modify the network each time a new sentence is processed. The radical view that Riesbeck advocates is really only radical within symbolic AI circles. Connectionists would feel quite at home with it.

To see how Riesbeck and Martin try to realize a recognize-and-record model using symbolic techniques, let's look at one of their example sentences. Here is a picture of DMAP's memory (see Figure 17).

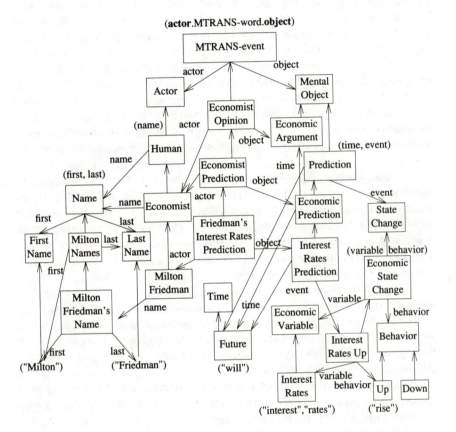

Figure 17 Understanding Milton Friedman

DMAP has some knowledge about newspaper articles taken from newspapers. The sentence we are now trying to understand is, "Interest rates will rise as an inevitable consequence of the monetary explosion." This is a quote from Milton Friedman in the *New York Times.* Figure 17 shows us the portion of DMAP's memory which is important for understanding "(Milton Friedman says) interest rates will rise ... ."

At the highest level of memory, we can characterize this sentence as a transfer of information. Somebody said something. This is a highly abstract characterization of the input sentence. As we move down to a more specific representation, we further understand the sentence to be an opinion by an economist. Even more specifically, a prediction by an economist. And more specifically again, a prediction by Milton Friedman about interest rates.

Looking at Figure 17, we can see an inheritance hierarchy that gives us all the further specifications needed to represent the input at various levels of abstraction. If we start at the top node for a communication event, filling in the details becomes something like a concretion problem. Of course, memory will only look like this if DMAP has already seen other stories about Milton Friedman making predictions about interest rates. Given such knowledge, the act of mapping our new input sentence into memory becomes an act of recognition: I see now... this is another interest rate prediction by Milton Friedman. DMAP shows how a sentence analyzer can work with memory in order to situate the content of a sentence within an existing framework for memory. The algorithm is a marker passing algorithm, and DMAP shows us what sentence analysis might look like within a memory-rich recognize-and-record paradigm.

Let's take one more look at the nodes in this tree structure (see Figure 17). Although the root node for a communication event looks very generic and therefore semantic, nodes further down the tree structure look more and more episodic. We have a node for all the names we know with the first name Milton. We have a node for economic predictions by Milton Friedman. This is completely episodic.

At some point, we've crossed the line and moved from nice, clean, semantic knowledge down to scruffy, first-hand experience knowledge of Milton Friedman and what he's said in the past. In fact, the marker passing algorithm in DMAP was designed with two kinds of memory organization in mind: abstraction hierarchies and packaging hierarchies [Schank, 1982]. The abstraction hierarchy is the traditional is-a hierarchy we see in semantic networks, and the packaging hierarchy handles stereotypic chronologies of the sort we first saw with scripts—this is clearly episodic knowledge.

So an interesting line gets crossed in DMAP, and there are important implications when you cross that line. One of the implications has to do with knowledge acquisition. If you are willing to cross that line and benefit from the advantages associated with it, then you necessarily have to worry about knowledge acquisition. Because every time you understand a sentence, you should add another instance of something to your knowledge framework. The tenth time you read about Milton Friedman predicting interest rates will rise, you should feel that the concept is somehow more familiar than it was the second time around. You are automatically in the learning business at that point. Earlier work on generalization and dynamic memory organization comes to mind [Lebowitz, 1983]. But this is a not a standard perspective on sentence analysis. Most researchers in natural language processing and even knowledge-based natural language processing would not claim to be working on learning or knowledge acquisition. So this is a really a radical view of language being promoted here.

7 *Conclusions*

That brings us to our wrap-up. I've tried to point out some trends over the last 15 years. It is possible to associate the trends with roughly five year cycles starting in 1972.

The first cycle (1972–77) was characterized by a preoccupation with strong methods addressing specific knowledge structures and processes of inference associated with specific knowledge structures. Ph.D. theses by Charniak and Rieger motivated much of this work, and Schank organized a large research group at Yale to identify knowledge structures for natural language processing.

The second cycle (1977–82) was characterized by a gradual appreciation for the implications of language processing based on strong methods alone. Dyer's thesis gave us a taste of the price we would have to pay in terms of system complexity if the strong methods continued to propagate without other kinds of processing techniques. At the same time, powerful ideas based on the earlier impetus toward strong methods were being pushed hard and refined in a number of computer implementations. Jaime Carbonell, Richard Cullingford, Gerald DeJong, Michael Dyer, Richard Granger, Janet Kolodner, James Meehan, Mallory Selfridge, Robert Wilensky, and I, all finished theses at Yale during this period. The pendulum was poised to swing back from there.

The third cycle (1982–87) fueled a renewed interest in weak methods—techniques for homogeneous inference generation, homogeneous memory organization, and broad processing techniques of great generality. Marker passing algorithms enjoyed a lot of attention during this period and progress by connectionists was greeted with cautious enthusiasm. Spreading activation became a common theme in a lot of the original research of this period. James Hendler, Graeme Hirst, Paul Jacobs, Peter Norvig, and Jordan Pollack, all completed theses consistent with the Zeitgeist of this cycle. Work by Gary Cottrell and Steve Small, which was completed before 1982, received recognition during this period for having surfaced "before its time."

So where are we going in the next five years? It's always safer to wait for 20–20 hindsight, but I'm willing to stick my neck out and imagine a future that would at least not surprise me.

- I expect to see a push toward knowledge acquisition as an active concern in knowledge-based natural language.

- The symbolic community will grapple with the questions raised by connectionist research: What are the essential issues in the symbolic/subsymbolic paradigm struggle? Should we all see the light and become connectionists? Should the connectionists see the light and forsake connectionism? Given the unlikelihood of those two scenarios, how will the two communities come to view each other and the relationship between their distinctive research paradigms?

- Somewhere in the midst of all this, theoretical progress might be made on the episodic/semantic distinction. More and more people will find it convenient to acknowledge the utility of both memory types and design algorithms that move freely between them. This will be viewed either in terms of an integration of two distinct memory types, or a demonstration that the original distinction cannot be supported by computational models (it was a bad idea in the first place).

- Finally, we may see some serious efforts aimed at evaluating our models and understanding the qualitatively different contributions that are being made by different research styles. The neat/scruffy dichotomy may give way to some other, more timely wedge, as more and more people find it difficult to pigeonhole themselves as card-carrying neats or free-spirited scruffies. Those who never liked this distinction in the first place will hold a workshop and burn all reprints that contain the keywords "neat" or "scruffy."

In closing I'll leave you with two of my favorite quotes. The first one is by Thomas Edison. Thomas Edison was born too early to be an AI person, but I think he would have been a good one if persistence counts for anything. He had a lot of trouble finding the right filament for the light bulb, and he tried a lot of filaments before he found a workable one. Whenever I see the following quote I like to mentally transport Edison into 1987 and place him in an NSF office where he's trying to convince a program manager to fund his research. Exasperated and impatient with the obvious difficulty of his situation, he says:

"I've tried everything. I have not failed. I've just found 10,000 ways that won't work."

I think anyone who's been in AI for more than ten years can probably relate to that scenario, but this is a rather pessimistic perspective on the state of the art, so I don't really want to leave you on that note. It makes the whole business sound like a simple brute-force search, and I think we're all at least a little smarter than that.

Here's a happier observation from Francis Bacon that seems closer to the true spirit of AI:

"Truth emerges more readily from error than from confusion."

Questions and Answers

(Q) I wonder if you might have seen the little note on USENET from Donald Norman about artificial intelligence as a science. Whether you have or not, let me ask the question. What, in your opinion, controls the development of this research from the point of view of both evidential support and falsification? I ask it because you didn't say anything about it.

(A) Well, I think there's a lot of soul searching that goes on in AI on this point, particularly within the machine learning community. Language researchers are perhaps less preoccupied with such concerns because it is very hard to design convincing experiments for processes of this complexity. However, one good collection of psychological experiments inspired by the knowledge structuring work at Yale is [Galambos et al., 1986].

I think a big part of our enterprise can be reasonably characterized as trying to understand the problem before we can presume to find solutions. For example, Rieger thought the inference problem was primarily a control issue. Schank says it's primarily an issue about knowledge and memory organization.

I think we understand a good deal more about language now than we did 15 years ago, but whether we're learning what we learn by practicing a normal science is another issue. Personally speaking, I don't really care if we're practicing science as long as we can say we're learning something.

How about an easy question?

(Q) I'll give you a technical question I have about the last point of your talk... where you describe the recent work by Riesbeck as an effort combining episodic memory with semantic memory. You said that would create a problem for knowledge acquisition. It seems to me that if you could store the sentences you understand in the same representation that you are using to parse them, then that would be a big windfall for knowledge acquisition, because once you parse it, you have it available as part of your episodic memory for use later on. So the impression I get is just the opposite of what you said. Can you clarify that?

(A) You have to be careful about exactly what it is you think you should learn. If you're interested in psychological validity, there's a lot of evidence that people are very bad at remembering sentences verbatim in long-term recall or recognition. Even so, the content of those same sentences can be recalled. This suggests that our episodic memory structures operate with some system of knowledge representation that is not dependent on sentences per se.

When we say that DMAP can "understand" a sentence better if it's seen the sentence before, we should keep in mind that DMAP will also understand a paraphrase of that sentence with equal advantage because the memory which facilitates understanding is based on a canonical form for meaning representation: All semantically invariant paraphrases are collapsed into a single meaning representation. So DMAP can't be expected to learn anything about syntax or the processes needed to handle syntactic information as long as its memory can't record distinctions specific to syntax.

It is very difficult to say how the learning associated with episodic domain knowledge relates to the problem of learning how to analyze sentences. Going back to psychological validity, children acquire the basics of sentence analysis very early on. By the time a child enters school, she's basically working on vocabulary acquisition and an increasing tolerance for syntactic complexity—the hard part of language acquisition is over and what remains is a lot of expansion within existing structures. This suggests that the mechanisms associated with adult language processing are probably not very plastic or sensitive to specific sentences on a case-by-case basis. It might therefore make sense to separate the two types of learning as distinct and separable problems (as DMAP does). Of course, there are plenty of connectionists who would disagree with me about this.

(Q) You spent some time talking about how one could use the same knowledge representation structures for representing the concept in the sentence and concepts of just verb and noun through grammatical terms, but I guess I missed something along the way. What power does that give you, what's the advantage of doing that?

(A) Ah. Well, the idea is that we should get away from that one slide I showed you from Dyer's thesis, where the 22 different knowledge structures interact with one another in very arbitrary and idiosyncratic ways. If we could find knowledge representation techniques and memory organization techniques that allow us to bring in all kinds of different knowledge structures under the same representational umbrella, then we could develop algorithms that manipulate that information in a uniform manner. So it's a question of finding uniform processing theories as opposed to allowing the whole enterprise to break down into 1,001 interacting experts who each speak different languages and talk about different things.

I should also point out that I'm only trying to identify some trends in our research. Time will tell whether or not this trend is justified. Maybe reality will ultimately reveal herself to be 1,001 different experts and we'll just have to develop appropriate techniques for dealing with that kind of complexity.

(Q) So in the case of Waltz and Pollack, we've really got sentences being parsed using only spreading activation? Some form of connectionism?

(A) In the case of Waltz and Pollack, that's exactly what we've got. In the case of Jacobs, who was working with KODIAK, we see another form of spreading activation called marker passing, which operates a lot like relaxation except it's just not numerical relaxation. In both the numeric and non-numeric approaches, a simple algorithm is iteratively applied to nodes in the network until a stable state is reached. A lot of people are playing around with marker passing these days, including Charniak.

(Q) And do those parsing algorithms duplicate the same phenomena that something like the Marcus parser does... garden path phenomena?

(A) Pollack and Waltz were very interested in garden path sentence processing and they have examples that simulate effects exhibited by human subjects.

(Q) Could you speak briefly about the current interaction between psycholinguistics and computer science in language understanding, because it seems like some of these models come from insights from psycholinguistics, but you didn't mention that.

(A) I think if you concentrate on the knowledge-based aspects of language processing, you find influence coming in from a number of places. For example, the Zernik work on frozen idioms and analogical mappings was, I suspect, heavily influenced, or at least inspired, by the work of George Lakoff.

Much of psycholinguistics, however, restricts its domain of inquiry to syntactic phenomena without appropriate concern for interactions between syntax and other knowledge structures. To the extent that this is true, many of the results we see from those experiments are not very illuminating for people working on knowledge-based natural language. Indeed, most of us argue rather vehemently against the segregation of syntactic processing.

(Q) No, but the psycholinguists do experiment on memory, and they're interested in memory, they're interested in semantic memory, they're interested in cross-cultural effects of understanding. I was just wondering if there are any active relationships between these bodies of research.

(A) There are scattered instances of influence. For example, Eugene Charniak was strongly influenced by the experiments of David Swinney in the late 70s. Experiments by Robert Milne are important for people working on lexical access. I'm not sure how much there is in terms of active collaboration, but it is always important to keep the channels of communication open.

(Q) I've noticed that the entire description stayed within the verbal domain, and I'm wondering if that reflects a supposition about how people really think. Or is that just a starting point that we might have to move away from at some later time?

(A) What do you mean by "verbal" domain?

(Q) Well, for instance, when you said, "Does a penguin have skin?" I immediately saw a picture of a penguin. As a matter of fact, it was superimposed on a map like an old Disney movie. Then I saw a few feathers removed and then I saw skin underneath. I didn't say, "Is this a bird?" There was no classification like that going on.

(A) Right. There are two things to say about that. First, a warning, and then an answer. It's a little dangerous to place a lot of credibility in your subjective experience of what happens when you answer questions or understand sentences. If we're conscious of anything, that's just the tip of the iceberg. In fact, we can't even say if it's a real piece of the iceberg or some completely misleading side effect caused by the iceberg. So that's the warning.

Having said that, I think there's a very serious question about whether or not the knowledge structures underlying language are in fact the same knowledge structures underlying visual information processing. If they aren't, then we should worry about which aspects of common sense reasoning would be better served by which structures.

And as far as I can tell, there's precious little interaction between high-level vision researchers and knowledge-based language researchers. This is too bad. Surely we both have needs related to spatial reasoning, although those concerns are probably much more central to vision processing than language processing.

There's been a certain amount of philosophical posturing around this question. Pylyshyn and Jackendoff come to mind. But it seems silly to jump to any conclusions given how little we really know about the whole business. I can't even say the jury is still out since the matter hasn't really come to trial.

Acknowledgments

This research was supported by DARPA contract #N00014-87-K-0238.

References

Abelson, R., 1981. Constraint, Construal, and Cognitive Science. *Proceedings of the Third Annual Conference of the Cognitive Science Society.* Berkeley, CA.

Alker, H. R., Jr., Lehnert, W. G., and Schneider, D. K., 1985. Two Reinterpretations of Toynbee's JESUS: Explorations in Computational Hermeneutics. In *Artificial Intelligence and Text-Understanding: Plot Units and Summarization Procedures, Quaderni di Ricerca Linguistica.* Graziella Tonfoni, ed.

Bobrow, D.G., and Winograd, T., 1977. An Overview of KRL-0, a knowledge representation language. In *Cognitive Science* **1**(1):3–46.

Charniak, E., 1972. *Toward A Model of Children's Story Comprehension.* Massachusetts Institute of Technology Artificial Intelligence Laboratory, Cambridge, MA. AI TR-266.

Cottrell, G.W. and Small, S.L., 1983. A Connectionist Scheme for Modeling Word Sense Disambiguation. *Cognition and Brain Theory* **6**(1).

Cullingford, R., 1978. *Script Application: Computer Understanding of Newspaper Stories.* Yale University, Department of Computer Science, Research Report #116. Dissertation.

Dreyfus H., 1987. Artificial Intelligence: Where Are We? *ABACUS* **4**(3):13. A collection of interviews edited by Bobrow, D.G. and Hayes, P.J.

Dyer, M., 1983a. *In-Depth Understanding.* MIT Press. Cambridge, MA.

Dyer, M., 1983b. The Role of Affect in Narratives. *Cognitive Science* **7**:211–242.

Galambos, J., Abelson, R., and Black, J., 1986. *Knowledge Structures.* Lawrence Erlbaum Assoc., Hillsdale, NJ.

Geisel, T., 1950. *If I Ran the Zoo.* Random House, New York.

Jacobs, P., 1987a. A Knowledge Framework for Natural Language Analysis. *Proceedings of the Tenth International Joint Conference on Artificial Intelligence.* Milan, Italy. 675–678.

Jacobs, P., 1987b. Knowledge-Intensive Natural Language Generation. In *Artificial Intelligence* **33**(3).

Lebowitz, M., 1983. Memory Based Parsing. *Artificial Intelligence* **21**(4):363–404.

Lehnert, W.G., 1981. Plot Units and Narrative Summarization. *Cognitive Science* **5**(4).

Lehnert, W.G., Dyer, M., Johnson, P. Yang, C. and Harley, S., 1983. BORIS—An Experiment in In-Depth Understanding of Narratives. *Artificial Intelligence*, **20**:15–62.

McClelland, J., and Kawamoto, A., 1986. Mechanisms of Sentence Processing: Assigning Roles to Constituents. In *Parallel Distributed Processing: Explorations in the Microstructures of Cognition—2.* Rumelhart and McClelland, ed. Bradford Books.

Norvig, P., 1987. *Unified Theory of Inference for Text Understanding.* Department of Computer Science, University of California, Berkeley. Dissertation.

Quillian, M.R., 1968. Semantic Memory. In *Semantic Information Processing.* Marvin Minsky, ed. MIT Press, Cambridge, MA.

Rieger, C., 1974. *Conceptual Memory: A Theory and Computer Program for Processing the Meaning Content of Natural Language Utterances.* Department of Computer Science, Stanford, Univ. Memo AIM-233, Stan-CS-74-419. Disseration.

Riesbeck, C. and Martin, C., 1986. Direct Memory Access Parsing. In *Experience, Memory and Reasoning*, Riesbeck, C. and Kolodner, J., ed. Lawrence Erlbaum, Hillsdale, NJ.

Schank, R., 1982. *Dynamic Memory: A Theory of Reminding and Learning in Computers and People.* Cambridge University Press.

Schank, R., 1975. *Conceptual Information Processing.* American Elsevier, New York.

Schank, R. and Abelson, R., 1977. *Scripts, Plans, Goals, and Understanding.* Lawrence Erlbaum, Hillsdale, NJ.

Small, S., 1980. *Word Expert Parsing: A Theory of Distributed Word-Based Natural Language Understanding.* Department of Computer Science, University of Maryland, TR-954. Dissertation.

Tulving, E., 1972. Episodic and Semantic Memory. In *Organization of Memory.* Tulving and Donaldson, ed. Academic Press, New York.

Waltz, D. and Pollack, J., 1985. Massively Parallel Parsing: A Strongly Interactive Model of Natural Language Interpretation. *Cognitive Science* **9**(1).

Wilensky, R., 1986. Knowledge Representation—A Critique, A Proposal. In *Experience, Memory, and Reasoning.* Kolodner, J. and Riesbeck, C., ed. Lawrence Erlbaum Assoc.

Wilensky, R., 1978. *Understanding Goal-Based Stories.* Department of Computer Science, Yale University Research Report #140. Dissertation.

Wilensky, R., Arens, Y., and Chin, D., 1984. Talking to UNIX in English: An Overview of UC. *Communications of the Association for Computing Machinery.*

Winograd T., 1987. Natural Language: The Continuing Challenge. *AI Expert* 2(5):7–8.

Winograd T., 1972. *Understanding Natural Language.* Academic Press, New York.

Winograd T., and Flores, F., 1986. *Understanding Computers and Cognition.* Ablex Publishing Corp., Norwood, NJ.

Zernik, U., 1987. *Strategies in Language Acquisition: Learning Phrases from Examples in Context.* UCLA-AI-87-1. Dissertation.

Chapter

4

Natural-Language Interfaces

C. Raymond Perrault and Barbara J. Grosz

SRI International

and Center for the Study of Language and Information

Menlo Park, California

Ann. Rev. Comput. Sci. 1986. 1:47–82

1 Introduction

Since the early 1960s when support decreased for machine translation, much of the research on natural-language processing (NLP) in North America has been motivated by its potential use for communicating with software systems.[1] Natural-language systems have been developed to extract information from databases, to control (simulated) robots [Winograd, 1972], to interact with graphic systems [Brachman et al., 1979], to specify simulation problems [Heidorn, 1976], and to communicate with systems embodying expertise in some task or problem area [Bobrow, 1977; A. Robinson, 1981].

In this article we focus on interfaces to database management systems (DBMS).[2] We use the term natural-language interface (or NLI) to refer to such interfaces, unless otherwise specified. In addition to being among the earliest interface systems developed, interfaces to databases account for most of the NLIs implemented to date and they are the subject of a substantial literature. Although some work has been done on the use of natural language to update

---

1 Notable exceptions include the story-understanding programs of Schank and his colleagues [Charniak, 1973; Schank, 1975].

2 We do not discuss commercial systems even though they are becoming increasingly available [Bates and Bobrow, 1983; Johnson, 1985]; the first was ROBOT/INTELLECT [Harris, 1977].

databases [Davidson and Kaplan, 1983] and on generating appropriate responses, most of the work on NLIs has been concerned with interpreting queries, and we will restrict ourselves to this problem area.

Besides discussing the main system architectures used in NLIs, we also sketch the body of techniques developed for them. In doing so, we distinguish between the task of an interface (the various functions of the underlying software system, such as answering questions, updating a database, or moving a robot) and its domain (the set of objects, properties, and relations denoted by the utterances it must interpret—e.g., employees and managers).

Natural language (NL) is but one of the methods available for human-machine interaction, but the reasons for its attractiveness are obvious:

- It provides an immediate vocabulary for talking about the contents of the database.

- It provides a means of accessing information in the database independently of its structure and encodings.

- It shields the user from the formal access language of the underlying system.

- It is available with a minimum of training to both novice and occasional user.

Although form-filling and menu-based techniques [Tennant et al., 1983] are appropriate to simple software systems whose structure is easily learned (and whose only user may be its designer), we conjecture that NL becomes more desirable as the following become true:

- The organization of the underlying information and procedures becomes more complex, so that the information necessary to process one query may be distributed widely throughout the system.

- The encoding of the information becomes more remote from everyday concepts, perhaps for the sake of retrieval efficiency.

- The problems the user wishes to solve become so complex that even writing a correct program in a formal query language may be difficult.

For example, the English query, "Who owns the fastest submarine," translates into over 20 lines of code [Hendrix et al., 1978] in the query language DATALANGUAGE. Even when compared to the more abstract relational query languages, NL is more concise. For instance, Warren and Pereira [1982] provide the following QUEL [Stonebraker et al., 1976] equivalent for the query "How many countries are there in each continent?"

```
range of C is countries
range of Cont is continents
range of I is inclusions
retrieve (Cont.name, count(C.name
where C.name = I.inside and I.outside = Cont.name))
```

As indeed they must, NLIs allow the same information to be requested in a variety of ways. For example, the following queries might all be used to ask a database to determine which manufacturers were known to have shipped equipment to Mexico:

Who sent equipment to Mexico?

Who sent Mexico equipment?

Mexico received equipment from which manufacturers?

Equipment was sent to Mexico by whom?

The function of an NLI is to translate utterances in NL to expressions of a more immediately interpretable form, such as the formal query language (QL) of a DBMS. In this regard the NLI is much like a programming-language (PL) compiler although differing from it in some important respects. The syntax of a PL is much simpler and the language is intentionally free of both syntactic and semantic ambiguities. PLs and their compilers assume certain primitive data types (e.g., numbers, strings). Although programs written in these PLs may be about other types of objects (e.g., employees, salaries), the syntax, the semantics, and the compiler of the PL are not sensitive to these types; the programmer must explicitly provide an ending for them into the data types provided by the PL. NLIs, on the other hand, are inherently sensitive to the types of objects in the domain. Thus, whereas with PLs the programmer must encode the objects in the datatypes of the PL, with NL the decoding burden is on the interface designer.

To simplify the discussion, we assume throughout that the underlying DBs are relational [Codd, 1970], and that the query language is relational calculus [Codd, 1972]. The relation between other DB models and the relational model is well understood [Ullman, 1982]; at worst they can be accommodated by building translators to them from relational calculus.

In the following section, we introduce a small database as the basis for the examples in this paper and we examine some of the more important problems of interpretation that an NLI must be designed to handle. We discuss the main sources of information available for the interpretation of utterances and outline the general features of the architecture of three classes of NLIs. We then offer a more detailed description of various NLI constituents, which shows how the sources of information are used by different systems to solve the various problems of interpretation. We conclude with a brief review of current research issues in NLP and their importance for more sophisticated interfaces to software systems.

2 *An Overview of the Problems*

The flexibility and succinctness of NL for querying DBs are achieved at the cost of problems in determining the interpretation of a query.[3]

Several of these problems, which we illustrate briefly here, have received interesting general treatments within the context of NLIs. For purposes of illustration, we consider a simple database containing information about employees and divisions in an organization. The information about an employee includes name, salary, division, and whether or not the employee was exempt from overtime pay. The information concerning a division includes its manager, its revenue, and its product.

The syntactic structure of a sentence is often ambiguous. For example, in the request, "Give me all the employees in a division making more than $50,000," it is unclear whether the modifying phrase "making more than $50,000" is meant to apply to employees or divisions. This may be termed the modifier attachment problem. In some cases, however, certain possibilities can be filtered out on semantic grounds. For example, while in general, "making shoes" in the query "Give me all the employees in a division making shoes" could modify either "employees" or "division," in a domain constrained by the information in our sample database, only divisions make shoes, not employees; thus the query in this specific case is unambiguous.

NL sentences with determiners—words such as "the," "each," and "what"—can have several readings, unlike the well-formed formulas of quantified logic. For example the query "What employee earns more than every division manager?" might be either a request to name the one employee whose salary exceeds that of any division manager or a request to name for each manager some employee who earns more than that manager. The relative scoping of the quantifiers corresponding to the different determiners depends on a number of factors, including the form of the utterance, the particular determiner, and the context of use. Various solutions to this problem, which is referred to as the quantifier scoping problem, are presented below.

The nominal compound problem is illustrated by the phrase "sales division" in the query "Who manages the sales division?" Such noun-noun combi-

---

3 Succinctness is certainly not a characteristic of all uses of NLP; for example, it is not a property of NL when used for the direct specification of low-level programs.

nations occur frequently in natural language. The syntax itself gives no clue as to the relationship between "sales" and "division." This kind of construction can be used to express arbitrary relationships (as illustrated by combinations like "wine glass," "oil pump," and "pump oil") and can be extended to longer concatenations of nouns "national park ranger station equipment procurement form"). The syntax does not even determine the direction of the modifier relationship (editors' attempts to encourage helpful hyphenation notwithstanding). For example, "Stanford Research Institute" formerly referred to a research institute associated with Stanford University, whereas "Computer Research Institute" would likely refer to an institute organized to conduct computer research. This problem is one of several related to modification discussed below.

The interpretation of a query may depend, in a number of different ways, on previous queries and their interpretations. Of these forms of dependency, elliptical utterances and certain uses of pronouns are prevalent in database querying.

Elliptical queries often arise because users are interested in obtaining similar information about different objects. After making a full request, they may ask for additional information with a single word or phrase. For example, Query 1, below, can be followed by either of the elliptical queries, 2a or 2b, which should then be interpreted as 3a or 3b, respectively.

1. Who is the manager of the automobile division?

2a. of aircraft?

2b. the secretary?

3a. Who is the manager of the aircraft division?

3b. Who is the secretary of the automobile division?

In these two examples, the "expanded" query is like the original one with but a single word (a different word in each case) replaced. The kind of expansion required may be much more complex, however. For example, a simple constituent may have to be replaced with a more complex one, as in Queries 4 and 5 below; or different parts of the original query may require replacement as in Queries 6 and 7.

4. What is Benson's salary?

5a. the sales division manager's?

5b. the highest revenue division's manager's?

6. What is the salary and title of the highest paid nonexempt employee?

7. Division of the lowest paid?

Note that Query 7 might be interpreted as either:

8a. What is the salary and division of the lowest paid nonexempt employee?

8b. What is the division of the lowest paid nonexempt employee?

Pronouns and other referring expressions provide one means of referring repeatedly to the same entities. For example, "they" in Query 9b must be resolved to refer to employees who earn more than the sales division manager.

9a. Can you tell me which employees earn more than the sales division
     manager?

9b. How much do they earn?

3 *Constraints on Interpretation*

In computational linguistics, as well as linguistics more generally, there is substantial disagreement (and no small amount of confusion) as to what interpretation actually is. Agreement has yet to be reached on answers to two fundamental questions:

- What receives interpretation? The alternatives include sentences, sentences in context, sequences of sentences, and dialogues.
- What is its object? Here alternatives include truth-values (especially for declarative sentences), answers (for questions), procedures for giving answers, or even the mental state the speaker must be in to make his utterance.

Within the restricted realm of interfaces to DBs, it is generally taken to be sentences and, occasionally, sequences of sentences that receive interpretations. The interpretation given to a query is taken to be a complex predicate; this predicate is satisfied by all the tuples of objects that are answers to the question. To allow for the possibility of ambiguity, we will take interpretation to be a relation between sentences and these complex predicates. For the interpretation relation to be specified, the following must be provided:

- A number of information sources,[4] each consisting of a class of objects and constraints on those objects. Thus, the syntactic information source

---

4 These are often called knowledge sources, but we prefer to reserve the term knowledge for other uses, as it suggests that the information is true; this is a connotation we wish to avoid.

might have words, phrases, and features as objects, and syntactic rules as constraints.

* Constraints that hold across information sources—expressing, for example, the relation between parse trees and their associated senses, or between sets of words (from the morphology) and sentences (from the syntax).

The NLI designer must also decide how the various objects and constraints will be represented, and how interpretations or, more accurately, their representations will be computed. One confusion that abounds in much of the computational-linguistics literature is the identification of interpretations with representations (i.e., interpretations are taken to be representations).

Although it is desirable for the overall theoretical account to be as modular as possible, computational efficiency may (and often does) suggest architectures where the various sources of information interact significantly. The kinds of information that are considered depend upon the kinds of tasks being performed by the NLI and the linguistic proficiency that is being sought. The standard information sources include morphology, syntax, the lexicon, illocutionary and discourse information, and encyclopedic information about the domain.

The objects of morphology are words, their roots, inflections, and derivations. Inflections in English include markers for number (to distinguish the singular "employee" from the plural "employees"), gender (to distinguish the masculine "him" from the feminine "her"), and case (to distinguish the nominative "who" from the accusative "whom"). Derivational morphology accounts for relationships among words of different syntactic classes, such as "inflate," "inflation," "inflationary," and "disinflate." Many NLIs include some treatment of inflectional morphology to minimize the size of the lexicon. Winograd [1983] provides a simple procedure. A more sophisticated computational treatment based on finite-state transducers is presented by Koskenniemi [1983].

The objects of syntax are words, phrases, and features. Of particular concern are phrase types (to distinguish noun phrases, prepositional phrases, and verb phrases), constraints on phrase structure (for example, that a prepositional phrase such as "in the auto division" consists of the preposition "in" and the noun phrase "the auto division"), and various phenomena collectively labelled as long-distance dependencies. These include constraints on complements (such as that John is the person doing the pleasing in "John is eager to please" but is the one who is pleased in "John is easy to please"). We include a brief review of various syntactic issues below; Winograd [1983] provides an excellent detailed treatment.

The illocutionary source is concerned with the actions (e.g., assertions, questions, requests) that can be performed using language, and with the indicators of those actions. In written language, the principal indicator is sentence mood—whether a sentence is indicative, interrogative or imperative. In spoken language, intonation is also important.

The discourse source specifies how the context established by sequences of utterances interacts with interpretation. It includes constraints on the structure of the sequence that are provided by linguistic expressions, as well as constraints on the interpretation of particular phrases that derive from the form and content of previous utterances.

The encyclopedia[5] contains constraints derived from the "real world"; it specifies its objects, relations, the structure of events, and the content of mental states. Of particular importance to NLIs is the domain model, that part of the encyclopedia describing the domain of the DB. The encyclopedia also encodes (a) restrictions on what word senses can modify or be modified by what others (e.g., that the adjective "solvent" can apply when "bank" denotes a financial institution but not when it denotes the side of a water course), and (b) sortal restrictions indicating that in "John paid Mary" the syntactic object "Mary" is the recipient of the payment, while in "John paid 5 dollars" the syntactic object "5 dollars" is the amount of the payment.

NLIs, unlike general linguistic theories, also need information about the software system to which they are interfaced. We simply call this database information.

Constraints are also necessary to relate information across information sources. The first set of these is the lexicon, which specifies relations between words and their senses (e.g., that the word "bank" has at least the two senses mentioned above). Also important are those constraints stating how to derive the interpretations of various syntactic constructions from those of their constituents. In some cases, these constraints relate parse (sub)trees with interpretations, while in others syntactic and semantic rules are linked.

Solutions to the interpretation problems mentioned in the previous section must typically make use of several information sources. The referent of a pronoun, for example, is constrained by syntactic, lexical, encyclopedic, and discourse information.

We have so far avoided the term semantics. In accordance with common practice in the field, we will use semantics in three ways, generally leaving it to the context to distinguish uses. By the model-theoretic semantics of an utterance we mean its interpretation, subject to the constraints of the information sources. We also refer loosely to the lexicon, encyclopedia, and illocutionary sources as semantic sources, or simply semantics. Finally, the process of finding a representation for what we call here the interpretation of an utterance is generally called semantic interpretation.

---

5 This is often called real-world or commonsense knowledge.

Most of the current attempts to develop a model-theoretic semantics for NL, roughly parallel to that given to artificial languages, are inspired by the work of Montague [1973]. Although Montague's interpretations could at least in principle be assigned directly to sentences, his formulation did make use of an unambiguous intermediate formal language—the language of intensional logic. In the computational framework such intermediate languages, or logical forms, are common. Moore [1981] examines various problematic NL constructions (e.g., adverbs, tense, quantification, and questions) and suggests ways of encoding them in a higher-order predicate calculus with intensional operators. Encoding of information in semantic sources lies at the very heart of artificial intelligence (AI) research. The articles in Hobbs and Moore [1985] discuss a number of such encoding problems, from the perspective of first-order logic and its extensions.

The use of logical languages for representation and of formal deduction as the means to draw inferences, as well as the desirability of a model-theoretic semantics for NL (and for the representations constructed in the process of interpreting utterances), are still controversial. Most studies in NL processing until the late 1970s, and many current efforts as well, stress the computational aspects of determining an interpretation rather than semantic issues [Schank, 1975; Wilks, 1975; Hirst, 1983; Palmer, 1983]. Much of this research emphasizes the role of implicatures based on stereotypical and salient information.

4 System Architectures

The various architectures in NLI systems reflect different choices of what information is to be applied (and thus what interpretation problems to attempt) and in what manner. After sketching the three main architectures, we discuss their differences and how these affect the range of natural language they can handle.

All systems must build at least one internal representation of a query, that is, an expression in QL. Some systems add an explicit, purely syntactic representation: One of the earliest and best known of these is Woods's LUNAR [Woods et al., 1972], described briefly in the following section. Semantic grammar systems, further discussed in the next section, also produce only a single intermediate representation, which in this case encodes constraints from several information sources. Finally, many systems produce a separate representation of the meaning of the query in terms of the concepts of the domain of the DB, independently of the DB structure.

We use the term intermediate representation language (or IRL) to refer in general to the languages in which these representations are expressed; the particular names of IRLs in individual systems (that is, meaning representation language, logical form) are used only when discussing the particular properties of those systems.[6]

4.1 *LUNAR*

The LUNAR system [Woods et al., 1972], based on earlier work by Woods [1967], pioneered many of the techniques that still underlie most NLIs. Designed as an interface to a two-file database containing information about chemical analyses of the Apollo-11 moon rocks and references to the literature on those analyses, LUNAR has three components: a parser, a semantic interpretation routine, and a query interpreter. The parser uses an augmented transition network grammar (discussed in more detail in the section on syntax) to produce parse trees in the form suggested by Chomsky [1965]. The grammar is a domain-independent grammar of English, which, through subsequent development as part of several systems, has become one of the most extensive computer-based English grammars ever constructed.

Semantic interpretation rules are used to map parse trees to QL expressions. Generally triggered by the head of a constituent (verbs for sentences, nouns for noun phrases), the rules obtain interpretations of the dependent and modifying constituents; they then combine these into the interpretation of the whole. Thus, there will be a set of semantic interpretation rules for each noun and verb in the sublanguage covered by the NLI.

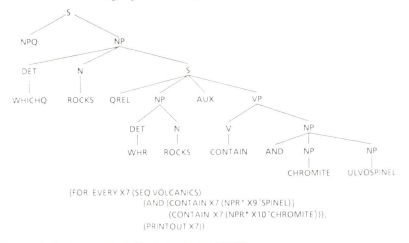

Figure 1 Parse tree and QL query from LUNAR.

---

6 The optimization of the generated queries is not discussed in this paper. Whether or not IRLs are used does not affect the question of whether, but only of when and in what manner optimization can be done.

The target of the semantic interpretation is an expression in a model first-order quantified language; this expression can be evaluated directly against the database to return a set of records. The vocabulary of the QL includes all the relations encoded directly in the DB, plus a number of derived relations. The only constraint on derived relations is that it should be possible to associate with each of them its own retrieval function, expressed in terms of the basic relations of the DB.

Figure 1 shows both the parse tree and the resulting QL query produced by LUNAR for the sentence "Which rocks contain chromite and ulvospinel?" LUNAR's parses are not surface structures, so in this query, the question-determiner noun phrase "which rocks" is taken to be the logical subject of the sentence and the analysis is analogous to that of "which rocks such that they contain chromite and ulvospinel exist?" The QL query includes two database-query specific constructs: SEQ, a general-purpose enumeration function that assumes its argument is a (precomputed) list, and PRINTOUT.

After LUNAR, architectures of natural language processors (NLPs) diverged in two directions: Systems were constructed in which either (a) syntactic, lexical, encyclopedic, and database information was encoded in one set of rules, or (b) the different information sources were kept quite separate. We examine each of these in turn.

4.2 Semantic-Grammar-Based Systems

The principal characteristic of a semantic grammar [Burton and Brown, 1979] is that it intentionally collapses distinctions among information sources. NLIs that incorporate semantic grammars vary somewhat in the details, but all classify words and phrases under a combination of syntactic, lexical, illocutionary, and database information. Exemplars of different approaches are PLANES [Waltz, 1978], LADDER [Hendrix et al., 1978], and REL [Thompson and Thompson, 1975]. The grammar rules incorporate categories that are oriented around a particular domain and task.[7]

For example, a semantic grammar for the domain of university life might contain the categories student, instructor, and course times; one for the domain of ships could include ships, officers, and ship locations. In contrast, typical categories of syntactic grammars are sentence and noun phrase. A semantic grammar for the task of database querying would have a category to cover the presentation of answers; this category might include various interrogatives (e.g., "what is") as well as certain imperatives (e.g., "show me"). In contrast, a semantic grammar for an experimental setting might include a category that

---

7 As there is nothing especially semantic about these grammars, the term aggregate grammar might be less confusing.

covered references to hypothetical situations (e.g., "if . . .," "what if . . .," "suppose that . . ."). Associated with each "syntactic" rule in the semantic grammar is a rule for combining the results of the interpretations of the sub-constituents into an interpretation of the constituent being analyzed.

As an example, we can consider a simple semantic grammar for handling queries about our sample database. To handle the query "Who manages the automobile division?" the grammar would include rules like the following:[8]

Grammar Fragment

<SENTENCE> → <PRESENT> <ATTRIBUTE> <DIVISION>

(db(subst(genvar '' 'DIVISION ATTRIBUTE')))*

<PRESENT> → who (is) / what (are) / show (me)

<ATTRIBUTE> → <ATTRNAME>

'return ATTRNAME.'*

<DIVISION> → the <DIVNAME> division

*'for each * in DIV file with DIV-NAME.*= 'DIVNAME' '*

Lexicon Fragment

manages: <ATTRNAME>
   'manages'
automobile: <DIVNAME>
   'auto'

Figure 2 shows the "syntactic analysis" and the interpretation for the above query. Each node of the tree is associated with an interpretation for the subtree below it; for example, the node labelled <ATTRNAME> would (from the lexical information) get the interpretation 'division,' and the node <ATTRIBUTE> would (from the third rule) get the interpretation 'RETURN MANAGER.X'.

Unlike the nodes in the parse tree produced by LUNAR, the nodes in this parse tree are not labelled with general syntactic categories. However, as in LUNAR (and to an even greater extent in some cases), the interpretation here assigned to a query is essentially a piece of code that states how to retrieve the answer to the query.

---

8 The grammar rules and lexical categories are in roman type, the associated interpretation is in italics.

As is evident from this example, a semantic grammar is both domain-and task-dependent; a different grammar must be constructed for each application. The LIFER system [Hendrix, 1977], on which LADDER was built, supplies a set of tools for building semantic-grammar-based NLIs. Although LIFER provides general capabilities for handling ellipsis and paraphrase (the first is done by the parser and hence works for all LIFER-defined grammars; paraphrases are handled by automatically modifying the language definition), it too requires a new grammar for each different application domain and task.

4.3 *IRL Systems*

IRL systems (CHAT-80 [Warren and Pereira, 1982], IRUS [Bates and Bobrow, 1983], PHLIQA1 [Scha, 1976; Landsbergen, 1976], TEAM [Grosz et al., 1986; Ginsparg, 1983]) construct at least three separate representations of a query: a parse tree, an IRL formula, and a QL query.[9] Each system separates the rules stating syntactic constraints from those that specify lexical, semantic, encyclopedic, and discourse constraints. Typically the objects, predicates, and relations of the encyclopedia furnish the IRL's basic vocabulary, and the representations used for encyclopedic constraints are quite close to those used for the QL. Encyclopedic constraints include at least taxonomic information (types and subtypes) and constraints on the arguments of predicates and relations.

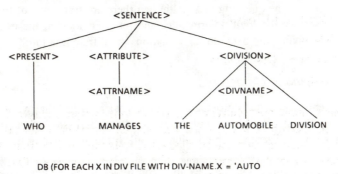

DB (FOR EACH X IN DIV FILE WITH DIV-NAME.X = 'AUTO
RETURN MANAGER.X)

Figure 2 Parse tree and QL query from a semantic grammar.

9 From this perspective, the PLANES system is a hybrid; it uses a semantic grammar but actually builds an intermediate representation of the "meaning" of the query from which it constructs the QL query. Because its IRL, like its grammar, is designed specifically for the task it undertakes (i.e., it comprises a collection of special-purpose "frames"), we have included it with the other semantic-grammar systems.

The differences between the IRL and other architectures can be clarified by an example. For the query "Which countries contain a volcano and a non-volcanic peak?" an IRL system[10] would produce a parse tree like the one in Figure 3 by using such grammar rules as the following:

```
SWHQ  →  WHNP PREDICATE
VP  →  VPT NP
NP  →  DETP NOMHEAD
NP  →  NPSERIES CONJ NP
```

The parse, like LUNAR's, is based on a general grammar of English. (However, it is a surface-structure, not a deep-structure, analysis, reflecting a change in underlying syntactic theory.) For example, the conjunction "a volcano and a nonvolcanic peak" is treated as a conjunction of noun phrases, as was the conjunction "chromite and ulvospinel" in the LUNAR example.[11] > → <DIVISION> and <DIVISION>.

The IRL representation of the interpretation of the query [in this case logical form] is shown in Figure 4 along with the QL [in this case an expression in SODA [Moore, 1979]. The IRL representation is a complex predicate composed of general predicates in the domain; it makes no reference to the actual database structures or any retrieval process. Only the QL representation reflects the database and the querying task. Although there are fragments of the LUNAR QL that resemble the logical form (e.g., the representation of the meaning of the conjoined NPs), the overall representations are different in kind.

4.4 Comparing Architectures

The different architectures provide for different ways of handling various interpretation problems. We leave until the next section discussion of the particular ways they do so. There are five major overall differences among the architectures.

First, the information sources that contribute to the interpretation of a query by the system are different. Many systems, for example, make little (or only ad hoc) use of morphological, illocutionary, or discourse constraints. In one way or another, however, they all utilize syntactic, lexical, and database constraints.

---

10 We will use an example produced by the TEAM system; the actual structures produced by other IRL systems would, of course, differ in detail.
11 In semantic-grammar-based systems, conjunction, if treated at all, is specialized for aggregate categories containing rules such as <DIVISION

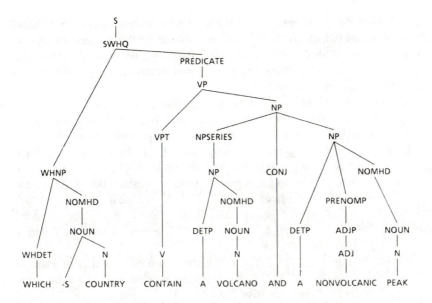

Figure 3 Parse tree from IRL system.

Second, there are different ways of combining the information sources into sets of rules. The semantic-grammar systems combine all sources into one set of rules. LUNAR distinguishes syntactic rules from the rest. IRL systems also separate database information and provide general constraints for mapping between syntactic constructions and their interpretations.

Third, the application of separate sets of rules may be sequential or interleaved. Although most systems apply the rules sequentially, IRUS uses the capabilities of the RUS parser [Bobrow and Webber, 1980] to interleave syntactic and semantic constraints; the interleaving is accomplished with cascaded ATNS [Woods, 1980]. Interleaving is done in Colmerauer's Prolog-based system [Colmerauer, 1979] and was also used in several speech-understanding systems [Lesser et al., 1975; Walker, 1978].

Fourth, the range of queries the systems can process at different stages is different. In semantic-grammar-based systems, any query that can be parsed can be translated into QL. In contrast, LUNAR and IRL systems can syntactically analyze some sentences for which they cannot construct a semantic interpretation. The range of concepts covered also differs. In semantic-grammar-based systems, only those queries that can be translated in QL can be interpreted at all. In contrast, in IRL systems, the concepts (i.e., objects, properties, relations) in the domain model provide the basic vocabulary for the IRL. A mapping from these concepts to DB structures provides the basis for translating IRL expressions (which are in terms of the concepts of the domain model) into QL expressions. With this sort of approach it is possible to supply interpretations of queries for which there is no QL representation (e.g., because the DB covers the domain only partially).

The IRL systems all take this type of approach; the actual coverage they offer, however, depends on how their domain models are defined. For example, the PHLIQA1, IRUS, and CHAT-80 domain models are provided completely independently of the DB (they are essentially "hand-built" by the system designers); it is therefore quite possible for them to construct IRL representations of queries for which there is no QL representation. In contrast, the TEAM system, which automates the process of adapting an NLI to a new domain and DB, constructs its domain model mechanically from information supplied about the DB; this restricts the concepts to those that can be generated from the DB concepts through relational calculus.

Finally, the architectures differ with respect to how easy it is to adapt an interface to a new domain or DB. As remarked previously, a semantic-grammar-based system requires extensive revision to be adapted to a new domain or task. Because all constraints are encoded in the grammar, the grammar itself must be rewritten or at least extensively revised. In contrast, adapting an IRL system to a new database requires little, if any, change in the syntax rules. In some systems (IRUS, Ginsparg's, PHLIQA1), modification of the semantic rules is required. In others (TEAM, CHAT-80), the semantic rules do not change; only the domain model and lexicon do.

```
(QUERY   (WH COUNTRY1
         (COUNTRY COUNTRY1)
         (SOME PEAK-VOL3
              (PEAK-VOL PEAK-VOL3)
              (SOME PEAK4
                   (AND (PEAK PEAK4)
                        (NONVOLCANIC PEAK4))
                   (AND (CONTAIN COUNTRY1 PEAK-VOL3)
                        (CONTAIN COUNTRY1 PEAK4))))))


((IN  # $1  PEAK)
    (( # $1  PEAK-VOL) EQ Y)
    (IN  # $2  PEAK)
         (( # $2  PEAK-COUNTRY)   EQ  # $1  PEAK-COUNTRY)  )
         (( # $2  PEAK-VOL) EQ N)
         (? ( # $1  PEAK-NAME))
         (? ( # $2  PEAK-NAME))
         (? ( # $1  PEAK-COUNTRY)))
```

Figure 4 IRL and QL representations from IRL system.

5 *Methods*

A number of techniques have been developed for encoding and applying the information sources needed to determine the interpretation of a query. In this section, we examine various methods used to handle the interpretation problems discussed earlier. We have chosen to focus on techniques sufficiently general for a wide range of natural-language-processing applications. As a result, certain problem areas are covered in more detail than others. This unequal treatment reflects, in part, a difference in the state of the art in the various areas of NLP. The usefulness of any specific method depends to some degree on a system's architecture; where it is relevant and not obvious, we will remark on the applicability of a method to different architectures.

5.1 *Syntactic Models*

With very few exceptions, phrase-structure grammars have provided the basis for the syntactic components of NLIs. Most of these grammars, in fact, are context-free (CF), with the possible addition of extra conditions on the subconstituents. The languages generated even by the extended grammars are, almost certainly, CF. In fact, the only solid arguments contending that NLs are not weakly CF are quite recent ([Shieber, 1985] for Swiss–German and [Culy, 1985] for Banbara). Both involve constructions not treated by grammars in existing NLIs. As with programming languages, non-CF grammars may be used to make the description of CF languages easier, especially when some constraints (subject-verb agreement, subject and object control) must be applied to nonadjacent nodes in the parse tree. Perrault [1984] surveys the known formal properties of some of the more common syntactic formalisms. Slocum [1981] compares the performance (on several hundred sentences) of various parsing strategies.

The first substantial extension of CF grammars widely used in NLP was the augmented transition network grammar (ATNG) of Woods [1970]. The ATNG is a two-step generalization of the Finite-State Automation (FSA) [Hopcroft and Ullman, 1979]. The FSA has a finite set of states; transitions among them are allowed when certain symbols appear in the input. One of the states is distinguished as the start state, one or more as final states. The input string is accepted if it leads to a sequence of acceptable transitions from the start state to a final state. The languages recognized by FSAs are the finite-state, or Type 3 languages. Recursive transition networks (RTNs) generalize FSAs by allowing a transition between two states to be taken via a recursive jump to a start state. RTNs recognize exactly the class of CF languages. Finally, the ATNG adds to the RTN a finite set of registers and actions that can set registers to words observed in the input, their corresponding lexical entries, or to some function of the contents of other registers; a recursive call to the network can pass values back to its calling level, which can in turn assign that value to a register. Transitions can be made conditional on register contents. ATNGs generate all recursively enumerable sets.

Because grammars for all but the smallest subsets of NLs are ambiguous, the LR(k) techniques often used for parsing PLs are generally not applicable to NLs. In their place, a number of parsing algorithms have been developed.

ATNGs are naturally implemented in recursive top-down parsers; in fact, in the early literature on the subject, grammars and parsers were hardly distinguishable from one another. The register assignment mechanism makes it difficult to conceive of using the grammar in other than a top-down left-to-right parsing scheme.

Much effort was devoted to efficient implementation of top-down ATN parsers. In the early implementations, the grammar and the lexicon were encoded as LISP data structures and interpreted by the parser. Burton and Woods [1976] then showed how to compile the parser and the grammar into a large LISP program and then, through the LISP compiler, into machine language. Compilation improved parsing performance by an order of magnitude.

However, pure top-down parsers suffer from some well-known problems. First, they cannot handle left-recursive constructions (as in "John's father's brother's book"), and second, their backtracking regimes may be very inefficient. The left-recursion problem can be solved by converting the grammar to a weakly-equivalent right-recursive one, but at the cost of complicating the process of deriving the interpretation.

The backtracking problem has been addressed in two quite different ways. The first has been through extensions of bottom-up [Younger, 1967 and Earley, 1970] parsing strategies to non-CF grammars. These methods include use of the well-formed substring table [Kuno and Oettinger, 1962; Wolf and Woods, 1980] and charts [Kay, 1980].

The second, and more radical, line is based on Marcus's determinism hypothesis. Marcus [1980] claims that English (and possibly other NLs) can be parsed by a mechanism that operates "strictly deterministically," in that:

- All syntactic structures created by the parser operating on an input string are permanent and must be included in the output produced for that input.

- The internal state of the mechanism is constrained so that it cannot encode temporary syntactic structures.

Marcus designed a parser satisfying these conditions (along with a small grammar for it) that captures interesting generalizations related to such phenomena as passives, imperatives, and yes/no questions. He also suggests a simple explanation for so-called garden path sentences, such as "The horse raced past the barn fell" and "Have the students who failed the exam take the supplemental" (closely related to "Have the students who failed the exam taken the supplemental?"). These sentences are perfectly grammatical, but their analysis by humans seems to require conscious backtracking. The determinism hypothesis is not without problems (for example, it depends essentially on an integration of syntactic and semantic analysis that remains to be demonstrated convincingly; moreover, no large deterministic grammar has yet been written). However, Marcus's work has influenced the design of some ATN parsers that now utilize look-ahead to reduce backtracking [Bobrow and Webber, 1980]. Recently Marcus et al., [1983] suggest representing syntactic analyses as logical formulas over the domain of syntactic nodes, in which the disjunction of the possible attachments can be stated, or in which no attachments are stated at all, save those that preserve the left-to-right order of constituents in the sentence.

Another problem with ATNs was that the dependence of the grammar on left-to-right processing made it very difficult to use the same grammar with different control regimes. For example, if subject-verb agreement was to be tested by having the parser assign to an ATN register the number of the subject noun phrase, so that this register could then be tested upon encountering the main verb, this procedure would fail if the parser encountered the verb before the subject. In doing research on speech-understanding systems, Paxton [1978] and Wolf and Woods [1980] investigated parsing "middle-out," that is, starting from the highly stressed parts of the sentence, and constructed parsers that were not order-dependent. In a different vein, some workers on language generation [Kay, 1979; Appelt, 1983] have argued that it is desirable to be able to make decisions about syntactic constituents independently of the order in which they are to appear in the utterance. It is not possible to do this, however, with an order-dependent ATN.

Although the need for order independence is still controversial (see [Wolf and Woods, 1980] for speech recognition and McDonald [1983] for language generation), several proposals to achieve it have been made, relying on unification of graphs as the main operation in parsing. One of the earliest proposals in this direction was Kay's functional-unification grammar (FUG) [Kay, 1985]. In several of these formalisms, grammatical rules are represented as formulas in first-order logic, or more accurately, in its Horn clause subset. In these logic grammars (under various guises known as metamorphosis grammars [Colmerauer, 1978], definite-clause grammars [Pereira and Warren, 1980], extraposition grammars [Pereira, 1981], modular grammars [McCord, 1985], and others), predicates are defined to be true of strings meeting certain conditions, such as NPs. Nonlocal syntactic constraints and semantic constraints can be imposed by allowing the predicates to take on extra arguments, enabling information to be propagated across the analysis. Subject-verb agreement provides a very simple example. Consider the following very simple grammar, expressed as first-order sentences. According to the conventions of PROLOG, identifiers starting with an upper-case letter are variables and all free variables are assumed to be universally quantified. The indices I, J, and K take integer values denoting positions between words in a sentence.

```
s(I,J,Number)  ←  np(I,K,Number) and vp(K+1,J,Number)
vp(I,K,Number)  ←  v(I,K,Number)
np(I,K,Number)  ←  occurs(I,I+1,the) and n(I+1,K,Number)
n(I,I+1,Number)  ←  occurs(I,I+1,X) and lex(X,n,Number)
v(I,I+1,Number)  ←  occurs(I,I+1,X) and lex(X,v,Number)
```

If the lexicon contains the assertions

```
lex(fish,  n,  singular)
lex(fish,  n,  plural)
lex(fish,  v,  singular)
lex(swim,  v,  plural)
lex(swims,  v,  singular)
```

then the sentence "the fish swims" can be recognized as generated by the grammar by asserting

```
occurs(1,2 the) and occurs(2,3,fish)
and occurs(3,4 swims)
```

and then proving that

```
(exists Number) s(1,4,Number).
```

The heart of logic grammars is their use of unification to test the compatibility of information and to propagate constraints. Although definite-clause grammars, for example, provide all the necessary expressive power within Prolog, this power is achieved at the cost of a certain lack of perspicuity. As a result, the constraining predicates have as many arguments as there are "pieces of information" that they control or that must be propagated through them. These arguments are all specified positionally; in the example above, the first two arguments denote the delimiting positions in the input string, while the third denotes the number feature of the subject and verb. This can easily lead to very long lists of arguments whose management is difficult.

In the last few years, several more perspicuous unification-based syntactic formalisms have been developed that derive their inspiration from both the linguistic and computational traditions. From pure linguistics have come lexical-functional grammar [Kaplan and Bresnan, 1982] and generalized phrase-structure grammar [Gazdar et al., 1985], which are full syntactic theories, including formalisms for representing rules and derivations and general constraints on the use of these formalisms. Coming from the computational perspective, the already mentioned FUG of Kay and PATR-II [Shieber, 1984] are formalisms only, without theoretical commitment.[12] The semantics of the formalisms has been studied with the tools of denotational semantics [Scott, 1982] by Pereira and Shieber [1984]. Kay has investigated the use of FUG for both generation and recognition.

Writing the extensive grammars needed by useful NLIs is still a difficult task that is normally performed only in research centers with substantial resources. Some examples are the LUNAR grammar, revised through several projects at Bolt, Beranek and Newman and now part of the IRUS system [Bates and Bobrow, 1983], the DIAGRAM grammar [J. Robinson, 1982], first developed at SRI as part of the SRI Speech-Understanding Project [Walker, 1978] and now included in the TEAM system, and the grammar of the Linguistic String Project [Sager, 1981].

Most "practical" grammar-writing exercises result in very liberal grammars that will accept sentences native speakers would not consider grammatical. There are three reasons for this. First, since grammars are devices that permit (rather than proscribe) membership in a language, it is often easier to write a small number of very general rules than a large number of specific ones. Second, it may be easier to exclude uninterpretable sentences on nonsyntactic grounds. Finally, one might want to allow certain nonstandard sentences (e.g., telegraphic speech) to be treated as if they were grammatical [Weischedel and Sondheimer, 1983], if there is reason to believe that users would want to express themselves that way. The main practical drawback in such a liberal position is that, by proliferating parses, it becomes much more difficult to select one that is semantically acceptable.

No discussion of syntactic models would be complete without mention of the transformational grammars (TG) introduced by Chomsky [1965]. They have provided the framework for much of the theoretical work on syntax since the 1960s. A TG has two main constituents: a base grammar, usually a phrase-structure grammar, and a set of transformations. The base grammar generates a class of trees, to which the transformations are applied to rearrange, copy, and delete constituents. The sentences of the language are the yield strings of the trees that result from all possible applications of the transformations to all

---

12 This is also the case with ATNGs and definite-clause grammars.

possible base trees. The details of the number and power of the transformations have changed considerably since their introduction in 1957, but, in some early versions of the theory, a passive sentence and its corresponding active sentence were transformationally related.

It therefore seemed plausible that one could build a parser that would take a sentence, construct a surface structure, and apply to it the transformations in reverse to obtain a base tree representing the interpretation of the sentence. This technique was first tried in a system built at MITRE [Zwicky et al., 1965] and then in the REQUEST and TQA systems built by Petrick, Plath, and Damerau at IBM [Damerau, 1981; Petrick, 1973]. One of the problems with the approach is that the inverse transformations can be applied only to the surface trees, even though the TG does not, in general, characterize those trees in any computable manner. The aforementioned systems dealt with this problem by handcrafting surface grammars. The TQA system is exceptional in that it is one of the very few to have been put to substantial use by bona fide users while it was undergoing development.

5.2 *Semantic Interpretation*

We turn now to semantic interpretation, the process of translating syntactic analyses into IRL.[13] The translation involves establishing three kinds of correspondences:

- Between the words of an NL and expressions in the IRL.

- Between various constituents of an NL phrase (e.g., head, subject, object, modifier) and the constituents of the expressions to which they correspond in the IRL (e.g., argument of a predicate, value of a field).

- Between the scope of determiners and other operators of an NL expression and the scope of the quantifiers to which they correspond in the IRL.

Vocabulary Correspondences   The first issue in semantic interpretation is the correspondence between words of the language and concepts in IRL. Some common nouns in English (such as "man" in "John is a man") correspond to one-place predicates in IRL, others (such as "manager" in "John is the manager of the sales department") correspond to relations. Verbs correspond to predicates (as in "John sleeps") or to relations (as in "John manages the sales department"). Some adjectives (such as "exempt" in our fragment) can be inter-

---

13 Some systems, including those using semantic grammars and several built by Schank and his colleagues [Schank, 1975; Lehnert and Shwartz, 1983], never construct an explicit representation of the syntactic analysis but go directly from NL to IRL.

preted as one-place predicates, although this solution is generally inadequate: Adjectives such as "tall" must be interpreted differently, so that "tall men" and "tall babies" do not refer to things that are independently tall and men, or tall and babies. "Former senators" and "alleged thieves" are certainly not senators and possibly not thieves. In systems in which the IRL is first-order logic, the presence of these adjectives may affect the interpretation of the nouns they modify; when this occurs, the lexical-assignment problem interacts with the modifier-attachment problem. In LUNAR, for example, "analyses" and "modal analyses" are translated by two unrelated predicates. Prepositions correspond in some instances to relations (as in "What employees are in the sales department?"), while in others they are markers of the case of arguments of other predicates (as in "Did Bill go to Boston?"). Their interpretation varies according to the situation of use; Herskovits [1986] provides an excellent discussion of locative prepositions (e.g., "on," "near," "beside") as well as a theoretical framework for handling them.

Modification and Attachment   There are various ways in which the meanings of constituents of a phrase can combine to determine, at least to some extent, the meaning of the entire phrase. Two special kinds of problems arise in computing these combinations:

- The surface form may not determine a unique association among the elements in a phrase; this happens, for example, with the attachment of prepositional phrases.

- Even when the association of constituents is clear, it may not be obvious exactly how the meanings combine; this may occur with combinations of adjectives and nouns, or with two nouns.

Proposed solutions to the attachment problem fall into three classes:

- The syntactic component makes direct use of lexical and encyclopedic constraints and produces only attachments that satisfy all of them simultaneously.

- The syntactic component produces structures corresponding to all possible attachments, which are then filtered by other constraints.

- The syntactic component proposes one attachment only, representing all the alternatives, and the semantic interpretation component is allowed to move the attached phrase so as to satisfy the other constraints as well.

Semantic grammar systems adopt the first approach. Some logic grammar systems [Colmerauer, 1979; Dahl, 1981] do likewise; these keep the syntactic categories separate, but have a single set of rules that constructs syntactic and

IRL representations simultaneously. The second approach has the simplest organization and is used in many large systems such as LUNAR and TEAM. The third is used by CHAT-80. The last two approaches use case frames [Bruce, 1975; Fillmore, 1977] to encode the relations between verbs, their syntactic cases, restrictions on the types of the fillers of the cases, the target language predicate, and the correspondence between the syntactic case fillers and the arguments of the target predicate. Reviews in Woods [1978] and Pereira [1983] contain excellent discussions of these topics.

The selection of IRL predicates to correspond to NL words has a considerable effect on the resolution of attachment problems. For example, the verb "have" can be used to express a have-as-part relationship ("A car has an engine"), an ownership relationship ("Susie has a Porsche"), and a have-as-property relationship ("Jack has red hair"), among others. This variety is also found with prepositions ("John is in the sales department," "John is in Europe"), genitives ("Joe's finger," "Joe's mother," "Joe's house," "Joe's friend"), and nominal compounds ("American ship," "American car," "American cooking").

Although different kinds of surface forms give rise to these semantic problems, their treatment is similar in two ways. First, the resolution of the indefiniteness requires a search for the most reasonable relationship that can hold between two concepts. In the case of nominal compounds and genitives, these are the immediate constituents of the phrase ("Joe" and "finger," "American" and "car"), whereas for verbs ("have" and "be") and prepositions (e.g., "employees in sales") the two concepts that are being related are structurally more distant from each other. Second, the larger context of the discourse may make possible interpretations that would not arise in isolation. For example, although the phrase "Boston flights" would not ordinarily be taken to refer to flights that are only passing through Boston, in the two-query sequence "Which flights from London to St. Louis enter the U.S. through Boston or Philadelphia? What times do the Boston flights leave?" the phrase receives precisely this interpretation.

Syntactic constraints determine which pairs of concepts need to be related for all of these constructs except nominal compounds that include more than two nouns, but they do not further constrain the particular relationship. Because the relationship that may hold between the two concepts may be arbitrarily complex, some proposals for handling noun-noun relations in general [Hobbs, 1980] depend on sophisticated inferential capabilities and a complex model of the domain. Several techniques have been developed for handling a narrow range of such expressions under the assumption that users will not create new constructions (e.g., using the phrase "toilet paper submarine" to refer to a recently mentioned submarine that needs a resupply of toilet paper). Isabelle [1984] surveys the nominal compound problem. Finin [1985] presents a set of rules for handling those nominal compounds that can be resolved in terms of case relationships or type hierarchies. The TEAM system includes a limited treatment for nominal compounds as well as several other related problems that uses relationships derived straightforwardly from the database structure.

Scoping   The third set of interpretation questions involves determination of the relative scope in the target language of quantifiers corresponding to such NL determiners as "a," "the," "each," and "most" as well as to such operators as negation, tense, modals, and superlatives ("most," "oldest"). Viewed syntactically, the determiners occur in noun phrases, within the scope of verbs, but in first-order representations the quantifiers must be given wider scope than the predicates. Syntactically again, determiners can occur within one another's scope, as in "each manager of some division," or in parallel, as in "each manager manages some division." Operators can occur at the noun-phrase level, such as in superlatives and in the negation in "none," or at the sentence level, such as in tense, modals, and sentential negation.

Even within noun phrases there may be changes in relative scope between the syntactic representation and the IRL: The interpretation of "Some employee of each manager is exempt" is that, for each manger, some employee of that manager is exempt. However, there are syntactic limits to how far up a quantifier can migrate: For example, no quantifier can move out of a relative clause, so that "Who is the manager who manages every employee?" cannot mean "For each employee, who is his manager?"

Aside from such syntactic constraints, all other relative scopings of the quantifiers are possible in certain circumstances, although some heuristics are useful for ranking the plausibility of the interpretations. Two can be mentioned. One simply gives preference to relative scopings, while preserving the left-to-right order of the corresponding determiners in the sentence. Thus, "Every manager manages some employee" would be read preferably as "For every manager m there is some employee e such that m manages e." Similarly, the preferred interpretation of "Some employee is managed by every manager" gives "some" wider scope than "every." Another heuristic, suggested by Hintikka [1974] and used by Hendrix [1978], associates with each determiner not only a corresponding quantifier but also a "strength." Interpretations in which stronger quantifiers outscope weaker ones are preferred. Thus "each" is stronger than "all," "any," and "some," so that in "Some manager manages each employee" there is a different manager for each employee, while in "Some manager manages every employee," either interpretation is possible, since "some" and "every" have similar strengths.

Presuppositions also affect scope. For example, in "What is the salary of all employees?" the determiner "all" probably should be given wider scope than "the," simply because it is unlikely that all employees would be receiving the same salary; the latter interpretation would violate the presupposition that the question has an answer. Although some computational work on presupposition has been done [Weischedel, 1979; S. J. Kaplan, 1982], it does not deal with scoping.

Woods [1978] proposed a compositional method for semantic interpretation in which phrases are assigned interpretations consisting of two constituents: a quantifier and a matrix proposition. The composition rules for a constituent combine the interpretations of the subconstituents by combining the matrix elements, nesting the quantifiers among themselves, or wrapping them around the matrices. This framework has been the basis for most scoping schemes since then. It has also been arrived at independently by theoretical linguists [Cooper, 1979]. Woods's rules in LUNAR produce only one scoping, which is obtained by pushing quantifiers up the parse tree past their weaker counterparts until they reach a "hard" boundary, such as the top of a relative clause or a conjunction. Arbitration between quantifiers of similar strength is done on the basis of the left-to-right heuristic. A similar strategy is used in CHAT-80. TEAM applies a generate-and-test algorithm, in which all scopings that are not disallowed by syntactic constraints are produced; these are ranked by a set of heuristics. This framework allows better use of the quantifier strength heuristics.

In practice, the treatment of quantifier scoping in semantic-grammar systems is very limited; they could use LUNAR-style rules, but tend not to. Lacking an intermediate representation, they have no way of applying more global scoping strategies.

5.3 *Discourse-Level Interpretation*

Users of an NLI are typically interested in getting information from a database to solve some problem. It is rare that a single piece of information is all that is required; even when such is the case, the user may not be able to request it in a single query. Although no NLI contains a sophisticated or general model of the query dialogue, most incorporate some capabilities for handling a limited range of these discourse-related expressions. Special attention has been paid to some kinds of referring expressions (pronouns) as well as to certain constrained uses of elliptical phrases. In this section, we describe the basic techniques used in NLIs and provide a brief overview of the techniques currently being investigated by researchers concerned with more general applications of NLP.

The Interpretation of Referring Expressions   There are two kinds of referring expressions prevalent in database queries: pronouns (especially, "it" and "they," but also "he" and "she") and definite descriptions ("the shoe department," "the U.S. peak"). To handle such expressions in a comprehensive manner requires a general model of the discourse context that takes into account the structure of the overall discourse and the purposes behind it [Grosz and Sidner, 1986; Litman, 1985]; in addition, the model must take into account the features of the immediate discourse context of neighboring utterances [Sidner, 1983; Grosz et al., 1983] as well as the structure and interpretation of an individual utterance [Webber, 1980; Heim, 1982]. Each of these aspects of discourse context constitutes an active area of investigation in NLP.

The techniques used in NLIs are aimed not at providing a general solution but at covering the most common uses of pronouns in database querying. Typically, the interpretation of pronouns is based on a "history list," which contains a record of the most recent preceding queries (i.e., some given number of these). The list distinguishes those expressions in each query that either introduce something new into the discourse or refer to something already introduced (these usually correspond to noun phrases), along with their interpretations and positions in the parse. When a pronoun is encountered, a search is made through the list (starting with the most recent entries) to find an expression or interpretation (depending on the type of system) that matches the pronoun (the same number and gender) and is compatible with the interpretation of the query.

For example, following the query "What is the division of the highest paid secretary?" the history list would include both "division of the highest paid secretary" and "highest paid secretary" (perhaps along with other information about each phrase). In interpreting the subsequent query "How many employees does it have?" the pronoun "it" is taken to refer to the same thing as "the division of the highest paid secretary" because divisions have employees and secretaries normally do not.

In semantic-grammar systems there are usually special rules that explicitly mention pronouns. For example, the following pair of rules might be used to provide an interpretation of the query "What is its revenue?" following the query "What department has the smallest number of employees?"

```
<SENTENCE>  →  what is <DEPT-POSSESSIVE> <ATTRIBUTE>
<DEPT-POSSESSIVE>  →  its
```

When a pronoun is encountered in a particular construction, one of these rules is matched. This triggers a search through the history list for an expression that matches a particular category; the category searched for depends on the matched rule.

LUNAR also allows for references to objects dependent on other quantified objects, as in "What is the silicon content of each volcanic sample? What is its magnesium content?" The most general treatment of pronouns in IRL systems takes into account the syntactic structure of preceding queries to give a preference ordering on candidates and omit certain of these on the basis of syntactic constraints [Hobbs, 1978]. Various aspects of the pronoun resolution problem have been treated more generally in NLP research; Hirst [1981] provides a good overview.

Because an adequate treatment of definite descriptions requires a model of discourse context, NLIs typically ignore the referring properties of such descriptions and take their interpretation to be all objects matching the description. In essence, these systems assume either a particular context in which there is only one object that matches a certain description or they assume that all items fitting that description are equally relevant. They ignore the difference between definitely and indefinitely determined noun phrases (e.g., "The G.M. employees" and "G.M. employees" are treated identically). Although this may be fine for an isolated query, it can lead to incorrect responses in context. For example, in isolation the query "Who manages the G.M. employees?" might be a request for a list of the managers of all G.M. employees; on the other hand, in a context in which the user has just asked for the names of all employees earning more than $30,000, it may be a request solely for the managers of those G.M. employees earning more than $30,000.

Ellipsis   The term ellipsis refers to the omission of certain elements from what would ordinarily constitute the full syntactically correct form of a phrase. The interpretation of an elliptical phrase depends on recovering the missing information from the context in which the phrase is used. The treatment of ellipsis in NLIs has been restricted to the use of elliptical queries like those given in the beginning of this paper.

Two different approaches to ellipsis have been taken. One is to encode elliptical phrases directly in the grammar; the other is to modify the parser. The second approach not only allows broader coverage but also is more easily adaptable to new domains and databases.

The encoding of elliptical fragments directly in the grammar has been done both for IRL systems [Walker, 1978] and for semantic-grammar systems [Burton and Brown, 1979]. In each case special grammar rules provide for incomplete phrases to be used in certain circumstances. For example, a syntactic grammar might include a rule like

```
S  →  NP
```

to allow a single noun phrase to be used in place of a complete sentence. Likewise a semantic grammar might include a rule such as

```
query  →  <division>
```

Such rules would cover a sequence like

```
Who are the secretaries in the sales department?
The research department?
```

The interpretation rules or processes attached to these fragment rules construct an interpretation of the fragment and then search through the history of previous interactions (in some cases, only the preceding query is considered; this is often correct) to find an interpretation into which this piece can fit; the match is determined on the basis of a number of constraints, typically including lexical and encyclopedic ones.

A more general solution is provided by modifying the parser. This has been done for semantic-grammar NLIs that are based on a top-down parse using an ATN [Hendrix, 1977], but not for NLIs with more general grammars. The resulting parser remains efficient for the semantic grammars because of the additional semantic and pragmatic information encoded directly in them.

5.4 *Semantic Coverage*

One of the most important questions in NLIs is the relation between the expressivity of NL, IRL, and QL. IRLs are less expressive than NLs, if only because their basic vocabularies (predicates and constants) are restricted to specific domains and tasks. They may, however, be more expressive than QLs in that they may admit logical concepts that are beyond the deductive abilities of the DBMS that interpret the QLs. The logical form of the TEAM system, for example, allows for modal operators (such as tense) and higher-order functions (such as maximum, count, and average) that lie beyond the deductive abilities of relational calculus, although their addition still leaves the QL decidable. This extra expressivity, often obtainable at little cost, makes it possible eventually for parts of the NLI to be used with software systems of greater deductive power.

There may be NL queries for which no corresponding QL representations exist. However, we claim that for any query that can be put to a DBMS in QL, there should be a corresponding query in NL that the NLI can translate into QL to generate the same answer. We call this the accessibility requirement. It is the analogue in NLIs of the Turing equivalence between a high-order programming language and the language into which it is compiled.

In the remainder of this section we show that NLIs in general do not meet the accessibility requirement. In the following section, we illustrate ways of regaining accessibility.

The translation from IRL to QL is usually done according to what we will call the rewrite method: Atomic elements of the IRL representation language are rewritten into possibly complex expressions of QL. Thus, for example, IRL atoms may be mapped into expressions in QL that contain references to various parts of the DB (files, fields, values, etc.) and operations upon them. In relational algebra, the set of such operations would include union, projection, and join—often enhanced by the so-called aggregate functions, such as maximum, minimum, average, and count. In logic-based systems, the operators are those of first-order logic.

Any NL query representable in QL has an answer in the DB, as all relational-calculus queries are decidable. There are, however, NL (or IRL) queries to which there exist answers in the DB, but which have no corresponding QL queries, at least none constructible under the rewrite method assumption. For example, the Navy Blue File, for which the LADDER system was written, contained a SHIP file in which a Boolean field DOB (for doctor-on-board) recorded whether or not a ship carried any doctors. The database contained no other mention of doctors, or of persons being on board ships. Thus, the IRL concepts doctor and on-board-of cannot be expressed separately as relational-calculus expressions in this database. As a result, the query "Is there a doctor on board the Fox?" can be interpreted only if the phrase "a doctor on board" (or its IRL equivalent) can be rewritten directly into a reference to the database field DOB.[14]

Introducing special translations for fixed phrases does not [14]n general. For example, the query "Is there a doctor within 500 miles of the Fox?" can be answered from the information in the Blue File, but it can be interpreted only by introducing translations for doctor and on-board-of separately.

The problem is not that the information is lacking in the database; that would explain why the query "How many doctors are on the Fox?" could not be answered. Neither is it only that the database does not represent certain objects, properties, and relationships directly (e.g., the Blue File does not explicitly represent doctors or indicate who is on what vessel), and that it is not possible, by means of relational algebra, to construct from the existing relations one that does represent these explicitly (doctors, for example). The problem is inherent in the assumption of the rewrite method that atoms of the IRL map to expressions in the QL; hence, this method does not provide a way to take expressions in IRL to atoms in QL. The deductive method described in the following section is one solution.

6 Future Directions

Thus far, we have focused our attention on natural-language interfaces to DBMS. More broadly, in the context of natural-language processing, it is important to consider what issues need to be addressed to provide capabilities for

---

14 A similar problem arises in a database in which every person is related directly to his or her grandfather, e.g., in the single relation GRANDFATHER (YOUNG, OLD). The query "Who is the father of the father of John?" has an answer in the DB, but "father" is not expressible as a function of GRANDFATHER.

users to communicate in natural language with a wider range of software. Two major obstacles stand in the way.

- Providing general procedures for bridging the gap between the concepts that can be expressed in natural language and the underlying software systems.
- Providing general mechanisms to allow the user and the computer system to cooperate in solving the user's problem by engaging in a dialogue.

One strategy for overcoming the first obstacle is suggested by a solution to the problem inherent in the use of the rewrite method, i.e., certain queries that can be made in QL cannot be asked in NL. Instead of placing the semantic burden on the QL, as most existing systems do, this strategy places it on the IRL.

The ability to sustain interaction requires a different perspective as to the function of the interface. It must be considered not merely as a translator of sentences of one language into those of another, but rather as a recognizer of the user's intentions and as a collaborator in bringing about their satisfaction.

6.1 *Putting Query Languages in their Place*

A solution to the doctor-on-board problem is readily available if two conditions are met: (a) first-order logic (FOL) is taken as the IRL, and (b) all the information in the database is encoded in IRL. The second condition can be relaxed, as we will do shortly. Under these assumptions, it is now possible to define the relations encoded in the DB directly in terms of the domain concepts in IRL, rather than vice versa. If the contents of the DB are now converted into ground literals in IRL, the answer retrieval process can be implemented as deduction in IRL. In the ship DB, this means including an axiom that defines the DOB field from the DB in IRL:

```
DOB(x)  →  ∃d ship(x) ∧ doctor(d) ∧ on-board(d,x)
```

where ship, doctor, and on-board are predicates of IRL. The query "Is there a doctor on board the Fox?" would be represented in IRL by

```
∃d x ∃ship(x) ∧ doctor(d) ∧ on-board(d,x) ∧ x = Fox
```

which is true if DOB(Fox) is true. Similarly, "Is there a doctor within 500 miles of the Fox?" would be represented in IRL by

```
∃d, dloc, sloc, s, dist doctor(d) ∧ location(d,dloc)
location(s,sloc) ∧ s = Fox
distance(dlock, sloc, dist) ∧ dist < 500 miles.
```

Obtaining the correct answer now depends on having axioms such as

```
on-board(d,x) ∧ location(d, dloc) ∧ location(s, sloc) →
dloc = sloc.
```

We will call this second view of the language-to-DB correspondence the deductive method.

Now, in a sense, the deductive method is an unacceptable solution to the answer retrieval problem, because it does not use the DBMS as an inference engine—all deduction is done directly in IRL. Konolige [1981] presents a better solution in which a QL query is actually constructed, but deduction rather than rewriting is used. The language in which deduction is performed contains IRL, but it also includes as terms the syntactic constructs of QL. Axioms are provided that express the relationships between the relations of IRL and the terms of QL.

Konolige's solution suggests a picture of the relation between an NLI and its underlying software that is rather different from the one suggested by analogy to programming-language compilers. The NLI must be able to draw inferences on its own, independently of whatever "black boxes" it may be connected to. Some of these boxes may themselves be specialized inference machines (DMSs are clear examples of this), but their operations and semantics must be subordinate to those of NL.

6.2 *Participating in a Dialogue*

Although superficially it may appear that users of NLIs are merely asking questions, at a deeper level they are almost always engaged in a problem-solving activity that requires them to obtain information from the DB. The view that interactive sessions with NLIs are instances of cooperative problem-solving behavior offers a more useful perspective not only on interaction with a database in particular but on human-machine interaction in general. From this perspective, a user is seen as interacting with a system to effect a certain change in the world. The user might intend to accomplish this directly by getting the system to do something, or indirectly by getting the system to communicate some fact. Utterances are actions that change the world and provide information about the mental state of the utterer—most notably, about certain of his or her beliefs and intentions [Austin, 1962; Searle, 1969].

When language use is examined from this perspective, discourses (i.e., extended sequences of utterances), not individual utterances, are the natural unit of analysis; what the user intends to do and not what he has said is ultimately what matters. This point of view may make a difference even for some simple database query applications (the need to take this view can be inferred somewhat from the range of constructions that most NLIs attempt to handle and that go beyond simple questions), but it is vitally important from the standpoint of providing NL interaction with a broader range of software systems (e.g., decision support systems). This point is nicely illustrated by the following short dialogue segment:

1. U: I need to know which divisions earned less than $500,000 in 1985.

2. S: The automobile division.

3. U: Consider its performance over the last five years.

4. Can you show me a histogram by month?

Although Utterance 1 is superficially a statement about U's mental state, it is intended as a request for some information. If it were merely a report on U's mental state, a response acknowledging that (e.g., "OK. I understand.") would suffice, but such a reply is clearly unreasonable. Utterance 3 demonstrates that, even in a simple query-like context, the system's responses are an important part of the dialogue. The "its" is used to refer to the automobile division, a singular entity; Utterance 1 contains only a plural noun phrase and, if Utterance 2 were ignored, it would seem that there was no compatible prior phrase supplying a referent. Furthermore, the considering to be done depends on both Utterances 1 and 2. Utterance 3 is not about the domain of discourse, nor is it even a query, but rather about the discourse per se: It establishes a particular focus of attention for the discourse, namely, the performance of the automobile division over the last five years. Utterance 4 can be treated properly only by taking the context of the preceding utterances into account. What we have here is a request for a histogram of the monthly performance of the automobile division over the last five years. Finally, Utterance 4 is a request for a particular action to be taken; although ostensibly it asks for a "yes" or "no" response, neither of these would be adequate in and of itself; the "yes" requires that the system supply the histogram and the "no" obligates it to explain why it cannot do so.

Several areas of active research are concerned with devising methods for supporting NL communication on a broader basis. Some of this research is directly concerned with natural language; natural language provides both a set of particular problems to be addressed and a set of constraints on the theories being developed. Other research involves more general study of theories and models of purposeful action but is nonetheless very relevant to work in NL. Activities in the following areas are of particular interest.

1. The connection between language and action: recognizing what a user intends (to do or have done) from what he says, as well as generating utterances that satisfy various intentions [Cohen and Perrault, 1979; Allen

and Perrault, 1980; Cohen and Levesque, 1985; Litman, 1985; Appelt, 1985].

2. The connection between the intentions of individual utterances and the overall purpose of a discourse [Hobbs and Evans, 1980; Grosz and Sidner, 1986].

3. Interactions among beliefs, desires, intentions, actions, and plans [Nilsson, 1980; Moore, 1985; Bratman, 1984; Konolige, 1984; Fagin and Halpern, 1985].

These issues are of interest to a broad range of intellectual communities: theoretical computer science (because of their relevance to distributed computing systems), artificial intelligence (with its long-standing interest in machine reasoning and planning), the philosophy of mind (especially practical reasoning), and the philosophy of language (in which speech acts and reference are of central concerns). There continues to be much more to the understanding of language than language.

Acknowledgments

Preparation of this paper was supported by the Defense Advanced Research Projects Agency under Contract N00039-84-K-0078 with the Naval Electronic Systems Command. We thank Martha Pollack and Jane Robinson for comments on earlier drafts.

References

Allen, J., Perrault, C. R., 1980. Analyzing intention in utterances. *Artificial Intelligence* **15**:143–78.

Appelt, D. E., 1983. TELEGRAM: a grammar formalism for language planning. In *Proceedings of the 8th International Joint Conference on Artificial Intelligence*. IJCAI, Karlsruhe, pp. 595–99.

Appelt, D., 1985. Planning English referring expressions. *Artificial Intelligence* **26**(10):1–33.

Austin, J. L., 1962. *How to Do Things with Words*. London: Oxford University Press.

Bates, M., Bobrow, R. J., 1983. A transportable natural language interface. In *Proceedings of the 6th Annual International SIGIR Conference on Research and Development in Information Retrieval*. ACM.

Bobrow, D., the PARC understander group, 1977. GUS-1, a frame driven dialog system. *Artificial Intelligence* **8**(2):155–73.

Bobrow, R. J., Webber, B. L., 1980. Knowledge representation for syntactic/semantic processing. In *Proceedings of the 1st Annual Natl. Conference on Artificial Intelligence.* AAAI pp. 316–23.

Brachman, R. J., Bobrow, R. J., Cohen, P. R., Klovstad, J. W., Webber, B. L., Woods, W. A., 1979. *Research in Natural Language Understanding—Annual Report.* Tech. Rep. 4274, Bolt Beranek And Newman Inc., Cambridge, Mass.

Bratman, M., 1984. Two faces of intention. *Philos. Rev.* **93**(3):375–405.

Bruce, B. C., 1975. Case systems for natural language. *Artificial Intelligence* **6**(4):327–60.

Burton, R. R., Brown, J. S., 1979. Toward a natural language capability for computer-aided instruction. In *Procedures for Instructional Systems Development.* Ed. H. O'Neil, New York: Academic Press. pp. 273–313.

Burton, R. R., Woods, W. A., 1976. A compiling system for augmented transition networks. In *Proceedings of the 6th International Conference on Computational Linguistics.* COLING. Ottawa.

Charniak, E., 1973. Jack and Jane in search of a theory of knowledge. In *Proceedings of the 3rd International Joint Conference on Artificial Intelligence.* IJCAI, Stanford, Calif., pp. 337–43.

Chomsky, N., 1965. *Aspects of the Theory of Syntax.* Cambridge, MIT Press.

Codd, E. F., 1970. A relational model for large shared data banks. *Communications of ACM* **13**(6):377–87.

Codd, E. F., 1972. Relational completeness of data base sublanguages. In *Data Base Systems.* Ed. R. Rustin, Englewood Cliffs, NJ: Prentice-Hall. pp. 65–98.

Cohen, P. R., Levesque, H. J., 1985. Speech acts and rationality. In *Proceedings of the 23rd Annual Meeting.* ACL, Chicago, pp. 49–60.

Cohen, P. R., Perrault, C. R., 1979. Elements of a plan-based theory of speech acts. *Cognitive Science* **3**:177–212.

Colmerauer, A., 1978. Metamorphosis grammars. In *Natural Language Communication with Computers.* Ed. L. Bolc, New York: Springer-Verlag. pp. 133–90.

Colmerauer, A., 1979. Un sous-ensemble interessant du Francais. *RAIRO* **13**(4):309–36.

Cooper, R., 1979. Variable binding and relative clauses. In *Formal Semantics and Pragmatics for Natural language.* Ed. F. Guenthner, S. J. Schmidt, The Netherlands: Reidel, Dordrecht. pp. 131–70.

Culy, C. D., 1985. The complexity of the vocabulary of Banbara. *Linguist. Philos.* **8**:345–51.

Dahl, V., 1981. Translating Spanish into logic through logic. *American Journal of Computational Linguistics* **7**(3):149–64.

Damerau, F. J., 1981. Operating statistics for the transformational question answering system. *American Journal of Computational Linguistics* **7**(1):30–42.

Davidson, J., Kaplan, S. J., 1983. Natural langauge access to databases: interpreting update requests. *American Journal of Computational Linguistics* **9**(2):57–68.

Earley, J., 1970. An efficient context-free parsing algorithm. *Communications of ACM* **13**(2):94–102.

Fagin, R., Halpern, J. Y., 1985. Belief, awareness, and limited reasoning. In *Proceedings of the 9th International Joint Conference on Artificial Intelligence*. IJCAI. Los Angeles, pp. 480–90.

Fillmore, C. J., 1977. The case for case reopened. In *Grammatical Relations*. Ed. P. Cole, J. M. Sadock, New York: Academic Press. pp. 59–81.

Finin, T. W., 1985. Constraining the interpretation of nominal compounds in a limited context. In *Analyzing Language in Restricted Domains*. Ed. R. Grishman, R. Kittredge. Hillsdale, NJ: Erlbaum.

Gazdar, G., Klein, E., Pullum, G. K., Sag, I., 1985. *Generalized Phrase Structure Grammar*. Oxford: Blackwell.

Ginsparg, J., 1983. A robust portable natural language database interface. In *Proceedings of the Conference on Applied Natural Language*. ACL, pp. 25–30.

Grosz, B. J., Joshi, A. K., Weinstein, S., 1983. Providing a unified account of definite noun phrases in discourse. In *Proceedings of the 21st Annual Meeting*. ACL. Cambridge, Mass., pp. 44–50.

Grosz, B. J., Sidner, C. L., 1986. The structures of discourse structure. *Computational Linguistics* **12**: In press.

Grosz, B. J., Appelt, D. E., Martin, P., Pereira, F., 1986. TEAM: An experiment in the design of transportable natural-language interfaces. *Artificial Intelligence*. In press.

Harris, L. R., 1977. User-oriented data base query with the Robot natural language query system. *International Journal of Man-Machine Studies* **9**:697–713.

Heidorn, G. E., 1976. Automatic programming through natural language dialogue: a survey. *IBM Journal of Research and Development* **20**(4):302–13.

Heim, I., 1982. *The Semantics of Definite and Indefinite Noun Phrases*. Ph.D. thesis. Univ. Mass., Amherst.

Hendrix, G. G., 1977. Human engineering for applied natural language processing. In *Proceedings of the 5th International Joint Conference on Artificial Artificial Intelligence*. IJCAI. Cambridge, Mass., pp. 183–91.

Hendrix, G., Sacerdoti, E., Sagalowicz, D., Slocum, J., 1978. Developing a natural language interface to complex data. *ACM Transactions on Database Systems* **3**(2):105–47.

Hendrix, G. G., 1978. Semantic aspects of translation. See Walker, 1978, pp. 193–226.

Herskovits, A., 1986. *Space and the Prepositions in English*. London/New York: Cambridge Univ. Press. In press.

Hintikka, J. K. K., 1974. Quantifiers vs. quantification theory. *Linguist. Inq.* **5**:153–77.

Hirst, G., 1981. Lecture Notes in Computer Science, Vol. 119: *Anaphora in Natural Language Understanding*. New York: Springer-Verlag.

Hirst, G., 1983. *Semantic Interpretation Against Ambiguity*. Ph.D. thesis. Brown Univ., Providence, RI.

Hobbs, J., 1978. Resolving pronoun references. *Lingua* **44**:311–38.

Hobbs., J. R., 1980. Selective inferencing. In *Proceedings of the 3rd Biennial Conference on of CSCSI*. Victoria, B.C., pp. 101–22.

Hobbs, J., Evans, D., 1980. Conversation as planned behavior. *Cognitive Science* 4(4):349–77.

Hobbs, J. R., Moore, R. C., 1985. *Formal Theories of the Commonsense World*. Norwood, NJ: Ablex.

Hopcroft, J. E., Ullman, J., 1979. *Introduction to Automata Theory, Languages and Computation*. Reading, Mass.: Addison-Wesley.

Isabelle, P., 1984. Another look at nominal compounds. In *Proceedings of the 10th International Conference on Computational Linguistics*. COLING. Stanford, Calif., pp. 509–16.

Johnson, T., 1985. *Natural Language Computing: The Commercial Applications*. London: Ovum.

Kaplan, R., Bresnan, J., 1982. Lexical-functional grammar: a formal system for grammatical representation. In *The Mental Representation of Grammatical Relations*. Ed. J. Bresnan, Cambridge, Mass.: MIT Press. pp. 173–281.

Kaplan, S. J., 1982. Cooperative responses from a portable natural language query system. *Artificial Intelligence* **19**(29):165–88.

Kay, M., 1979. Functional grammar. In *Proceedings of the Berkeley Linguistics Society* **5**:142–58.

Kay, M., 1980. Algorithm schemata and data structures in syntactic processing. *Nobel Symposium on Text Processing*. Gothenburg, Sweden.

Kay, M., 1985. Parsing in functional unification grammar. In *Natural Language Parsing*. Ed. D. R. Dowty, L. Karttunen, A. Zwicky, London: Cambridge University Press., pp. 251–78.

Konolige, K., 1981. *The Database as Model: a Metatheoretic Approach*. Menlo Park, Calif.: SRI International.

Konolige, K., 1984. *A Deduction Model of Belief and its Logics*. Ph.D. thesis. Stanford Univ., Calif.

Koskenniemi, K., 1983. *Two-level Model for Morphological Analysis*. Ph.D. thesis. Univ. Helsinki.

Kuno, S., Oettinger, A., 1962. Multiple path syntactic analyzer. *Information Process.* **62**:306–12.

Landsbergen, S. P. J., 1976. Syntax and formal semantics of English in PHLIQAI. See Burton and Woods, 1976.

Lehnert, W. G., Shwartz, S. P., 1983. EXPLORER: a natural language processing system for oil exploration. See Ginsparg 1983, pp. 69–72.

Lesser, V. R., Fennell, R. D., Erman, L. D., Eddy, D. R. 1975. Organization of the HEARSAY II Speech Understanding System. *IEEE Transactions on Acoustics, Speech, and Signal Processing* **23**(1):11–24.

Litman, D. J., 1985. *Plan Recognition and Discourse Analysis: An Integrated Approach for Understanding Dialogues.* Ph.D. thesis. University of Rochester, New York.

Marcus, M. P., 1980. *A Theory of Syntactic Recognition for Natural Language.* Cambridge, Mass.: MIT Press.

Marcus, M. P., Hindle, D., Fleck, M. M., 1983. D-Theory: talking about talking about trees. See Grosz et al., 1983, pp. 129–136.

McCord, M. C., 1985. Modular logic grammars. In *Proceedings of the 23rd Annual Meeting.* ACL, Chicago, pp. 104–17.

McDonald, D., 1983. Description directed control. *Comput. Math.* **9**(1):111–30.

Montague, R., 1973. The proper treatment of quantification in ordinary English. In *Approaches to Natural Language: In Proceedings of the 1970 Stanford Workshop on Grammar and Semantics.* Ed. J. K. K. Hintikka, J. Moravcsik, P. Suppes., The Netherlands: Reidel, Dordrecht. pp. 221–42.

Moore, R. C., 1979. *Handling Complex Queries in a Distributed Database.* Menlo Park, California: SRI International.

Moore, R., 1981. Problems in logical form. In *Proceedings of the 19th Annual Meeting.* ACL, Stanford, California, pp. 117–24.

Moore, R. C., 1985. A formal theory of knowledge and action. In *Formal Theories of the Commonsense Word.* Ed. J. R. Hobbs, R. C. Moore, Norwood, NJ: Ablex. pp. 319–58.

Nilsson, N. J., 1980. *Principles of Artificial Intelligence.* Morgan Kaufmann Publishers, San Mateo, California.

Palmer, M. S., 1983. Inference-driven semantic analysis. In *Proceedings of the 4th National Conference on Artificial Intelligence.* AAAI Washington, pp. 310–313.

Paxton, W. H., 1978. A framework for speech understanding. See Walker, 1978, pp. 17–120.

Pereira, F. C. N., Warren, D., 1980. Definite clause grammars for language analysis. *Artificial Intelligence* **13**:231–78.

Pereira, F. C. N., 1981. Extraposition grammars. *American Journal of Computational Linguistics* **7**(4):243–56.

Pereira, F. C. N., 1983. *Logic for Natural Language Analysis.* Ph.D. thesis. University of Edinburgh.

Pereira, F. C. N., Shieber, S. M., 1984. The semantics of grammar formalisms seen as computer languages. See Isabelle, 1984, pp. 123–29.

Perrault, C. R., 1984. On the mathematical properties of linguistic theories. *Computational Linguistics* **10**:165–76.

Petrick, S. J., 1973. Transformational analysis. In *Natural Language Processing*. Ed. R. Rustin, New York: Algorithmics Press. pp. 27–41.

Robinson, A. E., 1981. Determining verb phrase referents in dialog. *American Journal of Computational Linguistics* 7(1):1–16.

Robinson, J. J., 1982. DIAGRAM: a grammar for dialogues. *Communications of ACM* 25(1):27–47.

Sager, N., 1981. *Natural Language Information Processing*. Reading, Mass: Addison-Wesley.

Scha, R. J. H., 1976. Semantic types in PHLIQAI. See Burton and Woods, 1976.

Schank, R. C., 1975. *Conceptual Information Processing*. New York: American Elsevier.

Scott, D., 1982. Domains for denotational semantics. In *Proceedings of the ICALP-82, International Conference on Autom. Language Program.*. Heidelberg.

Searle, J. R., 1969. *Speech Acts: An Essay in the Philosophy of Language*. London: Cambridge University Press.

Shieber, S. M., 1984. The design of a computer language for linguistic information. See Isabelle, 1984, pp. 362–66.

Shieber, S. M., 1985. Evidence against the context-freeness of natural language. *Linguist. Philos.* 8:333–43.

Sidner, C., 1983. Focusing in the comprehension of definite anaphora. In *Computational Models of Discourse*. Ed. M. Brady, R. Berwick, Cambridge, MIT Press. pp. 267–330.

Slocum, J., 1981. A practical comparison of parsing strategies. See Moore, 1981, pp. 1–6.

Stonebraker, M., Wong, E., Kreps, P., Held, G., 1976. The design and implementation of INGRES. *ACM Transactions on Database Systems* 1(3):189–222.

Tennant, H. R., Ross, K. M., Saenz, R. M., Thompson, C. W., Miller, J. R., 1983. Menu-based natural langauge understanding. See Grosz et al., 1983, pp. 151–58.

Thompson, F. B., Thompson, B. H., 1975. Practical natural language processing: The REL system prototype. In *Advances in Computers*. Ed. M. Rubinoff, M. C. Yovits, New York: Academic Press. pp. 109–68.

Ullman, J. D., 1982. *Principles of Database Systems*. Rockville, Md.: Computer Science Press.

Walker, D., 1978. *Understanding Spoken Language*. New York: Elsevier.

Waltz, D. L., 1978. An English language question answering system for a large relational database. *Communications of ACM* 21(7):526–39.

Warren, D. H. D., Pereira, F. C. N., 1982. An efficient easily adaptable system for interpreting natural language queries. *American Journal of Computational Linguistics* 8(3-4):110–22.

Webber, B. L., 1980. *A Computational Approach to Discourse Anaphora.* New York: Garland.

Weischedel, R. M., 1979. A new semantic computation while parsing: presupposition and entailment. In *Presupposition.* Ed. C. K. Oh, D. A. Dinneen, New York: Academic Press. pp. 155–82.

Weischedel, R. M., Sondheimer, N. K., 1983. Meta-rules as a basis for processing ill-formed input. *American Journal of Computational Linguistics* **9**(3-4):161–77.

Wilks, Y., 1975. An intelligent analyzer and understander of English. *Communications of ACM* **18**(5):264–74.

Winograd, T., 1972. *Understanding Natural Language.* New York: Academic Press.

Winograd, T., 1983. *Language as a Cognitive Process Vol. 1: Syntax.* Reading, Mass., Addison-Wesley.

Wolf, J. J., Woods, W. A., 1980. The HWIM speech understanding system. In *Trends in Speech Recognition.* Ed. W. A. Lea, Englewood Cliffs: Prentice-Hall. pp. 1–24.

Woods, W. A., 1967. *Semantics for a Question Answering System.* Harvard University Computer Lab.

Woods, W. A., 1970. Transition network grammars for natural language analysis. *Communications of ACM* **13**(10):591–606.

Woods, W. A., Kaplan, R. M., Nashwebber, B. L., 1972. *The Lunar Sciences Natural Language Information System: Final Report.* BBN Rep. 2378, Bolt Beranek and Newman Inc., Cambridge, Mass.

Woods, W. A., 1978. Semantics and quantification in natural language question answering. In *Advances in Computers.* Ed. M. Yovits, New York: Academic Press. pp. 1–87.

Woods, W. A., 1980. Cascaded ATN grammars. *American Journal of Computational Linguistics* **6**(1):1–15.

Younger, D. H., 1967. Recognition and parsing of context-free languages in time n3. *Information and Control* **14**:189–208.

Zwicky, A. M., Friedman, J., Hall, B. C., Walker, D. E. 1965. The MITRE syntactic analysis procedure for transformational grammars. In *Proceedings of the Fall Joint Computer Conference.* AFIPS, pp. 317–26.

III

PLANNING AND SEARCH

5

Reasoning About Plans and Actions

Michael P. Georgeff

SRI International

Arltificial Intelligence Center and

Center for the Study of Language and Information

Menlo Park, California

1 *Introduction*

Humans spend a great deal of time deciding and reasoning about actions, some with much deliberation and some without any forethought. They may have numerous desires that they wish fulfilled, some more strongly than others. It is often necessary to accommodate conflicting desires, to choose among them, and to reason about how best to accomplish those that are chosen. This choice, and the means chosen to realize these ends, will depend upon currently held beliefs about present and future situations, and upon any commitments or intentions that may have been decided upon earlier. Often it will be necessary to obtain more information about the tasks to be performed, either prior to choosing a plan of action or during its execution. Furthermore, our knowledge of the world itself is frequently incomplete, making it necessary for us to have some means of forming reasonable assumptions about the possible occurrence of other events or the behaviors of other agents.

All this has to be accomplished in a complex and dynamic world populated with many other agents. The agent planning or deciding upon possible courses of action can choose from an enormous repertoire of actions, and these in turn can influence the world in exceedingly complicated ways. Moreover, because of the presence of other agents and processes, the environment is subject to continuous change—even as the planner deliberates on how best to achieve its goals.

2 The Representation of Actions and Events

2.1 Models of States and Events

To tackle the kind of problems mentioned above, we first have to understand clearly what entities we are to reason about. The traditional approach has been to consider that, at any given moment, the world is in one of a potentially infinite number of *states* or *situations*. A world state may be viewed as a snapshot of the world at a given instant of time.

The world can change its state only by the occurrence of an *event* or *action*. In this view, events can be modelled simply as state transitions (or, more generally, as certain sequences of state transitions). For example, in Figure 1, the occurrence of the event e_1 results in the world changing from state S_1 to state S_2, and event e_2 takes us then to state S_3. An *event type* is a set of event instances, representing all possible occurrences of the event in all possible situations. Thus, the event type "Put block A on top of block B" corresponds to all possible occurrences of the putting of block A upon B.

In domains in which there is no concurrent activity, it is only necessary to consider the initial and final states of any given event, as nothing can happen during the event to change its outcome. Consequently, an event (strictly, an event type) can be modeled as a set of pairs of initial and final states. If, in addition, we limit ourselves to deterministic events, this relation between initial and final states will be functional; that is, the initial state in which an event occurs will uniquely determine the resulting final state.

An *action* is a special kind of event, namely, one that is *performed* by some agent, usually in some intentional way. For example, a tree's shedding of its leaves is an event but not an action; John's running around a track is an action [in which John is the agent]. Philosophers make much of this distinction between actions and events, primarily because they are interested in activities that an agent decides upon, rather than those events that are not caused by the agent (such as leaves falling from a tree) or that involve the agent in some unintentional way (such as tripping over a rug) [Davis, 1979]. For our purposes, however, we can treat these terms synonymously.

We also want to be able to say that certain *properties* hold of world states. For example, in some given state, it might be that a specified block is on top of some other block, or that its color is red. But what kind of entities are such properties? For example, consider the property of redness. In a static world, we might model this property as a set of individuals (or objects), namely, those that are red. However, in dynamic worlds, the individuals that are red can vary from state to state; we therefore cannot model redness in this way.

One way to handle this problem is to introduce the notion of a *fluent* [McCarthy and Hayes, 1969], which is a function defined on world states. Essentially, a given fluent corresponds to some property of world states, and its value in a given state is the value of that property in that state. For example, the property of redness could be represented by a fluent whose *value* in a given state is the set of individuals that are red in that state.

STATES AND EVENTS

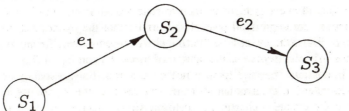

World States S

Event Instances e

Figure 1

Fluents come in a variety of types. A fluent whose value in a given state is either *true* or *false* is usually called a *propositional* fluent. For example, the property of it being raining could be represented by a propositional fluent that has the value *true* in those states in which it is raining and the value *false* when it is not raining [Dowty, Wall and Peters, 1981].

2.2 *The Situation Calculus*

Of course, in any interesting domain, it is infeasible to specify explicitly the functions and relations representing events and fluents. We therefore need some calculus or formal language for describing and reasoning about them.

McCarthy [McCarthy and Hayes, 1969] proposed a logic of situations (states) that has become the classical approach to this problem. In the variant we describe here, the logical terms of the calculus are used to denote the states, events, and fluents of the problem domain. For example, the event term *puton(A, B)* could be used to denote the action in which block A is placed on top of block B. Similarly, the fluent term *on(A, B)* could designate the fluent representing the proposition that A is on top of B.

The predicates in this situation calculus are used primarily to make statements about the values of fluents in particular states. For propositional fluents, we shall use the expression *holds(f, s)* to mean that the fluent f has value *true* in state s. For example, *holds(on(A, B), s)* will be true if the fluent denoted by *on(A, B)* has value *true* in state s; that is, if block A is on top of B in s.

We must also be able to specify the state transitions associated with any particular event in the problem domain. We shall do this by use of an *occurs* predicate, and write *occurs(e, s_1, s_2)* to mean that the performance of event e begins in state s_1 and ends in state s_2. (The more usual way to do this is to introduce the term *result(e, s)* to designate the state resulting from the performance of event e in state s, but this approach is not as expressive as the one I am proposing.) For example, *occurs(puton(A, B), s_1, s_2)* denotes the fact that the action *puton(A, B)* is initiated in state s_1 and terminates in state s_2. We can also use the *occurs* predicate to characterize those states that are *reachable* from some given state.

The well-formed formulas of this situation calculus may also contain the usual logical connectives and quantifiers. With this machinery, we can now express general assertions about the effects of actions and events when carried out in particular situations. For example, we can express the result of putting block A on top of block B as follows:

$$\forall s_1, s_2 . \ holds(clear(A) \wedge clear(B), s_1) \wedge occurs(puton(A, B), s_1, s_2) \supset$$
$$holds(on(A, B), s_2)$$

This statement is intended to mean that if blocks *A* and *B* are initially clear, then after the action *puton(A, B)* has been performed, block *A* will be on top of *B*.

One problem with the above approach is the apparently large number of axioms needed to describe what properties are *unaffected* by events. For example, if block *B* were known to be red prior to our placing block *A* on it, we would not be able to conclude, on the basis of the previous axiom alone, that block *B* would still be red afterward. To do so, we require an additional axiom stating that the movement of block *A* does not change the color of block *B*:

$$\forall s_1, s_2 \, . \, holds(color(B, red), s_1) \wedge occurs(puton(A, B), s_1, s_2) \supset$$
$$holds(color(B, red), s_2)$$

In fact, we would have to provide similar axioms for every property of the domain left unaffected by the action. These are called *frame axioms*; being forced to specify them is commonly known as the *frame problem* [Hayes, 1973].

Various other logical formalisms have been developed for representing and reasoning about dynamic domains. The most common are the *modal logics*, which avoid the explicit use of terms representing world state. One type of modal logic, called *temporal logic*, introduces various *temporal operators* for describing properties of world histories [Prior, 1967]. *Process logics* are another kind of modal logic in which explicit mention of state is avoided [Nishimura, 1980]. These logics are based on the same model of the world as described above, but introduce programs (or plans) as additional entities in the domain (see Section 3.1). *Dynamic logics* can be viewed as a special class of process logics that are concerned solely with the input-output behavior of programs [Harel, 1979]. While these various logics may vary in their expressive power, all suffer from the frame problem.

2.3 *The STRIPS Representation*

The STRIPS representation of actions, originally proposed by Fikes and Nilsson [1971], is one of the most widely used alternatives to the situation calculus. It was introduced to overcome what were seen primarily as computational difficulties in using the situation calculus to construct plans. The major problem was to avoid (1) the specification of a potentially large number of frame axioms, and (2) the necessity of having the planner consider these axioms in determining the properties that hold at each point in the plan.

In the STRIPS representation, a world state is represented by a set of logical formulas, the conjunction of which is intended to describe the given state. Actions or events are represented by so-called *operators*. An operator consists of a *precondition*, an *add list*, and a *delete list*. Given a description of a world state *s*, the precondition of an operator is a logical formula that specifies whether or not the corresponding action can be performed in *s*, and the add and delete lists specify how to obtain a representation of the world state resulting from the performance of the action in *s*. In particular, the add list specifies the set of formulas that are true in the resulting state and must therefore be added to the set of formulas representing *s*, while the delete list specifies the set of formulas that may no longer be true and must therefore be deleted from the description of *s*. This scheme for determining the descriptions of successive states is called the *STRIPS rule*.

For example, the following STRIPS operator can be taken to represent the action that moves block *A* from location zero to location 1.

Precondition: $loc(A, 0) \wedge clear(A)$
Add list: $\{loc(A, 1)\}$
Delete list: $\{loc(A, 0)\}$

Let's say that some world is described by the formulas $\{loc(A, 0),$ $clear(A),$ $red(A).\}$ Given this set of formulas, it is possible (trivially in this case) to prove that the precondition holds, so that the operator is then considered applicable to this world description. The description of the world resulting from application of this operator is $\{loc(A, 1), clear(A), red(A)\}$.

Although the operators in STRIPS are intended to describe actions that transform world states into other world states, they actually define *syntactic* transformations on *descriptions* of world states. STRIPS should thus be viewed as a form of logic and the STRIPS rule as a *rule of inference* within this logic. Given this perspective, it is necessary to specify the conditions under which the STRIPS rule is *sound*. That is, for each operator and its associated action, the formulas generated by application of the operator should indeed be true in the state resulting from the performance of the action. Surprisingly, only very recently has anyone attempted to provide such a semantics, though the importance of doing so has long been recognized.

The problem is that soundness is not possible to achieve if the STRIPS rule is allowed to apply to arbitrary formulas. For example, suppose in the case above I add to the description of the initial world state the formula:

$loc(A, 0) \wedge loc(A, 0)$

This is somewhat redundant, but from a logical point of view it is still a fine description of the initial state. The problem is that, when the STRIPS operator is now applied, this formula will not be deleted from the description of the successor state (because it does not appear in the delete list of the operator), yet of course it should be deleted.

Lifschitz [1987] was the first to describe a way of defining the kind of formulas allowable in world descriptions, and to prove soundness for such a system. In particular, soundness is guaranteed if, for every operator and its associated action: (1) Every allowable formula that appears in the operator's add list is satisfied in the state resulting from the performance of the action, and (2) Every allowable formula that is satisfied in the state in which the action is initiated, and that does not belong to the operator's delete list, is satisfied in the resulting state. The latter condition is commonly known as the *STRIPS assumption*.

The STRIPS representation thus avoids the specification of frame axioms that state what properties are left unchanged by the occurrence of actions. Furthermore, the lack of frame axioms allows a planner to better focus its search effort. On the other hand, STRIPS is not nearly as expressive as the situation calculus [Waldinger, 1977]. In particular, the STRIPS representation compels us to include in an operator's delete list all allowable formulas that could possibly be affected by the action, even if the truth value of some of these could be deduced from other axioms. For example, even if we were given an axiom stating that when Fred dies he stops breathing, an operator representing the fatal shooting of Fred would nonetheless have to include in its delete list *both* effects of the shooting.

To overcome this difficulty, it is tempting to modify the STRIPS rule so that formulas that can be *proved* false in the resulting state need not be included in an operator's delete list. This leads to the *extended STRIPS assumption*, which states that any formula that is satisfied in the initiating state and does not belong to the delete list will be satisfied in the resulting state, *unless* it is inconsistent to assume so. Unfortunately, no one has yet provided an adequate semantics for such an approach [Reiter, 1980].

Yet another variant representation is described by Pednault [1986]. Each action is represented by an operator that describes how performance of the action affects the relations, functions, and constants of the problem domain. As with the STRIPS representation, the state variable is suppressed and frame axioms need not be supplied. For a restricted but commonly occurring class of actions, the representation appears as expressive as the situation calculus.

3 *Plan Synthesis*

Plan synthesis concerns the construction of some plan of action for one or more agents to achieve some specified goal or goals, given the constraints of the world in which these agents are operating. In its most general form, it is necessary to take into account the various degrees to which the agents desire that their goals be fulfilled, the various risks involved, and the limitations to further reasoning arising from the real-time constraints of the environment. However, we shall begin by considering the simpler problem in which an agent's goals are consistent and all of the same utility. We shall disregard reasoning about the consequences of plan failure and we shall not concern ourselves with real-time issues. (In philosophy, this kind of planning is commonly called *means-ends reasoning*, and is considered to be just one of the many components comprising rational activity [Bratman, forthcoming; Davidson, 1980; Davis, 1979].)

3.1 *General Deductive Approaches*

Given a formulation of actions and world states as described in Section 2, the simplest approach to planning is to prove—by means of some automatic or interactive theorem-proving system—the existence of a sequence of actions that will achieve the goal condition. More precisely, suppose that we have some goal ψ that we want to achieve and that the initial state satisfies some condition φ. Then the theorem to be proved is:

$$\forall s \,.\, holds(\varphi, s) \,\supset\, \exists z \,.\, holds(\psi, z) \,\wedge\, reachable(z, s)$$

That is, we are required to prove that there exists a state z, reachable from s, in which the goal ψ holds, given that φ holds in the initial state s.

Green [1969] was the first to implement this idea. As he observed, however, it is essential to have the theorem prover provide the right kind of constructive proof. For example, consider being faced with a choice of two doors, behind one of which is a ferocious lion and the other a young maiden. In trying to maximize your lifespan, a theorem prover may well suggest that you simply open the door behind which lies the young maiden. Unfortunately, you may only be able to ascertain the maiden's location after opening the door—too late for you but of little concern to the planning system. This difficulty arises because the sequence of actions constructed by the planner can be conditional on properties of *future* states; that is, on properties that the agent executing the plan is not in a position to determine.

Manna and Waldinger [1987] consider many such problems and show how they can be solved. Unfortunately, while planners based on general deductive mechanisms are extremely elegant, no one has yet managed to produce one that can solve any interesting world problem within acceptable time limits.

3.2 *Planning as Search*

Instead of using some general deductive method, one can try *searching* for an appropriate plan in the space of all possible plans. There are two common ways of viewing plan search techniques. One is to perceive the process as searching through a space of world states, with the transitions between states corresponding to the actions performable by the agent. Another view is that the search takes place through a space of partial plans, in which each node in the search space corresponds to a partially completed plan. The latter view is the more general, as the first can be seen as a special case in which the partial plan is extended by adding a primitive plan element to either end of the current partial plan.

Thus, we can characterize most approaches to the planning problem as follows. Each node in the search space corresponds to some possibly partial plan of action to achieve the given goal. The search space is expanded by further elaborating some component of the plan formed so far. The plan space can be searched with a variety of techniques, both classical and heuristic [Nilsson, 1980; Tate, 1984].

Before we consider specific planning techniques, let us introduce some new terminology. Let us assume that, for some action a, if we initiate a in a state in which φ holds, ψ is guaranteed to hold at the completion of execution. If ψ is the strongest condition for which we can prove that this holds, we shall call ψ the *strongest provable postcondition* of a with respect to φ. We can similarly define the *weakest provable precondition* of a with respect to ψ to be the weakest condition φ that guarantees that ψ will hold if a is initiated in a state in which φ holds.

Now consider how we could find a sequence of actions p to achieve a goal ψ, starting from an initial world in which φ holds. Let's write $exec(p, \psi, \varphi)$ to mean that p satisfies this property. We now have that, for any primitive action a, $exec(p, \psi, \varphi)$ will hold if:

1. $p = \text{NO-OP}$ *and* $\forall s \, . \, holds(\varphi, s) \supset holds(\psi, s)$.

2. $p = a;q$, where q satisfies $exec(q, \gamma, \psi)$ and γ is the strongest provable postcondition of a. (I am here using the symbol *;* to denote sequencing of actions.)

3. $p = q;a$, where q satisfies $exec(q, \varphi, \gamma)$ and γ is the weakest provable precondition of a and ψ.

4. $p = q_1;a;q_2$, where, for some γ_1 and γ_2, a satisfies $exec(a, \gamma_1, \gamma_2)$, q_1 satisfies $exec(q_1, \varphi, \gamma_1)$, and q_2 satisfies $exec(q_2, \gamma_2, \psi)$.

Case (1) simply says that, if the goal condition is already satisfied, we need not plan anymore, i.e., the empty action (NO-OP) will do. Now consider case (2). Let's say that we are guaranteed that, if we execute some action a in a state in which φ holds, γ will be true in the resulting state. Thus, if the plan begins with the element a, the rest of the plan must take us from a state in which γ is true to one in which ψ is true. We can take γ to be any condition that is guaranteed to hold after the execution of a but, to spare ourselves from planning for situations that cannot possibly occur, it is best to take γ to be the strongest of these conditions. Thus, case (2) amounts simply to forward-chaining from the initial state and is usually called *progression*. Case (3) is similar to case (2), except that we chain backward from the goal. It is usually called *regression*; the condition γ is often called the *regressed goal*. Case (4) is tantamount to choosing a primitive plan element somewhere in the middle of the plan, then trying to patch the plan at either end. In fact, case (4) is a generalization of cases (2) and (3).

It is straightforward to construct a simple planner that uses these rules to build a plan. The planner simply applies rules (2), (3), or (4) recursively until, finally, rule (1) can be applied. Clearly, whether or not a solution is obtained will depend on the choice of rules and the choice of primitive plan elements at each step. The algorithm works for any plan or action representation, requiring only that we be able to determine action postconditions and preconditions, as described above. For example, GPS [Newell and Simon, 1963] and STRIPS [Fikes and Nilsson, 1971] use STRIPS-like action representations and rules (1) and (4), whereas Rosenschein [1981] employs dynamic logic to describe the effects of actions and uses rules (1), (2), and (3).

Unfortunately, this approach is too inefficient to be useful for most real-world planning problems. Thus, for the last 15 years or so, researchers in planning have attempted to make this process more efficient. One approach is to avoid fully instantiating the actions in the plan being formed (that is, to leave some of the parameters of the action free) until one is forced to make a commitment. Another approach is to allow the ordering of the actions to remain partial until sufficient information is available to make a wise choice (such planners are usually called *nonlinear planners*). Some planners form plans at one abstraction level, and only after that plan is complete do they consider elaborating it at lower levels of abstraction. The SIPE system, developed by Dave Wilkins at SRI, incorporates many of these ideas and is perhaps the most advanced of these planners [Wilkins, 1985].

However, it is often very hard to find practical real-world problems for which these planners are useful. What are the reasons for this? I believe there are two. First, the world modelled by these planners is assumed to be static, both during planning and during plan execution. They do not allow for the occurrence of events external to the planning agent, or the existence of other processes. Unfortunately, there are not many interesting applications where this assumption holds. Second, in those cases that are relatively static, there often exist special-purpose planners that can solve the problem more efficiently by taking account of the particular features of the problem domain for which they are designed. For example, specialized techniques have been developed for path planning in the presence of obstacles—these are far superior in performance to the general purpose planners I have discussed above (e.g., see the work of Gouzenes [1984] and Brooks [1983, 1985a]).

In the remainder of this paper, I want to look at two areas of planning that I believe are particularly rich in research problems and for which I believe there are a very large number of important applications. The first is what is commonly called *multiagent planning*, and the second involves the design of planning systems that are *embedded* in a dynamically changing environment.

4 *Multiagent Domains*

Most real worlds involve dynamic processes beyond the control of an agent. Furthermore, they may be populated with other agents—some cooperative, some adversarial, and others who are simply disinterested. The planners we have been considering are not applicable in such domains. These planners cannot reason about actions that the agent has no control over and that, moreover, may or may not occur concurrently with what the agent is doing. There is no way to express nonperformance of an action, let alone to reason about it.

We therefore need to develop models of actions and plans that are different from those we have previously considered. We need theories of what it means for one action to interfere with another. Many interactions are harmful, leading to unforeseen consequences or deadlock. Some are beneficial, even essential (such as lifting an object by simultaneously applying pressure from both sides). We should be able to state the result of the concurrence of two events or actions. We need to consider cooperative planning, planning in the presence of adversaries, and how to form contingency plans. In addition, we shall require systems capable of reasoning about the beliefs and intentions of other agents and how to communicate effectively both to exchange information and to coordinate plans of action. Furthermore, these systems will sometimes need to infer the beliefs, goals, and intentions of other agents from observation of their behaviors.

4.1 *Action Representations*

Multiagent domains are those having the potential for concurrent activity among multiple agents or other dynamic processes. The entities introduced in earlier sections—world states, fluents, actions, events, and plans—can also form the basis for reasoning in these domains. However, most of the simplifying assumptions made for handling single-agent domains cannot be usefully employed here. In particular, it is not possible to consider every action as a transition relation from an initial to a final state, as the effects of performing actions concurrently depends on what happens *during* the actions [Georgeff, 1983; Pelavin and Allen, 1986]. For example, in a production line making various industrial components, it is important to know what machines are used during each activity so that potential resource conflicts can be identified.

In addition, we need more powerful and expressive formalisms for representing and reasoning about sequences of states, or so-called *world histories*.

For example, we should be able to express environmental conditions such as "The bank will stay open until 3pm" and "If it rains overnight, it will be icy next morning." Similarly, we have to be able to reason about a great variety of goals, including goals of maintenance and goals satisfying various ordering constraints [Pelavin and Allen, 1986].

It is also important that the representation of events can model the simultaneous occurrence of events. One of the main reasons for doing so is simply that it is often the most natural way to describe some activities. For example, when two people are lifting a table together, it is very convenient to be able to describe the lifting of both ends of the table as occurring simultaneously. Furthermore, it is difficult to see how one could easily describe causal connections between processes without such a notion (and I will have more to say about this later). For example, consider two machines that are connected to one another in some way. Let's imagine that each machine has a lever, and that these levers are directly coupled together. Thus, the movement of one lever will directly cause a corresponding movement of the other. It would be difficult to describe this mechanism in a suitably simple way without the notion of simultaneity.

However, reasoning about the effects of actions is then much more complex, as the properties that are true of the world after the performance of an action will depend not only on what was true before the action was initiated but also on what events are occurring simultaneously with the given action. For example, consider the axioms regarding the action *puton(A, B)* that I gave earlier. The axiom concerning the fact that block *A* will be atop block *B* in the state resulting from performance of the action will clearly still hold. But none of the axioms concerning those properties that previously remained invariant throughout the action will hold if simultaneous actions are allowed! For example, the axiom concerning redness cannot be stated because it may be that, in some cases, someone throws a can of blue paint over block *B* just as I am putting block *A* atop it.

I believe that the solution to this problem rests on using the notion of *independence* to describe the region of influence of events and actions. This turns out to be critical for reasoning about the persistence of world properties and other issues that arise in multiagent domains. Indeed, what makes planning useful for survival is the fact that we can structure the world in a way that keeps most properties and events independent of one another, thus allowing us to reason about the future without complete knowledge of all the events that could possibly be occurring.

McDermott [1982] provides a somewhat different formalism for describing multiagent domains, although the underlying model of actions and events is essentially as described above. Allen and Pelavin [Allen, 1984; Pelavin and Allen, 1986] introduce yet another formalism based on a variation of this model of actions and events. The major difference is that fluents are viewed as functions on *intervals* of states, rather than as functions on states. Thus, in this formalism, *holds(raining, i)* would mean that it is raining over the interval of time *i*, which might be, for example, some particular time period on some specific day. The aim is that, by using intervals rather than states, we obtain a more natural and possibly more tractable language for describing and reasoning about multiagent domains. However, I think too much can be made of the difference between the state-based and interval-based approaches—both reduce one to the other, and the differences in expressive power or naturalness appear to me to be small.

Yet another approach is suggested by Lansky [1987], who considers events as primitive and defines state derivatively in terms of event sequences. Properties that hold of world states are then restricted to being temporal properties of event sequences. For example, one might identify the property "waiting for service" with the condition that an event of type "request" has occurred and has not been followed by an event of type "serve." Lansky uses a temporal logic for expressing general facts about world histories and, in part, for reasoning about them also.

If we are interested in constructing plans of action, one of the more important considerations is whether or not the actions constituting such plans are indeed performable. In single-agent planning, this question is quite easily handled by means of explicitly specifying preconditions that guarantee action performability. However, it is much more complex in multiagent domains.

The source of the problem in multiagent planning is that it is not possible to state simple preconditions for each individual action, the satisfaction of which would ensure its performability. In multiagent domains, whether or not an action can be performed will depend not only on the fulfillment of such preconditions, but also on which events or actions may (or are required to) occur simultaneously with the given action: It is, after all, of little use to form a plan that calls for the simultaneous or concurrent performance of actions that are inherently precluded from coexisting.

This problem is far more crucial than it may first appear. In particular, we are not concerned merely with issues of deadlock avoidance. In planning and other forms of practical reasoning, the failure of an action does not necessarily mean that the agent or device performing the action will thereafter be unable to proceed. Rather, such failure is usually taken to mean that the *desired* or *intended* effects of the action have not been achieved. Thus, though true deadlock may occur quite rarely, actions often fail to produce their intended effects because of interference with other, often unanticipated events.

Moreover, much of human planning revolves around the *coordination* of plans of action. Some of this is concerned with synchronizing the activities of agents so that tasks involving more than one agent can be carried out successfully. Such synchronization can be accomplished by specifying explicitly what temporal relations should hold among the activities of the various agents—

[Lansky, 1985; Stuart, 1985] the more difficult problem is to identify interactions among potentially conflicting actions. Indeed, the recognition of possible plan conflicts is considered by some philosophers to be at the heart of rational behavior [Bratman, forthcoming].

4.2 *Causality and Process*

One problem I have not yet addressed is the apparent complexity of the axioms that describe the effects of actions. For example, while it might seem reasonable to state that the location of block B is independent of the movement of block A, this is simply untrue, as everyone knows, in most interesting worlds. Whether or not the location of B is independent of the movement of A will depend on a host of conditions, such as whether B is in front of A, on top of A, atop A but tied to a door, and so on.

One way to solve this problem is by introducing a notion of *causality* (some philosophers, to avoid such a loaded term, prefer to use "generation" instead) [Allen, 1984; Georgeff, 1987; Lansky, 1987; McDermott, 1982; Shoham, 1986]. Two kinds of causality suggest themselves: one in which an event causes the simultaneous occurrence of another event; the other in which an event causes the occurrence of a subsequent event. We could denote these two causal relations by introducing two new predicates, $causes_s(\varphi, e_1, e_2)$ and $causes_n(\varphi, e_1, e_2)$, say, where φ is the condition under which event e_1 causes event e_2. These two kinds of causality are sufficient to describe the behavior of any procedure, process, or device that is based on discrete (rather than continuous) events.

Of course, we need to specify how causally related actions affect one another. The axiom expressing the effects of simultaneous causation can be written

$$\forall s_1, s_2, \varphi, e_1, e_2 \ . \ causes_s(\varphi, e_1, e_2) \wedge holds(\varphi, s_1) \wedge occurs(e_1, s_1, s_2) \supset$$
$$occurs(e_2, s_1, s_2)$$

This simply specifies that, if condition φ holds at the moment event e_1 is initiated, and if event e_2 is causally related to e_1 under these conditions, then e_2 will occur simultaneously with the occurrence of e_1. A similar axiom can be given for subsequent causation.

With such axioms, we are now in a position to write down the causal laws of the problem domain. For example, we might have a causal law to express the fact that, whenever a block x is moved, any block on top of x and not somehow restrained (e.g., by a string tied to a door) will also move. We could write this as

$$\forall x, y, l \ . \ causes_s((on(y, x) \wedge \neg \ restrained(y)), move(x,l), (move(y, l)))$$

While the introduction of causality can help simplify the descriptions of actions and events, we are still left with the problem of *specifying* the independence and causal relationships among events. Indeed, it would appear that the combinatorial difficulties in expressing all the required independence and causality axioms are no less formidable than those presented by the original frame problem.

One way to reduce the combinatorics of the problem is by introducing the notion of *process*. This notion can be used to specify the way in which groups or conglomerates of events depend on one another and the way in which they can interact with the external world. To do this, the problem domain is considered to be composed of a number of processes, and the events and fluents of the domains are classified as being either internal or external with respect to these processes [Georgeff, 1987; Lansky, 1987]. We then require that there be no *direct* causal relationship between internal and external events, so that the only way the internal events of a given process can influence external events (or vice versa) is through indirect causation by an event that belongs to neither category (Figure 2). Within the framework of concurrency theory, these intermediary events (more accurately, event types) are often called *ports*. Processes thus impose causal boundaries and independence properties on a problem domain, and can thereby substantially reduce combinatorial complexity [Georgeff, 1987; Lansky, 1987].

In this way I believe much of the difficulty surrounding the frame problem can be overcome. To make the point more strongly, consider the state of operating systems practice fifteen years ago, prior to the widespread use of the notion of process. In those days, the designer of an operating system had to consider, for every single program that the system might execute, whether or not such execution could interfere with the control state of other programs and thus affect their computation. But as soon as the formal notion of process was introduced—along the lines I sketched out above—the problem went away. I expect the same would happen in AI if we paid more attention to some of the concepts of operating systems theory and concurrent programming.

Of course, for the kind of problems we are concerned with, exploiting these ideas will not be easy. The identifiability of processes depends strongly on the problem domain. In standard programming systems (at least those that are well structured), processes can be used to represent scope rules and are fairly easy to specify. In complex physical systems, it is often the case that many of the properties of one subsystem will be independent of the majority of actions performed by other subsystems; thus these subsystems naturally correspond to processes as defined here. Lansky and Fogelsong [1987] give other examples in which processes are readily specified. In other situations, such specification might be more complicated. Moreover, in many real-world situations, dependence will vary as the spheres of influence and the potential for interaction change over time [Hayes, 1985].

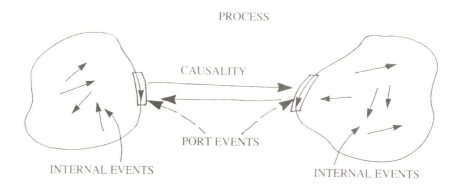

Figure 2

4.3 *Multiagent Planning*

Despite the variety of formalisms developed for reasoning about multiagent domains, relatively few planning systems have been fully implemented. Allen and Koomen [1983] describe a simple planner, based on a restricted form of interval logic [Allen, 1984]. While this technique is effective for relatively simple problems, it is not obvious that the approach would be useful in more complex domains.

Another issue concerns how separate plans can be combined in a way that avoids interference among the agents executing the plans. In such a setting, one could imagine a number of agents each forming their own plans and then, after communicating their intentions (plans) to one another or a centralized scheduler, modifying these to avoid interference. To solve this problem, it is necessary to ascertain, from descriptions of the actions occurring in the individual plans, which actions could interfere with one another and in what manner [Georgeff, 1984]. After this has been determined, a coordinated plan that precludes such interference must then be constructed. This plan can be formed by inserting appropriate synchronization actions (interagent communications) into the original plans to ensure that only interference-free orderings will be allowed [Georgeff, 1983]. Stuart [1985] formalized this approach and implemented a synchronizer based on techniques developed by Manna and Wolper [1981].

Lansky and Fogelsong [1987] have developed a multiagent planner that exploits causal independencies. Unlike the approaches described above, constraints between events have to be specified explicitly. However, the system accommodates a wide class of plan synchronization constraints. Also, the process of plan synchronization is not limited to a strategy of planning to separately achieve each component task and then combining the results. Instead, a more general, adaptable strategy is used that can bounce back and forth between local (i.e., single-agent) and global (multiagent) contexts, adding events where necessary for purposes of synchronization. Planning loci can be composed hierarchically or even overlap.

5 Embedded Systems

Of course, the ability to plan and reason about actions and plans is not much help unless the agent doing the planning can survive in the world in which it is embedded. This brings us to perhaps the most important and also most neglected area of planning research—the design of systems that are actually *situated* in the world and that must operate effectively given the real-time constraints of their environment.

5.1 Execution Monitoring Systems

Most existing architectures for embedded planning systems consist of a plan constructor and a plan executor. As a rule, the plan constructor plans an entire course of action before commencing execution of the plan [Fikes and Nilsson, 1971; Vere, 1983; Wilkins, 1985]. The plan itself is usually composed of primitive actions—that is, actions that are directly performable by the system. The rationale for this approach, of course, is to ensure that the planned sequence of actions will actually achieve the prescribed goal. As the plan is executed, the system performs the primitive actions in the plan by calling various low-level routines. Usually, execution is monitored to ensure that these routines achieve the desired effects; if they do not, the system may return control to the plan constructor so that it can modify the existing plan appropriately.

Various techniques have been developed for monitoring the execution of plans and replanning upon noticing potential plan failure [Fikes and Nilsson, 1971; Wilkins, 1985]. The basis for most of these approaches is to retain with the plan an explicit description of the conditions that are required to hold for correct plan execution. Throughout execution, these conditions are periodically checked. If any condition is discovered to be unexpectedly false, a replanning module is invoked. This module uses various plan modification operators to change the plan, or returns to some earlier stage in the plan formation process and attempts to reconstruct the plan given the changed conditions.

However, in real-world domains, much of the information about how best to achieve a given goal is acquired during plan execution. For example, in planning to get from home to the airport, the particular sequence of actions performed depends on information acquired on the way—such as which turnoff to take, which lane to get into, when to slow down and speed up, and so on. In such situations, one cannot use a system that plans in full down to the lowest level of detail. Of course, one might simply use a traditional planner at the higher levels of planning, but that avoids the issue—that is, how do we plan with incomplete information, how do we plan to gather information, and how do we elaborate our plans as we acquire this information.

5.2 *Reactive Systems*

Real-time constraints pose yet further problems for traditionally structured systems. First, the planning techniques typically used by these systems are very time consuming. While this may be acceptable in some situations, it is not suited to domains where replanning is frequently necessary and where system viability depends on readiness to act. In real-world domains, unanticipated events are the norm rather than the exception, necessitating frequent replanning.

A second drawback of traditional planning systems is that they usually provide no mechanisms for responding to new situations or goals during plan execution, let alone during plan formation. Indeed, the very survival of an autonomous system may depend on its ability to react quickly to new situations and to modify its goals and intentions accordingly. These systems should be able to reason about their current intentions, changing and modifying these in the light of their possibly changing beliefs and goals. While many existing planners have replanning capabilities, none have yet accommodated modifications to the system's underlying set of goal priorities.

A number of systems developed for the control of robots have a high degree of reactivity [Albus, 1981; Albus, Anthony, and Nagel, 1981]. Even SHAKEY [Nilsson, 1984] utilized reactive procedures (ILAs) to realize the primitive actions of the high-level planner (STRIPS), and this idea is pursued further in some recent work by Nilsson [1985]. Another approach is advocated by Brooks [1985], who proposes decomposition of the problem into *task-achieving* units in which distinct behaviors of the robot are realized separately, each making use of the robot's sensors, effectors, and reasoning capabilities as needed. This is in contrast to the traditional approach in which the system is structured according to *functional* capabilities, resulting in separate, self-contained modules for performing such tasks as perception, planning, and task execution. Kaelbling [1987] proposes an interesting hybrid architecture based on similar ideas.

Such architectures could lead to more viable and robust systems than the traditionally structured systems. Yet most of this work has not addressed the issues of general problem solving and commonsense reasoning; the work is instead almost exclusively devoted to problems of navigation and execution of low-level actions. It remains to extend or integrate these techniques with systems that have the ability to completely change goal priorities, to modify, defer, or abandon current plans, and to reason about what is best to do in light of the current situation.

5.3 *Rational Agents*

Another promising approach to providing the kind of high-level goal-directed reasoning capabilities, together with the reactivity, required for survival in the real world, is to consider planning systems as rational agents that are endowed with the psychological attitudes of belief, desire, and intention. The problem that then arises is specifying the properties we expect of these attitudes, the ways they interrelate, and the ways they determine rational behavior in a situated agent.

Amy Lansky and I have been largely concerned with means-ends reasoning in dynamic environments, and with the way partial plans affect practical reasoning and govern future behavior [Georgeff and Lansky, 1986; 1987]. We have developed a highly reactive system, called a Procedural Reasoning System (PRS), to which is attributed attitudes of belief, desire, and intention (Figure 3). Because these attitudes are explicitly represented, they can be manipulated and reasoned about, resulting in complex goal-directed and reflective behaviors. The system consists of a *data base* containing current *beliefs* or facts about the world, a set of current *goals* or *desires* to be realized, a set of *procedures* or *plans* describing how certain sequences of actions and tests may be performed to achieve given goals or to react to particular situations, and an *interpreter* or *reasoning mechanism* for manipulating these components. At any moment, the system also has a *process stack*, containing all currently active plans, which can be viewed as the system's current *intentions* for achieving its goals or reacting to some observed situation.

The set of plans includes not only procedural knowledge about a specific domain, but also *metalevel* plans—that is, information about the manipulation of the beliefs, desires, and intentions of the system itself. For example, a typical metalevel plan would supply a method for choosing among multiple relevant plans, for achieving a conjunction of goals, or for deciding how much more planning or reasoning can be undertaken, given the real-time constraints of the problem domain.

BDI ARCHITECTURE

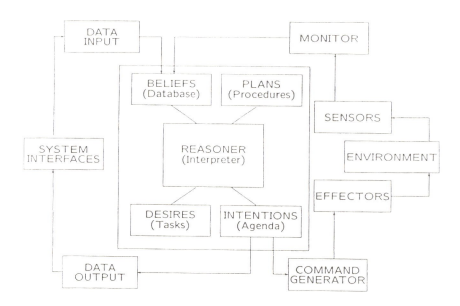

Figure 3

The system operates by first forming a partial overall plan, then figuring out near-term means, executing any actions that are immediately applicable, further expanding the near-term plan, executing further, and so on. At any time, the plans the system intends to execute (i.e., the selected plans) are structurally partial—that is, while certain general goals have been decided upon, specific questions about the means to attain these ends are left open for future reasoning.

While the above work attempts to show how means-ends reasoning may be accomplished by systems situated in real-world environments, little research has been done in providing theories of *decision making* that are appropriate to resource-bounded agents. Researchers in philosophy, as well as decision theory, have long been concerned with the question of how a rational agent weighs alternative courses of action [Jeffrey, 1983]. This work has largely assumed, either explicitly or implicitly, idealized agents with unbounded computational resources. In reality, however, agents do not have arbitrarily long to decide how to act, for the world is changing around them while they deliberate. If deliberation continues for too long, the very beliefs and desires upon which deliberation is based, as well as the real circumstances of the action, may change. Dean [1987] discusses some methods whereby a planning system can recognize the difficulty of the problems it is attempting to solve and, depending on the time it has to consider the matter and what it stands to gain or lose, produce solutions that are reasonable given the circumstances.

Systems that are situated in worlds populated with other agents also have to be able to reason about the behaviors and capabilities of these other systems. This requires complex reasoning about interprocess communication [Appelt, 1985; Cohen and Levesque, 1985], and the ability to infer the beliefs, goals, and intentions of agents from observations of their behavior [Pollack, 1986; 1987]. The challenge remains, however, to design situated planning systems capable of even the simplest kinds of rational behavior.

Acknowledgments

The views expressed here owe much to the insight and understanding of the researchers at SRI and CSLI. I wish to thank particularly Michael Bratman, David Israel, Amy Lansky, Nils Nilsson, Leslie Pack-Kaelbling, Martha Pollack, Stan Rosenschein, Richard Waldinger, and Dave Wilkins.

The writing of this paper has been made possible by a gift from the System Development Foundation, by the Office of Naval Research under Contract N00014-85-C-0251, and by the National Aeronautics and Space Administration, Ames Research Center, under Contract NAS2-12521.

References

Albus, J. S., 1981. *Brains, Behavior, and Robotics*. McGraw-Hill. Peterborough, New Hampshire.

Albus, J. S., A. J. Anthony, and R. N. Nagel., 1981. Theory and practice of hierarchical control. In *Proceedings of the Twenty-Third IEEE Computer Society International Conference*.

Allen, J. F., 1984. Towards a general theory of action and time. *Artificial Intelligence*. 23:123–154.

Allen, J. F. and J. A. Koomen., 1983. Planning using a temporal world model. In *Proceedings of the Eighth International Joint Conference on Artificial Intelligence*. 741–747. Karlsruhe, West Germany.

Appelt, D. E., 1985. Planning English referring expressions. *Artificial Intelligence*. 26:1–34.

Bratman, M. Forthcoming. *Intention, Plans, and Practical Reason*. Harvard University Press. Cambridge, Massachusetts.

Brooks, R. A., 1983. Planning collision-free motions for pick-and-place operations. *International Journal of Robotics Research*. 2(4):19–40.

Brooks, R. A., 1985. *A Robust Layered Control System for a Mobile Robot.* Technical Report 864. Artificial Intelligence Laboratory. Massachusetts Institute of Technology. Cambridge, Massachusetts.

Brooks, R. A., 1985. Visual map making for a mobile robot. In *Proceedings of IEEE Conference on Robotics and Automation.* St. Louis, Missouri.

Cohen, P. R. and H. J. Levesque., 1985. Speech acts and the recognition of shared plans. In *Proceedings of the Twenty-Third Conference of the Association for Computational Linguistics.* 49–59. Stanford, California.

Davidson, D., 1980. *Actions and Events.* Clarendon Press. Oxford, England.

Davis, L. H., 1979. *Theory of Action.* Foundations of Philosophy Series. Prentice-Hall. Englewood Cliffs, New Jersey.

Dean, T., 1987. Intractability and time-dependent planning. In *Reasoning about Actions and Plans: Proceedings of the 1986 Workshop.* 245–266. Morgan Kaufmann Publishers. San Mateo, California.

Dowty, D. R., R. E. Wall, and S. Peters., 1981. *Introduction to Montague Semantics.* Synthese Language Library. D. Reidel Publishing Company. Boston, Massachusetts.

Fikes, R. E. and N. J. Nilsson., 1971. STRIPS: a new approach to the application of theorem proving to problem solving. *Artificial Intelligence.* 2:189–208.

Georgeff, M. P., 1983. Communication and interaction in multiagent planning. In *Proceedings of the Third National Conference on Artificial Intelligence.* 125–129. Washington, D. C.

Georgeff, M. P., 1984. A theory of action for multiagent planning. In *Proceedings of the Fourth National Conference on Artificial Intelligence.* 121–125. Austin, Texas.

Georgeff, M. P. and A. L. Lansky., 1986. *A System for Reasoning in Dynamic Domains: Fault Diagnosis on the Space Shuttle.* Technical Note 375. Artificial Intelligence Center, SRI International. Menlo Park, California.

Georgeff, M. P., 1987. Actions, processes, and causality. In *Reasoning about Actions and Plans: Proceedings of the 1986 Workshop.* 99–122. Morgan Kaufmann Publishers. San Mateo, California.

Georgeff, M. P. and A. L. Lansky., 1987. Reactive reasoning and planning: an experiment with a mobile robot. In *Proceedings of the Sixth National Conference on Artificial Intelligence.* Seattle, Washington.

Gouzenes, L., 1984. Strategies for solving collision-free trajectories problems for mobile and manipulator robots. *The International Journal of Robotics Research.* 3(4):51–65.

Green, C. C., 1969. Application of theorem proving to problem solving. In *Proceedings of the First International Joint Conference on Artificial Intelligence.* 219–239. Washington, D. C.

Harel, D., 1979. *First Order Dynamic Logic.* Lecture Notes in Computer Science. 68. Springer-Verlag. New York, New York.

Hayes, P. J., 1973. The frame problem and related problems in artificial intelligence. In Elithorn A. and D. Jones, editors. *Artificial and Human Thinking.* 45–59. Jossey-Bass. San Francisco, California.

Hayes, P. J., 1985. The second naive physics manifesto. In *Readings in Knowledge Representation.* 467–485. Morgan Kaufmann Publishers. San Mateo, California.

Jeffrey, R., 1983. *The Logic of Decision.* University of Chicago Press. Chicago, Illinois.

Kaelbling, L. P., 1987. An architecture for intelligent reactive systems. In *Reasoning about Actions and Plans: Proceedings of the 1986 Workshop.* 395–410. Morgan Kaufmann Publishers. San Mateo, California.

Lansky, A. L., 1987. A representation of parallel activity based on events, structure, and causality. In *Reasoning about Actions and Plans: Proceedings of the 1986 Workshop.* 123–159. Morgan Kaufmann Publishers. San Mateo, California.

Lansky, A. L. and D. S. Fogelsong., 1987. Localized representation and planning methods for parallel domains. In *Proceedings of the Sixth National Conference on Artificial Intelligence.* Seattle, Washington.

Lifschitz, V., 1987. On the semantics of STRIPS. In *Reasoning about Actions and Plans: Proceedings of the 1986 Workshop.* Morgan Kaufmann Publishers. San Mateo, California.

Manna, Z. and R. J. Waldinger., 1987. A theory of plans. In *Reasoning about Actions and Plans: Proceedings of the 1986 Workshop.* Morgan Kaufmann Publishers. San Mateo, California,

Manna, Z. and P. Wolper., 1981. *Synthesis of Communicating Processes from Temporal Logic Specifications.* Technical Report STAN-CS-81-872. Computer Science Department, Stanford University. Stanford, California.

McCarthy, J. and P. J. Hayes., 1969. Some philosophical problems from the standpoint of artificial intelligence. *Machine Intelligence.* 4:463–502.

McDermott, D., 1982. A temporal logic for reasoning about processes and plans. *Cognitive Science.* 6:101–155.

Newell, A. and H. A. Simon., 1963. GPS, a program that simulates human thought. In E. A. Feigenbaum and J. Feldman, editors. *Computers and Thought.* 279–293. McGraw-Hill, New York.

Nilsson, N. J., 1980. *Principles of Artificial Intelligence.* Morgan Kaufmann Publishers. San Mateo, California.

Nilsson, N. J., 1984. *Shakey the Robot.* Technical Note 323. Artificial Intelligence Center, SRI International. Menlo Park, California.

Nilsson, N. J., 1985. *Triangle Tables: A Proposal for a Robot Programming Language.* Technical Note 347. Artificial Intelligence Center, SRI International. Menlo Park, California.

Nishimura, H., 1980. Descriptively complete process logic. *Acta Informatica.* 14:359–369.

Pednault, E. P. D., 1986. *Toward a Mathematical Theory of Plan Synthesis.* Ph.D. thesis. Department of Electrical Engineering, Stanford University. Stanford, California.

Pelavin, R. and J. F. Allen., 1986. A formal logic of plans in a temporally rich domain. *Proceedings of the IEEE. Special Issue on Knowledge Representation.* **74**:1364–1382.

Pollack, M. E., 1986. *Inferring Domain Plans in Question Answering.* Ph.D. thesis, Computer Science Department, University of Pennsylvania. Pittsburgh, Pennsylvania.

Pollack, M. E., 1987. A model of plan inference that distinguishes between the beliefs of actors and observers. In *Reasoning about Actions and Plans: Proceedings of the 1986 Workshop.* 279–295. Morgan Kaufmann Publishers. San Mateo, California.

Prior, A. N., 1967. *Past, Present and Future.* Clarendon Press. Oxford, England.

Reiter, R., 1980. A logic for default reasoning. *Artificial Intelligence.* **13**:81–132.

Rosenschein, S. J., 1981. Plan synthesis: a logical perspective. In *Proceedings of the Seventh International Joint Conference on Artificial Intelligence.* 331–337. Vancouver, British Columbia.

Shoham, Y., 1986. Chronological ignorance: time, nonmonotonicity, necessity and causal theories. In *Proceedings of the Fifth National Conference on Artificial Intelligence.* 389–393. Philadelphia, Pennsylvania.

Stuart, C. J., 1985. *Synchronization of Multiagent Plans Using a Temporal Logic Theorem Prover.* Technical Note 350. Artificial Intelligence Center, SRI International. Menlo Park, California.

Tate, A., 1984. *Planning in Expert Systems.* D. A. I. Research Paper 221. University of Edinburgh.

Vere, S., 1983. Planning in time: windows and durations for activities and goals. *IEEE Transactions on Pattern Analysis and Machine Intelligence.* **5**(3):246–267.

Waldinger, R., 1977. Achieving several goals simultaneously. *Machine Intelligence.* **8**:94–136.

Wilkins, D. E., 1985. Recovering from execution errors in SIPE. *Computational Intelligence.* **1**:33–45.

6

Search: A Survey of Recent Results

Richard E. Korf

Computer Science Department

University of California, Los Angeles

1 Introduction

This chapter surveys the literature of search in AI, with a focus on recent results in the field. The best reference for the state-of-the-art as of 1984 is Judea Pearl's book *Heuristics* [Pearl, 1984] A more recent survey of the field is an article in the *Annual Review of Computer Science* [Pearl and Korf, 1987].

Search has a long and distinguished history in artificial intelligence. The earliest AI programs were search programs. The reason behind this is that higher-level problem solving was the first aspect of intelligence to receive the attention of AI researchers. Problems such as theorem proving and playing chess were thought to embody the essence of intelligence. Problems such as vision and natural language didn't seem very difficult at first since young children could solve them. Paradoxically, we now have a situation where in certain domains, such as chess or symbolic mathematics, the best computer programs perform comparably to human experts, yet in areas such as language and vision, the best programs can't even reproduce the behavior of two-year-old children. This paradox becomes less surprising when we observe that problems such as vision have been attacked by evolution and natural selection over millions of years, while games such as chess are relatively recent inventions and performance in that domain doesn't convey any particular survival value.

1.1 *Early History*

The literature of heuristic search starts with an article by Claude Shannon, entitled "Programming a Computer for Playing Chess" [Shannon, 1950]. Even though he didn't actually implement a computer program, he laid out most of the theory of heuristic search for two-player games.

One of the earliest AI programs was the Logic Theorist of Newell and Simon [Newell et al, 1963]. The Logic Theorist proved theorems in propositional calculus using heuristic search.

Another very early effort, in the late 50s, was Samuel's pioneering program that played checkers as well as the best humans [Samuel, 1963]. What was especially notable about Samuel's program was that it was one of the first machine learning programs. It automatically improved its play with experience.

Other heuristic search programs prior to 1960 include Gelernter's geometry theorem proving machine [Gelernter, 1963], Slagle's symbolic integration program [Slagle, 1963], and Tonge's assembly-line balancing procedure [Tonge, 1963].

Thus, search is as old as AI, with the original efforts in artificial intelligence aimed at higher-level reasoning and problem solving [Newell, 1969]. It was thought at one point that expert performance would emerge from very general problem solving algorithms, the so-called *weak methods*. That view has shifted somewhat to focus on more knowledge-intensive efforts, but it's still the case that one of the important goals of AI is to develop and analyze general problem solving paradigms. Heuristic search is still one of the most successful.

1.2 *Problem Types*

The classic problems that have been attacked by search algorithms fall into three general classes: path-finding problems, two-player games, and constraint-satisfaction problems.

Canonical examples of pathfinding problems include puzzles such as the Eight Puzzle and Rubik's Cube, and the Traveling Salesman Problem. These are called pathfinding problems because the task is to find a sequence of operations that map an initial state to a goal state. Theorem proving is another example of a pathfinding problem, since the task is to find a sequence of primitive deductions that map the given state of knowledge of the problem to the statement to be proven.

Another class of search problems is two-player games. While chess, checkers, and othello have received the most attention by AI researchers, others including backgammon and go have been studied.

Constraint satisfaction is the third category of search problems, and forms a third parallel thread of the search enterprise. The classic example of a constraint-satisfaction problem is the Eight Queens Problem. The task is to place eight queens on a chessboard, such that no two queens are attacking each other along the same row, column, or diagonal. Another example is map coloring, where the task is to color the regions of a map with a minimum number of colors so that no two adjacent regions have the same color.

Research in all three of these areas has proceeded in parallel but somewhat independently, even though there are strong similarities among them. One of the open research problems is to unify all three areas into a single theory of heuristic search. We are closest to this goal with respect to path-finding problems and two-player games, and steps toward unifying these two will be discussed later.

This represents a top-level view of heuristic search. We will discuss path-finding algorithms in some depth, and treat two-player games and constraint satisfaction problems in less detail. This is less an indication of the relative importance of the areas than a reflection of the interests and expertise of this author. In any case, many of the same concepts that emerge from path-finding algorithms also surface in two-player games and constraint-satisfaction algorithms as well, and need not be revisited in each domain.

1.3 *Problem Spaces*

Why is search considered such a fundamental notion in AI? The reason is the *problem space hypothesis,* due to Allen Newell and Herbert Simon [1972]. The strong version of the hypothesis [Newell, 1980] says that *all goal-oriented symbolic activity occurs in a problem space.* The claim is that search in a problem space is a completely general model of intelligence. The General Problem Solver [Newell and Simon, 1963] was an early implementation of the theory, and the latest instantiation is the SOAR system [Laird et al., 1987], which completely embraces the problem space model, and seriously pursues the idea that everything that we think of as exhibiting intelligence can be cast as search in a problem space.

A *problem space* consists of two components: a set of states and a collection of operators. The states of the problem are configurations of the world or of the problem to be solved. The operators are the actions that map one state of the world to another state.

In addition to a problem space, a *problem instance* is a particular problem to be solved. A problem instance can be viewed as a problem space together with two additional components, an initial state that one starts out in, and a set of goal states or desired configurations of the world.

To be more precise, there are actually two different ways of characterizing a goal state. One is to explicitly give the goal state. For example, in a problem such as Rubik's Cube, the goal state is explicitly specified as that particular state in which every side of the puzzle shows only a single color. Another way of describing the goal state is to give a test for the solution. For example, in the Eight Queens Problem, the goal state isn't given explicitly, since there wouldn't be any problem if it was. Rather, a test or criteria for determining if one has reached the goal is given, namely that eight queens be on the board such that no two are attacking each other. Thus, all that is really needed is a test for a goal state, with an explicit goal state being a special case of such a test.

The task, in the pathfinding model, is to find a sequence of operations that maps the initial state to the goal state. The notion of search comes from the fact that in general there is more than one operator that can be applied to a given state. In order to find a solution, a systematic trial and error procedure is applied until a goal is reached.

If it were the case that from any given state there was exactly one operator to apply, then the problem would be quite easy. At any given state, one would simply determine which operator to apply, apply that operator, and continue until the problem was solved. A "search" in which exactly one operator is applicable to each state, is often called an algorithm. One can view search techniques as extending from brute-force techniques, where there is no information as to which operator to apply, to deterministic algorithms, in which there is sufficient knowledge of the problem to determine exactly what operator to apply to each state.

One normally doesn't think of sorting a list of numbers, for example, as a search problem. It does, however, exist in a problem space. The states are the different possible permutations of the list, the initial state is the current permutation of the elements, and the goal state is the sorted permutation. The operators might be to swap two elements, for example. What distinguishes this problem from traditional search problems is that we have enough knowledge of the problem that we know exactly which operator to apply at each stage to get to a solution. This knowledge is typically expressed as a deterministic algorithm for sorting.

While the problem space is a fairly general model, it will be illustrative to instantiate it with several examples. The first is the problem of road navigation, where the task is to plan a route to drive from one point to another on a network of roads. The states are the different locations one could be in. The primitive operators are sections of road between two adjacent intersections. A primitive operator is an operator that, when applied, doesn't admit any intermediate states from which other operators can be applied. Given that definition of a primitive operator, then a section of road between two adjacent intersections becomes a primitive, since we're not allowed to get off between intersections or drive on the sidewalk.

The initial state in such a problem is where we start out, and the goal state is where we want to end up. The reason that the problem is interesting is that for most intersections, there's more than one road to take. The problem is to find the right sequence of roads to get from the initial state to the goal state.

1.4 *Search Trees*

The standard abstraction of a problem space is a search graph. The nodes of the graph represent the states, and the edges of the graph represent the operators. A search tree is a special case of a search graph. The difference is that in general a graph may have cycles whereas a tree has no cycles. Most problems that we're actually interested in will have a graph structure, such as the network of roads in an area. Any graph, however, can be modelled by a tree, at the cost of introducing some duplicate nodes. When a cycle is encountered, two paths lead to the same state, but in the tree representation, that state will be represented by two different nodes that are different instances of the same data structure. Thus, any graph can be represented as a tree, with a consequent increase in the number of nodes. It's a reasonable simplification if there are few cycles in the graph or if they're fairly long. It's unreasonable if there are a very large number of fairly small cycles. The advantage of the tree structure over a general graph is that the absence of cycles simplifies many of the search algorithms.

Two important parameters of a search graph are called the *branching factor* and the *depth*. The reason they're important is that the performance of most search algorithms is characterized in terms of these parameters.

The branching factor is essentially the number of choices available at a given node. The branching factor of a node is the number of operators that can be applied to that node to yield a new state. Typically, the operator used to generate the given state is excluded, even if it's invertible. In other words, we look at the number of new states that can be generated from a particular node. In general, we're interested in an average branching factor computed by averaging the branching factors of all the nodes in the graph.

The other parameter of interest is the depth of the solution. The depth is the length of the shortest solution path, in terms of number of operator applications. Taken together, the branching factor and the depth characterize the difficulty of performing a search in a particular problem space.

Figure 1 is an example of a search tree. This is a classic problem called the Eight Puzzle. The puzzle is a 3×3 frame of movable square tiles, with one empty position called the blank. The legal operators are: to move a tile which is horizontally or vertically adjacent to the blank position into that position. The task is to rearrange the tiles from some given initial configuration to a particular goal configuration.

In the figure, we find nodes with branching factors of four, two, and one. The average branching factor for this problem turns out to be the square root of three, or about 1.7. If one of the nodes in the bottom row of the figure were the goal state, then the depth of solution for this problem instance would be three moves.

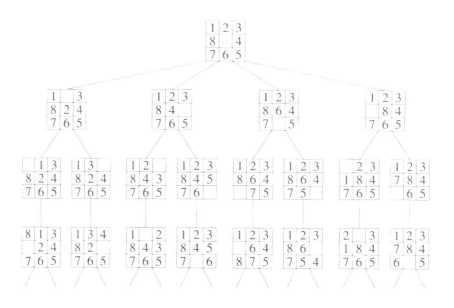

Figure 1 Eight Puzzle Search Tree

John Gaschnig [1979] called the Eight Puzzle the Drosophila or fruit fly of search in AI. The reason is that this toy problem serves as a useful experimental test bed for research on search algorithms. The features of this problem that make it suitable for such a role are that it is extremely simple to represent and manipulate, yet no efficient algorithms are known for finding optimal solutions. In fact, the generalization of the problem to arbitrary sizes was recently shown to be NP-complete [Ratner and Warmuth, 1986]. There do, however, exist heuristic evaluation functions that dramatically improve search efficiency in this problem.

1.5 *Search Efficiency*

The efficiency of algorithms is the central concern in heuristic search. The reason is that search is a completely general problem-solving algorithm. Any problem that can be formulated in a problem space can be solved by a search algorithm. Given claims for generality of problem spaces, then search becomes a very general mechanism for intelligence. What limits the applicability of heuristic search is the efficiency with which it can be performed. Thus, the central issue in search research, including single-agent problems, two-player games, and constraint satisfaction, is efficiency. The efficiency of search algorithms is typically measured along three dimensions: the cost of the solution generated, the time required for the search, and the memory required for the search.

If all of the edges or operators of the problem space have the same cost, then solution cost is characterized by the length of the solution path. More generally, however, operators may have different costs. For example, different sections of road may have different lengths or require differing amounts of time or fuel to traverse. In that case, all the relevant costs are lumped into a single parameter for each operator, depending on some utility function. The cost of a solution, then, becomes the sum of the edge costs along the corresponding path. An optimal solution is one whose cost is less than or equal to the cost of all possible solutions to a given problem instance.

Two other important measures of efficiency are the amount of time the algorithm takes to find the solution, and the amount of memory required to successfully execute the algorithm. The cost of the solution should not be confused with the time required for search. Even though they may be measured in the same units, in one case we're looking at the amount of time to plan a solution, whereas in the other case we are concerned with the cost of actually executing that solution.

1.6 *The Knowledge Dimension*

As mentioned above, the original goal of AI was to develop completely general problem-solving algorithms that would apply across a wide spectrum of domains. What has been discovered in almost every area of AI, however, is that in order to achieve better performance, one often needs more domain-specific knowledge. This gives rise to a spectrum of algorithms along what can be called the knowledge dimension. This spectrum ranges from very general and hence knowledge-poor algorithms to very specific but knowledge-rich methods. It amounts to the familiar trade-off between generality and power.

Search algorithms tend to be found near the general and knowledge-poor end of the spectrum. Even so, different search algorithms differ in their position on this spectrum. Three convenient points to discuss, in increasing order of knowledge, are the brute-force searches, the heuristic searches, and various abstraction techniques.

A brute-force search algorithm can be characterized as an algorithm that uses no knowledge about the problem other than the problem space itself. In other words, the set of states, the set of operators, the initial state, and a test for the goal state. As one would expect, these are very general but very inefficient algorithms.

The next point in the knowledge dimension includes heuristic search algorithms. The notion of heuristic search is to add a small amount of additional domain-specific information. That information, called a heuristic evaluation function, estimates the likelihood of success or the distance to the goal. These functions will be discussed in more detail below.

Many problem-solving techniques, such as subgoaling, macro-operators, and abstraction, can be viewed as search algorithms. What distinguishes them from more typical heuristic search algorithms is that other sources of knowledge are brought to bear. This also will be discussed in more detail.

2 *Brute-Force Searches*

We begin by looking at the brute-force search algorithms. A brute-force search algorithm uses no knowledge other than a set of states, a set of operators, an initial state, and a test for a goal. The classic algorithms are breadth-first search, and depth-first search. We'll also discuss uniform-cost search and depth-first iterative-deepening. Finally, we'll consider bidirectional search. In the descriptions of the algorithms, the term *generate* means to create the data structure corresponding to a particular node, whereas the term *expand* means to generate all the children of a node.

2.1 *Breadth-First Search*

Figure 2 shows a search tree along with the order in which the nodes would be generated by a breadth-first search. Breadth-first search explores the tree one level at a time, generating all the nodes at a given depth before generating any nodes at a greater depth.

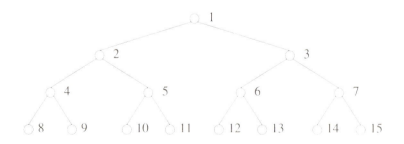

Figure 2 Breadth-First Search

What is the performance of breadth-first search? It should be clear that once the algorithm generates a goal node, the length of the path from the initial state to the goal node will be as short as possible. In this sense, breadth-first search finds an optimal solution.

In order to determine the running time, or time complexity, of the algorithm, let b be the branching factor and d the solution depth. The running time of the algorithm is proportional to the number of nodes generated, since each node can be generated in a fixed constant amount of time. The number of nodes at depth d is b^d. The number of nodes one level up is b^{d-1}, two levels up is b^{d-2}, and so on. The limit of the sum of these terms as d goes to infinity asymptotically approaches b^d, since all the smaller terms grow vanishingly small in relation to the dominant term. We say that the asymptotic time complexity is of order b^d, or $O(b^d)$.

The drawback of breadth-first search is its memory requirement. To run this algorithm requires $O(b^d)$ memory. The reason is that the space is proportional to the number of nodes saved, and in order to generate the next level of the tree, the entire previous level of the tree must be stored in memory. In practice, an implementation of breadth-first search on a typical computer usually exhausts the available memory quite quickly. This is due to the ratio of processor speed to the amount of memory on standard computer configurations. Computer designer Gene Amdahl is credited with coining what has been termed "Amdahl's law": For every million instructions per second (MIP) of processor speed, one needs approximately a million bytes of memory. This rough guideline balances the processing speed and memory capacity of a computer system. It is also a fairly good empirical generalization, in that if one examines a fairly wide range of machines, one finds for every MIP of processor speed about a megabyte of memory. Let's assume that a new state can be generated in a single instruction, and that it takes a byte of memory to store a state. Under these assumptions, memory is exhausted in one second. If we modify those numbers a little, then perhaps we run out of memory in ten seconds or a minute. In practice, however, breadth-first search tends to run out of space before we run out of patience.

2.2 *Uniform-Cost Search*

In the above discussion, we assumed that all edges had the same cost. If that is not the case, then breadth-first search can be generalized to uniform-cost search. Instead of expanding nodes in order of their depth from the root, uniform-cost search generates nodes in order of their total cost from the root. Thus, at each step the next node expanded is the one whose total cost from the root is lowest. If all edge costs are the same, then uniform-cost search degenerates to breadth-first search, and hence its performance is entirely analogous to that of breadth-first search. This algorithm is also known in the computer science community as Dijkstra's single-source shortest-path algorithm on a graph [Dijkstra, 1971]. It also suffers the same memory constraint as breadth-first search.

2.3 *Depth-First Search*

An algorithm that remedies the memory limits of breadth-first and uniform-cost search is depth-first search. Figure 3 shows the order in which nodes would be generated by a depth-first search. While breadth-first search always expands next the first unexpanded node generated, depth-first search always generates next a child of the last node to be generated. Both algorithms can be implemented using a list of unexpanded nodes, with the only difference being that managing the list as a first-in first-out queue produces breadth-first search whereas treating the list as a last-in first-out stack produces depth-first search.

The advantage of depth-first search is that its space requirement is proportional to the depth of the search. The reason is that the algorithm only needs to store a stack of the nodes on the path from the root to the current node. Thus, the memory is only linear in the search depth, as opposed to exponential for breadth-first search. The time complexity of depth-first search is still $O(b^d)$, since it generates the same set of nodes as breadth-first search, but simply in a different order.

The problem with depth-first search is that if the search tree doesn't have a natural termination, such as the Eight Puzzle tree, for example, then the algorithm may never terminate. It will proceed down the first branch forever, unless a solution happens to lie along that branch. In order to guarantee termination on infinite trees, an arbitrary cutoff depth must be imposed, beyond which the search will not extend.

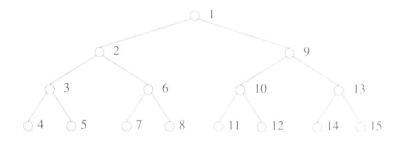

Figure 3 Depth-First Search

The question is how to choose that cutoff depth. Ideally, the cutoff depth c should equal the solution depth d, so that the solution will be found without expending any additional effort. The difficulty is that the solution depth is almost never known in advance of actually solving the problem. In fact, for problems that are too large to be searched exhaustively, the worst case optimal solution lengths are unknown. For example, in the Eight Puzzle, an exhaustive search of the entire state space shows that no two states are more than 31 moves apart. For a slightly larger problem, such as the 4×4 Fifteen Puzzle, the maximum distance between a pair of states is unknown, since an exhaustive search of the entire space is not feasible.

Given that the solution depth is not known a priori, a cutoff depth c must be chosen. If c is less than d, the algorithm terminates without finding a solution. If c is greater than d, then the first solution found may not be an optimal one. This can be remedied by completing the search to the depth of the last solution found, and returning the best solution. In that case, however, a very large price in running time may be paid relative to breadth-first search, since the time complexity grows exponentially with search depth.

2.4 Depth-First Iterative-Deepening

Depth-first iterative-deepening (DFID) [Korf, 1985b] is a brute-force search algorithm that resolves these problems. The intuition behind the algorithm is to dynamically set the cutoff depth c. At first, c is set to a very small value, and then incrementally increased until the solution is found.

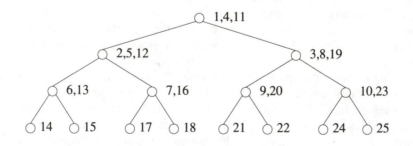

Figure 4 Depth-First Iterative-Deepening

DFID first appears in the literature in a description of the Northwestern Chess 4.5 program of Slate and Atkin [1977]. In a two-player game, a move must be made after a certain amount of time, and moves based on incomplete searches are very unreliable. The problem is how to set the search horizon so that the search will complete just as a move must be made. Since that's very difficult to do, Chess 4.5 first searched to a shallow horizon. If more time remained after that, the entire search was rerun with a horizon of one move deeper. These iterations continued until time ran out, at which point the move recommended by the last completed search was made. The application of DFID to single-agent problems was discovered independently by several researchers [Stickel and Tyson, 1985; Korf, 1985b].

The algorithm consists of a sequence of depth-first searches. The first iteration has a depth cutoff of one. If the solution is found, the algorithm terminates. Otherwise, the depth cutoff is increased by one and a complete depth-first search to the new depth is performed, ignoring the results of the previous search. While this seems a bit wasteful, we'll see below that it has a minimal impact on performance. The iterations continue, increasing the cutoff depth by one each time until the solution is found. Figure 4 shows the order in which nodes would be generated by a depth-first iterative-deepening search. Note that many nodes are generated by more than one iteration.

The first thing to observe about DFID is that the solution lengths it produces are optimal. One way to see this is that the order in which this algorithm generates new nodes is the same order as that of breadth-first search. In other words, with each iteration, another level of the tree is generated for the first time. Thus, once a solution is found, it's a shortest solution. If all edge costs are the same, this translates to an optimal solution. If the edge costs differ then DFID must be modified by replacing depth increments with cost increments. This modification will be discussed further in the context of heuristic search.

Since at any given point DFID is performing a depth-first search, it only maintains a stack of nodes. Furthermore, since the algorithm terminates when it finds a solution at depth d, the stack will never grow deeper than d. Thus, the memory required by DFID is linear in the solution depth d.

The remaining issue is the search time. On the surface it seems to be a very wasteful algorithm, since a large number of nodes are regenerated in each iteration. In fact, all the nodes except those at the final search frontier are generated more than once. This doesn't affect the asymptotic performance, however, because in an exponentially growing tree, most of the nodes are on the bottom level. Thus the extra work in the shallower levels doesn't affect the asymptotic complexity. Even with a branching factor of two, the number of nodes in the bottom level is one greater than all the nodes higher in the tree. With larger branching factors, the ratio is much higher.

One way of seeing that the asymptotic time complexity of DFID is $O(b^d)$ is that the final iteration has an asymptotic complexity of $O(b^d)$ since it's a depth-first search to depth d. The next to last iteration has a time complexity of $O(b^{d-1})$ since it's a depth-first search to depth $d-1$, and similarly for the remaining iterations. Summing each of these terms results in an overall asymptotic time complexity of $O(b^d)$ for DFID.

We can also prove that this algorithm is the best one can do under the assumptions of brute-force search. The precise statement of the theorem is that DFID is asymptotically optimal in time and space over all brute-force shortest path algorithms on a tree. Without going into all the details [Korf, 1985b], here's a sketch of the proof. The fact that it doesn't use any additional knowledge and finds an optimal solution qualifies it as a brute-force shortest path algorithm.

The time it takes is $O(b^d)$. How do we know that there isn't some other algorithm that is guaranteed to find an optimal solution and takes less time? Well, assume that there is such an algorithm. Since it takes less than b^d time, this hypothetical algorithm must examine less than b^d nodes. Then there must be at least one node at depth d in the tree that the algorithm doesn't examine. What we do is construct a problem in which the only solution is that one node that our algorithm misses, and hence it won't find the solution to that problem. Thus, our algorithm fails on at least one problem, disqualifying it from consideration. Therefore, any algorithm must take b^d time.

The memory required by DFID is $O(d)$. Again, how do we know that there isn't some algorithm that solves the same problem but uses less memory? From the above argument, we know that any algorithm for this problem has to take b^d time. A simple result from complexity theory says that any algorithm that takes $f(n)$ time must use at least log $f(n)$ space [Hopcroft and Ullman, 1979]. The reason is that in order to take $f(n)$ time and then terminate without looping, the algorithm must be able to store $f(n)$ distinct machine states, which requires log $f(n)$ bits of storage. Since any algorithm for our problem must take b^d time, then it must use log b^d or d space.

2.5 *Backward Chaining*

Since DFID is the best one can do without additional constraints on the problem, it's time to start adding such constraints. The first step in that direction leads to *backward chaining*. The idea of backward chaining is that instead of searching forward from the initial state to the goal state, one can search backward from the goal state until the initial state is reached. What's required to do backward chaining is an explicit goal state. One can't perform backward chaining on a problem such as the Eight Queens Problem, since we don't have an explicit goal state to work backward from. All we have is a test for the goal. Similarly, one can't do backward chaining on chess since there are a very large number of goal states or checkmate positions.

Given an explicit goal state, as in the Eight Puzzle for example, one can perform backward chaining. For problems such as the Eight Puzzle, in which forward and backward branching factors are the same, the search is equally efficient in either direction, hence it doesn't matter which direction one searches.

Other problems, however, have different forward and backward branching factors. Given a graph where the backward branching factor is less than the forward branching factor, then backward chaining is a good idea. The reason is that the solution depth is the same in either case, but the complexity of the search is a function of the branching factor and the solution depth.

An example where this occurs is the problem of theorem proving. In theorem proving, forward chaining amounts to starting with what's given in a particular problem, along with the axioms of the system, and seeing what can be deduced by the application of a single rule of inference. In general, there's a very large number of things that can be proved in one step from a given statement of a problem, most of them irrelevant to the particular problem at hand.

Backward chaining, on the other hand, corresponds to taking the statement that is to be proved, and determining what will allow us to conclude that statement in a single inference step. In theorem proving, backward chaining is almost always used in preference to forward chaining. The reason is that, in general, there are relatively few things that will imply a given statement in a single inference. Thus the backward branching factor is less than the forward branching factor, and backward chaining is more efficient.

2.6 *Bidirectional Search*

Even if the forward and backward branching factors are the same, one can combine forward chaining and backward chaining to produce *bidirectional search*. The study of bidirectional search was pioneered by Ira Pohl [1971].

The idea is to search forward from the initial state and backward from the goal state until the search frontiers meet in the middle. In principle, the two searches occur simultaneously, but in practice the algorithm timeshares between the two searches.

Bidirectional search still guarantees an optimal solution. By the time that each search reaches a depth of half the optimal solution, the frontiers will contain the end points of all paths of that depth, including two paths that together form an optimal solution. They will have a single node in common and the algorithm will return an optimal solution.

The time complexity of bidirectional search is significantly less than that of unidirectional search, however. Since two searches are performed to half the solution depth, the time is $O(2b^{d/2})$, which is $O(b^{d/2})$. Thus, bidirectional search cuts the exponent of the search time in half, a very significant savings.

The cost of that improvement, however, is memory. To implement a bi-directional search, at least one of the search frontiers must be stored in memory in order to know when a match has been found with the other search frontier. While the naive implementation stores them both, one can store only one and perform a depth-first search in the other direction. The memory required to store one of the frontiers is $O(b^{d/2})$.

Interestingly, multiplying the time and the space requirements of bi-directional search results in $O(b^d)$, which is the time requirement of uni-directional search. Thus, one way to think about bidirectional search is that it provides a multiplicative space-time trade-off. For problems and machines in which sufficient memory is available, bidirectional search reduces the amount of time drastically. The limiting factor, however, is memory, as is the case with breadth-first search. In both cases, the time and space complexities are equal, typically resulting in memory being exhausted before time.

2.7 *Combinatorial Explosion*

The problem with all brute-force search algorithms is that their time complexities grow exponentially with problem size. This is called *combinatorial explosion*, and its effect is that the size of problems that can be solved with these techniques is quite limited. For example, the Rubik's Cube problem space contains approximately 4×10^{19} nodes. If we want to solve this problem with brute-force search, even if we assume that we can manipulate a computer model of the puzzle at a rate of a million twists per second, on the average it would take almost a million years. Even worse, the complete chess tree is estimated to have about 10^{120} nodes in it. Even relatively small problems, such as the Fifteen Puzzle, generate search spaces that are large enough, ten trillion nodes in this case, to render brute-force search techniques completely impractical.

3 *Heuristic Search*

The standard AI technique for coping with combinatorial explosion is to add more knowledge to reduce the complexity. Heuristic search adds a small amount of knowledge to a problem space. Surprisingly, a small amount of knowledge often has a fairly dramatic effect on the efficiency of a search algorithm.

The term *heuristic search* has two somewhat different meanings in the AI literature: a general meaning, and a more specialized technical meaning. In a general sense, the term *heuristic* is often used for any advice or rule of thumb that is often effective, but isn't guaranteed to work in every case. For example, to drive from one point to another, a good heuristic is to select roads that go in the direction of the goal. While this is certainly a good general rule, it often must be violated due to various constraints. Much of artificial intelligence can be characterized as a collection of heuristic techniques of one sort or another.

3.1 *Heuristic Evaluation Functions*

In the heuristic search literature, however, the term *heuristic* has a more specialized technical meaning. In this context, a heuristic is a function that takes a state as an argument and returns a number that is an estimate of the merit of that state with respect to the goal. In the case of a single-agent problem, a heuristic is a function that returns an estimate of the cost of reaching the goal from a given state. In a two-player game, it is loosely interpreted as the relative strength of a position for one player or the other.

For example, in the road navigation problem, a standard heuristic evaluation function is the Euclidean or airline distance from a given state to the goal, which is an estimate of the distance to the goal in the road network. The reason it's only an estimate is that the road network prevents the problem solver from travelling directly as the crow flies. Euclidean distance does provide a reasonable estimate, however, and can be computed very efficiently. Given the x and y coordinates of the given state and the goal state, the Euclidean distance can be computed in constant time.

The important properties of a heuristic evaluation function are that it provide a reasonable estimate of the merit of a node, and that it be inexpensive to compute. One could compute the actual value of a node by solving the entire problem, but that would be prohibitively expensive. A key empirical result of heuristic search is that the trade-off of computational complexity versus accuracy of heuristic functions is very favorable. That is, giving up a small amount of accuracy often dramatically reduces the complexity of computing an estimate.

An example of a heuristic evaluation function for the Eight Puzzle is Manhattan distance. Manhattan distance is computed by determining, for each individual tile in the puzzle, how many grid units that tile is away from its goal position, and summing those values over all tiles.

An important property that both of these evaluation functions share is that they never overestimate actual distance. Airline distance never overestimates the road network distance between two points, since the shortest path between a pair of points is a straight line. Similarly, Manhattan distance never overestimates the actual number of moves necessary to solve an instance of the Eight Puzzle, since every tile must be moved as many times as its distance in grid units from its final position.

Another type of heuristic evaluation function is an estimate of the probability that a node will lead to a solution. In a situation where one has both an estimate of the probability of success and an estimate of the cost required to achieve it, Simon and Kadane [1975] have shown how to combine the two into a single evaluation function. Specifically, nodes should be ordered by the ratio of their probability of success to the cost of realizing it.

An important empirical result is that a wide range of different problem domains naturally give rise to heuristic evaluation functions. In other words, one can often find functions that are inexpensive to compute and give reliable estimates of the relative merits of different states. The main research issue is the design of algorithms that effectively use such functions to reduce the time complexity of search.

3.2 A^* Algorithm

The classical algorithm for single-agent heuristic search is called A^* [Hart et al., 1968]. The algorithm makes use of a heuristic evaluation function, labelled $h(n)$. If n is a node, then $h(n)$ returns the heuristic estimate of the cost of reaching the goal from node n. In addition, $g(n)$ is the actual cost incurred in going from the initial state to node n. The figure of merit that A^* uses for a node, $f(n)$, is the sum of these values, or $f(n) = g(n) + h(n)$. In other words, the merit of a node is the sum of the cost incurred in reaching that node from the initial state plus the estimate of the remaining cost to reach the goal from that node. The reason for this particular combination is that it represents the estimate of the total cost of a solution path from the initial state to a goal state that is constrained to go through node n.

A^* is a *best-first* search algorithm. It maintains an OPEN list of unexpanded nodes, sorted by cost, which contains only the initial state at first. At each cycle of the algorithm, a node on OPEN whose cost, $f(n)$, is lowest is chosen for expansion and removed from OPEN. It is expanded by generating each of its children, evaluating them according to the cost function, and inserting the children into the OPEN list. This continues until a goal state is chosen for expansion.

An important and well-known result is that if the heuristic function never overestimates actual cost, then when A^* terminates it will have found an optimal path to the goal [Hart et al., 1968]. For example, if A^* is used on the road navigation problem with Euclidean distance for the evaluation function, since Euclidean distance never overestimates road distance, then it will find a shortest route from the initial state to the goal. What's surprising about this result is that even though it makes use of inexact information, it still finds optimal solutions.

A more recent result [Dechter and Pearl, 1985] concerns the optimality of A^* in terms of time to find a solution as opposed to the cost of executing the solution. Informally, it says that A^* is the fastest algorithm for finding optimal solutions, for a given non-overestimating heuristic function. What this means is that the A^* cost function, $f(n) = g(n) + h(n)$, is the best way of combining the heuristic information with the other information available.

The drawback of A^* is the same as that of breadth-first search, namely its memory requirement. In every cycle of the algorithm, a new node is expanded, and its b children are added to the OPEN list, where b is the branching factor. Thus every cycle of the algorithm increases the size of the OPEN list by $b-1$ nodes. The space complexity of A^*, or of any other best-first search, is asymptotically the same as its time complexity. As mentioned previously, this causes memory to be exhausted rather quickly on typical computer configurations.

3.3 *Iterative-Deepening-A**

How do we get around this space limitation without sacrificing solution optimality or time complexity? The trick is to employ the same idea we used before for breadth-first search, namely iterative-deepening. The algorithm, called iterative-deepening-A^* (IDA^*) is similar to depth-first iterative-deepening, with the difference being the cutoff criterion [Korf, 1985b].. In the brute-force case, a path is cutoff when its depth exceeds a threshold c. In the heuristic case, a path is cutoff when its total cost, $f(n) = g(n) + h(n)$, exceeds a cost threshold.

IDA^* starts with an initial threshold equal to the heuristic estimate of the distance from the initial state to the goal. Each iteration of the algorithm is a pure depth-first search, cutting off a branch when its $f(n)$ value exceeds the threshold. If a solution is expanded, the algorithm terminates. Otherwise, the threshold is increased to the minimum f value that exceeded the previous threshold, and another complete depth-first search is started from scratch. This continues until a solution is found within the cost threshold.

As in the case of A^*, if the heuristic never overestimates actual cost, then IDA^* will find an optimal solution. The virtue of IDA^* is that its space complexity is linear in the solution depth instead of exponential. The reason is that at any point, the algorithm is executing a depth-first search, which requires only linear space. Furthermore, by the same argument used above for depth-first iterative-deepening, the space complexity of IDA^* is asymptotically optimal. For example, while A^* requires far too much space to solve typical instances of the Fifteen Puzzle on current machines, IDA^* can effectively solve this problem.

Finally, as was the case with depth-first iterative-deepening, IDA^* is asymptotically no slower than A^*. In the last iteration, the one that finds a solution, IDA^* does the same amount of work as A^*. In previous iterations, it does extra work that is wasted. But again, as long as the tree grows exponentially, most of the work goes into the final iteration. One can prove that under these conditions, IDA^* generates asymptotically the same number of nodes as A^*.

A surprising empirical result is that, even though IDA* generates more nodes than A*, it actually runs faster in practice than A*. The reason is that IDA* incurs less overhead per node. In addition, IDA* is easier to implement than A* since it is a depth-first search instead of a best-first search.

Combining the results on the time optimality of A* with the asymptotic time equivalence of IDA* allows us to conclude that, for a given non-overestimating heuristic function, IDA* is asymptotically optimal in time and space over all algorithms that are guaranteed to find shortest paths on an exponential tree.

One caveat that should be mentioned is that these results are for exponentially growing trees. If a problem space is not a tree, nor closely approximated by a tree, but rather contains many short cycles, then IDA* and DFID run into the same problem as any depth-first search algorithm. In particular, a depth-first search must explore all paths to a given node. Given a graph with a large number of cycles, there may be a large number of paths to any given node. Strictly speaking, therefore, our results for IDA* and DFID only apply on an exponential tree. In practice, however, as long as cycles in the problem space are relatively few and relatively long, then these algorithms are still effective.

3.4 *Running Time of Heuristic Search*

The reason that A* and IDA* are useful is that by using the information in the heuristic evaluation function, they are able to find solutions by examining a much smaller number of nodes than a brute-force search would. As a result, heuristic searches run much faster than brute-force algorithms and are able to solve larger problems within practical time constraints. This raises the obvious question of how much faster heuristic search is than brute-force search. The short answer is that the speed of the algorithm is a function of the accuracy of the heuristic function. The more accurate the heuristic function, the faster the algorithm. The problem really is to characterize the relationship between heuristic accuracy and time complexity.

The problem of trying to quantitatively characterize this relationship is one that has received a great deal of attention by Pearl [1984] and others. An easy and instructive way of approaching this is to examine various limiting cases. For example, if the heuristic evaluation function is exact, then A* runs in linear time. It goes straight to the solution, expanding only those nodes on an optimal path. Conversely, given a useless heuristic evaluation function, such as one that estimates zero everywhere, then A* degenerates to uniform-cost search, which has exponential complexity.

In between these two extremes are two other simple cases. If the heuristic function has constant absolute error, meaning that it never underestimates by more than a constant amount regardless of the magnitude of the estimate, then the running time of A* is linear in the solution depth [Gaschnig, 1979]. A more realistic assumption, however, is constant relative error, which means that the error is a fixed percentage of the quantity being estimated. In that case, the running time of A^* is exponential [Pohl, 1970].

In general, the time complexity of A^* is an exponential function of the error. If the error is constant, then a base raised to a constant exponent is still a constant. If the error is linear, as is the case with constant relative error, then a base raised to a linear exponent is an exponential function.

The difference is that, even though the complexity may be exponential, the base of the exponent will be significantly reduced by an accurate heuristic function. This means that one can solve larger problems with heuristic search than with brute-force search. For example, on current computers, brute-force search is sufficiently powerful to solve the Eight Puzzle in a reasonable amount of time, but not its larger relative the Fifteen Puzzle. With a heuristic function such as Manhattan distance, the Fifteen Puzzle can be solved with IDA^* in reasonable time on current machines. On the other hand, even though the heuristic allows somewhat larger problems to be solved, it doesn't allow the optimal solution of significantly larger problems, because of the limitation of exponential complexity. For example, IDA^* with the Manhattan distance heuristic function is not powerful enough to find optimal solutions to the 5×5 Twenty-Four Puzzle.

Summarizing then, the good news is that IDA^* is the best we can do for a given heuristic function. The bad news is that it often isn't good enough. The problem is that optimal heuristic searches don't actually defeat exponential complexity, but merely delay its effects.

4 *Abstraction*

In order to reduce exponential problems to polynomial complexity, we need to add more knowledge. Examples of the kinds of knowledge that can be utilized include subgoals, macro-operators, and abstract problem spaces [Korf, 1987]. We will briefly mention subgoals and macro-operators, and then discuss abstraction in more detail.

One caveat is that in using any of these techniques, we almost always sacrifice solution optimality. All of these methods involve solving a problem in multiple steps, and even if the individual steps are locally optimal, there is no guarantee that their combination will be globally optimal. One way of viewing this is that the loss of solution optimality is an unavoidable cost of reducing complexity.

The idea of subgoaling is that instead of solving a problem directly, we break the problem down into a sequence of subgoals, solve the subgoals one at a time, and then merge the solutions to the subgoals into a solution to the original problem. Subgoaling is used to solve almost every complex problem and dramatically reduces the time required to find a solution.

A macro-operator is a sequence of primitive operators that are stored and applied as if they were a single operator [Korf, 1985a]. A good example of their use is in road navigation. When one first moves into a new area, a search must be performed, either on a map or on the roads directly, to find a good driving route between home and work. After living in an area for a while, however, this search need not be repeated for every trip. Rather, one stores the route and repeats it from memory. The route may involve a fairly complex sequence of turns and utilize many different roads, but it is stored and executed as if it were a single operator. The result is to improve the efficiency of solving this task. As one becomes more familiar with an area, a large number of these different macro-operators are learned and stored, allowing navigation with almost no search.

4.1 *Single Level of Abstraction*

The idea of abstraction is that given a complex problem, one should at first ignore the low-level details of the problem and concentrate on the essential features, and then fill in the details later. Again, road navigation provides an excellent example. Consider the problem of finding a driving route between an address in Los Angeles and an address in New York. Given the size and density of the U.S. road network, brute-force or even heuristic search would require a significant amount of time to solve this problem. But we can do it quite quickly by hand. What we do first is consult a map of the Interstate Highway System. Since this is a much sparser problem space, we very quickly find a route in the Interstate System from the L.A. area to the N.Y. area. This leaves two subproblems to be solved. One is to find a route from the starting address in L.A., and the second is to find a route from the interstate in N.Y. to the destination address. These problems are also relatively easy since the distance that must be covered in each case is quite small. Thus, by ignoring the detail of all the roads in the country and first focusing only on the Interstate System, and then solving the relatively small problems of getting to and from the interstate, the overall complexity of the problem is greatly reduced. In this example, the Interstate Highway System serves as a more abstract problem space than the complete road network.

The idea of abstraction is well known. It is described in George Polya's book *How to Solve it* [Polya, 1945], a veritable fountain of ideas about problem solving. One of the first AI programs to make use of it was Earl Sacerdoti's NOAH system [Sacerdoti, 1974]. He found empirically that in robot problem solving, abstraction produces a large reduction in problem complexity.

How much does abstraction improve search performance in general? We'll answer this question by comparing it to brute-force search. In a brute-force search we don't have any knowledge to distinguish one state from another, other than the goal state, so all we can do is blindly examine one state after another until we stumble upon the goal. In the worst case, we'll have to look at all the states in the space, and in the average case we'll have to examine half of them. Thus the complexity of brute-force search is linear in the number of states in the problem space, which is usually an exponential function of the problem size.

The performance of a search using an abstract problem space depends on the density of the abstract space relative to the original problem space. By performance we mean the time required to find a solution, rather than the cost of executing that solution. What makes this problem interesting is that the two boundary conditions of density are equivalent to brute-force search. At one end of the spectrum is an abstract space that is so sparse that in the limit it doesn't exist at all, and hence the search must occur in the original space. At the other extreme is an abstract space that is so dense that it becomes equal to the original space. In that case as well one is stuck with searching in the original problem space. If abstraction is to help at all, there must be an optimal level of detail in between these two extremes.

One can prove that the optimal level of detail is for the number of states in the abstract space to be the square root of the number of states in the base space [Mackworth, 1977]. The effect of such an optimal abstraction is to reduce the running time to find a solution from linear in the number of states, to on the order of the square root of the number of states in the problem space.

4.2 *Multiple Hierarchical Levels of Abstraction*

Since one application of abstraction reduces the complexity of a search, will multiple applications reduce it even more? The idea is that given an abstract problem space, we could create yet a more abstract problem space on top of it. For example, in the road navigation problem, instead of having just a single level of abstraction that is the interstate highways, there are multiple hierarchical levels of abstraction, such as the interstate highways, the federal highways, state highways, county roads, municipal streets, etc. To solve a problem, we start with the base space and successively work our way up the abstraction hierarchy, and then work our way back down again into the base space.

With multiple hierarchical levels of abstraction, one can ask what is the optimal number of levels, what should the ratios of successive levels be, and what is the performance of the resulting problem solving. The answer is that an optimal abstraction hierarchy has $\log n$ levels where n is the number of states in the original space. Furthermore, in an optimal hierarchy the ratios of the number of states between successive levels is a constant. Finally, the running time of problem solving in such an optimal abstraction hierarchy is reduced from linear in the number of states to logarithmic in the number of states [Korf, 1987].

What's interesting about this result is that if the number of states is an exponential function of problem size, then using multiple hierarchical levels of abstraction actually defeats the combinatorial explosion, reducing the complexity as a function of problem size from exponential to polynomial. On further examination, it's not very surprising. The really complicated problems we solve, such as designing very complex circuits or writing very large computer programs, suffer from this exponential complexity if looked at naively. What we do in practice is use abstraction. For example, in programming, we build up multiple levels of subroutines, procedures, and high level language constructs. This allows us to solve such problems in time that is close to linear in the length of the program. As Simon points out in "The Architecture of Complexity," almost every artifact we encounter, either man-made or in nature, that is of sufficient complexity is hierarchically structured [Simon, 1981].

5 Two-Player Games

The second major application of heuristic search is two-player games. One of the original challenges of AI, which in fact predates AI by a few years, was to build a program that could play chess at the level of the best human players. Certainly a chess grand master exhibits at least some aspects of intelligent behavior, and hence a computer program playing at the same level would as well [Turing, 1950].

From the perspective of AI research, chess has some nice properties. First, it is a well-structured domain. There is a small, discrete board. There are a small number of different pieces. There is a small set of well-specified rules. Secondly, chess is a game of perfect information. Unlike most card games or games of chance, both chess players have all the information there is about a position. In spite of these nice properties, chess is a very difficult game to master. People spend their entire lives studying this game and still don't achieve the levels that they aspire to. This makes it a nearly ideal domain for studying certain aspects of intelligence.

5.1 Minimax Search

The standard algorithm for two-player games is called minimax search with static evaluation [Shannon, 1950]. The algorithm searches forward to some fixed depth in the game tree, limited by the amount of computation available per move. At this *search horizon*, a heuristic static evaluation function is applied to the frontier nodes. In this case, a heuristic evaluation is a function that takes a board position and returns a number that indicates how favorable that position is to one player or the other. For example, a very simple heuristic evaluator for chess would count the total number of pieces on the board for one player, appropriately weighted by their relative strength, and subtract the weighted sum of the opponent's pieces. Thus, large positive values would correspond to strong positions for one player whereas large negative values would represent advantageous situations for the opponent.

Unfortunately, while a heuristic function is well defined in a single-agent problem as an estimate of the cost of reaching a goal, there is no generally agreed upon precise formulation of the meaning of a heuristic function in a two-player game [Abramson and Korf, 1987].

Given the static evaluations of the frontier nodes, values for the interior nodes in the tree are computed according to the minimax rule. The player for whom large positive values are advantageous is called MAX, and conversely the opponent is referred to as MIN. The value of a node where it is MAX's turn to move is the maximum of the values of its children, while the value of a node where MIN is to move is the minimum of the values of its children. Thus, at alternate levels of the tree, the minimum and the maximum values of the children are backed up. This continues until the values of the immediate children of the current position are computed, at which point one move to the child with the maximum or minimum value is made, depending on whose turn it is to move.

The idea of minimax search comes from classical game theory, where it is assumed that the game tree is small enough to be exhaustively searched, and hence the values at the terminal nodes are assumed to be exact payoffs [Von Neuman and Morgenstern, 1944]. Claude Shannon adapted this idea to very large trees by introducing a fixed search horizon and a heuristic static evaluation function [Shannon, 1950]. Later we'll discuss some of the ramifications of this seemingly innocent modification.

5.2 *Alpha-Beta Pruning*

One of the most elegant ideas in all of heuristic search is the alpha-beta pruning algorithm. While it is not entirely clear who invented it, Pearl credits John McCarthy for coming up with the original idea [Pearl, 1984]. It first appeared in print in an MIT tech report by Hart and Edwards [1963]. The notion is that an exact minimax search can be performed without examining all the nodes at the search frontier.

Figure 5 shows an example of alpha-beta pruning. The square nodes represent moves for the maximizer while the circular nodes are moves for the minimizer. The search proceeds depth-first to minimize the memory requirement, and only evaluates a node when necessary. After statically evaluating nodes d and e to 6 and 5, respectively, we back up their maximum value, 6, as the

value of node *c*. After statically evaluating node *g* as 8, we know that the
backed up value of node *f* must be greater than or equal to 8, since it is the
maximum of 8 and the unknown value of node *w*. The value of node *b* must be
6 then, because it is the minimum of 6 and a value that must be greater than or
equal to 8. Since we have exactly determined the value of node *b*, we do not
need to evaluate or even generate node *w*. This is called an alpha cutoff. Similarly, after statically evaluating nodes *j* and *k* to 2 and 1, the backed-up value
of node *i* is their maximum or 2. This tells us that the backed-up value of node
h must be less than or equal to 2, since it is the minimum of 2 and the unknown value of node *x*. Since the value of node *a* is the maximum of 6 and a
value that must be less than or equal to 2, it must be 6, and hence we have
evaluated the root of the tree without generating or evaluating nodes *x*, *y*, or *z*.
This is called a beta cutoff.

Since alpha-beta pruning allows us to perform a minimax search while
evaluating fewer nodes, its effect is to allow us to search deeper with the same
amount of computation. This raises the question of how much deeper, or how
much does alpha-beta improve performance? This problem has been carefully
studied by a number of researchers and finally solved by Pearl [Knuth and
Moore, 1975; Pearl, 1982]. The best way to characterize the efficiency of a
pruning algorithm is in terms of its *effective branching factor*. The effective
branching factor is the dth root of the number of frontier nodes that must be
evaluated in a search to depth *d*.

The efficiency of alpha-beta pruning depends on the order of the node
values at the search frontier. For any set of frontier node values, there exists
some ordering of the values such that alpha-beta will not perform any cutoffs
at all. In that case, all frontier nodes must be evaluated and the effective
branching factor is *b*, the brute-force branching factor.

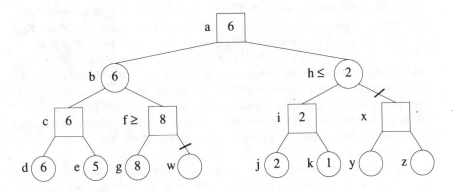

Figure 5 Alpha-Beta Pruning

On the other hand, there is an optimal or perfect ordering in which every possible cutoff is realized. In that case, the effective branching factor is reduced from b to $b^{1/2}$, which is the square root of the brute-force branching factor. Another way of viewing the perfect ordering case is that for the same amount of computation, one can search twice as deep with alpha-beta pruning as without. Since the search tree grows exponentially with depth, doubling the search horizon is quite a dramatic improvement.

In between worst-possible ordering and perfect ordering is random ordering, which is the average case. Under random ordering of the frontier nodes, alpha-beta pruning reduces the effective branching factor to approximately $b^{3/4}$. This means that one can search 4/3 as deep with alpha-beta, yielding a 33% improvement in search depth.

5.3 *Node Ordering, Quiescence, and Iterative-Deepening*

In practice, however, the effective branching factor of alpha-beta is closer to $b^{1/2}$ due to *node ordering*. The idea of node ordering is that instead of generating the nodes of the tree strictly left-to-right, the order in which paths are explored can be based on static evaluations of the interior nodes in the tree. In other words, the children of MAX nodes can be expanded in decreasing order of their static values while the children of MIN nodes would be expanded in increasing order of their static values.

Two other important ideas are quiescence and iterative-deepening. The idea of quiescence is that the static evaluator should not be applied to positions whose values are unstable, such as those occurring in the middle of a piece trade. In those positions, a small secondary search is conducted until the static evaluation becomes more stable.

Iterative-deepening is used to solve the problem of how to set the search horizon, as previously mentioned [Slate and Atkin, 1977]. In a tournament game, there is a limit on the amount of time allowed per move. Unfortunately, it is very difficult to accurately predict how long it will take to perform a complete search to a given depth. If one picks too shallow a depth, then time which could be used to improve the move choice is wasted. Alternatively, if the search depth is too deep, time will run out in the middle of a search, and a move based on an incomplete search is likely to be very unreliable. The solution is to perform a series of complete searches to successively increasing depths. When time runs out, the move recommended by the last completed search is made.

Iterative-deepening and node ordering can be combined as follows. Instead of ordering interior nodes based on their static values, the frontier values from the previous iteration of the search can be used to order the nodes in the next iteration. This produces much better ordering than the static values alone.

Virtually all performance chess programs in existence today use full-width, fixed-depth alpha-beta minimax search with node ordering, quiescence, and iterative-deepening.

5.4 *Special Purpose Hardware*

Another interesting development in the area of two-player games is the advent of special purpose hardware. This trend was started by Condon and Thompson at Bell Laboratories when they built the Belle machine [Condon and Thompson, 1982]. Up until that time, most entries in computer chess tournaments were general-purpose digital computers that were programmed to play chess. Condon and Thompson built a special-purpose machine that could only play chess. The advantage of this scheme is to be able to highly optimize the machine for chess with the result that it could search deeper than even very powerful general-purpose machines. In general, the deeper the search, the better the quality of play. What limits the search depth is the efficiency of the primitive operations of move generation and evaluation. By embedding these functions directly in hardware, they run much faster.

A more recent entrant in this category is Hitech, built by Hans Berliner and Carl Ebeling at Carnegie-Mellon University [Ebeling, 1987]. What's notable about Hitech is its use of a special purpose parallel architecture for playing chess, consisting of 64 processors arranged in an 8×8 array to match the chess board. Hitech can generate and evaluate over 200,000 nodes per second.

6 *Real-Time Single-Agent Search*

If one examines the history of research in single-agent problems and two-player games, one finds two parallel but distinctly different paths. In two-player games, the standard assumption is that it is completely impractical to search all the way to the end of the game. The effect of this is that research has focused on how to make the best decisions with a fixed amount of computation, with no serious thought devoted to making optimal decisions. In addition, tournament games require that individual moves be made within tight time constraints.

Conversely, in single-agent problems, researchers have long focused on finding optimal solutions. The challenge has been to increase the size of problems that can be solved optimally within practical computational limits. For example, the advent of iterative-deepening-A* increased the size of sliding tile puzzles for which optimal solutions could be found from 3×3 to 4×4.

6.1 *Limitations of A* and IDA**

One result of this preoccupation with optimal solutions is that search algorithms for single-agent problems, such as A^* and IDA^*, suffer from two fundamental limitations. One is that, even with the best heuristics available in practice, these algorithms take exponential time to run. The second problem is that to use these algorithms to solve a problem, the algorithm must be run to completion in a simulation mode before the first move can actually be made. The reason is that to guarantee an optimal solution, one can't be sure of even the first move until the entire solution is found and shown to be at least as good as any other possible solution.

Given this characterization, an obvious research direction is to look at single-agent problems under the ground rules of two-player games, namely limited search horizon and execution of moves based on incomplete information. The first assumption can be satisfied by picking a problem large enough that practical computational constraints prohibit the search from extending from an initial state to the goal node, such as, for example, the 5×5 Twenty-Four Puzzle. Alternatively, or in addition, there may be informational limits on the problem solver. For example, in the problem of autonomous navigation of a mobile robot, there is a limit on the range of data that can be gathered by the vision or other sensors of the robot. This suggests a literal interpretation of the term *search horizon*. In addition to limited information or computation, we assume that actions in the real world must actually be executed based on incomplete information. For example, the mobile robot must actually move in order to extend its search horizon in the chosen direction.

6.2 *Minimin Lookahead Search*

The research problem is to develop decision-making algorithms for a single problem-solving agent under such real-time constraints. The obvious approach is to try to adapt the algorithms for two-player games that were designed to solve a similar problem. This gives rise to a special case of minimax search called *minimin search* [Korf, to appear]. The idea is to search forward from the current state to a fixed depth determined by the informational or computational resources available. At the search horizon, the A^* heuristic evaluation function $f(n) = g(n) + h(n)$ is applied to the frontier nodes. Since only a single agent is making all the moves, the value of each interior node in the tree is recursively computed as the minimum of the values of its children. Finally, a single move is made in the direction of the immediate child of the current state with the minimum value. The reason for only making a single move instead of going directly to the frontier node with the minimum value is that since the values are based on fallible heuristic information, we should follow a strategy of least commitment. Further search from the new current state may indicate different choices for subsequent moves than originally anticipated.

6.3 *Alpha Pruning*

There exists an algorithm, called *alpha pruning* by analogy to alpha-beta pruning, that allows us to perform minimin search without evaluating all the nodes within the search horizon [Korf, to appear]. It is based on the heuristic function being a *metric*. A metric is a function that satisfies a set of properties that we normally associate with distance functions. In particular, a function h of two arguments is a metric if and only if (1) $h(x, x) = 0$, (2) $h(x, y) = h(y, x)$, and (3) $h(x, y) + h(y, z) \leq h(x, z)$. By adding the goal state as a second argument to h, we get a function of two arguments. Most naturally occurring heuristic functions, such as Euclidean distance and Manhattan distance, are metrics since they satisfy our intuitive and formal definitions of distance functions. If h is a metric, then the cost function $f = g + h$ is guaranteed to be monotonically non-decreasing along any path away from the initial state. Given a monotonic cost function, we can apply a technique known as branch-and-bound to significantly prune the search space.

The algorithm is as follows: Let α be the minimum cost of all frontier nodes encountered so far. Initially, α will be set to the cost of the first frontier node. In the course of the search, evaluate all interior nodes and whenever the cost of a node equals or exceeds α, abandon that path, pruning all nodes below it. The justification for this is that since the cost function can't decrease, all the frontier nodes below that node must have cost greater than or equal to the given node, and hence will not be less than the frontier node responsible for the current value of α. Finally, whenever a frontier node is encountered with a cost less than α, the value of α is reset to this new minimum.

The performance improvement of alpha pruning is quite dramatic, even when compared to alpha-beta pruning. In some cases, alpha pruning extends the achievable search horizon by a factor of five relative to brute-force search, with the same amount of computation [Korf, to appear].

Minimin lookahead search with alpha pruning is an algorithm for evaluating the immediate children of the current node. As such, the algorithm is run in a simulation or planning mode until the best child is identified, at which point the chosen move is executed in the real world. For simplicity of exposition, we can view the heuristic function combined with lookahead search and alpha pruning as simply a more accurate, but computationally more expensive heuristic function. In fact, it provides an entire spectrum of heuristic functions differing in accuracy and cost, depending on the search horizon.

6.4 *Real-Time-A**

Since minimin with alpha pruning only recommends a single move, the next question is how to determine the sequence of moves to be executed. The obvious approach of simply repeating the algorithm for each move won't work since it falls into infinite loops and doesn't benefit from the information gathered in previous lookahead searches. In addition, since the heuristic information is fallible, on occasion we may want to backtrack and undo the previous move. The question of how to allow intelligent backtracking while preventing infinite loops is the problem addressed next.

The principle of rationality is that backtracking should occur when the estimated cost of continuing the current path exceeds the cost of going back to a previous state plus the estimated cost of reaching the goal from there. One way to implement this policy would be to modify A^* so that the g value of every node is relative to the current position of the problem solver rather than the initial state. Unfortunately, this requires updating the g values of every node on the OPEN list with every move, and maintaining a path to every OPEN node from the current state. The following algorithm, called *real-time-A^** (RTA^*), produces the same behavior using only local information and control, and hence requires only constant time per move [Korf, to appear].

For each move, the $f = g + h$ value of each neighbor of the current state is determined, and the problem solver moves to the state with the minimum value. The second best f value, which is the best value among the remaining alternatives, is stored with the previous state. This represents the h value of the previous state from the perspective of the new current state. This is repeated until a goal is reached. To determine the h value of a neighboring state, if it has previously been visited, then the stored value is used, and otherwise the heuristic evaluator is called. Note that the heuristic evaluator may employ minimin lookahead search with alpha pruning in addition to the heuristic function itself.

One can prove that in a finite problem space in which there exists a path to a goal from every state, RTA^* is guaranteed eventually to find a solution, regardless of the initial heuristic values [Korf, to appear]. Of course, the speed with which a solution is found depends on the accuracy of the heuristic values. The algorithm, however, can be used effectively even in the absence of a heuristic function, for example, by setting h to zero for every node initially. Over the course of the problem-solving trial the algorithm learns more accurate h values.

7 *Constraint-Satisfaction Problems*

In addition to single-agent path-finding problems and two-player games, the third major application of heuristic search is constraint-satisfaction problems. The Eight Queens Problem mentioned previously is a classic example. More realistic examples include job shop scheduling, graph coloring, and applications in truth maintenance systems.

Constraint satisfaction problems are modelled as follows: There is a set of variables, a set of values, and a set of constraints on the values that the variables can be assigned. A unary constraint on a variable specifies a subset of all possible values that can be assigned to that variable. A binary constraint between two variables specifies which possible combinations of assignments to the pair of variables would satisfy the constraint. For example, in a map or graph-coloring problem, the variables would represent regions or nodes, and the values would represent colors. The constraints are binary constraints on each pair of adjacent regions or nodes that prohibit them from being assigned the same color.

7.1 *Brute-Force Backtracking*

The brute-force approach to constraint satisfaction is called *backtracking*. One selects an order for the variables, and an order for the values, and starts assigning values to the variables one at a time. Each assignment is made so that all constraints involving any of the variables that have already been assigned values are satisfied. The reason for this is that once a constraint is violated, no assignment to the remaining variables can possibly resatisfy that constraint. Once a variable is reached which has no remaining legal assignments, then the last variable that was assigned is reassigned to the next legal value. The algorithm continues until either a complete, consistent assignment is found resulting in success, or all possible assignments are shown to violate some constraint, resulting in failure.

The key property that makes this algorithm effective is that the constraints can be applied to partial assignments of variables, and that if a constraint is violated in a partial assignment, no complete extension of that partial assignment can satisfy the constraint. This makes backtracking much more efficient than trying all possible complete assignments. Backtracking is a brute-force depth-first search combined with a goal test that is applied to partial candidate solutions.

7.2 *Intelligent Backtracking*

Most of the interesting research in this area goes by the name of intelligent or heuristic backtracking. A short survey of the different techniques employed includes variable ordering, value ordering, going back to the source of failure, and constraint recording, including arc and path consistency.

The order in which variables are instantiated can have a large effect on the efficiency of backtracking. The idea of variable ordering is to choose an order that is likely to cause the least backtracking [Freuder, 1982; Purdom, 1983]. For example, one simple heuristic is to first instantiate the most tightly constrained variables, or to order the variables in increasing order of the number of possible values that can be assigned to them.

Similarly, the order in which the values of a given variable are chosen can significantly affect the efficiency of backtracking. The technique of value ordering is to choose the sequence of values for each variable that is likely to minimize backtracking [Dechter and Pearl, 1987a; Haralick and Elliott, 1980]. In general, one would like to order the values from most likely to succeed to least likely to succeed, in order to minimize the time required to find a complete solution.

An important idea that goes by a number of names, including dependency-directed backtracking, is that instead of simply undoing the last decision made, the decision that actually caused the failure should be modified [Gaschnig, 1979]. For example, consider a three-variable problem where the variables are instantiated in the order x, y, z. Assume that values have been chosen for both x and y, but that all possible values for z conflict with the value chosen for x. In pure backtracking, the value chosen for y would be changed, and then all the possible values for z would be tested again, to no avail. A better strategy in this case is to go back to the source of the failure and change the value of x, before trying different values for y.

In a constraint-satisfaction problem, some constraints are explicitly specified, and others are implied by the explicit constraints. Some implicit constraints may be discovered in the course of the backtracking search. The idea of constraint recording is that once these implicit constraints are discovered they should be saved explicitly so that they don't have to be repeatedly rediscovered. Constraint recording can occur during the backtrack search, or alternatively the problem can be preprocessed to record as many constraints as possible before beginning the search.

A simple example of constraint recording in a preprocessing phase is called *arc consistency* [Freuder, 1982; Mackworth, 1977; Montanari, 1974]. For each pair of variables x and y that are related by a binary constraint, we remove from the domain of x any values that do not have at least one corresponding legal counterpart in y and vice versa. In general, several iterations may be required to achieve complete arc consistency. *Path consistency* is a generalization of arc consistency where instead of considering pairs of variables, we examine triples of related variables, for example. The effect of performing arc or path consistency before backtracking is that the resulting search space can be dramatically reduced. In some cases, this preprocessing of the constraints can eliminate the need for search entirely.

7.3 *Network-Based Heuristics*

Another powerful set of techniques for constraint-satisfaction problems is grouped under the term *network-based heuristics* [Dechter and Pearl, 1987a].

Given a binary constraint-satisfaction problem, a corresponding *constraint graph* can be constructed as follows: Each variable is represented by a node and each constraint between a pair of variables is represented by an edge between the corresponding nodes. Higher-order constraints give rise to hypergraphs.

Network-based heuristics depend upon the structure of the resulting constraint graph. For example, if the graph is a tree, the problem can be solved in polynomial time Freuder, 1982]. One simply starts with the leaf variables, removes those values that do not have a consistent value in the parent variable, and repeats this process for each level of the tree. After a single complete pass over the tree, any choice of values from the remaining domains is guaranteed to be a solution. Only if some variable has no remaining values is the problem unsolvable.

If the constraint graph is not a tree, but contains only a small number of cycles, then the *cycle-cutset* method may be effective [Dechter and Pearl, 1987b]. The idea is to identify a small set of nodes that taken together would break every cycle in the graph if they were removed. Then the values of these variables are instantiated using a backtracking algorithm. For each instantiation of the cutset variables, the above technique for solving the resulting tree-structured graph is applied. The cycle-cutset method is exponential in the size of the cycle-cutset, as opposed to the complete graph, and hence is likely to be effective in a sparse graph.

8 *Major Open Problems*

Major open problems and new research directions in heuristic search include three general categories: parallel search algorithms, automatic learning of heuristic evaluation functions, and alternatives to full-width minimax search.

8.1 *Parallel Search Algorithms*

Since search is fundamentally constrained by its efficiency, an obvious question is how to effectively use parallel processing. There are basically three approaches to parallelizing a search algorithm. The first is to parallelize the primitive operations of node generation and evaluation. This is the approach taken by the Hitech machine [Ebeling, 1987]. Unfortunately, this approach is inherently domain specific. Some problems may be easy to parallelize this way and others may not, but the techniques applied will be specific to the particular application. Furthermore, the available parallelism is strictly limited by the domain. For example, it's difficult to see how Hitech processors could take advantage of *more than* 64 processors to speed up the machine any further.

A second approach is called parallel window search and was pioneered by Gerard Baudet [1978]. He parallelized alpha-beta minimax search by giving each processor the entire tree to search but different bounds for alpha and beta. The entire possible range for the minimax value was broken up into different windows bounded by different values of alpha and beta and distributed to different processors. All but one of the processors would return with the result that the minimax value was not within its window, and one would return the actual minimax value within its range. The virtue of the algorithm is that the successful processor would find the value more quickly by starting with a narrow range of alpha and beta and hence pruning many more branches than if it started with alpha and beta equal to negative and positive infinity. Unfortunately, this algorithm is limited in practice to a speedup of no more than five or six, regardless of the number of processors used. The reason is that even if a processor is given values of alpha and beta that equal the true minimax value, it still takes considerable time to verify that that is indeed the case.

The third approach is perhaps the most obvious, and that is to decompose the search tree so that different parts of the tree are searched by different processors. This provides potentially unlimited parallelism. The major challenge is load balancing. Since real search trees and particularly those pruned by heuristic techniques tend to be very irregular, there must be some mechanism to dynamically reallocate work to idle processors [Finkel and Manber, 1987; Rao et al., 1987; Ferguson and Korf, 1988].

A more challenging problem is to parallelize branch-and-bound searches such as alpha-beta or alpha pruning. The essential difficulty is that the work done by one processor may be wasted if its nodes are subsequently pruned by bounds obtained elsewhere in the tree. Effectively parallelizing alpha-beta pruning is a longstanding open problem [Finkel and Fishburn, 1982; Vornberger, 1987; Ferguson and Korf, 1988].

8.2 *Learning Heuristic Evaluation Functions*

Another very important open problem that has been around for quite a while is how to automatically learn heuristic evaluation functions.

Research on this problem started in the late 1950s with Arthur Samuel's checkers program [Samuel, 1963]. What was unique about that program was that it automatically learned to improve its performance by changing its evaluation function. This is the classic example of what is now called *parameter learning*. For purposes of exposition, let's consider chess, and assume that a program is told that a set of relevant features upon which to base a static evaluation is the numbers of different types of pieces. The learning task then is to figure out what the relative weights of those pieces ought to be, or the coefficients of a polynomial material evaluation function. The basic idea that Samuel originated and that has recently been improved by others [Christensen and

Korf, 1986] is that if the evaluation function were correct, then the static evaluation of a board should be equal to the backed-up minimax value from a lookahead search. This reduces the problem to finding a set of coefficients that is nearly invariant under lookahead search.

A more challenging problem is how to discover the features in the first place. Judea Pearl [1984] has suggested a rather compelling approach to this problem, based on some ideas of John Gaschnig [1979]. The claim is that heuristics are derived from simplified or relaxed problems. More specifically, the exact solution cost for a relaxed version of a problem is often a good heuristic evaluation function for the original problem. For example, consider the task of finding a good heuristic function for the road navigation problem. What makes this problem difficult is the constraint that one must travel along the given roads. If we remove this constraint and allow direct cross-country travel as in a helicopter, the resulting problem is very simple and can be solved by travelling in a straight line from the initial state to the goal state. The exact solution cost for any instance of this simplified problem is just the Euclidean distance. This suggests how Euclidean distance might be arrived at as a heuristic function for the original road navigation problem. As another example, if we remove the constraint on the Eight Puzzle that a tile can only be moved into the blank position, and allow tiles to be slid over one another, then the exact solution cost to this simplified problem is simply Manhattan distance.

While this theory provides a convincing explanation of the origin and nature of heuristic functions for single-agent problems, the challenge is to automate the process of going from an original problem to an effective heuristic function for that problem. This requires overcoming a number of difficulties and is still an open problem.

8.3 *Alternatives to Full-Width Minimax Search*

The final item on the list of open problems is alternatives to full-width minimax search. In Shannon's original paper [Shannon, 1950], he described two types of strategies that he labelled Type A and Type B. Type A is fixed-depth full-width search, with no pruning, since he didn't anticipate alpha-beta. When combined with alpha-beta pruning, this is the algorithm used by all current performance programs. Type B strategies included the use of additional heuristics to prune parts of the tree and search some lines of play more deeply than others. This is also called *selective search*.

The best current chess machines play better than 99% of all *rated* human players [Berliner and Ebeling, 1988]. In other games, such as Othello, computers play as well as the best humans [Rosenbloom, 1982]. However, when one realizes that these machines are looking at millions of positions per move, while human players only examine tens of positions, it becomes clear that humans must be doing something the machines are not. If one constrained

machines to only examine tens of positions, they would perform quite misera-
bly. The difference is that humans use a very selective search to rapidly prune
poor lines of play while exploring promising lines relatively deeply. Both
David McAllester [to appear] and Ron Rivest [1986] have recently proposed
interesting selective search algorithms. Unfortunately, the integration of selective search algorithms into successful performance programs has resisted most
efforts to date. This is likely to become an important research area in the near
future.

The other aspect of this problem is the minimax rule itself. Minimax has
long been the accepted way of backing up heuristic evaluations. It was originally invented by Von Neuman and Morgenstern in the 1940s in the context of
game theory [Von Neuman and Morgenstern, 1944]. In classical game theory,
it is assumed that the search can proceed all the way to the end of the game in
which case the values at the search horizon are exact payoffs. In that case,
minimax is provably the correct way to back up values. Shannon's contribution
was to recognize that this could not be done in a game like chess and to introduce the notion of a heuristic static evaluation function at the search frontier.
Then, for lack of anything better, he suggested using minimax to back-up the
heuristic values. Unfortunately, minimax is not justifiable as a backup rule
when the values are inexact.

As an example of this, consider a maximizer node with two children. Assume that the values of the two children are independent random variables that
are uniformly distributed between zero and one. The best heuristic estimate of
the values of the nodes would be their expected value which is one-half. Minimax would back-up the maximum of the two expected values and return one-
half as the backed-up estimate of the value of the maximizer node. However,
the expected value of the maximum of two independent random variables uniformly distributed between zero and one is not one-half but two-thirds. The
error is that we want the estimate of the maximum but we computed the maximum of the estimates instead.

As we continue to minimax values further up the tree, the error only increases, until the signal all but disappears in the noise due to minimaxing. The
result is that for certain analytic games with uniform branching factor, uniform
depth, and independent leaf values, occasionally searching deeper in the tree
leads to poorer play relative to shallower search. This phenomenon is called
pathology and was independently discover by Nau [1982] and Beal [1980]. The
dilemma is that for real games such as chess and checkers, it is almost always
the case that searching deeper improves play. This raises the question of which
assumptions in the analytic model are not valid for real games. The answer is
all of them, since removing any one of the above assumptions (uniform depth,
uniform branching factor, or independence of sibling nodes) causes pathology
to disappear [Nau, 1982; Pearl, 1983].

Nevertheless, the search for a better back-up rule than minimax continues. For example, when independence of sibling nodes is a reasonable assumption, and the heuristic function is interpreted as a probability of winning, then backing up heuristic values by multiplying them is often more effective than minimax [Nau et al., 1986]. Non-minimax rules have yet to find their way into performance chess programs, however.

9 *Conclusion*

In conclusion, search is a very general problem-solving technique. For any problem that can be represented as a problem space, search techniques can be used to solve it. The price of this generality is exponential complexity, with the result that many problems of practical interest are solvable in principle with search, but the limitations of computational capacity prevent them from being solved in practice. In order to reduce the complexity, more domain-specific knowledge must be added. The research challenge is to develop and analyze algorithms to acquire and use such knowledge. While this is true of heuristic search, it is also true of most work in artificial intelligence in general. What distinguishes work in search is an emphasis on domain-independent algorithms, even though the knowledge may be domain-specific, and a focus on analytical and quantitative performance results.

References

Abramson, B. and Korf, R. E., 1987. A model of two-player evaluation functions. In *Proceedings of the National Conference on Artificial Intelligence (AAAI-87)*, pp. 90–94, Seattle, Washington. San Mateo: Morgan Kaufmann.

Baudet, G., 1978. *The Design and Analysis of Algorithms for Asynchronous Multiprocessors*. Ph.D. dissertation. Dept. of Computer Science, Carnegie Mellon University, Pittsburgh, Pennsylvania.

Beal, D., 1980. An analysis of minimax. In *Advances in Computer Chess 2*, M. R. B. Clarke, ed., pp. 103–109. Edinburgh: Edinburgh University Press.

Berliner, H. and Ebeling, C., 1988. Pattern knowledge and search: The suprem architecture. Technical Report CMU-CS-109. Dept. of Computer Science, Carnegie Mellon University, Pittsburgh, Pennsylvania.

Christensen, J. and Korf, R. E., 1986. A unified theory of heuristic evaluation functions and its application to learning. In *Proceedings of the Fifth National Conference on Artificial Intelligence (AAAI-86)*, Philadelphia, Pennsylvania. San Mateo: Morgan Kaufmann.

Condon, J. H. and Thompson, K., 1982. Belle chess hardware. *Advances in Computer Chess 3*. Pergamon Press.

Dechter, R. and Pearl, J., 1985. Generalized best-first search strategies and the optimality of A*. *Journal of the Association for Computing Machinery* **32**(3):505–536.

Dechter, R. and Pearl, J., 1987a. Network-based heurestics for constraint-satis-faction problems. *Artificial Intelligence* **34**(1):1–38.

Dechter, R. and Pearl, J., 1987b. The cycle-cutset method for improving search performance in AI applications. In *Proc. 3rd IEEE Conf. on AI Applic.*, pp. 224–230, Orlando, Florida.

Dijkstra, E. W., 1971. A note on two problems in connection with graphs. *Numerische Mathematik* **1**:269–271.

Ebeling, Carl, 1987. *All The Right Moves*. Cambridge, Mass.: MIT Press.

Ferguson, C. and Korf, R. E., 1988. Distributed tree search and its application to alpha-beta pruning. In *Proceedings of the National Conference on Artificial Intelligence (AAAI-88)*, St. Paul, Minnesota. San Mateo: Morgan Kaufmann.

Finkel, R. and Fishburn, J., 1982. Parallelism in alpha-beta search. *Artificial Intelligence* **19**(1).

Finkel, R. and Manber, U., 1987. A distributed implementation of backtrack-ing. *ACM Transactions on Programming Languages and Systems* **9**(2).

Freuder, E.C., 1982. A sufficient condition for backtrack-free research. *Assoc. Comput. Mach* **29**(1):24–32.

Gaschnig, J., 1979. *Performance Measurement and Analysis of Certain Search Algorithms*. Ph.D. dissertation. Dept. of Computer Science, Carnegie Mellon University, Pittsburgh, Pennsylvania.

Gerlernter, H., 1963. Realization of a geometry-theorem proving machine. *Computers and Thought*, E. Feigenbaum and J. Feldman, ed. New York: McGraw-Hill.

Haralick, R. M. and Elliot, G. L., 1980. Increasing tree search efficiency for constraint satisfaction problems. *Artificial Intelligence* **14**:263–313

Hart, T. P. and Edwards, D. J., 1963. The alpha-beta heuristic. M.I.T. Artificial Intelligence Project Memo. Massachusetts Institute of Technology, Cam-bridge, Massachusetts.

Hart, T. P., Nilsson, N. J., and Raphael B., 1968. A formal basis for the heuris-tic determination of minimum cost paths. *IEEE Transactions on Systems Science and Cybernetics* SSC-4,**2**:100–107.

Hopcroft, J. E. and Ullman, J. D., 1979. *Introduction to Automata Theory, Languages, and Computation*. Reading: Addison-Wesley.

Knuth, D. E. and Moore, R. E., 1975. An analysis of alpha-beta pruning. *Artificial Intelligence* **6**(4):293–326

Korf, R. E., 1985a. A weak method for learning. *Artificial Intelligence* **26**(1):35–77.

Korf, R. E., 1985b. Depth-first iterative deepening: An optimal admissible tree search. *Artificial Intelligence.* **27**(1):97–109.

Korf, R. E., 1987. Planning as search: A quantitative approach. *Artificial Intelligence.*

Korf, R. E., In press. Real-time heuristic search. *Artificial Intelligence.*

Laird, J. E., Newell, A., and Rosenbloom, P. S., 1987. SOAR: An architecture for general intelligence. *Artificial Intelligence* **33**(1):1–64.

Mackworth, A. K., 1977. Consistency in networks of relations. *Artificial Intelligence* **8**(1):99–118.

McAllester, D. A., In press. A new procedure for growing min-max trees. *Artificial Intelligence.*

Montanari, U., 1974. Networks of constraints: Fundamental properties and applications to picture processing. *Inform. Sci.* **7**:95–132.

Nau, D.S., 1982. An investigation of the causes of pathology in games. *Artificial Intelligence* **19**:257–278.

Nau, D., Purdom, P., and Tzeng, C., 1986. An evaluation of two alternatives to minimax. *Uncertainty in Artificial Intelligence*, L. N. Kanal and J. F. Lemmer, ed. Amsterdam: Elsevier Science Publishers.

Newell, A., 1969. Heuristic programming: Ill-structured problems. In *Progress in Operations Research III*, J. Aronofsky, ed. pp. 360–414. New York: Wiley.

Newell, A., 1980. Reasoning, problem solving and decision processes: The problem space as a fundamental category. *Attention and Performance VIII*, R. Nickerson, ed. Hillsdale: Erlbaum.

Newell, A. and Simon, H. A., 1963. GPS, a program that simulates human thought. *Computers and Thought*, E. Feigenbaum and J. Feldman, ed. New York: McGraw-Hill.

Newell, A. and Simon, H. A., 1972. *Human Problem Solving.* Englewood Cliffs, New Jersey: Prentice-Hall,

Newell, A., Simon, H. A., and Shaw, J. C., 1963. Empirical explorations with the logic theory machine: A case study in heuristics. *Computers and Thought*, E. Feigenbaum and J. Feldman, ed. New York: McGraw-Hill.

Pearl, J., 1982. The solution for the branching factor of the alpha-beta pruning algorithm and its optimality. *Commun. of the Assoc. of Comput. Mach.* **25**(8):559–564.

Pearl, J., 1983. On the nature of pathology in game searching. *Artificial Intelligence* **20**(4):427–453.

Pearl, J., 1984. *Heuristics.* Reading: Addison-Wesley.

Pearl, J. and Korf, R. E., 1987. Search techniques. *Annual Review of Computer Science.* **2**.. Palo Alto, California: Annual Reviews Inc.

Pohl, I., 1970. First results on the effect of error in heuristics search. In *Machine Intelligence 5*, B. Meltzer and D. Michie, ed. pp. 219–236. New York: American Elsevier.

Pohl, I., 1971. Bi-directional search. In *Machine Intelligence 6*, B. Meltzer and D. Michie, ed. pp. 127–140. New York: American Elsevier.

Polya, G., 1945. *How to Solve It*. Princeton: Princeton University Press.

Purdom, P.W., 1983. Search rearrangement backtracking and polynomial average time. *Artificial Intelligence* **21**(1,2):117-133.

Rao, V. Nageshwara, Kumar, V., and Ramesh, K., 1987. A parallel implementation of iterative-deepening. In *Proceedings of the National Conference on Artificial Intelligence (AAAI-87)*, pp. 133–138. Seattle, Washington. San Mateo: Morgan Kaufmann.

Ratner, D. and Warmuth, M., 1986. Finding a shortest solution for the NxN extension of the 15-puzzle is intractable. In *Proceedings of the Fifth National Conference on Artificial Intelligence (AAAI-86)*, Philadelphia, Pennsylvania. San Mateo: Morgan Kaufmann.

River, R.L., submitted 1986. Game tree searching by min/max approximation. *Artificial Intelligence*.

Rosenbloom, P.S., 1982. A World-Championship-Level Othello Program. *Artificial Intelligence* **19**:279-320.

Sarcerdoti, E.D., 1974. Planning in a hierarchy of abstraction spaces. *Artificial Intelligence* **5**:115-135.

Samuel, A.L., 1963. Some studies in machine learning using the game of checkers. *Computers and Thought*. E. Feigenbaum and J. Feldman, ed. New York: McGraw-Hill.

Shannon, C.E., 1950. Programming a computer for playing chess. *Philosophical Magazine* **41**:256-275.

Simon, H. A., 1981. The architecture of complexity. *The Sciences of the Artificial*, 2nd edition. Cambridge, Mass.: M.I.T. Press.

Simon, H. A. and Kadane, J. B., 1975. Optimal problem-solving search: All-or-none solutions. *Artificial Intelligence* **6**(3):235–247.

Slagle, J. R., 1963. A heuristic program that solves symbolic integration problems in freshman calculus. *Computers and Thought*. E. Feigenbaum and J. Feldman, ed. New York: McGraw-Hill.

Slate, D. J. and Atkin, L. R., 1977. CHESS 4.5—the Northwestern University chess program. *Chess Skill in Man and Machine*, P.W. Frey, ed. New York: Springer-Verlag.

Stickel, M. E. and Tyson, W. M., 1985. An analysis of consecutively bounded depth-first search with applications in automated deduction. In *Proceedings of the International Joint Conference on Artificial Intelligence (IJCAI-85)*, Los Angeles, California. San Mateo: Morgan Kaufmann.

Tonge, F. M., 1963. A summary of a heuristic line balancing procedure. *Computers and Thought*, E. Feigenbaum and J. Feldman, ed. New York: McGraw-Hill.

Turing, A. M., 1950. Computing machinery and intelligence. *Mind* **59**:433–460. Also in *Computers and Thought*, E. Feigenbaum and J. Feldman, ed. New York: McGraw-Hill, 1963.

Von Neuman, J. and Morgenstern, O., 1944. *Theory of Games and Economic Behavior*. Princeton: Princeton University Press.

Vornberger, O., 1987. Parallel alpha-beta versus parallel SSS*. In *Proceedings of the IFIP Conference on Distributed Processing*. Amsterdam.

Waltz, D., 1975. Understanding line drawings of scenes with shadows. *Psychology of Computer Vision*, P. H. Winston, ed. New York: McGraw-Hill.

IV

REASONING ABOUT MECHANISMS AND CAUSALITY

7

Qualitative Physics: Past, Present, and Future

Kenneth D. Forbus

Qualitative Reasoning Group
Department of Computer Science
University of Illinois at Urbana, Champaign

1 *Introduction*

Qualitative physics is concerned with representing and reasoning about the physical world. The goal of qualitative physics is to capture both the common-sense knowledge of the person on the street and the tacit knowledge underlying the quantitative knowledge used by engineers and scientists. The area is now a little over ten years old, which, at least measured in the span of AI, is a long time. So it makes sense to step back and try to systematize the work in the field and describe the current state of the art.

I'll start by describing what qualitative physics is, why one should be doing it, and where it came from. Then I'll sketch the current state of the art, at least the part that is now fairly stable. Then I'll describe what I think lies around the corner, including some pointers to recent work and some interactions between qualitative physics and other fields. Finally, I'll describe some open problems, each of which will probably require quite a few inspired Ph.D. theses to crack.

Qualitative physics is growing rapidly, and thus any survey is likely to become quickly dated. For example, several problems which were described as virgin territory when this material was presented at AAAI-86 have now been at least partially explored. Nevertheless, I think the general framework for understanding the area that was presented then remains sound, and so I have remained faithful to that organization.

2 Why Qualitative Physics?

Consider what we need to know about the physical world to make coffee. We know that to pour coffee from the pot into a cup requires having the cup under the spout of the kettle, and that if we pour too much in, there will be a mess on the floor. We know all this without knowing the myriad equations and numerical parameters required by traditional physics to model this situation.

Suppose we were going to build a household robot that, among other duties, made coffee. We might start by using traditional physics to model the situation. Immediately several problems arise. There are few formal axiomatic theories of physics. The formal aspects of physics, the equations, do not by themselves describe when they are applicable. What, for example, is the equation for the cup? There isn't one, per se, but rather various aspects of the cup potentially participate in several different equations describing "what happens" in the world. Many everyday physical phenomena, such as boiling, are not easily described by a single equation. And even when equations exist, people who know nothing about them can often reason fluently about the phenomena. So equations cannot be necessary for performing such reasoning.

But suppose for a moment that we had such a set of equations. Could we use them? Realistic equations rarely permit closed-form, analytic solutions. Even when they do, the high computational complexity of symbolic algebraic means it's not the sort of computation you want going on inside a robot engaged in real-time activity. An alternate route is numerical simulation. By plugging in numerical values, we could generate a very precise description of what will happen. But such simulations require immense computational resources. Worse yet, it assumes the existence of a complete set of accurate values for all input parameters. Typically we just don't have such accurate information, thus forcing us to search a space of parameters corresponding to the ranges the various input parameters may take. This increases the amount of computation even more, making numerical simulation infeasible.

Even if numerical simulation were technologically feasible, by say shirt-pocket supercomputers, or by allowing rough approximations, it still would be insufficient for our robot. First, we still need to interpret the output of the simulation. A list of numerical state parameters is not the most perspicuous representation of an event. Second, any run of a numerical simulator provides a specific set of predictions about what the system being simulated will do. This will suffice for some tasks, but not for all. Often we want to characterize the possibilities that might occur, with some guarantee of completeness. For instance, a fault-tree analysis of a power plant that captured only a small fraction of the failure modes of the system would be inappropriate. With numerical simulations it is often hard to tell when one has captured all of the possible behaviors.[1] In many situations one needs a rapid and rough estimate of what is possible, rather than a very precise prediction based on many unsupported assumptions. A robot pouring coffee should be cognizant of the possibility of overflow, and not spend its time calculating just how big the resulting puddle might be.

These problems are not specific to making coffee; they hold more generally whenever one tries to reason about the physical world. To summarize, these problems are:

1. *The modeling problem:* How does one map from real-world objects to the abstractions of one's physics?

2. *The resolution problem:* Carrying out numerical simulations requires more detail than is often available. Reasoning techniques that can exploit low resolution, partial information are required for commonsense reasoning.

3. *The narrowness problem:* Traditional simulation provides precise answers given a particular set of assumptions. Many reasoning problems require knowing alternative possibilities, rather than a single projection.

At first these problems may seem surprising. Physics, one of the crowning successes of the scientific method, has been carried on for hundreds of years. But consider: Physicists already have commonsense theories of the world. Their goal is to create models capable of more precise explanations. With few exceptions, the focus of formalization lies with building new models that have significantly better predictive and explanatory power than our implicit commonsense models. Qualitative physics arises from the need to share our intuitions about the physical world with our machines.

There are many potential applications of qualitative physics. As argued elsewhere [Gentner and Stevens, 1983; de Kleer and Brown, 1984; de Kleer, 1984], the tacit knowledge of engineers and scientists rests on this shared framework. If we are to build programs that capture this expertise, we must understand the foundation qualitative physics provides. We will return to this point after briefly summarizing the essence of qualitative physics.

---

1 It is said that if the angular increment in the simulation of the aerodynamic properties of the Boston John Hancock building had been halved, the fact that the building's windows would tend to pop out in high winds could have been predicted. Instead, it was discovered empirically.

2.1 *The Essence*

The key to qualitative physics is to find ways to represent continuous properties of the world by discrete systems of symbols. One can always quantize something continuous, but not all quantizations are equally useful. One way to state the idea is the *relevance principle: The distinctions made by a quantization must be relevant to the kind of reasoning performed* [Forbus, 1984b].

The idea is simple, but few quantizations satisfy it. Rounding to fewer significant digits, replacing numbers by arbitrary intervals, using simple symbolic groups like TALL, VERY TALL, and fuzzy logic do not satisfy it. Signs generally do, since different things tend to happen when signs change (balls fly up and then down, different kinds of things can happen if the level of coffee in a cup is rising versus falling). Inequalities do, since processes tend to start and stop when inequalities change (heat flows occur when there is a temperature difference, boiling occurs when the liquid's temperature reaches its boiling point).

Good quantizations allow more abstract descriptions of state, which in turn make possible more concise descriptions of behavior. If our state parameters are elements of $\Re$, there are potentially an infinite number of states. Replacing state parameters by floating-point numbers makes the number of potential states finite, but still numbering in the billions for many systems. In the quantizations of qualitative physics there may be as few as a dozen, or a hundred, or in some cases thousands. Each state in a qualitative physics typically corresponds to many states in a traditional description, each distinguished by having the same "meaningful behavior pattern" occurring in them.

Abstraction is a two-edged sword. While these abstract state descriptions succinctly capture possible behaviors, they tend not to prescribe exactly which behavior will occur. By themselves they typically cannot, for we have thrown away just that information required to settle such questions. Thus qualitative simulations tend to be ambiguous. Often such answers suffice, e.g., if a household robot cannot imagine any way for the house to burn down as a consequence of its plan to cook supper, then its plan is reasonably safe. However, if a house fire is a possibility, more knowledge must be invoked. The ability of qualitative physics to represent this ambiguity explicitly is beneficial, since it provides a signal to indicate when more detailed knowledge is required.

A central goal of qualitative physics is to achieve a degree of systematic coverage and uniformity far in excess of today's knowledge-based systems. In today's expert systems, knowledge is encoded about a particular domain for a particular purpose. Instead of continuing to build such systems, qualitative physics strives to create *wide-coverage, multi-purpose domain models.* By wide-coverage, we mean that there is some large but precisely characterizable set of systems that can be described by the domain model. It is assumed that every model for a specific system is built by instantiating appropriate elements of the domain vocabulary in appropriate ways. This will reduce the amount of hand-crafting required for new programs and will hopefully lead to "off the shelf" knowledge bases.

By multi-purpose, we mean that a domain model (or a model for a specific situation) can be used for more than one inferential task. Characterizing these *styles of reasoning* is another goal of qualitative physics. These styles of reasoning include qualitative simulation, interpreting measurements, planning, comparative analysis, and others. Developing domain-independent characterizations of these styles will hopefully lead to generic algorithms that can be used as modules in a variety of larger systems.

2.2 *Potential Applications*

To turn robots loose in unconstrained environments, we must teach them qualitative physics. Often we must enlist physical processes to carry out our plans. For example, if I want to make coffee in the morning, I need to use the stove to make boiling water. This requires filling the kettle, putting the pot on the stove, turning the stove on, and waiting for it to boil. One could imagine writing a little expert system to do this. It wouldn't take many IF-THEN rules to express this particular procedure. However, if you lived in my house you would prefer a robot to be reasoning from first principles. My stove is a little unusual: The surface that contains the burners retracts into the wall, under the oven. When the stove is retracted, the burners are directly under the electrical wiring for the oven. Having been designed in the 50's, it has no safety cutoff switch. Turning the burner on when the stove is retracted, or retracting the stove when the burner is still hot, is likely to burn the house down. It is doubtful that the designer of the IF-THEN rules could have taken my stove into account, so I would be very nervous about turning such a machine loose in my house. And houses are fairly stereotyped; consider such machines loose in a construction site. Clearly, such robots will need some form of qualitative physics

But qualitative physics has many other potential applications as well. The subject matter of many expert systems includes aspects concerned with the physical world, particularly in the sciences and engineering. Diagnosis and design are two obvious examples. As remarked above, qualitative physics identifies the "tacit knowledge" that engineers and scientists use to ground the formalisms they learn in school and on the job.

Consider for example the problem of building an intelligent tutoring system for propulsion systems. Figure 1 shows a simplified layout of a Navy propulsion system. Distilled water is fed into the boiler, heated by oil-fired burners, and turned to steam. The system operates at very high temperature and pressure (950° F, 1200 psi) to increase the amount of energy transferred per pound of steam. The steam is heated in the superheater, to impart even more energy. (By the time it leaves the superheater in a shipboard system, it is travelling faster than the speed of sound.) Here is a hard problem that instructors routinely ask about this situation: Suppose the feedwater temperature increases, as might occur when travelling in a warmer part of the ocean. What happens to the temperature at the superheater outlet?

This is a complicated situation, and most of us haven't had a lot of experience with it, so it hardly qualifies as commonsense physics. Yet qualitative reasoning suffices to answer it. In fact, qualitative reasoning is crucial: While a few numerical values have been provided, many critical ones have not, including how much the feedwater temperature rises! Here is the solution, according to instructors at the Navy Surface Warfare Officer's school in Newport, Rhode Island. The water coming into the boiler is now hotter. The boiling will occur at the same temperature, so this means that the amount of heat that must be added to get a piece of water to boil is reduced. This means the water will boil sooner, which means the rate of steam production increases. Assuming a constant load, this means the steam spends less time in the superheater. Since the amount of heat transferred to the steam in the superheater is a function of the time it spends in the superheater, and the starting temperature of the steam is the same, less heat is transferred. Thus the steam temperature at the superheater outlet falls when the feedwater temperature rises.

The ability to make these subtle, yet human-like, deductions makes qualitative physics an excellent candidate for a knowledge component in intelligent tutoring systems [Forbus and Stevens, 1981; Forbus, 1984a] and plant monitors. For example, Figure 2 shows an explanation generated by one of my programs a long time ago, as part of the STEAMER system. The valve shown is a spring-loaded reducing valve, and it converts 1200 psi steam to 12 psi steam at constant pressure, for a wide range of loads. The important thing to notice is that the terms of the explanation are those which are easily understood by human students and operators. No numerical values were used to generate these conclusions—just a very simple qualitative physics.[2]

Qualitative physics also has many potential applications in other aspects of engineering [Forbus, 1987b]. Consider a really smart mechanical design assistant that could generate a description of possible behaviors before detailed parameters were chosen. Suppose the desired behavior exists in the space of behaviors predicted by a qualitative simulation. Then the design effort proceeds by choosing parameters to force the desired behavior, and not the alternatives, to occur. If the desired behavior is not even possible, then it is clear that the design must be changed, even without more details. It does not take detailed

---

2 The physics used was the early de Kleer and Brown physics, which provided only perturbation analysis, not full dynamical reasoning. The limitations of this approach inspired my own qualitative process theory (and their confluences theory).

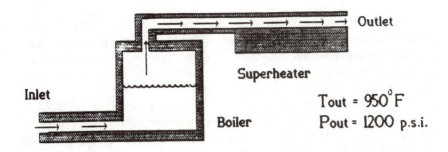

Figure 1. The SWOS Problem. Given that the temperature of the feedwater is increasing, what is the temperature at the superheater outlet? Instructors at the Navy Surface Warfare Officer's School say this is one of the hardest problems students are given, yet it can be answered with purely qualitative reasoning.

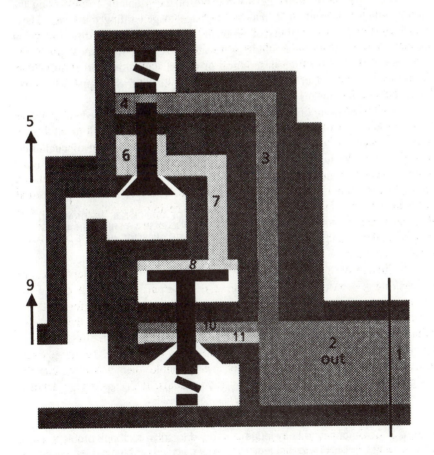

Figure 2. Qualitative physics can be used in intelligent tutoring systems

numerical simulation to ascertain, for example, that a pendulum is not a good oscillator to use in a wristwatch.

3 *The Past*

We will not attempt a complete historical survey or time line of qualitative physics. Instead, we will describe three early efforts, the "pre-history" of the area, that provide a background for making later work easier to understand.

Qualitative physics arose from attempts to build programs that could solve textbook physics and math problems. The earliest systems (STUDENT [Bobrow, 1968], CARPS [Charniak, 1968], MECHO [Bundy et al., 1979], ISSAC [Novak, 1976]) attempted to capture the full breadth of the problem, from parsing the initial problem description in natural language to generating diagrams. These programs could solve a variety of problems, but it was quickly discovered that the equations (explicit or implicit) were insufficient to solve most problems. Consider Figure 3 from the description of Charniak's CARPS program. To set up the equations properly required interpreting the phrase "approaching the dock," which here means the distance along the top of the water.

The easy answer, of course, is that more knowledge is needed. But what kind? de Kleer was the first person to characterize the relevant kind of knowledge. His work on the NEWTON program marked the beginning of qualitative physics. NEWTON was designed to solve problems concerning a single point mass sliding on a surface (see Figure 3).

A BARGE WHOSE DECK IS 10 FT BELOW THE LEVEL OF A DOCK IS BEING DRAWN IN BY MEANS OF A CABLE ATTACHED TO THE DECK AND PASSING THROUGH A RING ON THE DOCK. WHEN THE BARGE IS 24 FT FROM AND APPROACHING THE DOCK AT 3/4 FT/SEC HOW FAST IS THE CABLE BEING PULLED IN?

Make a sketch of this situation for yourself Most all people will draw

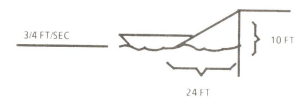

Clearly when we say APPROACHING THE DOCK we mean at the level of the boat. Once again information of gravity would lead to this result.

Figure 3 Commonsense knowledge is needed to solve textbook problems. In extending STUDENT's techniques to handle calculus problems, Charniak found that more world knowledge was needed to properly interpret these problems.

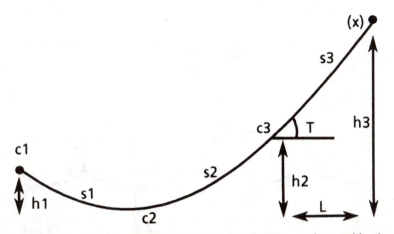

Figure 4 An example from NEWTON. de Kleer's NEWTON used a combination of qualitative and algebraic techniques to reason about a point mass moving on a surface.

When faced with a problem, NEWTON would begin by creating an *envisionment*, an explicit representation of all the different possible behaviors of the system. Figure 5 shows the envisionment for the problem in Figure 3. There are two things to note about this envisionment. First, in standard simulations there is a unique next state. In a qualitative simulation there can be more than one next state, due to the lack of resolution in the qualitative description. Second, the envisionment alone suffices to answer many questions about this domain. For example, if asked whether or not the mass could fly off segment S1 going to the right, NEWTON could answer "no," because no description matching that behavior can be found in the envisionment. To paraphrase de Kleer, an intelligent problem solver has to be able to answer stupid questions, and preferably with less work than it takes to answer subtle questions.

To answer more subtle questions, NEWTON performed algebraic manipulation. Consider the problem of determining conditions that will prevent the cart from flying off when it enters the right side of the track. There is a qualitative ambiguity in what happens after state S1, one branch corresponding to the cart flying off and the other branch to the cart sliding back. NEWTON used this qualitative ambiguity to index into a knowledge base of equations, which was then manipulated to derive an appropriate inequality.

The next event in the prehistory of qualitative physics was the Pat Hayes' Naive Physics Manifesto [Hayes, 1985]. This paper achieved wide informal circulation in 1978, and had a major impact. In particular, Hayes' notion of *histories* is central to qualitative physics. Figure 6 illustrates a fragment of the history for a liquid being poured from a container onto a table top. The basic idea of histories is that events should be represented as spatially bounded, but temporally extended, pieces of space-time. It is assumed that histories which do not intersect do not interact.

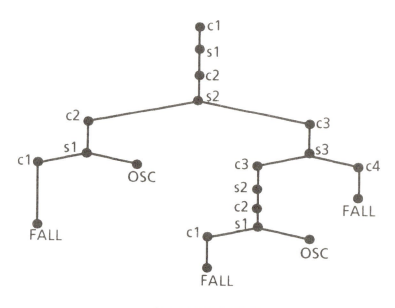

ENVISIONMENT

Figure 5. An Envisionment for a NEWTON problem.

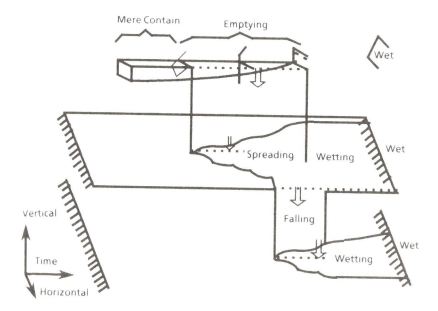

Figure 6 An example of Hayes' notion of histories.

Histories were designed to solve several problems with the situation calculus, especially the Frame Problem. Situation calculus provides no spatial boundaries for an event. In fact, the situation calculus describes what happens *between* events of some kind (such as the actions taken by an imaginary robot), not what happens *during* those events. This leads to several well-known problems, such as being forced to change situations whenever anything happens anywhere in the entire universe of discourse. There are two advantages to histories. Their being temporally extended means it is easier to talk about what is happening during some action (assuming appropriate temporal representations). Their being spatially bounded means that descriptions can be evolved locally, thus eliminating the requirement of global simulation (see [Hayes, 1979; Forbus, 1984b; Williams, 1986] for details).

While several aspects of Hayes' naive physics enterprise have been adopted enthusiastically in the qualitative physics enterprise, several have not. For instance, Hayes argued that implementation was an "unnecessary distraction." In qualitative physics, testing ideas via computer implementation is viewed as essential. As our models grow more complex, carrying out proofs by hand is burdensome. With abstruse mathematical constructs it is easy to maintain rigor, but with commonsense matters it is all too tempting to relax one's vigilance. Carefully written programs are superb bookkeepers, keeping one's theories honest. Furthermore, as discussed below, there are several *styles of reasoning* that use such knowledge. Identifying these problems and developing computational techniques to solve them is a worthwhile endeavor in its own right.

The third piece of prehistory is my FROB program [Forbus, 1980, 1981a] which reasoned about motion through free space. de Kleer's "roller-coaster" world was essentially one-dimensional, with the simulation halting whenever the cart left the surface. FROB worked with a true two-dimensional world, reasoning about balls bouncing around on surfaces (see Figure 7). The user could specify a scenario by drawing a diagram to specify the surfaces and introduce balls. The more information the user provides, the more FROB refines its descriptions. For example, FROB used a constraint language to determine, in conjunction with the diagram, the consequences of any numerical parameters provided. In addition to carrying out numerical analyses, FROB could answer questions like "where will this ball end up eventually?" and "can these two balls collide?" In all cases, FROB used minimal information to answer the question.

FROB's spatial reasoning worked by calculating a qualitative vocabulary of *places* from the surfaces in the diagram. Combined with symbolic descriptions of activity (such as FLY and COLLIDE) and velocity (e.g., (LEFT UP)), these places provided the framework for qualitative spatial analysis. Consider the problem of determining whether or not the two balls in Figure 8 will collide. To collide, two balls must be in the same place at the same time. If all we know is that both balls are going to the left, then they might collide, since the union of the places they might be overlap. But if we also assume that FRED never gets to S31, then a collision is ruled out, since the two balls can never be in the same place.

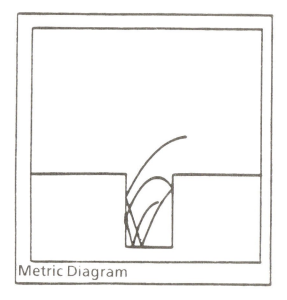

Metric Diagram

->> 'Motion-Summary-for b1)

FOR G0364
THE BALL WILL EVENTUALLY STOP
IT IS TRAPPED INSIDE (WELL0)
AND WILL STOP FLYING AT ONE OF (SEGMENT 11)
NIL

Figure 7 FROB reasoned about motion through space.

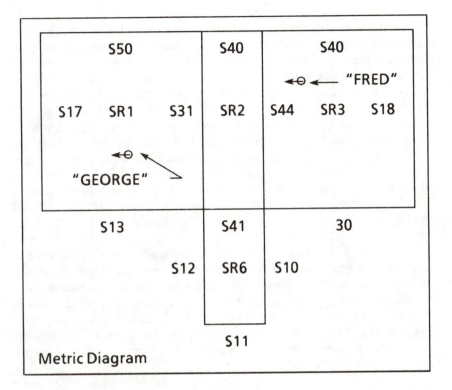

Metric Diagram

```
->>(collide? fred george)
(POSSIBLE AT SEGMENT 50 SEGEMNT 17 SEGMENT 13 SREGION)
->>(cannot-be-at fred segment 31)
(SEGMENT 31)
UPDATING ASSUMPTIONS FOR (>> INITIAL-STATE FRED)
CHECKING PATH OF MOTION AGAINST ASSUMPTIONS
->(collide? fred george)
NO
->>(what-is (>>state initial-state fred)
(>>STATE INITIAL-STATE FRED) = (FLY (SREGION3) (LEFT))
NIL
->>(what-is (>>state initial-state george))
(>>STATE INITIAL-STATE GEORGE) = (FLY (SREGION) (LEFT))
NIL
```

Figure 8 Collision problem.

FROB advanced the state of the art in several ways. First, it demonstrated that Hayes' notion of histories was indeed useful. There was perhaps more numerical information in FROB's histories than in Hayes' original conception, but they are histories nonetheless. Second, FROB was based on a theory of spatial reasoning that divided the problem into two parts, using a diagrammatic representation to provide quick answers to a class of geometric questions, and a qualitative description of places computed from the diagram. Third, it demonstrated that qualitative ambiguities could be resolved by numerical calculation, just as NEWTON demonstrated that symbolic algebra could resolve them. And finally, the notion of envisionments was generalized from the trees used in NEWTON to full graphs. This allows many properties of the behavior, such as final states and oscillations, to be characterized by properties of the envisionment graph (e.g., end states and cycles) rather than by explicit nodes as in NEWTON.

At this point we draw our pre-historic retrospective to a close. NEWTON and FROB were organized around using a combination of qualitative and quantitative techniques to solve particular classes of problems. It became clear around this time that simply understanding the nature of qualitative representation was a full-time effort, and that a domain-independent, general qualitative physics could exist. Research effort turned to finding such a physics—or, more correctly, understanding the space of such systems of physics—and we now turn to this exploration.

4 *The State of the Art*

Work in qualitative physics may be roughly divided into three areas: *qualitative dynamics*, *qualitative kinematics*, and *styles of reasoning*. In traditional physics,

> Dynamics deals with the causes of motion, as opposed to kinematics, which deals with its geometric description, and to statics, which deals with the conditions for the lack of motion [Considine, 1983].

Dynamics is used generically to describe the study of forces on systems (e.g., fluid dynamics), and typically includes statics. Hence qualitative dynamics is concerned with what causes systems to change over time, ignoring geometry except as a source of boundary conditions.

Qualitative kinematics is concerned with the spatial reasoning required by commonsense physics. Not all commonsense spatial reasoning is qualitative kinematics—counterexamples include navigation, spatial planning, and controlling arm motions. Carrying the distinction between dynamics and kinematics into qualitative physics is not an arbitrary choice, as we will argue in Section 4.2.

Styles of reasoning, of course, concern how to exploit the knowledge of qualitative physics. There is no direct analog in traditional physics, except insofar as physicists and educators have attempted to formalize their problem-solving methods in order to teach them more readily. But studying styles of reasoning is crucial for qualitative physics, since representation without reasoning is an idle exercise.

4.1 Qualitative Dynamics

Qualitative dynamics studies how physical systems change. It addresses the problem of how to represent differential equations qualitatively, and how to organize such knowledge in a usable form. We begin by surveying qualitative representations for numbers and time-varying differential equations. Ontological issues are discussed next, since providing a formalism for organizing knowledge is a central job of qualitative physics. Finally we take a brief look at two other issues, the role of continuity and how such equations are given causal interpretations, since these topics are often misunderstood.

But before we start: A variety of notations have been used in qualitative physics. While terminology differences can be bewildering to the uninitiated, and standardization has been suggested ([Bobrow, 1984], p. 5), it is doubtful that the situation will improve soon. In fact, two facts suggest that standardization is not an urgent issue. First, there is already significant overlap. Second, the lack of a single standardized notation has not seemed to retard progress in traditional mathematics, in which there are still over six different notations for derivatives, despite its being hundreds of years older than qualitative physics. We will sometimes point out variations, but will not attempt a complete concordance.

4.1.1 Numbers Three representations for number have proven useful so far in qualitative physics: *signs*, *inequalities*, and *orders of magnitude*. We describe each in turn.

Signs Reducing numbers to signs is the simplest qualitative representation for number [de Kleer, 1979b, 1984b; Williams, 1984]. For example, we might say that the level of water in a container is -1, 0, or 1, depending on whether or not the level is lower, the same as, or higher than a desired height. If the comparison is chosen carefully, we can satisfy our desiderata of capturing relevant distinctions while not introducing irrelevant ones.

Signs of derivatives form a natural indicator of change [Forbus, 1981b; de Kleer, 1984b; Williams, 1984]. We will use the notation of qualitative process (QP) theory and denote the sign of the derivative of a quantity Q by Ds[Q]. If the sign of the derivative is –1, then the quantity is decreasing, if 0 then it is constant, and if 1 then it is increasing. Since change is intuitively important, and the direction of change determines what boundary conditions might change, signs carry critical information about derivatives.

The earliest use of signs in qualitative physics was de Kleer's QUAL program [de Kleer, 1979a], where signs were interpreted as the difference between an original equilibrium value and the new equilibrium value reached as the result of a perturbation (the *incremental qualitative value* (IQ) interpretation). The semantics of this representation were slightly problematic: For example, it was not clear what the IQ value should be if the system went through several behavioral states before settling into an equilibrium value.

The major advantage of the sign representation is simplicity. We are taught the method of substitution very early in mathematics, and sign values provide a concrete object that may be "plugged in" to qualitative equations of whatever form. However, signs alone are often not enough. Consider the problem of figuring out what might happen if we have three tanks F, G, and H with pipes hooked up between them. Given some initial level of water in each, we turn on all the valves in the pipes between them. To determine how the water would flow requires comparing the pressures in the tanks that are linked together.

A sign value encodes a comparison of a magnitude with a single reference value. Suppose tank G is connected by pipes to both F and H. Clearly no sign representation of pressure will suffice for the pressure in G, since we must compare the pressure with two reference values, the pressures in F and G. The fact that these reference values are themselves changing is yet another complication. It seems counterintuitive to say that the value of pressure in G is changing simply because the pressure in F is changing.

One representational "trick" sometimes suggested to work around these problems, albeit unnaturally, is to rewrite a quantity as a constellation of signed quantities. For example, a given quantity Q might be represented by new quantities $Q_1 \ldots Q_n$, one for each comparison Q is involved in. This does violence to the notion of quantity. Furthermore, it makes the number of pseudo-quantities needed to describe a quantity vary with the situation, rather than with the type of object. The next section describes a more natural representation for such circumstances.

Inequalities Comparing the value of a quantity with several other parameters is a common occurrence in physics. For example, to determine the phase of a piece of stuff, one determines the relationship of its temperature to the boiling temperature and freezing temperature of that substance for the appropriate conditions (such as pressure). Worse yet, the parameters that it makes sense to compare a value with can change as conditions change. For example, if we discover a leak in tank G in the previous example, we should also consider the relationship between the pressure at the leak and the surroundings.

These considerations suggest collecting a set of inequalities to describe a quantity. This set of inequalities is called its *quantity space* [Forbus, 1981b]. Inequalities makes sense for several reasons. First, they provide a means to partition numerical values, and thus express boundary conditions for behavior. For example, when two objects in thermal contact are at different temperatures, there will be a heat flow from the object with higher temperature to the object with lower temperature. Second, a quantity can participate in any number of inequalities, thus providing the variable resolution we desire. Third, if numbers are combined by addition, inequality information often suffices to determine the sign of the outcome. If, for instance, there is flow into a tank and flow out, the relative magnitudes of the flows determine whether the level of the tank is rising or falling.

Here is a simple quantity space that describes the temperature of water W in a pot on the stove.

$$T_{freeze} \rightarrow T_W \begin{array}{l} \nearrow T_{stove} \\ \searrow T_{boil} \end{array}$$

A simple quantity space. The significant relationships involving the temperature of a piece of water (T_W) can be expressed as inequalities. Here, the temperature is above freezing (T_{freeze}) and less than the temperature of the stove and its boiling temperature.

The arrows represent inequalities, with the quantity at the head of the arrow being greater than the quantity at the tail of the arrow. Thus W is warmer than freezing, and cooler than both its boiling temperature and the temperature of the stove. Importantly, quantity spaces need not be complete—notice that in this diagram we do not know the relationship between the temperature of the stove and the boiling point of W. The ability to represent this ambiguity allows us to accumulate partial information, and detect when more information is required.

What should a number be compared to? One source of quantity space elements are parameters representing domain-specific boundary conditions. An example of such *limit points* are the boiling temperature of a substance or the fracture stress of a material [Forbus, 1981b]. Some comparisons are required due to the specifics of a situation, such as a comparison between the rate of flow into and out of a container. We will adopt the terminology of [Kuipers, 1986] and refer to the elements of a quantity space generically as *landmark values* for the quantity, whether or not they are limit points.

Landmarks versus limit points Two distinct semantics have been used for landmark values in the literature. The distinction has often been misunderstood, via a type/token confusion, and we undertake to clarify it here. We call a description *temporally generic* if it refers to a class of temporal behaviors, rather than just a single behavior. A description of a single behavior we will call *temporally specific*. The script of a play is a temporally generic description, while a videotape of its performance is temporally specific. Limit points are temporally generic, as are comparisons between rates, since there are classes of situations where liquids boil and flows occur. The value of the boiling temperature at 3 PM is temporally specific—we are referring to a single situation, and hence a single specific value.

Most systems of qualitative physics use only temporally generic landmarks. But temporally specific landmarks can be critical for many reasoning tasks: For example, it may be crucial for a doctor to compare a patient's cholesterol level today with the specific cholesterol level last week, not just with some generic "safe" value. Kuipers' QSIM generates such temporally specific landmarks. These landmarks do not correspond to "discovering" new limit points, as originally claimed. Rather, they are the equivalent of a qualitative "strip chart" that describes a specific behavior of a system. QSIM thus provides an automatic naming facility to support reasoning about temporally specific values.

Although temporally specific landmarks are essential for some inferences, they introduce a new level of computational complexity. Consider for example a decaying oscillation, such as a ball bouncing up and down, each time rising only some fraction of the height it reached before. Each height is a new landmark value. Thus an infinite behavior can sometimes lead to an infinite number of landmark values (see Section 4.3.2).

The quantity space is now a standard feature of qualitative physics [Kuipers, 1984, 1986; Simmons, 1983; Weld, 1986]. It addresses the resolution problem by providing the ability to incrementally accumulate information about a number, thus simplifying the modeling task. However, manipulating sets of statements describing a value is more complicated than treating values as atomic objects, as the sign representation allows. Quantity space implementations require efficient application of the laws of transitivity, typically obtained by separate inferential mechanisms [Forbus, 1984c; Simmons, 1983; Forbus, 1988].

Several useful variations of the quantity space have been developed. For instance, Kuipers requires quantity spaces to be totally ordered [Kuipers, 1984], which simplifies the representation into a collection of intervals. Simmons [1986] augments inequalities with numerical intervals, thus providing a simple way to integrate empirical bounds.

Orders of magnitude Sometimes saying that N_1 is greater than N_2 is not enough: One may need to say that N_1 is so large compared to N_2 that N_2 may be ignored. For instance, the effect of evaporation on the level of a lake may be ignored if the dam holding it has burst. In everyday life, engineers rely on the ability to distinguish a value that is significantly out of range from a normal variation. One way to represent such information is to extend the range of comparative relationships to include *orders of magnitude*. Three such representations, FOG [Raiman, 1986], O[M] [Mavrovouniotis and Stephanopolous, 1987], and Davis' infinitesimal theory [Davis, 1987] have been developed in qualitative physics. We begin with FOG and O[M] since they share intended use, and then describe Davis' system.

FOG introduces three new relationships, in addition to the traditional order relations. They are:

$A << B$: A is negligible compared to B.
$A \cong B$: A is very close to B.
$A \sim B$: A is the same order of magnitude as B.

Raiman has developed a consistent formalization that captures the intuitive meaning of these statements, using infinitesimals as a model. The effect of these relationships is to stratify values into equivalence classes, thus providing the means to say that values are very different. For example, in the DEDALE diagnosis system [Dauge et al., 1987], this vocabulary is used to describe the typical relationships between values in component models.

The O[M] is based on assigning labels to ranges of ratios. For example, the relationship

$A \sim\, < B$ (read A is slightly smaller than B)

is true exactly when

$$\frac{|A|}{|B|} < (1 + e)$$

where e is a domain-specific parameter. This mapping simplifies the laws of the system and potentially allows a variety of quantitative information to be easily incorporated. O[M] also uses physical units to reduce inferential complexity; only parameters of the same units may be compared.

The definition of orders-of-magnitude relations in O[M] in terms of ranges simplifies the mapping from numerical values, a problem for which FOG provides little guidance. However it also allows a large but finite number of negligible values to add up to something that is significant, which violates the intuitions underlying such reasoning. This cannot happen in FOG. The relative advantages of the two systems remain to be explored.

Davis [1987] describes another formalism for orders-of-magnitude which, like FOG, is based on infinitesimals. He reconstructs a qualitative calculus to include infinitesimal values for both numbers and as durations of intervals. Thus he can talk about changes taking infinite (or very short) time.

4.1.2 *Equations*

Equations are the hallmark of physics. Just as qualitative physics restricts the accuracy to which numerical values are known, the notions of equations developed in qualitative physics are also typically weaker. These weaker constraints can better capture partial knowledge and simplify inference, thus addressing the resolution problem.

Arithmetic operations Every system of qualitative physics includes at least addition and subtraction. Multiplication is often introduced as well. While the operations are familiar, the effects of weakening the values they are performed on has profound consequences. First, ambiguities can arise, even with complete initial information. If one only knows that A is greater than zero and B is less than zero, for instance, then the sign of $A + B$ cannot be determined. In this case knowing the relative magnitudes of A and B can provide the answer, but in general, algebraic inequalities are required. But since most qualitative values do not form a field, algebraic manipulations must be performed with care.

In [de Kleer and Brown, 1984], equations involving sign values are called *confluences*. Confluences are solved by propagation of constraints, using generate and test when unresolvable simultaneities occur. Under certain conditions, Dormoy has shown that sets of confluences can be solved by a variant of Gaussian elimination [Dormoy and Raimen, 1987]. Confluences have also been used with the FOG formalism, where the comparison is made between the actual value of a parameter and its nominal value [Dauge et al., 1987].

Monotonic functions One of the weakest statements that can be made about the relationship between two quantities is that when one increases, the other tends to increase. This level of knowledge is captured by *monotonic functions*, which are used as a primitive in several systems of qualitative physics and mathematics. Monotonic functions provide a means of approximating complicated or unknown functions with minimal commitment.

If $y = f(x)$ then $f(x)$ is *increasing monotonic* if whenever x increases, y increases. $f(x)$ is *decreasing monotonic* if whenever x increases, y decreases. Often there is no reason to name the function involved, so various notations for anonymous functions have been developed. For example, Kuipers [1984, 1986] uses $M^+(x, y)$ to denote an increasing monotonic connection between x and y, and $M^-(x, y)$ to denote a decreasing function.

QP theory allows the partial specification of monotonic functions through *qualitative proportionalities*. Formally, $y \; \alpha_{Q+} \; x$ indicates $y = f(. \; . \; ., x, \; . \; . \; .)$, where f is some function which is increasing monotonic in its dependence on x. Similarly, $y \, \alpha_{Q+} \, x$ indicates that the function involved is decreasing monotonic in x. To determine the complete specification of functional dependence in any particular situation requires a closed-world assumption.[3]

The advantage of qualitative proportionalities is composability; the knowledge of a function can be decomposed and distributed appropriately through a representation, to be assembled as needed by the reasoning system. For example, parameters may be selectively ignored (such as the effect of pipe resistance on the rate of liquid flow, if the fluid is moving very slowly) by "turning off" the description that contributes them to the function. Qualitative proportionalities can also be used to express intermediate hypotheses in a learning system. For example, ABACUS [Falkenhainer, 1985] searches for them as the first step in finding equations to describe numerical data. The disadvantage is that ambiguities arising from them cannot be settled by just inequality information. Consider for instance

$$C \, \alpha_{Q+} \, A \;\; \wedge \;\; C \, \alpha_{Q-} \, B \;\; \wedge \;\; \mathrm{Ds}[A] = \mathrm{Ds}[B] = 1$$

No additional sign or inequality information suffices to determine $\mathrm{Ds}[C]$, unlike subtraction or multiplication.

We have found it useful to allow two other kinds of information to be specified about monotonic functions. First, *correspondences* are introduced to propagate inequality information. Intuitively, a correspondence fixes a point on the curve relating two (or more) parameters. For instance, when a spring is at its rest length it exerts no force. Suppose the force is α_{Q-} its length (i.e., stretching it produces a force that tends to make it return to its rest length). These two facts together allow us to deduce that if we push a spring to be shorter than its rest length, we will cause it to exert a positive force (i.e., push against us). A detailed discussion of correspondences can be found in [Forbus, 1984b; Kuipers, 1986]. Second, functions can be named, so that inequality information can be propagated across distinct individuals [Forbus, 1984b]. For example, the function that determines the pressure of a contained liquid in terms of its level is the same for all containers, and hence information about differences in level can be mapped into differences in pressure.

Of course, many functions required in modeling the physical world are not monotonic. Such functions can be represented by decomposing them into monotonic segments. Providing a framework for explicitly describing the assumptions underlying this decomposition is one of the roles played by ontology in qualitative physics.

---

3 A language for framing more complete hypotheses about functional dependence is described in [Forbus, 1984b], Section 5.3.

4.1.3 *Ontology*

Ontological choices are central to qualitative physics. Along with space and time, ontology provides the organizational structure for everything else. Continuous properties are properties of something, and equations hold as a result of that. Usually developing the appropriate ontology is the most difficult part of formalizing a domain.

If we are to build a complete qualitative physics, one that covers the breadth and depth of our commonsense knowledge of the physical world, we must discover and utilize common abstractions. Generating an ad hoc model for each scenario is impractical and unreliable. Two such ontological abstractions, *devices* and *processes*, have been widely used in qualitative physics. We describe them here, after briefly reviewing a simple precursor.

4.1.4 *Qualitative State Vectors*

The *qualitative state vector* ontology was the earliest used in qualitative physics. It was the ontology used in both NEW-TON [de Kleer, 1975, 1979a], and FROB [Forbus, 1980, 1981a]. The idea is to decompose system behavior into segments, each described by a list of symbols. This symbolic state vector contains two types of elements:

1.   A quantization of the traditional state variables.

2.   A symbolic description of the type of activity.

In traditional physics, we might state informally what kind of system we are reasoning about (say, a ball bouncing on a surface), describe the initial values for the state parameters, and state what equations will be used to describe the different things a ball can do (i.e., fly through space and collide with surfaces). In the corresponding qualitative description, we would quantize position into symbolic places, velocities into symbolic directions, and add a symbol for the type of behavior. For example, we might say a ball is in REGION0, going (LEFT UP), and FLYing (see Figure 9).

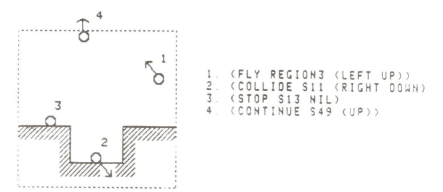

```
1.  (FLY REGION3 (LEFT UP))
2.  (COLLIDE S11 (RIGHT DOWN)
3.  (STOP S13 NIL)
4.  (CONTINUE S49 (UP))
```

Figure 9 An example of qualitative state vectors.

The need for the first class of constituent is obvious, since some representation of state variables is needed to capture the behavior. The second type explicitly describes that which is left implicit in the traditional representations. Roughly, the symbolic description of activity should change whenever the quantitative equations traditionally used to describe the behavior will change. Since we do not have equations, we must provide instead a set of *qualitative simulation rules*. These rules take a state and produce the set of states which can occur next. As mentioned previously, more than one state may be possible due to the coarse grain of the representation. The particular content of the rules is highly domain-specific, but typically a small set of rules suffices for each class of behavior. (Hayes' conception of reasoning with histories by "gluing them together" fits within this framework as well.)

The qualitative state vector representation has three useful properties. First, it is quite natural. The notion of state is central in any account of physics, traditional or qualitative. Second, it is very compact. Each state can be succinctly described by a short list of symbols, and hence envisioning is very cheap. Third, it provides an easy means to combine dynamic and kinematic representations, something which is more difficult with the other ontologies.

The difficulty with this ontology is that it lacks composability. To describe a complex system directly is often too difficult. Instead, one decomposes it into smaller parts, models each of those parts and the relationships between them, and then combines these models into a model of the whole system. The advantages of such modular approaches are well known; the pieces can often be re-used to describe yet more systems. But we have placed little constraint on the actual contents of states and simulation laws, and so we have no methodology for combining them.

For example, suppose we wish to combine the states in NEWTON and FROB. Each simulation stops when it reaches conditions that make the other appropriate, so one might imagine using the union of their simulation laws to more fully describe the behavior of a point mass. But not all combinations are so simple. If we glue the point mass onto a stick that is attached to a pivot (thus creating a pendulum), both sets of laws are simply wrong. Each new condition we add requires reorganizing our vectors and simulation laws in some ad hoc fashion.

Hayes' axioms for liquids do not escape this problem, either. First, Hayes himself points out there are many cases where his theory cannot make predictions (such as pouring water into a leaky cup). Second, adding new phenomena, such as solutions, would require wholesale reorganization of the theory. No theory is completely composable, of course. What we seek is an organizing principle, a methodology that simplifies combination as much as possible. Patterns of history combinations (or, equivalently, tables of qualitative simulation laws) are not constrained enough.

In traditional physics, composability is arranged by sharing parameters. The equations for distinct parts are combined by identity of names in some cases, and by new equations describing the relationship between the parts in others. Qualitative versions of such theories thus require both a qualitative representation of equations, and an organizing structure to place them in. This generative power is exactly what is required to provide composability. The other two ontologies exploit this idea.

4.1.5 *The Device Ontology* System dynamics [Shearer et al., 1971] is an engineering methodology which provides a common set of abstractions that encompass a variety of domains, including many electrical, thermal, mechanical, and acoustical systems. This modeling paradigm has been widely used in qualitative physics as well, the principle advocates being de Kleer and Brown [de Kleer, 1979b; de Kleer and Brown, 1984; de Kleer, 1984a] and Williams [1984]. These theories replace the quantitative equations of system dynamics with qualitative equations, and have developed new inference techniques for using these descriptions.

The basic idea is to view a system as constructed from a collection of *devices*, such as transistors and resistors. The behavior of a device is specified by internal laws, often decomposed into distinct states or operating regions. Each device has some number of *ports*, and all interaction between devices occurs through these ports. To model a particular system, one builds a network of devices. The device network is then analyzed by using the combined equations from the devices and interconnections, either by constraint propagation or symbolic relaxation.

Consider, for example, the bipolar transistor common emitter amplifier in Figure 10. The catalog of domain devices will include descriptions of transistors and resistors, and descriptions of what parameters are shared when terminals are connected together. A typical conclusion (but not the only kind) that can be reached with this description is how the circuit might respond to a change in input. This reasoning is accomplished by "perturbing" a declared input parameter, and using the laws associated with devices and interconnections to propagate effects through the system. For instance, suppose the input voltage increased. This will cause the base-emitter current to increase, which (due to the way transistors work) will cause the collector-emitter current to increase. This in turn will cause the collector voltage to drop, which will in turn cause the output voltage to go down.

This example has been deliberately simplified; detailed descriptions can easily be found in the literature (see [de Kleer and Brown, 1984; Williams, 1984]). However, it illustrates two important properties of this ontology. First, once a model is created, most inferential work occurs by local propagation within the model. Such antecedent reasoning is easy to control and can be made to work very efficiently. Second, we have assumed that *flow of informa-*

tion in the model of the system directly mirrors *flow of causality* in the world. The ramifications of this assumption are discussed in Section 4.1.7.

One additional complexity that bears mention is that devices can have *states*, corresponding to different modes of a device. For example, a valve may be OPEN, CLOSED, or PARTIALLY-OPEN. Each device state is characterized by a different set of laws (see Figure 11). The state of a device is invariably predicated on the (qualitative) value of a numerical parameter.

The device ontology has three advantages. First, the fixed network topology provides a substrate for efficient computations. All references within laws are strictly local, and hence resolving them is straightforward. This simplifies implementation. Second, composability is maintained by having all information transferred through local connections. Given a correct catalog of device models and interconnections, one could in principle model an arbitrarily complex system by connecting together the corresponding device models.

The third advantage is that system dynamics is a widely used traditional engineering methodology. Consequently, there are generally accepted standards for structural descriptions (i.e., schematics) and standard quantitative models for many domains which can be used as a starting point for creating qualitative models. The translation of such quantitative to qualitative models is not trivial, since new device states may have to be introduced (see [de Kleer and Brown, 1984] for details). However, most of the ontology can be inherited from system dynamics intact, thus simplifying the modeler's task and providing greater confidence in the result.

However, there are two serious disadvantages to this ontology. First, the device ontology provides no guidance for the construction of the network model itself. This is not a problem in some domains, such as electronics, where the mapping from objects and relationships in the world is straightforward. In manufacturing electronic components, great care is taken to ensure that the physical objects perform much like their idealizations, within reasonable limits. But for most domains this aspect of the modeling process is problematic.

Consider, for example, the block shown in Figure 12(a). If the block is sitting on a table and we push it, then we probably want to model it as an idealized mass. But if we push it while it is resting against a wall, then we will probably want to model it as an idealized spring (albeit very stiff). If we immerse the block in water and push on it, then we will probably model it as an idealized damper. Thus we see that the same physical object can be modeled by three distinct abstract devices, depending on the conditions in the system.

The advice given in system dynamics texts is to figure out how the object behaves, and then select the right device model. This advice is fine for human engineers, since their goal is to produce quantitative analyses and they presumably already have some idea of the system's qualitative behavior. But the goal of qualitative physics is to produce precisely those qualitative descriptions of behavior, and hence we are left in the position of needing the answer before

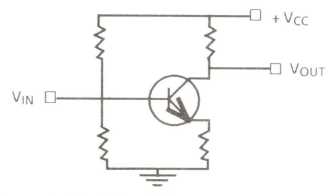

Figure 10 An example of the device ontology.

State	Condition		
OPEN:	$[A = A_{max}]$	$[P] = 0$	$\partial P = 0$
PARTIALLY-OPEN:	$[0 < A < A_{max}]$	$[P] = [Q]$	
CLOSED:	$[A = 0]$	$[Q] = 0$	$\partial Q = 0$

Figure 11 A device model for a valve. This simple model of a valve is drawn from *Confluences*. *A* refers to the area of the valve, relative to some maximum area A_{max}. *P* refers to the pressure across the valve, while *Q* refers to the flow rate of gas through the valve.

Acts like a mass   **Acts like a spring**   **Acts like a damper**

Figure 12 System dynamics doesn't capture modeling assumptions

we can compute it. Consequently, the standard device ontology fails to completely address the modeling problem, since it does not formalize the critical task of model creation.

The second disadvantage is that, in many cases, the device ontology is unnatural. Consider the situations in Figure 13. We can consider the water in the pot on the stove (Figure 13(a)) to be an object. If the water boils, this object will decrease in size until it vanishes. It is hard to think of this system as a collection of devices, since the reasoning requires "clipping" a device out of the network when the water vanishes. Such changes in the network topology lie outside the device formalism. Similarly, the bouncing ball in Figure 13(b) illustrates that what an object interacts with can change drastically. It is difficult to see any elegant representation for this system in the device ontology.

Figure 13 System dynamics cannot model many interesting systems.

4.1.6 *Processes* Informally, people often describe changes in the physical world in terms of *processes*. Examples include motion, liquid flow, heat flow, boiling, bending, compressing, and expanding. This notion has been formalized in qualitative physics as an ontological commitment. Consider a cup under a faucet. If the faucet is turned on, there will be a *process* of liquid flow occurring from the faucet, through the fluid path formed by the space above the cup, to the cup itself. This liquid flow is not a property of either the cup, the faucet, the water, or the space above the cup. It is a new type of entity, with properties of its own, such as the rate of water flow.

In this ontology, processes like liquid flow provide the notion of mechanism for physical situations. All changes, ultimately, are assumed to be caused directly or indirectly by physical processes. A model of a domain includes a description of the kinds of objects there are, the kinds of relationships that hold between them, and the kinds of processes that can occur. To describe a specific situation, models for each of the parts and relationships are asserted. Importantly, the modeler does not directly specify what processes are possible in each situation. Instead, the process specifications in the domain model state the conditions under which they can occur, and the inference system uses these specifications to automatically generate descriptions of the possible processes.

This notion of process was introduced by *qualitative process* (QP) theory [Forbus, 1981b, 1984b], and has been used in various forms by several researchers in qualitative physics, including Simmons [1983], Weld [1986], Mohammed and Simmons [1986], and Schmolze [1986]. Some of these theories describe the effects of processes continuously over time (such as QP theory), while others describe processes discretely by the net effect they have over an interval of time [Simmons, 1983; Weld, 1986]. (The earliest attempts to formalize physical processes in AI preceded qualitative physics. Hendrix [1973] described processes as STRIPS-like operators augmented with equations for use in planning. Brown, Burton, and Zdybel [1973] represented processes as finite-state automata, for instructional purposes. Neither representation used qualitative information, in the current technical sense of the term.)

Figure 14 illustrates a simple model of liquid flow expressed in QP theory. The *individuals* specification provides a form of quantification. An *instance* of a process is said to exist for every combination of objects in a scenario that matches the individual specifications. The *preconditions* and *quantity conditions* together determine when the process is active. Roughly, quantity conditions can be inequalities and whether or not other processes are active, and preconditions are external conditions. Aligned, for example, means that all valves in the path are open. A QP model can predict that pressures will change, but not that a sailor may walk by and close a valve.

The *relations* field describes what holds when the process is active. This field can declare local quantities and constraints, as well as information relevant to external representations (such as appearances). Here, the local quantity flow-rate is introduced and is declared to be equal to the difference in pressures. Together with preconditions, the relations field provides a means of interfacing QP theory to other representations.

The direct effects of a process are specified by the *influences* field. Every process must have at least one direct influence, and only processes can have direct influences. Direct influences, noted by *I+* and *I–*, specify the derivative of their first argument. Here, the amount of liquid in the source will tend to decrease, and the amount of liquid in the source will tend to increase. Like qualitative proportionalities, direct influences must be composed to compute the total derivative by making closed-world assumptions. But unlike qualitative proportionalities, where no commitment is made to the method of combination, direct influences are additive. So if we knew that in fact some other process were influencing the amount at the destination (an instance of liquid flow corresponding to a leak, say), then by knowing the relative flow rates we could predict how the amount of water in the destination will actually change. (This solves the problem with Hayes' leaky cup, mentioned earlier.)

The process ontology has several advantages. First, the notion of process is intuitively appealing for many domains. Objects can come into existence and vanish, for example, something that is not allowed in the device ontology. Second, processes provide a simple notion of causality by imposing a distinction between independent variables (those which are directly affected by processes) and dependent variables (those which are affected as a consequence of the independent variables changing). The next section examines this issue in detail.

The third advantage of the process ontology is that it allows explicit representation of modeling conditions and assumptions, via the individuals and preconditions fields. This means the program can take on more of the modeling burden. Instead of demanding a complete initial description, a program using the process ontology can "fill in" the user-supplied description of a particular situation with the kinds of processes that can occur. Potentially, this flexibility provides considerable power. For example, the *class-wide assumptions* described informally in [de Kleer and Brown, 1984] can be formally expressed by combinations of individuals and preconditions specifications in QP theory.

Of course, nothing comes for free—the process ontology also has some disadvantages. First, in some domains (like electronics) the distinction between dependent and independent parameters changes according to the kind of analysis being performed. Process descriptions are very hard to write for such cases. Second, the process ontology requires more inference, and the manipulation of quantified descriptions, to set up the model. This complicates the design of programs using the process ontology, and often results in longer run times. And third, the process ontology has not been formally explored as much as the device ontology. There is no process-oriented equivalent engineering formalism to system dynamics, no off-the-shelf models to adapt.

Process	Liquid-Flow(?src ?sub	?dst ?path)
	Individuals:	?src a container
		?dst a container
		?sub a substance
		?path a fluid-path,
		Connects(?path,?src,?dst)
	Preconditions:	Aligned(?path)
	Quantity Conditions:	A[Pressure(C-S(?sub,liquid,?src))]
		>A[Pressure(?dst)]
	Relations:	Quantity(flow-rate)
		flow-rate = Pressure(C-S(?sub,lqiuid,?src))
		-{ressire)?dst)
	Influences:	I+(Amount-of-in(?sub,liquid,?dst),A[flow-rate])
		I-(Amount-of-in(?sub,liquid,?src),A[flow-rate])

Figure 14 A description of liquid flow.

4.1.7 *Other Issues* A common misconception is that the different theories described in the literature are merely notational variants for "the" qualitative physics, or that eventually only one theory will be proven to be "right." Such a view ignores the rich variety of the phenomena we are trying to model (from the patchy, incomplete theories constructed on the fly by the person on the street to the integrated, broad theories formulated explicitly by world-class engineers and scientists) and the range of potential applications we are addressing (from student modeling in intelligent tutoring systems to monitoring process plants to scientific discovery).

As the earlier sections indicate, there are a variety of choices for representations of quantity, equation, and ontology. Different combinations of these choices correspond to different systems of qualitative physics. I claim the best way to view research in qualitative physics is to think of it as describing this space of possible theories and their properties. By understanding the alternatives and trade-offs, we can select the best combination of choices for particular purposes.

The next two issues apply this viewpoint to two controversial issues in the current state of the art: continuity and causality.

Continuity Continuity is a formal way of enforcing the intuition that things change smoothly. A simple consequence of continuity, respected by all systems of qualitative physics, is that, in changing, a quantity must pass through all intermediate values. That is, if $A < B$ at time t_1 then it cannot be the case that at some later time t_2 that $A > B$ holds, unless there was some time t_3 between t_1 and t_2 such that $A = B$.

This law has consequences for computing state transitions, since changing inequality relations (or just comparisons with zero, in the case of sign representations) herald state transitions. If $X > Y$ and $D[X] < D[Y]$, for instance, then the relation between X and Y could change to =. Similarly, if $X = Y$ and the same relationship held between their derivatives, then the relationship would change to <.

The details of computing state transitions are the same for all the existing theories, with one exception—how long these transitions will take. The second kind of transition, changes *from* equality, everyone agrees will occur in an instant. The first kind of transition, in every theory right now but QP, always takes an interval of time. In QP theory it takes an interval of time if the difference is finite, but only an instant if the difference is infinitesimal.

Invoking infinitesimals is an unusual step. The motivation is to capture the commonsense intuition that "if you kick something only for a moment, you can kick it back quickly," a kind of symmetry in duration. If you influence a quantity away from equality for only an instant, one should be able to push it back in an instant. In my first implementation of QP theory, GIZMO, this model caused cycles of behavior whose states only lasted for an instant (called *stut-*

ter). These cycles could then be merged into single states, expressing a changing equilibrium [Forbus, 1984b]. Unfortunately, in at least some of the examples studied the instant-instant transitions were violating continuity on derivatives, and a more accurate implementation (QPE) fails to show stutter. At this point it is not clear whether or not stutter will always be ruled out by such constraints,[4] and whether or not it will appear in "natural" models.

The more general question is, are infinitesimal models useful? Or should we simply adopt classical continuity universally? There are two arguments for continuing to pursue alternatives to classical continuity. The first is that infinitesimal models are proving their worth in other areas of qualitative physics (see Section 4.1.1 and [Weld, 1987]). The second is that classical continuity alone is inadequate to model the full range of phenomena in qualitative physics. Impulses, for instance, are part of every engineer's vocabulary. Yet they violate classical continuity, by allowing instantaneous transitions *to* equality. Other similar phenomena have been explored recently by Nishida and Doshita [1987]. Continuity, while significantly tamed through the efforts of a few hundred years of mathematics and physics, still has some unexplored territory.

Causality By any account, causality remains unruly, even after a long history of investigation. A recent public exchange between de Kleer and Brown and Iwasaki and Simon in the AI Journal unfortunately may have shed more heat than light on the matter. At the risk of unleashing yet more rhetoric, I will attempt to clarify the issues here.

The necessary framework to understand these issues appears in [Forbus and Gentner, 1986b], where Dedre Gentner and I analyze the various notions of causal reasoning about quantities used in qualitative physics. The goal of that analysis is to isolate some distinctions that may be useful in understanding human reasoning. Roughly, these distinctions are: the temporal aspects relating cause and effect (the *measurement scenario*), whether or not the ontology contains an explicit class of mechanisms or not, and whether or not the primitives for describing equations include presuppositions about the direction of effect (*directed* versus *non-directed primitives*). The second two factors will be the most relevant for this discussion.

We assume that some notion of *mechanism* underlies all causal reasoning (see [Forbus and Gentner, 1986a]). However, accounts differ in their construal of what mechanisms are. In *explicit-mechanism* theories, the notion of mechanism is tied to particular ontological classes. For example, in QP theory, processes are the mechanism; they are the source of all changes. In *implicit-mechanism* theories, such as de Kleer and Brown's confluence theory, the notion of mechanism arises from the interactions of the system's parts. They

---

4 Cycles of length 2 are forbidden, but longer sequences look plausible.

assume that flow of information in the model of the system directly mirrors "flow of causality" in the world. To see the differences, consider a liquid flow between two containers. In QP theory all changes would be caused by an instance of the `liquid-flow` process. In a confluence model the changes would arise from the interaction of the constitutive equations.

The difference between directed and non-directed primitives can be illustrated again by comparing QP theory and Confluence theory. The *influences* used in QP theory (and others) to represent equations are directed primitives. Influences include qualitative proportionalities and direct influences (`I+` and `I-`) needed to specify derivative relationships. We might represent the relationship between level and pressure in a contained liquid `WC` as:

$$\text{pressure(WC) } \alpha_{Q+} \text{ level(WC)}$$

indicating that a change in level could cause a change in pressure, but not the reverse. In Confluences (and others), the primitives are non-directed since they do not carry a presupposition of causality. Thus we might say

$$\text{pressure(WC) } = \text{ level(WC)}$$

but would be equally willing to say a change in pressure causes a change in level as the reverse. Notice that, at least in this case, there is a clear, intuitive direction.

Any causal analysis must determine which way the primitives in its representation are to be used. In theories with explicit mechanisms, what is an independent parameter is determined by what the mechanism directly affects. In QP theory, for instance, the *causal directedness hypothesis* [Forbus, 1984b] expresses causality:

> Changes in physical situations which are perceived as causal are due to our interpretation of them as corresponding either to direct changes caused by processes or propagation of those direct effects through functional dependencies.

A process directly affects something by supplying its derivative. (Since it can supply a derivative of 0, the same notion suffices to impose causality on static situations.)

By contrast, in theories with implicit mechanisms, some other means of specifying independent parameters must be found. For example, the confluence model critically relies on an input perturbation for causal analysis. The choice of input parameter provides significant constraint on the direction of propagation (which is interpreted as the direction of causation) in the system. This constraint is not quite sufficient, since it is necessary to annotate some parameters as independent, to prevent inappropriate causal deductions ([de Kleer and Brown, 1984], page 73).

Now we are in a position to understand the *causal ordering* proposal of Iwasaki and Simon [1986]: They propose to use directed primitives, similar to qualitative proportionalities, but without associating a sign of effect (i.e., α_Q , but not α_{Q+} or α_{Q-}). The exogenous variables of the system are used as the independent variables. Given these independent parameters, the technique of causal ordering will produce a graph of dependencies by manipulating the quantitative equations describing the system. To get the direction of change imposed by each connection, they propose to use the method of *comparative statics*, which uses quantitative information to produce a sensitivity analysis. The end result will be much the same as the graph of influences that holds for the corresponding situation in a QP model. The possibility of incorrect causal arguments seems to be avoided by detecting when the system of equations is underdetermined: It is exactly in such cases that an assumption must be made, and an external knowledge source (such as the user) can determine which assumption will lead to correct arguments.

Whether or not causal ordering is useful in analyzing a particular example depends on the availability of two things: a set of quantitative equations and knowledge about which variables are exogenous. For many circumstances equations are available, but for many simple circumstances (such as boiling) they aren't. Often the available equations are too complicated to use: A high-accuracy differential equation model of a coal-fired power plant, for instance, can be dozens of pages long. Basing the notion of causal independence on exogenous parameters limits causal ordering to creating models of specific systems in specific modes of behavior. The limitation to specific systems comes from the fact that what is exogenous often changes when a system becomes part of a larger system. Thus we cannot carry our analysis of, say, a heat exchanger, intact to the analysis of a larger system including it. The limitation to specific modes of behavior comes from the fact that the equations describing a system or object can change drastically (phase changes in fluids and turbulent versus non-turbulent flow are two examples).

While causal ordering satisfies several intuitions about commonsense reasoning, it also violates two others. First, since it requires quantitative equations, it cannot explain how commonsense physics comes about—after all, people reason causally about quantities long before they can do symbolic algebra. Second, it also does not assign causality in feedback systems ("a chicken and egg problem," [Iwasaki and Simon, 1986]), although such descriptions are common in informal descriptions of how systems work.[5]

---

5 There is no obvious reason why it couldn't; in classical simulation paradigms such "loops" in the equations are broken by delay elements (i.e., integration operators), and similar techniques can be used in qualitative equations (e.g., the QP theory notion of direct influence).

I believe that, while the techniques Iwasaki and Simon describe seem to have only limited usefulness as simulation tools, they could be quite valuable in the context of knowledge acquisition. Consider the problem of acquiring knowledge from textbooks. Two kinds of knowledge must be encoded. The formal aspects, the equations, must be transformed into qualitative laws. The informal aspects, the contents of the text, must be transformed into the organizational structure (typically ontological) that tells when these laws are appropriate and useful. Causal ordering and comparative statics may be useful techniques in translating the explicit, formal knowledge of a domain. By combining these techniques with a system that can induce representations for the implicit knowledge, we might be able to develop tools to semiautomatically acquire qualitative models by interacting with human experts.

4.2 *Qualitative Kinematics*

There has been significant progress in qualitative dynamics. Several representations for ontology, number, and equations have been explored, a number of successful programs developed to test these ideas, and there are high expectations of future progress. Unfortunately, the same cannot be said for qualitative kinematics. This section explores why, and describes some progress made since the original survey talk upon which this essay is based.

To begin with, we must refine what we mean by qualitative kinematics. We exclude problems like navigation, manipulator-level planning, and layout design simply because they overlap to a greater degree with robotics and engineering problem solving than with qualitative physics per se. By qualitative kinematics I mean the spatial reasoning aspects of qualitative physics. Examples include reasoning about motion, the geometry of fluid flow, the shape of charge distributions, and so forth. Most efforts have focused on the simplest of these, reasoning about motion. And recently, significant progress has been made on reasoning about *mechanisms*, in the classical sense—gears, transmissions, mechanical clocks, and the like.

I mentioned before that the dividing line between "prehistory" and the present in qualitative physics lay in the decision to explore purely qualitative representations. This tactic was reasonably successful in qualitative dynamics. I claim this hasn't happened in spatial reasoning because it cannot be done. We conjecture that there is no purely qualitative kinematics (the *poverty conjecture* [Forbus et al., 1987]).

This idea takes some explaining. Consider FROB. It did some fairly sophisticated spatial reasoning, including understanding collisions and the notion of being trapped in gravity wells. But to arrive at this understanding took a metric diagram, which contained a significant amount of quantitative information.

Thus FROB itself is not purely qualitative.[6] But in fact purely qualitative representations suffice for a surprising number of inferences about dynamics. Sadly, it just doesn't seem to be the case for qualitative kinematics.

The poverty conjecture is based on three arguments. First, no one to date has developed a purely qualitative kinematics. For example, I've spent years trying to develop one, and I've talked to a number of other people who have as well, with little success.

Naturally, this is a weak argument. Negation by failure is rarely safe scientifically, and part of my motivation for making this conjecture is the hope that someone will succeed in proving me wrong! But the second argument makes me skeptical. Much of the power of qualitative dynamics comes about from partial orders. Time, as Allen [1984] showed, can be nicely modeled in terms of temporal relations where transitivity provides significant constraint. Inequalities, while individually weak descriptions, combine via transitivity to yield often powerful conclusions. But these are both one-dimensional problems. There is a result in dimension theory which states that partial orders don't work for higher dimensions. Try it yourself: Create a vocabulary of spatial relationships between 2D figures like Allen's relationships for time, such as EQUAL, INSIDE, ABUT, OVERLAP, and so forth. You'll find the only entries in a transitivity table for such relationships that provide significant constraint are those which impose a partial order (in this case, EQUAL and INSIDE). With the others (e.g., ABUT, OVERLAP), just about anything is possible.

While stronger, this second argument still does not clinch the matter. After all, there might be some other powerful idea, some new formalism that will provide the "right" quantization for shape and space independent of an initial quantitative description.[7] But the third argument is that we have no reason to think that such a formalism necessarily exists, because people appear to perform poorly at spatial reasoning without the "moral equivalent" of a diagram. There is a large literature on the psychology of visual imagery, and while it must be interpreted with care, it seems to indicate that some kind of quantitative information plays an important role in human spatial reasoning. In addition to imagery, people resort to sketches, models, looking at the object itself, and so forth—in short, we harness our perceptual apparatus in service of spatial reasoning.

This apparent reliance on perceptual apparatus motivated FROB's metric diagram, and we believe that this model can be extended productively into a general model for qualitative kinematics (the *MD/PV model* [Forbus et al.,

6 If quantitative dynamics worked that way, there would be no qualitative simulators per se. Instead, we would always have to provide numerical simulation routines and lots of numerical parameters to get any predictions. (Or use symbolic algebra—as mentioned earlier, not every symbolic description is qualitative, and this is a good example.)

7 As shown previously, useful qualitative descriptions for space can be *computed* from quantitative ones—but the goal in this argument is to avoid using a metric diagram altogether.

1987]). By this account, spatial reasoning requires at least two representations. The first is a metric diagram, which includes quantitative information and can answer geometric questions by some form of calculation or measurement. The metric diagram attempts to describe the functionality of the visual system in human spatial reasoning. One operation that can be done with a metric diagram is computing a *place vocabulary*, which quantizes space by some relevance criteria. Figure 15 shows how this model was instantiated in FROB.

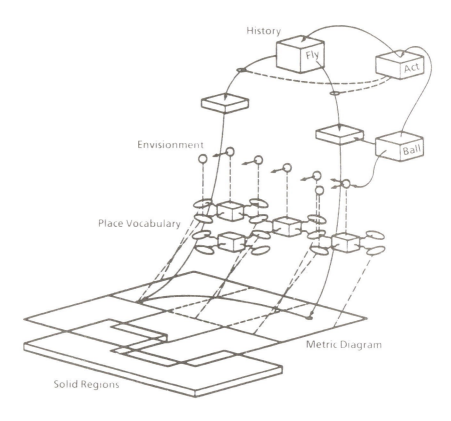

Figure 15 FROB illustrated the MD/PV model of spatial reasoning. This picture illustrates what is "under the hood" in FROB. The metric diagram provides a means of communicating with the user, a means of answering quantitative spatial queries, and a substrate for computing a qualitative description of space. The first step in computing this place vocabulary is to ascertain the *solid regions*, where free space isn't. Next, it breaks up the free space into regions, in a way that simplifies the description of possible motions. These regions plus symbolic descriptions of their connectivity form FROB's place vocabulary.

It seems that all spatial reasoning projects to date fit the MD/PV model fairly well. For example, the (earlier) natural language understanding program by Waltz and Boggess [1979] used a metric diagram in constructing models of sentences like "A fly is on the table." Geoff Hinton [1979] developed an elegant theory of imagery that used a mixture of propositional and numerical representations to explain phenomena that simpler theories based on array representations cannot explain. In reasoning about geological processes, Simmons [1983] compared quantitative calculations with a diagram to check the correctness of qualitatively plausible histories. Stanfill [1983] used symbolic descriptions with numerical parameters to reason about simple pistons and bearings. Davis [1987] argues that purely qualitative representations are "too weak" to support reasoning about motion involving solid objects.

4.2.1 *Reasoning About Mechanisms*

There has been renewed interest in spatial reasoning recently, particularly in understanding mechanisms. Gelsey [1987] uses a constructive solid geometry CAD description as his metric diagram, and computes motion envelopes to recognize kinematic pairs. The place vocabulary in his system consists of regions that involve interactions between parts. Joskowicz [1987] has proposed to analyze single interactions in a mechanism by recognition, describing kinematic pairs by patterns in configuration space. (Configuration space was first used in robotics for motion planning problems, see [Lozano-Perez, 1983]).

In our own CLOCK project, Faltings [1986, 1987a, 1987b] has developed a general theory of place vocabularies for mechanisms. Faltings observes that the important distinctions for quantizing shape must come from *pairs* of objects, rather than objects in isolation, since it is their interaction that determines whether or not a pair of objects will move together or bind. In mechanisms, each part has only one degree of freedom, so a configuration space for a pair of objects is two-dimensional. The place vocabulary for an entire mechanism (such as a clock) is the combination of the place vocabularies for the pairs of parts. Faltings also observes that symbolic algebra can be used to parameterize place vocabularies, thus increasing the potential for their use in mechanical design. Faltings's theory has been tested by an implementation on a wide range of examples, including gears, ratchets, escapements, and the complete set of kinematic pairs for a mechanical clock [Faltings, 1987b].

Of course, Faltings's theory only solves half of the problem: It describes what contact relationships are possible, and what might be reached if movement occurs in a particular direction. To integrate this information with a qualitative dynamics requires imposing reference frames in order to describe forces and motions. Nielsen, in his part of the CLOCK project, has developed a theory of qualitative vectors and reference frames. Such vectors are used for representing contact directions, forces, velocities, and other parameters. He has used these techniques in a qualitative theory of rigid-body statics [Nielsen, 1987], which can determine what directions an object is free to move in as well as what movement will occur. This theory has been implemented and has successfully answered questions about the stability of Blocks World structures, in addition to gears and escapements.

4.3 *Styles of Reasoning*

The purpose of representation is reasoning. This section describes some of the styles of reasoning that have been explored in qualitative physics to date. Because there has been confusion about the relationship between envisioning and other forms of qualitative simulation, this issue is discussed in detail. I will ignore diagnosis, since an adequate treatment is well beyond the scope of this survey.

4.3.1 *Qualitative Simulation*   The result of a standard numerical simulation is a list of state vectors, each vector representing the system being simulated at some particular Δt. Qualitative simulations differ from numerical simulations in two respects. First, time is individuated by the occurrence of interesting events, rather than some regular, fixed increment. Second, the reduced precision of qualitative representations often requires branching to represent alternate possible futures.

It is important to note that some qualitative simulators do not produce specific histories at all! This is a subtle point that is often misunderstood. A history describes a specific behavior of an object. While a history is (at least potentially) infinite, it typically consists of only a finite number of distinguishable episodes. Referring back to Section 4.1.1, we say that two episodes are distinguishable exactly when they differ in some limit point (i.e., temporally generic landmark). The implication is that each episode can be described as an occurrence of one of a finite set of abstract *qualitative states*. This assumes there are a finite number of properties, and a finite number of values for each property, and hence only a finite number of combinations of these properties. Similarly, for any finite collection of objects we can define qualitative states that describe consistent collections of every possible distinguishable episode for each object.

Qualitative states can be defined without recourse to histories. In fact, the notion of qualitative state was developed earlier than histories, as Section 3 indicates. The graph formed by the collection of all qualitative states of a system and the transitions between them is called an *envisionment*. The notion of envisionment is due to de Kleer [1975]. The process of constructing an envisionment, *envisioning*, was the first method of qualitative simulation. Roughly, each history corresponds to some path through the envisionment, but the converse is not true, as we will see shortly.

A further distinction between envisioners is whether they start from a given initial state or from all possible states. The former are said to produce *attainable* envisionments, the latter *total* envisionments. Total envisionments are usually larger than attainable envisionments, but are more useful for certain tasks. A number of envisioners of each type have been built for different theories. NEWTON [de Kleer, 1975] and FROB [Forbus, 1980] both produced attainable envisionments for different kinds of motion problems. QUAL [de Kleer, 1979b] produced attainable envisionments for electronics, while ENVISION produced total envisionments for system-dynamics-like models (see Section 4.1.5) For qualitative process (QP) theory, GIZMO [Forbus, 1984c] produced attainable envisionments, while QPE [Forbus, 1988] produces total envisionments.

Several programs produce histories directly. FROB, for instance, used a constraint-based numerical simulation to generate histories. In several important applications, histories are specified as part of the description of a problem, as in integrated circuit fabrication [Mohammed and Simmons, 1986] or hypothesized on the basis of other knowledge [Simmons, 1983]. Kuipers's QSIM system, of course, generates histories directly.

4.3.2 *Envisioning Versus History Generation*

The relationship between envisionments and histories is more subtle than first suspected, and is still being explored. Some aspects are clear; for instance, I've defined a *logic of occurrence* [Forbus, 1987a] that specifies how a history may be related to an envisionment so that general behavioral constraints (such as assuming classes of behavior must or may not occur) can be enforced. Sometimes there have been simple terminological confusions, such as de Kleer and Brown [1984] calling their qualitative states "episodes," Kuipers [1986] calling his account of history generation a "deeper semantics" for envisioning, or Collins and Forbus [1987] calling their MC envisioning a history. Other aspects, however, are genuinely problematic and have become fertile areas of research.

In a correct envisionment, every possible history can be expressed as a path. Various properties of the graph correspond to important behavioral distinctions. For example, states with no transitions from them represent final states for the system, and cycles correspond to oscillations.

Originally, de Kleer [de Kleer and Brown, 1984; de Kleer, 1984a] claimed that, just as every history corresponds to a path through the envisionment, so every path through the envisionment must correspond to a physically realizable history. Kuipers [1986] shows this is incorrect. The counterexample he uses is shown in Figure 16 (this envisionment was generated with QPE [Forbus, 1988]). The parameter Z is a function of position, and should be compared with Z', but is otherwise unconstrained. By declaring the comparison between

Z and Z' as interesting, we will cause a state transition to occur whenever the relationship between them changes. There are other transitions that will occur due to the way motion and acceleration are modeled (see [Forbus, 1984c] for details).

To generate a history from an envisionment, begin by selecting a start state. That state forms what occurs at the first episode in the history, the duration of the episode being the duration of the corresponding qualitative state (i.e., either an interval or instant). If there are no transitions from the chosen state, then that episode is the end of the history. If there are, select one of the transitions as representing what actually occurs. Then continue as before, starting from the state resulting from the transition.

Carrying out this procedure on the envisionment of Figure 16 reveals a variety of possible histories. For example, the sequence of states S_1, S_4, S_7, S_{10}, S_{13}, S_{16}, S_{19}, S_{22} corresponds to a legal history, as does S_3, S_6, S_9, S_{12}, S_{15}, S_{18}, S_{21}, S_{24}. Other legal histories correspond to variations of these where Z changes in its relationship to Z' within the range of variation for X. For example, the sequence S_3, S_6, S_8, S_{10}, S_{13}, S_{16}, S_{20}, S_{24} corresponds to the case where Z equals Z' when X equals zero.

All of the histories mentioned so far are legitimate. But consider again the transitions from, say, S_6. Each time around the cycle, one of these transitions must be chosen. In the algorithm specified, which corresponds to the original de Kleer claim, each such choice is independent. Thus we are free to choose another transition the next time we reach S_6, which will give us an illegitimate history. The problem can arise even on a single cycle; the sequence S_3, S_6, S_8, S_{10}, S_{13}, S_{16}, S_{17}, S_{18}, S_{21}, S_{24} is inconsistent because the S_6, S_8, S_{10} subsequence assumes $Z = Z'$ when $X = $ ZERO, while the S_{16}, S_{17}, S_{18}, S_{21} is based on the assumption that Z reaches Z'D before X reaches ZERO. The choices are not in fact independent, and treating them as such can lead to incorrect predictions.

In this simple case, the solution seems clear: Each choice of transition implies additional information about the functional relationship between X and Z. For example, assuming that the transition from S_6 to S_8 occurs "fixes" a point on the (implicit) graph defining their relationship: in particular, $Z = Z'$ when X = ZERO. (Assuming that one of the other transitions occurs requires introducing a new constant related either to X or to Z, but the principle is the same.) These constraints must then be respected in successive choices. For example, choosing the transition from S_{12} to S_{11} forces the later transition of S_{16} to S_{17}. However, it is not straightforward to generalize this technique to all situations.

To summarize: With no information, we can get incorrect predictions. If we had a fully specified correct quantitative model, there would be no ambiguity and hence we would always get correct histories. The open research question right now is, just how much information, and in what form, suffices to generate histories correctly from envisionments?

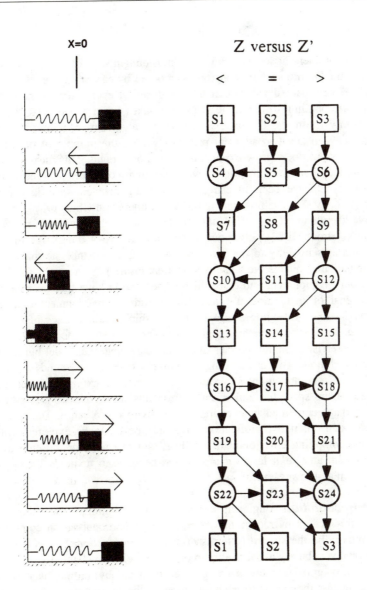

Figure 16 Generating histories from envisionments can be difficult. An envisionment for a modified spring-block oscillator is shown below. The modification consists of an extra parameter Z, which is a function of X and is compared with an arbitrary constant Z'. Each row is labelled with a picture indicating the general position and velocity of the block in the states of that row. Each column indicates the relationship Z has with Z' in those states. Arrows denote locally consistent transitions between states. Circles indicate states that last over an interval, while squares indicate states lasting only for an instant.

This problem arises even without envisionments; direct history generation must also take into account constraints imposed by earlier choices. In QSIM, for example, new named values can be introduced at every step of the computation, corresponding to the value a quantity takes on in a particular episode of the history (more on this below). Since the algorithm can introduce a new value between any two adjacent previous values, the number of possible episodes can (and does) grow exponentially without bound. This means that QSIM also produces incorrect histories. Several pruning techniques to weed out incorrect histories have been investigated, including problem-specific constraints [Lee et al., 1987], algebraic manipulation [Kuipers and Chiu, 1987], and quantitative knowledge [Chiu, 1987], but so far these results have been mixed. (For instance, Struss [1987] points out several limitations of qualitative mathematics, such as sensitivity to the form of equations, which indicate that algebraic manipulation of qualitative equations is often unsafe.)

Both envisionment and direct history generation have their role to play in the arsenal of qualitative physics. The notion of envisionment is a superb theoretical tool, providing a simple way to think about classes of behaviors. Envisioning is a good methodological tool for qualitative model development, since it exercises domain theories in obscure cases that the model builder might otherwise ignore. But envisioning is unlikely to be the desired solution for quick on-line computation: After all, it corresponds to explicitly generating the entire problem space for some class of problems! In such cases history generation, perhaps combined with heuristics, seems to make sense. The space/time trade-offs in qualitative simulation have only begun to be explored. One can imagine compiling envisionments "offline," for example, or the envisionment of a system at a high level of abstraction being used to guide direct history generation at a lower level.

4.3.3 *Recognition* Engineers are good at explaining how things work. Often, this occurs by recognition "Oh, it's a proportional-action controller"— they redescribe the system in terms drawn from a *functional vocabulary*. This functional vocabulary appears to help organize their knowledge for several purposes. In diagnosis, symptoms might be computed by comparing current behavior against the standard behavior stored with the functional description. In design, a functional vocabulary provides an intermediate goal that constrains the search space. The designer might decide what combination of functional blocks would achieve her purpose, and then figure out how to implement this functionality with the available components. Capturing this ability to map from *structure* to *function* was an early focus of qualitative physics.

The most successful work in this area is still that of de Kleer [1979b, 1984a], who originally pointed out the problem as well. His theory is that to perform recognition, engineers first figure out how the system behaves, and then use that description of behavior to "retrieve" into a functional vocabulary.

A transistor circuit that behaves in a particular manner, for instance, might be recognizable to an engineer as a "common-emitter amplifier." One elegant aspect of de Kleer's work was how he constrained the result of qualitative simulation. The simulation proceeded by determining how the system would respond to "poking" its input. He noted that any sensible engineer wouldn't include parts that didn't help the circuit perform its function. Thus, any interpretation of the circuit's behavior that did not include every component could be ruled out on *teleological* grounds. In almost all of the electronic circuits he examined, this principle sufficed to rule out all but one interpretation.

While this work was one of the early successes of qualitative physics, little has been done by way of follow-up. What is needed is the formalization of rich functional vocabularies, and this problem has received little attention. Recent work by Chandreskaran [Sembugamoorthy and Chandrasekaran, 1984] and Doyle [1986] can be viewed in this light.

4.3.4 *Measurement Interpretation* Ideally, we would like our programs to gather their own data about the world. A program that works in a power plant, for instance, should have the ability to "read the gauges" to find out what is happening inside the plant. This is the problem of *measurement interpretation*. My ATMI theory [Forbus, 1986a, 1987c] describes how to interpret measurements taken over a span of time in terms of qualitative states. This theory is very general, requiring only domain-specific procedures for performing an initial signal/symbol translation and that an envisionment (potentially) exists. An implementation has been demonstrated that works on multiple ontologies (i.e., both QP models and FROB models). However, at this writing it has only been tested on simulated data without gaps, and does not specify control strategies for handling noisy data.

Yet a different kind of measurement interpretation was studied by Simmons in the GORDIUS program [Simmons, 1983]. The specific problem he addressed was evaluating whether or not a hypothesized sequence of geological events could account for the strata at a particular place. Knowing how the sequence came about is important economically, since some sequences will result in oil as a byproduct and others won't. A map built up out of well measurements represents the final state of this behavior. The program accumulated constraints on the size and shapes of maps that could result from the proposed history, and checked the actual map to see if it was consistent with these constraints.

5 The Frontier

The previous sections examined where qualitative physics came from, and where it is now. I have tried to paint a coherent picture of the state of the art, indicating the alternatives that have been explored and where substantial progress has been made. But no survey is complete without looking at the boundaries: areas which right now are relatively unexplored, and are thus fertile ground for new investigations.

5.1 *The Near Future*

I'll begin by describing some areas that are likely to see rapid progress. It would surprise me to not see significant advances in these areas in the next three years or so.

5.1.1 *Improved Domain Models*

A central activity of qualitative physics is developing a variety of models for physical phenomena and engineered systems. However, building good domain models is very difficult, and even with good tools takes much longer than one would expect. Nevertheless, the next few years should see significant advances in the kinds of physical phenomena that we can represent. For example, initial forays into reasoning about granularity and composition [Bunt 1985; Schmolze, 1986; Raulefs, 1987] may provide tools for reasoning about nonrigid objects. I suspect that progress in modeling powders and clays will require developing more sophisticated geometric representations to describe deformations, sheer, stress planes, and the other constructs of materials science. In modeling fluids, we still do not have a good theory of mixtures that describes exactly how different stuffs affect each other inside a container. An especially fertile ground is chemistry, which is interesting both industrially and intellectually, since it requires integrating discrete structures and geometry with reasoning about continuous systems.

5.1.2 *Implementations*

I expect that implementations will steadily improve in performance and storage economy—we haven't been building qualitative simulators for very long, after all, and are still discovering the right techniques. This trend, combined with the rising tide of improvements in computer technology, suggests that the range of problems we can tackle will continue to expand.

As we understand styles of reasoning better, the kinds of programs used in qualitative physics will become more diverse as well. Problems like design, for instance, require a detailed accounting of how different properties of the components and their interconnections relate to properties of the behavior produced. Keeping track of these justifications, especially in the presence of feedback, is a difficult problem. Williams's [1986] temporal constraint propagator TCP is the first system that does this correctly. Widespread application of these techniques should improve the sophistication possible in qualitative analyses.

One of the advantages of envisioning is that it postpones worrying about control issues. Alas, such issues cannot be put off forever. Solving problems by explicitly generating the entire search space simply is not a viable long-range alternative. Notice that history generation, per se, is not the answer— these approaches are already plagued with control problems, since they can lead to infinite descriptions of behavior. (In fact, a resource limit is often imposed for control purposes.) An attractive alternative is to generate generic qualitative states by heuristic search, applying the standard AI techniques to minimize effort. This subset of the envisionment can then be used as a framework for constrained generation of temporally specific landmarks, if needed.

Of course, this is just one alternative. Another idea is to decompose a complex system (such as a power plant) into a collection of semi-independent pieces, produce envisionments for each of the pieces, and glue them together as needed to provide a description of the whole plant. A few theoretical ideas have been proposed for such decompositions (e.g., the notion of *p-component* in [Forbus, 1984b]), but the bulk of the work remains to be done.

Another control issue that must be faced concerns domain models which are potentially infinite. Consider this simple model: An object consists of a set of parts, each of which is itself an object. This simple recursive structure will kill every existing qualitative simulator in which it can be stated (it cannot even be stated in most), and hence such models have been avoided. However, such descriptions are sufficiently useful that techniques for controlling their instantiation should be explored.

5.1.3 *Ontological Shifts*   It is unlikely that we have exhausted the space of ontological choices. Furthermore, not much is known about the relationship between various ontologies. For example, aside from a few rules of thumb, we cannot precisely characterize when to use a device-centered ontology instead of a process-centered ontology.

In examining human reasoning, it seems ontological shifts occur in the course of solving a single problem. Recall the SWOS problem from Section 2.2. Most people implicitly use two distinct ways of looking at fluids to solve this problem. To establish directions of flow and the fact of boiling required looking at "the stuffs" in different parts of the system—the water in the boiler is turning into steam, the lower pressure in the load means there will be a flow of steam from the boiler through the superheater, and so on. To figure out how the temperature actually changed, however, required thinking of a little piece of stuff travelling through the system.

Early on, Hayes [1985] identified these ideas as the *contained liquid* ontology and *piece of stuff* ontology, respectively. Most qualitative physics work has used the contained liquid ontology. Recently John Collins and I developed a specialization of the piece of stuff ontology, the *molecular collection* ontology, to capture the kind of reasoning engineers do about thermodynamic cycles. The idea is to define a little piece of stuff, MC, which is large enough to have macroscopic properties yet small enough never to split up when traversing a fluid system.

How is an MC envisionment generated? Since qualitative representations are not detailed enough to provide local gradients, what MC does is computed from an envisionment generated using a contained stuff ontology. We suspect this is exactly the kind of ontological shift occurring in examples like the SWOS problem.[8]

Even considering fluids, many ontological questions remain open. For example, what other specializations of Hayes' piece of stuff ontology are useful? Spatially extended pieces of stuff appear essential to modeling mixing and weather patterns—how are they to be individuated and combined? I am sure that as we attempt to build more sophisticated domain models, we will uncover many new ontological issues, many of them revolving around spatial reasoning.

5.1.4 *Hypothesizer*

One particularly interesting potential application is a kind of monitoring task, using a module I call a hypothesizer.[9] The goal is to merge measurement interpretation with explanation in order to improve plant operations and fault management.

Suppose you have someone controlling a large, complicated system, such as a production line in a chemical plant, and some condition arises that must be dealt with. Operators in such circumstances will often seize upon the first theory they generate about what is going on, and stick with it even in the face of contradictory data. Imagine a program that could critique an operator's theory. Such a program, if done properly, could have two benefits. First, it would force the operator to be explicit about his theory of what is wrong. Second, the program could compare the consequences of the theory with measurements, point out discrepancies, and suggest further experiments and modifications. Besides being used for diagnosis, it would not surprise me if this kind of module became one of the first applications of qualitative physics. Providing human-understandable explanations is the forte of qualitative physics, after all.

5.1.5 *Planning*

Realistic planning requires knowing what the physical world will do, with and without the planner's actions. How can we best use qualitative physics in planning?

One way is to transform the domain model into something the planner can use. Hogge's *domain compiler* [Hogge 1987a, 1987b] takes as input a QP domain model, and produces rules suitable for a temporal planner. (The planner derives from [Allen and Koomen, 1983], adding inference rules and other extensions—see [Hogge, 1987c] for details.) Given a description of liquid

---

8 Techniques for comparative analysis in [Weld, 1987] provide another piece of the puzzle. It is not known at this writing if together these techniques are sufficient to solve the SWOS problem.

9 Mike Williams of IntelliCorp calls it a "Doubting Thomas" system.

flow, for instance, the domain compiler produces an inference rule describing what it takes to cause a liquid flow to happen. When these rules are added to other inference rules and a specification of the actions an agent may take, the planner can create plans which involve processes as intermediaries, such as filling a kettle by moving it under a faucet and turning it on.

While elegant, this approach requires more research to live up to its promise. The large descriptions produced by the domain compiler, and the complex inferences required (especially transitivity), tend to choke the temporal planner. Compiling can also produce oversimplified models. For instance, the rules implicitly assume that any influence they impose on a quantity will actually succeed in changing that quantity. Thus a planner using these rules might assume that it can prevent an ocean liner from sinking by bailing with a teaspoon. Such limitations do not appear impossible to overcome, and no doubt there are other valuable approaches to be explored as well.

There is also a second kind of planning problem that I think ultimately is going to be extremely important, yet has received little attention to date—the problem of *procedure generation.* When you design a new engineering system, you don't just design the object, you have to develop procedures for operating it, for maintaining it, for diagnosing problems with it. If we are trying to get our computers to help us design complex systems, we need to find ways to have them generate such procedures automatically. If the design system knew the kinds of actions the system operators can take and their limitations, its output could include not just the blueprint, but the operations manual, the maintenance manual, and the diagnosis manual (or expert systems that provided the same service). Furthermore, safe operation could be posted as an explicit constraint on the design of the plant.

5.1.6 *Connections with Traditional Physics*   Understanding the kind of reasoning scientists and engineers do was the original motivation for qualitative physics. To fully capture what they are doing, we must extend qualitative physics in the direction of traditional physics. This section describes two exciting recent efforts in this area.

In traditional physics, a set of equations can be solved analytically or by simulation to derive the behavior of a system. Similarly, qualitative equations are typically derived from an ontology in order to generate behavior via qualitative simulation (either envisioning or history generation, see above). Sacks [1985] has developed an analytic technique that generates qualitative descriptions from traditional equations. His initial QMR system could solve a variety of systems, including models of a dampened oscillator and heat dissipation. One limitation of this approach is that most interesting equations do not have analytic solutions. Sacks's [1987] solution is to decompose more complex systems into piecewise linear approximations, use QMR on each piece, and reconstruct the global solution from the local solutions.

Yip [1987] has a complementary approach to a similar problem. *Phase portraits* are a geometric technique traditionally used in mathematics to describe complex dynamics. Yip has created a vocabulary of qualitative descriptions of phase space that formalizes the intuitions mathematicians bring to bear in understanding such portraits. Given a numerical simulation of a non-linear system, he uses this vocabulary to interpret the particular behavior, and make predictions about what the other parts of phase space must be like. Ultimately, these predictions will form the basis of additional numerical experiments.

Williams [1988] has developed an elegant formalism that combines qualitative and quantitative algebra. Potentially, this theory could greatly extend the range of qualitative reasoning.

5.1.7 *Learning*   Creating a complete qualitative physics is a herculean task; it will become much easier if our machines can help. Several workers are tackling different aspects of this problem. Langley, Simon, Bradshaw, and Zytkow [1987] have studied various aspects of scientific discovery of physical laws. So far, their work has focused on equational and discrete symbolic (as opposed to qualitative) models. Kokar [1987] describes a methodology for determining limit points using dimensional analysis. Falkenhainer's ABACUS [Falkenhainer, 1985] program uses qualitative proportionalities as an intermediate representation in inducing equations from numerical data. Mozetic [1987] describes how hierarchy can be exploited in automatically acquiring qualitative models, demonstrating his techniques with a model of the heart. Rajamoney and De-Jong [1987] have tackled the problem of debugging qualitative theories, providing a theoretical classification of bug types, including strategies for detecting and fixing them.

At Illinois we are taking two different approaches to understanding learning in physical domains. The first is psychological; Dedre Gentner and I are combining QP theory and her Structure-Mapping theory of analogy [Gentner, 1983, 1987, 1988] in an attempt to account for experiential learning in physical domains [Forbus and Gentner, 1986a]. We suspect the kinds of representation and reasoning explored by qualitative physics to date actually appear rather late in human learning, with two other stages postulated for both computational reasons and to explain certain psychological findings. Right now we are exploring these ideas through both cognitive simulation (using SME, a cognitive simulation of Gentner's analogy theory [Falkenhainer et al., 1986, 1988]) and psychological experiments.

The other approach, the Automated Physicist project, is being carried out in collaboration with Jerry DeJong. The idea is to build a series of machine learning systems that learn by experimentation and observation and by solving textbook problems. The dream behind the AP project is to build a sort of "Sherlock Holmes" of physics—it it begins by sitting back in its armchair and trying to explain reported behavior in the physical world. If it can explain a report no learning takes place. But if it cannot, then it tries to fix its model. Our ultimate goal is to have a program which designs and builds its own experimental apparatus, analyzes real data, and so forth.

The first such programs are due to Falkenhainer and Rajamoney. Falkenhainer's PHINEAS program has demonstrated how QP models can be learned with his theory of *verification-based analogical learning* [Falkenhainer, 1987]. Given a new behavior, PHINEAS attempts to use its current domain model to explain the behavior. If it cannot, PHINEAS accesses a database of previously observed behaviors with associated explanations. An important aspect of PHINEAS is that it performs analogical matching on the *behaviors* first, to guide the transfer of a QP model from an understood domain to explain the new one. The new model is tested to see if it can explain the observations. Often, the model has to be "fixed up" in various ways. Rajamoney's ADEPT system provides exactly the right functionality, since it has the ability to generate potential improvements and the conceptual specifications of experiments required to decide between them. The two programs have been successfully linked and tested on several examples [Falkenhainer and Rajamoney, 1988].

5.2 *Open Problems*

I would like to finish with a set of open problems. While we will make significant progress on these problems in the near term, they are sufficiently deep and tough not to yield to short assaults. I suspect each of them will take a few generations of Ph.D. theses to solve.

5.2.1 *Spatial Quantities*
There are no doubt other representations lying between the poverty of signs and the richness of $\Re$ that remain to be discovered. And no doubt there will be advances in qualitative representations for time-varying differential equations as well. But the real frontier is now partial differential equations, especially quantities that vary by space instead of time. Formalizing these *spatial quantities* will allow us to describe a vastly wider range of phenomena than at present. These phenomena include the flow over an airplane wing, the distribution of electric fields due to a distribution of charges, and the stresses on different parts of a bridge.

I suspect the problem decomposes into two parts. The first is the formalization of partial derivatives in general. While this part may have many technical obstacles, it seems likely that the current theories can be gracefully extended in this direction. The second problem appears to me to be much harder: the problem of choosing the appropriate axes and frames of reference to simplify computations and produce perspicuous results.

5.2.2 *What Kinds of Numbers Are There?*
Imagine what we know about the space of representations for number. Let sign values be at the top and

elements of $\Re$ be at the bottom, so that increased height corresponds to increased degree of abstraction. Inequalities are high in this structure, almost up to sign values. Floating point numbers and other simple truncations of $\Re$ lie toward the bottom. You may choose for yourself where to put the order of magnitude formalisms that have been developed recently. The question is, what else is in there? How many different representations for number remain to be developed, and what do they look like?

It would not surprise me if several more useful representations of number were developed. Some, like fuzzy numbers [D'Ambrosio, 1987], will be imported from other branches of AI and mathematics. A better understanding of the tradeoffs and systems that integrate several types of numerical reasoning (like [Simmons, 1986]) are necessary.

5.2.3 *What Kinds of Functions Are There?* A related question is, what sort of functions are there? Traditional physics relies heavily on the *analytic functions*, i.e., combinations of +, −, *, polynomials, trigonometric functions, and so on. These lie at the most precise end of an abstraction continuum. At the other end are qualitative proportionalities, where a closed world assumption is required to even determine what parameters affect a given quantity. How many representations for functions remain to be developed?

I suspect the answer is very few, much fewer than for numbers. Functions and algebras have been well explored by mathematicians for a long time, and while we may harvest a few new things from their efforts, I doubt there will be much because the class of analytic functions is so large. But it is an empirical question.

5.2.4 *Large-Scale Organization of Qualitative Models* Almost all of the models we have built to date are quite simple (on the order of 300 or so axiom-equivalents) compared to the scope of human commonsense or expert knowledge of the physical world. Building such a massive knowledge base will be impossible on an ad hoc basis. Ontology provides one source of organizing principles, but there are no doubt others.

Hierarchy plays an important role in organizing many other AI knowledge bases, and it is likely to do so in qualitative physics as well. Making qualitative simulations work with multiple levels of detail is an important problem (see [Weld, 1986; Kuipers, 1987] for some initial forays).

At least two other organizational ideas appear necessary as well. First, we need to formalize the idea of *structural abstractions*, the conceptual objects used in our representations, as distinct from their real-world counterparts. This separation is needed in order to provide an input language for systems that is reasonably independent of the theoretical commitments of a particular model. It is seductive to consider a transistor as identical to our model of it, and as long as we limit our analysis to a particular frequency range this conflation does little harm. But more sophisticated reasoning about circuits, and any consideration of almost any other engineering domain (e.g., fluid systems, thermal systems, motion) requires more work to map from a relatively neutral description of the physical system to the kind of model used for a particular level of analysis.

The second organizational tool is a language of simplifying assumptions. Rather than build distinct models for different purposes, we should instead use explicit assumptions to turn off and on different parts of a model. For instance, in reasoning about thermodynamic cycles one often invokes a "steady-state assumption—the amount of fluid in each part of the system remains constant, despite flows. Human engineers constantly use assumptions like this to drastically reduce the number of possible states, making analysis of complex systems more feasible. Our models will have to be designed in a way that allows our programs to do the same. We have recently developed some conventions for representing such assumptions in QP theory, and tested them on a large multigrain, multiple perspective model of a Navy propulsion plant [Falkenhainer and Forbus, 1988]. These conventions are a solid first step, but much research remains.

As qualitative physics becomes ready for widespread application, we will face the same kinds of validation issues now confronting other kinds of expert systems. Most engineering disciplines have validation procedures in place, and standards on the quality of model that must be used for a particular level of safety desired. We will have to fit qualitative models into such schemes, somehow.

5.2.5 *Integration with Vision and Robotics* Vision and robotics are, in principle, closely tied to qualitative physics. Qualitative physics can tell a robot where something might go if it is dropped, and what it has to do in order to boil water. As mentioned in the introduction, some form of qualitative physics will be needed by robots that work in unconstrained environments (although in general the useful representations may be more like *protohistories* and the *causal corpus* [Forbus and Gentner, 1986a] than like the current state of the art). But qualitative physics also needs vision and robotics. The poverty conjecture suggests that advances in spatial reasoning and vision will help drive qualitative kinematics. For instance, Ullman's theory of visual routines [Ullman, 1985] can be viewed as a theory of human metric diagrams. Knowing what the visual system computes can suggest what primitives are likely to be useful, and conversely, knowing the computational requirements of qualitative kinematics may in turn suggest what spatial descriptions people might be computing. Eric Saud [1987] has in fact proposed an "information rich spatial representation," using the various representations postulated for human vision to support spatial reasoning.

5.2.6 *A Complete Qualitative Physics* Today qualitative dynamics and kinematics are typically pursued in isolation. Integrating them is crucial to building a complete qualitative physics. A full understanding of an internal combustion engine, for instance, cannot be gleaned without understanding how physical processes and geometry interact. Efforts like the CLOCK project are a step, but just a first step, in this direction.

And, finally, of course, there is the ultimate goal. The holy grail of qualitative physics is a complete set of models, spanning the space of all the physical domains people know, able to characterize human models from the person on the street up to the best experts, capable of supporting efficient application programs, and so forth. Like traditional physics, we will probably never get there. But we will certainly learn interesting things on the way.

Acknowledgments

I would like to thank Johan de Kleer, Dedre Gentner, Paul Nielsen, John Collins, Brian Falkenhainer, and Ernie Davis for useful comments and discussions. Support for this work has come from the Office of Naval Research (Contract No. N00014-85-K-0225, Contract No. N00014-85-K-0559), and the National Aeronautics and Space Administration (Contract No. NASA-NAG-9137).

References

Allen, J., 1984. Towards a general model of action and time. *Artificial Intelligence* **23**(2).

Allen, J. and Koomen, J., 1983. Planning using a temporal world model. In *Proceedings of IJCAI-83*, Karlsruhe, West Germany. San Mateo: Morgan Kaufmann Publishers.

Bobrow, D., 1968. Natural language input for a computer problem-solving system. *Semantic Information Processing*, M. Minsky, ed. Cambridge, Mass.: MIT Press.

Bobrow, D., ed., 1984. *Qualitative Reasoning About Physical Systems*. Cambridge, Mass.: MIT Press.

Brown, J., Burton, R. and Zdybel, F., 1973. A model-driven question-answering system for mixed-initiative computer-assisted instruction. *IEEE Transactions on Systems, Man, and Cybernetics*, SMC-**3**(2).

Bundy, A., Byrd, L. Luger, G., Mellish, C., Milne, R. and Palmer, M., 1979. MECHO: A program to solve mechanics problems. Working Paper 50, Department of Artificial Intelligence, Edinburgh University.

Bunt, H.C., 1985. The formal representation of quasi-continuous concepts. *Formal Theories of the Commonsense World,* R. Hobbs and R. Moore, ed. Norwood, N.J.: Ablex Publishing Corporation.

Charniak, E., 1968. CARPS, a program which solves calculus word problems. Technical Report MAC-TR-51, Project MAC, MIT.

Chiu, C., 1987. Qualitative physics based on exact physical principles. Paper presented at the First Qualitative Physics Workshop, Urbana, Illinois.

Collins, J. and Forbus, K., 1987. Reasoning about fluids via molecular collections. In *Proceedings of AAAI-87,* Seattle, Washington. San Mateo: Morgan Kaufmann Publishers.

Considine, D. M. ed., 1983. *Van Nostrand's Scientific Encyclopedia*, Sixth Edition. New York: Van Nostrand Reinhold.

D'Ambrosio, B., 1987. Extending the mathematics in qualitative process theory. In *Proceedings of AAAI-87,* Seattle, Washington. San Mateo: Morgan Kaufmann Publishers.

Dauge, P., Raiman, O. and Deves, P., 1987. Troubleshooting: When modeling is the trouble. In *Proceedings of AAAI-87,* Seattle, Washington. San Mateo: Morgan Kaufmann Publishers.

Davis, E., 1986. A logical framework for solid object physics. New York University Computer Science Department Technical Report No. 245. To appear in *International Journal of AI in Engineering*, 1988.

Davis, E., 1987. Order of magnitude reasoning in qualitative differential equations. New York University Computer Science Department Technical Report No. 312.

Davis, E., 1988. In press.

de Kleer, J., 1975. Qualitative and quantitative knowledge in classical mechanics. Technical Report No. 352, MIT AI Lab, Cambridge, Mass.

de Kleer, J., 1979a. The origin and resolution of ambiguities in causal arguments. In *Proceedings of IJCAI-79*, Tokyo, Japan. San Mateo: Morgan Kaufmann Publishers.

de Kleer, J., 1979b. Causal and teleological reasoning in circuit recognition. MIT AI Lab Technical Report No. 529.

de Kleer, J., 1984a. How circuits work. *Artificial Intelligence* **24**.

de Kleer, J., 1984b. Choices without backtracking. In *Proceedings of AAAI-84*, Austin, Texas. San Mateo: Morgan Kaufmann Publishers.

de Kleer, J., 1986. An assumption-based truth maintenance system. *Artificial Intelligence* **28**.

de Kleer, J. and Brown, J., 1984. A qualitative physics based on confluences. *Artificial Intelligence* **24**.

de Kleer, J. and Williams, B., 1986. Reasoning about multiple faults. In *Proceedings of AAAI-86*, Philadelphia, Pennsylvania. San Mateo: Morgan Kaufmann Publishers.

Dormoy, J. and Raiman, O., 1987. Assembling a device. Paper presented at the First Qualitative Physics Workshop, Urbana, Illinois.

Doyle, R., 1986. Constructing and refining causal explanations from an inconsistent domain theory. In *Proceedings of AAAI-86*, Philadelphia, Pennsylvania. San Mateo: Morgan Kaufmann Publishers.

Falkenhainer, B., 1985. Proportionality graphs, units analysis, and domain constraints: Improving the power and efficiency of the scientific discovery process. In *Proceedings of IJCAI-85*, Los Angeles, California. San Mateo: Morgan Kaufmann Publishers.

Falkenhainer, B., 1987. An examination of the third state in the analogy process: Verification-based analogical learning. In *Proceedings of IJCAI-87*, Milan, Italy. San Mateo: Morgan Kaufmann Publishers.

Falkenhainer, B., 1988. In press.

Falkenhainer, B. and Forbus, K., 1988. Setting up large-scale qualitative models. In *Proceedings of AAAI-88*, St. Paul, Minnesota. San Mateo: Morgan Kaufmann Publishers.

Falkenhainer, B., Forbus, K. and Gentner, D., 1986. The structure-mapping engine. In *Proceedings of AAAI-86*, Philadelphia, Pennsylvania. San Mateo: Morgan Kaufmann Publishers.

Falkenhainer, B., Forbus, K. and Gentner, D., 1987. The structure-mapping engine: Algorithm and examples. University of Illinois at Urbana-Champaign, Department of Computer Science Technical Report No. UIUCDCS-R-87-1361. To appear in *Artificial Intelligence*, 1988.

Falkenhainer, B. and Rajamoney, S., 1988. The interdependencies of theory formation, revision, and experimentation. In *Proceedings of the Fifth International Conference on Machine Learning*, Ann Arbor, Michigan. San Mateo: Morgan Kaufmann Publishers.

Faltings, B., 1986. A theory of qualitative kinematics in mechanisms. University of Illinois at Urbana-Champaign, Department of Computer Science Technical Report No. UIUCDCS-R-86-1274.

Faltings, B., 1987a. Qualitative place vocabularies for mechanisms in configuration space. University of Illinois at Urbana-Champaign, Department of Computer Science Technical Report No. UIUCDCS-R-87-1360.

Faltings, B., 1987b. Qualitative kinematics in mechanisms. In *Proceedings of IJCAI-87*, Milan, Italy. San Mateo: Morgan Kaufmann Publishers.

Forbus, K., 1980. Spatial and qualitative aspects of reasoning about motion. In *Proceedings of AAAI-80*, Palo Alto, California. San Mateo: Morgan Kaufmann Publishers.

Forbus, K., 1981a. A study of qualitative and geometric knowledge in reasoning about motion. MIT AI Lab Technical Report No. 615.

Forbus, K., 1981b. Qualitative reasoning about physical processes. In *Proceedings of IJCAI-81*, Vancouver, B.C. San Mateo: Morgan Kaufmann Publishers.

Forbus, K., 1984a. An interactive laboratory for teaching control system concepts. Bolt Beranek and Newman Technical Report No. 5511.

Forbus, K., 1984b. Qualitative process theory. *Artificial Intelligence* **24**.

Forbus, K., 1984c. Qualitative process theory. MIT AI Lab Technical Report No. 789.

Forbus, K., 1985. The problem of existence. In *Proceedings of the Cognitive Science Society*. Hillsdale: Lawrence Erlbaum.

Forbus, K., 1986a. Interpreting measurements of physical systems. In *Proceedings of AAAI-86*, Philadelphia, Pennsylvania. San Mateo: Morgan Kaufmann Publishers.

Forbus, K., 1986b. The qualitative process engine. Technical Report No. UI-UCDCS-R-86-1288. Also to appear, *International Journal of AI in Engineering*, 1988.

Forbus, K., 1987a. The logic of occurrence. In *Proceedings of IJCAI-87*, Milan, Italy. San Mateo: Morgan Kaufmann Publishers.

Forbus, K., 1987b. Intelligent computer-aided engineering. In *Proceedings of the AAAI Workshop on AI in Process Engineering*, Columbia University, New York. To appear in *AI Magazine*, Fall 1988.

Forbus, K., 1987c. Interpreting observations of physical systems. *IEEE Transactions on Systems, Man, and Cybernetics* SMC-**17**(3).

Forbus, K. 1988. In press.

Forbus, K. and Gentner, D., 1986a. Learning physical domains: Towards a theoretical framework. *Machine Learning: An Artificial Intelligence Approach, Volume II*, R. Michalski, J. Carbonell, and T. Mitchell, ed. San Mateo: Morgan Kaufmann Publishers.

Forbus, K. and Gentner, D., 1986b. Causal reasoning about quantities. In *Proceedings of the Eighth Annual Conference of the Cognitive Science Society*, Amherst, Mass. Hillsdale: Lawrence Erlbaum.

Forbus, K., Nielsen, P. and Faltings, B., 1987. Qualitative kinematics: A framework. In *Proceedings of IJCAI-87*, Milan, Italy. San Mateo: Morgan Kaufmann Publishers.

Forbus, K. and Stevens, A., 1981. Using qualitative simulation to generate explanations. Bolt Beranek and Newman Technical Report No. 4490. Also in *Proceedings of the Third Annual Meeting of the Cognitive Science Society*. Hillsdale: Lawrence Erlbaum.

Gelsey, A., 1987. Automated reasoning about machine geometry and kinematics. *Proceedings of the Third IEEE Conference on AI Applications*, Orlando, Florida.

Gentner, D., 1983. Structure-mapping: A theoretical framework for analogy. *Cognitive Science* **7**(2).

Gentner, D., 1987. Historical shifts in the use of analogy in science. University of Illinois Department of Computer Science Technical Report No. UI-UCDCS-R-87-1389.

Gentner, D., 1988. Mechanisms of analogical learning. To appear in Vosniadou, S. and Ortony, A. ed., *Similarity and Analogical Reasoning.* London: Cambridge University Press.

Gentner, D. and Stevens, A. ed., 1983. *Mental Models.* Hillsdale: Lawrence Erlbaum.

Hayes, P., 1979. The naive physics manifesto. *Expert Systems in the Microelectronic Age*, D. Michie, ed. Edingburgh: Edinburgh University Press.

Hayes, P., 1985. Naive physics 1: Ontology for liquids. *Formal Theories of the Commonsense World*, R. Hobbs and R. Moore, ed. Norwood: Ablex Publishing.

Hendrix, G., 1973. Modeling simultaneous actions and continuous processes. *Artificial Intelligence* **4**.

Hinton, G., 1979. Some demonstrations of the effects of structural descriptions in mental imagery. *Cognitive Science* **3**(3).

Hogge, J., 1987a. Compiling plan operators from domains expressed in qualitative process theory. In *Proceedings of AAAI-87*, Seattle, Washington. San Mateo: Morgan Kaufmann Publishers.

Hogge, J., 1987b. The compilation of planning operators from qualitative process theory models. Technical Report No. UIUCDCS-R-87-1368.

Hogge, J., 1987c. TPLAN: A temporal interval-based planner with novel extensions. Technical Report No. UIUCDCS-R-87-1367.

Hollan, J., Hutchins, E., and Weitzman, L., 1984. STEAMER: An interactive inspectable simulation-based training system. *AI Magazine.*

Iwasaki, I. and Simon, H., 1986. Causality in device behavior. *Artificial Intelligence* **29**.

James, G., and James, R., 1968. *Mathematics Dictionary.* New York: D. Van Nostrand Company.

Joskowicz, L., 1987. Shape and function in mechanical devices. In *Proceedings of AAAI-87*, Seattle, Washington. San Mateo: Morgan Kaufmann Publishers.

Kokar, M., 1987. Critical hypersurfaces and the quantity space. In *Proceedings of AAAI-87*, Seattle, Washington. San Mateo: Morgan Kaufmann Publishers.

Kuipers, B., 1984. Common sense causality: Deriving behavior from structure. *Artificial Intelligence* **24**.

Kuipers, B., 1986. Qualitative simulation. *Artificial Intelligence* **29**.

Kuipers, B., 1987. Abstraction by time-scale in qualitative simulation. In *Proceedings of AAAI-87*, Seattle, Washington. San Mateo: Morgan Kaufmann Publishers.

Kuipers, B. and Chiu, C., 1987. Taming intractable branching in qualitative simulation. In *Proceedings of IJCAI-87*, Milan, Italy. San Mateo: Morgan Kaufmann Publishers.

Langley, P., Simon, H., Bradshaw, G. and Zytkow, J., 1987. *Scientific Discovery: Computational Explorations of the Creative Processes.* Cambridge, Mass.: The MIT Press.

Lee, W. W., Chiu, C. and Kuipers, B. J., 1987. Developments towards constraining qualitative simulation. University of Texas at Austin Artificial Intelligence Laboratory Technical Report No. AI TR87-44.

Lozano-Perez, T., 1983. Spatial planning: A configuration space approach, *IEEE Transactions on Computers* C-**32**.

Mavrovouniotis, M. and Stephanopolous, G., 1987. Reasoning with orders of magnitude and approximate relations. In *Proceedings of AAAI-87*, Seattle, Washington. San Mateo: Morgan Kaufmann Publishers.

Mohammed, J. and Simmons, R., 1986. Qualitative simulation of semiconductor fabrication. In *Proceedings of AAAI-86*, Philadelphia, Pennsylvania. San Mateo: Morgan Kaufmann Publishers.

Mozetic, I., 1987. The role of abstractions in learning qualitative models. In *Proceedings of the Fourth International Workshop on Machine Learning*, Irvine, California. San Mateo: Morgan Kaufmann Publishers.

Nielsen, P., 1987. The qualitative statics of rigid bodies. University of Illinois at Urbana-Champaign, Department of Computer Science Technical Report No. UIUCDCS-R-87-1354.

Nishida, T. and Doshita, S., 1987. Reasoning about discontinuous change. In *Proceedings of AAAI-87*, Seattle, Washington. San Mateo: Morgan Kaufmann Publishers.

Novak, G., 1976. *Computer Understanding of Physics Problems Stated in Natural Language*. Ph.D. thesis, Department of Computer Science, University of Texas at Austin.

Raiman, O., 1986. Order of magnitude reasoning. In *Proceedings of AAAI-86*, Philadelphia, Pennsylvania. San Mateo: Morgan Kaufmann Publishers.

Rajamoney, S. and DeJong, G., 1987. The classification, detection, and handling of imperfect theory problems. In *Proceedings of IJCAI-87*, Milan, Italy. San Mateo: Morgan Kaufmann Publishers.

Raulefs, P., 1987. A representation framework for continuous dynamic systems. In *Proceedings of IJCAI-87*, Milan, Italy. San Mateo: Morgan Kaufmann Publishers.

Sacks, E., 1985. Qualitative mathematical reasoning. In *Proceedings of IJCAI-85*, Los Angeles, California. San Mateo: Morgan Kaufmann Publishers.

Sacks, E., 1987. Piecewise linear reasoning. In *Proceedings of AAAI-87*, Seattle, Washington. San Mateo: Morgan Kaufmann Publishers.

Saud, E., 1987. Presentation at the First Qualitative Physics Workshop, Urbana, Illinois.

Schmolze, J., 1986. Physics for robots. In *Proceedings of AAAI-86*, Philadelphia, Pennsylvania. San Mateo: Morgan Kaufmann Publishers.

Sembugamoorthy, V. and Chandrasekaran, B., 1984. Functional representation of devices and compilation of diagnostic problem-solving systems. Technical paper, AI Group, Ohio State University.

Shearer, J., Murphy, A., and Richardson, H., 1971. *Introduction to System Dynamics*. Reading: Addison-Wesley.

Simmons, R., 1983. Representing and reasoning about change in geologic interpretation. MIT Artificial Intelligence Lab Technical Report No. 749.

Simmons, R., 1986. Commonsense arithmetic reasoning. In *Proceedings of AAAI-86*, Philadelphia, Pennsylvania. San Mateo: Morgan Kaufmann Publishers.

Stanfill, C., 1983. The decomposition of a large domain: Reasoning about machines. In *Proceedings of AAAI-83*, Washington, D.C. San Mateo: Morgan Kaufmann Publishers.

Struss, Peter 1987. The limitations of qualitative mathematics. Paper presented at the First Qualitative Physics Workshop, Urbana, Illinois.

Ullman, S., 1985. Visual routines. *Visual Cognition*, S. Pinker, ed. Cambridge, Mass.: MIT Press.

Waltz, D. and Boggess, L., 1979. Visual analog representations for natural language understanding. In *Proceedings of IJCAI-79*, Tokyo, Japan. San Mateo: Morgan Kaufmann Publishers.

Weld, D., 1986. The use of aggregation in qualitative simulation. *Artificial Intelligence* **30**(1).

Weld, D., 1987. Comparative analysis. In *Proceedings of IJCAI-87*, Milan, Italy. San Mateo: Morgan Kaufmann Publishers.

Weld, D., 1988a. Exaggeration. In *Proceedings of AAAI-88*, St. Paul, Minnesota. San Mateo: Morgan Kaufmann Publishers.

Weld, D., 1988b. *Theories of Comparative Analysis*. M.I.T. Ph.D. thesis, May.

Williams, B., 1984. Qualitative analysis of MOS circuits. *Artificial Intelligence* **24**.

Williams, B., 1986. Doing time: Putting qualitative reasoning on firmer ground. In *Proceedings of AAAI-86*, Philadelphia, Pennsylvania. San Mateo: Morgan Kaufmann Publishers.

Williams, B., 1988. In press.

Yip, K., 1987. Extracting qualitative dynamics from numerical experiments. In *Proceedings of AAAI-87*, Seattle, Washington. San Mateo: Morgan Kaufmann Publishers.

Model-based Reasoning: Troubleshooting

Randall Davis
Walter Hamscher
Artificial Intelligence Laboratory
Massachusetts Institute of Technology

1 *Introduction*

To determine why something has stopped working, it's useful to know how it was supposed to work in the first place. That simple observation underlies some of the considerable interest generated in recent years on the topic of model-based reasoning, particularly its application to diagnosis and trouble-shooting. This chapter surveys the current state of the art, reviewing areas that are well understood and exploring areas that present challenging research topics. We begin by describing the nature of the task, exploring what is given and what we're trying to produce. Since, as will become clear, there are considerable advantages to reasoning from a model of structure and behavior, we need representations for both; we review the set of techniques in current use and examine their strengths and weaknesses.

A considerable part of the chapter is then devoted to how those representations are used to do model-based diagnosis. We view the fundamental paradigm as the interaction of prediction and observation, and explore it by examining its three fundamental subproblems: *generating* hypotheses by reasoning from a symptom to a collection of components whose misbehavior may plausibly have caused that symptom; *testing* each hypothesis to see whether it can account for all available observations of device behavior; then *discriminat-*

ing among those that survive testing. In any real system these three are likely to be intertwined for reasons of efficiency. We treat them independently to simplify the presentation and because our goal is a knowledge-level analysis— an understanding of what reasoning capabilities arise from the varieties of knowledge available to the program.

The presentation is structured as a sequence of increasingly elaborate examples, starting with the simplest approach and adding successively more knowledge, producing successively more constraints that can be brought to bear. This is useful both as a way of simplifying the presentation and as a way of making another of the major points of this chapter: While a wide range of apparently diverse model-based systems have been built for diagnosis and troubleshooting, they can all be seen as exploring variations on the basic paradigm outlined here. Their diversity lies primarily in the varying amounts of and kinds of knowledge they bring to bear at each stage of the process.

Our survey of this familiar territory leads to a second major conclusion of the chapter: Diagnostic reasoning from a tractable model is largely well understood. That is, given a model of structure and behavior of tolerable complexity, we know how to use it in a variety of ways to produce a diagnosis. Part of the evidence for this is the number of different applications of that same paradigm in a variety of domains.

There is, by contrast, a rich supply of open research issues in the modeling process itself. While to some degree we know how do model-based reasoning, we don't know how to model complex behavior, how to create models, and how to select the "right" one for the task at hand. The last major section of the chapter deals with these topics, exploring the kind of difficulties that arise and using them to outline some important research problems.

2 *The Basic Task*

The basic paradigm of model-based reasoning for diagnosis can best be understood as the interaction of observation and prediction (Figure 1). In one hand we have the actual device, typically some physical artifact whose behavior we can observe. In the other hand we have a model of that device that can make predictions about its intended behavior. Observation indicates what the device is actually doing, prediction indicates what it's supposed to do. The interesting event is any difference between these two, a difference termed a *discrepancy*.

A fundamental presumption behind model-based diagnosis is the notion that if the model is correct, all the discrepancies between observation and prediction arise from (and can be traced back to) defects in the device. Simply put, if the model is right, the device must be broken, and the discrepancies are clues to the character and location of the faults. This is a useful view of the process that will carry us through the first two-thirds of the chapter.

We will eventually see, however, that it is also a simplified view: The assumption that the model is correct is in fact *necessarily wrong in all cases*. It is wrong in ways that are sometimes quite obvious and sometimes quite subtle. Simply put, a model is a model precisely because it is not the device itself and hence must in many ways be only an approximation. There will always be things about the device that the model does not capture.

The *good* news is that the things the model fails to capture may have no pragmatic consequence. A schematic for a digital circuit will not indicate the color, smell, or coefficient of friction of the plastic used to package the chips, but this typically doesn't matter. In theory the model is always incomplete, and hence incorrect, in some respects, but it is a demonstration of the power and utility of engineering approximations that models are often pragmatically good enough.

The *less good* news comes in situations where the approximation is not good enough. In that case we need to ask the more difficult question of how to do model-based reasoning in the face of an incorrect model. What can be done when both the model and the artifact may have defects? We turn to this later in the chapter.

Turning back to the basic problem, the task can be specified slightly more precisely by saying that we are given:

- Observations of the device, typically measurements at its inputs and outputs (because these are often easiest to obtain; in fact measurements at any point will do and are handled identically).

- A description of the device's internal structure, typically a listing of its components and their interconnection.

- A description of the behavior of each component.

The task is then to determine which of the components could have failed in a way that accounts for all of the discrepancies observed. Figure 2, for example, shows a device made from three multipliers and two adders. We know the values at the five inputs; the value at output F was predicted to be 12 and observed to be 10 (observations are noted in square brackets). The value at G is predicted to be 12 and has not yet been measured. The overall task is to use knowledge about the structure and behavior of the components to determine which ones could have produced the discrepancy at F, a process explored in detail in Section 6.

This approach to troubleshooting has been called by a variety of names in addition to model-based, including "reasoning from first principles" because it is based on a few basic principles about causality, and "deep reasoning," an unfortunate term intended to distinguish it from the associational rules typically used in rule-based expert systems.

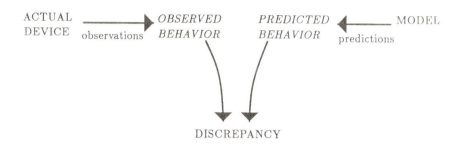

Figure 1 Diagnosis as the Interaction of Observation and Prediction.

Numerous model-based reasoners have been built, exploring a variety of problem domains. The illustrative sample given in Table 1 indicates the growth of interest in the area. Some of the earliest work dates from the mid-1970s, with a considerable growth of interest in the mid-1980s. Much of it has been directed to electronic circuits, both analog and digital, but there have also been applications to problems in neurophysiology, hydraulic systems, and other domains. In the remainder of this chapter we use digital circuits as a motivating example, largely because they are a familiar and important application that offers a range of examples from simple to quite complex.

Table 1   Sample Model-Based Troubleshooting Systems

INTER [de Kleer, 1976]
WATSON [Brown, 1976]
ABEL [Patil et al., 1981]
SOPHIE [Brown et al., 1982]
HT [Davis et al., 1982]
LOCALIZE [First et al., 1982]
IDS [Pan, 1984]
DART [Genesereth, 1984]
LES/LOX [Scarl et al., 1985]
GDE [de Kleer and Williams, 1987]
DEDALE [Dague et al., 1987]

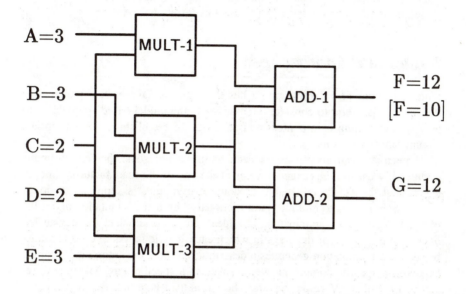

Figure 2 A Common Example.

The term *model* has been used widely to refer to a range of different things and is somewhat underdetermined. It is thus useful to review briefly some of the different kinds of models that have been used, to get a sense of the character of the information that models have supplied. As noted, the models used in this chapter contain information about the structure and correct behavior of the components in the device. Work in [Patil et al., 1981] describes a medical diagnosis system that used models of behavior without structure, models that indicated how one physiological event in the body could lead to another (e.g., low blood serum pH causes increased respiration, which causes decreased CO_2 concentration). Traditional circuit diagnosis has often relied on fault models, descriptions of the varieties of component misbehaviors typically encountered. Finally, work in [Pan, 1984] has attacked the problem of dependent failures by building models that capture the behavior of a component when it receives out-of-range inputs and itself begins to malfunction as a result. All of these are varieties of models, so a system built around any one of them could be termed model-based. Within the scope of this chapter we are concerned primarily with models of structure and correct behavior.

3 *Alternate Approaches*

Since a number of different approaches to diagnosis have been explored over the years, it is useful to consider alternatives to the model-based approach both as a way of setting it in context and as a way of establishing the appropriate circumstances for its use.

One traditional approach has been to use diagnostics, the test programs traditionally used on electronic devices at the end of the manufacturing line, to ensure that the device is capable of doing everything it's supposed to do. A second technique is to build a "fault dictionary" by using simulation and a list of the kind of faults anticipated. The idea here is to simulate the device behavior for every one of the ways in which each individual component can misbehave. Each simulation generates a description of how the entire device would behave if a specific component were broken in a specific way. The overall result is a list of fault/symptom pairs. The list is then inverted so that it is organized by symptom, providing a dictionary that indexes from observed symptom—the surface misbehavior—to one or more underlying faults capable of causing that misbehavior.

Third, we can build programs to do diagnosis by capturing the experience of experts, in the fashion widely used to build rule-based systems that employ empirical associations. Finally, decision trees are a long-standing approach to capturing diagnostic knowledge and offer a way of organizing a set of questions that leads methodically through the process of zeroing in on the faulty component.

Given the diversity of approaches to the problem, why and when does it make sense to use the model-based approach? One way to answer the question is to compare it against the alternatives.

3.1 *Compared to Diagnostics*

One problem with traditional diagnostics is that they are misnamed: Diagnostics don't do diagnosis, they do verification. As noted, their job is to ensure that a newly manufactured device will in fact do everything it's supposed to do. There is no misbehavior to diagnose, because there hasn't been any behavior yet. The fundamental task of verification is to exercise all the intended behaviors and make sure that they are all there. That's a different problem.

Model-based diagnosis, on the other hand, is both diagnostic and *symptom-directed*: It starts with the observed misbehavior and works back toward the underlying components that might be broken. As will become clear, whenever the behavior of a device is reasonably complicated, it's much easier to work from a specific symptom back to an underlying fault than to go exhaustively through all the expected behaviors until we find one that's aberrant.

3.2 *Fault Dictionaries and Diagnostics: Prespecified Fault Models*

As we explore in more detail later, the model-based approach also covers a wider class of faults than both fault dictionaries and traditional diagnostics, because both of those require a fixed, preselected class of relatively simple fault models. For fault dictionaries the task is to select a set broad enough to be useful in practice, yet simple enough that the simulation task is tractable. Writers of diagnostics typically have to settle on a small, fixed class of faults in order to create diagnostics that have acceptable coverage (the percent of possible faults actually detected), resolution (how precisely a detected fault can be localized), and efficiency. In the world of digital electronics the most common choices are the faults known as stuck-at-1 (a node in the circuit always exhibits the value 1) and stuck-at-0, largely because these are easily modeled, simulated, analyzed, and turn out to provide good coverage of other types of faults.

Whatever the faults chosen, the important point is that the fault dictionary creator or diagnostic writer must preselect a set of things that can go wrong and work from just those possibilities. As will become clear, the model-based approach takes a different view, defining a fault as "anything other than the intended behavior"; one consequence of this view is the ability to cover a wider class of possible misbehaviors.

Fault models do offer two useful abilities. First, as we explore in Section 6.3.1, they can provide an extra degree of specificity to the diagnosis. Where the model-based approach defines a fault by exclusion (anything other than expected behavior), fault models suggest specific misbehaviors that can aid in making the predictions necessary to design further tests.

Second, even though the set of pre-enumerated faults used may be small, it may be adequate for the task at hand. In digital circuits, for example, a large fraction of all faults can be detected (but not diagnosed) by checking just for stuck-ats. Hence two simple fault models turn out to be sufficient for determining that something is wrong (satisfying the verification task); determining the identity and location of the error (diagnosis), however, is more difficult.

3.3 *Compared to Rule-Based Systems*

Traditional rule-based systems have been built by accumulating the experience of expert troubleshooters in the form of empirical associations, rules that associate symptoms with underlying faults and that base those associations on experience with the device, rather than knowledge of structure or behavior. The problem here is the strong device dependence—a new rule set is required for every new device—and the time required to accumulate those rules. To the extent that the knowledge is an encapsulation of experience, a sizable body of experience may be necessary before the patterns emerge.

The issue becomes especially important in dealing with electronic devices, where the design cycle is getting short enough to be comparable to the time required to accumulate a new set of rules. This presents the difficult situation in which the device may be on its way to obsolescence by the time enough experience with it has accumulated to deal with the difficult faults.

The model-based approach is, by contrast, strongly device independent, works from an information source (the design) typically available when the device is first manufactured, and is far more likely to provide methodical coverage. Given a design description for a device, work can begin on diagnosing the device right away. Given a new design description for a different device, work can start on that one just as quickly.

The model-based approach can be less costly to use, because the model needed is often supplied by the description used to design and build the device in the first place. The increasing use of computer-aided design and manufacturing also means that those models are increasingly available as explicit descriptions in electronic form, rather than implicit in the head of the designer, or sketched informally on a scattered collection of paper.

The model-based approach is more likely to provide methodical coverage because the model-building process supplies a way of systematically enumerating the required knowledge. Systems built from empirical associations capture whatever experience has been encountered to date and offer far less guidance about what may be missing. As a result it is also more difficult to determine the coverage of such a system.

Finally, it may be claimed that rules need not be just empirical associations, they can also be written to take advantage of knowledge about device structure and behavior. But that's just the point: The relevant knowledge concerns structure and behavior. Given that, we ought next to ask what representations are well suited to capturing that information, and what representations offer us leverage in thinking about that knowledge. Rules, whether as empirical associations or viewed simply as if/then statements, offer us little or no help in thinking about or representing structure and behavior, or in using such descriptions to do diagnosis. Most fundamentally, they do not even lead us to think in such terms.

In slightly more general terms, the primary question is not whether some existing representation can in some fashion be made to do the task. The primary question is, what is the relevant knowledge?; and second, what does that content suggest about appropriate form? We consider such representations in Section 5.

3.4 *Compared to Decision Trees*

Decision trees provide a simple and efficient way to write down the sequence of tests and conclusions needed to guide a diagnosis. But the same simplicity and efficiency that is their strength is also an important weakness: They are a way of writing down the "answer" (a diagnostic strategy), but offer no indication of the knowledge used to create that answer. One consequence is a lack of transparency (the tree provides no indication why the diagnosis is what it is) and difficulty in updating (a small change to the device may mean a major restructuring of the tree). Like rule-based systems they are also device specific and must be recreated anew for each new device.

3.5 *When Not to Use the Model-based Approach*

Comparing the model-based approach to its alternatives provides some indication of its strengths and indications for its use. When does it make sense not to use this approach? The answer can be bracketed by examining problems that are too hard and problems that are too easy to be worth trying this way.

Problems that are too difficult are those involving subtle and complicated interactions in the device, interactions whose outcome is too hard to predict with current modeling technology. Consider, for example, a model of a computer that has been found through experience to have unreliable power supplies. The lack of reliability may arise from a sizable collection of interacting factors, like the heating and insulation patterns, air flow, electric and thermal properties of the materials used to build the power supplies, and so on. Predicting such behavior from the design description would very likely be pragmatically impossible, yet summarizing and using it once it has been noticed is quite easy ("if one of these machines is behaving erratically, it's likely to be the power supply"). We are in effect recognizing here that in some cases it's far easier to "let nature do the experiment," watch the outcome, and capture the experience in the form of rules, than it would be to predict the result from first principles.

Future advances in modeling and prediction will extend these limits, but the point remains that, given sufficient complexity, it is easier to let nature do the experiment. Reality is sometimes the cheapest simulator.

Problems that are too easy are those in which the device is so simple that we can model its behavior exhaustively and for which the set of faults to be considered is well enough known and well enough understood to be reliably pre-enumerated. In that case it may make sense simply to do exhaustive enumeration and create a fault dictionary.

We can thus approach the issue of when to use the model-based approach from two dimensions. First, the structure and behavior of the device should be reasonably well known and simple enough to model, but complex enough that exhaustive simulation is infeasible. Second, the set of possible faults should be difficult to reliably enumerate in advance.

4 *Organization and Vocabulary*

The discussion in this chapter uses several basic ideas as organizing principles. First, we view diagnosis in terms of the three stages of hypothesis *generation, test*, and *discrimination*. Second, we note that different amounts of knowledge can be brought to bear at each of these stages, producing more or less powerful approaches. Third, the range of programs that can be created by considering different amounts of knowledge at each stage maps out a space of possible program architectures. Finally, and perhaps most interestingly, we claim that this space of architectures captures the current set of programs that have been explored. That is, we can describe all the current model-based systems by characterizing them according to the amount and kind of knowledge they use at each of these three stages.

A number of basic vocabulary terms will facilitate later discussion. By "device" or "system," we mean the entire artifact, e.g., the entire device in Figure 2. By "component" we mean any one piece of it, in this case any of the adders or multipliers. (We may choose to represent wires as components as well; this is an issue of modeling choice discussed later.) By "structure" we mean the way things are interconnected, while "behavior" refers to what any one of these components is supposed to do. We use "discrepancy" to mean any of the differences between the behavior the device is supposed to exhibit (e.g., $F = 12$, predicted by the model) and what it is actually doing ($F = 10$, determined by observation). By "suspect" we mean any component identified in hypothesis generation as able to account for a discrepancy (e.g., MULT-1 can account for the discrepancy at F). Finally, by "candidate" we mean a component whose malfunction is consistent with all observations (i.e., a suspect that has survived hypothesis testing). When dealing with multiple faults, a candidate may consist of more than one component.

5 *Describing Structure and Behavior*

While a number of apparently different approaches to representing structure have been explored, there are several common themes that appear to be widely viewed as good ideas.

- Structure representation should be hierarchical.

Inside any of the boxes in Figure 2, for instance, there are more boxes and wires; look inside those and there are more of the same, until we arrive finally at primitive components. A hierarchical description permits hierarchical diagnosis: Work at the highest level initially until specific candidates have been isolated, then explore inside only those components, since there is no need to examine the substructure of components that are not candidates.

• Structure representation should be object centered and isomorphic to the organization of the device.

By "object centered" we mean that there are data objects corresponding to each of the components in the device; attached to each object is a description of its behavior. The representation should be isomorphic in the sense that the topology of interconnections between the objects should match the interconnections in the device. Hence the object associated with MULT-2, for instance, is connected in the LISP sense to the objects for ADD-1 and ADD-2.

One useful consequence of doing this is that it provides a single, unified representation that is both runnable and examinable. It is runnable in the sense that it can be used directly for simulation: If we supply values for the inputs to MULT-1, for instance, the object corresponding to it will discover that it has enough information to predict its output. It will do so, placing the result at its output, where the information will travel via the connections to the next component in line, which may now continue the process.

The same representation is examinable in the sense that it can be inspected to answer questions about device structure. Because it is in part a graph, questions about connectivity can be answered simply by traversing the representation.

• Behavior can be represented by a set of expressions that capture the interrelationships among the values on the terminals of the device.

The behavior of an adder, for example, can be captured with three expressions (Figure 3), indicating that:

• If we know the values at A and B, the value at C is $A + B$ (the solid arrow in Figure 3).

• If we know the values at C and A, the value at B is $C - A$ (the dashed arrow).

• If we know the values at C and B, the value at A is $C - B$ (the dotted arrow).

Interestingly these expressions capture both the causal behavior of the device (the bold arrow), as well as other things we can infer about the device (the other two arrows). The first of these indicates how it works, the other two are useful inferences we can make about what must have been at an input, given observations at other terminals. As we'll see, both kinds of information play an important role in supporting diagnosis.

While the expressions here are written in algebraic form, the important thing is the knowledge content, not form. Work in [Genesereth, 1984], for example, has explored the use of predicate calculus as a representation for both behavior and structure.

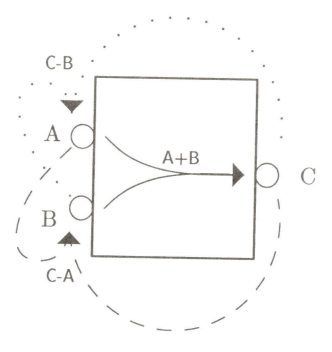

Figure 3 The Behavior Description of an Adder.

6 *Three Fundamental Tasks*

We consider next the three fundamental tasks of diagnosis and examine how each has been attacked in the model-based approach, using a variety of different kinds and amounts of knowledge. We consider each in turn, starting with the common simplifying assumption that there is only a single point of failure; as the discussion proceeds we show how some of the techniques can be extended to cover multiple points of failure.

- Hypothesis generation: Given one discrepancy, which of the components in the device might have produced it?

- Hypothesis testing: Given a collection of components implicated during hypothesis generation, which of them could have failed so as to account for all available observations of behavior?

- Hypothesis discrimination: When, as is almost inevitable, more than one hypothesis survives the testing phase, what additional information should be gathered to discriminate among them?

As noted, for the sake of presentation each of these is discussed independently, even though in most implementations they are interleaved for the sake of efficiency. While interleaving offers useful improvements in speed, it produces no fundamental changes to the paradigm.

6.1 *Hypothesis Generation*

The fundamental task here is, given a discrepancy, determine which components might have misbehaved in a way that can produce that discrepancy. Classical AI wisdom tells us that a good generator should be *complete* (i.e., capable of producing all the plausible hypotheses); *non-redundant* (i.e., capable of generating each hypothesis only once); and *informed* (i.e., able to produce few hypotheses that ultimately prove to be incorrect).

In the spirit of proceeding incrementally we consider a sequence of generators from the simplest and least informed, through successively smarter versions that bring additional kinds of knowledge to bear.

The simplest generator, guaranteed to be complete, is one that simply exhaustively enumerates the components in the device. For the device in Figure 2, for instance, the generator simply produces each of the five components one by one. This is trivially complete and not particularly intelligent.

We can improve on this with a succession of observations. For example:

- To be a suspect, a component must have been connected to a discrepancy.

That is, to plausibly explain a discrepancy, the suspect must have in some fashion been involved in it, have contributed to it. Our second generator takes advantage of the insight by traversing the structure description, working from a discrepancy (e.g., at *F* in Figure 2) to find all components connected to it. In the current case this provides no improvement, since the connections (wires) leading from *F* reach every component.

We next observe that:

• Devices often have distinguishable inputs and outputs.

This is clearly true for our adders and multipliers (Figure 4) and can be used to constrain the components considered: We need only consider components that are upstream of the discrepancy. In the current example this reduces the set of suspects to ADD-1, MULT-1, and MULT-2.

We can be a bit smarter yet, by observing that:

• Not every input to a device influences the output; there is no need to follow irrelevant inputs upstream.

The easiest example of this is an OR gate whose inputs are produced by two independent collections of components further upstream (Figure 5). Given inputs of 1 and 0, the model for the gate makes the obvious prediction at C. If the actual device is observed to be producing 0 there, three possibilities arise. First, the OR gate itself may be broken. Second, the gate may be working but input *A* is 0 rather than 1 and the problem lies further upstream in that direction, so we should continue tracing that way.

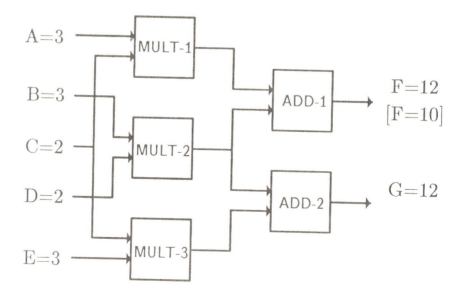

Figure 4 Taking Advantage of Direction of Information Flow.

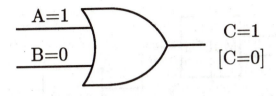

Figure 5 Not Every Input Influences the Output.

The third possibility, however, is problematic: It is contradictory to believe that the OR gate is working but that the problem lies further upstream of *B*. No matter what's going on upstream of *B*, if the OR gate is working, that is not going to account for the observed behavior. As a result we need not consider any components upstream of this point. More generally, the hypothesis generator can use knowledge about component behavior to determine which inputs are irrelevant and avoid tracing back through those.

Finally, we can observe that

- Information from more than one discrepancy can be used to further constrain suspect generation.

When there is more than one discrepancy, we can generate a set of suspects for each, then (assuming a single point of failure) intersect them, possibly reducing the number of suspects generated. Consider Figure 6, as an example. Tracing back from the discrepancy at *F* yields ADD-1, MULT-1, and MULT-2 as candidates; tracing from *G* yields ADD-2, MULT-1 and MULT-2. Assuming a single point of failure, the suspects lie in the intersection of these two sets.

This scheme is easily elaborated to deal with multiple points of failure by recognizing that the generalization of intersection in this case is set covering: We are trying to find a subset of components that accounts for (covers) all the discrepancies. To deal with the situation in Figure 6, for instance, we might select MULT-1 from the first discrepancy and ADD-2 from the second, yielding a hypothesized pair of faults that covers all the discrepancies.

6.1.1 Machinery One brief diversion into mechanism will make clear how to do this kind of reasoning easily and efficiently. The basic insight is to have the simulator record "reasons" as well as values. When the simulator predicts 1 at *C*, for instance, it records both that value and the expression from the behavior model for the component that produced the value (Figure 7). In this case the simulator would indicate that the value at *C* is 1 and the reason is *E1*.

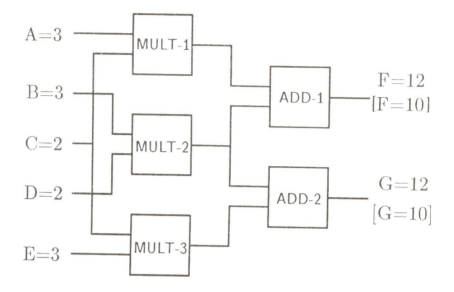

Figure 6 Polybox with Discrepancy at *F* and *G*.

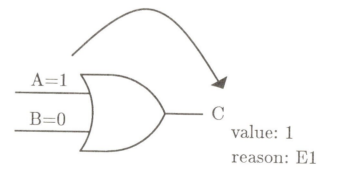

E1: If A=1 then C=1

E2: If B=1 then C=1

E3: If A=0 and B=0 then C=0

Figure 7 Recording Reasons as Well as Values.

This simple mechanism offers an easy way to determine which inputs to a component were relevant to its output, further constraining the search for hypotheses. All we need do is inspect the simulation record to determine what expression was used to predict a value, then inspect that expression to determine which inputs it used.[1] In Figure 7, for example, expression $E1$ uses only A, hence we need never consider hypotheses upstream of B.

This is a somewhat simplified but essentially correct view of the machinery in most model-based simulators in use today. The general notion is to have the simulator keep track of dependency records that indicate what information was used to determine each new value; generating candidates can then be done simply by tracing back through the dependencies.

A slightly more elaborate example will demonstrate why this technique can be very useful. Figure 8 shows a collection of gates with arrows indicating the records the simulator has kept as it made its predictions. Given a discrepancy at the output, the task of generating a complete, nonredundant and constrained set of hypotheses becomes simply a process of following the trail of electronic bread crumbs back along the reasons. Part of the overall insight here is that by using a reasonably sophisticated simulator—one that propagates reasons as well as values—the hypothesis generation task becomes relatively simple and straightforward (SOPHIE [Brown et al., 1982] provided one of the earliest examples of this approach).

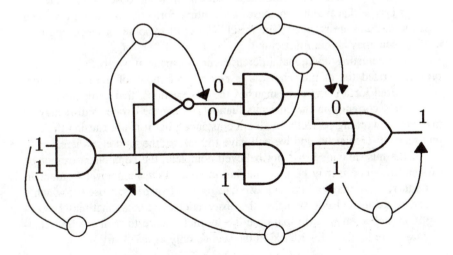

Figure 8a Dependency Traces Left by the Simulator.

---

1 Alternatively we could simply record which inputs were used. The scheme given is slightly more general, since the reasons can be useful in other ways, e.g., as a basis for explanation, and the inputs can be determined from them.

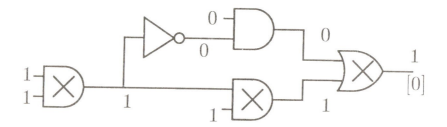

Figure 8b Candidates Selected by Tracing Back through the Dependency Traces.

6.2 Hypothesis Testing: A Simple Technique

In the second basic task of diagnosis—hypothesis testing—the goal is to test each suspect to see if it can account for *all* the observations made about the device. One simple approach is to use fault-model simulation on the suspects produced by the generator (as for example in [Brown et al., 1982] and [Pan, 1984]). We enumerate all the ways each specified component can malfunction, then simulate the behavior of the entire device on the original set of inputs under the assumption that the candidate is malfunctioning in the way specified. If the overall predicted behavior is inconsistent with the observations, the hypothesis can be discarded; hypotheses accounting correctly for the observations pass the test and are retained. The result is a set of hypotheses specifying how each suspect may be malfunctioning.

One interesting additional inference can be made if we believe that the pre-enumerated list of misbehaviors is *complete*: If none of the misbehaviors hypothesized for a component matches the observations, that component must be working correctly in the current situation and can be exonerated. It may or may not be working perfectly in all circumstances, but it is not causing the current set of discrepancies and we will have to look for the fault elsewhere.

If the misbehavior list is not believed complete, the component cannot be exonerated, since it may be misbehaving in some as yet unknown fashion. In this situation we may end up with two categories of suspects: those for which a hypothesized misbehavior matches the observations and those that may be failing in an unknown way. In that case it may make sense to treat the first category as more likely, falling back on the second only as necessary.

6.3 Hypothesis Testing: More Advanced Techniques

Three other slightly more advanced techniques use knowledge about device behavior to generate and test hypothesized candidates, yet do not require a pre-enumerated set of misbehaviors.

6.3.1 *Constraint Suspension* Constraint suspension [Davis, 1984] tests whether a suspect is consistent with all the observed behaviors of the device. The basic idea is to model the behavior of each component as a set of constraints, and test suspects by determining whether it's consistent to believe that only the suspect is malfunctioning. That is, given the known inputs and observed outputs, is it consistent to believe that all components other than the suspect are working correctly?

Consider the standard circuit as an example, in a situation in which the inputs are as shown in Figure 9 and where values at both outputs have been measured, yielding a discrepancy at F and the predicted value at G. The behavior of each component is modeled as a set of constraints of the sort shown previously in Figure 3; Figure 9 shows the entire device with the constraint network sketched in.

This network and set of values is clearly inconsistent. That is, given this set of constraints, if the values shown were inserted at the inputs and outputs, some constraint would soon encounter an inconsistency, i.e., attempt to fire and record a value at a node where there was already a different value recorded. Since constraints can propagate either from inputs to outputs or from outputs to inputs, the inconsistency might occur anywhere in the network (at the outputs, the inputs, or an interior node). The important point is that the network would report an inconsistency somewhere.

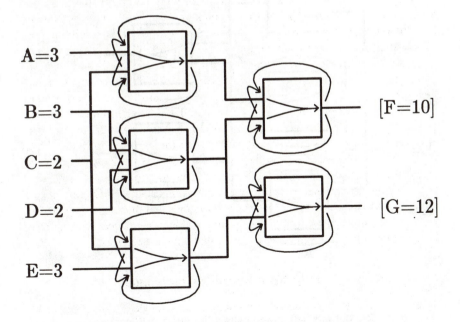

Figure 9 The Constraint Network View of the Device.

The traditional approach to handling inconsistencies in constraint networks is to find a value to retract. Here, however, we are sure of the values (the inputs sent in and the outputs measured); we are, however, unsure of the component behaviors. Constraint suspension thus takes the dual view: Rather than looking for a value to retract, it considers which constraint to retract to remove the inconsistency.

To put this back in hypothesis testing terms, recall the basic question stated above: Given the available observations, is it consistent to believe that all components other than the suspect are working correctly? "Working correctly" means the component is behaving as the model predicts; this is simulated by having the corresponding constraint "turned on." To say something is a suspect, by contrast, is to indicate that we don't know what it's doing, what its behavior is. In that case the most conservative stance is to retract all assumptions about its behavior. This is simulated by suspending its constraint, i.e., removing it from the network temporarily. Figure 10 shows the situation when testing the hypothesis that MULT-1 may be at fault.

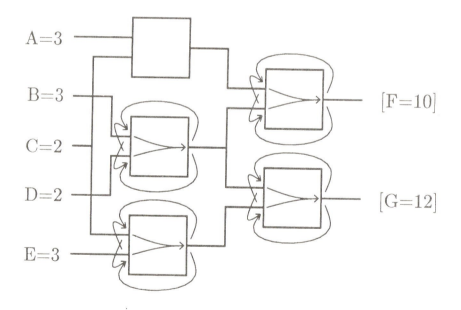

Figure 10 The Network with the Constraint for MULT-1 Suspended.

Hypothesis testing is thus accomplished by suspending the constraint for the suspect, leaving in place the constraints for everything else, then putting in the observed values and allowing the (reduced) constraint network to run to quiescence. If it does so without encountering an inconsistency, we get two interesting pieces of information. First, we know that the current suspect is in fact consistent with all the observations, i.e., there is some behavior for it that can account for all the observations. Second, the constraints often propagate values to the terminals of the suspect, supplying information about how it must be misbehaving. For example, the constraint network in Figure 10 will eventually determine that MULT-1 is a consistent candidate that could be multiplying 2 and 3 to produce 4. This ability to infer component symptoms is clearly dependent on the ability to propagate "backward," in this case inferring the upper input of ADD-1 from its output and lower input.

If the network is still inconsistent even with the suspect's constraint suspended, the current hypothesis can be rejected, exonerating the suspect: There is no set of assignments to the terminals of the suspect consistent with the observed values and the constraints currently in effect. This occurs when testing MULT-2, one of the three suspects produced by hypothesis generation for the situation in Figure 9. With only the constraint for MULT-2 suspended, there is no set of assignments to its terminals that is consistent with the inputs and outputs observed. It can thus be rejected.

There are several interesting properties of this technique. First, as noted, it not only indicates whether or not something is a consistent candidate, it can often specify the symptoms at the terminals of that component.

Second, the power of hypothesis testing and its ability to infer symptoms are dependent on the power of the propagation machinery. Current constraint systems are "local" in the sense that they propagate values through one component at a time, at each step solving one equation in one unknown. This style of propagation can stall when it encounters situations requiring more sophisticated algebra (e.g., solving two equations in two unknowns). Such situations are relatively common in domains with nondirectional components and can arise in domains with directional components in structures that have reconvergent fanout (i.e., a signal that branches and then rejoins at the inputs to a component).

The complexity of the algebra required depends on both the vocabulary used in the behavior language and the interconnection topology of the devices; it can quickly grow quite difficult. Some research has attacked the problem by propagating symbolic expressions rather than numbers (e.g., [Sussman and Steele, 1980]); exhaustive enumeration has also been explored where ranges are finite. If propagation does stall, the system will judge the candidate consistent because no contradiction was derived, even though there may in fact be one. Other work, relying on direct symbolic manipulation of expressions (e.g.,

[Genesereth, 1984], [Scarl et al., 1985]), encounters similar problems where symbolic solution methods are not complete.

Some candidates accepted as a result of stalled propagation are valid; in those cases there is no adverse consequence. Even when an invalid candidate is accepted, however, the only consequence is that the candidate set is larger than it should have been. The diagnosis is thus somewhat less precise, but at least no valid candidate is overlooked.

Third, where many traditional techniques require specifying how a component can fail, the reasoning above simply withdraws any commitment to how it might be behaving. That is an interesting property of model-based reasoning in general, not just the constraint suspension approach: Something is malfunctioning if it's not doing what it's supposed to, *no matter what else it may be doing*. As a result there is no need to prespecify how the component might fail; a fault is any behavior that doesn't match expectations.

It is in that sense that the model-based approach, using a model of correct behavior, covers a broader class of faults than traditional techniques that require prespecified fault models. Note for instance, that the device in Figure 10 may be misbehaving because the wrong kind of chip was inserted into the socket where the multiplier was supposed to go. In that case there is no simple model for the misbehavior and no plausible way to diagnose it in the traditional fashion. Yet the model-based approach handles this case because it need only observe that the component isn't doing what it's supposed to do.

The fault model approach falls short in this case because its models combine both physical and logical plausibility. The model-based approach by contrast deals only with logical plausibility, asking simply whether there is *any* set of values the component might display that can account for all the observations. The technique, by design, does not ask whether that set of values is in fact physically plausible.

As a result it can suggest candidates that, while logically plausible, are in fact physically unrealizable, requiring a second pass to filter them out. This can, however, be an advantage because physical plausibility is technology specific. A broken wire, for instance, can manifest differently depending on the technology; in TTL logic, for instance, it will appear as a high. Embodying this knowledge separately can both ease the initial construction task and reduce the difficulty of applying model-based reasoning to a new domain.

The traditional use of fault models can also be seen as trading off breadth for specificity: By committing to a pre-specified set of set of possible failures, we can gain in return greater specificity in the diagnosis. In the case of MULT-1, for instance, the model (of correct behavior) approach can say only that the component is multiplying 2 and 3 to get 4, while the fault model approach might indicate as one possibility that the 2-bit of the output is stuck at 0 (turning 6 into 4).

The model-based approach thus supplies a behavioral description of the misbehavior for this specific case, and, by design, says nothing about what the malfunctioning component would do with any other inputs. This permits it to cover a broad variety of possible failures. The fault model approach, on the other hand, precommits to a specific set of malfunction mechanisms and as a result can be more specific about what is wrong and can provide the basis for predictions of misbehavior for other inputs (e.g., if the 2-bit is stuck at 0, MULT-1 should produce 0 when given inputs of 2 and 1). The trade-off available thus asks whether we are willing to prespecify the faults and believe that the list is complete enough; if so, fault models might offer useful power.

Finally, we have so far been dealing with the single point of failure assumption. Multiple points of failure are trivial to check using constraint suspension: To check for a pair of failures, for instance, suspend the two corresponding constraints, then proceed as before. Generating multiple fault hypotheses efficiently, however, is somewhat more difficult; no simple extension of constraint suspension offers much leverage on this inherently exponential problem. This issue will resurface when we explore GDE [de Kleer and Williams, 1987] below.

6.3.2 *Combining Generation and Test* The two systems—DART [Genesereth, 1984] and GDE [de Kleer and Williams, 1987]—integrate hypothesis generation and testing sufficiently that when viewed in terms of generate and test they are best considered systems in which all of the testing knowledge has been integrated into the hypothesis generator.

6.3.2.1 *DART* The DART system illustrates the use of predicate calculus as a mechanism for model-based reasoning, with structure and behavior represented as axioms. The connection of MULT-1 to ADD-1, for instance, would be represented as

```
CONN(OUT(1,MULT-1), IN(1,ADD-1))
```

indicating that the first (only) output of MULT-1 is connected to the first input of ADD-1. Part of the behavior description of an adder would be

```
IF    ADDER(a) AND VAL(IN(1,a),x) AND VAL(IN(2,a),y)
THEN  VAL(OUT(1,a),x+y)
```

indicating that, if a is an adder with inputs x and y, its output will be x+y.

DART views diagnosis as a form of constrained theory formation. Starting with a set of observations of device misbehavior, the goal is to produce a description of its (faulty) structure. Given only the observations, the task would be the same as designing a device that exhibited the observed behavior. The design description is used to constrain the process by forcing the system to consider only propositions from the design description or their negation. A diagnosis in DART is thus a deduced proposition like

```
(OR(NOT(MULTIPLIER MULT-1))  (NOT(ADDER ADD-1)))
```

indicating which component might be misbehaving.

To arrive at these deductions the system uses a technique called resolution residue, a variation on resolution that works as a direct proof procedure (rather than a refutation method), guided by a number of strategies like unit preference for reducing the number of useless deductions. Details of the process can be found in [Genesereth, 1984]; at the knowledge level the deductions work much like the dependency tracing mechanism reviewed earlier, except in this case dependencies are deduced as needed (via the behavior descriptions) rather than automatically recorded when doing simulation. DART also uses the same resolution residue mechanism for test generation, providing a certain economy of machinery.

Among the limitations in this approach are the occasional difficulties in expression logic can present. The single point of failure assumption in [Genesereth, 1984], for example, requires five distinct axioms for a five component device, each stating that if one is broken the other four must be working. Further work in [Ginsberg, 1986] has demonstrated that reasoning from counterfactuals can produce a notion of minimal faults, at some increase in the complexity of the modeling and inference task.

One of the advantages of logic as a representation and reasoning mechanism is the potential for demonstrating the completeness of the inference procedure. While this can be useful, it does not imply that the resulting diagnostic process is complete. There are at least two sources of difficulty. First, as noted in [de Kleer and Williams, 1987], completeness of the inference procedure does not imply completeness of the prediction machinery. As one example, behavior descriptions for analog devices can involve higher-order differential equations; producing exact values for predictions in such devices means solving solutions of such equations, yet no general purpose technique exists.

Second, all of the inference, i.e., all of the candidate generation, is done with respect to the device model supplied, and completeness of the inference machinery is quite distinct from the completeness of the model. Simple examples of the problem arise when axioms are accidentally omitted; more subtle instances arise because, as we argue below, the model is necessarily incomplete. Thus while it can be useful to demonstrate completeness of the inference machinery with respect to the model, completeness of the diagnostic process is a distinct issue. Indeed, we argue below that the bulk of the work and difficult problems are in the modeling.

6.3.2.2 *GDE* The GDE system [de Kleer and Williams, 1987] provides a single mechanism for generating both single and multiple fault hypotheses, and presents a carefully constructed strategy for measurement selection. At this point we deal with a few of the ideas for hypothesis generation, illustrating the basic notions with a few simple examples; we return to the issue of measurement selection when discussing hypothesis discrimination in Section 6.5.1. A detailed picture and additional examples of GDE can be found in [de Kleer and Williams, 1987].

One important enabling technology for GDE is the use of an assumption-based truth maintenance system (ATMS), i.e., one that propagates both values and assumptions. The reasoning begins much like that done previously, with some difference in the record keeping. In Figure 11, for example, if we assume that MULT-1 is working, we can use its behavior description to predict the value at X, then record both the value and the set of underlying assumptions (in parentheses). Values that have been measured (in this case inputs and outputs) have no assumptions, indicated by the null set.

A particularly interesting event occurs when there are two contradictory predictions for the same point in the circuit, as in Figure 12, which shows the next step in the reasoning. The value at X is also predicted to be 4, this time using the (measured) value at F, the prediction at Y, and the assumption that ADD-1 is working. Note that assumptions accumulate: The prediction $X = 4$ carries all the assumptions it relies on.

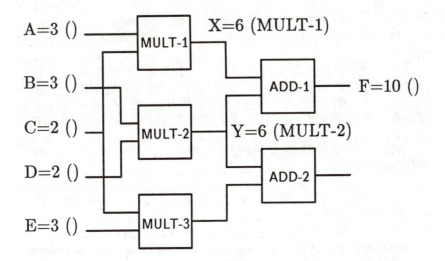

Figure 11 Values and Records Produced by an Assumption-Based TMS.

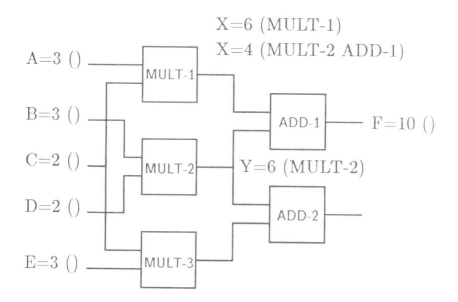

Figure 12 One More Step in the Propagation.

This is interesting because of the inference that can now be made: If all three assumptions so far were true, (i.e., MULT-1 *and* MULT-2 *and* ADD-1 were all working), there is an unavoidable contradiction—two different values at X. Taking the obvious step, we turn that around, inferring that one of the three assumptions must be wrong (i.e., one of the three components is not working correctly).

This is the process of constructing "conflicts": Whenever there are two different predictions for the same place in the circuit, collect all (i.e., take the union) of the assumptions underlying the conflicting predictions. The resulting conflict indicates that at least one of the components in it must be malfunctioning.

Continuing the propagation process in Figure 12 eventually yields a second conflict as well:

```
C1:  (MULT-1 MULT-2 ADD-1)
C2:  (MULT-1 MULT-3 ADD-2 ADD-1)
```

The second step in GDE is to generate a set of candidates that deals with all of the conflicts. MULT-1, for example, is a candidate because it can account for both C1 (one of (MULT-1 MULT-2 ADD-1) must be broken), and C2 (one of (MULT-1 MULT-3 ADD-2 ADD-1) is broken.) Since a single component is capable of accounting for all the conflicts, one of the hypotheses in this case happens to be a single point of failure. ADD-1 is a similar hypothesis; single point of failure hypotheses are produced by intersecting the conflicts.

Accounting for conflicts can be viewed more generally in mathematical terms as set covering: We want a collection of components that covers all the conflicts. Singleton covers like (MULT-1) produce single point of failure hypotheses; multiple point of failure hypotheses are generated by larger set covers like (MULT-2 ADD-2), which take MULT-2 from the first conflict and ADD-2 from the second.

This process is fairly intuitive, but it can be expensive—computing set covers is in the worst case exponential. One way to reduce the potential impact of this complexity is to use the notion of minimality in both conflicts and hypotheses. The basic intuition is the same in both cases: Any superset of a conflict is also a conflict; any superset of a hypothesis is also a hypothesis. GDE uses this to reduce the amount of work it does by generating and maintaining only minimal conflicts (i.e., no subset of one is also a conflict) and minimal hypotheses (i.e., no subset of one also covers all the conflicts). By doing this, the system need never examine any non-minimal conflict or hypothesis, saving a substantial amount of work. While the fundamental exponential character of the problem has not changed, the effect has been reduced, enabling the system to handle problems larger than might otherwise have been possible.

The candidate generation part of GDE thus offers an efficient and intuitive mechanism for generating both single and multiple fault hypotheses in a unified approach. The system also offers a degree of mechanism (and hence domain) independence, because the diagnostic process in GDE is separated from the machinery used to predict behavior (the ATMS).

6.4 *Hypothesis Testing via Corroborations*

It is useful to discuss briefly the notion of corroborations, the situation in which a measured value matches (corroborates) the prediction at that point. Using corroborations to do hypothesis testing is potentially useful, but must be approached with caution. The basic intuition is seductive: Having seen that any component involved in a discrepancy is a suspect, there is unfortunately a great temptation to construct an overly simplistic dual principle—any component involved in a corroboration must be innocent.

Figure 13 illustrates the difficulty in an example that has a discrepancy at F but a corroboration at G, where the observed value matches the predicted value. Straightforward topological tracing back from F yields the usual candidates (ADD-1, MULT-1, MULT-2). We are now, however, tempted to say that since the measurement at G matches the prediction, all components involved in that corroboration (i.e., MULT-2, MULT-3, and ADD-2) can be exonerated.

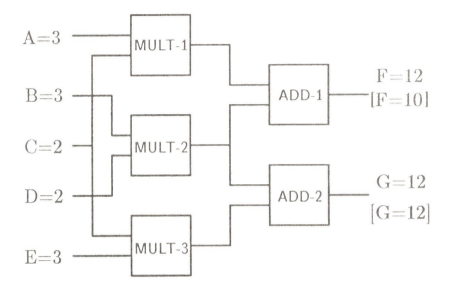

Figure 13 The Standard Example with a Corroboration at *G*.

The seductive part is that it works in this case and some others, leading at times to unjustified optimism that it is valid in general. The difficulty is illustrated by the simple counterexample in Figure 14, in which ADD-2 has been replaced by a component that computes the maximum of its inputs. Once again there is a conflict at *G*, and a corroboration at *G*, yet this time the exoneration is incorrect: MULT-2 might in fact be broken, producing 4 as its output.

In general the problem is fault masking, the situation in which a device receives incorrect inputs, yet produces the output that would have been expected with the correct inputs, masking further effects of the fault. Consider MAX-1 for instance: If it receives incorrect inputs of 6 and 4, it still produces the expected output, 6, that would have resulted from the correct inputs (6 and 6).

Fault masking can arise in several ways. Any component that can be insensitive to one of its inputs (e.g., MAX-1) can mask a fault on that input even when working correctly. Multiple points of failure can produce the problem, when one broken component outputs an incorrect value, but a second broken component further downstream masks some of the effects by producing the expected value despite the incorrect input. Finally, even with a single point of failure, the phenomenon of reconvergent fanout can produce fault masking.

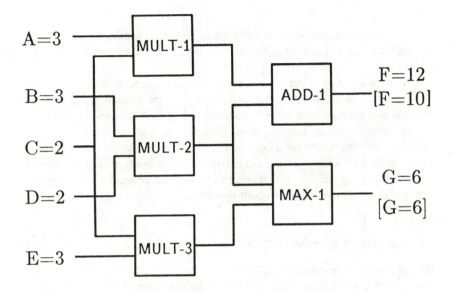

Figure 14 Counterexample Showing that Corroboration Is Not Valid in General.

In Figure 15, for example, component B computes the square of its input, component C computes $16 - 5x$, and ADD-1 is an adder. Component A is supposed to produce 3, which should eventually result in ADD-1 producing 10. If A instead incorrectly produces 2, B, working correctly, will produce 4, while C, also working correctly, produces 6. The final output at the adder is then the expected 10, despite the single fault present in the circuit. If the signal from A fans out to other places, its error would be manifest elsewhere, yet if we naively trace back from the corroboration at ADD-1 we would incorrectly exonerate A.

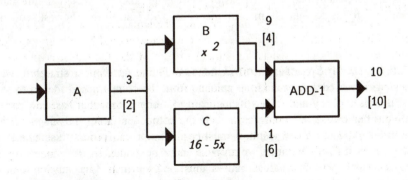

Figure 15 Reconvergent Fanout Can Produce Fault Masking.

One important reason to be wary about corroborations is thus the number and subtlety of the phenomena that can cause fault masking and invalidate corroborations as a heuristic.

A second reason is the asymmetry in the consequences of mistakes in hypothesis generation and in hypothesis testing. If the hypothesis generator is overzealous, we may have more hypotheses to test than are logically necessary, but the system will, at worst, be less efficient than it should have been. Overzealous exoneration, on the other hand, can cause the system to arrive at the wrong answer by ruling out a valid candidate. As a result, it may be plausible if desired to be aggressive with respect to hypothesis generation, but in general it is useful to be more cautious about hypothesis testing.

6.5 *Hypothesis Discrimination*

Having examined generation and testing, we next consider hypothesis discrimination, where the fundamental problem is how to distinguish among the hypotheses, when, as is almost inevitable, more than one survives testing. Distinguishing among competing hypotheses involves gathering new information about the behavior of the device, either by (i) making additional observations (probing), or (ii) changing the inputs and making observations in that new situation (testing). In both cases the goal is to gain the most information at the least cost.

6.5.1 *Probing* In considering probing strategies we proceed as before in steps from the most elementary approach to successively more sophisticated techniques. The simplest approach is to use only structural information to generate the set of all possible probe locations and pick any place that has not been measured previously. Refinements to this include (i) using knowledge about component behavior, (ii) using knowledge about expected failure rates, and (iii) trying to find the measurement that will lead to the shortest sequence of probes.

6.5.1.1 *Using Structure and Behavior* Perhaps the most straightforward and widely used approach is the guided probe. The fundamental idea is to start at the discrepancy and follow it upstream to a component that has an incorrect output but whose inputs are correct. If the component receives valid information but produces a bad result, it must be the culprit. Given the discrepancy in Figure 16 at F, for instance, we probe A and Z next, since if these are observed to have their predicted values, MAX-1 must be broken. If Z has any value other than 5, we probe upstream at both B and Y to see if they are 1 and 4 respectively, and so forth until we find the culprit.

6.5.1.2 *More Sophisticated Use of Behavior* Note that it was not in fact necessary to probe at *A*, since a discrepancy there alone could not have produced the observed value 3 at *F*. The guided probe technique can be extended to use information about component behavior to reduce the probes needed; Breuer, for example, shows how it can be applied to Boolean digital circuits. The reasoning involved is similar to that described earlier for using behavioral information to constrain hypothesis generation.

The guided probe approach is appealing in its simplicity and intuitive clarity. It is also, however, a linear time search, which, with even a little cleverness, can be turned into a much more efficient binary search. In the current example, for instance, simply examining the topology of the device makes clear that *Y* is a more effective probe. If the value there is bad, half the components are exonerated—all those downstream from it. In general the "half split" probe point can be found by considering for each probe point the value that would be predicted there given each suspect; the favored probe is the one that splits the set of current suspects. Figure 17 shows that *Y* is the best probe: *Y* will be 2 if MULT-1 or MIN-1 are broken, and 4 if ADD-1 or MAX-1 are broken; either outcome thus rules out half the suspects. Ideally, the process of cutting the search space in half can be continued at each step, producing the traditional binary search, with its potential increase in speed from linear in the number of suspects to be discriminated, to logarithmic. The maximal advantage arises in cases like this with a linear cascade of components, with somewhat less (but still useful) improvement in other cases.

6.5.1.3 *Using Failure Probabilities* The example above is particularly easy because one probe is clearly more informative than the others. In more realistic cases several places may be equally informative. If, for instance, we apply our methods so far to the example in Figure 18, *X* and *Y* turn out to be equally informative.

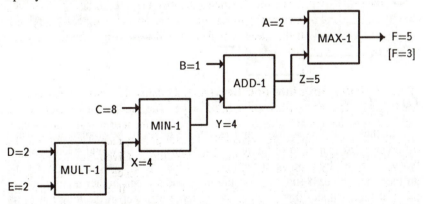

Figure 16 Guided Probe Example.

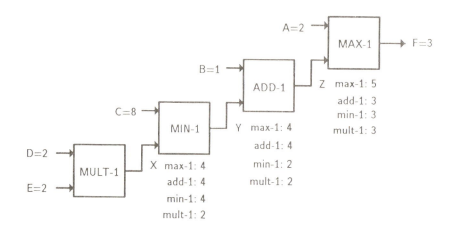

Figure 17 Half Split Strategy Example.

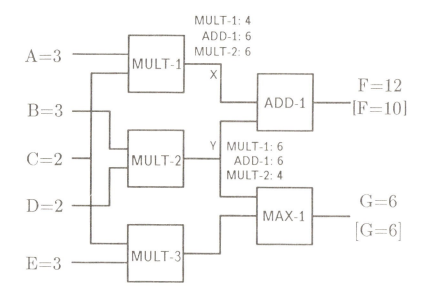

Figure 18 Two Equally Informative Probes.

In the event that MULT-1 and MULT-2 happen to be implemented using different chips that have different reliability histories, it would make sense to "play the odds" by probing at the place that has the greatest chance of having an incorrect value. If MULT-2, for instance, has a much higher *a priori* likelihood of failure than MULT-1, it would be more efficient in the long run to try probing at Y first.

While this example uses failure probabilities to help select among probe points that are indistinguishable using value predictions, the two are independent sources of information. We can in general combine information from predictions (about how discriminating a probe can be) with information from failure probabilities (about how likely it is that probe will encounter an incorrect value), to yield a measure of how informative a particular probe is likely to be.

6.5.1.4 *Selecting Optimal Probes* We have thus far used information about predictions and failure probabilities to look only one measurement ahead. The analysis in the previous section, for instance, considered what single measurement looked best. A more powerful strategy would determine what *sequence* of measurements was likely to be the most effective, since, as with any search problem, the best path is not always clear from a one-step lookahead.

One obvious approach is exhaustive lookahead: The current predictions indicate the potential places to probe first, we can then make new predictions based on the possible outcome of each of those probes, use that information to determine the set of possible places to probe second, make new predictions based on those, and so on, continuing until the sequence of hypothesized measurements would identify a unique fault. This is a classic decision tree analysis and as always the difficulty is the size of the search space.

As with any search problem, the challenge is to find a way of estimating the value of a path without having to explore it to the end. The GDE system takes an information theoretic approach, using the notion of minimum entropy as the basis for its evaluation function (see [de Kleer and Williams, 1987] for details). Part of the difficulty in applying this idea lies in determining the probability that a particular measurement will have a particular value when not every candidate predicts a value at that point. GDE develops a careful approximation and uses it to select a measurement that is, under a reasonable set of assumptions, optimal in the sense that it minimizes the expected total number of probes.

This approach is well suited to GDE because the assumption-based TMS that it uses maintains a substantial body of context information that includes the values predicted at each point in the device. Hence little additional machinery is needed to generate and keep track of the required information.

6.5.2 *Testing* Testing is the second basic technique for hypothesis discrimination. Here the fundamental idea is to select a new set of inputs to the device that will help reduce the suspect set by providing additional information about the behavior of the device. To remain valid, a suspect has to account for both the original symptoms and the behavior observed in response to the new inputs.

inputs. As with probing, the difficult task is selecting a set of inputs that is particularly informative.

If the set of tests that can be presented to the device is fixed in advance, the problem of selecting an informative test is essentially equivalent to probe selection. For each test, each suspect (ideally) predicts a certain outcome, hence the best test is the one which splits the set of suspects in half.

If, on the other hand, the set of possible tests is unknown or pragmatically infinite, it is necessary to generate an appropriate test. A simple, suboptimal technique will serve to illustrate the basic idea and difficulties: Design a test for each suspect in turn, that is, find a set of inputs that will give two different outputs depending on the condition of that one component. This will serve to determine whether the fault is in the current suspect or among those remaining.

As an example, assume that AND-gate AND-1 in Figure 19 is suspected of malfunctioning, in particular of taking in 1s and sending out 0. We want a set of inputs that will indicate whether that is really how the component is behaving.

To do that we need to get a 1 to both inputs to the gate, then ensure that its output is routed out to where it can be measured. The intuition is straightforward: Work backward from the inputs of AND-1 then forward from the output. We can get a 1 on the upper input by ensuring that OR-1 outputs a 1; this in turn can be ensured if the input to inverter I1 at A is 0. The value at B then does not matter. Similar reasoning from the lower input of AND-1 yields 0 at C. Then in order to ensure that the output of AND-1 can be measured accurately at the device output, we need a 1 at E, the lower input to AND-2. With that input vector it appears that the value at F will determine unambiguously whether AND-1 is malfunctioning in the manner noted.

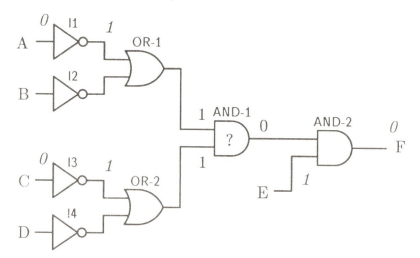

Figure 19 An Example of Test Generation.

This style of reasoning is the essence of test generation as traditionally practiced. While the approach is appealing in its intuitive clarity and simplicity, it has important limitations. For our purposes, the most significant limitation is its insensitivity to the presence of other suspects in the device and the resulting insufficient specificity. What if, in the current example, I1 and I3 also happen to be suspects? The test vector selected will generate a value at F that depends on the state of more than one suspect: If the value is incorrect any of the three components may be to blame.

Stated in this fashion the difficulty immediately suggests one plausible remedy: When routing signals through the device, whenever possible route the signal only through known good components (components that are not suspects). Using this strategy the test generation process would select I2 and I4 to provide the inputs to the OR gates, and end up producing a test that was completely specific, that is, dependent on the condition of only one suspect, AND-1. Work in [Shirley and Davis, 1983] describes a system that reasons in this fashion and that produces tests that are as informative and specific as possible.

A second substantial problem in testing arises in circuits with reconvergent fanout. If, for example, the lower input of AND-2 had been attached to input D (rather than having its own input E), the value at D would have entered into two different goals: establishing the lower input to AND-2 and routing the output through AND-2. It is thus a problem of planning in the face of interacting conjunctive subgoals, often resulting in backtracking and potentially involving a considerable amount of search, since test generation is in the worst case NP-complete.

6.5.3 *Cost Considerations* Underlying the preceding analysis are a number of assumptions about the relative costs of probing, test application, and computation, where the "cost" of an action is typically taken to mean the amount of time it takes to perform.

Analysis aimed at selection of optimal probes is useful only when computation is reasonably cheap compared to the probes themselves. There would, for example, be little point in waiting for a ten-minute computation to determine the optimal probe if all of the measurements are easily made in five minutes. In general the assumption holds true, partly because computation keeps getting cheaper, and gets cheaper faster than almost anything else. Probing, by contrast, typically means some sort of physical action (hence it is likely to be slower), and some of those actions may result in losing information (e.g., having to move boards to get access to probe points). Hence the assumption is typically valid, but it is important to be explicit about it.

Similarly, generation of distinguishing tests is useful only when the required computation is cheaper than probing or when probing is impossible. As above, there is little point in waiting for a computation to construct an informative test if many measurements that would eliminate suspects could be made in the meantime. Although this is an adequate working assumption, it is violated occasionally because test generation can be expensive (NP-complete for combinational digital circuits).

Finally, an assumption underlying the preceding discussion is that probes are independent of one another and all have equal cost. This assumption is violated if there is a range of technologies for probing the device, each with its own cost, resolution, and number of resulting observations. A digital logic analyzer, for example, yields detailed observations of several signals simultaneously, but requires much more setup time than a simple voltmeter. Hence the voltmeter may be preferable to the logic analyzer even if it yields less information about the currently outstanding suspects. Similarly, tests may have different setup costs—in fact they may have different setup costs depending upon the order in which they are applied— with analogous consequences. The potentially relevant literature on decision theory is too large to survey here, nevertheless it is important to be aware that subtleties of this kind are likely to arise in real applications.

7 Interim Conclusions

We have discussed a substantial collection of ideas and techniques that form the current basis for model-based diagnosis and troubleshooting. A brief review of the highlights will help set the stage for exploring the open research issues.

- Model-based troubleshooting is based on the comparison of observation and prediction.

Observation indicates what the device is actually doing; prediction describes the intended behavior. Discrepancies between the two provide the starting point for diagnosis. An important part of the diagnostic ability of model-based reasoning is provided by behavior descriptions that capture both the causal behavior of the device (predicting outputs from inputs) and inferences that can be made about its behavior (determining inputs from outputs). One of the important consequences of the model-based view is the ability to view misbehavior as anything other than what the device is supposed to do. We need not pre-enumerate the kinds of things that might go wrong.

- Model-based troubleshooting is device independent.

Given a new device description, work can begin immediately on troubleshooting the new device. Unlike rule-based approaches, there is no time-consuming accumulation of experience. These systems reason instead from engineering principles applicable to a wide variety of devices.

- Model-based troubleshooting is symptom directed.

It reasons from the observed misbehavior toward the underlying fault. This is particularly important for any device complex enough that the set of correct behaviors is too large to explore exhaustively. In that case it is infeasible to run the device through all its correct behaviors to see which one is not working; we work instead from the information supplied by the symptom. The technique is also familiar, in the sense that it captures some of the intuitions and reasoning that experienced people typically use.

Model-based diagnosis can be understood as a process of hypothesis generation, testing, and discrimination. Hypothesis generation works from a single symptom to determine which components might have caused that symptom. The key issue is providing a generator that is both complete and informed. We reviewed three different ways to do that, moving from the simplest version to more sophisticated approaches.

Where hypothesis generation works from a single symptom, the goal in hypothesis testing is to determine which candidates can account for all the observations available about the behavior of the device. We examined four approaches, ranging from straightforward fault simulation, to constraint suspension, DART's use of resolution residue, and the GDE approach.

In hypothesis discrimination the fundamental issue is finding inexpensive ways to gather additional information that will distinguish among the surviving hypotheses. In exploring probing strategies we looked at four ideas that used successively more information, beginning with structure, adding information about behavior, *a priori* failure probabilities, and finally ending with a means of estimating which probe will likely yield the shortest sequence of measurements. A brief review of test generation demonstrated that the traditional technique is indiscriminate in its selection of components to use in constructing a test; considerable advantage can therefore be gained by the simple expedient of using only known good components.

Two important elements of the analysis in this survey are the view of the basic task as a three-step process of generate, test, and discriminate, and the exploration of the character and amount of knowledge that can be brought to bear at each step. Dividing the task into those three steps provides an important form of mental hygiene, making it possible to understand each of these fundamentally different problems on its own terms, without being misled by the common implementation practice of intermingling them for efficiency. Exploring the kinds of knowledge used at each stage offers a sound basis for comparing different variations and understanding how and why one may be more powerful than another.

The combination of these two elements also maps out a sizable space of program architectures. This is valuable because it provides a way of unifying what might otherwise appear to be a diverse collection of systems. We claim in fact that the model-based systems built to date fit comfortably somewhere in that space, i.e., all the current systems can be characterized in this framework according to the amount and kind of knowledge they use at each stage.

One overall consequence evident at this stage is that model-based diagnosis is a fairly well-understood process. Part of the evidence for this is the character of the different programs that have been built: The variations in the way they work are minor in comparison with the common core of techniques in use. Additional evidence comes from recent success at recasting much of the reasoning in terms of formal logic. The work in [Reiter, 1987] and [Ginsberg, 1986], for instance, provides formal definitions of and proofs for some of the ideas presented in more intuitive form here.

All this has two interesting consequences. First, the technology is ready for application. A body of understanding is in place that is sufficient to attack modest-sized but real problems. Building these applications will no doubt raise additional interesting questions, but there is a sufficient base of knowledge available for us to begin to use it.

Second, the technology is well enough understood that the interesting research agenda now consists of either developing substantial advances beyond the techniques outlined earlier or finding fundamentally different ways to proceed. Interesting applications may result from constructing, tracing, and reasoning about dependencies, but research contributions arise by exploring problems for which the existing techniques are inadequate and finding ways to make substantial advances in them.

We consider next a number of problems that may help spur such results.

8 *The Research Issues*

Three categories of research issues seem particularly important and promising at this point in the evolution of the art: device independence and domain independence, scaling up to more complex behaviors, and selecting the "right" model. The first addresses the question of how broadly we can use the current set of ideas. The case for device independence is easily made, since nothing done so far is specific to the particular device(s) examined, but are the ideas more broadly applicable? What happens if they are applied to devices built with entirely different technologies?

Numerous questions arise in considering scaling up to more complex behaviors. At the most basic level, the question is how to represent and reason about the behavior of more complicated devices, in particular those that have memory and thus can present interesting dynamic behavior. A related question is the power of our predictive engines: How can we improve their performance so that predictions can still be made when dealing with complex devices or complex interaction topologies?

Finally, the question of selecting among models confronts a number of very difficult problems. As will become clear, the difficulties start with acknowledging the apparently simple observation that model-based reasoning is only as good as the models we provide to it. That will lead to an interesting and difficult challenge—the battle between complexity and completeness, where the desire to be complete in diagnosis seems directly contradicted by the impossibility of dealing with an unconstrained problem.

8.1 *Device Independence and Domain Independence*

It appears easy to argue that the technology reviewed so far has a strong degree of device independence—given a new description of a different circuit, the same reasoning process can begin immediately. It is not so obvious, by contrast, what degree of domain independence these techniques exhibit. While there has been a small amount of work done in other domains (e.g., neurophysiology, hydraulic systems), the vast majority has been aimed at relatively simple electronic circuits.

At this point an intriguing experiment would be to go out on the edge and apply this in a domain where it is not at all obvious that it will work. It would, for instance, be fun to try thinking about clock repair in this fashion. Not the modern digital kind, though; the interesting challenge would be the old-fashioned gear, wire, and spring-driven models. What would it take to describe the behavior and structure of such a device? Can the techniques reviewed above be used to reason about it? The intent here is to work on a problem that strains the state of the art, to teach us more about representing and reasoning about structure and behavior.

8.2 *Scaling*

In considering whether and how this technology can scale up to larger devices, it is important to recognize that there are at least two independent dimensions—size and complexity—and that size alone is not a particularly difficult issue. If the basic components are simple, it is possible to work with thousands of them without straining the current technology. One current program, for instance, models and diagnoses a system with a few thousand components [First et al., 1982]. Each of them is very simple, but nothing new is required to apply the existing ideas to this system of thousands of parts. The model entry task may be sizable, but it is an engineering challenge, not a fundamental advance in representation or reasoning.

More interesting challenges arise when we start to deal with devices with complex behavior. As one commonsense example, consider the behavior of a VCR that can be programmed to record two different broadcasts at different times in the future. Even this relatively modest-sized finite state machine can present apparently daunting problems of representing and reasoning about behavior.

As a somewhat more immediately useful example, consider the task of describing the behavior of an ALU (arithmetic/logical unit), using the behavior representation technology available today. If that seems tractable, imagine describing the behavior of a common microprocessor like the 80386. How might we describe what that device can do in a way that makes possible examining and reasoning about it? As long as we're at it, imagine describing the behavior of something genuinely complex, like a disk controller.

Nor is complexity solely the province of large-scale devices. Work at the other end of the scale has demonstrated how complex the behavior of a single transistor can be when coarse abstractions like "switch" or "amplifier" prove to be insufficiently detailed [Dague et al., 1987]. Many of the same issues arise here as well.

What might be done? One approach is to look for a new vocabulary, a new set of abstractions designed to deal with the kinds of complexity encountered. Imagine examining the data sheet for the 80386, making careful note of the vocabulary in use. That data sheet is a form of existence proof: With some degree of success it communicates what this device is supposed to do. The easy speculation is that its success arises in large part because it uses the "right" set of abstractions. The more difficult part is understanding what "right" means—what makes these abstractions effective? What is it that they ignore, what do they emphasize, and why are those effective selections?

Complex behavior also forces the question of the adequacy of our predictive engines. As noted earlier, the simpler local constraint propagators stall when encountering the need to deal with more than one equation in one unknown. Although some effort has been directed toward propagating symbolic expressions, the resulting algebra can be quite complex. One possible approach to the problem would be to guide the algebraic manipulations with some knowledge of the device structure and behavior, similar in spirit to the observation that a physicist guides his mathematics by an understanding of the problem and what he is trying to establish. The question is not how to be good at symbolic manipulation of complex expressions, so much as it is knowing what symbolic manipulation to do to avoid the complexity in the first place.

A third set of challenges arises in dealing with devices with memory. If, as is frequently the case with such devices, we know only the inputs supplied to it initially and the final output that results some time later, hypothesis generation and testing becomes truly indiscriminate. Work reported in [Hamscher and Davis, 1984], for instance, examined the task of diagnosing a sequential multiplier (a device that multiplies one digit at a time, shifting and adding in much the same way the problem is done by hand). If the multiplier's behavior is modeled using the technology reviewed above, candidate generation becomes indiscriminate—almost every component can account for the misbehavior. This is not a minor consequence of current implementations; the difficulty arises from the basic nature of the problem: If all we know is the input at the beginning and the output at the end, the problem is genuinely underconstrained in much the same way that two equations are insufficient to determine the value of three unknowns.

This is a second place in which new abstractions may prove to be the relevant tool, particularly temporal abstractions. Some early work in this direction has been done and seems promising: Hamscher [1988], for instance, demonstrates how temporal abstractions can be effective for such devices.

One other approach that may prove effective in reasoning about complex devices is the notion of "second principles of misbehavior." One example is the heuristic that, in a complicated device, fault manifestations will be obvious. To illustrate, imagine working with a device that includes a current generation microprocessor, one that happens to be broken in some fashion, and consider the consequences of that fault on the microprocessor's behavior. It is possible, but highly unlikely, that the consequences will be subtle: It is unlikely, for instance, that the device will exhibit only a very small perturbation in its expected behavior for only one of the instructions in its instruction set. It is much more likely that the fault will result in some obviously aberrant behavior every time the device is used. One common form of that aberration is for the device to stop producing any behavior at all, e.g., by hitting an illegal instruction and halting.

This is one example of the second principle that complicated devices don't break in subtle ways. It is a "principle" in the sense that it can be explained by (and perhaps eventually derived from) arguments about design. In this case, for instance, the argument is that complex designs often involve reuse of modules, both to simplify the design and reduce cost. Reuse of modules in turn means that any error in such a module will tend to have widespread consequences. In a microprocessor, for instance, a single ALU may be used both for the arithmetic required for an ADD instruction and the arithmetic needed to compute the next instruction address. Any error in that ALU will not only yield incorrect sums (which might be overlooked), it will also introduce instruction sequencing errors that are unlikely to be missed.

Since these principles can be grounded in knowledge about design, they are more than device-specific heuristics and are likely to have widespread applicability. They are also an important addition to the ideas explored thus far, because we are, as a field, a long way from being able to do such reasoning from a purely first principles approach. Second principles of misbehavior thus offer a way of summarizing what would otherwise be a long and difficult derivation.

One challenge we face is finding more of these principles; one obvious place to start is with experienced troubleshooters. Whenever a model-based system produces a diagnosis that is logical but strikes a human troubleshooter as inappropriate, there is the standard opportunity to find out what it is that the experienced troubleshooter knows that is still missing from the system. Some of that knowledge may point toward additional second principles of useful breadth and utility.

8.3 *Modeling Is the Hard Part*

The third and possibly most intriguing area of research is brought into focus by acknowledging that all model-based reasoning is only as good as the model. This observation is in some ways obvious and in some ways fairly subtle, but the consequences are interesting and present difficult problems.

To illustrate one version of the problem, note that all of the reasoning techniques reviewed earlier generate predictions by propagating along the pathways shown in the device description, then trace back from the discrepancies along those same pathways to find suspects. The crucial point is twofold: Suspects are found by tracing causal pathways back from a symptom, and all of the reasoning above accepted the device description as given, implicitly assuming that the pathways supplied accurately model causality in the device. Yet this can easily be false.

One commonplace example of this phenomenon is a bridging fault, the event that results when a chip is being soldered in place and enough solder accumulates at two adjacent pins to bridge the gap between them (Figure 20). The result is a connection—a causal pathway—where none was intended.

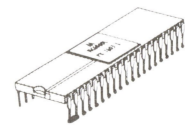

Figure 20 A Solder Bridge.

The possibility of faults of this sort has a particularly interesting consequence. Since candidates are found by tracing back along causal pathways, if the pathways indicated by the device description are different from those in the actual device, the tracing process will lead to the wrong components. Put somewhat more simply, the great virtue of the model-based approach is its ability to reason from the description of structure and behavior, yet the fatal flaw in the model-based approach is that it reasons from the description of structure and behavior, *and that description might not capture the actual causality in the device.*

8.3.1 *The Model Must Be Wrong*   How is it that the model might not be an accurate description of the causality in the device? One possibility is that the device isn't supposed to be that way. The bridge fault is one example of this, another is an error during assembly—the device is simply wired up incorrectly.

A second possibility is unexpected pathways of interaction. In an electronic circuit, a wire is the expected pathway of interaction; that's how components are supposed to affect one another. But there can be other, unexpected, pathways as well: One component may heat up another, two wires carrying high frequency signals may be so close that they affect one another via electromagnetic radiation, and so on. The important point is that the design description, by *intent*, only tells us about the pathways of interaction that are supposed to occur. In the device itself other unknown pathways may be operating. The consequences of this are particularly evident in DART's explicit statement that its diagnosis is restricted only to "... propositions from the design description or their negation." Hence the only kinds of diagnoses it can even consider are those stating that some component explicitly mentioned in the design description is malfunctioning.

Third, the model may not match the device because in our routine practice we explicitly decide not to represent a particular level of detail. In a large circuit, for instance, we may choose not to model every individual wire, settling instead for a slightly more coarse-grained model in which components are modeled as connected directly to one another.

But most importantly, it is in principle necessarily true that the model be different from the device. It is the fundamental nature of all models, all representations, that is at issue here: There is no such thing as an assumption-free representation. Every model, every representation contains simplifying assumptions. That's what models are, so in some ways this is perfectly obvious.

The perhaps less obvious part is the unavoidable impact this has on model-based reasoning. As noted, the fundamental idea behind the technique is the idea that, if the model is correct, then all the discrepancies between observation and prediction arise from, and can be traced back along causal pathways to, defects in the device. But the model is, inevitably and in principle, *never* correct.

To be more precise, the model is never *completely* correct. When it is a good enough approximation, the techniques described earlier are successful. But the inevitability of incorrectness in theory and the pragmatic reality of it in practice mean that this issue is real and crucial to the robustness of the systems we build. We need to understand both what effect it has on the systems we build and how to deal with it.

8.3.2 *Consequence: Complexity vs. Completeness*

One of the most important consequences of the phenomenon that a model is never *completely* correct is an inevitable tension between complexity and completeness. To be complete, diagnostic reasoning would have to consider all the things that may possibly go wrong, along every *possible* pathway of interaction. But such reasoning would be indiscriminate, implicating every component—there would always be some (perhaps convoluted) pathway by which that component might have caused the problem. Yet if we make any simplifying assumptions, i.e., omit any pathway, there will be entire classes of faults that the system will never be able to diagnose.

There is a fundamental problem here. If we make any simplifying assumptions we run the risk of being incomplete, because the simplifying assumption might be the one that encompasses the actual fault. Yet without some simplifying assumptions the reasoning drowns in complexity.

While this arises in a particularly immediate fashion here, it appears to be a fundamental issue for problem solving in general. Any time we set out to solve a problem, we need to make simplifying assumptions about the world in order to get started, yet sometimes those assumptions are wrong. Thus any techniques that can help us to select, organize, and manage the assumptions that will be of potentially broad utility.

8.3.3 *Consequence: Model Selection Is Fundamental*

Perhaps the most interesting implication of this line of argument is the significance of the problem of model selection. Since there are no assumption-free representations, one strategy would be to assemble a collection of them, each embodying a different set of assumptions, along with a body of knowledge about how to select carefully from among them. No one of them or any simple combination of them provides a complete representation, but progress might be made by selecting carefully from among them, attempting to make enough assumptions to keep the problem tractable, yet making as few as possible to reduce the chance of not being able to see the actual problem.

It is likely as well that the choice will not only have to be judicious, but repeated and dynamic as well, changing views on the fly as understanding of the problem evolves. One support for this approach is the observation that experienced engineers do something like this. We need to understand what it is they know and how they reason about model selection.

The problem seems to lie at the heart of engineering problem solving: Perhaps the most basic, most important decision made in starting to solve a problem is deciding "how to think about it." What is it that suggests modeling something as an analog device, a digital device, or a hydraulic device? How do we know what's relevant? How does the process begin? The problem seems difficult but particularly intriguing.

Three speculations suggest possible approaches to the problem. First, we might review the difficulties mentioned above that are encountered when using models, and reformulate them as heuristics for model design [Hamscher, 1988]. The difficulty presented by reconvergent fanout (i.e., causing local propagation to stall) can, for instance, be reduced to some degree by selecting module boundaries to encapsulate the fanout. Similarly, judicious selection of module boundaries can help reduce hidden state, the problem that makes diagnosis underconstrained in the case of the sequential multiplier. A set of such heuristics would assist in the design of models that reduce or avoid some of the problems encountered above.

A second speculation explores the problem of deciding how to model something by suggesting that different pathways of interaction define different kinds of models, different representations, which can then be layered to provide a sequence of successively more complex views [Davis, 1984]. A wire, for instance, is one pathway of interaction; it defines the traditional schematic. If heat is the relevant pathway, that defines a different representation of the device, one in which "distance" is defined in terms of how easily one device heats another. Electromagnetic radiation is a third pathway that defines yet another kind of model and another distance metric.

These multiple different kinds of models are then organized from simplest to more complex (defining "simplicity" is itself an open issue), so that the system starts by using the simplest and falls back on more complex models only as necessary. The technique has been used to diagnose a bridging fault successfully, demonstrating that multiple models using different representations and different definitions of distance can be used to reduce complexity without permanently losing completeness [Davis, 1984].

A third speculation begins with the observation that every model is defined by a set of simplifying assumptions. We might collect the set of all the simplifying assumptions routinely made and consider the space of models that are generated by it. For example, Figure 21 shows three different models of a NAND gate, beginning with the traditional transistor level model at the bottom.

Assuming that power can be ignored, then abstracting away from the specific subcomponents to the roles they play, produces the intermediate level representation in the middle. Two further simplifying assumptions—that current can be ignored and that all the subcomponents can be encompassed by a single box—yield the traditional representation at the top. Hence these two pairs of assumptions yield two successively simpler models of the device.

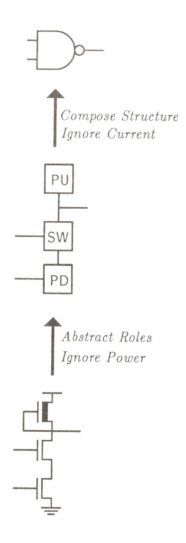

Figure 21 A Simple Hierarchy of Models.

But these are not the only models those assumptions can generate. The simple trick of changing the order in which the assumptions are made produces an entire lattice of different models (Figure 22).

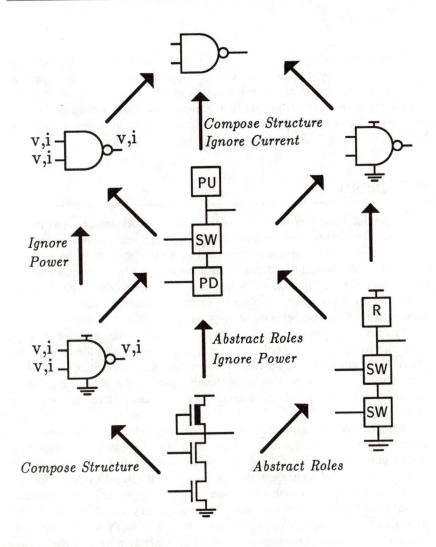

Figure 22 A More Complex Hierarchy of Models.

Some of them are admittedly rather obscure, but there are in fact (perhaps obscure) circumstances under which every one of them will be the "right" way to think about the device. One reason why some faults are so difficult to diagnose may be precisely because the "right" model in that case is a particularly unusual set of assumptions. Even faults as commonplace as bridges illustrate the issue: Part of the reason they are especially difficult to diagnose is that they require examining a less familiar representation—the physical layout of the chips. While the fault is "simple" in that representation (two adjacent pins), it can appear on the functional diagram as a connection between two widely separated points.

This is, of course, still speculation. Given that the lattice in Figure 22 was generated simply by changing the order of the assumptions, there's no particularly compelling reason to believe that it will work well. Nor have we answered the second half of the question: how to select from among the models, and how to know which to choose next when one of them begins to fail. This is only a beginning, but it may be worth further consideration.

9 *Summary*

We began this survey by viewing model-based diagnostic reasoning as the interaction of prediction and observation, and saw that one useful consequence was the chance to view misbehavior as anything other than what the device is supposed to do. Model-based reasoning thus covers a broader collection of faults than traditional approaches to diagnosis. A second virtue of the technique is its device independence, enabling us to begin reasoning about a system as soon as its structure and behavior description is available.

In examining how to represent structure, we noted the utility of descriptions that were hierarchic, object-centered, and topologically identical to the device being modeled. In examining behavior we noted the widespread use of constraint-like descriptions that allow both simulating the actual behavior of the device and making inferences about what the values at inputs must have been.

We explored diagnostic reasoning by viewing it in the three phases hypothesis generation, testing, and discrimination. This view allowed exploration of each of these fundamentally different problems on its own terms, made clear the common core of techniques that are in use, and offered evidence for the claim that model-based systems to date fit into the space of architectures characterized by the amount and kind of knowledge they use at each stage. The view also supports the claim that the process is reasonably well understood: Building a dependency-tracing model-based reasoner is now a fairly routine process.

Finally, we examined three major open research issues. We explored the question of domain independence, leading to the suggestion of trying these techniques on devices from widely different domains, to extend our ability to describe structure and behavior. We examined the difficulties in scaling up to devices with considerably more complex behavior, speculated about the possibility of finding a new vocabulary of effective abstractions, and touched on the difficulty of producing predictions in the face of complex behavior. And we emphasized the fundamental role and fundamental difficulty of model selection as the central problem in both extending the reach of these programs and ensuring their robustness.

Acknowledgments

Many people contributed useful suggestions aiding both the research and writing of this survey, including Johan de Kleer, Mike Genesereth, Paul Resnick, Mark Shirley, Howie Shrobe, Reid Simmons, Jeff Van Baalen, Dan Weld, Brian Williams, and Peng Wu.

References

Brown, A. L., 1976. Qualitative knowledge, causal reasoning, and the localization of failures. Technical Report AI-TR-362, MIT Artificial Intelligence Laboratory.

Brown, J. S., R. R. Burton, and J. de Kleer, 1982. pedagogical, natural language, and knowledge engineering techniques in SOPHIE I, II, and III. *Intelligent Tutoring Systems*, D. Sleeman and J. S. Brown (Eds.). New York: Academic Press, pp. 227–282.

Dague, P., O. Raiman, and P. Deves, 1987. Troubleshooting: When modeling is the difficulty. In *Proceedings of AAAI-87*, Seattle, Washington, pp. 600–605. San Mateo: Morgan Kaufmann.

Davis, R., 1984. Diagnostic reasoning based on structure and behavior. *Artificial Intelligence* 24(3):347–410.

Davis R., H. Shrobe, W. Hamscher, K. Wieckert, M. Shirley, and S. Polit., 1982. Diagnosis based on structure and function. In *Proceedings of AAAI-82*, Pittsburgh, Pennsylvania, pp. 137–142. San Mateo: Morgan Kaufmann.

de Kleer, J., 1976. Local methods for localizing faults in electronic circuits. Memo 394, MIT Artificial Intelligence Laboratory. (Out of print.)

de Kleer, J. and B. C. Williams, 1987. Diagnosing multiple faults. *Artificial Intelligence* 32(1):97–130.

First, M. B., B. J. Weimer, S. McLinden, and R. A. Miller, 1982. LOCALIZE: Computer-assisted localization of peripheral nervous system lesions. *Computers and Biomedical Research* 15(6):525–543.

Genesereth, M. R., 1984. The use of design descriptions in automated diagnosis. *Artificial Intelligence* 24(3):411–436.

Ginsberg, M., 1986. Counterfactuals. *Artificial Intelligence* 30(1):35–80.

Hamscher, W., 1988. *Representations for Model-based Troubleshooting*. Available from the author.

Hamscher, W. and R. Davis, 1984. Candidate generation for devices with state: an inherently underconstrained problem. In *Proceedings of AAAI-84*, Austin, Texas, pp. 142–147. San Mateo: Morgan Kaufmann.

Hamscher, W. and R. Davis, 1987. Issues in model-based troubleshooting. Memo 893, MIT Artificial Intelligence Laboratory.

Pan, J., 1984. Qualitative reasoning with deep-level mechanism models for diagnoses of mechanism failures. In *Proceedings of CAIA-84*, Denver, Colorado, pp. 295–301.

Patil, R., P. Szolovits, and W. Schwartz, 1981. Causal understanding of patient illness in medical diagnosis. In *Proceedings of IJCAI-81*, Vancouver, BC, pp. 893–899. San Mateo: Morgan Kaufmann.

Reiter, R., 1987. A theory of diagnosis from first principles. *Artificial Intelligence* **32**(1):57–96.

Scarl, E., J. R. Jamieson, and C. I. Delaune, 1985. A fault detection and isolation method applied to liquid oxygen loading for the space shuttle. In *Proceedings of IJCAI-85*, Los Angeles, California, pp. 414–416. San Mateo: Morgan Kaufmann.

Shirley, M. H. and R. Davis, 1983. Generating distinguishing tests based on hierarchical models and symptom information. In *IEEE International Conference on Computer Design*.

Sussman, G. J. and G. L. Steele, 1980. Constraints: A language for expressing almost-hierarchical descriptions. *Artificial Intelligence* **14**(1):1–40.

9

Artificial Intelligence Techniques for Diagnostic Reasoning in Medicine

Ramesh S. Patil

Clinical Decision Making Group
Laboratory for Computer Science
Massachusetts Institute of Technology

1 *Historical Perspective*

As early as the mid 1950s, physicians and computer scientists recognized that computers could assist in clinical decision making and began to analyze medical diagnosis with a view to the potential role of automating decision aids for that domain [Ladley and Lusted, 1959]. A variety of approaches were explored. They include: the use of *clinical algorithms* or *flowcharts* that encode the sequence of actions a good clinician would perform in the evaluation or management of some common disease [Bleich, 1972], the use of large *clinical databases* of previously studied groups of patients that are matched against the findings in a current case to suggest possible actions that have proved fruitful in similar cases in the past [Rosati et al., 1975], the use of *pattern recognition* techniques to classify the findings in a case into one of several predefined classes of diagnostic categories, and the use of *probability theory* and *decision analysis*, that allows the physician to assess the influence of available findings on the diagnostic likelihoods and to evaluate the merits of available alternatives [Gorry and Barnett, 1968b; de Dombal et al., 1972]. A good review of these early efforts can be found in [Reggia and Tuhrim, 1985].

Each of these approaches can be applied successfully to narrow and carefully chosen medical domains. However, they suffer from serious drawbacks when applied to a broad domain of medical diagnosis. For example, when faced with the outbreak of a new or rare disease, clinical algorithms (flowcharts) can be deployed effectively to codify and disseminate information on diagnosis and management. When applied to the broad domain of medicine, however, flow-charts become so enormous as to be unmanageable. When faced with the possibility of many diseases, the choice of an appropriate flow-chart becomes akin to the general problem of diagnosis. Furthermore, while following the flow-chart, if some unanticipated finding is observed or if the patient reacts unexpectedly to some therapeutic intervention, the clinician is faced with a difficult decision. Should the flow-chart be followed, ignoring the anomalous finding, or should some new decision procedure be adopted? To provide assistance in these difficult situations, it is essential that not only the sequence of actions but also the rationale underlying these actions be encoded in the program.

1.1 *Artificial Intelligence and Diagnostic Reasoning*

Because of various limitations of the existing techniques, a group of researchers turned to the expert physician as a resource that might provide detailed insights into the basic nature of clinical problem-solving and to the field of artificial intelligence in order to translate these insights into working programs. The field of Artificial Intelligence in Medicine (AIM) was formed around 1970 with near-simultaneous development of research groups at four institutions: Stanford University, Rutgers University, Massachusetts Institute of Technology (in collaboration with Tufts University School of Medicine) and University of Pittsburgh. Within approximately five years the early efforts came to fruition with the publication of seminal papers on MYCIN [Shortliffe, 1976], CASNET/Glaucoma program [Weiss and Kulikowski, 1984], Present Illness Program [Pauker et al., 1976b] and INTERNIST-I program [Pople, 1975; Miller et al., 1982]. All of these projects relied on human experts as the source of their knowledge and in one fashion or another have tried to incorporate the expertise of clinicians into computer programs with the long-term goal of creating programs that perform like experts.

The simulation of human expertise is, however, not the primary goal of the field. Rather, the primary goal of this field is to develop computer programs that perform efficiently and competently, and are able to interact and explain their reasoning and conclusions to their users (physicians) in a natural manner. It is believed that understanding human expertise will provide the foundation for the development of such sophisticated computer programs. Based on this assumption, researchers in the field of AIM have attempted to form theories of how physicians think about difficult medical problems and to implement computer programs that use similar organizations of medical knowledge and problem-solving methods. The principal methodology employed in understanding clinical cognition has consisted of introspection on the part of physicians and analysis of thinking-aloud protocols of physician performance during diagnostic encounters. The understanding of human cognitive processes and their implementation in computers is, however, a two-way street. As the existing theories of clinical cognition are formalized in the form of computer programs and certain aspects of clinical expertise are demystified, new and more subtle aspects of human cognition are identified, and the cycle repeats.

Furthermore, as experience is gained with computer models of cognitive processes, and their information processing characteristics are better understood, efficient data structures and algorithms are often developed to implement the same behavior on computers that bear little, if any, resemblance to the original models. This paper traces the evolution of some of these models and their implementations in the field of general medical diagnosis. Detailed descriptions of most of the systems drawn upon can be found in collections of papers edited by Szolovits [1982a], by Clancey and Shortliffe [1984], and by Reggia and Tuhrim [1985].

1.2 *The Hypothetico-Deductive Nature of Diagnostic Process*

Early analysis of clinical problem solving suggested that diagnosis is primarily a hypothetico-deductive process. In its simplest form such an hypothetico-deductive process can be implemented in a program using three steps: (1) Based on some initial findings, the program forms a first set of hypotheses. (2) These hypotheses suggest tests and observations leading to further information gathering. (3) The set of hypotheses is revised to account for new data.

The first programs built along such lines were extremely simple. Later programs developed to address weaknesses of earlier efforts have employed a wide variety of representation and reasoning techniques, ranging widely in degrees of sophistication. A hypothesis, for example, can be simply the name of a disease or an instance of a disease prototype with information on match between the observations and the findings predicted by the prototype disease. In a more sophisticated program, a hypothesis might include sets of co-occurring disorders whose predicted findings taken together cover the observations. A yet more sophisticated program might attempt to form parsimonious sets of hypotheses by taking into account knowledge of common complications and interactions among co-occurring diseases and how they account for the observed findings using a causal/temporal model of disease processes. Similarly, the strategies for gathering new information can range in complexity from simply asking a question to confirm the leading hypothesis or differentiate among the set of hypotheses, to intricate sequencing of questions (planning) that take into consideration the expected value of information, the risks of overlooking relevant data, common medical practice, and stylistic issues of interacting with the user.

Depending on the breadth of the program's domain and on its degree of refinement, the number of hypotheses represented could range from a few to many thousands. The most primitive representation of medical knowledge simply lists findings associated with a given disease. A more sophisticated program may describe the association between diseases and findings using frames and include the probability of occurrence of each finding, its import, and local criteria for concluding a diagnosis. A still more sophisticated representation may include a causal/temporal model of disease as well as a variety of ways in which a disease may present.

In this paper we will study the evolution of computational techniques in the area of medical diagnosis. I will present a number of systems with increasing capabilities and complexity with particular emphasis on the interaction between knowledge-representation and reasoning strategies, and on how our understanding of the nature of diagnostic expertise has changed over time. Let us begin this process with a brief description of a sequential diagnosis program using Bayesian probability theory.

2 Sequential Bayesian Diagnosis

A seminal paper in the sequential diagnosis was published by Gorry and Bennett [1968a]. This paper presented their work on a program for differential diagnosis of acute renal failure (called ARF). This program was designed to diagnose one of 14 specific causes of acute renal failure. It differed from earlier work in probabilistic diagnosis in its use of information theory to actively seek diagnostic information from its users. The differentiation among these 14 possible diagnostic outcomes was carried out using 31 clinical parameters with approximately three to four values for each parameter (approximately 100 findings). The medical knowledge of the program consisted of the prior probability of each disease and a table consisting of the conditional probabilities for findings in each of the 14 diseases. A fragment of the knowledge base for this program is shown in Figure 1. The algorithm used by the program is shown in Figure 2.

This program differed from its predecessors in a number of significant ways. It was based on a sequential algorithm that provided an interactive capability to the program. It was able to provide rudimentary explanation through a *what if* mechanism. For example, during the diagnosis a user could ask the program how the probabilities of different diseases would be affected by some unknown finding. Furthermore, unlike previous programs ARF took into consideration the cost of obtaining information and the cost of missing an important diagnosis. Finally, Gorry reports impressive success with this technique in several medical application domains [Betaque and Gorry, 1971; Gorry and Bar-nett, 1968a]. Using an average of only about seven to nine findings, the ARF program was able to arrive at the same diagnosis as expert clinicians in each of the thirty-three hypothetical cases on which it was initially tested [Gorry and Barnett, 1968b].

The question then arises—Why in spite of these successes did the team of original researchers turn to AI techniques?

The first and most commonly cited reason for this apparent move away from the Bayesian inference technique is its voracity for data. To overcome this problem, the ARF program assumed that the list of diseases under consideration was exhaustive and mutually exclusive. Furthermore, it assumed that findings are conditionally independent, that is, the probability of observing any finding depended solely on the current likelihood of the disease hypotheses but not on the knowledge of other findings. Thus, for example, using the framework of the ARF program it is not possible to state that the presence of nausea increases the chances of vomiting. Even for the small medical domain of the ARF program, approximately 750 conditional probability estimates had to be collected simply to permit the program to discriminate among fourteen causes of acute renal failure. Expanding the program's medical coverage would require a great deal more data. Even that, however, is likely to be insufficient because these antecedent assumptions begin to fail badly as the program's coverage increases. Furthermore, the database of the program is conditioned on the patient population from which it is derived. Thus, moving the program from one region of the country or a hospital to another region with a different patient population is likely to degrade the performance of the program.

Disease	Prior	Conditionals Proteinuria		
		none	trace	gross
FARF	0.4	0.8	0.2	0.001
ATN	0.25	0.1	0.8	0.1
AGN	0.1	0.01	0.2	0.8
OBSTR	0.1	0.7	0.3	0.001
⋮	⋮	⋮	⋮	⋮

Figure 1 An Example data table for the finding of Proteinuria used by the acute renal failure (ARF) program.

[Step 0:]   Construct a vector of probabilities for the fourteen possible hypotheses containing their initial probabilities in the general population of patients.

[Step 1:]   Using Bayes' theorem reevaluate the hypotheses based on newly available information:

$$P_i(H_j) = \frac{P_{i-1}(H_j)P(F/H_j)}{P_{i-1}(F)}$$

where

$$P_{i-1}(F) = \sum_{k=1}^{n} P_{i-1}(H_k)P(F/H_k)$$

Where $P_{i-1}(H_j)$ is the prior probability of hypothesis H_j before the ith finding is taken into account, and $P_i(H_j)$ is the probability after the ith finding is taken into account.

[Step 2:]   If any hypothesis reaches a predefined threshold probability (e.g., 95%), report the diagnosis and stop.

[Step 3:]   Identify the finding with maximum information: Consider each as yet undetermined finding and using each possible result of its determination, compute the resulting probability distribution and its information measure (entropy).

$$E(P_1,...P_n) = \sum_{j=1}^{n} - P_i(H_j)\log_2 P_i(H_j)$$

[Step 4:]   Ask about the finding with the maximum expected information content. Go back to **Step 1**.

Figure 2 Sequential Bayesian diagnosis algorithm used in the ARF program.

In spite of these difficulties, however, the use of Bayes' theorem (at least in spirit) remains at the heart of most diagnostic programs, although they are almost always augmented by other heuristic techniques that will be discussed later. Recent advances in the area of reasoning with uncertainty in AI, such as Bayesian networks, qualitative influence diagrams, and so on, have begun to provide new insights that overcome many earlier criticisms and are likely to lead to more principled use of incomplete probabilistic information in the future generation of AIM programs.

The second and more important problem with Bayesian technique is its computational requirement that the entire repertoire of hypotheses known to a program must be reevaluated each time a new finding is reported. For a small domain this is reasonable, but in a large domain such as internal medicine, where the number of hypotheses range into many thousands, such a process is tantamount to thumbing though the entire textbook of medicine for each finding. Such a process is computationally prohibitive. More important, however, is the fact that it is counter to the way clinicians perform diagnosis.

Furthermore, in choosing the next finding, a program must evaluate the information content of all remaining findings. The set of such findings is at least an order of magnitude larger than the number of possible diagnoses, making this process computationally prohibitive. Much more important, however, is the fact that these processes are clearly counter to the way clinicians approach diagnostic problem solving.

3 *Limiting the Number of Active Hypotheses*

Studies of clinical cognition suggest that clinicians generate only a very small number of hypotheses (no more than five or six) at any one time during the diagnostic process (see Figure 3). Furthermore, it has been observed that the number of hypotheses entertained by more expert clinicians tend to be smaller than those entertained by their less expert counterparts. Similarly limiting the number of hypotheses simultaneously entertained by the program at any one time has significant advantages. Focusing the program's attention on a small number of relevant hypotheses saves much of the effort expended in continually reevaluating all possible diseases. Thus, the program can devote a larger share of its computational resources to each of the hypotheses considered. These resources can then be applied to more sophisticated strategies for evaluating individual hypotheses, forming new hypotheses, and differential diagnosis. Furthermore, by mimicking human information processing characteristics, the program is better able to communicate its reasoning to its users.

How can a similar reduction in the number of hypotheses under consideration be achieved in computer programs without sacrificing performance?

The first step in limiting the number of hypotheses consists of activating from the database only those hypotheses for which at least some evidence has been obtained (reported). A set of hypotheses called the *active hypothesis set* can now be created and maintained by adding the set of diseases supported by each new finding to the existing active hypothesis set.

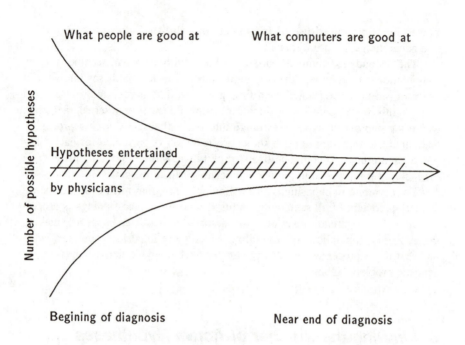

Figure 3 Space of possible hypotheses during diagnostic process. Adapted from an article by M. S. Blois [1980].

A second step, necessary to prevent the active hypothesis set from growing continually as new findings are obtained, consists of removing from consideration those hypotheses that are judged to be no longer viable on the basis of the total available information. This can be accomplished by scoring each active hypothesis based on total available information and *deactivating* those hypotheses whose score falls below a threshold. The threshold used could be predetermined or determined dynamically relative to the best hypothesis in the active set.

The activation/deactivation process described above provides the basic mechanism for a program containing a very large set of potential hypotheses in its knowledge-base to focus on the subset of hypotheses relevant to the situation at hand. The specific technique for activation of hypotheses described above, however, is inadequate. It does not limit the number of hypotheses to the small numbers typically entertained by human clinicians. One source of this inadequacy is the presence of so called *nonspecific findings*, i.e., findings such as weakness that can be caused by a very large number of diseases and thus can result in the activation of a very large set of hypotheses. One solution to this problem is to allow activation of hypotheses only in response to findings highly suggestive of a particular disease.

This strategy can be implemented in several ways. A simple approach would divide the findings associated with a disease into two separate groups, the *trigger findings* and the *non-trigger* findings and use only the trigger findings for the purpose of activation [Pauker et al., 1976b]. Findings other than the trigger findings would be utilized in the diagnostic process only when a particular hypothesis has already been activated. For example, the finding of acute chest pain will activate the hypothesis of "myocardial infarct," whereas the complaint of occasional headaches will not trigger the hypothesis of "brain tumor" but lend support to the hypothesis once it is activated. This approach could be refined to include with each finding associated with a disease a number, called the *evoking strength*, representing the degree of suggestiveness of a finding to the disease. A disease will then be activated only when the total evoking strength of all its findings exceeds a predetermined threshold [Miller et al., 1982]. Unfortunately, both of these strategies are found wanting, because a single finding or combination of independent findings often leads to the generation of an unmanageably large set of hypotheses [Sherman, 1981].

One proposed refinement makes the triggering heuristic more specific by the use of a cluster of related findings rather than a single finding as a trigger. For example, the pattern of "hematuria and flank pain" suggests a much narrower set of hypotheses than either one alone. By varying the size of the triggering cluster, a range of behavior can be achieved.[1,2] Generally, clusters of two or three findings are probably the right size to achieve adequate specificity without risking the chance of missing an important diagnosis [Sherman, 1981].

But even the use of compound triggers can fail to reduce sufficiently the number of hypotheses that must be considered. Often, a cluster of related findings, arising from a shared clinical state or syndrome, is strongly indicative of a fairly large number of underlying diseases, and therefore triggers them all. In the next section we will focus on ways to exploit the source of this problem— commonality among diseases—to further reduce the number of hypotheses considered by the diagnostic process.

3.1 *Hierarchic Organization of Hypotheses*

Cognitively it is much simpler to deal with a single disease hypothesis embodying a large number of possibilities than to deal with each possibility in-

---

1 A compound trigger could, in theory, be made so large as to encompass all the findings relevant to a disease. This would make triggering a disease tantamount to confirming the disease hypothesis. This approach, however, would circumvent the hypothetico-deductive nature of the diagnosis and fail to support the needs of information gathering activity.

2 Alternately, a compound trigger could be viewed as a data-driven rule which suggests the disease in response to the presence of a specific pattern of findings.

dividually. Firstly, because of the shared structure, we can easily identify the commonality among the diseases. Secondly, an aggregate hypothesis can sometimes be ruled out using a few observations, thus simultaneously ruling out all the alternatives within the class. Furthermore, the aggregate may suggest a small set of findings or a preferred method for carrying out differentiation among alternatives without the program having to commit itself to any one of the individual diseases in that aggregate. Such an ability can be implemented easily in a program by hierarchically organizing disease hypotheses.

Hierarchic organization of hypotheses in a program has many advantages. First, it allows the program flexibility in controlling the number of active hypotheses. If too many hypotheses are activated, the program can move up the hierarchy and group the hypotheses together. If on the other hand, too few hypotheses are activated, the program can move down the hierarchy and refine the hypothesis to expand the set of hypotheses. Secondly, each aggregate node in the hierarchy itself represents a frequently encountered differentiation problem. Problem solving knowledge and heuristics specific to that differentiation problem can now be stored with the aggregate node and retrieved efficiently to tailor the diagnostic process. Finally, hierarchic organization provides a systematic basis for organizing a knowledge-base of hypotheses that aids not only in reasoning by the program but also in the construction and maintenance of the knowledge-base.

Use of hierarchic organization of disease hypotheses was first explored in the INTERNIST-I program [Miller et al., 1982]. To evaluate potential advantages of hierarchic reasoning, a version of the INTERNIST-I diagnostic algorithm was implemented in our laboratory (at MIT) and employed using a knowledge-base of approximately 100 birth defects. The performance of the program with and without the use of a hierarchic database was evaluated on 32 cases. Figure 5 shows the number of hypotheses generated by the program after the presentation of findings for each of the 32 cases. Surprisingly, the figure shows that the use of hierarchy did not have significant effect on the number of hypotheses generated [Sherman, 1981]. There are three main reasons for the ineffectiveness of hierarchic reasoning in the INTERNIST-I program.

The first reason stems from the use of a definitional inheritance hierarchy for organizing disease hypotheses similar to those used in other fields of artificial intelligence [Brachman, 1979]. Each node in the hierarchy is defined using features that are common to all its children. Thus, for example, if the nodes labeled *Hepatitis-A*, *Hepatitis-B* and *Infectious Mononucleosis* had findings F1, F2, F3; F1, F2, F4; and F2, F3, F4 respectively as shown in Figure 4, their common superior, *Hepatocellular Infection*, would only have F2 in common. This method of defining aggregate hypotheses is, however, inappropriate for diagnostic knowledge, as the relation between diseases and findings is evidential or associational rather than definitional. Thus, for example, even though the finding of jaundice is present in most liver diseases, there are some liver diseases that do not cause jaundice. In other words, jaundice, although common in liver diseases, is not a necessary or definitional attribute of liver diseases. Thus, jaundice cannot be associated with the description of liver disease. As a result, most disease finding associations in the knowledge-base are concentrated at or near the leaf nodes in the taxonomy, leaving most aggregate disease descriptions without a sufficient number of features for adequate diagnostic reasoning.

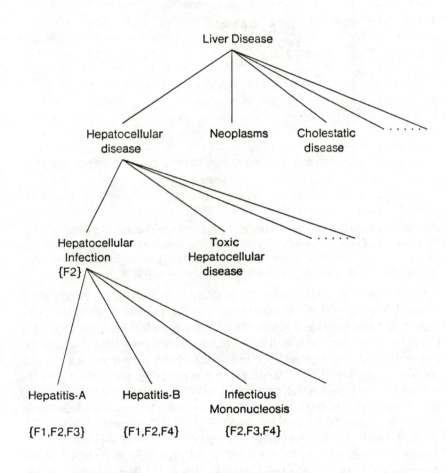

Figure 4 A fragment of INTERNIST-I disease hierarchy.

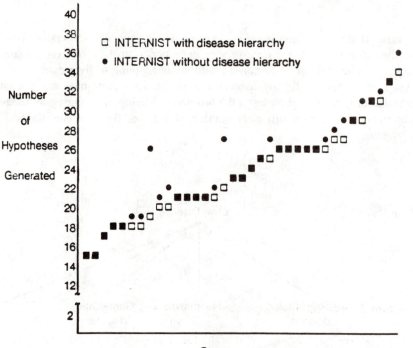

Figure 5 A comparision of the number of hypotheses generated by the INTERNIST-I algorithm implemented in the BDDS program on 32 cases using birth defects database. Adapted from Sherman [1981]. Note: Places where the two symbols □ and ● overlap have been signified with a ■ .

One approach to overcoming this problem is to abandon the notion of inheritance hierarchy. This approach is taken by the developers of the MDX program [Chandrasekaran and Mittal, 1983]. MDX organizes its knowledge as a hierarchy of decision nodes with the leaf nodes representing ultimate diagnostic outcomes. Each intermediate node is associated with only those features that are heuristically useful for either confirming or ruling out that node. One problem with this approach is that the features to be associated with each node and, more importantly, features of lower level nodes that are to be excluded from consideration must be determined individually on an ad hoc basis, placing considerable burden on the knowledge-base designers. Another approach to overcoming this problem is to form a hierarchy of symptoms in parallel with the hierarchy for diseases, that allows aggregate diseases to be associated with abstract findings as shown in Figure 6, and to use heuristic classification technique described by Clancey [1985] for diagnostic reasoning. Both these techniques overcome the problem described above. Neither can, however, deal with the remaining two problems described below.

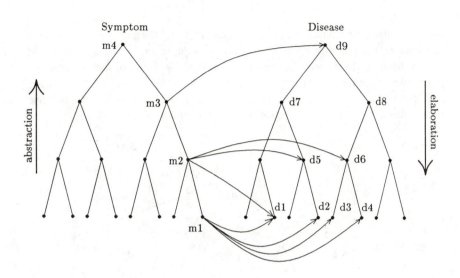

Figure 6 Heuristic-classification using disease and finding hierarchies.

A second problem stems from the fact that there is no one correct way of organizing diseases into a single hierarchy. There are many diseases that involve multiple organ systems or regulatory mechanisms. These diseases share findings with diseases widely dispersed in the hierarchy. Furthermore, because of their many-faceted character, they cannot be placed adequately in any one branch in the hierarchy. Finally, when confronted with a case of one of these multi-system diseases, the program is unable to focus on the appropriate hypothesis in exclusion of sub-components of the disease or other diseases that cover only part of the overall presentation.

Finally, the third problem arises from the fact that hypotheses may be organized hierarchically based on a number of different commonalities. In organizing disease knowledge using a single hierarchy, the designer of the knowledge base must choose one refinement for each disease from among a number of possible refinements. This takes away the ability to choose *at runtime* the commonality that allows the program to operate most efficiently for the case at hand. For example, consider an organization (shown in Figure 7) in which the hypothesis "kidney disease" is first refined using anatomical structure into glomerular, tubular, and cortical kidney diseases and, then using temporal patterns, each of these is further refined into "acute" and "chronic," e.g., acute glomerular disease and chronic glomerular disease. Given this organization, the program can, if it chooses, suppress the temporal ambiguity between acute and chronic glomerular disease into a single hypothesis. When faced with an acute disease of either glomerular or tubular origin, however, the program is unable to aggregate them into acute kidney disease. Of course, if the hierarchy were organized first based on temporal character and then anatomy (as shown in Figure 8), the program could easily deal with the second situation, but would fail on the first. As a consequence of this problem inherent in the organization of disease hypotheses in a single hierarchy, researchers have turned to using multiple hierarchies, making it possible for the program to choose the one among them that is the most appropriate for the case at hand.

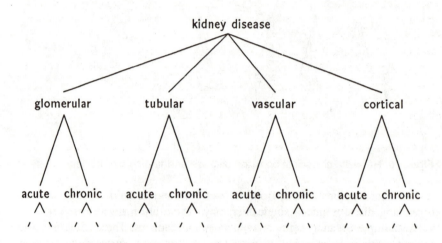

Figure 7 A hierarchic organization for kidney diseases.

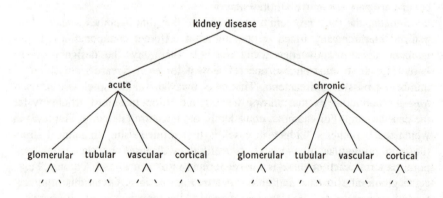

Figure 8 An alternate organization for kidney diseases.

4 *Diagnostic Reasoning Using Multiple Hierarchies*

Diseases can be organized along many dimensions: They are caused by an inciting cause (etiology), they act on an organ (anatomy), the body mounts a physiologic response (pathophysiology) which results in varying degrees (severity) of dysfunctions (signs and symptoms) expressed over a period of time, and so on. It is often possible, even desirable in the early phase of diagnosis, to characterize a clinical problem along these dimensions without committing to any one of a large number of specific disease entities that may underlie a patient's illness. For example, presented with a patient with fever and headache, it is quite reasonable to suspect that the patient's illness is of infectious origin. It is, however, inappropriate to consider specific hypotheses such as meningitis without more information. Working with these dimensions individually, the program can approach clinical problems from a number of different directions. In other words, the program can choose among a number of available viewpoints in working toward its goal—a better characterization of the disease process. When a sufficiently good characterization has been obtained, such that only a small number of specific disease entities are possible, the program can turn its attention to discriminating among them. However, this requires the program to combine different characterizations of the disease processes to identify specific disease hypotheses consistent with all of them.

Combining different characterizations of diseases into a specific differential diagnosis can be achieved through an *intersection heuristic*. If the disease is known to be of infectious etiology and is known to affect the kidney (anatomy), then specific diseases can be identified by intersecting the etiologic hierarchy below infectious diseases with the anatomic hierarchy below kidney diseases, resulting in a differential set containing infectious kidney diseases.[3]

The intersection heuristic works on the assumption that each aggregate hypothesis is providing a different characterization of the same underlying disease. If the available findings identify the etiology for one component disease and anatomy for the other, intersecting the two will result in an empty hypothesis set. In such a situation, the program must conclude either that the patient is suffering from two independent problems or that the two problems are manifestations of some larger multifaceted problem. In either case, the program must abandon the single disease assumption and explore the possibility of multiple disorders.

In the present section we have focused on limiting the number of hypotheses under consideration through a number of mechanisms such as the triggering heuristic, which allows us to focus our attention on those hypotheses that are relevant to the case at hand, and the grouping heuristic, which uses a hierarchy

---

3 Intersection can be achieved efficiently using greatest lower bound algorithm on lattices, similar to the realization algorithm used in Kandor [Brachman et al., 1983].

to aggregate possible hypotheses into a small and manageable number of aggregate hypotheses. Finally, we have considered the use of multiple hierarchies and the use of intersection heuristics for dynamically combining multiple hierarchies. With the number of active hypotheses under consideration limited to a range similar to that used by a clinician, we now turn our attention to the more difficult problem of dealing with the diagnosis of a patient suffering from multiple diseases.

5 Problems in Dealing with Multiple Disorders

The most difficult problem faced by diagnostic programs is to decide whether a patient under consideration is suffering from just one or several disorders (or perhaps none). Most of the programs discussed above allow several diagnoses to be made in a single case. During the process of diagnosis, however, they focus their efforts on identifying the single most likely diagnosis. Only after the first diagnosis is confirmed do they attempt to make the second diagnosis based on the residual findings, and the process is repeated until either all findings are exhausted or the user explicitly terminates the diagnostic process. Such a sequential approach suffers from serious deficiencies. The program does not consider the possibility of multiple disorders at any one time, and it is forced to attribute all observed findings to the primary diagnosis it is trying to establish. As a result, findings that are not in fact relevant to the primary diagnosis can easily confound the diagnostic process.

Assuming just one disease considerably simplifies the diagnostic task, because the program can assume that the hypothesis that is finally accepted must account for all the known data. Thus each finding either favors or acts against a hypothesis, and a finding that favors one hypothesis automatically argues against the others. Furthermore, each disease hypothesis corresponds to a disease description in the program's knowledge base. Thus the process of hypothesis activation is equivalent to instantiating a disease description in the knowledge base. In reality, however, patients often suffer from several disorders, either because they have several independent problems (e.g., an acute infection superimposed on a chronic heart condition), or because one disease may often induce or complicate another.

Algorithms developed to deal with multiple disorders can be divided into two groups. The first group deals with the case of several independent problems. They consider multiple disorders whose findings may overlap but do not interact with each other, that is, the presence of one disease does not alter the features associated with a second concomitant disease. The second group deals with situations when the two diseases may interact with each other giving rise to additional findings not manifested by either of the two diseases or when presence of one disease may occlude some of the findings of the second disease.

5.1 *Dealing With Multiple Disorders Whose Findings Do Not Interact*

The earliest technique for dealing with this problem, called the *partitioning heuristic*, was developed and used in the INTERNIST-I program. The partitioning heuristic is based on the premise that the symptoms associated with coexisting diseases are set additive. This heuristic was used to separate the active diagnostic hypotheses into two groups. First, the *competing group,* containing hypotheses that competed with the leading hypothesis, i.e., explained only a subset of findings explained by the leading hypothesis. Second, the *complementary group*, containing hypotheses that complemented the leading hypothesis, i.e., explained some finding(s) not explained by the leading contender. The program then focused its diagnostic activities on the competing group, setting aside the hypotheses in the complementary group for later consideration. In a study of the INTERNIST-I and PIP diagnostic algorithms by Sherman [1981], the partitioning heuristic was found to be a key to INTERNIST-I's superior performance over the Present Illness Program.

The partitioning heuristic fails to deal adequately with the problem of multiple disorders for two reasons. The first problem results from the program's inability to properly account for findings. In the presence of multiple disorders it is not clear when a program can reasonably conclude that some finding has been successfully accounted for. A finding that has already been accounted for by a confirmed diagnosis can either be allowed to continue to lend support to additional diagnoses or not. Both of these choices lead to problematic behavior. The first leads the program to continue its diagnostic activity interminably in pursuit of ever-more implausible combinations of diagnoses that would account in new ways for findings that have already been accounted for adequately. The second, on the other hand, can often prevent the program from correctly diagnosing a co-occurring disease that shares a significant fraction of its findings with an already confirmed diagnosis.

A second problem results from the ephemeral nature of the competing and complementary hypotheses in INTERNIST-I. During each cycle of the information gathering process, the program reevaluates all hypotheses and re-partitions them from scratch. The partitioning is based primarily on the leading hypothesis. As a result, the differentiation problem formed by the INTERNIST-I program changes radically with each change in the leading hypothesis. This problem is particularly acute in dealing with two or more diseases whose findings overlap appreciably, such as, urinary tract infection and pyelonephritis.

Over the last several years, a number of techniques have been developed to deal with multiple disorders [Reggia et al., 1983; de Kleer and Williams, 1987; Reiter, 1987]. They overcome the problems resulting from the ephemeral nature of problem formulation by directly representing and manipulating the competing hypotheses. Each competing hypothesis, also called a candidate hypothesis, is represented as a set of individual disease hypotheses which when taken together explain all of the observed symptoms. Following the *principle of parsimony* [de Kleer and Williams, 1987; Reiter, 1987], only minimal candidate sets are considered during the diagnostic process. A candidate set is considered minimal if no subset of the set can completely account for all observed anomalies.

The space of possible candidate hypotheses is the power set of individual disease hypotheses, and is thus very large. Nevertheless, programs dealing with them can be made efficient because during the process of sequential diagnosis, the candidate sets can be refined incrementally. That is, when presented with a new finding, the existing minimal candidate sets can be refined efficiently to produce new sets that take the new finding into account. Whenever a new symptom is presented that is not explained by a candidate set, it is replaced by one or more new minimal candidate sets, each of which contains the old candidate plus one additional disease hypothesis accounting for the newly observed symptom. Any new candidate that is subsumed or duplicated by another is eliminated; the remaining candidates are added to the set of new minimal candidates.

The generalized set cover techniques have been applied widely in electronics and other engineering domains [Davis and Hamscher, 1988]. This technique is particularly suited for diagnosis from first principles reasoning using the structure and function of a healthy system. Our understanding of the human body is, however, sufficiently incomplete to allow us to deduce human physiology from the knowledge of human anatomy. As a result, the use of structure and function reasoning in medicine has been limited to areas such as localization of neurological defects. Generalized set cover technique does not, however, require reasoning from structure and function and thus can be used with experiential knowledge of disease-finding associations described earlier. Furthermore, the generalized set cover techniques can also exploit hierarchic organization of diseases by allowing candidate hypotheses to use aggregate disease nodes as their elements [Davis, 1984]. The candidates formed using aggregates must, however, be refined during the process of diagnosis. When dealing with tree-structured hierarchies, such a refinement can be achieved in a straightforward manner by applying the algorithm recursively in the limited context of the symptoms explained by the aggregate hypothesis being refined and the diseases subsumed by the aggregate. Special care must be taken to guarantee that the candidates formed using aggregates are minimal, that is, no two aggregate elements of the candidate have a common descendant.[4]

---

4   If two aggregate elements of a candidate have a common descendant then the candidate is not minimal, as replacing the two aggregates with their common descendant would result in a better candidate hypothesis.

The situation where one disease may cause or precipitate another can also be incorporated within the generalized set cover techniques by extending the definition of minimality of candidates. Consider, for example, two candidate hypotheses where the elements of the first are causally related and the second are not. Intuitively, the first candidate is much more appealing than the second. This notion can be captured in the principle of parsimony by minimizing the number of causally related clusters or ultimate etiologies[5] in a candidate. Note that when the elements of a candidate set are causally unrelated, this definition reverts to the original definition of minimal candidate. A causal relation, once established, can also be exploited during the refinement process in a manner as illustrated by the following example.

Consider a patient with anemia and hepatobiliary involvement (liver disease) in whom the anemia is caused by the hepatobiliary disease (as shown in Figure 9). Let us assume that the program has identified a candidate set containing anemia and hepatobiliary involvement. The number of possible pairs of diseases (two levels below the starting nodes shown in the two hierarchies) ranges in the hundreds, while only two of them are consistent with causal assumption. If the program assumes that the two are causally related, it need consider only those two hypotheses that are compatible with the causal assumption. Figure 10 illustrates the process of identifying these two hypotheses by alternately refining the anemia and the hepatobiliary involvement nodes. Figure 11 shows the two composite hypotheses resulting from this process. Furthermore, the hypotheses considered are precisely those that can occur in practice. A program (called CADUCEUS) that embodies a similar strategy is currently under development at the University of Pittsburgh [Pople, 1982].

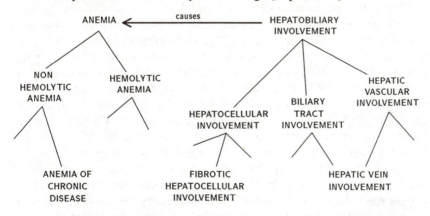

Figure 9 Fragments from two hierarchies below anemia and hepatobiliary disease where anemia is suspected to be caused by the hepatobiliary disease.

---

5 Ultimate etiologies can be defined as elements that do not have causal antecedents in the candidate hypothesis.

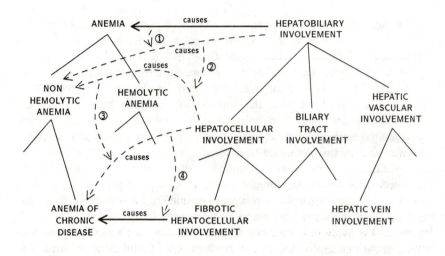

Figure 10a

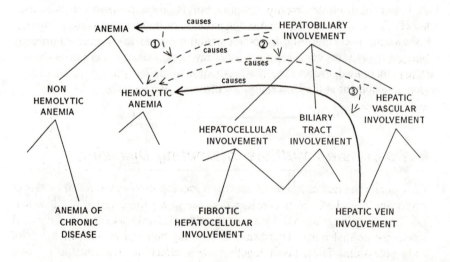

Figure 10b

Figure 10 Two possible refinements of the causal relation between anemia and hepatobiliary disease. Circled numbers show the sequence of intermediate refinements.

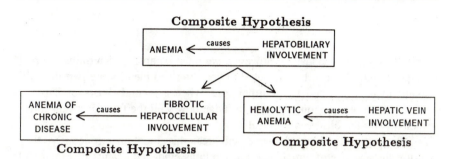

Figure 11 Two successful refinements of the hypothesis that the observed anemia is caused by a hepatobiliary disease.

In this section we have reviewed a number of strategies for going beyond the single disease assumption by directly generating and manipulating sets of compatible hypotheses. Furthermore, we have observed that causal relation can be used effectively in limiting the space of possible combination of hypotheses. Throughout this section we have made the assumption that the findings of two or more co-occurring diseases are set additive. Such an assumption can be justified in diagnosis from structure and function where any deviation from the normal behavior is considered a conflict (symptom) and no further distinction among symptoms need be made. Significantly richer characterization of a symptom based on its severity, temporal evolution, precipitating circumstance, and so on, is necessary for proper diagnosis in medicine. Furthermore, because homeostatic processes responsible for maintaining life are comprised of many intricate feedback loops, malfunction of any organ system can potentially influence the proper functioning of almost all other systems in the body. As a result, interactions among co-occurring diseases are common in medicine and must be addressed.

6 Diagnosing Multiple Interacting Diseases

To illustrate the rich character of clinical reasoning involved in the diagnosis of interacting disorders, let us consider the case of a patient suffering from diarrhea and vomiting who is hypovolemic, hypokalemic and has a serum pH within the normal range. Diarrhea and vomiting both cause substantial loss of body potassium. Thus, taken together, their effect on hypokalemia is compounded. On the other hand, diarrhea results in loss of alkalis, vomiting results in loss of body acids. Therefore, taken together they tend to offset each other's effect on serum acidity. For the sake of example, let us suppose that we know about the vomiting but are not aware of the diarrhea. In such a situation, the observed hypokalemia is too severe to be accounted for properly by the vomiting alone; vomiting cannot be considered a complete explanation for the observed severity of hypokalemia. Therefore, a program must consider vomiting either as not responsible for hypokalemia or only partially responsible for it. If vomiting is partly responsible, however, we must be able to determine the part of hypokalemia that can be attributed to vomiting and identify the part that still remains to be accounted for. Furthermore, when a second cause for hypokalemia is identified, we must be able to judge how well the two causes taken together explain the observed hypokalemia.

The programs discussed above will treat this situation erroneously; they will use the absence of anticipated alkalemia as evidence against vomiting and lower their belief in it. They will, therefore, fail to identify the second disorder, namely diarrhea, that is surreptitiously masking the effects of vomiting on serum alkalinity. Even if diarrhea were activated through some other finding, these programs would consider the normal value of serum pH as evidence against the hypothesis. A program that allows a proper accounting for the findings will, however, attribute only a part of the hypokalemia and hypovolemia to the vomiting and will be able to identify an as yet unknown factor compensating for the effects of vomiting on serum acidity. It will thus be able to hypothesize the presence of a second disorder that in the absence of vomiting should lead to hypokalemia, hypovolemia, and acidosis.

To capture the richness of medical knowledge and clinical reasoning illustrated above, we have been developing an experimental program called ABEL [Patil, 1981]. ABEL's knowledge base includes descriptions of causal mechanisms that capture the relation between the severity and duration of cause and effect. It uses composite hypotheses that are capable of representing multiple concomitant disorders, and it can deal with interactions among diseases through the use of detailed pathophysiologic models of disease processes. Finally, ABEL combines the shallow experiential knowledge of association between diseases and findings with deep pathophysiologic knowledge for efficient diagnostic reasoning.

6.1 *Organization of Medical Knowledge in* ABEL

The basic medical knowledge in ABEL consists of hierarchical representations of anatomic, physiologic, etiologic, and temporal knowledge. A disease is characterized in terms of its anatomic involvement, its temporal character, its etiologic origin, and the functional derangement resulting from it. As each element of anatomic, etiologic, and pathophysiologic knowledge is organized in a taxonomic hierarchy, the projection of a disease description along each of these dimensions can be used to derive a unique lattice structure, based on the subsumption relation [Brachman and Schmolze, 1985], so that a general description of a disease or clinical state appears above more specific descriptions. The disease descriptions are then augmented using causal relationships.

The causal knowledge in the program is organized at several levels of detail. At the shallowest level this knowledge is in terms of diseases and their clinically observable manifestations. At the deepest level this knowledge includes detailed biochemical and pathophysiologic mechanisms that provide quantitative relations among normal and abnormal physiologic parameters and processes. Additional information is also provided to describe the connection of knowledge at one level to that at adjacent levels.

The causal knowledge at each level of detail is organized in terms of nodes and links. Nodes are clusters of information that describe physiologic and clinical states. Nodes are linked to one another by causal links or by links that describe associations when underlying causal mechanisms are not clear. Causal links may connect a node describing a disease or a clinical state to one or more nodes that describe its effects. They specify the relationship between the severity, duration, and other relevant aspects of the cause and the effect nodes, that is, given a cause and an effect node it is possible to compare the two for causal consistency. Furthermore, reasoning may be carried out in the forward or the reverse direction; a cause may be used to predict the effects or an effect used to deduce the necessary severity and duration of a cause. Additional information is also provided to permit the combining of separate effects into a joint one when multiple causes are present or suspected.

Multi-level representation of nodes allows the knowledge base to describe a high level node (called a *composite node*) in terms of a network of states and causal relations at the next lower level (Figure 12). One of the nodes in this causal network is designated as the *focus node*. The focus node identifies the essential part of the causal structure (called the *elaboration*) of the node above it. Indeed, the collection of focal nodes acts to align the causal network representing the medical knowledge at different levels of detail. Nodes that do not play a role as a focal definition of any node at a higher level are called *non-aggregable* nodes. They represent the detailed aspects of the causal model introduced at the given level that was subsumed under other nodes with different foci at less detailed levels of description. Finally, nodes that are not described at the next lower level of detail are called *primitive nodes*. Such a situation arises when either the pathophysiology of a given state is not available, or it is not medically relevant.

Multi-level representation of links allows the knowledge base to describe a high-level relation between two clinical or pathophysiologic states at the next more detailed level using a chain of causal relations. Similar to nodes, links described in such a manner are called *composite links*, and links that do not contain such structure are called *primitive links*. A schematic causal relation described at multiple levels of detail is shown in Figure 13.

Causal knowledge organized as above plays two important roles in the diagnostic reasoning processes. The causal pathways associated with links play a key role in elaborating clinical level descriptions to the detailed pathophysiologic level, whereas the causal network associated with a node plays a central role in identifying clusters that can be meaningfully aggregated in developing a coherent diagnosis.

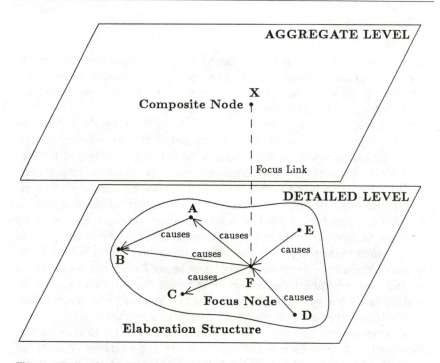

Figure 12 A schematic description of the multilevel node structure in ABEL.

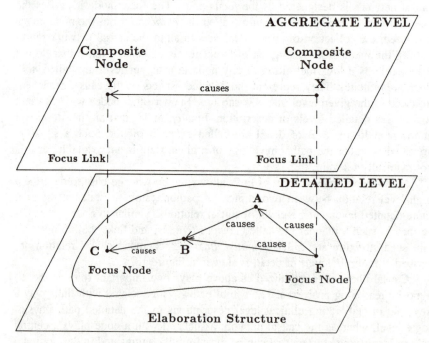

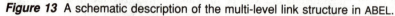

Figure 13 A schematic description of the multi-level link structure in ABEL.

6.2 *Composite Hypotheses*

To deal effectively with diagnoses involving multiple interacting disorders, a program must have the capability to develop composite hypotheses that include not only the list of individual disorders thought to be simultaneously present but also an account of which disorder explains what finding and how the presence of one disorder modifies the expression of another. Unlike individual disease descriptions, that can be stored in the knowledge base and activated directly to form individual disease hypotheses, the number of possible composite hypotheses is so large that to store them directly in the knowledge base is impractical. They must therefore be constructed. This process of constructing composite hypotheses, each of which provides an alternate comprehensive account of observed manifestations of the patient's illness, is akin to the process of constructing scientific theories to explain observed phenomena [Pople, 1982; Patil et al., 1982a,b]. Thus in a process similar to scientific theory formation, the program's composite hypotheses must be refined and debugged to accommodate new data and abandoned only when significant contradictions are discovered.

Composite hypotheses in ABEL are described using a set of patient-specific models (PSMs), each of which attempts to explain all the known facts about a patient. Furthermore, each PSM is itself a multi-level structure, describing the same diagnostic explanation (composite hypothesis) at varying levels of detail, starting at the top from a clinical level summary to the detailed pathophysiology of the patient's illness. A PSM is created by instantiating portions of ABEL's medical knowledge. Much of the meaning of an observation depends on the context provided by the PSM; conversely, the PSM is created by assimilating many observations. As the PSM is multi-level, this assimilation requires the ability to summarize detailed pathophysiologic descriptions into concise clinical summaries and the ability to disaggregate summaries into detailed descriptions. This is achieved in the program using *aggregation* and *disaggregation* operators. An example of a composite hypothesis is shown in Figure 14.

A critical feature of the PSM is its ability to determine interactions among multiple diseases. This is achieved by a pair of operators: *component summation* and *decomposition*. Efficient implementation of these operators in ABEL depends critically on its ability to expand a high-level clinical description down to the pathophysiologic level and vice versa. When an interaction between disorders is identified at the clinical level, ABEL disaggregates the relevant clinical context to the detailed pathophysiologic level, which includes quantitative parameters that can be added or subtracted without any special case knowledge. It then aggregates the result back to the clinical level. The program can thus circumvent the combinatoric explosion that would result if each possible interaction among diseases were stored individually.

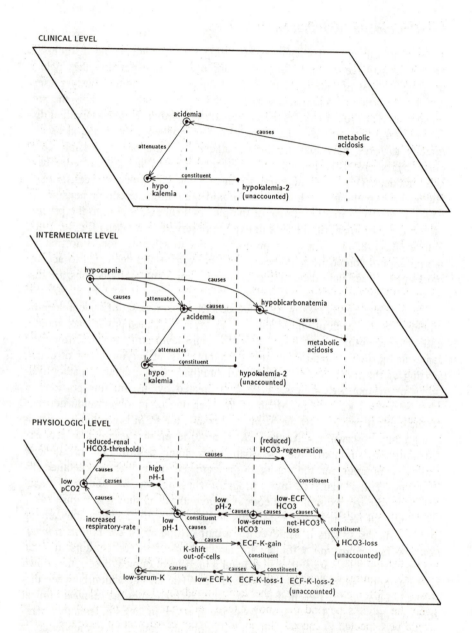

Figure 14 A fragment from the multi-level patient-specific model for a patient suffering from metabolic-acidosis and hypokalemia.

6.3 *Diagnostic Problem Solving in* ABEL

ABEL takes a radically different view of diagnosis from the other programs discussed above. Unlike most previous systems that view diagnosis as a process of classifying a patient's illness into one or more disease categories, ABEL views diagnosis as a process of constructing a model or a theory that can explain a given patient's illness. The process of diagnosis in ABEL is carried out by first constructing a small number of PSMs that provide consistent (if partial) interpretations of the known facts about a patient's illness. Each of these PSMs is then used to construct a possible scenario of the patient's illness by identifying those elements in the PSM that need further explanations, identifying additional diseases (causes) that could explain them, and for each such additional disease, identifying additional findings that would be observed if the patient in fact had the hypothesized disease. An example scenario for the PSM shown in Figure 15.

Having developed individual scenarios, the program turns its attention to the process of planning its information gathering strategy. To this end, the program compares different scenarios. It identifies key differences among the scenarios under consideration and makes these the top-level goal for further investigation. Each of these goals is then decomposed into sub-goals. This process is repeated until each of the terminal goals can be confirmed directly through one or more questions. This plan is then refined and reorganized based on other considerations, such as the cost of gathering each piece of information and common medical practice. This plan is then used to gather new information. Existing patient-specific models are revised on the basis of this information and the process is repeated until a working diagnosis is reached.[6]

In summary, ABEL goes beyond the existing medical diagnosis programs by taking into consideration the severity and duration of each disease and by formulating detailed models of the patient's illness. Such models allow the program to reason with the details of the disease process, to recognize how one disease can alter the presentation of another, and to sort out component elements due to each disease. This capability is achieved through the use of causal reasoning. The results we have obtained cannot be achieved by probabilistic techniques. ABEL's models (PSMs) are built using a knowledge base that encodes the various ways in which a disorder presents and quantitative information that captures an understanding of the severity of the illness. For the purposes of differential diagnosis the same knowledge base is used again to expand the models beyond the known facts, playing out scenarios of what else would be expected if, indeed, the etiology under consideration were the correct

---

6   A more complete description of this information gathering process is available in [Patil et al., 1982a,b].

one. On the basis of these scenarios, the program identifies the critical diagnostic points on which to focus its questioning of the physician.

Because ABEL builds detailed causal models for each diagnosis under consideration, it can also explain the logical processes by which it arrived at its diagnostic assessment. Such an explanation, in our view, is critical if the user is to have any faith in the program's recommendations. Just as in the case of any consultant, the reasonableness of the diagnostic conclusions must be assessed by the physician seeking help. This requirement becomes especially important as programs become larger and more complex, because they will, in all likelihood, make occasional mistakes. The ability to explain itself will also be critical to "debugging" the program when it has made an error and to updating the program in light of new clinical or physiologic information.

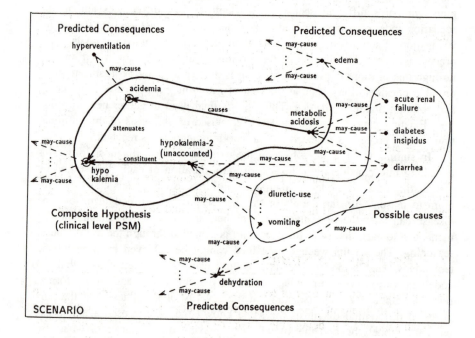

Figure 15 Set of scenarios consistent with the PSM of Figure 14.

There are several key problems. The first problem with ABEL arises from its reliance on knowledge of detailed quantitative pathophysiology. In most areas of medicine, however, such detailed understanding of quantitative relations among physiologic parameters is not available. The techniques developed in ABEL could still be applied using more aggregate quantitative or qualitative relations, but their effectiveness is likely to degrade rapidly. A second problem arises due to the lack of probabilistic reasoning in ABEL, particularly in situations where a unique working diagnosis cannot be established on the basis of clinical data. The lack of an ability to estimate the relative likelihood of the alternative composite hypotheses thus prevents ABEL from resolving such situations and from planning the optimal course of treatment.

Finally, in designing ABEL to deal with complex clinical situations, we have built a program that reasons extremely carefully with all cases presented to it, be they simple or complex. The cost incurred in running ABEL can be justified for a complex case, but for a routine case this cost must be viewed as excessive, since such a straightforward case could be solved much more efficiently by a program such as CADUCEUS or INTERNIST-I.

Thus, we are faced with the challenge of developing a new program that meets the following criteria: It can deal with a broad domain such as internal medicine; while it solves routine cases efficiently, it can increase the level of its analysis as the cases become more complex, using the best available pathophysiologic knowledge when necessary. We believe that such a challenge can be met by synthesizing many of the techniques described in this paper with a number of recent AI advances in the areas of reasoning with uncertainty, temporal reasoning, qualitative reasoning, compilation of causal knowledge, and case-based reasoning. Of course, such an exercise in synthesis will necessarily involve a number of modifications and reorganizations of the existing techniques. More importantly, it will require development of large new knowledge-bases of medicine, a long and arduous task that in itself is likely to challenge the state-of-the-art in knowledge acquisition and acquisition techniques.

7 Where Do We Stand?

We have discussed a number of techniques that have evolved over the last two decades in the field of medical diagnosis. We have been able to capture the clinician's expertise in being able to narrow down the scope of diagnostic hypotheses from many thousands to a handful through the use of hypothesis activation and hierarchic problem-reformulation heuristics. We have been able to achieve a very high level of performance comparable to the best experts in analyzing complex clinical situations in some limited fields through the use of causal knowledge. The field of Artificial Intelligence in Medicine has provided inspiration and technology for the development of expert systems in many fields outside of medicine, through exemplary projects such as MYCIN [Buchanan and Shortliffe, 1984], CASNET [Weiss and Kulikowski, 1984], and INTERNIST [Miller et al., 1982]. Why is it, then, that very few programs, if any, are currently in use?

First, most of the successes of the expert system technology have come in commercial tasks such as configuring computers (R1/XCON [McDermott, 1982]) and scheduling maintenance of telephone networks (ACE [Vesonder et al., 1983]). These successes have been possible largely because of the well-defined character of the problem and the knowledge needed to solve the problem. Furthermore, these programs could be deployed gainfully even though they are unable to perform at a near-perfect level. An occasional failure to identify an impending problem in a telephone network or to configure a customer order can be measured in terms of dollars lost and traded against efficiency and cost savings achieved through the program more readily than the consequences of a misdiagnosis in a seriously ill patient. Unrealistic expectations about the performance of programs in the medical field in conjunction with a lack of technology for evaluating and certifying these programs has been a great impediment to the utilization of the programs [Schwartz et al., 1987].

Lack of adequate inroads by information support technology (such as patient information management systems) into the practice of medicine has continued to keep the cost of interacting with expert computer programs unreasonably high. For example, most consulting programs require, at minimum, 15 to 30 minutes of interaction to provide routine clinical facts about a case.[7] On the other hand, for most complex cases requiring expert attention, a clinician in a major medical center can obtain an expert opinion with a phone call lasting just a few minutes.

Finally, the choice of expert consultation as the model for interaction between the clinician and the program itself leads to some impediments. Such a model tends to raise expectations about a program's performance, inspiring fear among clinicians that if such a technology becomes commonplace it would affect their job security and earning potential. To address this issue the field has more recently turned to the exploration of less threatening models for interaction that assist a clinician in resolving difficult clinical problems by meeting his problem-specific informational needs (INTERNIST/QMR [Miller et al, 1986]), aiding in the evaluation of alternative treatment modalities (CHF [Long et al., 1984]), and critiquing patient management plans [Miller (Perry), 1986]. These and other similar approaches give promise of being more acceptable and thus playing a larger role in the everyday practice of medicine.

---

7 Only by extracting needed information directly from patient records can a system reduce the cost to the clinician of using these systems.

Acknowledgments

The author's research is supported by National Institutes of Health grants R24 RR 01320 from the Division of Research Resources and R01 LM 04493 from the National Library of Medicine.

References

Betaque, Norman E. and G. Anthony Gorry, 1971. Automating judgmental decision making for a serious medical problem. *Management Science* **17**:B421–B434.

Bleich, Howard L., 1972. Computer-based consultation: Electrolyte and acid-base disorders. *AJM* **53**:285.

Blois, Marsden S., 1980. Clinical judgement and computers. *New England Journal of Medicine* **303**:192–197.

Brachman, Ronald J., 1979. A structural paradigm for representing knowledge.

Brachman, Ronald J., Richard E. Fikes, and Hector J. Levesque, 1983. Krypton: A functional approach to knowledge representation. *Computer* **16**(10):67–73.

Brachman, Ronald J. and James G. Schmolze, 1985. An overview of the kl-one knowledge representation system. *Cognitive Science* **9**:171–216.

Buchanan, Bruce G. and Edward H. Shortliffe, ed., 1984. *Rule-Based Expert Systems: The MYCIN Experiments of the Stanford Heuristic Programming Project*. Reading: Addison-Wesley.

Chandrasekaran, B. and S. Mittal, 1983. Conceptual representation of medical knowledge for diagnosis by computer: MDX and related systems. *Advances in Computers*, M. Yovits, ed., pp. 217–293. New York: Academic Press.

Clancey, William J., 1985. Heuristic classification. *Artificial Intelligence* **27**:289–350.

Clancey, William J. and Edward H. Shortliffe, ed., 1984. *Readings in Medical Artificial Intelligence: The First Decade*. Reading: Addison Wesley.

Davis, Randall, 1984. Diagnostic reasoning based on structure and behavior. *Artificial Intelligence* **24**:347–410.

Davis, Randall and Walter Hamscher, 1988. Model-based reasoning: Troubleshooting. Chapter 8, this volume.

de Dombal, F. T., D. J. Leaper, J. R. Staniland, A. P. McCann, and Jane C. Horrocks, 1972. Computer-aided diagnosis of abdominal pain. *British Medical Journal* **2**:9–13.

de Kleer, Johan and Brian C. Williams, 1987. Diagnosing multiple faults. *Artificial Intelligence* **32**:97–130.

Gorry, G. A. and G. O. Barnett, 1968a. Experience with a model of sequential diagnosis. *Computers and Biomedical Research* **1**:490–507.

Gorry, G. A. and G. O. Barnett, 1968b. Sequential diagnosis by computer. *Journal of the American Medical Association* **205**(12):849–854.

Ladley, R. S. and L. B. Lusted, 1959. Reasoning foundations of medical diagnosis. *Science* **130**:9–21.

Long, W. J., S. Naimi, M. G. Criscietello, S. G. Pauker, and P. Szolovits, 1984. An aid to physiological reasoning in the management of cardiovascular disease. In *Proceedings of the Computers in Cardiology Conference*, pp. 3–6. IEEE.

McDermott, J., 1982. R1's formative years. *Artificial Intelligence Magazine* **2**(2):21–29.

Miller, Perry L., 1986. *Expert Critiquing Systems: Practice-based Medical Consultation by Computer*. New York: Springer-Verlag.

Miller, Randolph A., Harry E. Pople, Jr., and Jack D. Myers. 1982. INTERNIST-I, an experimental computer-based diagnostic consultant for general internal medicine. *New England Journal of Medicine* **307**:468–476.

Miller, R.A., M. A. McNeil, S. M. Challinor, F. E. Masari, Jr., and J. D. Myers, 1986. The INTERNIST-I/quick medical reference project—status report. *Western Journal of Medicine* **145**:816–822.

Patil, Ramesh S., 1981. Causal representation of patient illness for electrolyte and acid-base diagnosis. Technical Report No. 267, Massachussetts Institute of Technology, Laboratory for Computer Science, 545 Technology Square, Cambridge, MA, 02139.

Patil, R. S., P. Szolovits, and W. B. Schwartz, 1982a. Information acquisition in diagnosis. In *Proceedings of the National Conference on Artificial Intelligence*, Pittsburgh, Pennsylvania, pp. 345–348. San Mateo: Morgan Kaufmann.

Patil, Ramesh S., Peter Szolovits, and William B. Schwartz, 1982b. Modeling knowledge of the patient in acid-base and electrolyte disorders. *Artificial Intelligence in Medicine*, Peter Szolovits, ed., pp. 187–222. Boulder: Westview Press.

Pauker, S. G., P. Szolovits, H. Silverman, W. Swartout, and G. A. Gorry, 1976a. A computer program that captures clinical expertise about digitalis therapy and provides explanations of its recommendations. In *Computer Networking in the University: Success and Potential; Proc. of the EDUCOM Fall Conference*, pp. 187–189. EDUCOM.

Pauker, Stephen G., Anthony Gorry, Jerome P. Kassirer, and William B. Schwartz, 1976b. Towards the simulation of clinical cognition: Taking a present illness by computer. *American Journal of Medicine* **60**:981–996.

Pople, Harry E. Jr., 1975. The dialog model of diagnostic logic and its use in internal medicine. In *Proceedings of the Fourth International Joint Conference on Artificial Intelligence*, Tibilisi, USSR, pp. 1030–1037.

Pople, Harry E. Jr., 1982. Heuristic methods for imposing structure on ill-structured problems: The structuring of medical diagnostics. *Artificial Intelligence in Medicine*, Peter Szolovits, ed., pp. 119–190. Boulder: Westview Press.

Reggia, James A., Dana S. Nau, and Pearl Y. Wang, 1983. Diagnostic expert systems based on a set covering model. *International Journal of Man-Machine Studies* **19**:437–460.

Reggia, James and Stanley Tuhrim, ed., 1985. *Computer-assisted Medical Decision Making*. New York: Springer-Verlag.

Reiter, Raymond, 1987. A theory of diagnosis from first principles. *Artificial Intelligence* **32**:57–96.

Rosati, R. A., J. F. McNeer, C. F. Starmer, B. S. Mittler, J. J. Morris, and A. G. Wallace, 1975. A new information system for medical practice. *Archives of Internal Medicine* **135**:1017–1024.

Schwartz, W.B., R. S. Patil, and P. Szolovits, 1987. Artificial intelligence in medicine: Where do we stand. *New England Journal of Medicine* **316**:685–688.

Sherman, Howard Bruce, 1981. A comparative study of computer-aided clinical diagnosis of birth defects. Technical Report No. 283, Massachussetts Institute of Technology, Laboratory for Computer Science, 545 Technology Square, Cambridge, MA, 02139.

Shortliffe, Edward Hance, 1976. *MYCIN: Computer-based Medical Consultations*. New York: American Elsevier.

Szolovits, Peter, ed., 1982a. *Artificial Intelligence in Medicine*. Volume 51 of *AAAS Selected Symposium Series*. Boulder: Westview Press.

Vesonder, Gregg T., Salvatore J. Stolfo, John E. Zielinski, Frederick D. Miller, and David H. Copp, 1983. Ace: An expert system for telephone cable maintenance. In *Proceedings of the Eighth International Joint Conference on Artificial Intelligence*, Karlsruhe, West Germany, pp. 116–121. San Mateo: Morgan Kaufmann.

Weiss, Sholom and Casimir Kulikowski, 1984. *A Practical Guide to Designing Expert Systems*. Totowa, N. J.: Rowman and Allanheld.

THEORETICAL UNDERPINNINGS

10

Evidential Reasoning Under Uncertainty

Judea Pearl

Cognitive Systems Laboratory
Computer Science Department
University of California, Los Angeles

1 *Introduction*

1.1 *Overview*

One can hardly identify a field in AI that doesn't use some sort of evidential reasoning, namely, processes leading from evidence or clues to guesses and conclusions under conditions of partial information. Therefore, to avoid having to cover the entire field of AI, the topic will be limited to evidential reasoning tasks in which the uncertainty is given a specific notation, namely, it is represented explicitly by some sort of measure or degree.

Constrained by this guideline, I will not be able to give a full account of the heuristic approaches to evidential reasoning [Cohen, 1985; Clancey, 1985] nor to works in truth-maintenance systems and nonmonotonic reasoning that, essentially, address the same sort of problems. The latter are given full coverage by other surveys (see this volume), and will only be touched on briefly to point out their fundamental ties to other formalisms.

Additionally, it will not be possible to survey everything that anyone has said or written about uncertainty, nor would I be able to summarize the intricacies of powerful programs such as MYCIN [Shortliffe, 1976], INTERNIST [Miller et al., 1982], PROSPECTOR [Duda et al., 1976], MEDAS [Ben-Bassat et al., 1980], RUM [Bonissone et al., 1987], MUM [Cohen et al., 1987a] and MDX [Chandrasakaran and Mittal, 1983] that have embodied practical solutions to various aspects of reasoning with uncertainty. This survey focuses on a select set of issues, trends, and principles that have emerged from these past works and which I hope to describe in a unifying perspective and in greater depth than a more general survey would permit. For more extensive surveys, the reader is referred to [Thompson, 1985; Prade, 1983; Stephanou and Sage, 1987], and the works collected in [Kanal and Lemmer, 1986]. Expanded technical treatments of the topics discussed in this survey can be found in [Pearl, 1988a].

The thrust of this survey is shown in Figure 1—it depicts my perception of current approaches to evidential reasoning and is, in fact, a summary of this discussion. I will spend the first part discussing the general needs and difficulties of managing uncertainty, and then talk about two diametrically opposed approaches to the problem; one called *extensional*, the other *intensional* .[1] The extensional approach, also known as production systems, rule-based systems, or procedure-based systems, treats uncertainty as a generalized truth value attached to formulas and, following the tradition of classical logic, computes the uncertainty of any formula as a function of the uncertainties of its subformulas. It is characterized by computationally attractive features, but is semantically sloppy. In the intensional approach, also known as declarative or model-based approach, uncertainty is attached to "states of affairs" or subsets of "possible worlds." It is semantically clear but computationally clumsy. Naturally, there have been attempts from both sides to rectify their respective deficiencies. I will briefly discuss (Section 2) some movements from the extensional to the intensional, and will spend most of the time on movements with which you are more familiar, namely, attempts to make intensional approaches computationally more attractive (Section 3).

In this vein, I will discuss the central role of *belief networks* representations, both the Bayesian type and the Dempster-Shafer type. Finally, I will speculate (Section 4) on the middle ground toward which the two approaches will hopefully converge in the next few years. This area, I believe, will involve the issues of encoding context-dependent information, the formalization of relevance, and network decomposition techniques.

---

1   This terminology is due to [Perez and Jirousek, 1985].

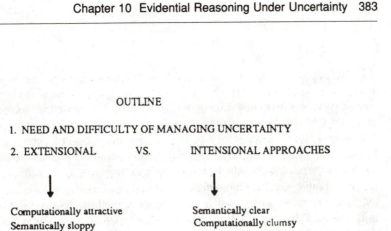

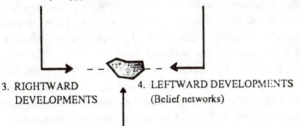

OUTLINE

1. NEED AND DIFFICULTY OF MANAGING UNCERTAINTY

2. EXTENSIONAL   VS.   INTENSIONAL APPROACHES

Computationally attractive   Semantically clear
Semantically sloppy   Computationally clumsy

3. RIGHTWARD   4. LEFTWARD DEVELOPMENTS
   DEVELOPMENTS   (Belief networks)

5. MEETING GROUNDS?

Figure 1 Outline of survey and relationships between extensional and intensional approaches to uncertainty.

1.2 *Why Bother with Uncertainty?*

Reasoning about any realistic domain always requires that some simplifications be made. By necessity, we leave many facts unknown, unsaid, or crudely summarized. For example, most rules used to encode knowledge and behavior have exceptions that one cannot afford to enumerate, and the situations in which the rules apply are usually ambiguously defined or hard to satisfy precisely in real life. Reasoning with exceptions is like navigating through a minefield; most steps are safe but some can be devastating. Given its location, each mine can be avoided or diffused, but we must start our journey with a map the size of a postcard, with no room to mark down the exact location of every mine or the way they are wired together. An alternative to the extremes of ignoring or enumerating exceptions, is to *summarize* them, i.e., provide some warning signs to indicate which areas of the minefield are more dangerous than others. Such summarization is essential if we wish to find a reasonable compromise between safety and speed of movement.

1.3 *Why Is It Hard?*

One way of summarizing exceptions is to assign to propositions numerical measures that combine according to uniform syntactic principles, similar to the way truth values are combined in logic. This approach has been adopted by first-generation expert systems, but often yields unpredictable and counterintuitive results, examples of which will soon be demonstrated. As a matter of fact, it is remarkable that this combination strategy went as far as it did, in view of the fact that uncertainty measures stand for something totally different than truth values. While truth values in logic characterize the formulas under discussion, uncertainty measures characterize exceptions, i.e., the invisible facts *not* shown in the formulas. Accordingly, while the syntax of the formula is a perfect guide for combining the visibles, it is close to useless when it comes to combining the invisibles. For example, the machinery of Boolean algebra gives us no clue as to how the exceptions to $A \rightarrow C$ interact with those of $B \rightarrow C$ to yield the exceptions to $(A \wedge B) \rightarrow C$. These invisible exceptions may interact in very intricate and clandestine ways, as a result of which we lose most of the computationally attractive features of classical logic, e.g., modularity and monotonicity.

Although in logic, too, formulas interact in intricate ways, the interactions are visible. This enables us to calculate the impact of each new fact *in stages,* by a process of derivation that resembles the propagation of a wave: We first compute the impact of the new fact on a set of syntactically related sentences, S_1, store the results, then propagate the impact from S_1 to another set of sentences, S_2, and so on, without having to come back and redo S_1. Unfortunately, this computational scheme, so common to logical deduction, cannot be justified under uncertainty unless one makes restrictive assumptions, that, in probabilistic terms, amount to *conditional independence.*

Another feature we lose in going from logic to shaded uncertainties is *incrementality.* What we would like to do when we have several items of evidence is to account for the impact of each of them individually: Compute the effect of the first item, then attend to the next, absorb its added impact, and so on. This, too, can only be done after making restrictive assumptions of independence. Thus, it appears that uncertainty reasoning represents a hopeless case of having to compute the impact of the entire set of past observations on the entire set of sentences in one global step. This, of course, is an impossible task.

1.4 *Three Approaches to Uncertainty*

AI researchers tackling these problems can be classified into three schools, which I will call: logicist, neo-calculist, and neo-probabilist. The logicist school attempts to deal with uncertainty using nonnumerical techniques. The neo-calculist school uses numerical representations of uncertainty but, believing that probability calculus is inadequate for the task, invents entirely new calculi, such as the Dempster-Shafer calculus, fuzzy logic, certainty factors, and so on. Finally, the neo-probabilists remain within the traditional framework of probability theory, while attempting to equip the theory with computational facilities needed to perform AI tasks. This taxonomy, however, is rather superficial as it captures the notational rather than the semantical variations among the various approaches. A more fundamental taxonomy can be drawn along the dimensions I mentioned in the outline, namely, the extensional vs. the intensional approaches. For example, it is possible to use probabilities either extensionally (e.g., in PROSPECTOR [Duda et al., 1976]) or intensionally (e.g., in MUNIN [Andreassen et al., 1987]). Similarly, one can use the Dempster-Shafer notation either extensionally (as in [Ginsberg, 1984]) or intensionally (as in [Lowrance et al., 1986]).

1.5 *Extensional vs. Intensional Approaches*

1.5.1 *The Role of Connectives* Extensional systems, a typical representative of which is the certainty-factors calculus used in MYCIN [Shortliffe, 1976], treat uncertainty as a generalized truth value, i.e., the certainty of a formula is defined to be a unique function of the certainties of its subformulas. Thus, the connectives in the formula serve to select the appropriate weight-combining function. For example, the certainty of the conjunction $A \wedge B$ is given by some function (e.g., the minimum, or the product) of the certainty measures assigned to A and B individually. By contrast, in intensional systems, a typical representative of which is probability theory, certainty measures are assigned to sets of worlds and the connectives, too, combine sets of worlds by set theoretical operations. For example, the probability of $P(A \wedge B)$ is given by the weight assigned to the intersection of two sets of worlds, those in which A is true and those in which B is true, but cannot be determined from the individual probabilities $P(A)$ and $P(B)$.

1.5.2 *What's in a rule?* Rules, too, have different roles in these two systems. The rules in extensional systems provide licenses for certain symbolic activities. For example, the rule $A \rightarrow B(m)$ may mean: If you see A, then you have the license to update the certainty of B by a certain amount that is a function of the rule strength m. The rules are interpreted as a summary of past performance of the problem solver, describing the way an agent normally reacts to problem situations or to items of evidence. In intensional systems, the rules denote elastic constraints about the world. For example, in the Dempster-Shafer formalism the rule $A \rightarrow B(m)$ does not describe how an agent reacts to the finding of A, but asserts that the set of worlds in which A and $\neg B$ hold simultaneously is rather unlikely and hence should be excluded with probability m.

In the Bayesian formalism the rule $A \rightarrow B(m)$ is interpreted as a conditional probability statement $P(B \mid A) = m$ asserting that among all worlds satisfying A, those that also satisfy B constitute a majority of proportion m. Although there exists a vast difference between these two interpretations (as will be shown in Sections 3.2.2 and 4.1.1), they both represent summaries of factual or empirical information, rather than summaries of past decisions.

2 Extensional Systems: Merits, Deficiencies, and Remedies

2.1 Computational Merits

A good way to present the computational merits of extensional systems is to examine the way rules are handled in the certainty-factors formalism [Shortliffe, 1976] and contrast it with that dictated by probability theory. Figure 2 depicts the combination functions that apply to series and parallel rules, from which one can form a rule-network. The result is a modular procedure for determining the certainty factor of a conclusion, given the credibility of each rule, and the certainty factor of the premises (i.e., the roots of the network). To complete the calculus we also need to define combining functions for conjunctions and negation. However, ignoring mathematical details, the important point to notice is that the same combination function applies uniformly to all rules in the system, regardless of the topology of the network that surrounds them.

Computationally speaking, this uniformity mirrors the modularity of inference rules in classical logic. For example, the logical rule "If A then B" has the following procedural interpretation: "If you see A anywhere in the knowledge base, then, regardless of other things the knowledge base contains, and regardless of how A was derived, you have the license to assert B and add it to the database." This combination of *locality:* "regardless of other things," and *detachment:* "regardless of how it was derived," constitutes the principle of *modularity*. The numerical parameters that decorate the combination functions in Figure 2 do not alter this basic principle. The computational license provided by the rule $A \rightarrow B(m)$ reads: "If you see the certainty of A undergoing a change δ_A, then, regardless of other things the knowledge base contains, and regardless of how δ_A was triggered, you have an unqualified license to modify the current certainty of B by some amount, δ_B, that may depend on m, δ_A, and on the current certainty of B.[2]

---

2   The observation that the rules refer to changes, rather than absolute values, was made by [Horvitz and Heckerman, 1986].

EMYCIN CERTAINTY MANAGEMENT

Rules:
- If A then C (x)
- If B then C (y)
- If C then D (z)

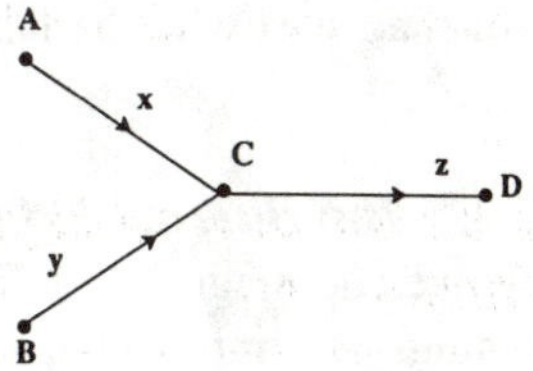

1. **Parallel Combination**

$$CF(C) = \begin{cases} x + y - xy & x, y > 0 \\ (x + y) / (1 - \min(x, y)) & x, y \text{ different sign} \\ x + y + xy & x, y < 0 \end{cases}$$

2. **Series Combination**

$$CF(D) = z \cdot \max(0, CF(C))$$

3. **Conjunction, negation ...**

Figure 2 Functions combining certainty factors in EMYCIN—an extensional system.

To appreciate the power of this interpretation, let us compare it with that given by an intensional formalism such as probability theory. Interpreting rules as conditional probability statements, $P(B \mid A) = p$, does not provide us with a license to do anything. Even if we are fortunate to find A true in the database, we still cannot assert a thing about B or $P(B)$, because the meaning of the statement is: If A is true, and A is the only thing that you know, then you can attach to B a probability p. As soon as we have other facts, K, in the database, the license to assert $P(B) = p$ is automatically revoked, and we need to look up $P(B \mid A, K)$ instead. Therefore, such a statement leaves one totally impotent, unable to initiate any computational activity, unless one can verify that all the other things in the knowledge base are irrelevant. It is for this reason that verification of irrelevancy is so crucial in intensional systems.

In truth, such verifications are also crucial in extensional systems, except that the computational convenience of the latter and their striking resemblance to logical derivations tempts people to neglect the importance of the former. We shall next demonstrate what semantic penalties are paid when relevance considerations are ignored.

2.2 Semantic Deficiencies

The price tag attached to the computational advantages of extensional systems is that they often yield incoherent updating, i.e., they are subject to surprises and counter-intuitive conclusions. These surface in several ways; the most notable are:

1.   difficulties in retracting conclusions,

2.   improper treatment of correlated sources of evidence, and

3.   improper handling of bidirectional inferences.

We shall start with the latter.

2.2.1 *The Role of Bidirectional Inferences*   The ability to use both predictive and diagnostic information is an important component of plausible reasoning, and improper handling of such information leads to rather strange results. A common pattern of normal discourse is that of *abductive* reasoning: If
A implies *B*, then finding the truth of *B* makes *A* more credible [Polya, 1954].
This pattern involves reasoning both ways, from *A* to *B*, as well as from *B* to
A. Moreover, it appears that people do not require two separate rules for performing these inferences; the first provides the license to invoke the second.
Extensional systems, on the other hand, require that the second rule be stated
explicitly and, what is more disturbing, that the first rule be removed. Otherwise, a cycle is created where any slight evidence in favor of *A* would be
amplified via *B* and fed back to *A*, quickly turning into a stronger confirmation
(of *A* and *B*), with no apparent basis. The prevailing practice in such systems
(e.g., MYCIN) is to cutoff cycles of that sort, permitting only diagnostic reasoning but no predictive inferences.

   Cutting off its predictive component, prevents the system from exhibiting
another important pattern of plausible reasoning, one that we name "Explaining
away": If *A* implies *B*, and *C* implies *B*, and *B* is true, then finding that *C* is
true makes *A* *less* credible. In other words, finding a second explanation to an
item of data, makes the first explanation less credible. Such interaction among
multiple causes appears in many applications. When a physician discovers evidence in favor of one disease, this reduces the credibility of other diseases, although the patient may as well be suffering from two or more disorders simultaneously. A suspect who provides an alternative explanation for being at the
scene of the crime appears less likely to be guilty, even though the explanation
furnished does not preclude his having committed the crime.

   To exhibit this sort of reasoning, a system must use bidirectional inferences—from evidence to hypothesis (or explanation), as well as from hypothesis to evidence. While it is sometimes possible to use brute force (e.g., enumerating all exceptions) and restore "explaining away" without the dangers of
circular reasoning, we shall see that any system that succeeds in doing that
must compromise the principles of modularity, i.e., locality and detachment.
More precisely, every system that updates beliefs modularly at the natural rule
level and that treats all rules equally, is bound to behave contrarily in prevailing patterns of plausible reasoning.

2.2.2 *The Limits of Modularity* The principle of locality attains its ultimate realization in the inference rules of monotonic logic. The rule "If P then Q" means that if P is found true, we can assert Q with no further analysis, even if the database contains some other knowledge K. In plausible reasoning, the luxury of ignoring the rest of the database can no longer be maintained. For example, suppose we have a rule

R_1 = "*If the ground is wet, then assume it rained (with certainty c_1).*"

Finding the ground wet does not permit us to raise the certainty of "rain" because the knowledge base might contain strange items such as K = "the sprinkler was on last night." These strange items, called *defeaters*, are sometimes easy to discover (as in the case of K' = "the neighbor's grass is dry," which directly opposes "rain"), but sometimes hide cleverly behind syntactical innocence. The neutral fact K = "sprinkler on" neither supports nor opposes "rain," yet K manages to undercut the rule R_1. This undercutting cannot be implemented in an extensional system; once R_1 is invoked, the increase in the certainty of "rain" will never be retracted, because, normally, no rule exists that directly connects "sprinkler on" to "rain." Forcing such a connection by proclaiming "sprinkler on" as an explicit exception to R_1, again defeats the spirit of modularity; it forces the rule-author to pack together items of information that are only remotely related to each other, and, moreover, it loads the rules with an unmanageably large number of exceptions.

Violation of detachment can also be demonstrated in this example. In deductive logic, if K implies P and P implies Q, then finding K true permits us to deduce Q by simple chaining; a derived proposition *(P)* can trigger a rule with the same vigor as a directly observed proposition. However, chaining does not apply in plausible reasoning. The system may contain two innocent looking rules: "If wet-ground then rain" and "If sprinkler-on then wet-ground"; you find that the sprinkler is on and, obviously, you do not want to conclude that it rained. On the contrary, finding that the sprinkler is on only takes away support from "rain."

As another example, consider the relationships shown in Figure 3. Normally an alarm sound alerts us to the possibility of a burglary. If somebody calls you at the office and tells you that your alarm system is on, you would surely rush home, even though there could be other causes for the alarm. If you further hear a radio announcement that there was an earthquake nearby, and if the last false alarm you recall was triggered by an earthquake, then your certainty of a burglary would diminish. Again, this requires going both ways, from effect to cause (radio → earthquake), cause to effect (earthquake → alarm), and then back from effect to cause (alarm → burglary). However, notice what pattern of reasoning results from such a chain: We have a rule "If A (alarm) then B (burglary)," you listen to the radio, A becomes more credible, and the conclusion B becomes less credible. Overall, we have: "If $A \rightarrow B$ and A becomes more credible, then B becomes less credible." This behavior is clearly contrary to everything we expect from local belief updating.

In conclusion, we see that the difficulties that plague classical logic do not stem from its nonnumeric, bi-value character. Equally troublesome difficulties emerge when truth and certainty are measured on a gray scale, whether by a point estimate, by interval bounds, or by linguistic quantifiers such as "likely" or "credible." There seems to be a basic struggle between procedural modularity and semantic coherence, independent of the notational system used.

2.2.3 Correlated Evidence Extensional systems, greedily exploiting the licenses provided by locality and detachment, respond only to the magnitudes of the weights but not to their origins. As a result they will produce the same conclusions regardless of whether the weights originate from identical or independent sources of information. An example due to Henrion [1986b] helps demonstrate the problems encountered by such local strategy. Figure 4 shows how multiple, independent sources of evidence would normally increase the confirmation of a hypothesis (e.g., "thousands dead"), yet, upon discovering the common origin of these sources, the confirmation should be reduced. Extensional systems are too local to recognize the common origin of the information, and will update the confirmation of the hypothesis as if supported by three independent sources.

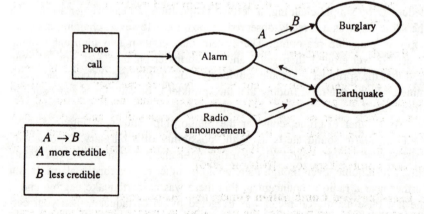

Figure 3 Making the antecedent of a rule more credible can cause the consequent to become less credible.

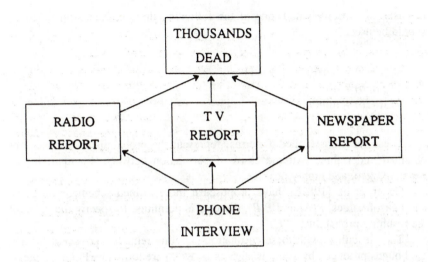

Figure 4 The Chernobyl disaster example (after Henrion) shows why rules cannot combine locally.

2.2.4 *Attempted Remedies and Their Limitations* The developers of extensional systems have proposed and implemented powerful techniques to remedy some of the semantic deficiencies discussed in the preceding subsections. Most have focused on the issue of correlated evidence and fall into two approaches:

1. **Bounds Propagation**—Since most correlations are unknown, certainty measures are combined under two extreme assumptions; one, that the components are highly positively correlated, the other that they are negatively correlated. This gives rise to upper and lower bounds on the combined certainty, which enter as inputs to subsequent computations and produce new bounds on the certainty of the conclusions. This approach has been implemented in INFERNO [Quinlan, 1983] and represents a local approximation to Nilsson's probabilistic logic [Nilsson, 1986].

2. **User-Specified Combination Functions**—Bonissone et al. [1987], in a system named RUM, has permitted the rule-author to specify the combination function that should apply to the rule's components. For example, if *a, b, c* stand for the weights assigned to propositions *A, B, C* respectively, in the rule

$$A \wedge B \rightarrow C$$

the user can specify which one of the following three combination functions should be used:

$$T_1(a, b) = \max(0, a + b - 1)$$
$$T_2(a, b) = ab$$
$$T_3(a, b) = \min(a, b)$$

These functions (called T norms) represent the probabilistic combinations obtained under three extreme cases of correlation between A and B: highly negative, zero, and highly positive.

Cohen et al. [1987b], have proposed a more refined scheme, where, for any pair of values, $P(A)$ and $P(B)$, the user is permitted to specify the value of the resulting probability, $P(C)$.

The difficulties with these correlation-handling remedies are several. First, the bounds produced by systems such as INFERNO are too wide. For example, if we are given $P(A) = p$ and $P(B \mid A) = q$ then the bounds we obtain for $P(B)$ are

$$pq \leq P(B) \leq 1 - p(1 - q)$$

that, for small p, approach the unit interval [0, 1]. Second, the user-specified approaches are plagued by the problem that pair-wise correlations are generally not sufficient to handle the intricate dependencies that may occur among rules; higher-order dependencies are often necessary [Bundy, 1985]. Finally, even if one succeeds in specifying higher-order dependencies, a much more fundamental limitation exists: dependencies are dynamic relationships, that are created and destroyed as new evidence obtains. For example, the dependence between a child's shoe size and reading ability is destroyed once we find out the child's age. A dependency between the propositions "it rained last night" and "the sprinkler was on" is created once we find out that the ground is wet. Thus, whatever correlations and/or combination functions are specified at the knowledge-building phase, these may quickly become obsolete once the program is put into use.

Heckerman [1986a, 1986b] delineated precisely the range of applicability of extensional systems of the MYCIN type. He proved that any system that updates certainty weights in a modular and consistent fashion can be given a probabilistic interpretation in which the certainty update of a proposition A is some function of the likelihood ratio

$$\lambda = \frac{P(Evidence \mid A)}{P(Evidence \mid \neg A)}.$$

In MYCIN, for example, the certainty update *CF* can be interpreted to stand for

$$CF = \frac{\lambda - 1}{\lambda + 1}$$

Once we have a probabilistic interpretation, it is easy to determine the set of structures within which the update procedure will be semantically valid. It turns out that a system of such rules will produce coherent updates if and only if the rules form a directed tree, i.e., no two rules may diverge from the same premise. This limitation explains why strange results were obtained in the burglary example of Figure 3. There the alarm event points to two possible explanations, "Burglary" and "Earthquake," giving rise to two evidential rules diverging from the premise "Alarm," in violation of the tree restriction.

Hajek [1985] and Hajek and Valdes [1987] have developed an algebraic theory that characterizes an even wider range of the extensional systems and combining functions, including, for example, those based on Dempster-Shafer intervals. The unifying properties common to all such systems is that they form an ordered Abelian group. Again, the knowledge base must form a tree in order that no evidence is double counted via alternative paths of reasoning.

2.3 *Conclusions*

Handling uncertainties is a rather tricky enterprise. It requires a very fine balance between our desire to use the computational permissiveness of extensional systems and our ability to refrain from committing semantical sins. It is like crossing a minefield with an untrained wild horse. You can make believe that your horse is smart and, being decorated with certainty weights, will keep you out of trouble. However, the danger is real, and highly skilled knowledge engineers are needed to prevent it from turning into a disaster. The other extreme is to try and work your way by foot with a semantically safe system, such as probability theory, but then you can hardly move—every step seems to require that you examine the entire field, afresh. We shall now examine means for making this movement brisker.

3 *Intensional Systems and Network Representations*

In intensional systems, the syntax consists of declarative statements and, hence, mirrors world knowledge fairly nicely. For example, conditional probability statements are both empirically testable and conceptually meaningful parameters. Additionally, the problems of handling bidirectional inferences and correlated evidence do not arise; these are obtained as built-in features of one globally coherent model. However, since the syntax does not point to any useful procedures, we need to construct special mechanisms that convert the declarative input into query-answering routines.

A solution, or at least part of a solution, is offered by techniques based on *belief networks*. The idea is to make intensional systems operational by making relevance relationships explicit, thus curing the impotence of declarative statements such as $P(B \mid A) = p$. As we mentioned earlier, the reason one cannot act on the basis of such declarations is that one must first make sure that other things contained in the knowledge base are irrelevant to B, hence can be ignored. The trick is, therefore, to encode knowledge in such a way that the ignorable be recognizable or, better yet, that the nonignorable be quickly identified and readily accessible. Belief networks encode relevancies as neighboring nodes in a graph, thus ensuring that by consulting the neighborhood you have taken everything into account and gain a license to act; what you don't see locally won't matter any way. In summary, what network representations offer is a dynamically updated list of all currently valid permissions to ignore, and permissions to ignore amount to permissions to act.

Network representations are not foreign to AI systems. Most reasoning systems encode relevancies using intricate systems of pointers, i.e., networks of indices that group facts into structures, such as frames, causal chains, and inheritance hierarchies. These structures, while shunned by pure logicians, have proven to be indispensable in practice, because they make the information required to perform an inference task reside "in the vicinity" of the propositions involved in the task. Moreover, many patterns of human reasoning can be explained only by people's tendency to seriously conform to the pathways laid out by such networks.

The special feature of the networks discussed in this survey is that they have clear semantics. In other words, they are not auxiliary devices, contrived to make reasoning more efficient but, rather, are an integral part of the semantics of the knowledge base and, to a certain degree, can even be derived from the knowledge base.

I will first discuss the nature of these networks in two uncertainty formalisms: probability theory, where they are called *Bayesian networks, causal nets*, or *influence diagrams*, and the Dempster-Shafer theory, where they are referred to as *galleries* [Lowrance et al., 1986], *qualitative Markov networks* [Shafer et al., 1987], or *constraint networks* [Montanari, 1974]. In Section 4.1 I will briefly discuss the theory of *graphoids*, which provides an axiomatic characterization of the notion of relevance and its relation to network representations.

3.1 *Evidential Reasoning with Bayesian Networks*

3.1.1 *Network Construction and the Role of Causality* Defined formally, Bayesian networks are directed acyclic graphs in which each node represents a random variable, or uncertain quantity, that can take on two or more possible values. The arcs signify the existence of direct influences between the linked variables, and the strengths of these influences are quantified by forward conditional probabilities. Informally, the structure of a Bayesian network can be determined by a simple procedure: we assign a vertex to each variable in the domain and draw arrows toward each vertex X_i from a select set S_i of vertices perceived to be "direct causes" of X_i. The strength of these direct influences is then quantified by a link matrix $P(x_i \mid s_i)$, that represents (judgmental estimates of) the conditional probabilities of the event $X_i = x_i$, given any value combination s_i of the parent set S_i. The ensemble of these local estimates specifies a complete and consistent global model (i.e., a joint distribution function), on the basis of which all probabilistic queries can be answered. The overall joint distribution function on the variables $X_1, \ldots, X_n$, is given by the product:

$$P(x_1, x_2, \ldots, x_n) = \prod_{i=1}^{n} P(x_i \mid s_i)$$

So, for example, the joint distribution corresponding to the network of Figure 5 is given by:

$$P(h, e, r, s, d, w, g) = P(h)P(e)P(r \mid e)P(s \mid e, h)P(d \mid s)P(w \mid s)P(g \mid s)$$

where lowercase symbols stand for any particular value (i.e., true or false) of their corresponding variables.

To pacify the mathematicians among us, note that, conversely, the structure of the network can be determined by the joint distribution function, if such is ever available. Once we agree on a total order (e.g., temporal precedence) for the variables involved, the set of parents S_i of variable X_i is chosen from its predecessors by the criterion that

$$P(x_i \mid s_i) = P(x_i \mid x_1, \ldots, x_{i-1})$$

In other words, knowing the parents renders all other predecessors of X_i irrelevant relative to our belief in X_i. In principle, any choice S_i satisfying this criterion will define an adequate network, but, of course, choosing minimal sets of parents will be more efficient, and ordering the variable chronologically would probably result in sparser networks than otherwise.

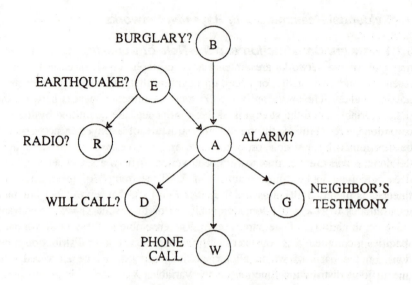

Figure 5 The Bayesian network associated with the burglary alarm story.

Figure 5 depicts the burglary alarm story of Figure 3, with two added variables D and G. D describes the event that your daughter, having been surprised by the alarm, will try to reach you at the office. G stands for the testimony of another neighbor relative to the alarm sound S. The transition from Figure 3 to Figure 5 demonstrates the incremental nature of the process of constructing the knowledge base. Adding the facts about D only requires that one identifies the possible causes of D (in our case, S) and estimates two parameters:

$P(D \mid S)$ = How likely is it that your daughter will try to call, given that she hears the alarm sound, and

$P(D \mid \neg S)$ = How likely is it for her to call, assuming there is no alarm.

The addition of the link $S \rightarrow G$ requires similar parameters, except that, if the testimony G is available (even if it is nonpropositional, say, a lengthy conversation [Pearl, 1987b]), it can be summarized by a single parameter; the likelihood ratio:

$$\lambda = \frac{P(G \mid S)}{P(G \mid \neg S)}$$

The advantage of a network representation is that it allows people to directly express the fundamental qualitative relationship of "direct dependency"; the network then displays a consistent set of many additional direct and indirect dependencies and preserves them as a stable part of the model, independent of the numerical estimates. For example, Figure 5 displays the fact that the radio report *(R)* would not change the prospects of the daughter's phone call *(D)*, once we verify the actual state of the alarm system *(S)*. This fact is conveyed via the network topology—showing *S* intercepting the path between *R* and *D*—despite the fact that it was not considered explicitly during the construction of the network. It can be inferred visually from the linkages used to put the network together and, moreover, will remain part of the model regardless of the numerical estimates that are assigned to the links.

The directionality of the arrows is essential for displaying nontransitive dependencies, e.g., *S* depends on both *E* and *H* and, yet, *E* and *H* are independent; they become dependent only if *S* or any of its descendants is known. Had the arcs been stripped of their arrows, some of these relationships would be misrepresented. This role of identifying what information is or is not relevant in any given state of knowledge is an important feature of causal schemata. In this role, causality serves as a lubricant that modularizes experience. By displaying a high number of legitimate irrelevancies in the domain, causal schemata minimize the number of relationships that need to be considered while the model is constructed. Thus, causality also operationalizes our experience, because modularity authorizes a high number of licenses to perform local inferences. The currently prevailing practice in rule-based expert systems, of encoding knowledge by evidential rules (i.e., if effect then cause), is deficient in this respect. It normally fails to account for intercausal dependencies (e.g., an earthquake explaining away the alarm sound), and if one ventures to encode these interactions by direct rules, legitimate independencies are no longer represented, such as between earthquakes and burglaries (see [Shachter and Heckerman, 1988]).

There is a long and rich tradition of Bayesian belief networks, starting in 1921 with a geneticist named Wright. He developed a method called *path analysis* [Wright, 1934], that later on, became an established representation of causal models in economics [Wold, 1964], sociology [Kenny, 1979; Blalock, 1971] and psychology [Duncan, 1975]. *Influence diagrams* represent another component in this tradition [Howard and Matheson, 1981; Shachter, 1988]. These were developed for decision analysis and contain both event nodes and action nodes. *Recursive models* is the name given to such networks by statisticians seeking meaningful and effective decompositions of contingency tables [Lauritzen, 1982; Wermuth and Lauritzen, 1983; Kiiveri et al., 1984].

The next subsection illustrates the role of networks as a representation capable of converting declarative knowledge to answer-producing procedures. The illustration will focus on Bayesian networks, but similar techniques have been developed for constraint networks in the Dempster-Shafer formalism [Shafer et al., 1987; Kong, 1986].

3.1.2 *Belief Propagation by Message Passing*   Since a fully specified Bayesian network constitutes a complete probabilistic model of all variables in the domain, it contains the information necessary to answer all probabilistic queries about these variables. Such queries include, for example, "what are the chances of a burglary, given that the radio announced an earthquake and the daughter did not call?" or "what is the most likely explanation for your daughter's not having called?" Additionally, due to the relevance information conveyed by their links, belief networks can also be used as inference engines, i.e., the nodes can be regarded as processors and the links as communication channels that provide the (storage locations of the) inputs and outputs as well as the timing information necessary for sequencing the computational steps. In other words, many of the computations can be conducted by a local and parallel message-passing process, with minimum external supervision, similar to the derivational steps taken by extensional systems.

The advantages of this distributed, message-passing paradigm is that it provides a natural mechanism for exploiting the independencies embodied in sparsely constrained systems and translating them, by subtask decomposition, into substantial reduction in complexity. Additionally, distributed propagation is inherently "transparent"; namely, the intermediate steps, by virtue of their reflecting interactions only among semantically related variables, are conceptually meaningful. This facilitates the use of natural, object-oriented programming tools and helps establish confidence in the final result.

Distributed schemes for belief *updating* and belief *revision* are described in [Pearl, 1986, 1987a]. Belief updating aims at assigning each variable a posterior probability that correctly accounts for the evidence at hand. The aim of belief revision is to identify a composite set of propositions (one from each variable) that "best" explains the evidence at hand, i.e., attains the highest posterior probability. These involve the updating and transmittal of two types of messages:

λ—the strength of evidential support that a variable obtains from its descendants, and

π—the strength of causal support that a variable obtains from its nondescendants.

This separation into causal and evidential components permits the execution of bidirectional inferences without the dangers of circular reasoning (see Section 2.2.1).

Figure 6 shows six successive stages of belief propagation through a simple binary tree, assuming that all activities are triggered by changes in the parameters of neighboring processors. Initially (Figure 6a), the tree is in equilibrium, representing the state of belief due to all prior information. As soon as two nodes are activated by new information (Figure 6b), white tokens (representing λ) are placed on their links, directed toward their parents. Activated by these tokens, the parents compute their degree of belief, and manufacture the appropriate number of tokens for their neighbors (Figure 6c): white tokens for their parents and black tokens (representing π) for the children. (The links through which the absorbed tokens have entered do not receive new tokens, thus reflecting the feature that a π-message is not affected by a λ-message crossing the same link). The root node now receives two white tokens, one from each of its descendants. That triggers the production of two black tokens for top-down delivery (Figure 6d). The process continues in this fashion until, after six cycles, all tokens are absorbed, and the network reaches a new equilibrium, where each variable is assigned a probability measure reflecting the new information.

The updating scheme possesses the following properties:

1. New information diffuses through the network in a single pass, i.e., equilibrium is reached in time proportional to the diameter of the network.

2. The primitive processors are simple, repetitive, and they require no working memory except that used in matrix multiplication.

3. The local computations and the final belief distribution are entirely independent of the control mechanism that activates the individual operations. They can be activated by either data-driven or goal-driven (e.g., requests for evidence) control strategies, by a clock, or at random.

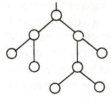

(a)

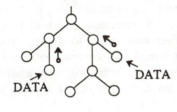

(b)

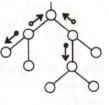

(c)

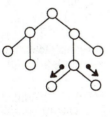

(f)

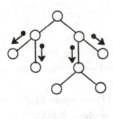

(e)

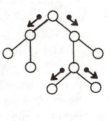

(d)

Figure 6 The impact of new data propagates through a tree by a message-passing process.

As soon as a node posts a token for its parent, it is ready to receive new data, and when this occurs, a new token is posted on the link, replacing the old one. In this fashion the network can track a changing environment and provide coherent interpretation of signals emanating simultaneously from multiple sources. Having an efficient mechanism of updating and/or revising beliefs also facilitates various control functions such as, for example, selecting the next best test in diagnosis. This can be done by the method of "hypothesizing"; we imagine what impact the outcome of various tests would have on some target hypothesis, and select the test with the highest impact.

The objective of updating beliefs coherently by purely local computations can be fully realized if the network is singly-connected, i.e., if there is only one undirected path between any pair of nodes. These include trees, where each node has a single parent, as well as networks with multi-parent nodes, representing events with several causal factors, as in Figure 5.

Here the π message transmitted from "Earthquake" to "Alarm" interacts with the λ message that "Alarm" receives from "Phone call" to produce a reduction of the evidential support (λ) the "Alarm" lends to "Burglary." This distinction between causal (π) and evidential (λ) supports identifies the origin of beliefs and permits the system to treat multiple causes differently than multiple symptoms; the former compete with each other, the latter support each other. It is due to this distinction that the system obtains coherent updating via modular computations, dispensing with the need to specify direct inhibitory connections from one cause to another [Pearl, 1988b].

The profile of π and λ messages that load the network at any given time also provides the information needed for generating explanations, similar to the justification network in truth-maintenance systems. Tracing the most influential π and λ messages back to their origins yields a skeletal subgraph from which verbal explanations can be structured, clearly reflecting the distinction between causal and evidential supports.

3.1.3 *Coping with Loops*

When loops are present, as in Figure 3, the network is no longer singly-connected, and local propagation schemes invariably run into trouble. Several methods have been developed that extend the propagation method to networks containing loops while still maintaining global coherence relative to probability theory. The most notable are conditioning, clustering, and stochastic simulation.

Before describing each of these methods, one should not overlook a simple but important approximation method called "ignore the loops," namely, propagate the π and λ messages according to the equations developed for a singly-connected network. If loops are present, this strategy will cause the messages to circulate indefinitely until their magnitude becomes insignificantly small (this will always be the case because the conditional probabilities on the links tend to attenuate the messages). If the loops are long, ignoring them is not going to introduce a significant error because the degree of inter-message correlation, created by multiple paths, diminishes with the lengths of such paths. At any rate, the results obtained after relaxation should be closer to the theoretical results than those obtained by extensional updating strategies, because the latter totally ignore the distinction between causal and evidential supports, while the former account for it in an approximate way.

The method of conditioning involves identifying a set of variables (called cycle cutset) that, if known with certainty, would render the network singly-connected, instantiate these variables to some values, conduct the propagation on the rest of the network, repeat for all possible instantiations, then combine the results by taking their weighted average. In Figure 3, for example, we would run two propagation exercises, one under the assumption "Thousands dead" = true, the other under "Thousands dead" = false. The evidential supports obtained under these two assumptions would then be combined to yield the overall, unconditioned results.

The effectiveness of conditioning depends heavily on the topological properties of the network. In general, the number of instantiations required is 2^c, where c is the size of the cycle cutset chosen for conditioning. Since each propagation phase takes only time linear with the number of variables in the system (n), the overall complexity is exponential with the size of the cycle cutset that we can identify. If the network is sparse, topological considerations can be used to find a small cycle cutset and render the interpretation task tractable.

A second method of sidestepping the loop problem is that of stochastic simulation [Henrion, 1986a]. It amounts to generating a random population of scenarios agreeing with the evidence, then answering queries on the basis of this population. This is accomplished distributedly by having each processor inspect the current state of its neighbors, compute the belief distribution of its host variable, then randomly select one value from the computed distribution, to be inspected by its neighbors in their turn [Pearl, 1987c]. Probabilities are calculated by counting the frequency at which a proposition obtains the value *true*. The advantages of this method are that it is purely distributed, and that the rate of convergence does not depend on the topology of the network. Unfortunately, the rate of convergence deteriorates when the links convey logical constraints, i.e., extreme probabilities [Chin and Cooper, 1987].

The third technique, and currently the most promising, is that of *clustering*. It involves forming local groups of variables in such a way that the topology of the resulting network (treating each group as a single compound node), is singly-connected. For example, grouping the three intermediate nodes in Figure 3 into one compound variable will result in a three-node causal chain. Once a clustered configuration is found, the propagation method described in the preceding subsection is applicable with a processor assigned to each cluster. The complexity of this scheme is exponential with the size of the largest cluster found, because the processor assigned to manage that cluster must handle that many value combinations (e.g., eight in Figure 3).

A popular method of selecting clusters is to form *join trees*, i.e., trees made up of overlapping clusters in such a way that all links are contained within the clusters. The network of Figure 3, for example, will be decomposed into two overlapping clusters, one comprising the top four nodes, the other the bottom four nodes. The merit of join tree representations have been recognized by statisticians for over 25 years [e.g., Vorobev, 1962; Goodman, 1970; Haberman, 1974]. Their applications to databases are discussed in [Beeri et al., 1983 and Malvestuto, 1986] and they also have been suggested for Bayes inferences [Lemmer, 1983] and constraint processing [Pechter and Pearl, 1987b]. A systematic method of finding such clusters and a thorough analysis of the updating scheme are described in [Lauritzen and Spiegelhalter, 1988]. The method involves triangularizing the network [Tarjan and Yannakakis, 1984], identifying the maximal cliques of the triangularized (or chordal) graph, organizing the cliques in a tree structure, and assigning a processor to each clique. Beliefs can then propagate by the message-passing mechanism described in Section 3.1.2.

The attractive feature of clustering schemes is that, once the clusters are formed and their tree organization established, the resulting structure offers an effective database that can be amortized over many evidential reasoning tasks. A large variety of queries could be answered swiftly by unsupervised, local and parallel processes. Therefore, if one takes seriously the paradigm that unsupervised parallelism is one capability that human learning aspires to achieve [Pearl, 1986], then it is quite reasonable to speculate that the clusters found for join tree representations form the nuclei around which higher cognitive concepts normally evolve.

It is important to note that the difficulties associated with the presence of loops are not unique to probabilistic formulations but are inherent to any problem where globally defined solutions are produced by local computations, be it probabilistic, deterministic, logical, numerical, or hybrids thereof. Identical computational issues arise in Dempster-Shafer's formalism [Kong, 1986], constraint-satisfaction problems [Dechter and Pearl, 1987a], truth-maintenance systems [Doyle, 1979], diagnostic reasoning [Geffner and Pearl, 1987a], relational databases [Beeri et al., 1983], matrix inversion [Tarjan, 1976], and network reliability [Arnborg et al., 1987]. The importance of network representation, though, is that it uncovers the core of these difficulties, and provides a unifying abstraction that encourages the exchange of solution strategies across domains.

3.2 *Dempster-Shafer Theory and Constraint Networks*

Pure Bayesian theory requires the specification of a complete probabilistic model before reasoning can commence, namely, determining for each variable X the conditional probabilities that govern the values of X, given their causal factors. When a full specification is not available, Bayes practitioners have devised approximate methods of completing the model. For example, if we are given the strength of each individual cause but not the combined impact of several causes, we assume that they combine disjunctively, and that all exceptions are independent [Peng and Reggia, 1986; Pearl, 1987a].

An alternative method of handling partially specified models is provided by the Dempster-Shafer (D-S) theory [Shafer, 1976]. Rather than completing the model, the D-S theory sidesteps the missing specifications, and is resigned instead to less ambitious inference tasks: computing probabilities of provability rather than probabilities of truths. The partially specified model is idealized by qualitative relationships of compatibility constraints, and these qualitative relationships are then used as a logic for assembling proofs of various propositions. Items of evidence are modeled as probabilistic modifications of the available constraints, and the support they lend to a given hypothesis H is defined as the probability that a proof of H can be assembled.

The current popularity of the D-S theory stems both from its readiness to admit partial models and its compatibility with the classical, proof-based style of logical inference. As such, the approach matches the syntax of deductive databases and logic-programming languages but may inherit many of the problems associated with monotonic logic, some of which will be discussed in Section 4.1.1.

3.2.1 Belief Functions as Probabilities of Provability

I will introduce the D-S theory from a rather unconventional perspective, one that I hope will be more meaningful to AI researchers, especially those versed in constraint processing, truth-maintenance systems and logical programming. Our starting point will be a static network of logical constraints that represents generic knowledge about the world. Each constraint is a declarative statement on a group of variables specifying what is and what is not permitted to hold in the domain. For example the rule $A \rightarrow B$ forbids the simultaneous assignment of *true* to A and *false* to B. A collection of such constraints yields a (possibly empty) set of *extensions* or *solutions*, i.e., assignments of values to all variables that simultaneously satisfy all constraints.

In addition to this static network, we also have items of evidence that provide direct but partial support to a select set of propositions in the system. Each such item of evidence is modeled as a randomly fluctuating constraint, that, for a certain fraction of the time m, imposes the value *true* on the propositions supported by that item. The larger the m the stronger the support. To compute the overall support that several items of evidence impart to a given proposition, say A, we subject the static network to the corresponding set of externally imposed, randomly fluctuating constraints, assume that they act independently of each other, and ask for the probability (or fraction of the time) that A can be proven true. This probability defines the belief function $Bel(A)$, and similarly, a plausibility function $Pl(A) = 1 - Bel(\neg A)$ is defined by the probability that A is not proven false.

This scheme is illustrated metaphorically in Figure 7. It shows a static network of variables $X, Y, Z, V. . .$ (the nodes) interacting via local constraints (the arcs), subject to the influence of two switches that impose additional time varying constraints on various regions of the network. The switches represent two independent items of evidence, each characterized by the fraction of time spent in each position.

To illustrate the analysis of belief functions, let us assume that the static network represents the familiar graph-coloring problem: Each node may take on one of three possible colors, 1, 2, or 3, but no two adjacent nodes may take on identical colors. The position of the switches represents additional constraints e.g., C_{XY}: either X or Y must contain the color 1, or C_Z: Z cannot be assigned the color 2, and so on. The relative time that a switch spends enforcing each of the constraints is indicated by the weight measures $m_1(C_X)$, $m_1(C_{XY})$, $m_2(C_Z)$, and so on. Our objective is to compute $Bel(A)$ and $Pl(A)$, where A stands for the proposition $V = 1$, namely, variable V is assigned the color 1.

Figure 8 represents typical sets of solutions to the coloring problem under different combinations of the switches (the actual values are fictitious).

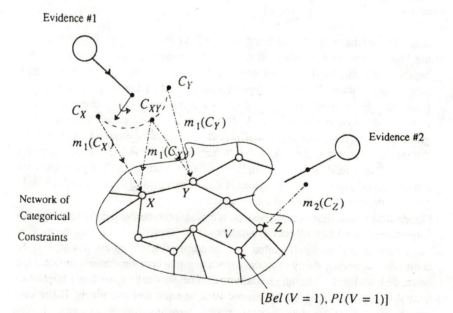

Figure 7 Multiple evidence modeled as random switches, imposing additional constraints on a static network of compatibility relations.

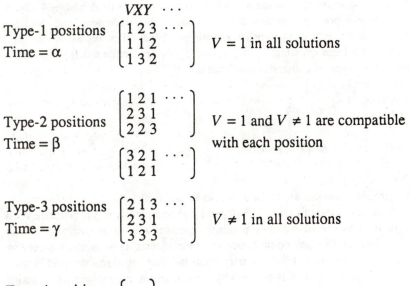

$$VXY \cdots$$

Type-1 positions
Time $= \alpha$
$\begin{bmatrix} 1\,2\,3 \cdots \\ 1\,1\,2 \\ 1\,3\,2 \end{bmatrix}$ $V = 1$ in all solutions

Type-2 positions
Time $= \beta$
$\begin{bmatrix} 1\,2\,1 \cdots \\ 2\,3\,1 \\ 2\,2\,3 \end{bmatrix}$ $V = 1$ and $V \neq 1$ are compatible
$\begin{bmatrix} 3\,2\,1 \cdots \\ 1\,2\,1 \end{bmatrix}$ with each position

Type-3 positions
Time $= \gamma$
$\begin{bmatrix} 2\,1\,3 \cdots \\ 2\,3\,1 \\ 3\,3\,3 \end{bmatrix}$ $V \neq 1$ in all solutions

Type-4 positions
Time $= \delta$
$\begin{bmatrix} \text{Nil} \end{bmatrix}$ no solution

(a)

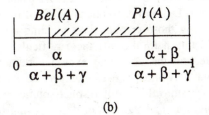

$$\overset{Bel(A)}{} \qquad \overset{Pl(A)}{}$$

$$0 \quad \frac{\alpha}{\alpha + \beta + \gamma} \qquad \frac{\alpha + \beta}{\alpha + \beta + \gamma} \quad 1$$

(b)

Figure 8 (a) Four types of constraints in the graph coloring problem and (b) the resulting belief interval for the proposition $A: V = 1$.

Each row represents one extension (or solution) where the entries indicate the value assigned to the variables (columns). The first set of solutions is characterized by having the value 1 assigned to V in each and every row. If the system spends a fraction α of the time in such combinations of switches, we say that $P(e \mathrel{\vert=} A) = \alpha$, namely, the proposition $A:$ "$V = 1$" can be proven true with probability α, given the evidence e. A type-2 position is characterized by the column of V containing 1s as well as alternative values, e.g., 2 or 3. Each such position (or position combination) is compatible with both A and $\neg A$. Similarly, a type-3 position permits only extensions that exclude $V = 1$, while a type-4 position represents conflict situations; there exists no extension consistent with all the constraints. $Bel(A)$ and $Pl(A)$ are computed from the time spent in each type of constraint combination:

$$Bel(A) = \frac{\alpha}{\alpha + \beta + \gamma}$$

$$Pl(A) = 1 - Bel(V \neq 1) = 1 - \frac{\gamma}{\alpha + \beta + \gamma} = \frac{\alpha + \beta}{\alpha + \beta + \gamma}$$

These are illustrated as a belief interval in Figure 7(b).

The assumption of evidence independence, coupled with the normalization rule above, leads to an evidence pooling procedure known as *Dempster's Rule of Combination*. For any combination of the evidential constraints, we need to examine the set of extensions permitted by that combination and decide whether the proposition A is entailed by the set, i.e., if every extension contains A and none contain $\neg A$. The total time that a system spends under constraint combinations that compel A, divided by the total time spent in no-conflict combinations, yields $Bel(A)$.

The preceding analysis can be rather complex. The graph-coloring problem, even with only three colors, is known to be NP complete. Moreover, if each item of evidence is modeled by a 2-position switch, and if we have n such switches, then a brute force analysis of $Bel(A)$ would require solving 2^n graph-coloring problems. Listing the solutions obtained under every switch combination and identifying those combinations yielding $e \models A$ seems hopeless. Fortunately, two factors help alleviate these difficulties: the sequential nature of Dempster's rule and the ability to exploit certain topological properties of sparse constraint networks. The former permits us to combine evidence incrementally if we store the set of distinct solution sets produced in the past. The latter revolves around the idea of decomposing the network into a tree of clusters, where solutions can be obtained in linear time [Dechter and Pearl, 1987b]. The use of tree decomposition techniques for belief function computations are reported in [Shafer et al., 1987] and [Kong, 1986].

3.2.2 *Comparing Bayes and Dempster-Shafer Formalisms*   We   see
that the D-S theory differs from probability theory in several aspects. First, it accepts an incomplete probabilistic model where some parameters (e.g., the prior or conditional probabilities) are missing. Second, the probabilistic information that is available, like the strength of evidence, is not interpreted as likelihood ratios but rather as random epiphenomena that impose truth values

on various propositions for a certain fraction of the time. This model permits a proposition and its negation to be simultaneously compatible (with the evidence) for a certain portion of the time, and this may permit the sum of their beliefs to be smaller than unity. Finally, due to the incompleteness of the model, the D-S theory does not pretend to provide full answers to probabilistic queries, but rather, is resigned to providing partial answers. It estimates how close the evidence is to forcing the truth of the hypothesis, instead of estimating how close the hypothesis is to being true.

Phrased another way, the D-S theory computes the probability that some set of hypotheses suggested by the evidence would materialize from which the truth of A can be derived out of logical necessity. Thus, instead of the conditional probability $P(A \mid e)$, the D-S theory computes the probability of the logical entailment $e \models A$. The entailment $e \models A$ is not a proposition in the ordinary sense, but a meta-level relationship between e and A, requiring a logical, object-level theory by which proofs from e to A can be assembled. In the D-S scheme the object-level theory consists of categorical *compatibility* constraints, for example, that it is incompatible for an alarm system to turn off unless either a burglary or an earthquake occurred (see Figure 5). It is remarkable that, while the calculation of $P(A \mid e)$, and even the probability of the material conditional $P(e \supset A)$, require complete probabilistic models, $P(e \models A)$ does not.

At this point, it is worthwhile reflecting on the significance of the interval $Pl(A) - Bel(A)$ in the D-S formalism. This interval is often interpreted to portray the degree of ignorance we have about probabilities, namely, the amount of information needed in order to construct a complete probabilistic model. Such intervals would have been a useful supplement to Bayes methods, which always provide point probabilities and so might give one a false sense of security in the model.

Unfortunately, the D-S intervals have little to do with ignorance, nor do they represent *bounds* on the probabilities that would ensue once ignorance is removed. For example, the disappearance of the interval $Pl(A) - Bel(A)$ often vanishes when the model is far from being complete. The equality $Bel(A) = Pl(A)$ simply means that, based on the categorical abstraction captured by the compatibility constraints, the available evidence could not simultaneously be compatible with A and its negation $\neg A$. It is curious to note that applying the same interpretation to noncategorical models yields an interval that *never* vanishes because, barring extreme probabilities, a body of evidence is always compatible with both a proposition and its negation. For example, if in the model of Figure 5 we assume that all rules have exceptions (e.g., there is a nonzero chance of a false alarm, a nonzero chance of a prank phone call, and so on), then all propositions will be assigned zero belief and unit plausibility, because none can actually be *proven* true. Thus, the choice of a categorical abstraction is a crucial one.

3.2.3 *Relations to Truth Maintenance Systems and Incidence Calculus*   The readiness of the D-S formalism to accept knowledge in the form of logical constraints, rather than conditional probabilities, renders it close to uncertainty management technique developed in the logicist camp of AI, most notably truth-maintenance systems (TMS) [Doyle, 1979] and incidence calculus [Bundy, 1985]. These two approaches can be regarded as cousins to the Dempster-Shafer theory because, like the latter, they are based on *provability* as the basic relationship connecting evidence with a conclusion.

Truth-maintenance systems also use logical rules as their elementary units of knowledge, and, similar to our treatment in Section 3.2.1, conclusions are drawn by piecing together rules to form proofs. Likewise, rules may have exceptions that may cause the expected conclusion of the proof to clash with observed facts or with other deductions. However, whereas the exceptions and/or assumptions in the D-S theory were summarized numerically, using the evidence weight m, the TMS approach maintains an explicit list of the main assumptions and exceptions that are involved in each rule.

In the ATMS approach [de Kleer, 1986] one further maintains for each conclusion c, a list $L(c)$ of nonredundant sets of assumptions called *environments*, each of which is sufficient to support a proof of c. Thus $L(c)$ is a Boolean expression whose truth signifies the existence of a proof for c. If we are given probabilities on the assumptions that appear in $L(c)$ and if we further assume that they are independent, then we can obtain $Bel(c)$ by simply computing the probability of $L(c)$:

$$Bel(c) = P[L(c)]$$

Moreover, the computation can be done symbolically, which might be more efficient than the computations method shown in Section 3.2.1. Thus, the ATMS can be used as a symbolic engine for computing the belief functions sought by the D-S theory. Steps in this direction have been taken by D'Ambrosio [1987].

Incidence calculus [Bundy, 1985] suggests a method of computing belief functions by logical sampling, similar in spirit to the method of stochastic simulation [Henrion, 1986a; Pearl, 1987c]. A probabilistic model is used to generate random samples of truth values (bit strings) for a select set of propositions representing uncertain facts. These values are presented as assumptions, or axioms, to a theorem prover. Different sets of assumptions give rise to different theorems and $Bel(c)$ is given by that fraction of the time that c can be proven. This scheme is a physical embodiment of the random switch model described in Figure 7. The random position of each switch is replaced by a random bit string assigned to the propositions impacted by the evidence.

The advantage of this scheme is that the theorem prover can be general purpose (e.g., First Order Logic), not limited to propositional constraint networks. Moreover, the scheme is not limited to simulating independent switches; dependencies can be simulated by having the bit strings generated by a complete probabilistic model (e.g., a causal network) in which these dependencies are encoded.

4 Lessons and Open Issues

4.1 Relations to Nonmonotonic Logic

4.1.1 Softened Logic vs. Hardened Probabilities
The ills of monotonic logic have often been attributed to its coarse and sharp, bi-valued character. Indeed, when one tries to figure out why logic would not predict the obvious fact that penguin birds do not fly, the first thing that one tends to blame is the sharp, uncompromising stance of the rule "birds fly" toward exceptions. It is natural, therefore, to assume that once we soften the constraints of Boolean logic and allow truth values to be measured on a gray scale, these problems will disappear. There have been several attempts along this line. Rich [1983] has proposed a likelihood-based interpretation of default rules, managed by certainty-factors calculus. Ginsberg [1984], and Baldwin [1987] have, likewise, pursued similar aspirations using the Dempster-Shafer notion of belief functions. While these attempts produce valuable results, revealing, for instance, how sensitive a conclusion is to the uncertainty of its premises, the fundamental problem of monotonicity remains unresolved. For example, regardless of the certainty calculus used, these analyses always yield an increase in the belief that penguins can fly, if one adds the superfluous information that penguins are birds and birds normally fly. Identical problems surface in the use of incidence calculus and softened versions of truth-maintenance systems [D'Ambrosio, 1987].

Evidently, it is not enough to add a soft probabilistic veneer on top of a system that is basically structured after hard monotonic logic. The problem with monotonic logic lies not in the hardness of its truth values, but rather in its inability to process context-dependent information. Logic does not have a device equivalent to the conditional probability statement "$P(B \mid A)$ is high," whose main function is to identify the context A where the proposition B can be believed, and to make sure that only legitimate changes in that context (e.g., going from A = penguins to A' = bird-penguins or $A'' $ = white penguins) will be permitted without significant changes in the belief of B.

Lacking an appropriate logical device for conditionalization, the natural tendency is to interpret the English sentence "If A then B" as a softened version of the material implication constraint $A \supset B$. A useful consequence of such softening is allaying the fears of outright contradictions. For example, while the classical interpretation of the three rules: "penguins do not fly," "penguins are birds" and "birds fly," yields an unforgivable contradiction, the uncertainties attached to these rules now render them manageable. Still, they are managed in the wrong way, because the material implication interpretation of if-then type rules is so fundamentally wrong that its maladies cannot be rectified by simply allowing exceptions in the form of shaded truth values. The source of the problem lies in the property of transitivity, $(a \rightarrow b, b \rightarrow c) \Rightarrow a \rightarrow c$, that is inherent to the material-implication interpretation.

There are occasions where rule transitivity must be totally suppressed, not merely weakened, or else strange results will surface. One such occasion occurs in property inheritance, where subclass specificity should override superclass properties. Another occurs in causal reasoning where predictions should not trigger explanations, (e.g., "sprinkler-on" predicts "wet-ground," "wet-ground" suggests "rain," yet "sprinkler-on" should not suggest "rain"). In such cases, softening the rules only weakens the flow of inference through the rule chain but does not bring it to a dead halt, as it should.

Apparently, what is needed is a new interpretation of "if-then" statements, one that does not destroy the context-sensitive character of probabilistic conditionalization. McCarthy [1986] remarks that circumscription indeed provides such an interpretation. In his words:

> Since circumscription doesn't provide numerical probabilities, its probabilistic interpretation involves probabilities that are either infinitesimal, within an infinitesimal of one, or intermediate—without any discrimination among the intermediate values. The circumscriptions give conditional probabilities. Thus we may treat the probability that a bird can't fly as an infinitesimal. However, if the rare event occurs that the bird is a penguin, then the conditional probability that it can fly is infinitesimal, but we may hear of some rare condition that would allow it to fly after all.

Rather than contrive new logics and hope that they match the capabilities of probability theory, an alternative approach would be to start with probability theory and, if we can't get the numbers or find their use inconvenient, we can extract qualitative approximations as idealized abstractions of the latter, while preserving its context-dependent properties. In this way, nonmonotonic logics should crystallize that are guaranteed to capture the context-dependent features of natural defaults [Pearl, 1988a].

4.1.2 The Logic of "Almost True"   This program had in fact been initiated over twenty years ago by the philosopher Ernest Adams [1966] who developed a logic of conditionals based on probabilistic semantics. The sentence "If A then B" is interpreted to mean that the conditional probability of B given A is very close to 1, short of actually being 1. An adaptation of Adams'

logic to default schema of the form *Bird (x) → Fly (x)*, where *x* is a variable, is reported in [Geffner and Pearl, 1987b]. The resulting logic is nonmonotonic relative to learning new facts, in accordance with McCarthy's desiderata. For example, learning that Tweety is a bird would yield the conclusion that Tweety can fly; subsequently learning that Tweety is also a penguin would yield the opposite conclusion: Tweety can't fly. Further, learning that Tweety is white will not alter this belief, because white is a typical color for penguins. However, and this is where it falls short of expectations, learning that Tweety is clever would cause Adams' logic to retract all previously held beliefs about Tweety's flying and answer: "I don't know." The logic is so conservative that it never jumps to conclusions that some new rule schema might invalidate (e.g., that clever penguins can fly). In other words, the logic does not capture the usual convention that, unless we are told otherwise, properties are presumed to be *irrelevant* to each other.[3]

Attempts to enrich Adams' logic with *relevance*-based features are described in [Pearl, 1987d], [Geffner and Pearl, 1987b], and [Geffner, 1988]. The idea is to follow a default strategy similar to that of belief networks (Section 3.1); dependencies exist only if they are mentioned explicitly or if they logically follow from other explicit dependencies. However, whereas the stratified method of constructing belief networks ensures that all relevant dependencies are already encoded in the network, this can no longer be assumed when knowledge is presented in the form of isolated default rules and logical constraints. A new logic is needed to tell us when one relevancy follows from others. This issue is further discussed in the Section 4.2.

4.1.3 *The Issue of Consistency* There is another dimension along which probabilistic analysis can assist current research in nonmonotonic logics. The latter do not provide any criterion for testing whether a database comprising default rules is internally consistent. The prevailing attitude is that once we tolerate exceptions we might as well tolerate anything [Brachman, 1985]. However, there is a sharp qualitative difference between exceptions and outright contradictions. For example, the statement "red penguins can fly" can be accepted as a description of a world in which redness defines an abnormal type of penguins. However, the statements "typically birds fly" and "typically birds do not fly" stand in outright contradiction to each other; since there is no world in which the two can hold simultaneously, they will invariably lead to strange, inconsistent conclusions. While such obvious contradictions can easily be removed from the database (e.g., [Touretzky, 1986]), more subtle ones might escape detection, e.g., "birds fly," "birds are feathered animals," "feathered animals are birds," and "feathered animals do not fly."

---

3 Grosof [1986] discusses this convention in terms of a principle of maximizing conditional independencies, similar in spirit to the maximum entropy principle [Cheeseman, 1983].

Adams' logic provides a criterion for detecting such inconsistencies, in the form of three axioms that should never be violated. In inheritance hierarchies this criterion yields a simple graphical test [Pearl, 1987e] that is a generalization of Touretzky's: A network N is consistent iff for every pair of conflicting rules $p_1 \rightarrow q$ and $p_2 \rightarrow \neg q$, p_1 and p_2 are distinct and there is no cycle of rules that embraces both p_1 and p_2. For more intricate structures of default rules the test becomes more involved.

4.2 Graphoids and the Formalization of Relevance

A central requirement in several topics of this survey has been to articulate the conditions under which one item of information is considered relevant to another, given what we already know, and to encode knowledge in structures that vividly display these conditions as the knowledge undergoes changes. Different formalisms give rise to different definitions of relevance. For example, in probability theory, relevance is identified with dependence; in constraint-based formalisms (and in relational databases) relevance is associated with induced constraints—two variables are said to be relevant to each other if we can restrict the range of values permitted for one by constraining the other.

The essence of relevance can be identified with a structure common to all these formalisms. It consists of four axioms that convey the simple idea that when we learn an irrelevant fact, the relevance relationships of all other propositions remain unaltered; any information that was irrelevant remains irrelevant and that which was relevant remains relevant. Structures that conform to these axioms are called *graphoids* [Pearl and Paz, 1987]. Interestingly, both undirected graphs and directed acyclic graphs conform to the graphoids axioms (hence the name) if we associate the sentence "variable x is irrelevant to variable y once we know z" with the graphical condition "every path from x to y is intercepted by the set of nodes corresponding to z." (A special definition of "intercept" is required for directed graphs.)

With this perspective in mind, graphs, networks, and diagrams can be viewed as inference engines devised for efficiently representing and manipulating relevance relationships: The topology of the network is assembled from a list of local relevance statements (e.g., direct dependencies), this input list entails (using the graphoids axioms) a host of additional statements, and the function of the graph is to ensure that a substantial portion of the latter can be read off by simple graphical criteria. Such a mapping will enable one to determine, at any state of knowledge z, which information is relevant to the task at hand and which can be ignored. Permissions to ignore, as we saw in Section 3.1, are the fuel that gives intensional systems the power to act.

An important result from the theory of graphoids states that Bayesian networks constitute a sound and complete inference mechanism relative to probabilistic dependencies, i.e., it identifies, in polynomial time, each and every conditional-independence relationship that logically follows from those used in the construction of the network [Pearl and Verma, 1987; Geiger and Pearl, 1988]. Similar results hold for other types of relevance relationships, e.g., partial correlations and constraint-based dependencies. However, the essential requirement for soundness and completeness is that the network be constructed *causally*, i.e., that we specify, recursively, the relationship of each variable to its predecessors in some total order. (Once the network is constructed, the original order can be forgotten; only the partial order displayed in the network matters).

One can speculate whether it is this soundness-completeness feature that renders causal schemata so important in knowledge organization. More generally, the precise relationship between causality as a representation of irrelevancies and causality as a commitment to a particular inference strategy (e.g., chronological ignorance [Shoham, 1986]) is yet to be fully investigated. A different notion of relevance has been explored by Subramanian and Genesereth [1987], based on logical derivability. The latter takes propositions, rather than variables, as the atomic entities in the relevance relationships, and, again, the connection to graphoid structures is not fully understood.

References

Adams, E., 1966. Probability and the Logic of Conditionals. In *Aspects of Inductive Logic*, J. Hintikka and P. Suppes, ed. North-Holland, Amsterdam.

Andreassen, S., Woldbye, M., Falck, B., and Andersen, S. K., 1987. MUNIN— A Causal Probabilistic Network for Interpretation of Electromyographic Findings. In *Proceedings of the Tenth International Joint Conference on AI*, Milan, Italy. pp. 366–372.

Arnborg, S., Corneil, D. G. and Proskurowski, A., 1987. Complexity of Finding Embeddings in a K-Tree. *SIAM Journal on Algebraic and Discrete Methods* **8**(2):277–284.

Baldwin, J. F., 1987. Evidential Support Logic Programming. *Fuzzy Sets and Systems* **24**:1–26.

Beeri, C., Fagin, R., Maier, D., and Yannakakis, M., 1983. On the Desirability of Acyclic Database Schemes. *Journal of ACM* **30**:479–513.

Ben-Bassat, M., Carlson, R. W., Puri, V. K., Lipnick, E., Portigal, L. D., and Weil, M. H., 1980. Pattern-based Interactive Diagnosis of Multiple Disorders: The MEDAS System. *IEEE Transactions on Pattern Analysis and Machine Intelligence* **PAMI-2**(2):148–160.

Blalock, H. M., 1971. *Causal Models in the Social Sciences*. London, Macmillan.

Bonissone, P. P., Gans, S. S., and Decker, K. S., 1987. RUM: A Layered Architecture for Reasoning with Uncertainty. In *Proceedings of the Tenth International Joint Conference of Artificial Intelligence*. Milan, Italy. pp. 891–898.

Brachman, R. J., 1985. I Lied About the Trees, or, Defaults and Definitions in Knowledge Representation. *AI Magazine* 6(3):80–93.

Bundy, A., 1985. Incidence Calculus: A Mechanism for Probabilistic Reasoning. *Journal of Automated Reasoning* 1:263–283.

Chandrasakaran, B., and Mittal, S., 1983. Conceptual Representation of Medical Knowledge for Diagnosis by Computer: MDX and Related Systems. *Advances in Computers* 22:217–293.

Cheeseman, P., 1983. A Method of Computing Generalized Bayesian Probability Values for Expert Systems. In *Proceedings of the Sixth International Joint Conference on AI*, Karlsruhe, W. Germany. pp. 198–202.

Chin, H. L. and Cooper, G. F., 1987. Stochastic Simulation of Bayesian Belief Networks. In *Proceedings of the Uncertainty in AI Workshop*, Seattle, Washington. pp. 106–113.

Clancey, W. J., 1985. Heuristic Classification. *Artificial Intelligence* 27(3):289–350.

Cohen, P. R., 1985. *Heuristic Reasoning about Uncertainty: An Artificial Intelligence Approach*. Pitman, Boston.

Cohen, P., Day, D., Delisio, J., Greenberg, M., Kjeldsen, R., Suthers, D., and Berman, P., 1987a. Management of Uncertainty in Medicine. *International Journal of Approximate Reasoning* 1(1):103–116.

Cohen, P. R., Shafer, G., and Shenoy P. P., 1987b. Modifiable Combining Functions. In *Proceedings of the Uncertainty in AI Workshop*. Seattle, Washington. pp. 10–21.

D'Ambrosio, B., 1987. Truth Maintenance with Numeric Certainty Estimates. In *Proceedings of the 3rd Conference on AI Applications*. Orlando, Florida, 244–249.

de Kleer, J., 1986. An Assumption-Based Truth Maintenance System. *Artificial Intelligence* 29:241–288.

Dechter, R., and Pearl, J., 1987a. Network-Based Heuristics for Constraint-Satisfaction Problems. *Artificial Intelligence* 34(1).

Dechter, R., and Pearl, J., 1987b. *Tree-Clustering Schemes for Constraint-Processing*. UCLA Cognitive Systems Laboratory Technical Report 870054 (R-92). Also in *Proceedings of AAAI-88*. Minneapolis, Minnesota.

Doyle, J., 1979. A Truth Maintenance System. *Artificial Intelligence* 12(3).

Duda, R. O., Hart, P. E., and Nilsson, N. J., 1976. Subjective Bayesian Methods for Rule-Based Inference Systems. In *Proceedings of the National Computer Conference*. AFIPS. 45:1075–1082.

Duncan, O. D., 1975. *Introduction to Structural Equation Models*. New York, Academic Press.

Geffner, H., and Pearl, J., 1987a. An Improved Constraint-Propagation Algorithm for Diagnosis. In *Proceedings of the Tenth International Joint Conference on AI*. Milan, Italy. pp. 1105–1111.

Geffner, H., and Pearl, J., 1987b. *A Sound Framework for Reasoning with Defaults*. UCLA Cognitive Systems Laboratory Technical Report 870058 (R-94).

Geffner, H., 1988. On the logic of defaults. In *Proceedings of AAAI-88*. Minneapolis, Minn.

Geiger, D. and Pearl, J., 1988. On the logic of influence diagrams. In *Proceedings of AAAI-88 Workshop on Uncertainty in AI*. Minneapolis, Minn.

Ginsberg, M. L., 1984. Nonmonotonic Reasoning Using Dempster's Rule. In *Proceedings, 3rd National Conference on AI*. AAAI-84. Austin, Texas. pp. 126–129.

Goodman., 1970. The Multivariate Analysis of Qualitative Data: Interaction among Multiple Classifications. *Journal of the American Statistics Association* **65**:226–256.

Grosof, B. N., 1986. Nonmonotonicity in Probabilistic Reasoning. In *Proceedings of AAAI Workshop on Uncertainty in AI*. Philadelphia, Pennsylvania. pp. 91–98.

Haberman, S. J., 1974. *The General Log-Linear Model*. Ph.D. thesis, Department of Statistics, University of Chicago.

Hajek, P., 1985. Combining Functions for Certainty Degrees in Consulting Systems. *International Journal Man-Machine Studies*. **22**:59–65.

Hajek, P., and Valdes, J. J., 1987. *Algebraic Foundations of Uncertainty Processing in Rule-Based Expert Systems*. Ceskoslovenka Akademie Ved, Matematicky Ustav.

Heckerman, D., 1986a. A Probabilistic Interpretation for MYCIN's Certainty Factors. In *Uncertainty in Artificial Intelligence*. North-Holland, Amsterdam.

Heckerman, D., 1986b. *A Rational Measure of Confirmation. Medical Computer Science Group*. Technical Report, Memo-KSL-86-25. Stanford University.

Henrion, M., 1986a. *Propagation of Uncertainty by Logic Sampling in Bayes Networks*. Technical Report, Department of Engineering and Public Policy, Carnegie-Mellon.

Henrion, M., 1986b. Should We Use Probability in Uncertain Inference Systems? In *Proceedings, Cognitive Science Society Meeting*. Amherst. pp. 320–330.

Horvitz., E. J. and Heckerman, D. E., 1986. The Inconsistent Use of Measures of Certainty in Artificial Intelligence Research. In *Uncertainty in Artificial Intelligence*. Kanal, L., Lemmer J., ed. North-Holland, Amsterdam. pp. 137–151.

Howard, R. A., and Matheson, J. E., 1981. Influence Diagrams. In *Principles and Applications of Decision Analysis*. Menlo Park, California: Strategic Decisions Group.

Kanal, L. N., and Lemmer, J. F., ed., 1986. *Uncertainty in Artificial Intelligence*. North-Holland, Amsterdam.

Kenny, D. A., 1979. *Correlation and Causality*. John Wiley and Sons

Kiiveri, H., Speed, T. P., and Carlin, J. B., 1984. Recursive Causal Models. *Journal of Australian Math Society* **36**:30–52.

Kong, A., 1986. *Multivariate Belief Functions and Graphical Models*. Ph.D. Thesis, Department of Statistics, Harvard University.

Lauritzen, S. L., 1982. *Lectures on Contingency Tables*. Second edition. University of Aalborg Press, Aalborg, Denmark.

Lauritzen, S. L., and Spiegelhalter, D. J., 1988. Local Computations with Probabilities on Graphical Structures and their Applications to Expert Systems. To appear in *Journal of the Royal Statistics Society Bulletin*. **50**.

Lemmer, J., 1983. Generalised Bayesian Updating of Incompletely Specified Distributions. *Large Scale Systems* **5**:51–68.

Lowrance, J. D., Garvey, T. D., and Strat, T. M., 1986. A Framework for Evidential-Reasoning Systems. In *Proceedings of the Fifth National Conference on AI*. AAAI-86, Philadelphia, Pennsylvania,. pp. 896–901.

Malvestuto, F. M., 1986. Decomposing Complex Contingency Tables to Reduce Storage Requirements. In *International Workshop on Scientific and Statistical Database Management*. R. Cubitt et al., ed. Luxembourg. pp. 66–71.

McCarthy, J., 1986. Applications of Circumscription to Formalizing Common-Sense Knowledge. *Artificial Intelligence* **28**(1):89–116.

Miller, R. A., Poole, H. E., and Myers, J. P., 1982. INTERNIST-1, An Experimental Computer-Based Diagnostic Consultant for General Internal Medicine. *New England Journal of Medicine* **307**(8):468–470.

Montanari, U., 1974. Networks of Constraints, Fundamental Properties and Applications to Picture Processing. *Information Science* **7**:95–132.

Nilsson, N., 1986. Probabilistic Logic. *Artificial Intelligence*. **28**(1):71–87.

Quinlan, J. R., 1983. Inferno: A Cautious Approach to Uncertain Inference. *The Computer Journal* **26**:255–269.

Pearl, J., 1986. Fusion, Propagation and Structuring in Belief Networks. *Artificial Intelligence* **29**(3):241–288.

Pearl, J., 1987a. Distributed Revision of Composite Beliefs. *Artificial Intelligence* **33**(2):173–215.

Pearl, J., 1987b. Bayes Decision Methods. *Encyclopedia of AI*. Wiley Interscience, New York. pp. 48–56.

Pearl, J., 1987c. Evidential Reasoning Using Stochastic Simulation of Causal Models. *Artificial Intelligence* **32**(2):245–258.

Pearl, J., 1987d. *Probabilistic Semantics for Inheritance Hierarchies with Exceptions*. UCLA Cognitive Systems Laboratory Technical Report 870052 (R-93). Also in [Pearl, 1988a].

Pearl, J., 1987e. *Deciding Consistency in Inheritance Networks*. UCLA Cognitive Systems Laboratory Technical Report 870053 (R-96).

Pearl, J., 1988a. *Networks of Belief: Probabilistic Reasoning in Intelligent Systems*. Morgan Kaufmann Publishers, San Mateo, California.

Pearl, J., 1988b. Embracing Causality in Formal Reasoning. *Artificial Intelligence* 35(2):259–271.

Pearl, J., and Paz, A., 1987. Graphoids: A Graph-Based Logic for Reasoning about Relevance Relations. In *Advances in Artificial Intelligence-II*. B. Du Boulay et al., ed. North-Holland, Amsterdam.

Pearl, J., and Verma, T., 1987. The Logic of Representing Dependencies by Directed Graphs. In *Proceedings of the AAAI Conference*. Seattle, Washington. pp. 374–379.

Peng, Y., and Reggia, J., 1986. Plausibility of Diagnostic Hypotheses. In *Proceedings of the Fifth National Conference on AI*. AAAI-86. pp. 140–145.

Perez, A., and Jirousek, R., 1985. Constructing an Intensional Expert Systems (INES). In *Medical Decision Making*. Elsevier Scientific Publishers. pp. 307–315.

Polya, G., 1954. *Patterns of Plausible Inference*. Princeton University Press.

Prade, H., 1983. A Synthetic View of Approximate Reasoning Techniques. In *Proceedings of the Eighth International Joint Conference of Artificial Intelligence*. Karlsruhe, West Germany. pp. 130–136.

Rich, E., 1983. Default Reasoning as Likelihood Reasoning. In *Proceedings of the International Joint Conference of Artificial Intelligence*. pp. 348–351.

Shachter, R. D. and Heckerman, D. V., 1987. A Backward View for Assessment. *AI Magazine* 8(8):55–62.

Shachter, R. D., 1988. Probabilistic Inference and Influence Diagrams. To appear in *Operations Research*.

Shafer, G., 1976. *Mathematical Theory of Evidence*. Princeton University Press.

Shafer, G., Shenoy, P. P., and Mellouli, K., 1987. Propagating Belief Functions in Qualitative Markov Trees, working paper no. 190. To appear in *International Journal of Approximate Reasoning*.

Shoham, Y., 1986. Chronological Ignorance: Time, Nonmonotonicity, Necessity and Causal Theories. In *Proceedings of AAAI-86*. Philadelphia, pp. 389–393.

Shortliffe, E. H., 1976. *Computer-Based Medical Consultation:* MYCIN. Elsevier Scientific Publishers.

Stephanou, H., and Sage, A., 1987. Perspectives on Imperfect Information Processing. *IEEE Transactions on Systems, Man, and Cybernetics* SMC-17(5):780–798.

Subramanian, D., and Genesereth, M., 1987. The Relevance of Irrelevance. In *Proceedings of the Tenth International Joint Conference on Artificial Intelligence*. Milan, Italy. pp. 416–422.

Tarjan, R. E., 1976. Graph Theory and Gaussian Elimination. In *Sparse Matrix Computations*. D. J. Rose, ed. Academic Press, New York. pp. 3–22.

Tarjan, R. E., and Yannakakis, M., 1984. Simple Linear-Time Algorithms to Test Chordality of Graphs, Test Acyclicity of Hypergraphs, and Selectively Reduce Acyclic Hypergraphs. *SIAM Journal on Computing* 13:566–579.

Thompson, T. R., 1985. Parallel Formulation of Evidential Reasoning Theories. In *Proceedings of the Eighth International Joint Conference of Artificial Intelligence*. Los Angeles, California. pp. 321–327.

Touretzky, D. S., 1986. *The Mathematics of Inheritance Systems*. Morgan Kaufmann Publishers, San Mateo, California.

Vorobev, N. N., 1962. Consistent Families of Measures and Their Extensions. *Theory of Probability and Applications*. 7:147–163.

Wermuth, N., and Lauritzen, S. L., 1983. Graphical and Recursive Models for Contingency Tables. *Biometrika* 70:537–552.

Wold, H., 1964. *Econometric Model Building*. North-Holland, Amsterdam.

Wright, S., 1921. Correlation and Causation. *Journal Agricultural Research* 20:557–585.

Wright, S., 1934. The Method of Path Coefficients. *Ann. Math. Statist.* 5:161–215.

11

Temporal Reasoning in Artificial Intelligence

Yoav Shoham
Nita Goyal
Computer Science Department
Stanford University

1 Introduction

In one way or another, every area of AI has to do with time. Medical diagnosis systems reason about the time at which a virus infected the blood system. Device troubleshooting systems look at how long it takes a capacitor to saturate. In automatic programming the time at which a variable becomes bound is important. In robot planning one wants to achieve one goal before another, to meet deadlines and so on. In qualitative physics the concept of time is essential: We speak of a bucket eventually filling, and we talk about race conditions. In speech-act theory, it is really crucial *when* the speaker and hearer know or believe something. Even in domains that seem inherently atemporal, such as mathematical theorem proving, meta-level reasoning about how long to continue along a line of proof involves time.

One can identify several classes of tasks in AI that require reasoning about time:

1. *Prediction:* Given a description of the world over some period of time, and the set of rules governing change, predict the world at some future time.

2. *Explanation:* Given a description of the world over some period of time and the rules governing change, produce a description of the world at some earlier time that accounts for the world being the way it is at the later time.

3. *Planning:* Given a description of some desired state of the world over some period of time, and the rules governing change, produce a sequence of actions that would result in a world fitting that description.

4. *Learning new rules:* Given a description of the world at different times, produce the rules governing change which account for the observed regularities in the world.

These classes of tasks, though related, have given rise to by and large disjoint fields of research. These disjoint research areas can be unified to some extent by providing a uniform framework for temporal reasoning. The somewhat mythical area of "temporal reasoning" aims to provide such a framework.

Representation of temporal information, and reasoning about such information, requires a language which can capture the concept of change over time and can express the truth or falsity of statements at different times. This language should not only be well-defined, but also have a clear meaning. This has led researchers to develop temporal logics.

The passage of time is important only because *changes* are possible with time. The sun moving across the sky or advances of program counters all involve changes with time. The concept of time would become meaningless in a world where no changes were possible. In Sections 2 and 3 we explain two different approaches to reasoning about change, *change-based* and *time-based*. The change-based approach is discussed first with two representative formalisms: situation calculus and dynamic logic. We point out some of the limitations of this approach. Then we introduce the time-based approach; after considering the various issues involved in constructing a temporal logic, we introduce a representative temporal logic with formal syntax and semantics. This solves several of the problems with change-based logics, but some problems such as the qualification, ramification and the frame problems still remain unsolved. A common framework to solve these problems is nonmonotonic reasoning. We end with an overview of the problems and the advances made in nonmonotonic temporal reasoning.

2 Change-based Approach

The change-based approach concentrates on the entities that signify a change having taken place; that is, *change-indicators*. Situation calculus in AI, and dynamic logic in theoretical computer science, are prototypes of this approach.

Actions in situation calculus, and *programs* in dynamic logic, are the basic change-indicators.

2.1 *Situation Calculus*

Situation calculus was introduced by McCarthy and Hayes in 1969 [McCarthy and Hayes, 1981]. It views the world as a set of *states* or *situations*, each of which is a "frozen" snapshot of the world. At different points in time, the world can be in different states.

The world persists in one state until an action is performed that changes it to a new state. Consider the example of starting a car. Initially the world is in state S1 where the motor is off; and the action of switching on the car, Switchon, results in the state S2 where the motor is on. This can be expressed in logic using the Result function, which takes an action and a state and produces the state the world will be in after performing the given action in the given state.

To see what happens across actions we have the truth operator True.

$\forall s$ True(s,Off) $\supset$ True(Result(Switchon,s),On)

$\forall s$ True(s,Off)

$\qquad \supset$ True(Result(Hitpedal,Result(Switchon,s)),Move)

The first sentence says that in all states in which the engine is off, if the action of switching on the engine is performed then in the resulting state the engine is on. The results of the actions can be nested as in the second sentence. This is a basic kind of formalism which gave rise to much work, particularly the STRIPS planner and its derivatives [Fikes and Nilsson, 1971; Fikes et al., 1972; Sacerdoti, 1974].

2.2 *Dynamic Logic*

Dynamic logic, introduced by Pratt [1976], is a framework for reasoning about programs based on modal logic (refer to [Chellas, 1980; Hughes and Cresswell, 1969; Kripke, 1963] for modal logic). The idea is to integrate programs into an assertion language by allowing programs to be modal operators. In dynamic logic, programs are the change-indicators, which when applied to a *program state* change it to another program state. Propositional dynamic logic (PDL), as defined by Fischer and Ladner [1979], has a set of *atomic formulas* Φ_0 which are propositional variables and a set of *atomic programs* Σ_0 which are indivisible statements in a programming language. The set of programs, Σ, and the set of formulas, Φ are inductively defined as follows.

Programs:

1.   Atomic programs and θ are programs;

2.   If *a* and *b* are programs and *p* is a formula, then (*a*;*b*), (*a*∪*b*), *a**, and *p*?
     are programs.

   θ   means "abort" or "blocked."
   (*a*;*b*)   means "execute *a* followed by *b*."
   (*a*∪*b*)   means "nondeterministically do *a* or *b*."
   *a**   means "repeat *a* a nondeterministically chosen number of times."
   p?   means "test *p* and proceed only if true."

Formulas:

1.   Atomic formulas, *true* and *false*, are formulas;

2.   If *p* and *q* are formulas and *a* is a program, then (*p* ∨ *q*), ¬*p*, and ⟨*a*⟩*p* are
     formulas.

Informally, ⟨*a*⟩*p* means that it is possible for the program *a* to terminate with
assertion *p* holding on termination. The dual notion [*a*]*p* defined as ¬⟨*a*⟩¬*p*
means that *p* must hold when *a* terminates.

   The effect of these programs is to change one program state into another.
Like the situation calculus, dynamic logic has no concept of time except that
which is implicit in the sequencing of change-indicators (actions for situation
calculus and programs for dynamic logic).

2.3 Limitations of the Change-based Approach

The change-based approach has several limitations:

1.   *Instantaneous actions*: In the change-based systems, the actions do not
     have any duration. Sentences such as "The robot should move the vase to
     the table slowly so that it does not break, but move the book to the table
     fast to save as much time as possible" cannot be expressed because we
     cannot define the notion of performing an action slow or fast. Even
     sentences such as "The robot should get to Little Nell before the train
     arrives" are not directly expressible in this framework.

2.   *Instantaneous and immediate effects*: The fact that the result of an action
     is immediate gives rise to two problems.

     • *Delayed effects*: It is not necessary in the real world for an action to
       produce an effect immediately. It could take place after a while,
       during which period other actions could take place. For instance, there

is no way to express in the system, the sentence "30 seconds after you press the button at the crosswalk, the pedestrian light turns to green."

- *Natural death*: This refers to the phenomenon in which the effects of an action have only a certain duration, such as "When you press the button of the hand-drying machine at the airport, it emits hot air for 30 seconds." Here the state of the world changes after 30 seconds without any action which makes it do so. There is no mechanism for expressing such phenomena.

3. *Concurrent or overlapping actions*: Simultaneous actions cannot be expressed in the change-based formalism. For example, suppose we have two actions, `Pushright` and `Pushleft`, referring to pushing a block to the right or to the left. If the situation is idealized to accommodate concurrent actions, the concurrent action {`Pushright,Pushleft`} results in neither. Similarly, overlapping actions are not expressible. A situation like "While Robot1 painted the body of the car, Robot2 finished inspecting the transmission, and so by the time Robot2 was done the car was ready for assembly" is not expressible.

4. *Continuous processes*: In change-based systems, the only notion of time possible is the discrete view, with states corresponding to different time points. This is sufficient for many purposes, but in the areas of naive physics or qualitative physics we might want to say something like "Turning on the tap resulted in the level of water growing steadily, until the cup overflowed." Such continuous processes are not expressible in change-based systems.

5. *The qualification problem*: This is best illustrated by an example. We have the knowledge that when nothing is wrong, the result of turning the ignition key of the car on is to start the engine. "Nothing is wrong" requires a richer knowledge of the world about dead batteries, empty gas tanks, of bananas in tailpipes and so on. This can be expressed as:

$$\text{True}(s,\text{Batteryok}) \land \text{True}(s,\text{Gas}) \land$$
$$\text{True}(s,\text{No\_bananas\_in\_tailpipes}) \land \ldots$$
$$\supset \text{True}(\text{Result}(\text{Switchon},s),\text{On})$$

As long as nothing is wrong, all this information is irrelevant, but if something does go wrong then we need this information to find out what has gone wrong. We would not like to drown in this long chain of reasoning every time we start the car, yet we would like to tap this information when necessary. In the context of predicting the future, it is the problem of making sound predictions about the future without taking into account everything in the past. This is called the qualification problem.

6.   *The ramification problem*: The problem is that the results of an action may be very complex. For example, if you drive your car from A to B, then as a result it is in B and so are its tires, engines. . .

```
Car(x) ⊃ True(Result(Move(x,A,B),s), At(x,B) ∧
        At(Engine(x),B) ∧ At(Wheels(x),B) ∧. . .)
```

We would like to state that as a result of moving the car from A to B, everything contained in the car moves to B without having to explicitly state all the details as done here. This is the ramification problem.

7.   *The frame problem*: Suppose a block is moved from A to B. The moving action changes the location but it does not change its color or size, it does not change the President of the United States and so on. We have to write down this information in the form of *frame axioms* such as

```
True(s,Green(x)) ⊃ True(Result(Move(x,A,B),s),Green(x)).
```

The frame problem is the problem arising due to the complexity of representing the things that remain *unchanged* as the result of an action.[1]

Among the seven problems listed above, the first four arise due to the choice of the particular formalism, the change-based approach. A lot of effort went into trying to get around these problems in dynamic logic. The best known attempt is the *process logic*, introduced by Pratt a few years later [Pratt, 1979]. It is a language which enables one to say what happens while an action is taking place. This was a minor improvement, but it did not come close to solving all these problems. Dynamic logic is not used much nowadays, and we predict the same fate for situation calculus in AI.

The alternative to the change-based approach is to have only one basic kind of change, namely, the passage of time. This gives rise to the time-based approach which is discussed in the next section.

The last three problems have a global nature and do not result from a particular choice of formalism. Therefore, as we will see, the qualification, ramification and frame problems show up in the time-based approach too; the attempts to solve them are discussed in Section 4.

---

1 Shoham and McDermott suggest a more general version of the frame problem, called the "extended prediction" problem [Shoham and McDermott, 1988].

3 Time-based Approach

The time-based approach recognizes only one fundamental change, the passage of time, which is a constant change unaffected by anything else. There is a time structure, and the assertions are either true or false at various points on this time structure. To construct a temporal logic, we have to make decisions about this structure, and about the language used to express assertions. These issues are discussed in the following subsections.

Philosophy has the longest tradition of developing temporal logics. The most up-to-date survey of this work is in van Benthem's book [1983]. Previous books include those by Prior [1967] and Rescher and Urquhart [1971]. Theoretical computer scientists borrowed from that tradition. Pnueli [1977] was the first to use it to reason about properties of programs. In AI, the best known temporal logics are the ones due to Allen [1984] and McDermott [1982]. Since these early systems, however, much work has been done by Vilain [1982], Shoham [1987], Ladkin [1986], Haugh [1987], Reichgelt and others.

We will bring out the issues in developing temporal logics by actually constructing a representative logic. This logic follows the development in [Shoham, 1987]. It is a crystallization and generalization of the ideas proposed by Allen [1984] and McDermott [1982].

3.1 Representational Issues in Temporal Logics

To construct a temporal logic, certain decisions have to be made about temporal representation. The first issue to resolve is over what entity we interpret assertions. Should this be a time *point*, a time *interval*, perhaps neither, or maybe both? The answers to these questions have varied in philosophy, theoretical computer science and in AI. In AI, one finds all three kinds of formalisms: point-based, interval-based and mixed. Allen's formalism [Allen, 1984] allowed statements to be interpreted only over time intervals. In McDermott's formalism [McDermott, 1982b], there are two kinds of statements; those interpreted over time points are *facts* and others referring to intervals are *events*. The situations that we are interested in require reasoning about time intervals and therefore we will interpret assertions over intervals. There will be no assertions interpreted over time points. Instead, we will allow interpretations over intervals of zero duration.

The second important decision to be made is about the primitive temporal elements in our ontology of time. The major contenders are again, points and intervals. We can take intervals as primitives and have a calculus of intervals in which two intervals can abut, overlap or one can be a subinterval of the other. Such a calculus was proposed by Allen [1984]. We can also take points as primitive objects and define intervals in terms of their endpoints. In the

Allen formalism [Allen, 1984] intervals are the primitives, whereas in the McDermott formalism [McDermott, 1982b] an interval is an ordered pair of points. We will follow McDermott and have points as basic temporal objects. An interval will be represented as a pair of its endpoints.

The third important question is whether truth over one interval constrains truth over other intervals. For example, in the Allen formalism [Allen, 1984], if a property holds over an interval, then it must hold over all subintervals. On the other hand, if an event holds over an interval, then it does not hold over any overlapping interval. In philosophy, an assertion is *homogeneous* if the following is true: for any interval $\langle$ P1, P2 $\rangle$, the assertion holds over $\langle$ P1, P2 $\rangle$ iff it holds over every subinterval of $\langle$ P1, P2 $\rangle$. In theoretical computer science, an interval-based logic is *local* if an assertion holds over $\langle$ P1, P2 $\rangle$ iff it holds over P1 (or over the interval $\langle$ P1, P1 $\rangle$). We shall not make any *a priori* associations between the truth of an assertion over an interval and its truth over other intervals.

The fourth decision to be made is about the structure of time. Some of the issues involved here are:

- *Precedence:* Time is usually considered to be linear, that is, a total order. Sometimes, though, it is considered only to be a partial order. Time can branch; it can branch only into future, or into past, or both. There are philosophical formulations which permit circular time. Most AI formalisms have assumed linear time, though there are some exceptions such as McDermott's logic [McDermott, 1982b].

- *Discrete vs. dense*: Time is *discrete* if between every pair of time points there are a finite number of time points. It is *dense* if between every pair of points there is another point. Discrete time has been popular in computer science since one has to reason mostly about digital devices. However, many temporal logics now view time as dense.

- *Complete vs. incomplete:* A structure is *complete* if for every series of points that is bounded from above by another point, there exists a point that is the least upper bound of the series. This is the property that distinguishes reals from rationals. If time is dense, is it complete too?

- *Bounded vs. unbounded*: A stucture is *unbounded* if every point has a later point or an earlier point, corresponding respectively to being unbounded in the future or unbounded in the past.

-

So far we have decided that the time structure will have time points as the primitive temporal entities. A time interval will be represented as a pair of time points which are its end-points. We will allow intervals that have zero duration and these will represent points. We have not committed ourselves on any other issues at this time, though most of the time we will view time to be *linear* and *dense*. The assertions will be interpreted over time intervals.

Now that we have defined the time structure, we address the question of the logical form to be used to express temporal information. We have three primary options for the logical form:

1. *Classical First Order Logic*: We can simply include time as an argument or two arguments to a predicate. For example, if M is an interpretation then,

   M ⊨ Color(House17,Red,T1,T2)

   says that over the interval ⟨ T1,T2 ⟩, House17 had color Red in M. The problem with this approach is that we have not accorded time any special status. We cannot say anything about the temporal aspects of an assertion. Without any further restrictions, there is nothing to disallow formulas with many time arguments or none at all. For instance, there is nothing to disallow Color(House,Red,Cat,Mouse) as a legal formula.

2. *Reified sentences*: In this representation, we separate the atemporal component of assertions from their temporal component. The atemporal component is also called a *proposition type*. This can be done by using something like a "truth" predicate, which will take three arguments; two time points denoting an interval and a proposition type. For example, if M is an interpretation, the expression

   M ⊨ True(T1,T2,Color(House17,Red))

   associates the proposition type Color(House17,Red) with an interval from time T1 to T2. Note that True is not really a predicate, but only a notational convenience to express this association. This approach is prevalent in AI, and we will return to it shortly.

3. *Modal Temporal Logic*: Another way to associate a proposition type with time is by taking the modal route (refer to [Chellas, 1980; Hughes and Cresswell 1969; Kripke, 1963] for modal logic). This can be done by not mentioning time at all, but instead complicating the interpretation of our formulas. Here the temporality enters not in the syntax but in the semantics. In philosophy, modal temporal logics in which time points correspond to possible worlds, the so-called tense logics, have been prevalent. Interpretation of formulas in such a logic is explained below. If

in classical logic a formula φ is true in an interpretation M (written M $\vDash$ φ) or false in it, now a formula would be either true in M *at a given point of time* T (written M, T $\vDash$ φ) or false there. Each time point would then correspond to a possible world. The modal operator $\Box\varphi$ can mean "φ is true at all future times" and $\Diamond\varphi$ can mean "φ is true at some future time." In our red house example, we would have M, T $\vDash$ Color(House17,Red). We can have other interpretations too for these modal operators. For example, $\Box\varphi$ can also mean "φ is true at all times in the past, present and future" and $\Diamond\varphi$ can mean "φ is true at some time in the past, present or future." Note that we can also interpret statements over time intervals rather than time points. Then the intervals would correspond to possible worlds. There has been a growing interest in interval-based modal temporal logics in the recent past. Halpern and Shoham [1986] illustrate one such approach.

The classical first-order logic does not accord any special conceptual or notational status to time, and is thus insufficient for our purposes. The reified first-order logic and the temporal modal logic are closely related. In particular, it can be shown that any assertion in modal temporal logic can be transformed into an equivalent assertion in the reified first-order logic. We will, therefore, use the reified first-order logic. Based on the assumptions made in this subsection, a sample temporal logic is constructed in the next subsection.

3.2 *A Sample Temporal Logic*

We want to associate an atemporal assertion with a time interval. The most straightforward way of doing so is to form an interval/assertion pair: each *primitive formula* will be a pair $\langle i, p \rangle$, where i is an interval symbol and p is a primitive propositional symbol. Since we treat time points rather than time intervals as basic, an interval symbol i is really a pair $\langle t_1, t_2 \rangle$, where the t_i are the time point symbols. For notational convenience, we will replace the formula $\langle\langle t_1, t_2 \rangle, p \rangle$ by the more appealing True(t_1, t_2, p). The precise syntax and semantics for both the propositional and the first-order cases are given below.

3.2.1 *Propositional Case*

Syntax   Given P, a set of *primitive propositions*; T, a set of *time point symbols*; V, a set of *temporal variables*, TV = T $\cup$ V, and $\leqslant$, a binary relation symbol; the set of well-formed formulas (wffs) is defined recursively as follows:

1. If $tv_1 \in$ TV and $tv_2 \in$ TV, then $tv_1 = tv_2$ and $tv_1 \leqslant tv_2$ are wffs.

2. If $tv_1 \in$ TV, $tv_2 \in$ TV and $p \in$ P, then $\text{True}(tv_1, tv_2, p)$ is a wff.

3. If φ_1 and φ_2 are wffs, then so are $\varphi_1 \wedge \varphi_2$ and $\neg\varphi_1$.

4. If φ is a wff and $v \in$ V, then $\forall v \ \varphi$ is a wff.

We assume the usual definition of $\vee, \supset, \equiv, \exists$ and other logical operators. We can also use the following syntactic sugar: $\text{True}(tv_1, tv_2, \varphi_1 \wedge \varphi_2)$ is shorthand for $\text{True}(tv_1, tv_2, \varphi_1) \wedge \text{True}(tv_1, tv_2, \varphi_2)$, $\text{True}(tv_1, tv_2, \neg\varphi)$ is shorthand for $\neg \text{True}(tv_1, tv_2, \varphi)$, and so on.

Semantics An *interpretation* is a tuple $\langle$ W, $\leq$, M $\rangle$, where W is a nonempty universe of time points, $\leq$ is a binary relation on W, M $= \langle$ M$_1$, M$_2$ $\rangle$ is a meaning function M$_1$: T $\rightarrow$ W and M$_2$: P $\rightarrow 2^{W \times W}$.

(We can require that $\langle w_1, w_2 \rangle \in$ M$_2$(p) iff $\langle w_2, w_1 \rangle \in$ M$_2$(p). This convention makes explicit the intuition that a pair of time points denotes a single interval. Alternatively, we can omit this requirement, and simply pay no attention to the truth value of the formulas $\text{True}(t_1, t_2, p)$ such that M$_1(t_1) \not\leq$ M$_1(t_2)$.)

A *variable assignment* is a function VA : V $\rightarrow$ W. An interpretation S $= \langle$ W,$\leq$,$\langle$ M$_1$, M$_2$ $\rangle \rangle$ satisfies a wff φ under the variable assignment VA (S $\models \varphi$ [VA]) given the following inductively defined conditions (in the following, for any $tv \in$ TV, VAL(tv) is defined to be M$_1(tv)$ if $tv \in$ T, and VA(tv) if $tv \ll$ V):

> S $\models$ $(tv_1 = tv_2)$ [VA] iff VAL(tv_1) = VAL(tv_2).
>
> S $\models$ $(tv_1 \leqslant tv_2)$ [VA] iff VAL(tv_1) $\leq$ VAL(tv_2).
>
> S $\models$ $\text{True}(tv_1, tv_2, p)$ [VA] iff $\langle$ VAL(tv_1), VAL(tv_2) $\rangle \in$ M$_2$(p).
>
> S $\models$ $(\varphi_1 \wedge \varphi_2)$[VA] iff S $\models \varphi_1$[VA] and S $\models \varphi_2$[VA].
>
> S $\models \neg \varphi$ [VA] iff S $\not\models \varphi$ [VA].
>
> S $\models (\forall v\varphi)$[VA] iff S $\models \varphi$ [VA$'$] for all VA$'$ that agree with VA everywhere except possibly on v.

An interpretation S is a *model* for a wff φ if S $\models \varphi$[VA] *for all* variable assignments VA. A *sentence* is a wff containing no free variables. Clearly, if a sentence φ is satisfied by an interpretation S under some variable assignment then φ is satisfied by S under *any* variable assignment, and therefore S is a model for φ. A wff is *satisfiable* if it has a model. A wff φ is *valid* (written $\models \varphi$) if its negation is not satisfiable.

3.2.2 *First-Order Case*

The propositional nature of the logic presented in the previous section restricts one to basic assertions that are "structureless": the assertion "House17 is Red" collapses into a single propositional letter p, and so on. We cannot say something about all houses. Therefore, the logic is now generalized to a first-order one.

Syntax   Given TC, a set of *time point symbols*; C, a set of *constant symbols* that is disjoint from TC; TV, a set of *temporal variables*; V, a set of *variables* that is disjoint from TV; TF, a set of *temporal function symbols* (typical ones being the arithmetic operators); F, a set of *function symbols* that is disjoint from TF; and R, a set of *relation symbols*.

The set of *temporal terms* is defined inductively as follows:

1.   All members of TC are temporal terms.

2.   All members of TV are temporal terms.

3.   If $trm_1, \ldots, trm_n$ are temporal terms, and $f \in TF$ is an *n*-ary function symbol, then $f(trm_1, \ldots, trm_n)$ is a temporal term.

The set of *nontemporal terms* is defined in exactly the same way, with TC replaced by C, TV replaced by V and TF replaced by F.

The set of well-formed formulas (wffs) is defined inductively as follows:

1.   If trm_a and trm_b are temporal terms, then $trm_a = trm_b$ and $trm_a \leqslant trm_b$ are wffs.

2.   If trm_a and trm_b are temporal terms, $trm_1, \ldots, trm_n$ are nontemporal terms, and $r \in R$ an *n*-ary relation symbol, then $True(trm_a, trm_b, r(trm_1, \ldots, trm_n))$ is a wff.

3.   If φ_1 and φ_2 are wffs, then so are $\varphi_1 \wedge \varphi_2$ and $\neg \varphi_1$.

4.   If φ is a wff and $z \in TV \cup V$ is a variable, then $\forall z \varphi$ is a wff.

Again, we assume the usual definitions of $\vee, \supset, \equiv, \exists$, and so on. Below are some examples of sentences (or wffs with no free variables):

```
True(T1,T2,Color(House17,Red))
∃u True(T3,T4,On(u,B))
∀v(1984 ≤ v ∧ v ≤ 1988)
    ⊃ True(v,v,Gender(President(USA),Male))
∀v1,u ∃v2 (v2 ≤ v1 + 30min
    ∧ ((True(v1,v1,Solid(u))
    ∧ True(v1,v2,Heating(u))
        ⊃ True(v2,v2, Liquid(u))))).
```

Notice that in the third example above, the term President(USA) contains the function symbol President that depends implicitly on time (in addition to its dependence on the explicit argument). Such functions, which were called *fluents* by McCarthy and Hayes [1981], will therefore be interpreted in a way that takes time into account. In fact, the interpretation of all function symbols will be time-dependent; of course, the value of the function along the time dimension may be constant. The same applies to the interpretation of relation symbols. Constant symbols, on the other hand, will be interpreted in a time-independent fashion. For example, the symbol USA will denote the same object at all times. In other words, we will assume that constant symbols are what philosophers have called *rigid designators.*

The respective intended meanings of the sentences above are that House17 is Red from T_1 to T_2, that there is something on B from T_3 to T_4, that at no time between 1984 until today has the USA had a woman president, and that if you heat a solid object then it melts within half an hour. Next we guarantee that these indeed *are* the meanings.

Semantics An *interpretation* is a tuple $\mathfrak{I} = \langle$ TW, $\leq$, W, TFN, FN, RL, M $\rangle$, where TW is a nonempty universe of time points, $\leq$ is a binary relation on TW, W is a nonempty universe of individuals that is disjoint from TW, TFN is a set of total functions in $\cup_k$ (TW$^k \to$ TW), FN is a set of total functions in $\cup_k$ (W$^k \to$ W), RL is a set of relations over W, and M $= \langle$ M$_1$, M$_2$, M$_3$, M$_4$, M$_5$ $\rangle$ is a meaning function as follows. M$_1$: T $\to$ TW, M$_2$: C $\to$ W, M$_3$: TF $\to$ TFN, M$_4$: TW $\times$ TW $\times$ F $\to$ FN, and M$_5$: TW $\times$ TW $\times$ R $\to$ RL. (Again, we require that M$_4$ and M$_5$ be commutative in the first two arguments: that is, M$_4$(w$_1$,w$_2$,f) = M$_4$(w$_2$,w$_1$,f) and similarly for M$_5$. Alternatively, we can ignore the truth value of formulas over "reversed" interval, that is, over pairs $\langle$ w$_1$,w$_2$ $\rangle$ s.t. w$_1 \not\leq$ w$_2$.)

A *variable assignment* is a function VA $= \langle$ VAT, VAV $\rangle$, such that VAT : VT $\to$ TW and VAV : V $\to$ W. M and VA induce a time-independent meaning MVA on arbitrary terms in the following way.

We first define the meaning of arbitrary temporal terms. That meaning is the same regardless of when the terms are interpreted: the terms 1.1.2000 and (12:00 + 12$_{min}$) each denote a single, unambiguous absolute time. The precise meaning of temporal terms is as follows. If $vt \in$ VT, then MVA(vt) = VAT(vt). If ct $\in$ CT, then MVA(ct) = M$_1$(ct). If f $\in$ TF and trm = f(trm$_1$,...,trm$_n$) is a temporal term, then

$$\text{MVA(trm)} = \text{M}_3(\text{f})(\text{MVA(trm}_1),\ldots,\text{MVA(trm}_n)).$$

The meaning of arbitrary nontemporal terms is slightly trickier since it is time-dependent: the meaning of President(USA) depends on the time of interpretation. We therefore make the following definition. If $v \in$ V, then for all w$_1$,w$_2 \in$ WT, MVA(w$_1$,w$_2$,v) = VAV (v). If c $\in$ C, then MVA(w$_1$,w$_2$,c) = M$_2$(c). The temporal dependence of the interpretation enters in the following definition: if $f \in F$ and $\text{trm} = f(\text{trm}_1, \ldots, \text{trm}_n)$ is a nontemporal term, then[2]

$$\text{MVA}(w_1, w_2, \text{trm}) = M_4(w_1, w_2, f)(\text{MVA}(w_1, w_2, \text{trm}_1), \ldots,$$
$$\text{MVA}(w_1, w_2, \text{trm}_n)).$$

The interpretation $\Im$ and the variable assignment VA satisfy a wff φ (written $\Im \models \varphi[\text{VA}]$) under the following inductively defined conditions.

$\Im \models \text{trm}_1 = \text{trm}_2[\text{VA}]$ iff $\text{MVA}(\text{trm}_1) = \text{MVA}(\text{trm}_2)$.

$\Im \models \text{trm}_1 \leq \text{trm}_2[\text{VA}]$ iff $\text{MVA}(\text{trm}_1) \leq \text{MVA}(\text{trm}_2)$.

$\Im \models \text{True}(\text{trm}_a, \text{trm}_b, r(\text{trm}_1, \ldots, \text{trm}_n))[\text{VA}]$ iff
$\quad \langle \text{MVA}(\text{MVA}(\text{trm}_a), \text{MVA}(\text{trm}_b), \text{trm}_1), \ldots,$
$\quad \text{MVA}(\text{MVA}(\text{trm}_a), \text{MVA}(\text{trm}_b), \text{trm}_n) \rangle$
$\qquad \in M_5(\text{MVA}(\text{trm}_a), \text{MVA}(\text{trm}_b), r)$.

$\Im \models (\varphi_1 \wedge \varphi_2)[\text{VA}]$ iff $\Im \models \varphi_1[\text{VA}]$ and $\Im \models \varphi_2[\text{VA}]$.

$\Im \models (\neg \varphi)[\text{VA}]$ iff $\Im \not\models \varphi[\text{VA}]$.

$\Im \models (\forall z \, \varphi)[\text{VA}]$ iff $\Im \models \varphi[\text{VA}']$ for all VA' that
$\quad$ agree with VA everywhere except possibly on z.

The next few definitions are identical to those made in the propositional case. An interpretation $\Im$ is a *model* for a wff φ (written $\Im \models \varphi$) if $\Im \models \varphi[\text{VA}]$ for *all* variable assignments VA. A *sentence* is a wff containing no free variables. Again, it is clear that if a sentence φ is satisfied by an interpretation $\Im$ under some variable assignment then φ is satisfied by $\Im$ under *any* variable assignment, and therefore that $\Im$ is a model for φ. A wff is *satisfiable* if it has a model. A wff φ is *valid* (written $\models \varphi$) if its negation is not satisfiable.

3.3 *Ontology: Facts, Properties, Events, and Other Animals*

We now have a temporal logic that enjoys both clear syntax and precise semantics. But all we have are *temporal propositions*, which associate a *proposition type* with a time interval. These temporal propositions do not have the structure of Allen's *properties, events*, and *processes* [Allen, 1984] or McDermott's *facts* and *events* [McDermott, 1982b]. We will now provide the means for distinguishing between fact-like (or property-like) proposition types and event-like proposition types. In fact we will be able to construct a categorization of proposition types that is richer and more flexible than the fact/event dichotomy or the property/event/process trichotomy. For example, the assertions "I ran more than two miles" and "I ran less than two miles" do not fit into either of those two categorization schemes; they will into the following one.

---

2 Note that a certain problem still remains here. How would you represent the sentence "From 1776 to 1976, the president of the United States has always been a male?"

The way we will distinguish between different kinds of propositions is by specifying how the truth of the proposition over one interval is related to its truth over other intervals. For the propositional logic, interpret a proposition type to mean a primitive propositional symbol. For the first-order case, interpret a proposition type to be a relation symbol with the appropriate number of arguments. We have defined below a few concepts based on this principle to illustrate the power we have at our disposal.

- A proposition type **x** is *downward-hereditary* (written ↓ **x**) if whenever it holds over an interval it holds over all of its subintervals, possibly excluding the two end points. *Example*: "The robot traveled less than two miles" is downward-hereditary.

- A proposition type *x* is *upward-hereditary* (written ↑ *x*) if whenever it holds for all proper subintervals of some nonpoint interval (except possibly at its end points), it also holds over the nonpoint interval itself. *Example*: "The robot traveled at a speed of two miles per hour" is upward-hereditary.

- A proposition type is *liquid* (written ↕ *x*) if it is both upward-hereditary and downward-hereditary. *Example*: "The robot's arm was in the GRASPING state" is liquid.

- A proposition type is *clay-like* if whenever it holds over two consecutive intervals it holds also over their union. *Example*: "The robot started and ended at the same place" and "The robot traveled an even number of miles" are clay-like.

- A proposition type is *gestalt* if it never holds over two intervals one of which properly contains the other. *Example*: "Exactly six minutes passed" is gestalt.

- A proposition type is *solid* if it never holds over two properly overlapping intervals. *Example*: "The robot executed the NAVIGATE procedure (from start to finish)" is solid.

4 Nonmonotonic Temporal Reasoning

We have identified seven problems with the change-based approach in the beginning. Of these, the first four are solved by the time-based system proposed here. What about the rest, that is, the qualification problem, the ramification problem, and the frame problem? The answer is they are still with us. Let us reexamine the car-starting scenario, which ought to be expressed as

```
True(T,T,Switchon) ∧ True(T,T,Gas)
    ∧ True(T,T,Battery) ∧ . . . ⊃ True(T + ε,T + ε,On).
```

The qualification problem still exists since we still have to specify all the conditions for the car to start in the antecedent. Another problem is that we cannot say anything about the engine after the time point $T + \epsilon$. That is, for $\epsilon < \delta$, nothing can be said about $\texttt{True}(T + \delta, T + \delta, \texttt{On})$; this is exactly the frame problem. Much work recently has addressed these problems using nonmonotonic logics.

Nonmonotonic logics permit "jumping to conclusions," or assigning sentences "default truth values," or reaching conclusions which rely in part on the "absence of evidence to the contrary." The three best-known nonmonotonic logics are *circumscription* by McCarthy [1980], *default logic* by Reiter [1980], Etherington [1983], and the modal family of logics by McDermott and Doyle [1980], McDermott [1982a], Moore [1983], Halpern and Moses [1985], Shoham [1987c], Levesque [1984] and others. We will not discuss these since they are covered elsewhere in the book.

Since nonmonotonic logics permit "jumping to conclusions," it is natural to expect that they will be useful for solving the qualification and frame problems. For example, given the fact that the car ignition has been switched on, one might expect such a logic to allow jumping to the conclusion that the car starts, and retracting that statement when told that the battery is dead. Indeed, until recently, such wishful thinking was common. That ended with the well-known paper by Hanks and McDermott [1987], which introduced what is now known as the Yale shooting problem. The moral of the paper was that the naive use of *any* of the standard nonmonotonic logics gave bad results in a temporal setting. We will describe the Yale shooting problem and the proposed solutions in brief.

The Yale shooting problem concerns a person often named Fred, and a gun. At any time, Fred may or may not be alive and the gun may or may not be loaded. In the initial situation Fred is alive and the gun is loaded. Also in any situation in which the gun is loaded, firing it will kill Fred (that is, cause Fred to cease being alive). Finally we are given a frame axiom which says that unless an action a is abnormal in that it reverses the sentence p in situation s, p will persist through the execution of the action. We will presumably minimize the extension of the abnormality predicate using one of the formal approaches to nonmonotonic reasoning.

Now suppose that in the initial situation, we wait and then fire the gun. Our *intuition* says that as a result of the shooting action, Fred should die since waiting does not change anything. Unfortunately, none of the existing nonmonotonic logics can derive this. All of them derive the fact that *either* Fred is killed as the result of the shooting action, *or* the waiting action causes the gun to become unloaded. If our intention is merely to minimize abnormality, there is no way to select between these two possibilities. As this sort of minimization is all that is effected by any of the existing formalizations of nonmonotonic logics, all of them are incapable of concluding that Fred is dead after we shoot him.

One set of solutions suggested appealed to the temporal information. These were *chronological ignorance* by Shoham [1987c], *pointwise circumscription* by Lifschitz [1986] and the logic of *persistence* by Kautz [1986]. The idea is that the set of situations can be partially ordered in time, so that we can say that something happened *later* or *before* something else. Then we try to delay the occurrence of abnormality to as late in the time as possible. This way the gun cannot be unloaded during the course of the first waiting action; the only abnormal action is that of the gun being fired after the wait action and successfully killing Fred. Unfortunately, this approach gives unintuitive answers in some cases. Suppose we are told that if we wait twice, the gun becomes unloaded for some reason or other. Combining this with our existing domain description, we are able to conclude that one of the waiting actions must have been abnormal, since the gun became unloaded during it. Now the approach based on temporal ordering forces us to break this ambiguity by concluding specifically that the gun became unloaded at the last possible moment. Intuitively, this is not justified by the information available to us.

There has also been a causal approach to the solution typified by the logic of *causal minimization* proposed independently by Lifschitz [1987] and Haugh [1987]. This approach suggests modifying the domain description so as to capture the notion of causality. It *explicitly* states that the shooting action causes Fred to become not alive, and that no change can occur unless there is a causal explanation for that change. There are technical difficulties with this approach too that we will not go into here.

The nonmonotonic solutions have so far been only partial. They are useful in some respects, but not others. For instance, they allow us to predict the future without drowning in details, but they do not allow us anything more complex. This is currently a very active research area and proposed solutions to the Yale shooting problem are still pouring in.

5 Conclusion

To summarize, we introduced a distinction between the change-based and time-based systems for representing change. We discussed some change-based systems like the situation calculus and dynamic logic, pointing to the problems in the change-based approach. Some of these problems, which were formalism-dependent, can be solved by using the time-based approach. After consideringseveral alternatives, a reified temporal logic with formal syntax and semantics was constructed. This solved the formalism-dependent problems, but some formalism-independent problems such as the qualification problem and the frame problem, were still unsolved. We mentioned the usefulness of nonmonotonic logics in solving these problems. We then briefly discussed the Yale shooting problem and the solutions proposed to it based on nonmonotonic temporal reasoning.

6 *References*

Allen, J. F., 1984. Towards a general theory of action and time. *Artificial Intelligence* **23**(2):123–154.

Chellas, B. F., 1980. *Modal Logic*. London: Cambridge University Press.

Etherington, D. W., 1983. *Formalizing Nonmonotonic Reasoning Systems*, p. 83. Computer Science Department, University of British Columbia.

Fikes, R. and N. J. Nilsson, 1971. STRIPS: A new approach to application of theorem proving to problem solving. *Artificial Intelligence* **2**:189–208.

Fischer, M. J. and Ladner, R. E., 1979. Propositional dynamic logic of regular programs. *Journal of the Computer Science Society* **2**(18):194–211.

Halpern, J. Y. and Moses, Y., 1985. A guide to the modal logics of knowledge and belief: Preliminary draft. In *Proceedings of the Ninth International Joint Conference on Artificial Intelligence*, Los Angeles, California, pp. 480–490. San Mateo: Morgan Kaufmann.

Halpern, J.Y. and Shoham, Y., 1986. A propositional modal logic of time intervals. In *Proceedings of the Symposium on Logic in Computer Science*, Boston, Mass. New York: IEEE.

Hanks, S. and McDermott, Drew V., 1987. Nonmonotonic logics and temporal projection. *Artificial Intelligence* **33**:379–412.

Haugh, B., 1987. Simple causal minimizations for temporal persistence and projection. In *Proceedings of the Sixth National Conference on Artificial Intelligence*, Seattle, Washington, pp. 218–223. San Mateo: Morgan Kaufmann.

Kautz, H.A., 1986. The logic of persistence. In *Proceedings of the Fifth National Conference on Artificial Intelligence*, Philadelphia, Pennsylvania, pp. 401–405. San Mateo: Morgan Kaufmann.

Lifschitz, V., 1987. Formal theories of action. In *The Frame Problem in Artificial Intelligence: Proceedings of the 1987 Workshop*, Frank L. Brown, ed. San Mateo: Morgan Kaufmann.

Levesque, H.J., 1984. A logic of implicit and explicit belief. In *Proceedings of the Fourth National Conference on Artificial Intelligence*, Austin, Texas. San Mateo: Morgan Kaufmann.

Moore, R.C., 1983. Semantical considerations on nonmonotonic logic. In *Proceedings of the Eighth International Joint Conference on Artificial Intelligence*, Karlsruhe, West Germany, pp. 272–279. San Mateo: Morgan Kaufmann.

Ladkin, P., 1986. Primitives and units for time specification. In *Proceedings of the Fifth National Conference on Artificial Intelligence*, Philadelphia, Pennsylvania, pp. 354–359. San Mateo: Morgan Kaufmann.

Ladkin, P., 1986. Time representation: A taxonomy of interval relations. In *Proceedings of the Fifth National Conference on Artificial Intelligence*, Philadelphia, Pennsylvania, pp. 360–366. San Mateo: Morgan Kaufmann.

Hughes, G. E. and Cresswell, M. J., 1969. *Introduction to Modal Logic*. London: Methuen.

Kripke, S. 1963. Semantical considerations on modal logic. *Acta Philosophica Fennica* **16**:83–94

Sacerdoti , E. D., 1984. Planning in hierarchy of abstraction spaces. *Artificial Intelligence* **5**:115–135

Lifschitz, V., 1986. Pointwise circumscription. In *Proceedings of the Fifth National Conference on Artificial Intelligence*, Philadelphia, Pennsylvania. San Mateo: Morgan Kaufmann.

McCarthy, J. M., 1980. Circumscription—A form of non monotonic reasoning. *Artificial Intelligence* **13**:27–39.

McCarthy, J. M. and P. J. Hayes, 1981. Some philosophical problems from the standpoint of artificial intelligence. *Readings in Artificial Intelligence*, pp. 431–450. San Mateo: Morgan Kaufmann.

McDermott, D. V., 1982b. A temporal logic for reasoning about processes and plans. *Cognitive Science* **6**:101–155.

McDermott, D. V., 1982a. 29. Nonmonotonic logic II: Nonmonotonic modal theories. *Journal of the Association for Computing Machinery* **1**:33–57.

McDermott, D. V. and J. Doyle 1980. Nonmonotonic logic I. *Artificial Intelligence* **13**:41–72.

Pnueli, A., 1977. A temporal logic of programs. In *Proceedings 18th FOCS*, pp. 46–57. New York: IEEE.

Pratt, V. R., 1976. Semantical considerations on Floyd-Hoare logic. In *Proceedings 17th FOCS*, pp. 109–121. New York: IEEE.

Pratt, V. R., 1979. Process logic. In *Proceedings 6th POPL*, pp. 93–100. New York: ACM.

Prior, A. N., 1967. *Past, Present and Future*. Oxford: Clarendon Press.

Fikes, R. E., Hart, P., and Nilsson, N. J., 1972. Learning and executing generalized robot plans. *Artificial Intelligence* **3**:235–246

Reiter, R., 1980. A logic for default reasoning. *Artificial Intelligence* **13**:81–132.

Rescher, N. and Urquhart, A., 1971. *Temporal Logic*. New York: Springer-Verlag.

Shoham, Y., 1987a. Temporal logics in AI: Semantical and ontological considerations. *Artificial Intelligence* **33**.

Shoham, Y., 1987b. A semantical approach to nonmonotonic logics. In *Proceedings IEEE Symposium on Logic in Computer Science*, Ithaca, New York. New York: IEEE.

Shoham, Y., 1987c. *Reasoning about Change*. Cambridge, Mass.: MIT Press.

Shoham, Y. and D. McDermott, 1988. Problems in temporal reasoning. *Artificial Intelligence*. To appear.

van Benthem, J. F. A. K., 1983. *The Logic of Time*. D. Reidel.

Vilain, M. B., 1982. A system for reasoning about time. In *Proceedings of the Second National Conference on Artificial Intelligence*, Pittsburgh, Pennsylvania, pp. 197–201. San Mateo: Morgan Kaufmann.

12

Nonmonotonic Reasoning

Raymond Reiter[1]
Department of Computer Science
University of Toronto
Ontario, Canada

Ann. Rev. Comput. Sci. 1987. 2 : 147–86
Copyright © 1987 by Annual Reviews Inc. All rights reserved

1 *Introduction*

If Artificial Intelligence (AI) researchers can agree on anything, it is that an intelligent artifact must be capable of reasoning about the world it inhabits. The artifact must possess various forms of knowledge and beliefs about its world, and must use this information to infer further information about that world in order to make decisions, plan and carry out actions, respond to other agents, and so on. The technical problem for AI is to characterize the patterns of reasoning required of such an intelligent artifact, and to realize them computationally. There is a wide range of such reasoning patterns necessary for intelligent behavior. Among these are:

- Probabilistic reasoning (e.g., [Bundy, 1985; Nilsson, 1986]), in which probabilities are associated with different items of information. Reasoning requires, in part, computing appropriate probabilities for inferred information, based upon the probabilities of the information used to support the inference.

- Fuzzy reasoning (e.g., [Zadeh, 1981]), designed to characterize vague concepts like "tall" or "old" and to assign degrees of vagueness to conclusions inferred using such concepts.

---

1 Fellow of the Canadian Institute for Advanced Research.

- Inductive reasoning (e.g., [Michalski, 1983]), which is concerned with determining plausible generalizations from a finite number of observations.

- Deductive reasoning, the concern of mathematical logic, which characterizes, among other things, the axiomatic method in mathematics.

This is far from a complete enumeration of human reasoning patterns. The most recent addition to this list in nonmonotonic reasoning, the study of which appears to be unique to AI. In order to convey an intuitive sense of what this is all about, it is first necessary to consider what has come to be known in AI as the knowledge representation problem.

Because an agent must reason *about* something (its knowledge, beliefs), any consideration of the nature of reasoning requires a concomitant concern with how the agent represents its knowledge and beliefs. The stance adopted by AI research on nonmonotonic reasoning is in agreement with the dominant view in AI on knowledge representation; the "knowledge content" of a reasoning program ought to be represented by data structures interpretable as logical formulas of some kind. As Levesque [1986] puts it:

> For the structures to represent knowledge, it must be possible to interpret them *propositionally*, that is, as expressions in a language with a *truth theory*. We should be able to point to one of them and say what the world would have to be like for it to be true.

The province of nonmonotonic reasoning is the derivation of plausible (but not infallible) conclusions from a knowledge base viewed abstractly as a set of formulas in a suitable logic. Any such conclusion is understood to be tentative; it may have to be retracted after new information has been added to the knowledge base.

In what follows, I assume the reader is logically literate, at least with respect to the fundamental ideas of first-order logic (with a smattering of second-order) and the familiar modal logic of necessity (e.g., $S4$ and $S5$).

2 Motivation

Nonmonotonic reasoning is a particular kind of plausible reasoning. Virtually every example in AI that calls upon such reasoning fits the following pattern:

Normally, A holds.

Several paraphrases of this pattern are commonly accepted:

Typically, A is the case.

Assume A by default.

The remainder of this section is devoted to a number of examples of this pattern as it arises in various settings of special concern to AI. The ubiquity of this pattern is remarkable. Once one learns to look for it, one discovers it virtually everywhere.

2.1 *The Canonical Example*

The standard example in AI of a nonmonotonic reasoning pattern has to do with flying birds. The sentence "Birds fly" is not synonymous with "All birds fly" because there are exceptions. In fact, there are overwhelmingly many exceptions—ostriches, penguins, Peking ducks, tar-coated birds, fledglings, etc., etc.—a seemingly open-ended list. Nevertheless, if told only about a particular bird, say Tweety, without being told anything else about it, we would be justified in assuming that Tweety can fly, *without knowing that it is not one of the exceptional birds*. In other words, we treat Tweety as a *typical* or *normal* bird.

We can represent the sentence "Birds fly" by instances of our patterns of plausible reasoning:

"Normally, birds fly."

"Typically, birds fly."

"If *x* is a bird, then assume by default that *x* flies."

We can now see why these are *plausible* reasoning patterns. We wish to use them to conclude that Tweety can fly, but should we subsequently learn information to the contrary—say, that Tweety is a penguin—we would retract our earlier conclusion and conclude instead that Tweety cannot fly. Thus initially we *jumped to the conclusion* or made the *default assumption* that Tweety can fly. This, of course, is what makes our rule patterns plausible rather than deductive; they sanction assumptions rather than infallible conclusions.

Notice also that there is another possible paraphrase of our reasoning pattern. In the case of Tweety the bird we were prepared to assume that Tweety can fly provided we knew of no information to the contrary, namely that Tweety is a penguin or an ostrich or the Maltese Falcon or... . So one possible reading of our pattern of plausible reasoning is:

In the absence of information to the contrary, assume *A*.

What is problematic here (as it is for notions like "typically" and "normally") is defining precisely what one means by "absence of information to the contrary." A natural reading is something like "nothing is known that is inconsistent with the desired assumption *A*." As we shall see later, this consistency-based version of the pattern motivates several formal theories of nonmonotonic reasoning. We shall also see that other intuitions are possible, leading to formalism that apparently have little to do with consistency.

2.2 *Databases*

In the theory of databases there is an explicit convention about the representation of negative information that appeals to a particular kind of default assumption. To see why negative information poses a problem, consider the simple example of a database for an airline flight schedule representing flight numbers and the city pairs they connect. We certainly would not want to include in this database all flights and the city pairs they do *not* connect, which clearly would be an overwhelming amount of information. For example, Air Canada flight 103 does not connect London with Paris, or Toronto with Montreal, or Moose Jaw with Athens, or. . . . *There is far too much negative information to represent explicitly*, and this will be true for any realistic database.

Instead of explicitly representing such negative information, databases *implicitly* do so by appealing to the so-called *closed world assumption* [Reiter, 1978b], which states that all relevant positive information has been explicitly represented. If a positive fact is not explicitly present in the database, its negation is assumed to hold. For simple databases consisting of atomic facts only, e.g., relational databases, this approach to negative information is straightforward. In the case of deductive databases, however, the closed world assumption (CWA) is not so easy to formulate. It is no longer sufficient that a fact not be explicitly present in order to conjecture its negation; the fact may be *derivable*. So in general we need a closed world rule that, for the flight schedule example, looks something like:

If f is a flight and c_1, c_2 are cities, then in the absence of information to the contrary, assume $\neg$ CONNECT(f, c_1, c_2).

Here, by "absence of information to the contrary" we mean that

CONNECT(f, c_1, c_2)

is not derivable using the database as premises. As we shall see below, there are formal difficulties with this version of the CWA; but on an intuitive level the CWA conforms to the pattern of plausible reasoning we are considering in this section. When we consider various proposed formalization for nonmonotonic reasoning, below, we shall return to the question of the CWA since it plays a dominant role in many approaches.

2.3 *Diagnosis from First Principles*

There are two basic approaches in the AI literature to diagnostic reasoning. Under the first approach, which might be called the experiential approach, heuristic information plays a dominant role. The corresponding systems attempt to codify the rules of thumb, statistical intuitions, and past experience of human diagnosticians considered experts in some particular task domain. In particular, the structure or design of the object being diagnosed is only weakly represented, if at all. Successful diagnoses stem primarily from the codified experience of the human expert being modeled rather than from detailed information about the object being diagnosed. This is the basis of so-called rule-based approaches to diagnosis, of which the MYCIN system [Buchanan and Shortliffe, 1984] is a notable example.

Under the second approach, often called *diagnosis from first principles*, or *diagnosis from structure and behavior*, the only information at hand is a description of some system, say a physical device or setting of interest, together with an observation of that system's behavior. If this observation conflicts with intended system behavior, then the diagnostic problem is to determine which components could by malfunctioning account for the discrepancy between observed and correct system behavior. Since components can fail in various and often unpredictable ways, their normal or default behaviors should be described. These descriptions fit the pattern of plausible reasoning we have been considering. For example, an AND-gate in a digital circuit would have the description:

> Normally, an AND-gate's output is the Boolean *and* function of its inputs.

In a medical diagnostic setting, we might want the description:

> Normally, an adult human's heart rate is between 70 and 90 beats per minute.

In diagnosis, such component descriptions are used in the following way: We first assume that all of the system components are behaving normally. Suppose, however, the system behavior *predicted* by this assumption conflicts with (i.e., is inconsistent with) the *observed* system behavior. Thus some of the components we assume to be behaving normally must really be malfunctioning. By retracting enough of the original assumptions about correctly behaving components, we can remove the inconsistency between the predicted and observed behavior. The retracted components yield a diagnosis. This approach to diagnosis from first principles forms the basis for several diagnosis reasoning systems [de Kleer and Williams, 1986; Genesereth, 1985; Reiter, 1987]. Poole [1986] took a somewhat different but closely related approach.

2.4 *Prototypes, Natural Kinds, and Frames*

Nonmonotonic reasoning is intimately connected to the notion of prototypes in psychology [Rosch, 1978] and natural kinds in philosophy [Putnam, 1970]. To see the connection, observe that both these notions concern concepts that cannot be defined via necessary and sufficient conditions. We cannot, for example, define the natural kind "bird" by writing something like

$$(\forall x)\ BIRD(x) \equiv BIPED(x)\ \&\ FEATHERED(x)\ \&\ldots$$

because we can always imagine a bird that lacks one or more of the defining properties, say a one-legged bird. The best we seem capable of doing is to describe one or more "typical" members of the concept, and to define the concept as the set of individuals that do not deviate too far from the typical member(s). This notion of a "typical" member of such a concept provides the link with nonmonotonic reasoning. The rest of this section elaborates on this link.

The concepts that concern us are those lacking necessary and sufficient defining conditions. Recall that N is said to be a *necessary condition* for a predicate P if the following formula holds:

$$(\forall x)P(x) \supset N(x).$$

S is said to be a *sufficient condition* for P if the following holds:

$$(\forall x)S(x) \supset P(x).$$

Finally, P possesses a *classical definition* if there are formulas $D_1, \ldots, D_n$ that are both necessary and sufficient for P—i.e., if the following holds:

$$(\forall x)P(x) \equiv D_1(x)\ \&\ldots\ \&\ D_n(x).$$

As we have seen, commonsense concepts like "bird," "chair," "game," and so on, are not like mathematical concepts; they lack classical definitions based on necessary and sufficient conditions. Nevertheless, by appealing to conventional logic together with our pattern of plausible reasoning, we can define notions that correspond to normal necessary and sufficient conditions. For example, we have the following "necessary conditions" for the concept "bird":

If $BIRD(x)$ then $VERTEBRATE(x)$.
If $BIRD(x)$ then normally $FLY(x)$.
If $BIRD(x)$ then assume by default $BIPED(x)$.
If $BIRD(x)$ then typically $FEATHERED(x)$.
If $BIRD(x)$ then typically $HAS\text{-}AS\text{-}PART(x, beak(x))$.
and so on.   (1)

It is natural to define a *prototypical bird* as one that enjoys all of the consequences, including the default assumptions, of the above "necessary conditions": It is a beaked, bipedal, feathered vertebrate that flies, and so on.

The bird concept also possesses "sufficient conditions," some of which are logical implications while other fit our pattern for default reasoning:

> If SPARROW(x) then BIRD(x).
> If FLY(x) & CHIRP(x) then assume by default that BIRD(x).
> IF FLY(x) & FEATHERED(x) then assume by default that BIRD(x)
> and so on. $\qquad\qquad$ (2)

It is natural, then, to take the concept of a bird to be defined by the above "necessary and sufficient conditions."

Now the obvious problem for AI knowledge representation is this: How do we characterize, represent, and compute with prototypes, or concepts like natural kinds, where defaults assumptions play such a prominent role? In his very influential "frames paper," Minsky [1975] proposed the notion of a frame, a complex data structure meant to represent certain stereotyped information. While Minsky's description of a frame is informal and often impressionistic, central to his notion are the issues we have just considered: prototypes, default assumptions, and the unsuitability of classical definitions for commonsense concepts like natural kinds. A few quotations from Minsky ([1975], p. 212) serve to illustrate this point.

> Here is the essence of the theory: When one encounters a new situation (or makes a substantial change in one's view of the present problem) one selects from memory a substantial structure called a frame. This is a remembered framework to be adapted to fit reality but changing details as necessary. . . .
>
> A *frame* is a data-structure for representing a stereotyped situation, like being in a certain kind of living room, or going to a child's birthday party. . . .
>
> We can think of a frame as a network of nodes and relations. The "top levels" of a frame are fixed, and represent things that are always true about the supposed situation. The lower levels have many *terminals*— "slots" that must be filled by specific instances or data. . . .
>
> Much of the phenomenological power of the theory hinges on the inclusion of expectation and other kinds of presumptions. A frame's terminals are normally already filled with "default" assignments. Thus, a frame may contain a great many details whose supposition is not specifically warranted by the situation.

Frames, therefore, are representations of stereotyped information. As Hayes [1979] points out, formally a frame has a logical status consisting of a collection of "necessary and sufficient" conditions on the concept defined by the frame. (Here, the quotation marks remind us that these conditions may be default assumptions.) Thus, a frame for the concept of a bird might contain bundle 1 above, of "necessary conditions" and bundle 2, of "sufficient conditions." What Minsky called the "top levels" of a frame, which represent things always true of the frame, are logical implications like the first formula of the bundle 1 or 2. The lower-level terminals or slots are predicated representing the default assumptions normally made of an instance of the frame. Thus FLY(.) and HAS-AS-PART(.,.) are slots of our BIRD(.) frame. The arguments of these slot predicates are the "fillers" in Minsky's description, so that if Tweety is an instance of the bird frame, i.e., BIRD(Tweety) holds, then the frame instance's terminals FLY(.), HAS-AS-PART(.,.), and so on, will be filled by Tweety, so that the default assignments FLY(Tweety), and HAS-AS-PART(Tweety, beak(Tweety)) will be assumed.

We can now see that the "necessary and sufficient" conditions defining a frame play different roles. "Necessary conditions" are used for frame institution. Given an instance, say BIRD(Tweety), of the BIRD(.) frame, we can infer some of Tweety's other properties, many of them default values. These are the expectations or presumptions referred to by Minsky, the "details whose supposition is not specifically warranted by the situation." Because some of these default assumptions may be specifically contradicted in certain cases, e.g., in the case of a bird that doesn't fly, not all the frame's terminals will be assumed. This corresponds to Minsky's assertion that "the default assumption are attached loosely to their terminals, so that they can be easily displaced by new items that better fit the current situation." "Sufficient conditions" are used for frame *selection* or *recognition*. Here recognition means determination of what kind of thing one might have in hand based upon knowledge of some of its properties. Of what frame might this thing be an instance? For example, the BIRD frame has as one of its sufficient conditions:

If CHIRP(x) and FLY(x) then assume by default BIRD(x).

If we have in hand something that we know chirps and flies, then we might select and initiate the bird frame. This frame-selection or concept-recognition process is determined by some of the concept's sufficient conditions. These are normally taken to be *criterial*; chirping and flying are taken here to be criterial properties for BIRDness. The understanding that such properties do not guarantee the concept—it might be a flying cricket for example—is reflected in the default character of the sufficient condition.

3 *The Need for a Formal Theory*

Having isolated a common pattern of reasoning, namely "Typically *A* holds," or "Assume *A* by default," we are still left with the problem of defining what this means. In addition, we shall need a theory of so-called *truth maintenance*. While an exploration of truth-maintenance systems is beyond the scope of this paper, it is important to note their intimate connection with the kinds of plausible reasoning considered thus far. Because our reasoning pattern sanctions default assumptions, some of these assumptions may have to be retracted in the light of new information. But these retracted assumptions might themselves have supported other conclusion, which therefore also ought to be retracted, and so on. It is the job of truth-maintenance system, in the style of Doyle's [1979], to manage this retraction process. One reason that truth-maintenance systems are as complex as they are is that default conclusions are normally based on two things: *(a) the presence*, either explicit or inferred, of certain information (e.g., the presence of the fact that Tweety is a bird), and *(b)* the *absence* of certain information, either explicit or inferred (e.g., the absence of ¬ FLY(Tweety)). A truth-maintenance system must maintain a dependency record with each inferred fact indicating its justification in terms of both the presence and absence of information. This will obviously complicate both the system's bookkeeping and its process of belief revision whenever the knowledge base is modified.

One reason a formal account is required for default-reasoning is that the inferences they sanction can be complicated [Reiter and Criscuolo, 1983]. For example, two default assumptions can conflict, as the following example shows:

> The typical Quaker is a pacifist.
>
> The typical Republican is not a pacifist.

Suppose Dick is both a Quaker and a Republican. Then he inherits contradictory default assumptions, so that intuitively neither should be ascribed to him.

A second example illustrates that typically is not necessarily transitive, in the sense that "Typical *A*s are *C*s" need not follow from both "Typical *A*s are *B*s" and "Typical *B*s are *C*s." For if typicality were transitive, then from

> "Typical high-school dropouts are adults"

and

> "Typical adults are employed"

we could conclude the intuitively incorrect

"Typical high-school dropouts are employed."

As a final example of the complexities of reasoning about typicality, consider inheritance hierarchies, which form the backbone of almost all semantic networks and knowledge-representation languages. The classes in any such hierarchy are organized into a taxonomy via ISA links. These classes normally also have attributes. Now, suppose one wants to find out whether an individual in class *C* has attribute *A*. To do this, simply search from the node *C* up the hierarchy via ISA links to find if there is a higher node with attribute *A*. If so, then the individual inherits this attribute. Unfortunately, this simple graphical processing fails when exceptions to attributes are allowed in the hierarchy. In a nice example of this, provided by Fahlman et al., [1981], we have an exception to an exception to an exception:

A mollusc typically is a shell-bearer.

A cephalopod ISA mollusc except it typically is not a shell-bearer.

A nautilus ISA cephalopod except it typically is a shell-bearer.

A naked nautilus ISA nautilus except it typically is not a shell-bearer.

Here, the class mollusc has a default attribute shell-bearer. The class cephalopod has a default attribute non-shell-bearer, and so on. Now, suppose all we know of Fred is that he is a nautilus. Fred gets the default attribute shell-bearer by virtue of being a nautilus. But Fred is also a cephalopod via an ISA link, so at the same time he gets to be a non-shell-bearer by default. To deal with this kind of problem, most implementations adopt a shortest-path heuristic. A concept inherits the attribute nearest it in the hierarchy. Unfortunately, this can be shown to fail [Reiter and Criscuolo, 1983], so other criteria are necessary. Any formal theory of default reasoning must allow us to sort out inheritance problems like this.

4 *Classical Logic Is Inadequate*

There are two arguments against classical logic for formalizing the reasoning patters we have been considering. The first simply notes that even if we could enumerate all exceptions to flight with an axiom of the form

$$(\forall x)\ \mathrm{BIRD}(x)\ \&\ \neg\ \mathrm{EMU}(x)\ \&\ \neg\ \mathrm{DEAD}(x)\ \&\dots \supset \mathrm{FLY}(x)$$

we still could not derive FLY(Tweety) from BIRD(Tweety) alone. This is so since we are not given that Tweety is not an emu, or dead, and so on. The antecedent of the implication cannot be derived, in which case there is no way of deriving the consequent of the implication.

The second argument against classical logic is the so-called *monotonicity argument*. Classical logics share a common property of being monotonic. This means that whenever T is a set of sentences in such a logic and w is a sentence, then $T \models w$ implies $T \cup N \models w$ for any set N of sentences. In other words, new information N preserves old conclusions w.

Now suppose default reasoning could be represented in some classical logic, and T are axioms entailing that Tweety flies—i.e., $T \models$ FLY(Tweety). If later we learn that Tweety is an ostrich, we want the enlarged axiom set not to entail that Tweety flies, i.e., we want

$$T \cup \{OSTRICH(Tweety)\} \not\models FLY(Tweety).$$

But this is impossible in a classical logic. So whatever the logical mechanism that formalizes default reasoning, it must be *nonmonotonic*; its conclusions must be retractable or *defeasible*.

5 *Procedural Nonmonotonicity in AI*

AI researchers have routinely been implementing nonmonotonic reasoning systems for some time, usually without consciously focussing on the underlying reasoning patterns on which their programs rely. Typically these patterns are implemented using the so-called negation-as-failure mechanism, which occurs as an explicit operator in AI programming languages like PROLOG, or in rule-based systems. In PROLOG, for example, the goal *not G* succeeds iff *G* finitely fails. Since failing on *G* amounts to failing to find a proof of *G* using the PROLOG program as axioms, the *not* operator implements finite nonprovability. From this observation we can see that PROLOG's negation is a nonmonotonic operator. If *G* is nonprovable from some axioms, it needn't remain nonprovable from an enlarged axiom set.

Procedural negation is almost always identified with real—i.e., *logical*—negation. The way procedural negation is actually used in AI programs amounts to invoking the rule of inference "From failure of *G*, infer ¬ *G*." This is really the closed world assumption, which we encountered earlier in the context of representing negative information in databases. Partly because is a nonmonotonic operator, procedural negation can often be used to implement other forms of default reasoning. The following example, a PROLOG program for reasoning about flying birds, illustrates this.

```
fly (X) ← bird (X) & not ab(X).

bird (X) ← emu (X).

bird (X) ← canary (X).

ab (X) ← emu (X).

emu (fred).

canary (tweety).

Goal: not fly (fred) succeeds.

Goal: fly (tweety) succeeds.
```

Notice that the first rule uses a predicate *ab*, standing for abnormal. So this rule says that *X* flies if *X* is not an abnormal bird, in other words if *X* is a normal bird. The fourth rule describes a circumstances under which something is abnormal, namely when it is an emu. This device of the *ab* predicate for representing defaults is due to McCarthy, who introduced it in conjunction with his circumscription formalism for nonmonotonic reasoning. We shall see it again in Section 6.3.1, where circumscription is described. Continuing with the current example, we see that by identifying procedural negation with real negation we can derive that the emu *fred* doesn't fly, while the bird *tweety* does.

For a nontrivial, formally precise application of procedural negation for reasoning about time and events see Kowalski and Sergot [1986].

6 *Some Formalizations of Nonmonotonic Reasoning*

The need for nonmonotonic reasoning in AI had been recognized long before formal theories were proposed. In support of his argument against logic in AI, Minsky invoked the nonmonotonic nature of commonsense reasoning in one version of his 1975 "frames" paper (reprinted in [Haugland, 1981]). Partial formalization for such reasoning were proposed by McCarthy and Hayes [1969], Sandewall [1972], and Hayes [1973]. Several knowledge-representation languages, most notably KRL [Bobrow and Winograd, 1977], specifically provided for default reasoning. Hayes [1979] emphasized the central role of defaults in Minsky's notion of a frame and in KRL in particular. Reiter [1978a] described various settings in AI where default reasoning is prominent.

The rest of this section is devoted to a critical examination of several formalization of nonmonotonic inferences.

6.1 *The Closed World Assumption*

As we remarked earlier, the closed world assumption (CWA) arises most prominently in the theory of databases, where it is assumed that all of the relevant positive information has been specified. Any positive fact not so specified is assumed false. In the case of deductive databases it is natural to understand that a positive fact has been specified if it is entailed by the database, and that any fact not so entailed is taken to be false. This is the intuition behind Reiter's [1978b] formalization of the CWA. Let **DB** be a first-order database (i.e., any first-order theory). Reiter defines the closure of **DB** by

CLOSURE(DB) = **DB** $\cup$ {$\neg P(\mathbf{t})$ | **DB** $\not\models P(\mathbf{t})$ where P is an n-ary predicate symbol of **DB** and **t** is an n-tuple of ground terms formed using the function symbols of **DB**}.[2]

In other words, the implicit negative information of a database sanctioned by the CWA are those negative ground literals whose (positive) ground atoms are not entailed by the database. Under the CWA, queries are evaluated with respect to **CLOSURE(DB)**, rather than **DB** itself.

There are several problems with this view of the CWA. The most obvious is that the database closure might be inconsistent, as would be the case for

DB = {$P \vee Q$}.

[In the case of Horn databases, Reiter [1978b] shows that closure preserves the consistency of **DB**.] Even for nondeductive relational databases consisting only of ground atoms, Reiter's notion yields incorrect results in the presence of so-called null values. A null value is a constant symbol meant to denote an existing individual whose identity is unknown. For example, if SUPPLIES(s, p) denotes that supplier s supplies part p, then the following is a simple database **DB**, where ω is meant to denote a null value:

SUPPLIES(Acme, p_1) **SUPPLIES**(Sears, p_2) **SUPPLIES**(ω, p_1)

So we know that some supplier, possibly the same as Acme or Sears, possibly not, supplies p_1. Since **DB** $\not\models$ SUPPLIES(ω, p_2), Reiter's CWA sanctions $\neg$ SUPPLIES(ω, p_2) which, coupled with SUPPLIES(Sears, p_2) entail $\omega \neq$ Sears. But this violates the intended interpretation of the null value as a totally unknown supplier; we have inferred *something* about ω, namely that it is not Sears.

---

2 In this paper [Reiter, 1978b] the database is taken to be function-free, so that **t** is an n-tuple of constant symbols; but this restriction is unnecessary in general.

A different formalization of the CWA was proposed by Clark [1978] in connection with his attempt to provide a formal semantics for negation in PRO-LOG. Clark begins with the observation that PROLOG clauses, being of the form $\alpha \supset P(\mathbf{t})$, provide sufficient but not necessary conditions on the predicate P. Such clauses are said to be *about P*. Clark's intuition is that the CWA is the assumption that these sufficient conditions are also necessary. In other words, the implicit information in a PROLOG database sanctioned by the CWA consists of the necessary conditions on all of the predicated of the database. Clark provides a simple effective procedure for transforming a set of clauses defining sufficient conditions on a predicate P into a single formula representing its necessary conditions. We illustrate this procedure with the following example:

$$P(a, b) \tag{3}$$

$$P(a, c) \tag{4}$$

$$(\forall u, v, w) \neg Q(u, v) \& R(v, w) \supset P(g(u), w) \tag{5}$$

$$(\forall u)Q(u, f(u)) \tag{6}$$

Clauses 3–5 are the only ones in the database about *P*. These are logically equivalent, respectively, to

$$(\forall x, y)x = a \& y = b \supset P(x, y)$$

$$(\forall x, y)x = a \& y = c \supset P(x, y)$$

$$(\forall x, y)((\exists u, v, w)x = g(u) \& y = w \& \neg Q(u, v) \& R(v, w)$$
$$\& P(u, w)) \supset P(x, y),$$

and these three clauses are in turn logically equivalent to

$$(\forall x, y)[(x = a \& y = b) \vee (x = a \& y = c) \vee ((\exists u, v, w)x = g(u) \&$$
$$y = w \& \neg Q(u, v) \& R(v, w) \& P(u, w))] \supset P(x, y). \tag{7}$$

This is a single formula representing all the sufficient conditions on *P* given by the original database. Similarly, clause 6 is logically equivalent to

$$(\forall x, y)((\exists u)x = u \& y = f(u)) \supset Q(x, y), \tag{8}$$

and this represents *Q*'s sufficient conditions. Finally, we must determine *R*'s sufficient conditions. No clause of the database is about *R*, so we take *R*'s sufficient conditions to be

$$(\forall x, y) \text{ false} \supset R(x, y). \tag{9}$$

Formulas 7, 8 and 9 are logically equivalent to the original database and represent that database's sufficient conditions on, respectively, the predicates P, Q, and R. To determine the implicit information about the predicates P, Q, and R sanctioned by Clark's CWA, assume that these sufficient conditions are also necessary—i.e., simply reverse the implications of formulas 7, 8, and 9. The resulting completed database represents the closure of the original database according to Clark. For the example at hand, the completed database is:

$$(\forall x, y)\mathrm{P}(x, y) \equiv [(x = a \ \& \ y = b) \vee (x = a \ \& \ y = c) \vee ((\exists u, v, w)x = g(u)$$
$$\& \ y = w \ \& \ \neg \ Q(u, v) \ \& \ R(v, w) \ \& \ P(u, w))]$$

$$(\forall x, y)Q(x, y) \equiv (\exists u)x = u \ \& \ y = f(u)$$

$$(\forall x, y)R(x, y) \equiv \text{false}.$$

On Clark's view of the CWA, queries are evaluated with respect to the completed databases, rather than the original database.

As intuitively appealing as Clark's notion is, it suffers from a number of problems. To begin, it lacks generality. It is defined only for PROLOG-like databases and hence is restricted to universally quantified formulas. Moreover, each clause must be about some predicate, so for example $\neg P$, which cannot be construed as being about P, cannot be accommodated. The approach is also sensitive to the syntactic form of the database clauses. Thus $\neg P \supset Q$ is about Q, while its logically equivalent form $\neg Q \supset P$ is about P. In particular, as Shepherdson [1984] observes, the completed database corresponding to

$$\neg P \supset P \text{ is } P \equiv \neg P,$$

which is inconsistent.

6.2 Consistency-based Approaches

Some of the early attempts at formalizing nonmonotonic reasoning ground this notion in logical consistency. They interpret the pattern "In the absence of information to the contrary, assume A" as something like "If A can be consistently assumed, then assume it."

6.2.1 Nonmonotonic Logic   McDermott and Doyle's *nonmonotonic logic* [1980] appeals to a modal operator M in conjunction with the language of first-order logic. MA is intended to mean "A is consistent," so the flying birds example translates in their logic to

$$(\forall x) \ \mathrm{BIRD}(x) \ \& \ M \ \mathrm{FLY}(x) \supset \mathrm{FLY}(x).$$

The technical problem is to make precise this notion of consistency, since we want consistency with respect to the entire knowledge base. But this means that a formula involving the M operator is in part referring to itself since as a formula it is part of the very knowledge base with respect to which it is claiming consistency. McDermott and Doyle capture this self-referential property by a fixed-point construction, and they define the theorems of a nonmonotonic knowledge base to be the intersection of all its fixed points. Specifically, if A is a nonmonotonic theory, then T is a *fixed point* of A if

$$T = Th(A \cup \{Mw \mid \neg w \notin T\}).^3$$

The intuition behind this definition is to capture the notion that if $\neg w$ is not derivable, then Mw (whose intended meaning is "w is consistent") is.

As a simple example, consider the nonmonotonic theory $A = \{E \ \& \ MC \supset \neg D, F \ \& \ MD \supset \neg C, E, E \supset F\}$. The first formula says that if E is the case and if C is consistent then conclude $\neg D$, so we do conclude $\neg D$. Now $\neg D$ prevents D being consistent in the second formula, so this blocks concluding $\neg C$ using the second formula. Thus one fixed point is obtained by adding $\neg D$ to A. Similarly, adding $\neg C$ to A gives a second fixed point. Thus, A has two fixed points:

> $Th(A \cup \{\neg D\})$
> $Th(A \cup \{\neg C\}).$

The theorems of A are therefore the intersection of these two fixed points.

This formalism turns out to have several problems. Because of the consistency requirement, neither the fixed points nor the theorems are recursively enumerable. A proof theory is known only for the propositional case. There are also serious difficulties with the semantics, the M operator fails to adequately capture the intuitive concept of consistency. For example, the nonmonotonic theory $\{MC, \neg C\}$ is consistent.

In response to this latter difficulty, McDermott [1982a] attempted to develop several stronger versions of the logic based on the entailment relation of various standard modal logics (T, $S4$, and $S5$) instead of, as in the 1980 version, first-order logic. Unfortunately, these attempts turned out either to be too weak to adequately characterize the M operator (in the case of T and $S4$), or to "collapse" the logic to (monotonic) $S5$ when $S5$'s entailment relation was used.

6.2.2 Default Logic   The other most prominent consistency-based approach to nonmonotonic reasoning is Reiter's [1980] default logic. It differs from the

---

3 Here *Th* denotes closure under first-order logical consequence.

nonmonotonic logic of McDermott and Doyle in that default statements are formally treated as rules of inference, not as formulas in a theory. The flying birds default is represented by the rule of inference (actually a rule schema because of the variable x)

$$\frac{\text{BIRD}(x) : \text{FLY}(x)}{\text{FLY}(x)}$$

This may be read as

> If x is bird and it can be consistently assumed to fly, then you can infer that x flies.

More generally, rule schemas of the following form are permitted:

$$\frac{\alpha(\mathbf{x}) : \beta(\mathbf{x})}{\gamma(\mathbf{x})}$$

which can be read as:

> If $\alpha(\mathbf{x})$ holds and $\beta(\mathbf{x})$ can be consistently assumed, then you can infer $\gamma(\mathbf{x})$.

The approach is to begin with a set of first-order sentences. These are things known to be true of the world. This knowledge is normally incomplete; we are not omniscient, so there are gaps in our world knowledge. Default rules act as mappings from this incomplete theory to a more complete *extension* of the theory. They partly fill in the gaps with plausible conclusions. So if such an incomplete first-order theory contains BIRD(Tweety), and if FLY(Tweety) is consistent with the theory, then by the above default schema for flying birds we can extend this theory by adding FLY(Tweety) to it.

As in McDermott and Doyle's approach, the extensions are defined by a fixed-point construction. For simplicity, we consider only *closed* default rules, namely rules of the form $\alpha : \beta/\gamma$ for first-order sentences α, β, and γ. A *default theory* is a pair (D, W) where D is a set of closed default rules and W a set of first-order sentences. For any set of first-order sentences S, define $\Gamma(S)$ to be the smallest set satisfying the following three properties:

1. $W \subset \Gamma(S)$.

2. $\Gamma(S)$ is closed under first-order logical consequence.

3. If $\alpha : \beta/\gamma$ is a default rule of D and $\alpha \in \Gamma(S)$ and $\neg \beta \notin S$, then $\gamma \in \Gamma(S)$.

Then E is defined to be an *extension* of the default theory (D, W) iff $\Gamma(E) = E$, i.e., iff E is a fixed point of the operator Γ.

The following example corresponds closely to that used to illustrate McDermott and Doyle's logic.

$$W = \{E, E \supset F\}$$

Defaults: $\dfrac{E : C}{\neg D}$ $\dfrac{F : D}{\neg C}$

Here E and $E \supset F$ are the two things we know about a world W. The first default can be invoked since C is consistent with W, so we infer $\neg D$. $\neg D$ prevents the second default from applying, so no further inferences are possible. This yields an extension $Th(W \cup \{\neg D\})$. A second (and only other) extension $Th(W \cup \{\neg C\})$ is obtained similarly.

As we have just seen, multiple extensions are possible. The perspective adopted on these [Reiter, 1980] is that any such extension is a possible belief set for an agent, although one could, as do McDermott and Doyle, insist that an agent's beliefs are defined by the intersection of all extensions.

One advantage of default logic is that there is a "proof theory" in the case that all default rules are *normal*, namely, of the form

$$\frac{\alpha(\mathbf{x}) : \beta(\mathbf{x})}{\beta(\mathbf{x})}$$

for arbitrary first-order formulas α and β with free variables $\mathbf{x}$. This turns out to be an extremely common default pattern; all of the examples of Section 2 conform to it. The sense in which normal defaults have a "proof theory" is the following: Given a set of first-order sentences W, a set of normal defaults D, and a first-order sentence β, then β is in some extension of W wrt the defaults D iff the "proof theory" sanctions this. The quotation marks indicate that in general the consistency condition prevents the default rules from being effectively computable. So one problem with default logic is that its extensions are not recursively enumerable. Another is that as yet there is no consensus on its semantics (see [Etherington, 1987; Sandewall, 1985; Shoham, 1986]). Moreover, because the defaults are represented as inference rules rather than object language formulas as in McDermott and Doyle [1980], defaults cannot be reasoned about within the logic. For example, from "Normally canaries are yellow" and "Yellow things are never green" we cannot conclude "Normally canaries are never green." Notice that whether McDermott and Doyle's non-monotonic logic can support such reasoning is debatable. From

$$(\forall x) \text{ CANARY}(x) \And M \text{ YELLOW}(x) \supset \text{YELLOW}(x)$$
$$(\forall x) \text{ YELLOW}(x) \supset \neg \text{ GREEN}(x)$$

we can indeed infer

$(\forall x)$ CANARY(x) & M YELLOW$(x) \supset \neg$ GREEN(x).

However, it is unclear whether this last formula can legitimately be interpreted to mean "Normally canaries are not green."

Despite these shortcomings of default logic, analyses using the logic have been applied to several settings in AI: inheritance hierarchies with exceptions, as described in Section 3 [Etherington and Reiter, 1982], diagnostic reasoning [Poole, 1986; Reiter, 1987], and the theory of speech acts [Perrault, 1987].

Etherington [1986] provides a number of properties of default logic, together with various results on its relationship to other nonmonotonic formalisms. Lukaszewicz [1984] proposes a modification of default logic with several desirable properties.

6.3 *Approaches Based upon Minimal Models*

A promising way of achieving nonmonotonicity is to treat as theorems those sentences true in all suitably distinguished models of a logical theory. Provided that enlarging the theory can lead to new distinguished models, then what was once a theorem may no longer remain so; it may be falsified by one of the new models. Approaches that adopt this perspective on nonmonotonicity require that these preferred models respect some minimality property.

6.3.1 *Circumscription* McCarthy [1980, 1986] has proposed basing nonmonotonic reasoning on the notion of truth in all minimal models of a first-order theory. ! 4 Since his 1986 approach generalizes that of his 1980 paper, we shall focus on his more recent theory. The notion of minimality to which McCarthy appeals is as follows [Lifschitz, 1985b]:

Assume L is a first-order language. Suppose **P** and **Z** are tuples of distinct predicate symbols of L. For any two structures Σ_1 and Σ_2 for L, define

$\Sigma_1 \leq^{P;Z} \Sigma_2$ if

i.   domain(Σ_1) = domain(Σ_2);

ii. Σ_1 and Σ_2 interpret all function symbols and predicate symbols other than those of **P** and **Z** identically; and

iii. for each predicate symbol P of **P**, P's extension in Σ_1 is a subset (not necessarily proper) of its extension in Σ_2.

---

4 McCarthy [1986] actually treats second-order theories. For simplicity of exposition, we shall restrict ourselves to first-order theories. The more general case is elaborated by Lifschitz [1985b, 1986a].

Notice that the relation $\leq^{P;Z}$ places no restrictions on how Σ_1 and Σ_2 interpret the predicates of $\mathbf{Z}$.

Suppose now that $A(\mathbf{P}; \mathbf{Z})$ is a sentence of L that mentions the predicate symbols of $\mathbf{P}$ and $\mathbf{Z}$. $A(\mathbf{P}; \mathbf{Z})$ may mention predicate symbols other than those of $\mathbf{P}$ and $\mathbf{Z}$. In McCarthy's circumscription theory, the distinguished models of interest are those models of $A(\mathbf{P}; \mathbf{Z})$ that are minimal wrt $\leq^{P;Z}$. The sentences true in all such minimal models are taken to be the nonmonotonic entailments of $A(\mathbf{P}; \mathbf{Z})$ of interest.

The above focus on minimal models and their entailments is not the approach emphasized by McCarthy [1986]. McCarthy actually focussed on a syntactic approach, as follows:[5]

The circumscription of $\mathbf{P}$ *in* $A(\mathbf{P}; \mathbf{Z})$ *with variable* $\mathbf{Z}$ is defined to be the (second-order) sentence

$$A(\mathbf{P}; \mathbf{Z}) \ \& \ [\forall \mathbf{P}', \mathbf{Z}'] \neg [A(\mathbf{P}'; \mathbf{Z}') \ \& \ \mathbf{P}' \ \mathbf{P}]. \tag{10}$$

Here, for predicates Q and R of the same arity, $Q < R$ is defined to be

$$(\forall \mathbf{x})(Q(\mathbf{x}) \supset R(\mathbf{x})) \ \& \ \neg (\forall \mathbf{x})(R(\mathbf{x}) \supset Q(\mathbf{x})).$$

If we define $Q \leq R$ to be the formula $(\forall \mathbf{x})Q(\mathbf{x}) \supset R(\mathbf{x})$, then $Q < R$ is logically equivalent to the formula $Q \leq R \ \& \ \neg (R \leq Q)$. When $(Q_1, \ldots, Q_n)$ and $(R_1, \ldots, R_n)$ are tuples of predicate symbols with correspondingly equal arities, $(Q_1, \ldots, Q_n) (R_1, \ldots, R_n)$ is defined to be the formula

$$Q_1 \leq R_1 \ \& \ldots \& \ Q_n \leq R_n \ \& \ \neg [R_1 \ Q_1 \ \& \ldots \& \ R_n \leq Q_n].$$

The second conjunct in sentence 10 is called the *circumscription axiom of* $A(\mathbf{P};$ $\mathbf{Z})$. It says that the extensions in $A(\mathbf{P}; \mathbf{Z})$ of the predicates P cannot be made smaller, even when the $\mathbf{Z}$ predicates are allowed to vary; or more succinctly, $\mathbf{P}$ is minimal in A with $\mathbf{Z}$ varying. Sentence 10 thus expresses the original sentence A further constrained by the requirement that $\mathbf{P}$ be minimized with $\mathbf{Z}$ variable.

In McCarthy's formulation, the nonmonotonic consequences of $A(\mathbf{P}; \mathbf{Z})$ of interest are those sentences entailed by 10. Because of what the circumscription axiom actually says, it is not surprising that the semantic and syntactic accounts of circumscription coincide. In other words as proved independently by Lifschitz [1985b] and Etherington [1986], the sentences true in all models of $A(\mathbf{P}; \mathbf{Z})$ minimal wrt $\leq^{P;Z}$ are precisely the sentences entailed by 10.

---

5 We adopt here the equivalent formulation of Lifschitz [1985b].

The circumscription axiom has the character of a second-order induction axiom in mathematics. In fact, McCarthy [1980] shows that, when sentence A defines a fragment of number theory, the circumscription axiom reduces to conventional Peano induction on the natural numbers. In arriving entailments of sentence 10, the circumscription axiom is used precisely the way induction axioms are used to prove theorems in mathematics. Since the predicate variables $\mathbf{P}'$ and $\mathbf{Z}'$ are universally quantified, we can substitute for them arbitrary formulas (provided they have suitable numbers of free individual variables). The entailments of any such instantiated version of sentence 10 will be some of the consequences of 10 itself.

Because of the extreme generality of sentence 10 (for example, which predicates $\mathbf{P}$, $\mathbf{Z}$ of A do we focus on?), McCarthy [1986] proposes a uniform principle for representing knowledge by sentences A in order to capture the pattern "Normally, such and such is the case." His approach appeals to a distinguished unary predicate AB (or often several such predicates $AB_1, \ldots, AB_n$) standing for "abnormal." In circumscribing the sentence A, it is these unary predicates that are minimized. The following example illustrates this use of the AB predicates, together with how the circumscription axiom is used as an induction axiom for deriving consequences of sentence 10.

$$(\forall x)\ \text{THING}(x)\ \&\ \neg AB_1(x) \supset \neg \text{FLY}(x) \tag{11}$$

$$(\forall x)\ \text{BIRD}(x) \supset \text{THING}(x)\ \&\ AB_1(x) \tag{12}$$

$$(\forall x)\ \text{BIRD}(x)\ \&\ \neg AB_2(x) \supset \text{FLY}(x) \tag{13}$$

$$(\forall x)\ \text{EMU}(x) \supset \text{BIRD}(x)\ \&\ \neg \text{FLY}(x) \tag{14}$$

Formula 11 is intended to express that normal (i.e., not AB_1 normal) things don't fly. Thus $\neg AB_1$ restricts THINGs to being normal wrt not flying. Formula 12 states that birds are abnormal things wrt not flying and 13 has intent of describing birds that are normal wrt being able to fly. Finally, axiom 14 distinguishes a subclass of nonflying birds.

Denote the conjunction of sentences 11–14 by $A(AB_1, AB_2; \text{FLY}]$ so that we shall minimize AB_1 and AB_2 with FLY variable using the circumscription axiom for $A(AB_1, AB_2; \text{FLY})$. The point of minimizing AB_1 and AB_2 is to allow as few abnormal individuals as possible, namely those forced by the theory A to be abnormal. The circumscription axiom is:

$$(\forall AB'_1, AB'_2, \text{FLY}')\ \neg\ [A(AB'_1, AB'_2; \text{FLY}')$$
$$\&\ AB'_1 \leq AB_1$$
$$\&\ AB'_2 \leq AB_2$$
$$\&\ \neg\ (AB_1 \leq AB'_1\ \&\ AB_2 \leq AB'_2)] \tag{15}$$

In this axiom, we have three universally quantified predicate variables AB'_1, AB'_2, and FLY', so we can choose these to be any fixed predicates we like. Suppose we cunningly choose

$AB'_1(x) \equiv \text{BIRD}(x)$
$AB'_2(x) \equiv \text{EMU}(x)$
$\text{FLY}'(x) \equiv \text{BIRD}(x) \;\&\; \neg \text{EMU}(x).$

If we make this substitution for the universally quantified predicate variables of the circumscription axiom 15, then from this instance of 15 together with $A(AB_1, AB_2; \text{FLY})$ we can derive, in first-order logic alone, the following:[6]

$(\forall x)AB_1(x) \equiv \text{BIRD}(x)$
$(\forall x)AB_2(x) \equiv \text{EMU}(x)$

i.e., the only abnormal things wrt flightlessness are birds, and the only abnormal birds wrt flight are emus. From this it follows easily that

$(\forall x)\; \text{THING}(x) \;\&\; \neg \text{BIRD}(x) \supset \neg \text{FLY}(x)$
$(\forall x)\; \text{BIRD}(x) \;\&\; \neg \text{EMU}(x) \supset \text{FLY}(x)$

neither of which is entailed by the original (uncircumscribed) theory.

As one can see from the example, it is not obvious in general how to initiate the circumscribed theory. Lifschitz [1985b] provides some results about computing circumscription for various interesting special cases. Another formal problem is that, because circumscribed theories are second order, their valid formulas are not in general recursively enumerable. Note that this is also the case for nonmonotonic and default logic. In addition, it can happen that a satisfiable theory has an unsatisfiable circumscription, although this cannot be in the case of theories all of whose sentences are universal in the prenex normal form [Etherington et al., 1985]. Lifschitz [1986a] generalizes this result on when circumscription preserves satisfiability.

Of all the formalisms proposed for nonmonotonic reasoning, circumscription appears to be the richest. It is certainly the most amenable to mathematical analysis. As a result, its formal properties have been extensively studied. Some completeness results are known [Perlis and Minker, 1986]. Its relationship to Reiter's notion of the closed world assumption of Section 6.1 has been analyzed by Lifschitz [1985a] and Gelfond et al., [1986]. Reiter [1982] shows that for a certain class of first-order theories, Clark's notion of theory completion (Section 6.1) is a consequence of circumscribing the theory. Lifschitz [1985b] provides the same result for a different class of first-order theories. A modifi-

---

6 The derivation itself is straightforward but tedious so we omit the details.

cation of McCarthy's circumscription, called pointwise circumscription [Lifschitz, 1986b], together with priority orderings on the predicated to be minimized [McCarthy, 1986], has been used to provide a semantics for negation for a large class of PROLOG programs [Lifschitz, 1986c]. All of this suggests that circumscription is a rich formalism whose full potential is far from being realized.

Independently of McCarthy, Bossu and Siegel [1985] have provided a semantic account of nonmonotonic reasoning for a special class of minimal models of a first-order theory. In the notation introduced above, their notion of minimality turns out be based on the ordering $\leq^{\mathbf{P};\{\}}$, where $\mathbf{P}$ is the set of all predicate symbols mentioned by the theory. In other words, they minimize all predicates, with no variable predicates. Their analysis is strictly semantic, which is to say they provide nothing corresponding to McCarthy's circumscription axiom. Most significantly, Bossu and Siegel provide a decision procedure for first-order theories and queries of a certain kind. More specifically, suppose

1. the only function symbols are constants (the normal state of affairs in database theory),

2. the prenex form of each formula of the theory is universally qualified and satisfies a further natural syntactic constraint (which turns out to be a reasonable assumption for a database), and

3. the prenex form of the query is universally quantified (a reasonable assumption for some but far from all database queries) and satisfies a further simple syntactic constraint.

Under these conditions it is decidable whether the query is true in all minimal models of the theory (and hence is circumscriptively entailed by the theory). The decision procedure is based upon a particular resolution theorem-proving strategy.

Minker [1982] provides a closely related [4]ysis of the closed world assumption for database theory.

6.3.2 *Minimality and the Frame Problem* The frame problem [McCarthy and Hayes, 1969] concerns the representation of those aspects of a dynamically changing world that remain invariant under state changes. For example, walking to your front door or starting your automobile will not change the colors of any objects in the world. In a first-order representation of such worlds, it is necessary to explicitly represent all of these invariant under all state changes by so-called *frame axioms*. Thus, to represent the fact that turning on a light switch does not alter the colors of objects requires, in the situational calculus of McCarthy and Hayes [1969], a frame axiom of the form

$$(\forall x, c, s, l) \; \textbf{COLOR}(x, c, \text{s}) \supset \textbf{COLOR}(x, \text{c}, \text{result(turn-on, } l, s))$$

where s is a state variable, x an object, c a color, and l a light switch.

The problem is that in general a vast number of such axioms will be required; object colors also remain invariant when lights are switched off, when someone speaks, and so on, so there is a major difficulty even articulating a complete set of frame axioms for a given world, not to mention the computational problems associated with deduction in the presence of so many axioms.

A solution to the frame problem is a representation of the world that provides correct conclusions to be drawn about the dynamics of that world without explicitly representing, or reasoning with, the frame axioms. One of the principle motivations for the study of nonmonotonic reasoning was the belief that it would provide a solution to the frame problem [McCarthy, 1977; Reiter, 1978a]; we required some way of saying that in the absence of information to the contrary a state-changing event preserves the truth of an assertion.

Hanks and McDermott [1986] have investigated various nonmonotonic proposals for solving the frame problem and conclude that the apparently natural approaches fail. Specifically, they consider the simple setting where in initial state s_0, a person is alive, then a gun is loaded, some time passes, and the gun is fired at the person. They ask whether the person's resulting death can be deduced nonmonotonically, i.e., without explicit use of frame axioms. The axiomatization used appeals to McCarthy's AB predicate. It also appeals to a binary predicate T (for true) where $T(f, \text{s})$ denotes that fact f is true in world state s. Syntactically, facts are first-order sentences and so are treated as terms. Their axioms for the shooting scenario are simple and seemingly natural:

$T(\text{alive}, s_0)$

$(\forall s) \; T (\text{loaded, result (load, } s))$

$(\forall s) \; T (\text{loaded}, s) \supset AB(\text{alive, shoot}, s) \; \& \; T(\text{dead, result(shoot}, s))$

$(\forall f, e, s) \; T(f, s) \; \& \; \neg AB(f, e, s) \supset T(f, \text{result}(e, s)).$

Here $AB(f, e, s)$ means that fact f is abnormal when event e occurs in world state s. The last axiom, intended to circumvent the need for frame axioms, says that normally a fact f, true in state s, will remain true in the state that results from event e occurring in state s.

Hanks and McDermott consider circumscribing the above axioms, minimizing AB with T varying and ask us to consider the following situations:

$$s_0, \; s_1 = \text{result(load, } s_0), \; s_2 = \text{result(wait, } s_1), \; s_3 = \text{result(shoot, } s_2).$$

Intuitively, we want $T(\text{dead}, s_3)$ to be circumscriptively derivable. Somewhat surprisingly, it is not. The reason is that the circumscribed theory has two models minimal in AB. In one, $AB(\text{alive, shoot}, s_2)$ is the only true AB atom, and it is easy to see that $T(\text{dead}, s_3)$ is true in this model, as required. But there is another model minimal in AB, namely that in which $AB(\text{loaded}, \text{wait}, s_1)$ is the only true AB atom, and in this model, corresponding to the gun mysteriously being unloaded during the wait event, $T(\text{alive}, s_3)$ is true. It follows that $T(\text{dead}, s_3)$ is not circumscriptively derivable from the above theory. Hanks and McDermott also show that default logic leads to an analogous result, in the sense that the above axioms, together with the default rule schema

$$\frac{:\neg AB(f, e, s)}{\neg AB(f, e, s)}$$

has two extensions, one containing $T(\text{dead}, s_3)$, the other containing $T(\text{alive}, s_3)$.

One might argue that this failure to solve the frame problem stems from an inappropriate set of axioms. Indeed, Lifschitz [1986d] has proposed an axiomatization that circumscriptively does yield the correct conclusions. Others, e.g., Kowalski and Sergot [1986], have argued that time plays a distinguished role in the frame problem, and that any nonmonotonic approach must respect this special status of time. It is towards this perspective that we now turn.

By explicitly providing for time, we obtain a finer-grained representation of dynamically changing worlds than with the situational calculus. We can, for example, represent overlapping events, event durations, and so on [Allen, 1984; Kowalski and Sergot, 1986; McDermott, 1982b]. In such temporal representations the frame problem becomes the persistence problem—determining that a fact known to be true at time t remains true over a future time interval provided no event is known to occur during that time interval to change the fact's truth value. In the case of the shooting scenario, assuming discrete time, we have that a $t = 0$ the person is alive and the gun is loaded at $t = 2$ the gun is fired.[7] The problem is to infer that at $t = 2$ the person is still alive and the gun still loaded, i.e., that the truth of the fact "alive" and "loaded" persists from $t = 0$ to $t = 2$. Intuitively, since we were not informed of an unloading event occurring at $t = 1$, we want to infer that at $t = 2$ the gun is still loaded. This, of course, must be defeasible inference since it could have been the case that the gun was unloaded at $t = 1$.[8]

Kautz [1986] proposes a minimal model solution to the persistence problem, and shows that there is a second-order circumscription-like axiom corresponding to this semantics. Shoham [1986] adopts an $S5$ modal logic for representing an agent's knowledge, proposing a minimal knowledge semantics for the persistence problem. Kowalski and Sergot [1986] propose a PROLOG-based

---

7 Recall that in the scenario we wait some time before firing the gun.
8 Recall that in Hanks and McDermott's situational calculus version, the undesired model was one in which the gun was mysteriously unloaded during the wait event.

temporal calculus of events that addresses the nonmonotonic character of the persistence problem using PROLOG's negation-as-failure-mechanism. This is currently perhaps the most sophisticated approach to the persistence problem and the representation of events. It suffers primarily form its reliance on negation-as-failure, whose semantics is far from clear, so that is it somewhat closer to an implementation than a specification.

Shoham [1986] speculates on foundations for nonmonotonic reasoning for general settings, not just the temporal domain. He argues two perspectives.

1.   There should be a shift in emphasis away from syntactic characterizations [as in default and nonmonotonic logic, or autoepistemic logic (Section 6.4.1, below] in favor of semantic ones. This means that, having first fixed upon a logical language (not necessarily first order) one next provides a semantics for this language appropriate to the intended entailment relation for the application in mind.[9]

2.   This entailment relation will be defined in terms of truth in all those models of a given axiomatization minimal with respect to some application dependent criterion. The ability to characterize such minimality criteria axiomatically (as is the case for example with a circumscription axiom in McCarthy's theory), while perhaps desirable, is not essential. In effect, on Shoham's view, an axiomatization of an application domain coupled with a characterization of its preferred minimal models is a sufficient specification of the required entailments.

In support of his conclusion that nonmonotonicity necessarily involves minimality of one kind or another, Shoham offers his own theory of temporal minimization, as well as McCarthy's minimal semantic of circumscription. In addition, he proposed a minimal model semantics for a modification of Reiter's default logic.

Shoham's thesis—that nonmonotonic reasoning can be identified with truth in minimal models of one kind of another—is attractive. It provides a unifying perspective. Moreover, it suggests a methodology with which one can approach novel applications by considering which notion of minimality is to be preferred. The considerable successes of different forms of circumscription is strong evidence in its favor. Nevertheless, the fact that so few applications have been thoroughly explored, coupled with the unexpected difficulty of the frame problem, should caution us against overly hasty generalizations when it comes to nonmonotonic reasoning.

---

9 Such an approach to knowledge representation was earlier provided by Levesque [1984].

6.4 *Epistemic Approaches*

A number of approaches to nonmonotonic reasoning appeal to logic of belief or knowledge. The intuitive idea behind these is that a possible paraphrase of our favorite "Typically, birds fly" is something like "If x is a bird and if you don't believe (know) that x cannot fly, then x can fly." Since the standard epistemic logics ($S4$, $S5$ and so on) are all monotonic, direct appeals to these cannot work. However, nonmonotonicity can be achieved by a logic that sanctions $\neg Ba$[10] whenever α is absent from an agent's belief set, a property possessed by none of the standard epistemic logics. Under these circumstances, if an agent's belief set contains BIRD(Tweety) together with the default sentence

$$(\forall x)\ \text{BIRD}(x)\ \&\ \neg B \neg \text{FLY}(x) \supset \text{FLY}(x)$$

but not $\neg$ FLY(Tweety), then the belief set will contain $\neg B \neg$ FLY(Tweety) whence, by modus ponens, the belief set will contain FLY(Tweety)

This, then, is the basic intuition behind epistemic approaches to nonmonotonicity. Notice that nonmonotonicity is achieved by virtue of endowing an agent with the ability to reflect on its pen beliefs in order to infer sentences expressing what it doesn't believe. The sentences contained in such a belief set depend on the entire belief set and hence are indexical.

We now consider several proposals for nonmonotonic epistemic logics.

6.4.1 *Autoepistemic Logic*   In response to the semantic deficiencies of McDermott and Doyle's nonmonotonic logic, Moore [1984, 1985] provides a reconstruction of their logic based upon belief rather than consistency, which he calls autoepistemic logic. Recall that the former logic appeals to a modal operator M with consistency as its intended meaning. Autoepistemic logic invokes a dual operator B[11] corresponding (roughly) to $\neg M \neg$. Moore's is a propositional logic only with the usual formulas formed from a propositional logic only with the modal operator B. Given some set of premises A, a set T of formulas is a *stable expansion of A* just in case

$$T = Th(A \cup \{Bw \mid w \in T\} \cup \{\neg Bw \mid w \notin T\}).\text{[12]}$$

Notice that this is a fixed-point definition much like that of McDermott and Doyle. In fact, under the dual correspondence of B with $\neg M \neg$ Moore's definition of a stable expansion differs from the fixed points of McDermott and Doyle (Section 6.2.1) only by the inclusion of $\{Bw \models w \in T\}$ in his fixed-point

---

10 We use to denote that an agent believes.

11 We use B here for belief. In his papers, Moore uses the symbol L.

12 Here Th denotes closure under the entailment relation of propositional logic.

construction. This set provides for an agent's perfect positive introspection; if w is in its belief set, then it believes w so that Bw is also in its belief set. The second set in the definition provides for perfect negative introspection; if w is not in an agent's belief set, the agent does not believe w.

Levesque [1987] generalizes Moore's notion of a stable expansion to the full first-order case (which includes quantification into modal contexts). He also provides a semantic account of stable expansions in terms of a second modal operator O, where Ow is read as "w is all that is believed." Levesque then goes on to characterize stable expressions as follows: Ow is true exactly when all the formulas that are believed form a stable expansion of $\{w\}$.

As observed by Konolige [1987], stable expansion have some undesirable properties. Konolige note that there are two stable expansions of $\{Bp \supset p\}$, one containing $\neg Bp$ but not p, the other containing both Bp and p. The first expansion is intuitively appropriate; an agent whose only initial belief is $Bp \supset p$ has no grounds for entering p into her belief set and should therefore enter $\neg Bp$. The second expansion, containing both Bp and p, is intuitively unacceptable. It corresponds to an agent arbitrarily entering p, hence also Bp, into her belief set.

To eliminate this undesirable property of Moore's autoepistemic logic, Konolige proposes the notion of a strongly grounded expansion of a set of premises A.[13] For any set Σ of formulas of our modal propositional language, denote by Σ_0 those formulas of Σ with no occurrence of the modal operator B, i.e., Σ_0 is the purely propositional part of Σ. Call a stable expansion T of A *minimal* iff there is no stable expansion S of A such that S_0 is a proper subset of T_0. Finally, call a set of formulas a *strongly grounded expansion* of A iff it is a minimal stable expansion of A. Konolige [1987] proposes strongly grounded expansions "as candidates for ideal introspective belief sets, because they limit the assumptions an agent makes about the world." Notice that the premise set $\{Bp \supset p\}$, which was problematic under Moore's account, has just one strongly grounded expansion, namely, the intuitively appropriate expansion containing $\neg Bp$ but not p.

Konolige provides several characterizations of strongly grounded expansion of A, all appealing to fixed-point constructions. Perhaps the most interesting characterization is in terms of the modal logic $KU45$, which is axiomatic $S5$, with $S5$'s axiom schema $B\varphi \supset \varphi$ replaced by the weaker $B(B\varphi \supset \varphi)$. Denote $KU45$'s provability relation by $\vdash_{KU45}$. Konolige shows that T is a strongly grounded expansion of A iff T satisfies the fixed point equation

---

13 Konolige [1987] calls these "strongly grounded autoepistemic extensions of A." He also deals with a first-order modal language, generalizing Moore's [1984, 1985] propositional language, but without quantifying into modal contexts. Here I continue to use a propositional modal language since the differences are inessential when quantification into modal contexts is forbidden.

$T = \{w \models A \cup \{B\alpha \models \alpha \in A\} \cup \{\neg B\alpha \models a \gg T_0\} \vdash_{KU45}w\}.$

Suppose (D, W) is a default theory (Section 6.2.2). Define its *auto-epistemic transform* to be

$$W \cup \left\{B\alpha \& \neg B \neg \beta \supset \gamma \middle| \frac{\alpha : \beta}{\gamma} \in D\right\}.$$

Thus, the transform translates default rules to sentences of autoepistemic logic. Konolige proves that autoepistemic logic is at least as expressive as default logic in the following sense:

Let A be the autoepistemic transform of a default theory. Then E is an extension of this default theory iff $E = S_0$[14] for some strongly grounded expansion S of A.

The question remains whether autoepistemic logic is strictly more expressive than default logic. Is there a set A of sentences with a strongly grounded expansion S for which S_0 is not an extension of any default theory? Surprisingly, the answer is no; Konolige shows:

For any set A of sentences there is an effectively construable default theory such that E is an extension of this theory iff $E = S_0$ for some strongly grounded expansion S of A.

The above two results yield the unexpected conclusion that there is an exact correspondence between the extensions of default logic and strongly grounded expansions of autoepistemic logic.

6.4.2 *Self-Knowledge and Ignorance*

Levesque [1982, 1984] is concerned with the following question: What is an appropriate notion of knowledge that would endow with self-knowledge a database *KB* of information about a world? Levesque's concept of self-knowledge includes knowledge about lack of knowledge; not only should *KB* know the information (and the entailments thereof) it contains, it should also know that it doesn't know a fact when indeed that fact is unknown to it.

---

14 Recall that S_0 is the purely propositional part of S.

To simply the discussion, we shall consider a knowledge language called KFOPCE by Levesque [1982] which, though elementary, is sufficient to convey how nonmonotonicity and default reasoning can be achieved. In a subsequent paper Levesque [1984] treats a much richer such language.

KFOPCE is a first-order modal language with equality and with a single modal operator K (for "know"), constructed in the usual way from a set of predicate and variable symbols and a countably infinite set of symbols called *parameters*. Parameters can be thought of as constants. Their distinguishing feature is that they are pairwise distinct and they define the domain over which quantifies range, i.e., the parameters represent a single universal domain of discourse.

A database *KB* of information about a world is a first-order sentence, i.e., a sentence of KFOPCE with no occurrence of the K operator. We consider how Levesque defines the result of querying *KB* with a sentence of KFOPCE. This requires first specifying a semantics for KFOPCE. A *primitive sentence* (of KFOPCE) is any atom of the form $P(p_1, \ldots, p_n)$, where P is an n-ary predicate symbol and $p_1, \ldots, p_n$ are parameters. A *world structure* is any set of primitive sentences that includes $p = p$ for each parameter p, and that does not include $p_1 = p_2$ for different parameters p_1 and p_2. The effect of this requirement on the equality predicate is that semantically the parameters are all pairwise distinct. A world structure is understood to be a set of true atomic facts. A *structure* is any set of world structures. The truth value of a sentence of KFOPCE with respect to a world structure W and a structure Σ is defined as follows:

1. If p is a primitive sentence, p is true wrt W and Σ iff $p \in W$.

2. $\neg w$ is true wrt W and Σ iff w is false wrt W and Σ.

3. $w_1 \vee w_2$ is true wrt W and Σ iff w_1 or w_2 is true wrt W and Σ.

4. $(\forall x)w(x)$ is true wrt W and Σ iff for every parameter p, $w(p)$ is true wrt W and Σ.

5. Kw is true wrt W and Σ iff for every $S \in \Sigma$, w is true wrt S and Σ.

Notice that condition 4 implies that, insofar as KFOPCE is concerned, the parameters constitute a single universal domain of discourse. The parameters are used to identify the known individuals. Notice also that when f is a first-order sentence (so that condition 5 need never be invoked in the truth recursion for f) then the truth value of f wrt W and Σ is independent of Σ, and we can speak of the truth value of f wrt W alone.

Given this semantics, Levesque defines the result of querying *KB* with an arbitrary sentence of KFOPCE as follows:

Let $M(KB)$ be the set of the world structures W for which KB is true wrt W. $M(KB)$ is thus the set of models of KB. The result of querying KB with a sentence k of KFOPCE is defined to be

ASK(KB, k)   = *yes* if for all $W \in M(KB)$ k is true wrt W and $M(KB)$.

= *no* if for all $W \in M(KB)$ k is false wrt W and $M(KB)$.

= *unknown* otherwise.

Notice that this is an $S5$ semantics with $M(KB)$ the equivalence class of mutually accessible possible worlds. It is this semantics that justifies interpreting the modal operator K of KFOPCE as a knowledge operator.

As an example, suppose KB is the conjunction of the following formulas:

ENROLLED(Bill, cs100)
TEACH(Mary, cs100) $\vee$ TEACH(SUSAN, cs100)
$(\exists x)$ TEACH(x, math100)

Here, Bill, Mary, cs100,..., are among the parameters. The following are some sample queries, together with the answers sanctioned by the above definition:

1. Is anyone known to be enrolled in cs100?

    $\neg (\exists x)K$ ENROLLED(x, cs100): yes

2. Does anyone teach cs100?

    $(\exists x)$ TEACH(x, cs100): yes

3. Is anyone known to teach cs100?

    $(\exists x)K$ TEACH(x, cs100): no

4. Is anyone known to teach math100?

    $(\exists x)K$ TEACH(x, math100): no

5. Is there a course in which Bill is enrolled and in which he is not known to be enrolled?

    $(\exists x)$ ENROLLED(Bill, x) $\& \neg K$ ENROLLED(Bill, x): unknown.

Notice that ASK is nonmonotonic. For example, updating KB with TEACH(Sam, math100) would change the answer to question 4 from no to yes.

Levesque provides a noneffective way, requiring only an oracle for first-order theoremhood, of determining the result of ASKing KB an arbitrary sentence of KFOPCE.

In order to represent defaults like flying birds Levesque proposes

$$(\forall x)\ \mathrm{BIRD}(x)\ \&\ \neg\ \mathrm{K}\ \neg\ \mathrm{FLY}(x) \supset \mathrm{FLY}(x). \tag{16}$$

This creates a technical problem; we must be able to update *KB* with non-first-order formulas like this, which requires first specifying the semantics of such updates. Levesque provides such a semantics, whose details we omit here. He then shows how to (noneffectively) determine a first-order formula $\models \alpha_{KB}$ such that the result of updating *KB* with α is *KB* & $\models \alpha_{KB}\models$. Thus, updating *KB* with a default like statement 16 has the effect of conjoining with *KB* a certain first-order formula.

Levesque's approach to (nonmonotonically) querying a first-order database haw several advantages. It is semantically precise and well motivated. It allows one to ASK a database about its states of knowledge (witness the above simple example of an educational database), thus providing a far more expressive query language than conventional approaches using first-order logic [Green, 1969]. Moreover, the ASK operator can be realized in terms of first-order theoremhood, albeit by appealing to an oracle.

On the other hand, Levesque's treatment of default reasoning is problematic. Because defaults like statement 16 are assimilated into *KB* as suitable first-order formulas, they lose their character as defaults and hence cannot be reasoned about within the logic. In this respect they are akin to the default rules of default logic (Section 6.2.2). Moreover, inconsistencies can arise when intuitively they should not. For example, using the default sentence 16 to update the following *KB* leads to an inconsistent database:

$$\mathrm{BIRD}(\mathrm{Tweety})\ \ \mathrm{BIRD}(\mathrm{Opus})\ \ \neg\ \mathrm{FLY}(\mathrm{Tweety}) \vee \neg\ \mathrm{FLY}(\mathrm{Opus}).$$

Intuitively, this is so since *KB* does not know FLY(Tweety), and it does not know FLY(Opus), so by sentence 16 it deduces both FLY(Tweety) and FLY(Opus). Most other formalisms for handling defaults—e.g., circumscription, nonmonotonic logic, and default logic—do not lead to inconsistencies like this.

Despite such problems, Levesque [1982] provides a variety of interesting ideas for representing and structuring default information, including a proposal that, in many respects, anticipates McCarthy's [1986] use of the *AB* predicate for representing typicality. In its simplest form, Levesque's proposal is to introduce the concept of a typical-*P*, written ∇P, understood to be a new predicate. Thus ∇BIRD denotes a typical bird, and we can write a first-order axiom.

$$(\forall x)\ \nabla\mathrm{BIRD}(x) \supset \mathrm{FLY}(x).$$

Certain birds are not typical:

$(\forall x)$ OSTRICH$(x) \supset \neg \nabla$ BIRD(x).

Defaults now state conditions under which instances of typical-birds may be inferred.

$(\forall x)$ BIRD(x) & $\neg$ K $\neg \nabla$BIRD$(x) \supset \nabla$BIRD(x).

Using such representations for typicality, Levesque [1982] shows how to structure these to deal with many problems involving interacting defaults [Reiter and Criscuolo, 1983] like the Quaker-Republican and shell-bearing examples of Section 3.

There have been a few other theories of knowledge in which an agent's ability to introspect on his ignorance leads to nonmonotonicity. Halpern and Moses [1984] propose a propositional approach very like Moore's auto-epistemic logic (Section 6.4.1) but based upon an agent's knowledge rather than (as in Moore's case) belief. Unfortunately, as Halpern and Moses observe, their formalism cannot accommodate default reasoning. Konolige [1982] proposes a multi-agent logic of knowledge grounded in the propositional modal logic $S4$. This achieves nonmonotonicity by means of a closed world rule of inference based upon $S4$ nonprovability. Using this logic, Konolige solves the Wise Man Puzzle, which requires a wise man to reason about the states of knowledge of two other wise men. However, the logic does not allow an agent to conclude that he does not know some fact, and hence it cannot provide a theory for default reasoning.

6.5 *Conditional Logics*

A few recent attempts to formalize nonmonotonic reasoning have been based upon conditional logics, which have been studied by several philosophical logicians, e.g., Lewis [1973] and Stalnaker [1968].

We shall focus here on *subjunctive conditionals*, i.e., statements of the form "If A were the case, then B would be the case," which we denote by $A \Rightarrow B$. The classic example from the philosophical literature is "If a match were to be struck, then it would light," which intuitively we all take to be true. But we also take to be true that "If a wet match were to be struck, then it would not light." and there is nothing peculiar about these two statements in the presence of a wet match. This means that the subjunctive if–then, $\Rightarrow$, is not the same as $\supset$, material implication, for otherwise the match example would have the form $A \supset C$ and A & $B \supset \neg C$ which, in the presence of A & B, a wet match, leads to a contradiction.

Now all of this certainly feels nonmonotonic. We can rephrase our bird example by subjective conditionals like "If x were a bird then x would fly," whereas "If x were a featherless bird then x would not fly." It is this intuition that suggests appealing to a suitable logic of conditionals to formalize nonmonotonic reasoning.

Such logics do exist (e.g., [Delgrande, 1986]). Typically, these are based upon a possible-worlds semantics in which the truth value of a conditional $A \Rightarrow B$ in a world depends on a subset of those worlds in which A is true. Conditional logics differ primarily in how these worlds-in-which-A-is-true are distinguished. Axiomatizations of conditional logics correspond to these different semantics—e.g., Delgrande's [1986].

As Delgrande [1986] observes, one motivation for considering conditional logics is that they allow us to reason about typicality within the logic. For example, "Typical canaries are not green" should be derivable (see Section 6.2.2). The logic should mandate the inconsistency of "All ravens are birds" with "Typical ravens are not birds," provided some raven exists. Indeed, Delgrande's logic has these properties.

Unfortunately, for our proposes, these logics have a fatal flaw; they are monotonic. Moreover, they are extremely weak. For example, modus ponens cannot be a rule of inference for conditional statements. This is so since otherwise, in our wet match example, from $A \Rightarrow C$, $A \& B \Rightarrow \neg C$, and $A \& B$ we could derive both C and $\neg C$. This failure of modus ponens means that we cannot infer default conclusions. BIRD(Tweety) and $(\forall x)$ BIRD(x) $\Rightarrow$ FLY(x) does not entail FLY(Tweety) in any conditional logic.

Despite these shortcomings, a few researchers [Delgrande, 1986; Ginsberg, 1986; Nute, 1984] have proposed basing nonmonotonic reasoning systems on such logic. In all cases, nonmonotonicity is achieved by pragmatic considerations affecting how the logic is used. Unfortunately, this destroys the principled semantics on which these logics were originally based, so it is unclear what the advantages are of pursuing this approach to nonmonotonic reasoning.

7 Some Objections

Formalisms for nonmonotonic reasoning, grounded as they are in more or less conventional logics, have often been criticized. The most common objection is that probability theory is more appropriate (e.g., [Cheeseman, 1985]). Numerically inclined nonprobabilists argue in favor of fuzzy reasoning [Zadeh, 1985] or likelihood reasoning [Rich, 1983], etc. In effect, all such proposals identify statements like "Typically birds can fly" with "Most birds fly." In other words, they identify prototypical properties with statistical properties. Now, in certain settings a statistical reading is warranted. Regardless of my concept of a prototypical bird, if I find myself lost and hungry in a remote part of the world, my design of a bird-catching trap will depend upon my observation of the frequency with which the local birds fly. But to appeal exclusively to a statistical reading for plausible inference is to misunderstand the intended purpose of nomonotonic reasoning.

In a wide variety of settings, nonmonotonic reasoning is necessary precisely because the information associated with such settings requires that certain *conventions* be respected. Such conventions may be explicit, as in the closed world assumption for the representation of negative information in databases. More commonly, these conventions are implicit, as in various principles of cooperative communication of information where it is understood by all participants that the informant is conveying all of the relevant information. Any relevant item of information not so conveyed is justifiably infer that John was beating the rug despite the fact that the original statement might be true precisely because John never was beating the rug to begin with.[15] The point is that if this were the case, your informant should have told you. Since she didn't, convention dictates the appropriateness of your conclusion, despite its defeasibility.

Pictures and diagrams provide another interesting example. There is a kind of closed world convention to the effect that if an entity is not depicted in a picture or diagram, then it is not present in the world or the device the diagram represents.

It would seem that with such respect to such conventions, statistical reasoning has no role to play whatsoever. It is difficult to imagine, for example, what it could mean to assign a probability to the failure of a circuit diagram to depict a device's power supply, or what advantage there could possibly be in doing so. McCarthy [1980] makes a similar point in discussing the missionaries-and-cannibals problem; he observes that the situation described by the puzzle is so wildly implausible that it would be meaningless to try to assign a conditional probability to the proposition that the boat is not leaky. In this connection, notice that puzzle solving is perhaps the clearest example of how convention sanctions and nonmonotonic reasoning independently of any probabilistic interpretation. In fact, the preceding discussion suggests that much of what passes for human commonsense reasoning may at heart be puzzle solving.

The above argument from convention does not address all objections to logically based formalizations of nonmonotonic reasoning. Many nonmonotonic inferences are *abductive* in nature, which is to say they provide plausible explanations for some state of affairs. In this settings, an explanation can be taken to be a set of formulas that, together with the available background knowledge, entails the given state of affairs. The problem, of course, is that not just any explanation will do; it must, in some sense, be a "best" explanation. An explanation might be judged "best" because it is simplest, most general, or most probable, or because it is the outcome of weighing explicit evidence pro

---

15 In linguistics, the original statement is said to *presuppose* the conclusion that John was beating the rug. Presupposition is well known to involve defeasible inferences ([Levinson, 1983] Ch. 4).

and con, etc. No such criteria are embodied in any current formalism for non-monotonic reasoning.

Israel [1980] criticizes nonmonotonic formalism on similar, though more general grounds. He objects to the centrality of deductive logic in these formalisms as a mechanism for justifying an agent's beliefs. For Israel, "a heuristic treatment [of nonmonotonic reasoning], that is a treatment in terms of rational epistemic policies, is not just the best we could hope for. It is the only thing that makes sense." Abductively reasoning to a best explanation would, in Israel's view, require rational epistemic logic. McDermott [1986] levies a similar criticism (among others) but is pessimistic about the very existence, currently, of formal theories of such rational epistemic policies for abductive reasoning. Nevertheless, as he observes:

> This state of affairs does not stop us from writing medical diagnosis programs. But it does keep us from understanding them. There is no independent theory to appeal to that can justify the inferences a program makes. . . these programs embody *tacit* theories of abduction; these theories would be the first nontrivial formal theories of abduction, if only one could make them explicit.

We shall pursue McDermott's example of diagnostic reasoning because it will allow us to draw an important distinction. This, in turn, will reveal a significant role for nonmonotonic logic in situations requiring Israel's rational epistemic policies.

The proper way of viewing diagnosis is as a process of theory formation [Poole, 1986]: What is the best theory that accounts for the given evidence? But if there is a best theory, there must be poor ones; so diagnostic reasoning really consists of two problems: (*a*) What is the space of possible theories that account for the given evidence? (*b*) What are the best theories in this space? Most rule-based diagnostic systems conflict these two questions, attempting to converge on a best theory (usually by statistical means) without explicitly accounting for the space of possible theories through which they are searching. However, once this distinction is revealed: They can characterize the space of possible theories that explain the evidence. This is seen most clearly in papers by Poole [1986] and Reiter [1987]. For example, Reiter shows that the space of possible theories is precisely the set of extensions of a suitable formalization in default logic (Section 6.2.2) of the diagnostic setting. Poole's characterization, while somewhat different, is also based on default logic. Other approaches to diagnosis that emphasize characterizing the space of all theories are give by de Kleer and Williams [1986] and Reggia et al., [1985].

The second problem—choosing a best theory from the space of possible theories—is currently beyond the province of nonmonotonic logic. In this respect, Israel's criticism is correct. However, given the space of possible theories as provided by nonmonotonic logic, we can at least begin a principled study of the rational epistemic policies for theory selection that Israel rightly emphasizes. This is the approach of de Kleer and Williams [1986] and Peng and Reggia [1986], who provide probabilistic grounds for diagnostic theory preference. In a different setting Poole [1985] proposes a preference ordering on theories that favors the most specific theories.

In brief, a proper analysis of diagnostic reasoning, and more generally abductive reasoning, must address two distinct problems. The first—that of characterizing the space of possible explanatory theories—is an appropriate role for nonmonotonic logic. The second—that of determining theory preference—requires rational epistemic policies that appear to have little to do with current approaches to nonmonotonic reasoning.

8 Conclusions

Nonmonotonicity appears to be the rule, rather than the exception, in much of what passes for human commonsense reasoning. The formal study of such reasoning patterns and their applications has made impressive, and rapidly accelerating progress. Nevertheless, much remains to be done.

The unexpected complexity of the frame problem suggests that many more non-toy examples need to be thoroughly explored in order for us to gain a deeper understanding of the essential nature of nonmonotonic reasoning. In this connection, note that most potential applications have barely been touched, if at all. Apart from those discussed in this paper, examples include implicatures and presuppositions in natural language, high-level decision, qualitative physics, and learning.

With the possible exception of PROLOG's negation-as-failure mechanism, we know almost nothing about reasonable ways to compute nonmonotonic inferences. Truth maintenance systems must be integrated components of nonmonotonic reasoners, yet we have no adequate formal account of such systems. All current nonmonotonic formalism deal with single agent reasoners. However, it is clear that agents must frequently ascribe nonmonotonic inferences to other agents, for example in cooperative planning or speech acts.[16] Such multi-agent settings require appropriate formal theories, which currently we lack.

The ultimate quest, of course, is to discover a single theory embracing all the seemingly disparate settings in AI where nonmonotonic reasoning arises.

---

16 See Perrault [1987]. Incidentally, the requirement that an agent must be able to ascribe default rules to another agent argues for an epistemic approach to nonmonotonic reasoning (Section 6.4). See Halpern and Moses [1985] for a (monotonic) multi-agent logic of knowledge.

Undoubtedly, there will be surprises en route, but AI will profit from the journey, in the process becoming much more the science we all wish it to be.

Acknowledgments

Many thanks to David Etherington, Russ Greiner, and Hector Levesque for providing valuable suggestions on improving an earlier draft of this paper. My thanks also to Teresa Miao for carefully and patiently preparing this manuscript. This research was done with the financial support of the National Sciences and Engineering Research Council of Canada, under operating grant A9044.

References

Allen, J. F., 1984. Towards a general theory of action and time. *Artificial Intelligence* **23**:123–54.

Bobrow, D. G. and Winograd, T., 1977. An overview of KRL, a knowledge representation language. *Cognitive Science* **1**:3–46.

Bossu, G. and Siegel, P., 1985. Saturation, non-monotonic reasoning and the closed-world assumption. *Artificial Intelligence* **25**:13–63.

Buchanan, B. G. and Shortliffe, E. ed., 1984. *Rule-Based Expert Systems: The MYCIN Experiments of the Stanford Heuristic Programming Project*. Reading, Mass: Addison-Wesley.

Bundy, A., 1985. Incidence calculus: A mechanism for probabilistic reasoning. *Journal of Automated Reasoning* **1**:263–83.

Cheeseman, P., 1985. In defense of probability. In *Proceedings of the Ninth International Joint Conference on Artificial Intelligence*, Los Angeles, pp. 1002–9. San Mateo: Morgan Kaufmann Publishers.

Clark, K., 1978. Negation as failure. See Gallaire and Minker, pp. 293–322.

de Kleer J. and Williams, B. C., 1986. Reasoning about multiple faults. In *Proceedings of the Fifth National Conference of the American Association for Artificial Intelligence*, Philadelphia, pp. 132–45. San Mateo: Morgan Kaufmann Publishers.

Delgrande, J. P., 1986. A first-order conditional logic for reasoning about prototypical properties. Simon Fraser University Department of Computer Science Technical Report. Burnaby.

Doyle, J., 1979. A truth maintenance system. *Artificial Intelligence* **12**:231–72.

Etherington, D. W., 1986. *Reasoning with Incomplete Information: Investigations of Non-monotonic Reasoning*. PhD thesis. University of British Columbia, Vancouver.

Etherington, D. W., 1987. A semantics for default logic. In *Proceedings of the Tenth International Joint Conference on Artificial Intelligence*, Milan. San Mateo: Morgan Kaufmann Publishers.

Etherington, D., Mercer, R., and Reiter, R., 1985. On the adequacy of predicate circumscription for closed world reasoning. *Computational Intelligence* **1**:11–15.

Fahlman, S. E., Touretzky, D. S., and van Roggen, W., 1981. Cancellation in a parallel semantic network. In *Proceedings of the Seventh International Joint Conference on Artificial Intelligence*, Vancouver, pp. 257–63. San Mateo: Morgan Kaufmann Publishers.

Genesereth, M. R., 1984. The use of design descriptions in automated diagnosis. *Artificial Intelligence* **24**:411–36.

Gallaire, H., Minker, J., ed., 1978. *Logic and Data Bases*. New York/London: Plenum.

Gelfond, M., Przymusinska, H., Przymusinska, T., 1986. The extended closed world assumption and its relation to parallel circumscription. University of Texas, Department of Math. Sci. Work. Pap. El Paso.

Ginsberg, M. L., 1986. Counterfactuals. *Artificial Intelligence* **30**:35–79.

Green, C., 1969. *The Application of Theorem-Proving to Question Answering Systems*. Ph.D. thesis. Stanford University.

Halpern, J. Y. and Moses, Y., 1984. Towards a theory of knowledge and ignorance: Preliminary report. In *Proceedings of the AAAI Workshop Non Monotonic Reasoning*, New Paltz, pp. 125–43.

Halpern, J. Y. and Moses, Y., 1985. A guide to the modal logics of knowledge and belief: Preliminary draft. In *Proceedings of the Ninth International Joint Conference on Artificial Intelligence*, Los Angeles, pp. 480–90. San Mateo: Morgan Kaufmann Publishers.

Hanks, S. and McDermott, D., 1986. Default reasoning, nonmonotonic logics, and the frame problem. In *Proceedings of the Fifth National Conference of the American Association for Artificial Intelligence*, Philadelphia, pp. 328–33. San Mateo: Morgan Kaufmann Publishers.

Haugland, J., 1981. *Mind Design*. Cambridge, Mass: MIT Press.

Hayes, P. J., 1973. The frame problem and related problems in artificial intelligence. *Artificial and Human Thinking*, ed. A. Elithorn and D. Jones, pp. 45–59. San Francisco: Jossey-Bass.

Israel, D. J., 1980. What's wrong with non-monotonic logic? In *Proceedings of the First National Conference of the American Association for Artificial Intelligence*, Stanford, pp. 99–101. San Mateo: Morgan Kaufmann Publishers.

Kautz, H. A., 1986. The logic of persistence. In *Proceedings of the Fifth Natioanl Conference of the American Association for Artificial Intelligence*, Philadelphia, pp. 401–5. San Mateo: Morgan Kaufmann Publishers.

Konolige, K., 1982. Circumscriptive ignorance. In *Proceedings of the Second National Conference of the American Association for Artificial Intelligence*, Pittsburgh, pp. 202–4. San Mateo: Morgan Kaufmann Publishers.

Konolige, K., 1987. On the relation between default theories and autoepistemic logic. SRI International Artificial Intelligence Center Technical Report. Palo Alto.

Kowalski, R. and Sergot, M., 1986. A logic-based calculus of events. *New Generation Computing* **4**:67–95.

Levesque, H. J., 1982. A formal treatment of incomplete knowledge bases. Fairchild Lab. Artificial Intelligence Research Technical Report 3.

Levesque, H. J., 1982. Foundations of a functional approach to knowledge representation. *Artificial Intelligence* **23**:155-212.

Levesque, H. J., 1986. Knowledge representation and reasoning. *Annual Review of Computer Science* **1**:255–87.

Levesque, H. J., 1987. All I know: Preliminary report. University of Toronto, Department of Computer Science Technical Report. Toronto.

Levinson, S. C., 1983. *Pragmatics*. London: Cambridge University Press.

Lewis, D., 1973. *Counterfactuals*. Cambridge, Mass: Harvard University Press.

Lifschitz, V., 1985a. Closed-world databases and circumscription. *Artificial Intelligence* **27**:229–35.

Lifschitz, V., 1985b. Computing circumscription. In *Proceedings of the Ninth International Joint Conference on Artificial Intelligence*, Los Angeles, pp. 121–27. San Mateo: Morgan Kaufmann Publishers.

Lifschitz, V., 1986a. On the satisfiability of circumscription. *Artificial Intelligence* **28**:17–27.

Lifschitz, V., 1986b. Pointwise circumscription: A preliminary report. In *Proceedings of the Fifth National Conference of the American Artificial Intelligence*, Philadelphia, pp. 406–10. San Mateo: Morgan Kaufmann Publishers.

Lifschitz, V., 1986c. On the declarative semantics of logic programs with negation. Stanford University Computer Science Department Technical Report. Stanford.

Lifschitz, V., 1986d. Formal theories of action. Stanford University Computer Science Department Technical Report. Stanford.

Lukaszewicz, W., 1984. Consideration on default logic. In *Proceedings of the AAAI Workshop Non-Monotonic Reasoning*, New Paltz, pp. 165–93.

McCarthy, J., 1977. Epistemological problems of artificial intelligence. In *Proceedings of the Fifth International Joint Conference on Artificial Intelligence*, Cambridge, Mass., pp. 223–27. San Mateo: Morgan Kaufmann Publishers.

McCarthy, J., 1980. Circumscription—a form of non-monotonic reasoning. *Artificial Intelligence* **13**:27–39.

McCarthy, J., 1986. Applications of circumscription to formalizing common-sense knowledge. *Artificial Intelligence* **28**:89–116.

McCarthy, J. and Hayes, P. J., 1969. Some philosophical problems from the standpoint of artificial intelligence. *Machine Intelligence 4,* ed. B. Meltzer and D. Michie, pp. 463–502. Edinburgh: Edinburgh University Press.

McDermott, D., 1982a. Non-monotonic logic II: Non-monotonic modal theories. *Journal of ACM* **29**:33–57

McDermott, D. V., 1982b. A temporal logic for reasoning about processes and plans. *Cognitive Science* **6**:101–55.

McDermott, D., 1986. A critique of pure reason. Yale University Department of Computer Science Technical Report. New Haven

McDermott, D. and Doyle, J., 1980. Non-monotonic logic I. *Artificial Intelligence* **25**:41–72

Mercer, R. E. and Reiter, R., 1982. The representation of presuppositions using defaults. In *Proceedings of the Can. Soc. Computat. Stud. Intell. National Conference*, Saskatoon, pp. 103–7.

Michalski, R. S., 1983. A theory and methodology of inductive learning. *Machine Learning* ed., R. S. Michalski, J. G. Carbonell, T. M. Mitchell, pp. 83–129. San Mateo: Morgan Kaufmann Publishers.

Minker, J., 1982. On indefinite databases and the closed world assumption. In *Proceedings of the 6th Conference on Automated Deduction*, New York, pp. 292–308.

Minsky, M., 1975. A framework for representing knowledge. *The Psychology of Computer Vision*, ed. P.H. Winston, pp. 211–77. New York: McGraw-Hill.

Moore, R. C., 1984. Possible-world semantics for autoepistemic logic. In *Proceedings of the AAAI Workshop Non-Monotonic Reasoning,* New Paltz, pp. 396–401.

Moore, R. C., 1985. Semantical consideration on nonmonotonic logic. *Artificial Intelligence* **25**:75–94.

Nilsson, N., 1986. Probabilistic logic. *Artificial Intelligence* **28**:71–87.

Nute, D., 1984. Non-monotonic reasoning and conditionals. University of Georgia Advanced Comput. Methods Center for Research Report 01-0002. Athens, GA.

Peng, Y. and Reggia, J. A., 1986. Plausibility of diagnostic hypotheses: The nature of simplicity. *Proceedings of the Fifth National Conference of the American Association for Artificial Intelligence*, Philadelphia, pp. 140–45. San Mateo: Morgan Kaufmann Publishers.

Perlis, D. and Minker, J., 1986. Completeness results for circumscription. *Artificial Intelligence* **28**:29–42.

Perrault, C. R., 1987. An application of default logic to speech act theory. SRI International Artificial Intelligence Center Technical Report. Palo Alto.

Poole, D. L., 1985. On the comparison of theories: Preferring the most specific explanation. In *Proceedings of the Ninth International Joint Conference on Artificial Intelligence*, Los Angeles, pp. 144–47. San Mateo: Morgan Kaufmann Publishers.

Poole, D., 1986. Default reasoning and diagnosis as theory formation. University of Waterloo Department of Computer Science Technical Report CS-86-08.

Putnam, H., 1970. Is semantics possible? *Language, Belief, and Metaphysics*, ed. H. E. Kiefer and M. K. Munitz, pp. 50–63. Albany: State University of New York Press.

Reggia, J. A., Nau, D. S., Wang, Y., and Peng, Y., 1985. A formal model of diagnostic inference. *Information Science* **37**:227–85.

Reiter, R., 1978a. On reasoning by default. In *Proceedings of TINLAP-2, Theoretical Issues in Natural Language Processing 2*, pp. 210–18. University of Illinois, Urbana-Champaign.

Reiter, R., 1978b. On closed world data bases. See Gallaire and Minker, pp. 55–76.

Reiter, R., 1980. A logic for default reasoning. *Artificial Intelligence* **13**:81–132.

Reiter, R., 1982. Circumscription implies predicate completion (sometimes). In *Proceedings of the Second National Conference of the American Association for Artificial Intelligence*, Pittsburgh, pp. 418–20. San Mateo: Morgan Kaufmann Publishers.

Reiter, R., 1987. A theory of diagnosis from first principles. *Artificial Intelligence*.

Reiter, R., Criscuolo, G., 1983. Some representational issues in default reasoning. *Journal of Computer Mathematics Applications* **9**:1–13 (Special issue on computational linguistics).

Rich, E., 1983. Default reasoning as likelihood reasoning. In *Proceedings of the Third National Conference of the American Association for Artificial Intelligence*, Washington D. C., pp. 348–51. San Mateo: Morgan Kaufmann Publishers.

Rosch, E., 1978. Principles of categorization. *Cognition and Categorization*, ed. E. Rosch, B. B. Lloyds. Hillsdale: Lawrence Erlbaum Assoc.

Sandewall, E., 1972. An approach to the frame problem and its implementation. *Machine Intelligence 7*, ed. B. Meltzer, D. Michie, pp. 195–204. Edinburgh: Edinburgh University Press.

Sandewall, E., 1985. A functional approach to non-monotonic logic. *Computational Intelligence* **1**:80–87.

Shepherdson, J. C., 1984. Negation as failure: A comparison of Clark's completed data base and Reiter's closed world assumption. *Journal of Logic Programming* **1**:51–79.

Shoham, Y., 1986. *Reasoning About Change: Time and Causation from the Standpoint of Artificial Intelligence*. PhD thesis. Yale University, New Haven.

Stalnaker, R., 1968. A theory of conditionals. *Studies in Logical Theory*, ed. N. Rescher, pp. 98–112. Oxford: Blackwell.

Zadeh, L., 1981. PRUF—a meaning representational language for natural languages. *Fuzzy Reasoning and its Applications*, ed. E. Mamdani, B. Gaines. New York: Academic.

Zadeh, L.., 1985. Syllogistic reasoning as a basis for combination of evidence in expert systems. In *Proceedings of the Ninth International Joint Conference on Artificial Intelligence*, Los Angeles, pp. 417–19. San Mateo: Morgan Kaufmann Publishers.

13

A Survey of Automated Deduction[1]

Woody Bledsoe
University of Texas
Computer Sciences Department

Richard Hodges
Oakland, California

1 Introduction

1.1 What Is Automated Deduction?

It includes many things. A part of it involves *proving theorems by computer*, theorems like the Pythagorean theorem from plane geometry (Figure 1) or the theorem: If an equilateral triangle is inscribed in a circle, and lines are drawn from its corners to a point on the circumference, then the length of the longest such line is equal to the sum of the lengths of the others (Figure 1).

Or theorems from algebra such as:

A group for which $x^2 = e$ for each of its elements x, is commutative.
A ring for which $x^3 = x$ is commutative.

---

1 This is an enlarged version of a survey talk given by Woody Bledsoe at the Sixth National Conference on Artificial Intelligence, Seattle, Washington, July 16, 1987.

Or theorems from analysis such as the *maximum value theorem* and the *intermediate value theorems*, depicted in Figure 2:

EXAMPLE THEOREMS FROM GEOMETRY

Pythagorean Theorem:

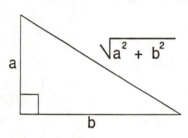
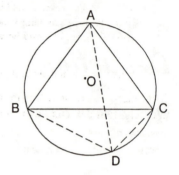

Figure 1

EXAMPLES FROM ANALYSIS

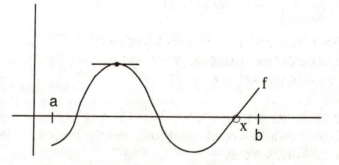

Maximum Value Theorem and Intermediate Value Theorem, for continuous functions.

Figure 2

A continuous function f defined on a closed interval $[a, b]$, attains its maximum (and minimum) on that interval.

And if $f(a) < 0$ and $f(b) > 0$, then $f(x) = 0$ for some x in $[a, b]$.

Also puzzles such as the *truthtellers and liars* one, can be solved by theorem proving. See [Lusk and Overbeek, 1985].

> On a certain island the inhabitants are partitioned into those who always tell the truth and those who always lie. I landed on the island and met three inhabitants A, B, and C. I asked A, "Are you a truthteller or a liar?" He mumbled something which I couldn't make out. I asked B what A had said. B replied, "A said he was a liar." C then volunteered, "Don't believe B, he's lying!"

> What can you tell about A, B, and C?

The halting problem theorem (Figure 3) shows how complicated these theorems can get, and others more so.

HALTING PROBLEM IS UNSOLVABLE
(Burkholder)

(1) $(Ex)[Gx \ \& \ (Ay)(Py \longrightarrow (Az)Dxyz)] \longrightarrow (Ew)[Pw \ \& \ (Ay)(Py \longrightarrow (Az)Dwyz)]$

(2) $(Aw)([Pw \ \& \ (Ay)(Py \rightarrow (Az)Dwyz)] \rightarrow (Ay)(Az)([Py \ \& \ H_2yz) \rightarrow (H_2wyz \ \& \ Owg)]$
  $\& \ [(Py \ \& \ \neg H_2yz) \longrightarrow (H_3wyz \ \& \ Owb)]))$

(3) $(Ew)[Pw \ \& \ (ay)([Py \ \& \ H_2yy) \longrightarrow (H_2wyy \ \& \ Owg)] \ \& \ [(Py \ \& \ \neg H \ yy)$
  $\longrightarrow (H_2wyy \ \& \ Owb)])] \longrightarrow (Ev)[Pv \ \& \ (Ay)([Py \ \& \ H_2yy) \longrightarrow (H_2vy \ \& \ Ovg)]$
  $\& \ [(Py \ \& \ \neg H_2yy) \longrightarrow (H_2vy \ \& \ Ovb)])]$

(4) $(Ev)[Pv \ \& \ (Ay)([Py \ \& \ H_2yy) \rightarrow (H_2vy \ \& \ Ovg)] \ \& \ [(Py \ \& \ \neg H_2yy) \rightarrow (H_2vy \ \& \ Ovb)])]$
  $\longrightarrow (Eu)[Pu \ \& \ (Ay)([(Py \ \& \ H_2yy) \longrightarrow \neg H_2uy] \longrightarrow \neg H_2uy] \ \& \ [(Py \ \& \ \neg H_2yy)$
  $\longrightarrow (H \ yy) \longrightarrow (H_2uy \ \& \ Oub)])].$

$\longrightarrow$

(5) $\neg(Ex) \ [G \ x \ \& \ (Ay) \ (Py \longrightarrow (Az) \ DxyZ)]$

Figure 3

1.2 *Facets of Automated Deduction*

What is *automated deduction*? It is a number of things. But in all cases one is *making deductions* by computer. It is often called *automated theorem proving* (ATP), or *automatic reasoning* (AR). We will use these terms interchangeably. Let me list some of the *facets* and *applications* of automated deduction. See Figure 4.

We consider *proof discovery* to be the major component of ATP, because every application of ATP uses some amount of automatic proof discovery. We will tend to concentrate on it in this talk, since we are personally interested in it, and will discuss the others only briefly, if at all. There are a number of review papers and references for each of these areas. One might add to this list: *all nonnumeric programming*, since some form of inferencing is involved in all of it.

Automatic proof checking is a very important part of AR (see, for example, [Boyer and Moore, 1982; Constable et al., 1986; Hunt, 1985; Weyhrauch, 1977]) but will be discussed only briefly here. The reader is referred to [McDonald and Suppes, 1984] for a report on using ATP in computer-aided instruction.

We will also not discuss *interactive provers*, but consider this to be one of the most important areas of ATP. See [Bledsoe and Bruell, 1973; Boyer and Moore, 1979].

APPLICATIONS OF ATP

Proof Discovery

Proof Checking: Including Computer–Aided Instruction

Interactive Provers   (Man–machine)

Logic Programming & Programming Languages

Deductive Data Bases

Program Verification & Automatic Programming

Expert–Systems Inferencing

Algebraic Manipulation   (such as Macsyma)

Proof Representation & Manipulation

Figure 4

We will discuss *logic programming* shortly. Many efforts are underway to combine logic and functional programming languages such as PROLOG and LISP, and to join this with *rapid type inheritance*, to make it easier to write AI applications, and attain greater speed. See, for example, [Ait-Kaci and Nasr, 1985].

In the near future we expect to see an increased research effort on *deductive databases*, especially for very large collections of *facts* and *rules*, written in logic, and requiring *a great deal of inferencing* to answer a query. See [Gallaire and Minker, 1978] for a review and also [Henschen et al., 1984] for an example of *compiling* database queries, to speed up retrieval.

Such a database might contain the facts about a corporation and its operating "rules." Similarly for a political situation, such as the Middle East (will country *X* cut off the oil or go to war), and for military situations. We believe that a structured knowledge base of *general* (commonsense) knowledge, such as [Lenat et al., 1986], will play a big role in these efforts.

Program verification (e.g., [Good, 1985; Boyer and Moore, 1979]) and automatic programming [Manna and Waldinger, 1985] continue to be significant application areas for ATP. Algebraic manipulation [Buchberger et al., 1983], as represented by MACSYMA [1983] and other systems, has grown to be a sizable part of AR.

Of most interest to the AI community is automatic inference associated with expert systems and related "intelligent" programs. In this conference alone there were 46 papers (out of 150) related to automatic reasoning. We expect that trend to continue, especially as AI programs are being based more on traditional logic and extensions of it. Here we could include *nonmonotonic* reasoning (e.g., circumscription) [McCarthy, 1980; Brown, 1986] truth maintenance [Doyle, 1979; de Kleer and Brown, 1984], commonsense reasoning [McCarthy, 1968; Lenat et al., 1986], qualitative reasoning, (see, for example, [de Kleer and Brown, 1984; Forbus, 1984]), Metareasoning [Genesereth et al., 1983, 1987].

1.3 *Proof Representation and Manipulation*

Another branch of automated deduction studies methods of representing and transforming proofs. Human mathematicians seem to be able to understand a proof as a whole, whereas automated deduction systems tend to have a very narrow view, centered around a single clause or a small group of clauses at any one time.

One reason for wanting to be able to manipulate proofs is to facilitate higher-level strategies for proof discovery. The method of proof by analogy is an area which needs the ability to transform proofs, to extract the abstract content of a proof, and to annotate proofs with additional information such as the "motivation" for a given step. (See Section 5.2.1.)

The internal representations used in automated deduction are often not very easy for people to understand. Many theorem provers use clausal Resolution. But putting a theorem into clauses often introduces redundancy and obscures the logical structure of the theorem and its proof. Observing that it is often much easier to understand a proof in natural deduction format, Peter Andrews and Dale Miller have developed algorithms for transforming Resolution proofs into an intermediate form called an "expansion tree" and then into a natural deduction proof [Andrews, 1981]. Amy Felty, a student of Miller, has recently developed a system to translate proofs into natural English. These systems use "Higher Order Logic" (see Section 3.3) and have automatically proven Cantor's theorem and a version of Russell's paradox.

A group of systems [Gordon et al., 1982; Nederpelt, 1980; Cardelli, 1986; Coquant and Huet, 1985; Constable, 1986; deBruijn, 1980] have been developed for representing and checking mathematical proofs using a Higher Order Logic based on the Curry-Howard isomorphism between propositions and lambda-types (see Section 3.4) These systems have also been used for verifying software and hardware [Gordon, 1987]. Proofs often can be written in a form much closer to that used by a human mathematician than by employing first-order predicate calculus and Resolution. So far, little work has been done on proof-discovery in these systems.

McAllester (MIT) has developed a theorem prover with set theory "built-in" and with a novel concept for proof guidance: The user specifies a "focus object" and the prover tries to forward chain from established facts to prove everything it can about the selected object. The prover can then search using patterns to see if anything useful has been proved. This seems potentially useful as a representation for motivation in proofs. His ONTIC has been used to proof-check the Stone Representation Theorem as well as others [McAllester, 1987].

Weyrauch [1977, 1982] has developed a system called FOL in which the syntax and reasoning rules of a deductive system can be formalized in First Order Logic (FOL). In particular, FOL can formalize its own logic. It can conduct reasoning about proofs and about its own rules of inference. New rules can be verified using the deductive capabilities of FOL and can be added declaratively to the set of metatheorems representing facts FOL knows about itself.

2 References

There have been a number of excellent *review papers* of ATP during the last few years. Perhaps the review by Loveland [1984] or [Bledsoe and Henschen, 1985] in the first issue of the *Journal of Automated Reasoning*, 1985, would be the best for the beginner. In that same issue is an extended review of AR. Those interested in the prehistory and early history of ATP should see Martin

Davis's [1983] article. Also see [Wos and Henschen, 1983]. Bill Pase, of I. P. Sharp Associates, has recently revised his 70-page bibliography of automated deduction, which is very useful for those serious about this subject [Pace, 1987].

There are a number of books and collections of important papers which are introductory to the subject. For example, [Chang and Lee, 1973; Loveland, 1978; Bibel, 1982, 1987; Wos et al., 1984a; Genesereth and Nilsson, 1987; Kowalski, 1979; Bundy, 1983; Andrews, 1986; IEEE, 1976; Wos, 1987; Boyer and Moore, 1979; Siekmann and Wrightson, 1983; Bledsoe, 1984]. Also there are chapters on ATP in various books on AI such as [Nilsson, 1980; Rich, 1983], and various journals and conference proceedings *(Journal of Automated Reasoning*, AAR Newsletter, CADE Reports, *AI Journal*, MI Series, AAAI, IJCAI, *IEEE Transactions*, *PAMI* and SSC, etc.).

Other books of related interest include Konolige [1986a] on representing the capabilities of intelligent agents with imperfect knowledge; and Smullyan's books of logic puzzles, especially [Smullyan, 1985], a good source of challenge problems for ATP systems.

3 *Brief History of Automated Deduction*

Modern ATP was born in the middle 1950s with the "Logic Machine" of Newell, Shaw, and Simon [1956]. Gelernter's "Geometry Machine" [Gelernter, 1959], followed in the late 1950s, as well as other interesting work by Hao Wang [1960], Davis and Putnam [1960] and many others (see [Davis, 1983]). But it was the advent of J. A. Robinson's *Resolution* paper [Robinson, 1965a] that forever changed this field.

Also note that Maslov's *inverse method* [Maslov, 1968] stems from the mid 1960s. Vladimir Lifschitz [1987] has recently completed an excellent paper simplifying the presentation of this powerful method.

Other proof procedures, such as the so called "Natural Deduction" provers [Wang, 1960; Bledsoe, 1975; Loveland, 1978; Bledsoe, 1977; Plaisted, 1982], model elimination, connection and mating methods [Andrews, 1981; Bibel, 1982], interconnectivity graphs [Kowalski, 1975; Sickel, 1976], semantic tableaux [Oppacher and Suen, 1986; Smullyan, 1968], and the earlier "inverse methods" of Maslov [1968], have much in common with Resolution and also suffer many of its shortcomings.

Still, we believe that the introduction of Resolution represents the single most important event in ATP so far. What is it?

3.1 *Resolution*

The basic idea of Resolution is simple and is very easy to learn. See, for example, the presentation in [Chang and Lee, 1973]. It is based upon the *modus ponens* rule, or more generally the *chain rule*. Referring to Figure 5, if the chain rule is converted to *clausal form* (by replacing an expression $x \rightarrow y$ by $(\neg x \lor y)$) then the rule is effected by cancelling the q and $\neg q$ in the upper clauses. Shown at the bottom of Figure 5 is the *resolvent rule* for first order logic, where *unification* is required; here the variable x is bound to the term a.

Figure 6 shows a Resolution proof of a simple theorem. Note that the hypotheses are converted to clausal form and the conclusion is negated. Then clauses are resolved until a contradiction, ☐, is reached.

For Propositional Logic (where no variables are to be bound), Resolution is quite simple:

Resolution Rule

1. Negate theorem

2. Put in "clausal form" (i.e., conjunctive normal form, CNF)

3. Resolve until a contradiction, ☐, is obtained

Now let us look at Resolution for First Order Logic (FOL). Figure 7 shows some expressions in FOL and a theorem. One is dealing here with quantifiers and variables. In order to prove this by Resolution we must convert it to *clausal* form (Figure 8). First each hypothesis is *skolemized* by removing the quantifiers.

RESOLVENT RULE

OD

MODES PONENS	CHAIN RULE	RESOLVENT RULE
$\dfrac{p, \quad p \rightarrow q}{q}$	$\dfrac{p \rightarrow q, \quad q \rightarrow r}{p \rightarrow r}$	$\dfrac{\neg p \lor q, \quad \neg q \lor r}{\neg p \lor r}$

$$\frac{\neg p(x) \lor q(\neg x), \quad \neg q(a) \lor r}{\neg p(a) \lor r}$$

Figure 5

EXAMPLE Resolution Proof

Theorem: $[(p \rightarrow q) \ \& \ p] \longrightarrow q$

Use CONTRADICTION.   (Clauses)

1. $\neg p \lor q$ 4. q 1, 2

2. p 5. $\square$ 3, 4

3. $\neg q$ "box"

Actually: $\left\{ \begin{array}{c} \neg p \lor q \\ p \\ \neg q \end{array} \right\} \Rightarrow \left\{ \begin{array}{c} \neg p \lor q \\ p \\ \neg q \\ q \end{array} \right\} \Rightarrow \left\{ \begin{array}{c} \neg p \lor q \\ p \\ \neg q \\ q \\ \square \end{array} \right\}$

Figure 6

In the first hypothesis, the expression is true for all x and y, so we discard the quantifiers, and remember that we can replace x and y by any term we please in the proof. We also convert the implication as before. Similarly in the next hypothesis, except that we require a skolem function. For each p, there exists a z such that Mother(z, p). It is clear that z *depends* on p, so we show that dependence by replacing z by the expression $m(p)$. The conclusion is negated (since Resolution uses Contradiction). The z remains a variable that also might be replaced with a term. Figure 9 shows the corresponding clauses and the derivation of $\square$ by Resolution. There, x, y, p, and z are variables, and *John* and m are constants. The proof goes as before except that some of the variables are *bound* in the process. These bindings are called a *substitution*. The process of determining the substitution is called *unification*. Two formulas are *unified* (made one) in the process.

For example, the pair

$P(g(x), x)$
$P(y, x0)$

FIRST ORDER LOGIC

Girl (x),   Female (x), Person (p)

THEOREM:

$\forall$x $\forall$ y [Mother (x,y) $\longrightarrow$ Female (x)] &

$\forall$p [Person (p) $\longrightarrow$ $\exists$ z Mother (z,p)] &

Person (John)

$\longrightarrow$ $\exists$ z Female (z)

Figure 7

is unified by the substitution $[x \leftarrow x0, y \leftarrow g(x0)]$ (where x and y are variables and g and $x0$ are function symbols). But the pair

$P(g(x), x)$
$P(y, h(y))$

has no unifier. Why?

The first step in trying to unify

$P(g(x), x)$
$P(y, h(y))$

yields

$P(g(x), x)$
$P(g(x), h(g(x)))$.

CLAUSES

∀ x   ∀ y [Mother (x, y) ⟶ Female (x)] &

¬ Mother (x, y)   v Female (x)

∀ p [Person (p)   ⟶ ∃ z Mother (z,p)]

¬ Person (p) v Mother (m(p), p)
Note: m(p) is a "skolem" expression

Person (John)

Person (John)

⟶   ∃ f Female (z)

¬ Female (z)

Figure 8

But we cannot finish, because x occurs in $h(g(x))$. If we tried to continue by substituting $[x \leftarrow h\,(g(x))]$ we would get into an infinite loop. We prevent this kind of error by what is called the " occurs-check" in the unification algorithm. If we don't use such occurs-check, we could "prove" nontheorems, such as

$\forall x\,\exists y\,P(y,\,x) \to \exists y\,\forall x\,P(y,\,x).$

We will see more on the *occurs-check* problem when we discuss *logic programming*.

Resolution is *complete* for first order logic; i.e., any theorem expressed in FOL can be proved by Resolution. This is an important result since FOL includes much of mathematics (indeed, can include *all* of mathematics).

However, Resolution is not a *decision procedure* for FOL, there is no guarantee that it will detect nontheorems in finite time; in fact FOL has no decision procedure. Higher Order Logic (HOL), which we will discuss shortly, has *no* complete proof procedure, let alone a decision procedure.

PROOF

1. ¬Mother (x, y)   ∨ Female (x)

2. ¬Person (p)   ∨ Mother (m(p), p)

3. Person (John)

4. ¬Female (z)

---

5. Mother (m(John), John)   3, 2, p ← John

6. Female (m(John))   5, 1, y ← John,

                                          x ← m(John)

7. ☐   4, 6 z ← m(John)

Figure 9

3.2 Completeness

Completeness is a desirable property of a proof procedure such as Resolution; we want to know what it *can* and *cannot* do before we employ it. But completeness alone is not enough. We also need *speed* as well. But Resolution—as well as other proof procedures for FOL—tend to be slow when attempting the discovery of proofs of hard theorems.

We are faced with the classic *combinatorial explosion* problem when we automatically search a *proof tree*, such as the one depicted in Figure 10a. The prover searches down along the branches looking for the *goal nodes*, indicated by the asterisks. Finding such a goal finishes the proof.

Actually, in standard Resolution, the search space is not really a tree, since branches often rejoin other branches. Linear formats for organizing Resolution search (such as SL-Resolution, Model Elimination, problem reduction) make the search more tree-like. In any case, the "tree" metaphor in the following discussion is useful for intuition.

PROOF SEARCH TREE

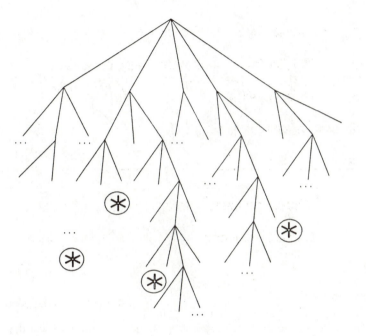

Figure 10a

The number of branches in the tree increases at least exponentially with depth. When the solution nodes lie even moderately deep, brute-force search methods quickly exhaust available resources.

Professional mathematicians have an uncanny way of excluding much of the "brush" of the tree by heading directly toward one of these solution nodes. But the computer—though a million times faster—tends to thrash hopelessly around through all the branches (using depth-first or breadth-first search methods). The *challenge of this age* for this field is to *shorten* the search time. Attempts to do so can be classified into two categories.

1. Methods that speed up the *inherent reasoning process* by

    (a) Using faster *hardware*, or by

    (b) Clever programming *tricks*, such as *clause compiling*

2. Those that *prune* the search tree.

PROOF SEARCH TREE

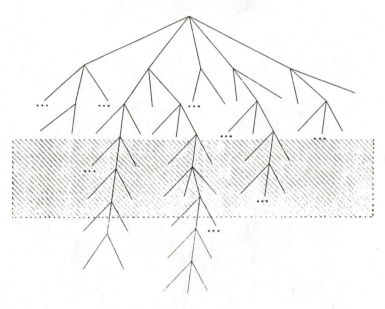

Figure 10b

The effect of the first category is to push down a few layers in the search tree (see Figure 10b). The swath indicates how a *faster* prover might *push farther down* in the tree. This may or may not help, depending, of course, on the positions of the goal nodes in the tree. For *many applications* in AI and related fields, it *does* help. A speed up of *one* or *two orders of magnitude*, that seems to be attainable by the new *clause-compiling* techniques coming from the PROLOG community, has made possible the proofs of many theorems previously unattainable by automatic methods. This is good news for many workers in AI who are beginning to use logic more extensively for *representing rules* for *expert systems*, and for entries in *logic databases*, etc.

This extended use of logic is placing a greater load on the *"inference engine"* of these systems, and these new *compiling techniques* will help greatly with that load. But it is through the *second category*, the *pruning* strategies, that we can expect satisfactory solutions for the long run. *speed alone* cannot replace the judicial use of *knowledge*. (See our recent paper, *Some thoughts on proof discovery* [Bledsoe, 1986a], for a further articulation of this argument.) There were many early attempts to *prune* the search tree. Most of these are *syntactic* in nature, applying equally well from one subfield to another. Some refinements of Resolution to speed up proof discovery are:

- Set-of-Support Resolution
- Hyper-Resolution
- SL-Resolution (= Model Elimination)
- Connection Method, Matings
- Interconnectivity Graphs
- Locking
- Dozens more.

One such method, an important one, is the *set-of-support* strategy [Wos, 1965], whereby the program works back from the desired goal, and avoids generating unmotivated lemmas that may or may not contribute to the final solution.

Another important one is called *Hyper-Resolution* [Robinson, 1965b] in which a number of Resolution steps are combined into one *larger step*, with the program keeping *only* the final resolvent and discarding the intermediate resolvents ("fragments"). (See Section 5 below.) This method has been especially powerful in the hands of the Argonne Group headed by Larry Wos. Many other pruning strategies have been tried, but these will not be reviewed here [Kowalski and Kuehner, 1971; Loveland, 1968; Andrews, 1984; Bibel, 1982; Kowalski, 1975; Sickel, 1976; . . .].

It should be noted the *ground* proofs (proofs in which no binding of variables takes place) are hardly ever difficult. It is only when we allow the *binding of variables* (i.e., the replacement of variables by other terms), through the unification process, that we encounter the combinatorial explosions that so hamper our provers. There have been developed ground provers which are enormously fast, and it is questionable whether further progress in this area is necessary.

We will return to the problem of speeding-up proof discovery shortly, but we first briefly discuss other logics and equality.

3.3 *Higher Order Logic*

In first order logic we do *not* quantify *function* symbols, *predicate* symbols, or symbols representing *higher* order objects. For example, the formula

$$\forall a \, [\forall x \, P(x) \rightarrow P(a)] \tag{1}$$

is from the first order logic because only the a and x are quantified. But the formula

$$\forall a \, \exists Q [\forall x \, P(x) \rightarrow Q(a)] \tag{2}$$

is not, because the predicate symbol Q has been quantified.[2]

Actually, (2) is an *easy theorem* for people or machines: We simply replace "*Q*" by "*P*," and "*x*" by "*a*," but it is part of Higher Order Logic (HOL), which is not even complete, let alone decidable. Inherently, HOL is *harder* than FOL. However, the methods of Unification and Resolution have been extended to HOL [Huet, 1973; Andrews, 1984] with a certain amount of success. For example, Andrew's Prover, based on the Huet Unification Algorithm has proved:

> **Cantor's Theorem**: If *N* is the set of integers, and *SN* is the set of subsets of *N*, then there is no one-to-one function from *N* to *SN*.

More difficult theorems, such as

> **Intermediate Value Theorem**: If *f* is a continuous function on a nonempty closed interval [*a*, *b*], $f(a) < 0$, and $f(b) > 0$, then $f(x) = 0$ for some *x* in [*a*, *b*]. (Using the Least Bound Axiom.)

have been proved by special purpose provers such as the one described in [Bledsoe, 1979], but that prover has limited generality. General purpose provers tend to be SLOW, especially for HOL.

3.3.1 *Propositions as Types*

An interesting approach to HOL has been developed from the so-called Curry-Howard isomorphism. This is an elegant relationship between the typed lambda-calculus and intuitionistic logic. It has been championed, primarily by Martin-Lof [1984], as a basis for abstract computer science.

Basically, the idea is that if a proposition is viewed as a type and the proof of a proposition is viewed as an object having that type, lambda conversion is formally the same as *modus ponens*. If *A* and *B* are propositions (types) and *f* is a term of type *B*, the expression

$$(\lambda (x : A) f)$$

is a function mapping the type *A* into the type *B*. The type of this function is symbolized as $A \rightarrow B$, which can be thought of as expressing the implication $A \rightarrow B$, with the meaning that given a proof *p* of *A*, we can get a proof

$$(\lambda (x) f) (p)$$

for *B*. To prove $A \rightarrow B$ means to demonstrate an object of type $A \rightarrow B$, i.e., an effective procedure for obtaining a proof of *B* from a proof of *A*.

---

2 The predicate symbol *P* is also universally quantified (implicitly) in (1) and (2), it is only when "existential" type quantifiers are used, where the quantified predicate symbol is to be replaced (bound) in the proof process, that we enter true Higher Order Logic.

This calculus is a sufficient starting point to do mathematics. It is possible to construct definitions of all the usual logical connectives (and, or, not), quantifiers, and equality (using Leibniz's definition of substitutivity of equals). See [Coquand and Huet, 1985] for an example of how this is done in one system.

The resulting logic is intuitionistic; all objects purported to exist must be constructed, and there is no law of excluded middle. However, if desired, logical connectives and quantifiers obeying the usual nonintuitionistic rules can be constructed from the intuitionistic ones.

A branch of category theory, the theory of Topoi [Goldblatt, 1979] leads naturally to the same intuitionistic logic and is a convenient abstract setting for foundational questions in this kind of logic.

Potential advantages of Curry-Howard systems for ATP include: higher order quantifiers are naturally available; we can get a lot of security in the logic from the strong typing; and there is a natural mapping between proofs and programs for constructing objects. So far the only provers using such representations are proof checkers, having very limited search capabilities.

3.4 *Other Logics*

Many sorted logic brings the idea of typed variables and terms into First Order Logic. Walther [1983] (see Section 6.9) has developed a complete many sorted extension of Resolution. Mathematical problems can often be expressed more compactly in many-sorted logic than in standard FOL. There is a significant gain in efficiency of search for proofs, since the types attached to the terms place restrictions on permissible unifications.

An example which has been widely used as an ATP benchmark is "Schubert's Steamroller" (see below). Figure 11 shows how many sorted logic can improve the proof length and input sizes for this problem, and also includes data on further improvements which are possible using Cohn's LLAMA logic [Cohn, 1987].

Schubert's Steamroller Problem

Wolves, foxes, birds, caterpillars, and snails are animals, and there are some of each of them. Also there are some grains, and grains are plants. Every animal either likes to eat all plants or all animals much smaller than itself that like to eat some plants. Caterpillars and snails are much smaller than birds, which are much smaller than foxes, which in turn are much smaller than wolves. Wolves do not like to eat foxes or grains, while birds like to eat caterpillars but not snails. Caterpillars and snails like to eat some plants. Therefore there is an animal that likes to eat a grain eating animal.

STEAMROLLER PROBLEM
STATISTICS

	FOL	Walter's logic	LLAMA
No. of clauses initially	27	12	3
No. of possible inferences	102	12	7
Length of proof	33	10	5

Figure 11

For reasoning about the commonsense world, for planning actions, and for communicating with agents (including people), it is necessary to express and reason about ideas like possibility, belief, knowledge, successiveness (in time), etc. Modal logics and temporal logics have been developed for this purpose. Proof procedures based on connection methods [Wallen, 1986] and semantic tableaux [Smullyan, 1968] have been developed.

Others, particularly Kowalski [1979], have argued that modal and temporal logics are unnecessary and that the corresponding reasoning can be formulated and carried out entirely in FOL. The *situation calculus* [McCarthy, 1963; McCarthy and Hayes, 1969; Brown, 1986] formulates actions and their effects on states in FOL. Green [1969] developed a large working system based on Resolution for performing such reasoning.

For recent work in applications of these methods, see [Konolige, 1986a, 1986b; Appelt, 1982; Moore, 1985]. An excellent textbook covering this area is [Genesereth and Nilsson, 1987].

3.5 *Equality*

An early problem, a persistent one, is that involving *equality*, the "substitution of equals." For example, the theorem

$$(a = b \land P(a)) \to P(b)$$

is rather easy, one simply substitutes a for b, or vice versa (assuming of course that "=" has its traditional meaning). But in more complex examples, like the following theorems,

A group for which $x^2 = e$, is commutative, (Hard)
A ring for which $x^3 = x$, is commutative, (Very Hard)

the proof discovery process is difficult for a computer program, because there are so many ways in which one term can be replaced by another.

The problem arises because, if $a = b$ is hypothesized, then we can replace either a by b, or b by a. This branching factor of 2, when invoked many times, leads to a serious combinatorial explosion. Paramodulation [Wos and Robinson, 1970] and E-Resolution [Morris, 1969], provided *complete* solutions to the equality problem, but brought very little to prevent the inherent explosion. Some ATP researchers have greatly tamed the problem by the use of *rewrite rules*. Called *demodulators* by Wos [Wos et al., 1967] and *reductions* by Bledsoe [1971], these procedures rewrite a formula using a set of *reducers* or *rewrite rules*. For example, if we have the rewrite rules

$$x + 0 \rightarrow x$$
$$t \in (A \cap B) \rightarrow t \in A \ \& \ t \in B$$
$$\cdots$$

we would rewrite the formula

$$f(t) \in (A(x) \cap B(x + 0))$$

as

$$f(t) \in A(x) \ \& \ f(t) \in B(x).$$

The great advantage here is that the substitution on *one-way* only. We replace "$x + 0$" by "x," but do *not* replace "x" by "$x + 0$," as might be possible by paramodulation and E-Resolution. Thus a branching factor of 2 is replaced by 1! However, the disadvantage is that such procedures are *incomplete*, some theorems cannot be proved by rewriting alone.

3.5.1 *Term Rewriting Systems*

An exciting advancement in this area was an attempt to enlarge these sets of rewrite rules to *complete* sets, the so called *complete sets of reductions*. A signal paper in this subarea was [Knuth and Bendix, 1970], that provided a set of ten rewrite rules which constitute a *complete set of reductions* (CSOR) for (noncommutative) group theory (see Figure 12). These can be used, by rewriting alone, to prove a variety of theorems in group theory. Knuth and Bendix also offered a procedure for *completing* an incomplete set, where that is possible.

This is part of a rapidly growing subfield of ATP called *term rewriting systems*, which includes work on *narrowing* [Slagle, 1974] and *unification algorithms with built-in theories* [Fay, 1979].

The first studies concerning the use of complete sets of reductions in Resolution were conducted by Dallas Lankford [1975]. They brought together the notion of complete sets of reductions with that of "narrowing" introduced by Slagle [1974].

The connection between CSORs and the study of unification algorithms became closer when independently, Peterson and Stickel [1981] and Lankford and Ballantyne [1977] used the commutative associative unification algorithm [Stickel, 1981] to extend the Knuth-Bendix completion algorithm to handle commutative associative functions. Conversely, Fay [1979] used the narrowing algorithm to generate unification algorithms for theories which could be represented by CSORs. Fay's work was extended by Hullot [1980]. The study of unification algorithms is now being actively pursued by several research groups, at SRI International [Smolka et al., 1987] and Kirchner [1986] in particular. See also [Ait-Kaci and Nivat, 1987].

COMPLETE SET OF REDUCTIONS
For a Group

KB1	$x + 0 \to x$
KB2	$0 + x \to x$
KB3	$x + (-x) \to 0$
KB4	$(-x) + x \to 0$
KB5	$(x + y) + z \to x + (y + z)$
KB6	$-(-x) \to x$
KB8	$-(x + y) \to (-y) + (-x)$
KB9	$x + ((-x) + y)) \to y$
KB10	$(-x) + (x + y) \to y$

Figure 12

A good survey of the field up to 1980 is found in [Huet and Oppen, 1980]. A more up-to-date survey on completion can be found in [Derschowitz, 1987a], and an equally recent survey on the termination of systems of reductions can be found in [Derschowitz, 1987b].

4 *Logic Programming and Clause-Compiling*

Another giant subarea of ATP is represented by the PROLOG community, or more correctly, *logic programming*. During the early 1970s Kowalski, Colmereauer, Roussel and others [Kowalski, 1974; Roussel, 1975], discovered that one could use a theorem proving system as a programming language. This is in the spirit of earlier work by Green [1969], where an *answer-clause* was used to return the list of bindings of variables, resulting from the proof of a theorem. For example, if one asserts the facts

> Father(Frank, Mary)
> Mother(Mary, Ted)
> Grandfather(x, z) ← father(x, y) & Mother(y, z),

and proves the theorem

> $\exists x$ Grandfather(x, Ted),

he can obtain the binding

> x ← Frank,

which gives an answer to the question, "Who is Ted's Grandfather?"

PROLOG is widely used as a programming language, especially in AI, and there are a number of implementations of it. The "standard" version employs ordinary Resolution, but

1. allows only Horn clauses,[3]
2. does not do the "occurs-check" during unification.

By restricting use to Horn clauses, the implementation can employ a depth-first search, which greatly simplifies the storage allocation problem, and enables high performance via *clause-compiling* (which we will discuss shortly).

---

3 A clause is Horn if it has at most one positive literal. e.g., $\neg P(x) \vee Q(x) \vee \neg R(x, y)$

There is no apparent difficulty with ignoring the occurs-check when PRO-LOG is used as programming language. But it is unsound as a theorem prover, because it would allow the unification of formulas such as

$$P(g(x), x) \ \& \ P(y, h(y)),$$

thereby (as we saw earlier), "proving" nontheorems such as

$$\forall x \ \exists y \ P(y, x) \rightarrow \exists y \ \forall x \ P(y, x)$$

It is also incomplete for FOL, because it employs a depth-first search, and is restricted to Horn clauses.[4] So why are we interested in PROLOG as a reasoning mechanism, since it is unsound and incomplete? The reason is that during the last few years David Warren (for DEC10 PROLOG) and others have used some compiling techniques (clause-compiling, or rule-compiling) to greatly speed up the process—by orders of magnitude.

Shortly we will (very) briefly describe how clause-compiling is done for PROLOG, and how that is extended to speed up proofs in full first order logic.

Our interest is in automatic deduction more than programming, so we will not report on the enormous literature in logic programming and PROLOG. Those with further interest should consult review papers such as those found in [Clark and Tarnlund, 1982].

4.1 *Clause Compiling in PROLOG*

Clause compiling is like ordinary compiling (of say LISP), in that it involves structure sharing, clever use of the stack, open coding of unification, and much more. See papers by Warren [1987] and Stickel [1986].

A key to clause-compiling is to have an unchanging set of (original) clauses which will not be enlarged during the proof. So that these can be compiled *once and for all* at the beginning, in a way that makes their use extremely fast. Additionally, there will be one goal literal which continually changes (during the proof search). These original clauses are compiled by anticipating how unification might be accomplished with each of their literals, and constructing a computer program by open coding to carry out that unification and other tasks.

This program can be written in some computer language such as C, LISP, or an abstract machine language such as Warren's WAM [Warren, 1987], and

---

4 Of course PROLOG, like any other programming language, can be used to implement a sound and complete theorem prover. What is more, Plaisted's SPRF [Plaisted, 1987] (see Section 6.11) gains much of the speed of PROLOG for ATP.

then compiled (ordinary compiling) into machine code. See [Warren, 1987; Stickel, 1986] for details.

Suppose we have the following input clauses (and others)

1. $(P \ x \ 1) \leftarrow (Q \ x \ z) \ (S \ z)$

2. $(P \ (fz) \ y) \leftarrow (R \ y \ z)$

3. . . .

The clause compiler will compile each of the predicates $P, Q, S, R, \ldots$, by constructing a LISP[5] function for each of them, and other supporting functions (not shown here).

Shown here is the function, FUN-P, which has been constructed for the predicate P.

```
(DE FUN-P (u v CONTINUATION) (GOAL)
    (PROG (z)
        (COND((UNBOUND-VARIABLE v) (ASSIGN V 1))
             ((NOT (= V 1)) (GO OUT)))
        (... Allocate, etc...)
        (... Alter CONTINUATION to include the further goal(S z))
        (Q u z CONTINUATION)
    OUT
        (COND((=(FCN-SYM u) 'f) (SETQ Z (ARG1 u)))
             (T (go OUT2)))
        (R v z CONTINUATION).
    OUT2 .... ))
```

Much has been left out, but the main idea is that when a goal literal of the form $(P \ u \ v)$ is encountered, to determine whether Clause 1 will apply to it (i.e., whether $(P \ x \ 1)$ will unify with $(P \ u \ v)$), we can ignore u since x is a variable and hence can be bound to any term; we need only check whether v is 1 or is a variable, and then accomplish the further goal $(Q \ u \ z)$.

The *continuation* parameter refers to any additional goals that were carried over from a previous call; we must add to it the subgoal $(S \ z)$ getting *continuation'* before proceeding to the goal $(Q \ u \ z)$. If $(Q \ u \ z \ continuation')$ succeeds, i.e., the goal $(Q \ u \ z)$ is accomplished plus the goals of *continuation'*, then the proof is finished; if not, then it attempts to apply Clause 2 to the goal literal $(P \ u \ v)$. This is done at the point OUT in the program.

---

5 Or a C program, etc. We have used LISP here to simplify the presentation.

Similar LISP functions are constructed by the clause-compiler for the other predicates Q, R, S, and any others that appear in the original clause set. All of these LISP functions are then compiled (traditional compiling) *to C code or machine code. Of course, as mentioned earlier, the clause-compiler could avoid* LISP altogether. But LISP offers a convenient tool for the clause-compiler and a convenience to us for explaining how this part of clause-compiling works.

4.2 *Clause-Compiling for First Order Logic*

The phenomenal speeds gotten by clause-compiling in PROLOG were not lost on the rest of the ATP community—they wanted this performance too, but could not use the results from PROLOG unless three major difficulties with it were overcome:

1.   the Horn clause restriction
2.   the depth-first search problem
3.   the occurs-check problem

Work on these problems, to bring clause-compiling (and its inherent speeds) to all of first order logic, represents some of the most exciting work in ATP right now. Some systems which extend the PROLOG compiling techniques as follows:

*   Stickel's PROLOG Technology Prover [Stickel, 1986]
*   Plaisted's Simplified Problem Reduction Format [Plaisted, 1987]
*   Loveland's Near PROLOG [Loveland, 1987]
*   Overbeek and Lusk's New Argonne Prover
*   Munich Group's PROTHEQ [Bayerl et al., 1986]

There are probably a number of others. How do these systems overcome the restriction, 1–3? Let us consider them in order.

The *Horn clause* restriction (1) was used in PROLOG to allow a linear search mechanism: once a proof-search is started it can proceed to success or failure without having to backtrack, as is necessary when using ordinary-clauses Resolution. This linear format greatly simplifies the search mechanism; one only needs a "stack" and no auxiliary clause storage; only the original clauses are retained, and they can be compiled before the proof search starts.

The way that Stickel [1986] avoids the Horn clause restriction for full Resolution is to employ a variation of Resolution called *Model Elimination* (which is essentially *SL-Resolution*),[6] which uses chains instead of clauses.

These chains act like clauses, with extra data in them which code the history of how they were constructed in the proof process. This allows a linear format similar to that used in PROLOG, but requires the addition of many contrapositives[7] of input clauses.

Plaisted avoids the Horn clause restriction by using a form of "case-splitting," which does not require contrapositives [Plaisted, 1987].

Loveland uses "multiple-head Horn clauses" e.g. $P, Q \leftarrow R$, with no contrapositives needed. His technique is similar to Model Elimination but it greatly reduces the amount of extra "history information" recorded with clauses [Loveland, 1987].

The *depth-first* search problem (2), is avoided by "iterative deepening," i.e., by repetitively searching to deeper and deeper levels of the search tree. The added cost for recomputing the top parts of the tree is minimal when the search tree is branchy, which is usually the case.

There have been two ways used for avoiding the *occurs-check* problem:

(3.i) by detecting at compile time those literals which can possibly have an occurs-check problem, e.g., $P(x, f(x))$, tagging them, and handling only them during the proof.

(3.ii) by examining the substitution resulting from any successful unification to determine if there was a problem, and rejecting substitutions with "cyclic" terms, like $x \leftarrow h(g(x))$ (Plaisted, Overbeek and Lusk).

Both methods cause a loss of speed, but not a severe one because such problems rarely occur. (e.g., it is necessary for a variable to occur twice in such a literal for it to present an occurs-check problem.)

We believe that clause-compiling will be very important for the future of ATP. These great speeds cannot be ignored. Granted that the ultimate solution is not in speed, but in the better use of knowledge to prune the search tree. Nevertheless, fast reasoning components will be important parts of future technology.

Also, compiling methods of the kind that we have described, are useful for other components of the reasoning process. For example, similar improvements in performance have been obtained for forward chaining [Forgy, 1980], rewriting

---

6 Model elimination was discovered by Loveland [1968, 1969]; it is essentially equivalent to SL-Resolution, developed independently by Kowalski and Keuhner [1971].

7 E.g., for the clause $P \leftarrow Q \wedge R$, we would add the contrapositives $\neg Q \leftarrow (\neg P \wedge R)$ *and* $\neg R \leftarrow (\neg P \wedge Q)$.

or demodulation [Boyer, 1986a], inheritance [Ait-Kaci and Nasr, 1985], and database indexing [Butler, 1986].

5 *Overview of Proof Discovery*

Now let us give an overview of (our version) of automated proof discovery. How do we classify the research that is being done and should be done?

We feel that building a program for discovering proofs is like designing an autonomous vehicle to cross the USA, say from Atlantic City to Fresno. See Figure 13. To do so one needs:

1. Fast cars;

2. Tactics: For getting from city to city;

3. Strategy: An overall plan of action.

And one needs a map.

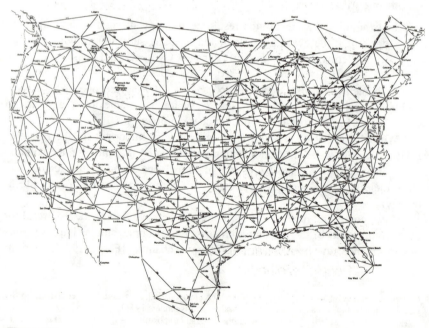

Figure 13

But note that speed alone is not enough; dashing off in more less the right direction will not lead to a distant goal without some guidance, no matter how fast the car.

One could liken this to the way that automated proof discovery is being attacked. See Figure 14. Here again we have "fast cars" (fast inference vehicles), tactics and strategy. Let us break this down into more detail.

Category 1 is easy to define, it consists of those efforts which produce *speed* of inferencing. They are *essential* to the success of ATP. Whatever else we do to prune the tree, it is absolutely necessary that we have great speeds for the "vehicle."

Examples of parallel processing in ATP, are the efforts of Overbeek et al., at Argonne National Lab [Lusk, 1982], the Munich Group [Bibel, 1987], and Waltz and Stanfield at Thinking Machines [Stanfield, 1986].

But speed alone is not enough. Again we need overall guidance that comes from tactics and strategy.

It is not so clear what to put in Category 2, tactics, but we feel that those methods which employ "large inference" steps tend to have the "city to city" flavor, as do the special purpose provers. We will discuss these in more detail shortly.

OVERVIEW OF AUTOMATED PROOF DISCOVERY

1. Fast Inference Vehicles:

> Faster Hardware, Parallel Processing
>
> Clause–Compiling (and Compiling Rewrite–rules, etc.)

2. Tactics:

> Large Inference Steps
> Semantic Methods
> Special Purpose Provers

3. Strategy:

> Analogy, Abstraction, etc.
> "People" Methods

(and a "MAP": Knowledge Base)

Figure 14

But what do we put in Category 3, strategy? Is there any method being used, that takes an overall, *global* view, that provides and uses an overall strategy? Probably not. Perhaps *analogy* comes the closest to it; whereby, the (complete) proof of one theorem acts as an *overall guide* to finding the proof of another. *Abstraction* is surely another. All such methods that are used or appear to be helpful, can be classified under the heading of "people methods," methods *routinely* used by practicing mathematicians, but hardly used at all by existing programs. And it is quite clear that there is an *absolute requirement* for a *structural knowledge base* of mathematical knowledge (a "map" if you will), if we are to attain substantial success at this field.

5.1 *Tactics*

5.1.1 *Large Inference Steps*   Under tactics, we have listed *large inference steps* (or multi-steps), where the prover tries to accomplish its goal (discover the proof) by a few large steps rather than a whole bunch of small ones.

The *key* here is to *discard* the intermediate results. Many current provers "choke" from retaining unneeded proof fragments, such as intermediate clauses.

Another key point is to identify for each such large step, the *objective* of that step. The prover then sets out to achieve that objective, and if it succeeds it retains only the objective and discards all intermediate results. In fact it discards the intermediate results even if it *fails* to achieve the desired objective. Thus it keeps only a few powerful results for further use. These results act as a kind of *subsumers* to those discarded.

Some examples of systems using large inference steps are:

- Hyper-Resolution (J. A. Robinson)
- Linked-UR-Resolution (Wos, et al.)
- Terminator (Antoniou and Ohlbach, Kaiserslautern, Germany)
- Variable Elimination (Bledsoe and Hines)
- Hyper-Chaining (Hines)
- Theory Resolution (Stickel)
- Complete Sets of Resolutions (see Section 3 [Knuth and Bendix, 1970], etc.)

Hyper-Resolution [Robinson, 1965b]. As mentioned earlier, Hyper-Resolution has been extensively used for a number of years. Figure 15a gives an example of its use, showing also the *objective*, and the discarded intermediate clause. The example shown is from propositional logic, but the method works equally well for full FOL, using unification.

Linked-UR-Resolution [Wos et al., 1984a]. Linked-UR-Resolution is somewhat like Hyper-Resolution. The idea is depicted in Figure 15b, where a *nucleus* is given which contains a *goal literal*. The *objective* is to obtain a *unit clause* by a set of resolutions, which eliminates all literals except (possibly) one, the goal literal. A variation allows the goal literal to occur in one of the satellite clauses. Also an *initiating* satellite (a unit clause) might be used to start the process. The goal literal can also be required to satisfy a given predicate P. "This allows the use of semantic criteria for guiding the proof discovery."

Terminator [Antoniou and Ohlback, 1983]. The *objective* is to try for a *unit* proof of ☐, at various points in the proof.

Variable Elimination [Bledsoe and Hines, 1980]. This procedure is designed for the field of real analysis, where the inequality predicates ≤ and < are used.

LINKED UR–RESOLUTION [Wo7]

Initiating Satelite:

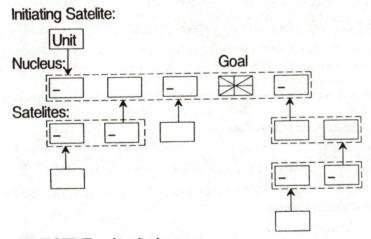

OBJECTIVE: A unit clause

Allows the use of Semantic Criteria for guiding proof discovery.
It is related to other Connection Methods.

Figure 15a

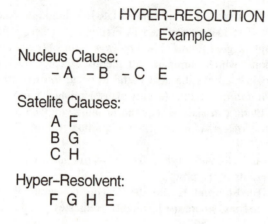

HYPER–RESOLUTION
Example

Nucleus Clause:

$-A \quad -B \quad -C \quad E$

Satelite Clauses:

A F
B G
C H

Hyper–Resolvent:

F G H E

Three Resolution steps in one.

Discard intermediate Resolvents

$F \quad -B \quad -C \quad E, \quad F \quad G \quad -C \quad E$

OBJECTIVE: Remove all negative literals from a clause

Figure 15b

Figure 16 shows an example where the variable x is eliminated from the target Clause 1 to obtain the VE-Resolvent 2. The *objective* is to remove an eligible[8] variable from a target clause.

In this example, the one large step is equivalent to six Resolution steps. The method implicitly uses the axioms of real inequality theory, including those for transitivity and interpolation.

This method has greatly helped with proofs in intermediate analysis. For example, the proof of *lim+*, a limit theorem for sums,

$$\lim_{x \to a} f(x) = l \; \& \; \lim_{x \to a} g(x) = k \; \to \; \lim_{x \to a} [f(x) + g(x)] = l + k$$

took only 13 steps instead of an estimated 100,000 or more by Resolution.

---

8 A variable x is eligible in a clause C if it does not occur within the scope of any uninterrupted function of predicate symbol.

VARIABLE ELIMINATION

Target Clause:

1. $a < x$ $x < b$ Q

      x is a variable not occurring in Q

VE–Resolvent:

2. $a < b$ Q   1, VE x

Six Resolution steps in one.

Implicitly uses the axioms of Real Inequality theory, including:

    Transivity: $x < y \wedge y \leq z \longrightarrow x < z$, etc.

    Interpolation: $u < v \longrightarrow \exists\, w\, (u < w < v)$

OBJECTIVE: Remove a variable from a clause (if eligible)

Figure 16

Hyper-Chaining [Hines, 1987]. Hyper-Chaining is an extension of variable elimination, wherein the variable x being removed does *not* need to be *eligible* in the target clause. The Hyper-Chain rule works to *make* the variable eligible (using other Hyper-rules) and then eliminates it.

Figure 17 shows Hyper-Chaining on a simple example. A much harder example, the limit of a sum theorem, lt, shown above, is proved in three steps. See Figure 18. The *objective* is to remove the variable δ from the target Clause 10, which is done in one step to obtain Clause 11. This large step also utilizes Clauses 2, 3, 5, 6, 8, 9, and is equivalent to at least 22 Resolution steps. Two more uses of Hyper-Chaining yields ☐. Figure 19 shows a few of the intermediate steps which were discarded.

Theory Resolution [Stickel, 1985]. Stickel's Theory Resolution encompasses many of the ideas from the other large inference steps methods discussed above. It incorporates a *theory* (or theories) into a Resolution theorem prover, thereby making it unnecessary to resolve directly upon the axioms of that theory. Two or more clauses are resolved *with respect* to that theory. Intermediate results are discarded.

HYPER–CHAINING
Example

Target Clause:

$$1. \quad a < x \qquad x < b \qquad f(x) \le c$$

x is a variable, not occuring in a, b, or c

Supporting Clauses:

$$2. \quad d \le f(y)$$

Hyper–Chain Resolvent:

$$3. \quad a < b \qquad d \le c \qquad\qquad 1, 2 \qquad\qquad x$$

OBJECTIVE: Remove a variable from a clause.

USES: Variable Elimination, Chaining, . . .

Figure 17

Hyper-Chaining Rule
Proving Sum-of-Limits Theorem

1. $0 < \delta'_{\varepsilon'}$ $\varepsilon' \le 0$
2. $\delta'_{\varepsilon'} + x' < x_0$ $\delta'_{\varepsilon'} + x_0 < x'$ $(f x_0) \le (f x') + \varepsilon'$ $\varepsilon' \le 0$
3. $\delta'_{\varepsilon'} + x' < x_0$ $\delta'_{\varepsilon'} + x_0 < x'$ $(f x') \le (f x_0) + \varepsilon'$ $\varepsilon' \le 0$
4. $0 < \delta''_{\varepsilon''}$ $\varepsilon'' \le 0$
5. $\delta''_{\varepsilon''} + x'' < x_0$ $\delta''_{\varepsilon''} + x_0 < x''$ $(g x'') \le (g x_0) + \varepsilon''$ $\varepsilon'' \le 0$
6. $\delta''_{\varepsilon''} + x'' < x_0$ $\delta''_{\varepsilon''} + x_0 < x''$ $(g x_0) \le (g x'') + \varepsilon''$ $\varepsilon'' \le 0$
7. $0 < \varepsilon_0$
8. $x_0 \le x_\delta + \delta$ $\delta \le 0$
9. $x_\delta \le x_0 + \delta$ $\delta \le 0$
10. $\varepsilon_0 + (f x_0) + (g x_0) < (f x_\delta) + (g x_\delta)$
    $(f x_\delta) + (g x_\delta) + \varepsilon_0 < (f x_0) + (g x_0)$
    $\delta \le 0$

(Hyper-Chain 10 [δ]: 3, 2, 6, 5, 9, 9, 8, 8)

11. $\varepsilon_0 < \varepsilon' + \varepsilon''$ $\delta' \le 0$ $\varepsilon' \le 0 \quad \delta''_{\varepsilon''} \le 0$ $\varepsilon'' \le 0$
    (Hyper-Chain 11 [ε']: 1)
12. $\varepsilon_0 < \varepsilon''$ $\delta''_{\varepsilon''} \le 0$ $\varepsilon'' \le 0$
    (Hyper-Chain 12 [ε']: 4)
13. □.

Figure 18

discarded

(Chaining 10 3)
$(g\, x_0) + \varepsilon_0 < (g\, x_\delta) + \varepsilon'$ $\quad (f\, x_\delta) + (g\, x_\delta) + \varepsilon_0 < (f\, x_0) + (g\, x_0)$ $\qquad \delta \le 0$
$\delta'_{\varepsilon''} + x_\delta < x_0 \quad \delta'_{\varepsilon'} + x_0 < x_\delta \quad \varepsilon' \le 0$

(Chaining ... 2)
$(g\, x_0) + \varepsilon_0 < (g\, x_\delta) + \varepsilon'$ $\quad (g\, x_\delta) + \varepsilon_0 < (g\, x_0) + \varepsilon'$ $\qquad\qquad \delta \le 0$
$\delta'_{\varepsilon'} + x_\delta < x_0 \quad \delta'_{\varepsilon'} + x_0 < x_\delta \quad \varepsilon' \le 0$

(Chaining ... 6)
$(g\, x_0) + \varepsilon_0 < (g\, x_\delta) + \varepsilon'$ $\quad\quad \varepsilon_0 < \varepsilon' + \varepsilon''$ $\qquad\qquad\qquad\qquad \delta \le 0$
$\delta'_{\varepsilon'} + x_\delta < x_0 \quad \delta'_{\varepsilon'} + x_0 < x_\delta \quad \varepsilon' \le 0 \quad \delta''_{\varepsilon''} + x_\delta < x_0 \quad \delta''_{\varepsilon''} + x_0 < x_\delta \quad \varepsilon'' \le 0$

(Chaining ... 5)
$\varepsilon_0 < \varepsilon' + \varepsilon''$ $\qquad\qquad\qquad\qquad\qquad\qquad\qquad\qquad\qquad \delta \le 0$
$\delta'_{\varepsilon'} + x_\delta < x_0 \quad \delta'_{\varepsilon'} + x_0 < x_\delta \quad \varepsilon' \le 0 \quad \delta''_{\varepsilon''} + x_\delta < x_0 \quad \delta''_{\varepsilon''} + x_0 < x_\delta \quad \varepsilon'' \le 0$

(Chaining ... 9)
$\varepsilon_0 < \varepsilon' + \varepsilon''$ $\qquad\qquad\qquad\qquad\qquad\qquad\qquad\qquad\qquad \delta \le 0$
$\delta'_{\varepsilon'} + x_\delta < x_0 \quad \delta'_{\varepsilon'} < \delta \quad\quad \varepsilon' \le 0 \quad \delta''_{\varepsilon''} + x_\delta < x_0 \quad \delta''_{\varepsilon''} + x_0 < x_\delta \quad \varepsilon'' \le 0$

(Chaining ... 9)
$\varepsilon_0 < \varepsilon' + \varepsilon''$ $\qquad\qquad\qquad\qquad\qquad\qquad\qquad\qquad\qquad \delta \le 0$
$\delta'_{\varepsilon'} + x_\delta < x_0 \quad \delta'_{\varepsilon'} < \delta \quad\quad \varepsilon' \le 0 \quad \delta''_{\varepsilon''} + x_\delta < x_0 \quad \delta''_{\varepsilon''} < \delta \quad\quad \varepsilon'' \le 0$

(Chaining ... 8)
$\varepsilon_0 < \varepsilon' + \varepsilon''$ $\qquad\qquad\qquad\qquad\qquad\qquad\qquad\qquad\qquad \delta \le 0$
$\delta'_{\varepsilon'} < \delta \qquad\qquad\qquad\qquad \varepsilon' \le 0 \quad \delta''_{\varepsilon''} + x_\delta < x_0 \quad \delta''_{\varepsilon''} < \delta \quad\quad \varepsilon'' \le 0$

(Chaining ... 8) [before variable elimination of δ]
$\varepsilon_0 < \varepsilon' + \varepsilon''$ $\qquad\qquad\qquad\qquad \delta \le 0$
$\delta'_{\varepsilon'} < \delta \qquad\qquad\qquad\qquad \varepsilon' \le 0 \quad \delta''_{\varepsilon''} < \delta \qquad\qquad\qquad \varepsilon'' \le 0$

11. $\varepsilon_0 < \varepsilon' + \varepsilon'' \quad \delta'_{\varepsilon'} \le 0 \qquad\qquad \varepsilon' \le 0 \quad \delta''_{\varepsilon''} \le 0 \qquad\qquad\qquad\qquad \varepsilon'' \le 0$

Figure 19

Figure 20 shows two simple examples from taxonomic theory and inequality theory. See [Stickel, 1985] for other examples, especially for useful applications in AI. Figure 21 lists some of the other work that resembles theory Resolution.

Complete Sets of Reductions [Knuth and Bendix, 1970, etc.]. See Section 3. The *objective* is to reduce a target formula (e.g., clause) as far as possible by applying to it a (complete) set of rewrite rules.

THEORY RESOLUTION EXAMPLES

1. Taxonomic Theory:
    1. Boy(x) $\longrightarrow$ Person(x)
    6. NoDaughter(x) & Child(x,y) $\longrightarrow$ Boy(y)

    Resolve: 11. Child(Chris, sk2) with
       10. NoDaughter(Chris) to get
       _____

    13. Boy(sk2)   in one step.

2. Inequality Theory:

    1. $\neg (x < x)$
    2. $x < y$ & $y < z \longrightarrow x < z$
    . . . .

    Resolve: 6. $a < b$,   7. $b < c$,   & 8. $\neg(a < c)$
       to get 9. $\square$

Figure 20

OTHER WORK RESEMBLING THEORY RESOLUTION

Hyperresolution   (J. A. Robinson) [Ro65A]

Z–resolution   (Dixon) [Dix73]

U–generalized resolution   (Harrison and Rubin)   [HR]

E–resolution   (J. Morris) [Mo69]

Linked inference Principle   (Wos, et al)   [Wo84]

General Inequality Prover   (Bledsoe and Hines)   [BH80]
   Variable Elimination
   Shielding Term Removal
   Attached ground Prover

Figure 21

5.1.2 *Semantic Methods* One of the most characteristic methods employed by people is to use semantics to guide proof; A mathematician knows what his symbols mean (for example, he knows that x is a real number when doing analysis). He also knows many examples of predicatively defined structures (such as groups, continuous functions, etc.). He uses this knowledge in at least two ways: (1) by extending known examples (closely related to analogy; see Section 5.2.1 below); and (2) by not attempting to prove intermediate goals for which he has a counterexample.

Method 2, checking for reasonableness seems to be extremely powerful—it probably accounts for a major portion of the mental effort used by human mathematicians. Several researchers have attempted to apply this principle with varying success ([Gelernter 1959; Ballantyne and Bledsoe, 1982; Bledsoe, 1983; Wang, 1985] and Section 6.3 below).

It appears to be quite challenging both to represent and to access the large variety of examples the human has available.

5.1.3 *Special Purpose Provers* We list here areas for which a few special purpose provers have been developed, and which are classified under "tactics."

- Inequalities—Ground [Nelson and Oppen, 1978; Shostak, 1977, 1979; Bundy, 1983; Sacks, 1987]
- Inequalities—General [Bledsoe and Hines, 1980; Bledsoe et al., 1985; Hodes, 1972]
- Geometry (Wu and Chou, see this survey, Section 6)
- Nonstandard Analysis [Ballantyne, 1982]
- Algebraic Manipulation [MACSYMA, 1983]
- Equality Subsystems

5.2 *Strategy*

5.2.1 *Analogy* Analogy is the heart and soul of intelligent behavior. We do very little that is absolutely new. Somehow intelligent machines (including reasoners) must make use of analogy, but success with it has been limited, so far. It is closely related to the field of *machine learning* [Michalski et al., 1983, 1986].

There have been a number of AI researchers working on analogy, including Winston, Carbonell, Gentner, Greiner, Russell, and others. I will not review all of that literature here. A good review, with an extensive set of references, is given by Hall [1985].

There are many aspects of analogy, but we are concerned here only with the situation where the *solution of one problem* is used as *guide* to the solution of another, or the proof of one theorem as guide to the proof of another.

A signal paper of this sort, is that of Bob Kling [1971], in which he used the proof of a theorem in Group Theory to guide the search for an analogous proof in Ring Theory.

Figure 22 depicts this idea. The *guiding* proof proposes actions to the prover. If the proposed action fails, then the prover must somehow recover, to get the process back on track. Also a *fetching* mechanism is needed to automatically select, from a database, proofs that might be used as a guide to the current endeavor.

An example of this is an analogy prover based on Resolution and Chaining [Brock et al., 1986], which has used the proof of *lim+* as a guide for proving *lim**. See Figure 23. Since the proof of *lim** makes some major detours from that of *lim+*, it was necessary to rely on its "expert system" component for recovery from failed actions, and to also rely on its stand-alone proving capability. See [Brock et al., 1986] for details. This same prover handled other pairs of theorems, including those depicted in Figure 24, and has been extended and converted to a *natural deduction format* [Brock et al., 1987], which we feel will be better able to handle more complex proofs, especially where *parts of proofs* are needed as guides.

ANALOGY FORMAT

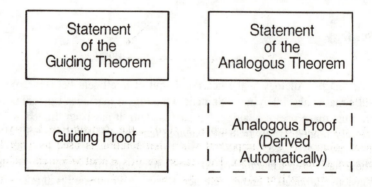

Figure 22

AN EXAMPLE

LIM +

$$\lim_{x \to a} f(x) = l \ \land \ \lim_{x \to a} g(x) = k \ \longrightarrow \ \lim_{x \to a} [f(x) + g(x)] = l + k$$

LIM*

$$\lim_{x \to a} f(x) = l \ \land \ \lim_{x \to a} g(x) = k \ \longrightarrow \ \lim_{x \to a} [f(x) \cdot g(x)] = l \cdot k$$

Figure 23

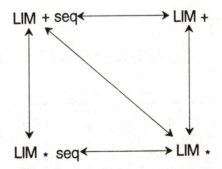

Figure 24

As was pointed out by Carbonell [1983], the *derivational history* of a problem solution is very important when that solution is used as a guide to solving an analogous problem. The reason for this is that when an analogous action fails, the problem solver needs to "know" what was the *intended goal* of the action, so that it can try to attain that goal by another action (through analogy, or by stand-alone methods). Such a derivations history provides for *annotating* a proof, with *motivational* information.

Another reason for the natural deduction format, is that subgoals of the proof can be treated in a hierarchical way. Thus, in Figure 25, suppose the hierarchical structure represents the *proposed* proof of a new theorem (as proposed by a guiding proof). Now if, for example, goal G23 fails, then the prover can execute the following strategy:

1. Fetch another guiding proof and try to apply it to G23.

2. If step 1 fails, try to prove G23 by a stand-alone prover.

3. If step 2 fails, fail the goal, backtrack and try steps 1–2 on goal G2.

Such a hierarchical structure helps make use of the derivational history (annotated proof) that is needed. (Other useful information could also be included in the derivational history.)

A problem with this is that one must collect and store this additional information (i.e., not just proofs, but annotated proofs) if it is to be used to guide new proof searches.

A HIERARCHICAL PROOF

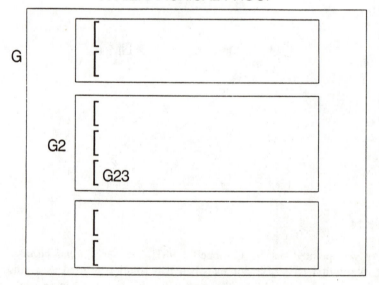

Figure 25

Some possible mechanisms for these annotated proofs are:

- Expansion Trees (Andrews, Miller, Section 1)
- Proof Parsers (Simon, Section 6.9.2)
- Requirement Graphs [Bledsoe, 1986a]
- Multi-step Rules (Hines, Section 5.1.1)
- Other formal representations (Section 1)

We believe that in the long term a large structured knowledge base will be needed, such as CYC, the commonsense knowledge base being built by Doug Lenat and his team at MCC (Microelectronics and Computer Technology Corporation) [Lenat et al., 1986; Lenat and Feigenbaum, 1987]. See also [Hobbs and Moore, 1985]. Indeed, analogy plays a central role in the building and use of CYC.

5.2.2 *Abstraction* The idea here is to prove an abstraction of a theorem, as a subgoal, and use that proof as a guide for proving the theorem itself. For example, one could abstract a formula $P(x, y)$ by suppressing the second argument and retaining only $P(x)$.

Such an idea was first introduced by Newell, Shaw, and Simon [1956], but the best work in this area is by Plaisted [1981, 1982], in which he suggests and uses a number of kinds of abstraction, and uses a number of layers of abstraction.

5.2.3 *Other "People" Methods* We list here some other methods in addition to analogy and abstraction, that are extensively used by professional mathematicians, with some references to machine implementation:

- Generating and using examples in proof discovery [Ballantyne and Bledsoe, 1982; Bledsoe, 1983]
- Using counter-examples to prune search trees [Gelernter, 1959; Ballantyne and Bledsoe, 1982] (See Section 5.1.2)
- Automatic conjecturing of lemmas and subgoals
- Automatic fetching of useful lemmas and definitions from a large knowledge base
- Agenda mechanisms for controlling the proof search [Tyson, 1981]
- Higher-level reasoning, Metareasoning [Genesereth, 1983], Higher Order Logic [Andrews et al., 1984]

6 Contemporary Provers, Centers, People

We describe here the work of a few groups and individuals conducting ATP research. Some of the efforts of others are described in other parts of this survey. This list is by no means complete, nor is it ordered by importance. For example, much of the work in expert systems is not included, as well as the work in PROLOG and commonsense reasoning. See also [Pastre, 1987]. See [Lusk and Overbeek, 1988] pp. 735–775, for abstracts of other prover systems.

6.1 Argonne Laboratory Theorem Provers, L. Wos, E. Lusk, R. Overbeek, et al., [Wos et al., 1984a; Wos, 1987]

Argonne is one of the most prolific center for ATP research in the world. Researchers there have implemented a series of systems including AURA [Wos, 1981] and ITP [Lusk, 1984]. Currently, [Butler, 1986] they are implementing a new system aimed largely at getting an increase of speed (> 100 times) compared to ITP. This system will use implementation techniques from PROLOG (e.g., clause compiling), multiprocessors, associative-commutative unification, and database indexing techniques (for clause retrieval). McCune also has implemented an interactive Resolution proof checker. With Boyer, this system was used to prove some basic mathematical theorems from Gödel's axiomatization of set theory [Boyer et al., 1986b].

The Argonne group has used ITP extensively in ATP research, proving many theorems, verifying software and hardware, solving word problems using ATP methods (AAR newsletter often reports examples of this work), and solving open questions in mathematics. They have distributed ITP to over 200 sites (it is written in Pascal for portability).

The basic technique is clausal Resolution with set-of-support, paramodulation, demodulation, and subsumption (all optional). Elaborate data structures are used to permit full structure-sharing for terms and literals (only one copy of each unique object is kept). Indexing techniques allow efficient access to terms which might unify with a given term. A complex evaluation function is used for prioritizing the next Resolution step. A "user friendly" interface is provided for interactive or batch use.

6.2 KLAUS Automated Deduction system (originally called CG5): Mark Stickel (SRI) [Stickel, 1985, 1986, 1986a]

This large system implements a number of techniques of ATP. The basis is a connection graph encoding possible Resolution steps between nonclausal first-order formulae. Special techniques include:

- Control of inference direction (a formula may be restricted to forward or backward chaining);

- Theory Resolution [Stickel, 1985] which increases efficiency by allowing a single Resolution step to incorporate a whole "theory" such as rewriting (demodulation), associative-commutative unification, many-sorted unification, taxonomic hierarchies, etc. (See Section 5.11);

- a Knuth-Bendix algorithm is provided for completion of sets of rewrite rules;

- a priority control mechanism employing evaluation function;

- a PROLOG Technology Theorem Prover (PTTP) component. Using Loveland's Model Elimination style of PROLOG-like linear search, PTTP compiles each clause into LISP functions which carry out the search corresponding to that clause. Iterative deepening is the search strategy. Occurs-check is used except in cases where it can be determined that it is necessary (see Section 4.2).

Stickel has proved a good collection of standard ATP test theorems and theorems from mathematicians.

6.3 *Kaiserslautern: N. Eisenger, H. J. Ohlbach, J. Siekmann, Universitat Kaiserslautern*

The Margraf Karl Refutation Prover (MKRP) [Blasjus et al., 1981, 1984] is a powerful system developed over many years at Kaiserslautern and Karlsruhe. It uses connection graphs, due originally to Kowalski [1975]. Each possible inference step (Resolution, paramodulation, factoring) in the clause set is represented as a link in a graph. After performing a chain of inference steps, it is often possible to "reduce" the graph, removing irrelevant and redundant links [Ohlback, 1987]. This is the source of efficiency of the algorithm, but it is also the source of a problem: there is no completeness theorem for connection-graph Resolution with inference restriction strategies typically used (In practice, this does not seem to be a problem).

Unification in MKRP is many-sorted [Walther, 1983] (see Section 3.4). Further research on unification theory promises to add the capabilities for handling equational theories and structured sorts.

An important technique in MKRP is the "terminator module" [Antoniou and Ohlback, 1983] which quickly detects situations where the refutation of a set of clauses can be completed immediately. Extensive input and output translation facilities are provided.

The Kaiserslautern group is currently working on a successor system called HADES (Highly Automated Deduction System). Among other features, it attempts to incorporate higher-level links as atomic inference steps in the connection graph. They aim to encode and prove all theorems in a standard textbook on semigroups and automata.

6.4 *Munich: W. Bibel* [9]

The Munich group has implemented as a project within ESPRIT, a PROLOG-like theorem prover called PROTHEQ based on Bibel's connection method [Bibel, 1982]. Special hardware including associative memory for accessing connections and highly parallel multiprocessing is under development.

Available input preprocessing includes translation to clausal form. Lemmas are generated and retained. Depth bound search is used. The system is complete for first order logic.

Special reductions of the clause set [Bibel et al., 1987] are used for efficiency; for example, Schubert's Steamroller is proved in 7 steps.

6.5 *University of North Carolina: David Plaisted*

Plaisted's Simplified Problem Reduction Format prover (SPRF) [Plaisted, 1982, 1987] is written in PROLOG and obtains efficiency by encoding first-order formulae as PROLOG clauses. A special splitting rule is used for non-Horn clauses for completeness. Contrapositives of the input clauses are not required, but help in some cases. Rewrite rules can also be given and Knuth-Bendix completion is available.

The search strategy is depth-limited with iterative deepening. Solutions to subgoals are cached.

The code is noteworthy for its conciseness, about 15 pages of PROLOG. Speed is competitive with major Resolution based provers such as ITP, Stickel, etc.

6.5.1 *Greenbaum* The Illinois prover was written by S. Greenbaum [1986; Greenbaum and Plaisted, 1986] as a test-bed for Plaisted's abstraction methods [Plaisted, 1981]. It became a general purpose prover of considerable power, employing many interesting implementation techniques.

A special refinement of locking Resolution and unit preference is used which simulates backwards and forward chaining. Complex data structures are used for structure sharing and indexing speed.

The aim is uniformly good performance with minimal user guidance. Schubert's Steamroller is obtained in about 1 minute on a VAX 11/780.

---

9 Bibel is now at the University of British Columbia.

6.6 *Edinburgh: A. J. Milner, M. J. Gordon, et al.*

Logic for Computable Functions (LCF) [Gordon et al., 1982] is a large system for verifying properties of computable functions defined in typed lambda calculus. It is efficiently implemented in ML [Cardelli, 1982].

LCF has been used to verify thousands of standard mathematical theorems. It has recently been enhanced by Larry Paulson to include higher order deduction [Paulson, 1986].

6.7 *Boyer-Moore Prover: University of Texas [Boyer and Moore, 1979]*

This is a large system for verifying properties of recursive functions defined by lambda expressions in "pure LISP." Structural induction on the size of the input is used, with many heuristics available.

The prover has been implemented in several dialects of LISP and is widely distributed, referenced and used by others. Applications, some of commercial importance, have included program verification [Boyer and Moore, 1981], hardware verification [Hunt 1986; Borrione, 1987], verification of compilers, and verification of the proofs of many theorems in mathematics and meta-mathematics including the uniqueness of prime factorization for natural numbers, Wilson's Theorem [Rusinoff, 1985], The Church-Rosser theorem for pure lambda calculus, and Gödel's Incompleteness Theorem [Shankar, 1986, 1987].

One of the commendable features of this prover is its ability to automatically carry out the proof of a theorem when given the necessary lemmas by the user. Another is its ability to automatically construct a *generalized* induction hypothesis when the obvious one does not suffice.

Boyer has also done important work on compiling rewrite rules [Boyer, 1986a].

6.8 *The Wu-Chou Geometry Provers*

An interesting proof procedure for theorems in geometry has been given by the Chinese mathematician, Wen-Tsun Wu [1978, 1984]. Shang-Ching Chou (University of Texas) has extended and refined that work and used his implementation to prove a number of difficult theorems in plane geometry (about 2000 Theorems), some of which are new [Chou, 1985, 1986, 1987; Chou and Schelter, 1986].

The procedure is as follows:

Transform the Hypotheses and Conclusion of a theorem in Geometry to sets of Algebraic equations. Show that the conclusion follows from the hypotheses by performing a series of "divisions" (somewhat like Matrix operations). This requires factoring of polynomials over algebraic extensions of fields of rational functions (very difficult in some cases).

The method does not apply to all areas of plane geometry, only to cases where hy potheses and conclusions can be expressed as equalities, not inequalities. The general method can be applied to other areas, such as Differential Geometry. Figure 26 shows drawings from two examples from [Chou, 1987], the first of which was given in Section 1 of this survey.

6.9 *Bledsoe, et al., (University of Texas and MCC)*

Figure 27 shows some provers from this group. See also [Bledsoe, 1984, 1986a].

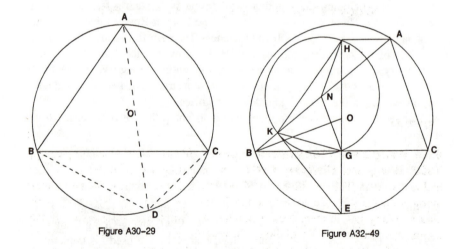

EXAMPLES USING THE WU–CHOU PROVER

Figure A30–29   Figure A32–49

Figure 26

BLEDSOE, et al (UTexas and MCC)

IMPLY – Natural Deduction Style Prover [Bl75]
      – Regular and Interactive Versions

General Inequality Prover [Bl84]
      – Proofs in Analysis

Wang's Hierarchical Prover [WaT87]

Building–in Multistep Axiom Rules – Larry Hines

Gazing – Plummer (U. Edinburgh)

Proof Checking in Number Theory – Don Simon

Analogy Prover – Brock, Cooper, and Pierce

Figure 27

6.9.1 Wang's SHP (Semantically-guided Hierarchical Prover) [Wang, 1985; Wang and Bledsoe, 1987]

An interesting aspect of SHP is the hierarchical format. This is similar to SL-Resolution, recording extra information along with each clause to record the history of subgoals which led to the clause. Wang has implemented a number of completeness-preserving refinements (restrictions on Resolution) allowed by this implementation. For example, redundant subgoals can be avoided, certain forms of subsumption can be checked quickly, etc.

A number of heuristic methods for assigning priority to subgoals are available, and a user interface allows control of parameters affecting these heuristics.

Another goal of Wang's prover was to provide a base for semantic guidance to the proof process. A partial model of the axioms of the input theorem may be provided by the user. The user specifies a finite set of (ground) terms from the Herbrand universe and provides effective procedures for evaluating predicates built on these terms. Candidate subgoals are only attempted if they are acceptable in the model.

Several difficult theorems have been proved, such as IMV (a first-order form of the intermediate value theorem).

6.9.2 *Proof Checking Number Theory: Don Simon* This system accepts a proof in its natural language form (Figure 28) exactly as it is written by the mathematician.[10] The proof is then parsed: First the sentences are parsed, then the whole proof (see Figure 29, 30), using a proof grammar. This enables the deduction component to verify the statements in the proof. A powerful reducer for number theory [Simon, 1984] is used.

ELEMENTARY THEORY OF NUMBERS – W. J. Leveque

THEOREM 1–1.   If a is positive and b is arbitrary, there is exactly one pair of integers q, r such that the conditions

$$b = qa + r, \quad 0 \quad \le r < a, \qquad (6)$$

hold.

Proof: First, we show that (6) has at least one solution.

OMITTED

To show the uniqueness of q and r, assume that q' and r' also are integers such that

$$b = q'a + r', \quad 0 \quad \le r' < a.$$

Then if q' < q, we have

$$b - q'a = r' \ge b - (q - 1) a = r + a \ge a,$$

and this contradicts the inequality r' < a. Hence q' $\ge$ q.

Similarly, we show that q $\ge$ q'. Therefore q = q', and consequently r = r'. ▲

Figure 28

10 The system is currently working on proofs from LeVeque's book on Numbered Theory [LeVeque, 1962]

```
PROVE (UNQ (Q,R) (B = Q*A+R & 0 <= R & R < A))
|-TO
|-SHOW
|-UNIQUENESS
|-IMPLICITLY-SUPPOSE (B = Q*A+R & 0 <= R & R < A)
|-SUPPOSE (B = Q1*A+R1 & 0 <= R1 & R1 < A)
| |-ASSUME
| |-THAT
| |-(FORMULA (B = Q1*A+R1 & 0 <= R1 & R1 < A))
| |-BREAK
|-PROVE (Q = Q1 & R = R1)
  |-PROVE Q = Q1
  | |-PROVE (Q1 >= Q & Q >= Q1)
| | |-PROVE Q1 >= Q
  | | | |-SUPPOSE Q1 < Q
  | | | |-THEN
  | | | |-IF
  | | | |-(FORMULA (Q1 < Q))
  | | | |-CONTRADICTION
  | | | |-PROVE R1 >= A
  | | | | |-WE
  | | | | |-HAVE
  | | | | |-(FORMULA (B-Q1*A = R1 & R1 >= B-(Q-1)*A
  | | | | |     & B-(Q-1)*A = R+A & R+A >= A))
  | | | | |-DEDUCE B-Q1*A = R1
  | | | | |-DEDUCE B-Q1*A >= B-(Q-1)*A
```

Figure 29

All proofs in Chapters 1 and 2 of LeVeque's book are in the process of being proof checked [Simon, 1988].

6.9.3 *Building-In Multi-step Axiom Rules: Hines [1986, 1987]* This system compiles multi-step actions into a single rule, thereby attaining higher-level objectives. Interim results are discarded.

Examples of these are the VE rule and Hyper-Chaining rules described in Section 5.1 above. Each rules has restricted entry points, and other restrictions on their use. Most rules will not apply, but when one does, it can give sizable results. They are somewhat like expert systems rules in that respect. The rules are built up in a hierarchical way, some rules are subparts of others.

```
| | | | | |-DEDUCE B-(Q-1)*A = R+A
| | | | | |-DEDUCE R+A >= A
| | | | | |-AND
| | | | | |-THIS
| | | | | |-CONTRADICTS
| | | | | |-(FORMULA (R1 < A))
| | | | | |-DEDUCE R1 < A
| | | | | |-DEDUCE R1 >= A <=> NOT(R1 < A)
| | | | | |-BREAK
| | | | |-HENCE
| | | | |-(FORMULA (Q1 >= Q))
| | | | |-DEDUCE Q1 < Q <=> NOT(Q1 >= Q)
| | | |-BREAK
| | | |-PROVE Q >= Q1
| |  |-SIMILARLY
| |  |-WE
| |  |-SHOW
| |  |-(FORMULA (Q >= Q1))
| |-BREAK
| |-THEREFORE
| |-(FORMULA (Q = Q1))
| |-DEDUCE (Q1 >= Q & Q >= Q1) => Q = Q1
|-AND
|-CONSEQUENTLY
|-(FORMULA (R = R1))
|-BREAK
|-DEDUCE Q = Q1 => R = R1
```

Figure 30

6.9.4 *Gazing: Dave Plummer [1987]* Plummer's system, VOYER, is a natural-deduction style prover, which uses the concept of *gazing* to control the use of rewrite rules. Abstractions of rules are used, stored in a concept hierarchy graph, to facilitate the proper acquisition and use[11].

---

11 Plummer, a visitor at the University of Texas, finished his Ph.D. thesis under Bundy at Edinburgh.

7 *Concluding Remarks*

Logic is emerging as a foundation for AI and all of computer science. The consequence of this is that some form of *automatic reasoning* is a *requirement* for most AI programs. Much of the research in ATP over the last thirty years is applicable to this need.

As these programs grow more complex, the corresponding inference problems will become more difficult, comparable in difficulty to the proof substantial theorems in mathematics.

We have reviewed the current research on automated reasoning and given a proposed classification of that work. We note that some research areas, such as *clause-compiling* and *parallel processing*, are very exciting, and this is rightly so. But we wonder whether these efforts on *fast implementation*, which are very important in their own right, might divert us from the even more important areas (in the long run) of *tactics* and *strategy*.

Under tactics, we are especially hopeful about the work on *larger-inference-steps*, and the work on special purpose systems such as those for the use of rewrite rules.

We believe that more *large-scale experiments* are needed, wherein researchers exercise their provers on worthwhile examples, rather than play with toy problems and/or a couple of harder problems (such as the Steamroller problem or the Intermediate Value Theorem).

What about strategy? Are we to soon attain "over all" strategies for our provers? There has been some promising work on analogy and machine learning; a little on conjecturing, abstractions, and using examples to guide proof discovery, but not much else.

We feel that fundamental progress will require advances in representing and accessing the knowledge used by human mathematicians. This knowledge includes examples, rules, heuristics, and motivations, in addition to the more commonly recognized declarative facts represented by axioms and lemmas. The experiments we have reported on demonstrate simplified approaches to representing one or more forms of mathematical knowledge, but the realization of an integrated truly powerful system remains for the future.

References

Ait-Kaci, H. and Nasr, R., 1985. LOGIN: A logic programming language with built-in inheritance. Technical Report MCC-AI-068-85, Microelectronics and Computer Technology Corporation, Austin, Texas. Also to appear in *Journal of Logic Programming*.

Ait-Kaci, H. and Smolka, G., 1987. *Feature Unification*.

Ait-Kaci, H. and Nivat, M., ed., 1987. *Preliminary Proceedings of CREAS Workshop*, Lakeway, Texas. Also forthcoming book: *Resolution of Equations in Algebraic Structures*, Academic Press, 1988.

Andrews, P. B., 1980. Transforming matings into natural deduction proofs. In *Proceedings of the Fifth International Conference on Automated Deduction*, Les Arcs, France. Bibel and Kowalski, ed. *Lecture Notes in Computer Science* **87**:281–292. Springer-Verlag, New York.

Andrews, P. B., 1981. Theorem proving via general matings. *Journal of ACM* **28**:193–214.

Andrews, P. B., et al., 1984. Automating higher order logic. In Bledsoe, 1984, pp. 169–192.

Andrews, P. B., 1986. *An Introduction to Mathematical Logic and Type Theory: To Truth Through Proof*. Academic Press, New York.

Antoniou, G. and Ohlback, H. J., 1983. TERMINATOR. In *Proceedings of the Eighth International Joint Conference on Artificial Intelligence*, Karlsruhe, West Germany, pp 916–919. Morgan Kaufmann Publishers, San Mateo, California.

Appelt, D. E., 1982. Planning natural-language utterances to satisfy multiple goals. SRI International Technical Note 259.

Ballantyne M. and Bledsoe, W. W., 1977. Automatic proofs of theorems in analysis using non-standard techniques. *Journal of ACM* **24**:353–374.

Ballantyne, M. and Bledsoe, W. W. 1982. On generating and using examples in proof discovery. In *Machine Intelligence 10*, pp. 3–39. Harwood, Chichester.

Bayerl, S., Eder, E., Kurfess, F., Letz, R., and Schumann, J., 1986. An implementation of a PROLOG-like theorem prover based on the connection method. In *AIMSA'86*, P. Jorrand, ed. North Holland, Amsterdam.

Bibel, W., 1982. *Automated Theorem Proving*. Vieweg Verlag, Braunschweig. Second Edition, 1987.

Bibel, W. Kurfess, F., et al., 1986. Parallel inference machines. In *Future of Parallel Computers*, J. de Bakker, P. Trealeven, ed. Springer-Verlag, New York.

Bibel, W., Letz, R., and Schumann, J., 1987. Bottom-up enhancements of deductive systems. *AI and Robotics I*, Plander, ed. North Holland, Amsterdam.

Biundo, S., et al., 1986. The Karlsruhe induction theorem proving system. In *Proceedings of the Eighth International Conference on Automated Deduction*, Oxford, UK.

Blasjus, K., Eisinger, N., Siekmann, J., Smolka, G., Herold, A., and Walther, C., 1981. The Markgraf Karl refutation procedure. In *Proceedings of the Seventh International Joint Conference on Artificial Intelligence*, Vancouver, B.C., Canada, pp 511–518. Morgan Kaufmann Publishers, San Mateo, California. Also Seiki-84-08-K1, FB Inf., Universitat Kaiserslautern. 1984.

Bledsoe, W. W., 1971. Splitting and reduction heuristics in automatic theorem proving. *Artificial Intelligence* **2**:55–77.

Bledsoe, W. W. and Bruell, P., 1973. A man-machine theorem proving system. In *Proceedings of the Third International Joint Conference on Artificial Intelligence*, Stanford University. Morgan Kaufmann Publishers, San Mateo, California. Also in *Artificial Intelligence* **5**:51–72.

Bledsoe, W. W. and Tyson, M., 1975. The UT interactive prover. Memos ATP17A and ATP17B, Department of Mathematics, University of Texas, 1983.

Bledsoe, W. W., 1979. A maximal method for set variables in automatic theorem proving. *Machine Intelligence* **9**:53–100.

Bledsoe, W. W. and Hines, L., 1980. Variable elimination and chaining in a resolution-based prover for inequalities. In *Proceedings of the Fifth International Conference on Automated Deduction*, Les Arcs, France. Bibel and Kowalski, ed. *Lecture Notes in Computer Science* **87**:281–292. Springer-Verlag, New York.

Bledsoe, W. W., 1983. Using examples to generate instantiations of set variables. In *Proceedings of the Eighth International Joint Conference on Artificial Intelligence*, Karlsruhe, Germany. Morgan Kaufmann Publishers, San Mateo, California.

Bledsoe, W. W., 1984. Some automatic proofs in analysis. In Bledsoe and Loveland, 1984, pp. 89–118.

Bledsoe, W. W. and Loveland. D., ed., 1984. *Automated Theorem Proving: After 25 Years. Contemporary Mathematics Series* **19**. American Mathematics Society.

Bledsoe, W. W., and Henschen, L., 1985. What is Automated theorem proving? *Journal of Automated Reasoning* **1**:23–28.

Bledsoe, W. W., Kunen, K., and Shostak, R., 1985. Completeness proofs for inequality provers. *Artificial Intelligence* **27**:225–288.

Bledsoe, W. W. 1986a. Some thoughts on proof discovery. In *Proceedings of the 1986 Symposium on Logic Programming*, Salt Lake City, Utah, pp. 2–10. Also Technical Report MCC-AI-208-86. Microelectronics and Computer Technology Corporation, Austin, Texas.

Bledsoe, W. W., 1986b. The use of analogy in proof discovery. Technical Report MCC-AI-158-86. Microelectronics and Computer Technology Corporation, Austin, Texas.

Book, R. and Siekmann, J., 1985. On the unification hierarchy. In *Proceedings of the Ninth German Workshop on Artificial Intelligence*. Springer-Verlag, New York. Also published as SEKI-Report, Universitat Kaiserslautern, 1985.

Borrione, D., ed., 1987. *From HDA Description to Guaranteed Correct Circuit Designs*. North Holland, IFIP.

Boyer, R. S., 1971. *Locking: a Restriction on Resolution*. Ph.D. thesis. University of Texas, Austin.

Boyer, R. S. and Moore, J. S., 1979. *A Computational Logic*. Academic Press, New York.

Boyer, R. S. and Moore, J. S., 1981. A verification condition generator for FORTRAN. *The Correctness Problem in Computer Science*, Boyer and Moore, ed. Academic Press, London.

Boyer, R. S. and Moore, J.S., 1982. Proof checking the RSA public key encryption algorithm. University of Texas Technical Report ICSCA-CMP-37.

Boyer, R. S., 1986a. Rewrite rule compilation. Technical Report MCC-AI-194-86. Microelectronics and Computer Technology Corporation, Austin, Texas.

Boyer, R. S., et al., 1986b. Set theory for first order logic: Clauses for Gödel's axioms. *Journal of Automated Reasoning* 2:287.

Brock, B., Cooper, S., and Pierce, W., 1986. Some experiments with analogy in proof discovery. Technical Report MCC-AI-347-86. Microelectronics and Computer Technology Corporation, Austin, Texas.

Brock B., Cooper, S., and Pierce, W., 1987. Analogical reasoning and proof discovery. Submitted to the *Ninth International Conference on Automated Deduction*.

Brown, F. M., 1986. An experimental logic based on the fundamental deduction principle. *Artificial Intelligence* **30**.

Buchberger, B., Collins, G. E., and Loos, R., 1983. *Computer Algebra, Symbolic and Algebraic Manipulation*. Springer-Verlag, New York.

Bundy, A., 1983. *The Computer Modelling of Mathematical Reasoning*. Academic Press, New York.

Burckert, H.-J., 1986. Some relationships between unification, restricted unification and matching. In *Proceedings of the Eighth International Conference on Automated Deduction. Lecture Notes in Computer Science* **230**. Springer-Verlag, New York.

Burckert, H.-J., 1987. Matching—A special case of unification? In *Report of the First Workshop on Unification*, ed. C. Kirchner, Universite de Nancy, Val d'Ajol. Also published as SEKI-Report, Universitat Kaiserslautern, 1987.

Butler, R., Lusk, E., McCune, W., and Overbeek, R., 1986. Paths to high-performance automated theorem proving. In Siekmann, 1986, pp. 588–597.

Carbonell, J. G., 1983. Learning by analogy: Formulating and generalizing plans from past experience. In *Machine Learning*, ed. Michalski, Carbonell, Mitchell, pp. 137–161. Morgan Kaufmann, San Mateo, California.

Cardelli, L., 1982. *ML under Unix*. Bell Laboratories, Murray Hill, New Jersey.

Cardelli, L., 1986. A polymorphic Lambda-calculus with Type:Type. DEC SCR Report, Digital Equipment Corporation, Palo Alto California.

Chang, C. C. and Lee, R. C. T., 1973. *Symbolic Logic and Mechanical Theorem Proving*. Academic Press, New York.

Chou, S. C., 1985. *Proving and Discovering Theorems in Elementary Geometries Using Wu's Method*. Department of Mathematics, University of Texas, Austin.

Chou, S. C., 1986. Proving geometry theorems using Wu's method: A collection of geometry theorems proved mechanically. Technical Report 50, Institute for Computing Science, University of Texas at Austin. Note: 366 theorems.

Chou, S. C. and Schelter, W. F., 1986. Proving geometry theorems with rewrite rules. *Journal of Automated Reasoning*. 2(4):253–273.

Chou, S. C., 1987. *Mechanical Geometry Theorem Proving*. Reidel Publishing Company.

Clark, K., and Tarnlund, S. A., ed., 1982. *Logic Programming*. Academic, New York.

Cohn, A. G., 1987. A more expressive formulation of many sorted logic. *Journal of Automated Reasoning* 3:113–200.

Constable, R. L., 1985. Constructive mathematics as a programming logic I: Some principles of theory. *Annals of Discrete Mathematics* 24:21–38.

Constable, R. L., et. al., 1986. *Implementing Mathematics with the Nuprl Proof Development System*. Prentice-Hall, Englewood Cliffs, New Jersey.

Coquand, Th. and Huet, G., 1985. Constructions: A higher order proof system for mechanizing mathematics. In *EUROCAL85, Linz. Lecture Notes in Computer Science 203*. Springer-Verlag, New York.

Coquand, Th., 1986. An analysis of Girard's paradox. In *Symposium on Logic in Computer Science*, Cambridge, Massachusetts, pp. 227–236.

Davis, M., 1983. The prehistory and early history of automated deduction. In Siekmann and Wrightson, 1983.

de Bruijn, N. G., 1980. A survey of project Automath. *To H. B. Curry: Essays on Combinatory Logic, Lambda Calculus, and Formalism*, ed. J. P. Seldin and J. R. Hindley. Academic Press, New York.

de Kleer, J. and Brown, J. S., 1984. A qualitative physics based on confluences. *Artificial Intelligence* 24:7–83.

de Kleer, J., 1984. Choices without backtracking. In *Proceedings of the Fourth National Conference on Artificial Intelligence*, Austin, Texas. pp. 79–85. Morgan Kaufmann Publishers, San Mateo, California.

Derschowitz, N., 1987a. Completion and its applications. In Ait-Kaci and Nivat, 1987.

Derschowitz, N. 1987b. Termination of rewriting. *Journal of Symbolic Computation*.

Dixon, J. K., 1973. Z-Resolution: Theorem-proving with compiled axioms. *Journal of ACM* 20:127–147.

Doyle, J., 1979. A truth maintenance system. *Artificial Intelligence* **12**:231–272.

Eisenger, N., 1986. What you always wanted to know about Clause Graph Resolution. In *Proceedings of the Eighth International Conference on Automated Deduction.*

Evans, T. 1951. On multiplicative systems defined by generators and relations. In *Proceedings of the Cambridge Philosophical Society* **47**:637–649.

Fay, M., 1979. First order unification in equational theories. In *Proceedings of the Fourth International Conference on Automated Deduction. Lecture Notes in Computer Science* **87**:161–167. Springer-Verlag, New York.

Forbus, K. D., 1984. Qualitative process theory. *Artificial Intelligence* **24**:65–168.

Forgy, C. L., 1980. RETE: A fast algorithm for the many pattern/many object pattern match problem. Technical Report 309, Carnegie Mellon University.

Gallaire, H. and Minker, J., 1978. *Logic and Data Bases*. Plenum.

Geissler, C. and Konolige, K., 1986. A resolution method for quantified modal logics of knowledge and belief. In *Proceedings of the Conference on Theoretical Aspects of Reasoning about Knowledge*, pp. 309–324. Morgan Kaufmann Publishers, San Mateo, California.

Gelernter, H., 1959. Realization of a geometry-theorem proving machine. In *Proceedings of the International Conference on Information.* UNESCO House, Paris, 1979. Also in *Computers and Thought*, ed. Feigenbaum, Feldman. McGraw-Hill, 1963, pp. 134–152.

Genesereth, M. R., Greiner, R., and Smith, D. E., 1983. A meta-level representation system. Stanford University Memo HPP-83-28.

Genesereth, M. R. and Nilsson, N. J. 1987. *Logical Foundations of Artificial Intelligence*. Morgan Kaufmann Publishers, San Mateo, California.

Goguen, J., 1980. How to prove algebraic induction hypotheses without induction. In *Proceedings of the Fifth International Conference on Automated Deduction.*

Goldblatt, Robert, 1979. *Topoi: The Categorial Analysis of Logic*. North Holland, New York.

Gordon, M., Milner, A., Wadsworth, C., and Edinburgh, L. C. F., 1982. *A Mechanized Logic of Computation. Lecture Notes in Computer Science* **78**. Springer-Verlag, New York.

Gordon, Michael, 1987. HOL, a proof generating system for higher-order logic. To appear in *VLSI Specification, Verification, and Synthesis*.

Green, C., 1969. Theorem proving by resolution as a basis for question-answering systems. In *Machine Intelligence 4*. American Elsevier, New York, pp 183–205.

Greenbaum, S., 1986. *Input Transformations and Resolution Implementation Techniques for Theorem Proving in First Order Logic*. Ph.D. thesis. University of Illinois at Urbana-Champaign.

Greenbaum, S., and Plaisted, D., 1986. The Illinois prover: A general purpose resolution theorem prover, extended abstract. In *Eighth International Conference on Automated Deduction*.

Greiner, R., 1985. *Learning By Understanding Analogies*. Ph.D. thesis. Stanford University Technical Report STAN-CS-1071.

Hall, R. P., 1985. Analogical reasoning in artificial intelligence and related disciplines. Irvine Computational Intelligence Project, University of California, Irvine.

Halpern, J. Y. and Rabin, M. O., 1987. A logic to reason about likelihood. *AI Journal* **32**:379–405.

Harper, R. and Mitchell, K., 1986. Introduction to standard ML. Laboratory for Foundations of Computer Science, University of Edinburgh.

Harper, Honsell, and Plotkin, 1987. A framework for defining logics. *Second Annual Conference in Logic in Computer Science*. Cornell University.

Harrison, M. C. and Rubin, N., 1978. Another generalization of resolution. *Journal of ACM* **25**:341–351.

Henschen, L. J. and Naqvi, S. A., 1984. On compiling queries in recursive first order databases. *Journal of ACM* **31**:47–84.

Hines, L. M., 1987. Hyper-chaining and knowledge-based theorem proving. Submitted to the *Ninth International Conference on Automated Deduction*.

Hines, L. M., 1988. *Building-in Knowledge of Axioms*. Ph.D. thesis, University of Texas.

Hoare, T. and Shepardson, J. C., ed., 1985. Mechanical proof about computer programs. In *Mathematical Logic and Programming Languages*, International Series in Computer Science. Prentice-Hall, Englewood Cliffs, New Jersey.

Hobbs, J. R., and Moore, R. C., 1985. *Formal Theories of the Commonsense World*. Ablex Publishing Corporation, Norwood, New Jersey.

Hodes, L., 1972. Solving problems by formula manipulation in logic and linear inequalities. *Artificial Intelligence* **3**:165–174.

Huet, G. P., 1973. A mechanization of type theory. In *Proceedings of the Third International Joint Conference on Artificial Intelligence*, Stanford. pp. 139–146. Morgan Kaufmann Publishers, San Mateo, California.

Huet, G. and Oppen, D. C., 1980. Equations and rewrite rules: A survey. In *Formal Languages: Perspectives and Open Problems*, ed. R. Book, pp. 348–405. Academic Press, New York.

Hullot, J.-M., 1980. Canonical forms and unification. In *Proceedings of the Fifth International Conference on Automated Deduction. Lecture Notes in Computer Science* **87**:318–334.

Hunt, W. A., Jr., 1986. The mechanical verification of microprocessor design. In Borrione, 1987, pp. 89–129.

IEEE, 1976. *IEEE Transactions on Computers* **C-25**(8). Special issue on Automated Theorem Proving.

Kirchner, C., 1987. Computing unification algorithms. In *Proceedings of the First IEEE Symposium on Logic in Computer Science* 206–216.

Kling, R. E., 1971. A paradigm for reasoning by analogy. *Artificial Intelligence* **2**:147–178.

Knoblock, T. B., and R. L. Constable, 1986. Formalized metareasoning in type theory. In *LICS 86*, ed. A. K. Chandra and A. R. Meyer, pp. 237–248.

Knuth, D. and Bendix, P., 1970. Simple word problems in universal algebras. *Computational Problems in Abstract Algebra*, ed. J. Leech. Pergamon Press, Oxford. pp 263–297.

Konolige, K., 1986a. *A Deduction Model of Belief*. Research Notes in Artificial Intelligence Series. Morgan Kaufmann Publishers, San Mateo, California.

Konolige, K., 1986b. Resolution and quantified epistemic logics. In *Proceedings of the Eighth International Conference on Automated Deduction*. Oxford, England.

Kowalski, R. and Keuhner, D., 1971. Linear resolution with selected functions. *Artificial Intelligence* **2**:227–260.

Kowalski, R., 1974. Predicate logic as a programming language. *Information Processing*.

Kowalski, R., 1975. A proof procedure using connection graphs. *Journal of ACM* **22**(4):424–436.

Kowalski, R., 1979. *Logic for Problem Solving*. North-Holland, New York.

Lankford, D. S., 1975. Canonical inference. Memo ATP-32, Automatic Theorem Proving Project, University of Texas, Austin.

Lankford, D. S. and Ballantyne, A. M., 1977. Decision procedures for simple equational theories with commutative-associative axioms: Complete sets of commutative-associative reductions. Memo ATP-39, Automatic Theorem Proving Project, University of Texas, Austin.

Lenat, D., Prakash, M., and Shepherd, M., 1986. CYC: Using common sense knowledge to overcome brittleness and knowledge acquisition bottlenecks. *AI Magazine* **6**(Winter).

Lenat, D. and Feigenbaum, E. A., 1987. On the thresholds of knowledge. In *Proceedings of the Tenth International Joint Conference on Artificial Intelligence*, Milan, Italy. Morgan Kaufmann Publishers, San Mateo, California.

LeVeque, W. J., 1962. *Elementary Theory of Numbers*. Addison-Wesley, Reading, Massachusetts.

Lifschitz, V., 1987. What is the inverse method? Memo, Stanford University Computer Science Department.

Loveland, D. W., 1968. Mechanical theorem proving by model elimination. *Journal of ACM* **15**:236–251.

Loveland, D. W., 1969. A simplified format for the model elimination procedure. *Journal of ACM* **16**:349–363.

Loveland, D. W., 1978. *Automated Theorem Proving: A Logical Basis*. North-Holland, Amsterdam.

Loveland, D. W., 1984. Automated theorem-proving: A quarter-century review. In Bledsoe, 1984.

Loveland, D. W., 1986. Automated theorem proving: Mapping logic into AI. Invited paper, *International Symposium on Methodologies for Intelligent Systems*. Z. Ras and M. Zemankova, ed. Knoxville, Tennessee, pp. 214–229.

Loveland, 1987. Near-Horn PROLOG. Duke University Report CS-1987-14.

Lusk, E. L. and Overbeek, R. A., 1982. An LMA-based theorem prover. Report ANL-82-75, Argonne National Laboratory.

Lusk, E. and Overbeek, R. A., 1985. Non-Horn problems. *Journal of Automated Reasoning* **1**.

Lusk, E., McCune, W., and Overbeek, R. A., 1986. ITP at Argonne National Laboratory. In *Proceedings of the Eighth International Conference on Automated Deduction*, Oxford, England, pp. 697–698.

Lusk, E., 1987. Private communication.

Lusk, E. and Overbeek, R. A., ed., 1988. *Proceedings of the Ninth International Conference on Automated Deduction*, Argonne, Illinois. Springer-Verlag, New York.

MACSYMA Reference Manual, 1983. Laboratory for Computer Science, Massachusetts Institute of Technology.

Manna, Z. and Waldinger, R., 1985. *The Logical Basis for Computer Programming* **1**. Addison-Wesley, Reading, Mass.

Martin-Lof, P., 1984. *Intuitionistic Type Theory*. Studies in Proof Theory Lecture Notes, Bibliopolis.

Maslov, S. J., 1968. The inverse method for establishing deducibility for logical calculi, In *Proceedings of the Steklov Institute of Mathematics*. **98**.

McAllester, D. A., 1987. *ONTIC: A Knowledge Representation System for Mathematics*. Ph.D. thesis, MIT. AI Laboratory Technical Report 979.

McCarthy, J., 1963. Situations, actions, and causal laws. AI Memo **2**. Stanford University AI Project.

McCarthy, J., 1968. Programs with common sense. *Semantic Information Processing*, ed. Marvin Minsky. MIT Press, Cambridge, Mass.

McCarthy, J., Hayes, P., 1969. Some philosophical problems from the standpoint of artificial intelligence. *Machine Intelligence 4*, ed. Melzer and Michie, pp. 463–502. Edinburgh University Press, Edinburgh, Scotland.

McCarthy, J., 1980. Circumscription—A form of nonmonotonic reasoning. *Artificial Intelligence* **13**:27–39.

McDermott, J., 1979. Learning to use analogies. In *Proceedings of the Sixth International Joint Conference on Artificial Intelligence*, Tokyo, Japan, pp. 568–576. Morgan Kaufmann Publishers, San Mateo, California.

McDonald, J. and Suppes, P., 1984. Student use of an interactive theorem prover. In Bledsoe, 1984, pp. 315–360.

Michalski, R. S., Carbonell, J. C., and Mitchell, T. M., 1983. *Machine Learning: An Artificial Intelligence Approach.* Morgan Kaufmann Publishers, San Mateo, California.

Michalski, R. S., Carbonell, J. C., and Mitchell, T. M., 1986. *Machine Learning: An Artificial Intelligence Approach, Volume 2.* Morgan Kaufmann Publishers, San Mateo, California.

Milner, R., 1983. A proposal for standard ML. Report CSR-157-83, Computer Science Department, University of Edinburgh. Also published in *Conference Record of 1984 ACM Symposium on LISP and Functional Programming,* Austin, Texas.

ML, 1986. *The ML Handbook.* Internal Document, Project Formel, INRIA.

Moore, R. C., 1985. A formal theory of knowledge and action. In Hobbs and Moore, 1985.

Morris, J. B., 1969. E-Resolution: Extension of resolution to include the equality relation. In *Proceedings of the First International Joint Conference on Artificial Intelligence.* Washington, D. C., pp 287–294. Morgan Kaufmann Publishers, San Mateo, California.

Nederpelt, R. P., 1980. An approach to theorem proving on the basis of a typed lambda-calculus. In *Proceedings of the Fifth International Conference on Automated Deduction,* pp. 182–194.

Newell, A., Shaw, J. C., and Simon, H. A., 1956. The logic theory machine. *IRE Trans Information Theory IT-2.* Also in *Computers and Thought,* ed. Feigenbaum, Feldman. McGraw-Hill, 1963.

Nilsson, N. J., 1980. *Principles of Artificial Intelligence.* Morgan Kaufmann Publishers, San Mateo, California.

Nelson, G. and Oppen, D. C., 1978. A simplifier based on efficient decision algorithms. In *Fifth ACM Symposium on Principles of Programming Languages,* pp. 141–150.

Ohlback, H. J., 1987. Link inheritance in abstract clause graphs. *Journal of Automated Reasoning* 3:1–34.

Oppacher, F., and Suen, E., 1986. Controlling deduction with proof condensation and heuristics. In Siekmann, 1986.

Pace, B., 1987. A bibliography of automated deduction. Technical Report No. 87-5400-08, I. P. Sharp Associated Limited, Ottawa, Ontario, Canada.

Pastre, D., 1987. *MUSCADET: An Automatic Theorem Proving System using Knowledge and Metaknowledge in Mathematics.* Ph.D. thesis, University of Paris.

Paulson, L., 1986. Natural deduction as higher-order resolution. *Journal of Logic Programming* 3(3):237–258.

Petrie, C. J., Russinoff, D. M., and Steiner, D. D., 1986. PROTEUS: A default reasoning perspective. Technical Report MCC-AI-352-86. Microelectronics and Computer Technology Corporation, Austin, Texas.

Plaisted, D., 1981. Theorem proving with abstraction. *Artificial Intelligence* **16**:47–108.

Plaisted, D. A., 1982. A simplified problem reduction format. *Artificial Intelligence* **18**:227–261.

Plaisted, D. A., 1987. Non-Horn clause logic programming without contrapositives. Memo, Department of Computer Science, University of North Carolina.

Plummer, D., 1986. *Gazing: A Technique for Controlling the Use of Rewrite Rules in a Natural Deduction Theorem Prover*. Ph.D. thesis, Department of Artificial Intelligence, University of Edinburgh.

Rich, E., 1983. *Artificial Intelligence*. McGraw-Hill, New York.

Robinson, J. A., 1965a. A machine-oriented logic based on the resolution principle. *Journal of ACM* **12**:23–41.

Robinson, J. A., 1965b. Automatic deduction with hyper-resolution. *International Journal of Computer Mathematics* **1**:227–234.

Ross, K., 1986. *Elementary Analysis: The Theory of Calculus*. Springer-Verlag, New York, New York.

Roussel, P., 1975. *PROLOG: Manuel de Reference et d'utilisation*. Groupe d'Intelligence Artificielle, Universite d'Aux-Marseille, Luminy.

Russinoff, D., 1985. An experiment with the Boyer-Moore theorem prover: A proof of Wilson's theorem. *Journal of Automated Reasoning* **1**:121–139.

Sacks, E., 1987. Hierarchical reasoning about inequalities. In *Proceedings of the Sixth National Conference on Artificial Intelligence*, Seattle, Washington, pp. 649–654. Morgan Kaufmann Publishers, San Mateo, California.

Schroeder-Heister, P. 1984. A natural extension of natural deduction. *Journal of Symbolic Logic* **49**(4):1284–1300.

Shankar, N., 1986. *Proof-checking Metamathematics*. Department of Computer Science, University of Texas.

Shankar, N., 1987. A machine-checked proof of Gödel's incompleteness theorem. In *Proceedings of the Eighth International Conference on Logic, Methodology and Philosophy Computer Science Congress*.

Shostak, R. E., 1977. On the SUP-INF method for proving Presburger formulas. *Journal of ACM* **24**:520–543.

Shostak, R. E., 1979. A practical decision procedure for arithmetic with function symbols. *Journal of ACM* **26**:351–360.

Sickel, S., 1976. Interconnectivity graphs. *IEEE Transactions on Computers* C-25.

Siekmann, J. and Wrightson, G., 1979. Paramodulated connection graphs. *Acta Informatica*.

Siekmann, J. and Wrightson, G., 1983. *The Automation of Reasoning I*. Springer-Verlag, New York.

Siekmann, J. and Wrightson, G., 1986. *The Automation of Reasoning II*. Springer-Verlag, New York.

Simon, D., 1984. A linear time algorithm for a subcase of second-order instantiation. In *Seventh International Conference on Automated Deduction*, Napa, California.

Simon, D., 1988. Checking rational proofs. Submitted to the *Ninth International Conference on Automated Deduction*.

Slagle, J. 1974. Automated theorem proving with simplifiers, commutativity, associativity. *Journal of ACM* **21**:622–642.

Smolka, G., Nutt, W., Meseguer, J., and Goguen, J. A., 1987. Order sorted equational computation. In Ait-Kaci and Nivat, 1987.

Smullyan, R., 1968. *First Order Logic*. Springer-Verlag, Berlin.

Smullyan, R., 1985. *To Mock a Mockingbird*. Alfred Knopf, New York.

Stanfield C., Waltza, D., 1986. Toward memory-based reasoning. Technical Report. Thinking Machines.

Stickel, M. E., 1981. A unification algorithm for associative-commutative functions. *Journal of ACM* **28**(3):423–434.

Stickel, M. E., 1984. A case study of theorem proving by the Knuth-Bendix method: Discovering that $x_{[3]} = x$ implies ring commutativity. In *Seventh International Conference on Automated Deduction*, Napa, California.

Stickel, M. E., 1985. Automatic deduction by theory resolution. In *Proceedings of the Ninth International Joint Conference on Artificial Intelligence*, Los Angeles, California, pp. 1181–1186. Morgan Kaufmann Publishers, San Mateo, California.

Stickel, M. E., 1986. A PROLOG technology theorem prover: Implementation by an extended PROLOG compiler. In *Proceedings of the Eight International Conference on Automated Deduction. Lecture Notes in Computer Science* **230**:573–587. Springer-Verlag, New York.

Tyson, M., 1981. *APRVR: A Priority-ordered Agenda Theorem Prover*. Ph.D. thesis. University of Texas Computer Science Department. Also in *Proceedings of the Second National Conference on Artificial Intelligence*, Pittsburgh, Pennsylvania, 1982. Morgan Kaufmann Publishers, San Mateo, California.

Wallen, L., 1986. Chapter in *Modal Logic in Artificial Intelligence and its Applications*. A. G. Cohn and J. R. Thomas, ed. John Wiley and Son, New York.

Walther, C., 1983. A many-sorted calculus based on resolution and paramodulation. In *Proceedings of the Eighth International Joint Conference on Artificial Intelligence*, Karlsruhe, West Germany, pp. 882–891. Morgan Kaufmann Publishers, San Mateo, California.

Walther, C., 1984. A mechanical solution of Schubert's Steamroller by many-sorted resolution. In *Proceedings of the Fourth National Conference on Artificial Intelligence*, Austin, Texas, pp. 330–334. Morgan Kaufmann Publishers, San Mateo, California.

Wang, H., 1960. Toward mechanical mathematics. *IBM Journal of Research and Development* **4**:2–22. Also see Siekmann and Wrightson, 1983, pp. 244–264.

Wang, T. C., 1985. Designing examples for semantically guided hierarchical deduction. In *Proceedings of the Ninth International Joint Conference on Artificial Intelligence*, Los Angeles, California, pp. 1201–1207. Morgan Kaufmann Publishers, San Mateo, California.

Wang, T. C. and Bledsoe, W. W., 1987. Hierarchical deduction. *Journal of Automated Reasoning* **3**:35–77.

Warren, D. H. D., 1987. Implementing PROLOG—compiling predicate logic programs. University of Edinburgh Department of Artificial Intelligence Research Reports **39**(40).

Webber, N. J., ed., 1977. Non-resolution theorem proving. *Artificial Intelligence* **9**:55–77. Also in *Readings in Artificial Intelligence*. Morgan Kaufmann, San Mateo, California, 1981. .

Weyhrauch, R., 1977. FOL: A proof checker for first order logic. Stanford AI Memo AIM-235.1.

Winker, S., 1976. An evaluation of an implementation of qualified hyper-resolution. *IEEE Transactions on Computers* **C-25**(8):835–843.

Winston, P. H., 1980. Learning and reasoning by analogy. *CACM* **23**(12):689–703.

Wos, L., Robinson, G., Carson, D. F., 1965. Efficiency and completeness of the set of support strategy in theorem proving. *Journal of ACM* **12**:536–541.

Wos, L., Robinson, G., Carson, D., Shalla, L., 1967. The concept of demodulation in theorem proving. *Journal of ACM* **14**:698–709.

Wos, L., Robinson, G., 1970. Paramodulation and set of support. *Symposium on Automatic Demonstration. Lecture Notes in Mathematics* **125**:276–310. Springer-Verlag, New York.

Wos, L. and Henschen, L., 1983. Automated theorem proving 1965-1970. In Siekmann and Wrightson, 1983.

Wos, L., Overbeek, R., Lusk, E., and Boyle, J., 1984a. *Automated Reasoning: Introduction and Application*. Prentice-Hall, Englewood Cliffs, New Jersey.

Wos, L., Veroff, R., Smith, B., and McCune, W., 1984b. The linked inference principle, II: The user's viewpoint. In *Proceedings of the Seventh International Conference on Automated Deduction*, Napa, California, pp 316–332.

Wos, L., 1987. *Automated Reasoning: 33 Basic Research Problems*. Prentice-Hall, Englewood Cliffs, New Jersey.

Wu, 1978. On the decision problem and the mechanization of theorem proving. *Elementary Geometry Scientia Sinica* **21**:157–179.

Wu, 1984. Basic principles of mechanical theorem proving in geometries. *Journal of Sys. Sci. and Math. Sci* **4**(3):207–235. Republished in *Journal of Automated Reasoning* **2**(4):221–252. 1986.

VI

ARCHITECTURE AND SYSTEMS

14

Symbolic Computing Architectures

Howard E. Shrobe

Symbolics Incorporated
Cambridge, Massachusetts

Introduction

In this survey, I'll be looking at the evolution of computer architectures that have been developed in and for the AI community. These are known as symbolic computing architectures, because they emphasize the manipulation of symbolic as opposed to numeric entities. The road map for this survey is as follows: First, we'll discuss what is meant by symbolic computing; I'll try to give you a sense of how this style of computation differs from conventional computing. Hopefully this will help develop an appreciation of the unique demands that symbolic computing places upon a systems architecture. Then we'll spend some time reviewing the history of symbolic computing. We'll look at how the earliest LISP systems matured as sophisticated hardware became available. Today's LISP Machine systems represent the culmination of this history; I'll spend some time trying to show what's really important in these systems. Next we'll look at several efforts to push symbolic computing into the future with parallel processing. Finally, we'll take a quick peek at neural networks and some other ideas that are pretty speculative.

Throughout this survey I will emphasize a theme that one might expect to hear from a physicist more than from a computer scientist; this is the search for symmetry and coherence. I'm using the word "symmetry" in the same sense that a physicist would: A symmetry is an abstract structure that we can impose on reality to reveal a uniformity and simplicity that would otherwise be hidden. The notion of coherence will become particularly important when we turn to parallel symbolic computing. Allowing many symbolic processors to operate in parallel forces us to worry about whether all of them share a common perception of the system's state. One example of this problem is that of cache coherence; if each processor has a private cache-memory, how do we make sure that they all agree about what's actually in main memory?

As we'll soon see, the applications for which symbolic computing is the technique of choice are characterized by their complexity and heterogeneity; it is because of this that we need to find ways to structure problems so that hidden uniformities become apparent. That is why symmetry and coherence are such important architectural goals.

1 What is Symbolic Computing?

1.1 A Simple Example

First of all, just exactly what do we mean by symbolic computation? Let's take a quick look at a very simple but nevertheless very paradigmatic program: a symbolic differentiator. Such a program is given a mathematical expression as input; it is supposed to return another mathematical expression which is the derivative of the input with respect to some particular variable. Although we are used to writing these expressions using infix mathematical operators, it is actually more convenient for the program to manipulate them in prefix form, leaving the conversion to a simple parser. By a mathematical expression I might mean something like the following:

```
(Plus (expt x 4) (times 2 (expt x 3)))
```

which is the internal form for

$$x^4 + 2x^3$$

If one were going to write such a program in a conventional programming language like FORTRAN or C, you'd have to spend a lot of time building all the facilities needed to represent expressions like these. The list processing capabilities of LISP (or PROLOG) make this work unnecessary.

Also, if you were writing this program in FORTRAN or ADA or C, you'd probably be forced to structure it as a single big CASE statement (or a bunch of nested IF statements). The CASE would test in turn whether the expression is a PLUS expression, or a TIMES expression or an exponentiation or a constant, or any of the other special rules we learn in first year calculus about differentiation. Such a program is shown in LISP notation in Figure 1. There are two problems with such a program. First, it's inefficient. Second it's unmaintainable.

1.1.1 *Data-driven Programming* In a symbolic computing environment we would structure this program quite differently as a large collection of very small routines (as shown in Figure 2). The core routine (called DIFF) only checks a few of the simplest cases, for example, differentiating a constant. If the expression is not any of these trivial cases, DIFF determines what kind of expression it is and, based on this, dispatches to a specialized routine, say, a PLUS differentiator or a TIMES differentiator. The specialized routines, of course, can and do call DIFF to recursively differentiate their subexpressions.

How does the core DIFF function known which routine to call? In this program, expressions are represented as lists; the first element of each expression is a symbol that indicates the type of the expression. DIFF simply looks on the property list of this symbol for a *differentiator* property; this property should index the procedure appropriate for that type of expression. For example, if the expression is a *plus* expression, DIFF should look for the *differentiator* property of *plus* which should contain the function which "knows how to" differentiate *plus* expressions.

Notice that the differentiator decides which procedure to call by looking inside a data structure (i.e., the property list). The specific data being processed (i.e., the expression being differentiated) tells it which data structure to look in. This is an example of *data-driven programming*, one of the hallmarks of

```
(defun Diff (expression)
    (cond ((numberp expression) 0)
      ((eq expression 'x)  1)
      ((symbolp expression) 0)
      ((eq (car expression) 'plus)
          '(plus ,(diff (second expression))
              ,(diff (third expression))))
      ((eq (car expression) 'times)
      . . .Code to differentiate products. . .)
      ((eq (car expression) 'exp)
      . . .Code to differentiate exponentials. . .)
      (  . . .etc.. . .)))
```

Figure 1 A naive differentiation program.

symbolic computing; this type of technique is very difficult or impossible to implement in conventional programming languages.

1.1.2 *Embedded Languages*   One interesting thing to notice about this program is that it has exactly the same structure as an interpreter for a programming language; it's actually quite similar to the LISP interpreter itself. Both a language interpreter and the differentiation program are presented with an expression (a program in one case, a mathematical expression in the other); they both traverse the tree-like structure of the expression and at each level each of them lets the data dictate the flow of control (see Figure 3).

Because of this structural similarity to a language interpreter, we are inclined to think of the DIFF program as if it actually is a specialized programming language: the DIFF language. In more complicated forms of data-driven programming, such as rule-based inference systems, the similarity to a programming language is even clearer and we almost always refer to them as languages. Such data-driven interpreters are specialized to their domain and make expressing problems in that domain much simpler than if one had to express everything in LISP alone. However, one does not lose the power of LISP by building such data-driven interpreters since they are *embedded* in LISP. Although DIFF has its own control regime and data structures it also has access to all the facilities of LISP. Similarly, rule systems implemented in LISP typically allow the body of the rule to use all the facilities LISP has to offer.

```
(defun Diff (expression)
   (cond ((numberp expression) 0)
      ((eq expression 'x)   1)
      ((symbolp expression) 0)
         (t (apply (get (car expression) 'differentiator)
            (cdr expresion)))))


(defun (:property plus differentiator) (addend augend)
   '(plus ,(diff addend) (diff augend)))


(defun (:property times differentiator) (multiplier
      multiplicand)
   . . .Code to differentiate products. . .)


      . . .etc.. . .
```

Figure 2 A better way to organize the differentiator.

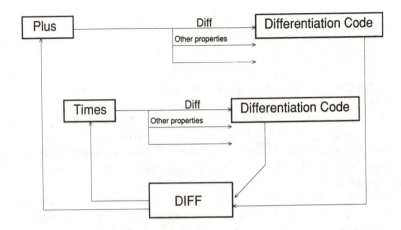

Figure 3 The similarity of DIFF to an Interpreter.

So we've identified a second very common technique of symbolic programming, *language embedding*. Rule-based inference engines and frame systems are typical more sophisticated examples of this technique.

1.1.3 *Heterogeneity* It should be clear that these tasks for which symbolic computing is uniquely qualified are different in kind from those served well by conventional numerical computing. Conventional programs tend to be uniform, simple, homogeneous, and numerically intensive. Symbolic programs, instead, are diverse and heterogeneous, involving a variety of mechanisms and conceptual tasks within a single program. A single symbolic computing application, for example the manager of an autonomous space vehicle, will have to perform a variety of tasks such as hierarchical classification, signal interpretation, hypothesis formation, matching, and logical inference not to mention conventional numerical tasks. It will have to employ a variety of different mechanisms such as rule-based programming, frame instantiation, constraint propagation, numerical simulation, object-oriented programming, symbolic mathematics, and truth maintenance; all within a single large system.

Finally, this single system may well employ several different embedded languages. In AI applications, the most common embedded languages will be rule-based inference systems and object-oriented programming languages. But we may also need a symbolic manipulation language, for example MACSYMA. All of these languages will need to share data and be able to call upon one another's capabilities in a variety of ways; the fact that they are all embedded in a common base language (which is typically LISP) makes this possible.

It should be clear that the popular notion of an AI program as a single, simple rule interpreter is a gross oversimplification. In fact, symbolic computing places much more serious demands on the system architecture than would be presented by the need simply to to support a simple rule interpreter.

1.2 *Characteristics of Symbolic Computing*

So far we have seen that symbolic computing is aimed at solving large and complex problems. To do this several programming techniques have been developed. Data-driven programming and language embedding are two of the most important of these techniques, because they allow the problem to be structured and abstracted. In a sense, they are examples of my theme of the search for symmetry. They impose a structure on the problem which would otherwise be hidden. Without this structure, the program would be longer and more complex, assuming that the complexity didn't overwhelm the programmer altogether.

However, these techniques of symbolic computing present challenges for the hardware because they make the flow of both data and control hard to predict. The fact that symbolic computing is diverse and heterogenous also presents a challenge to the architecture, since it means that there will be no single facility which will always be in the inner loop of the computation. Techniques used to optimize highly regular numeric computations, such a vector pipelines, are not particularly useful in the domain of symbolic computations.

There are two other characteristics of symbolic computations that present challenges to the system architecture. The first is that the program typically works on very large knowledge representations; this necessitates a large and uniform address space. In the absence of this, some of the knowledge simply will not fit into the address space (by address space I mean the size of *virtual memory*) and will have to be treated asymmetrically. Such an asymmetry shows up as added complexity in the program since it necessitates special procedures to deal with those dafa structures that don't happen to fit in the address space along with all the others.

Secondly, symbolic computations tend to create temporary data structures whose lifetime is difficult to predict through static analysis. Our differentiator, for example, produces intermediate expressions representing the derivatives of the subexpressions. But if two subexpressions both differentiate to 2x, then their sum can be simplified to 4x and the data structures for the original subexpressions will no longer be needed. But it is impossible to predict this in advance; other inputs would create different subexpressions that can't be simplified and thrown away. Unless you know the specific data that the program will work on, you can't tell what intermediate results will be needed.

A more realistic example occurs in the Boyer benchmark from the Gabriel [1985] set of symbolic computing benchmarks. This program creates about a half million words of temporary storage every 10 seconds of execution (see [Moon, 1984] for this data). Most of that is volatile and unneeded by the end of the 10 seconds, but the programmer can't predict in advance which specific pieces of data will be needed and which won't. So, the system must provide the ability to find the storage which is no longer needed and make it available for further allocation; this task is usually called *garbage collection.*

1.3 *Desiderata*

We can now summarize all this into a set of desiderata for a symbolic computing system. First and foremost, because of the complexity of the task, we need to raise the abstraction level of the languages we use to express our solutions so that we can program closer to the knowledge level. We want to leave as many of the details as possible to the system (by which I mean both the hardware and the lower levels of system software).

Secondly, we want the system to provide a broad range of ready-to-use facilities and a powerful program development environment to ease the task of creating the code.

Finally, and most importantly, we want the system to support *incrementality.* By incrementality, I mean the ability to make a small modification to the program while it's running (for example to replace a rule in a rule-based system). This is usually facilitated by decomposing the system into modular units such as rules, frames, semantic network nodes, etc. Any of those can be changed while the program is running without interrupting the program or losing its state.

This is an extremely powerful capability because it lets you examine and characterize a bug within the context of the failing program: the stack, symbol table, and the global state of the computation are there to help you understand what went wrong. Furthermore, you can examine all this information while running within an error handler and come up with a fix on the spot. Incrementality then allows you to replace the offending procedure with a better version and to proceed from the error as if it had never occured. This dramatically speeds up the rate of program development.

Because symbolic computations are evolved rather than designed, and because of their size and complexity, they're never really done. Even when the program is deployed, you need to be able to modify it, and you sometimes need to do that quickly.

There are many stories of software systems that have been deployed in critical applications where an entire mission depends on the program. Now, suppose that there is a bug in the program which is only triggered once the program is fielded. Certainly in such a case you'd like to be able to patch the program without taking it down to run some long and time-consuming Sysgen activity. After all, there might be people's lives at stake during the entire time you're doing this.

The ability to support incrementality does not come for free because it means that virtually anything can change under you. Therefore, many more decisions must be postponed until runtime.

1.4 *The Object-oriented Viewpoint*

What this leads to is a viewpoint of a computer that's characteristic of symbolic computation which I call *Object-oriented Viewpoint*. In this viewpoint, the memory doesn't consist of a stream of raw bits organized into bytes or words. Rather, it consists of much larger conceptual entities which we can think of as objects. An object might be something simple like a list, an array, an integer or it might·be something with higher semantic content, for example, a node in a semantic network or a data structure representing an entity in the real world.

We want these objects to have identity. This means that just by looking at an object you should be able to tell what kind of object it is; in addition, you should be able to tell its extent in memory. The techniques that are used to do this are called *storage conventions*. Ideally, the hardware should guarantee that the storage conventions are never violated. As we'll see later, this is precisely what modern LISP Machines do. Notice that guaranteeing storage conventions is an example of the need to preserve coherence.

The object-oriented viewpoint depends upon the ability to make memory seemingly infinite, in the sense that there will always be room for allocating new objects. Indeed, the goal is to free the programmer from worrying about where objects are allocated and when they are deallocated. In practice, this means that the system needs to support *garbarge collection*, the process of reclaiming unused storage at a rapid enough rate so that you never run out of free storage. Garbage collection means that the symmetry of storage is maintained; to the programmer all storage is the same, and it's always available.

The second major feature of the object-oriented viewpoint is that the programmer codes using *generic operations*. By a generic operation, I mean an abstract, conceptual operation which does not reflect the limitations of the hardware. For example, addition is a conceptual operation which is meaningful to apply to integers, floating-point numbers, vectors, polynomials, etc. Ideally, there should be a single operation, called PLUS, which does all of these, dispatching on the type of the objects being added to determine how to perform the operation.

In conventional programming languages the types of the language reflect the limitations of the hardware. The reason why you have integer types and floating-point types in most languages is because that's what the hardware has; the programming language is designed to make the programmer worry about things like this so that the compiler can generate reasonably efficient code. In symbolic computing, we would ideally like to free the programmer from these details by emphasizing the abstract unity (or symmetry) of all the different forms of addition.

As we'll see, modern symbolic computing hardware allows this viewpoint to be supported efficiently. It is the hardware's job to check every operation and decide how to perform it based upon the types of the operands. So in effect that hardware will tell itself: "That's a fixed-point number and therefore I should do integer adds," or "That's a floating-point number, I should be doing floating-point adds." Or, "It's an extended number that I can't directly support at all, but I can support it by this sequence of other instructions."

In addition to higher level code, this approach leads to better debugging and incrementality. Any attempt to do an invalid operation on any particular piece of data is detected by the hardware, allowing the programmer to enter a debugging sessions in the context of the error.

Figure 4 shows an example of a generic operation. Here we have the single generic function *plus*, which when applied to two integers just adds them using the fixed point adder. When applied to a mix of integer and floating-point operands, it converts one datum to the type of the other (for example, it converts the integer to floating point) and then uses a floating-point coprocessor to compute the result. When presented with two vectors to add, (notice that these are not hardware primitives), it traps out and performs a complex computation that makes a vector which is the vector sum of the two operands. Presumably, this operation is performed in software, but the way you get to that software is by the hardware trapping you to it.

2 The Historical Evolution of Symbolic Computing

We've seen so far that symbolic computing is concerned with organizing large, complex heterogenous computations into structures that have uniformity and coherence. The conceptual core of symbolic computing is the object-oriented viewpoint, which structures memory and abstracts the primitive operations. Key to providing this conceptual viewpoint is the ability to tag objects with their types, to delineate their extent in memory, to reclaim unused storage making it available for reuse, and finally to support generic operations.

(+ 3 4)   Use hardware to add 3 and 4 -> 7

(+ 3.0 4)   Use hardware to convert 4 to 4.0
             Use hardware to add 3.0 and 4.0 -> 7.0

(+ V1 V2)   (MAKE-VECTOR (+ (VECTOR-DELTA-X V1)
                             (VECTOR-DELTA-X V2))
                          (+ (VECTOR-DELTA-Y V1)
                             (VECTOR-DELTA-Y V2)))

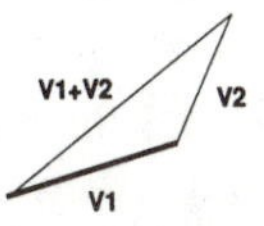

Figure 4 The generic Add operation.

Now that we have an understanding of the nature of symbolic computing and of the challenges that it creates for the computer architect, I'd like to lead you on a tour through the evolution of symbolic computing technology. As we'll see, the central theme of this history is the attempt to efficiently support the object-oriented viewpoint; this goal has been achieved reasonably well in modern symbolic computing systems. After we complete this tour we'll look at current day attempts to exploit parallelism in symbolic computing.

2.1 *Homeric Times*

Long ago, in the pre-history of symbolic computing, a few heroic individuals, using tiny and weak vehicles, set forth on a journey through storms and monsters and attempted to build the first truly powerful computing environments. Although the people who pioneered these efforts are all still alive and active, they are surrounded by an aura of mystery in the popular mythology of the major centers of symbolic computing research.

This was in the late 1950s and the machines were tiny by today's standards; the early work was done on the PDP-1 [Deutsch and Berkeley] (and later the PDP-6 [Samson, 1966] and the SDS-930 [Deutsch and Lampson] (later the XDS-940) both of which are long since dead. LISP 1.5 [McCarthy et al., 1962] (preceded by LISP 2 [McCarthy et al., 1960] and followed by LISP 1.6 [White, 1967]) was the first true LISP language, although it was preceded by a variety of other symbolic computing languages such as the IPL series [Newell, 1961] in which the Logic Theorist and GPS were implemented. There has been incredible progress since those days, but it's striking how many of the good ideas were there in the original LISP language. McCarthy [1978] is a history of these developments, told as only John McCarthy can.

2.2 *Ancient Times*

In the early recorded history (i.e., the mid-1960s) computing hardware evolved enough to provide a significant base for serious research. Most significant was the evolution from the PDP-6 to the DEC-10 which was the first machine big enough and fast enough to provide adequate support for symbolic computing.

This hardware facilitated the development of three symbolic computing environments each contributing a major theme whose importance continues to this day.

2.2.1 *MACLISP* The LISP environment that evolved at MIT on the DEC-10 eventually became known as MACLISP [Moon, 1976]. MACLISP was the "lean and mean" approach to LISP implementation. It was low on frills, but it was a very high-performance system. In particular, its numerical performance was as good as the FORTRAN supplied by DEC. In parallel with MACLISP, a powerful editor known as EMACS [Stallman, 1984] was developed by Richard Stallman which had considerable support for editing LISP programs and which was loosely coupled to the MACLISP environment. In particular, one could go from MACLISP to EMACS to edit a single LISP definition and then return this definition to the LISP environment. To the programmer it appeared as if this took place within a single environment; in fact, the two systems ran in separate address spaces.

The MACLISP environment continued to evolve forming the basis for the MIT LISP Machine. The LISP dialect that continued to evolve in the LISP Machine environment provided one of the strongest influences in the standardization of Common LISP [Steele, 1984].

2.2.2 Interlisp The original SDS-940 LISP was ported to the DEC-10 at BBN, assuming the name BBN LISP [Bobrow et al., 1966]; it continued to evolve at BBN and took on the name Interlisp [Teitelman, 1978]. Many of the developers moved from BBN to Xerox PARC which continued to champion Interlisp. PARC developed a series of machines know as the D-Machines that were microcoded to provide an Interlisp environment known as Interlisp-D [Burton, 1981]. Interlisp implementations were also built for the VAX architecture [Bates et al., 1982] and other machines. I think it's fair to say that DEC-10 Interlisp was the first example of an integrated programming environment in the sense described in Sandewall [1978]. It was a fairly large and complex software system in which the compiler, editor, debugger, etc. all shared a common environment and set of conventions. Each of these facilities embedded considerable knowledge about the syntax and semantics of LISP and each was capable of using the others as subroutines. Its major drawback was its relatively low performance, particularly as compared to the MACLISP implementation on the same hardware.

2.2.3 PROLOG In roughly the same time period, David Warren at the University of Edinburgh implemented a high-performance compiler for the logic programming language PROLOG [Warren, 1977]. Most of the interest in PROLOG initially was confined to Europe, but it spread from there to Japan where logic programming ideas are central to the Fifth Generation project [Moto-Oka and Fuchi, 1983; Moto-Oka and Stone, 1984]. Warren's DEC-10 PROLOG introduced the idea of compiling the unification pattern matching that is central not only to PROLOG but also to many other rule-based languages used for expert system development. The concept of a logic variable data type is central to this scheme, but I'll delay talking about this idea until later.

2.2.4 BIBOP Data Typing As I've emphasized, the object-oriented viewpoint is the central concern of symbolic computing and the key to this viewpoint is the ability to tell the type of an object just by looking at it. This capability underlies the notion of generic operations and is crucial for all garbage collection schemes. It is not surprising, therefore, that during this period a very clever scheme was developed to facilitate data typing even on a machine that provided no special data typing features in its architecture. This scheme came to be known as BIBOP (for **BI**g **B**ag **O**f **P**ages) and was pioneered in MACLISP [Steele, 1977b].

The BIBOP scheme tries to reconcile the lack of any extra bits in the hardware with the need to encode typing information. The DEC-10 was a 36 bit machine and all 36 bits were used. BIBOPing is based on the observation that we can encode the typing information in the way we refer to an object, i.e., in its address. This dictates a set of storage conventions in which only objects of a single data type are allocated on any particular page of virtual memory. For example, there will be pages that only contain integers, pages that contain only floating-point numbers, pages of arrays, and so on. Notice that it isn't the necessary for all data of a particular type to be contiguous. The only requirement is that each page contain objects of a single data type; the next page containing similar objects can be far removed.

To figure out the type of a particular datum, we need to consult the *master type table*, which maps page numbers to data types (see Figure 5). A pointer (for example the CAR half of a CONS cell) in this scheme is simply an address. The BIBOP scheme gets the page number from this address and uses it to index into the master type table and retrieve the data type. So by knowing the location of an object, we also know what kind of object it is.

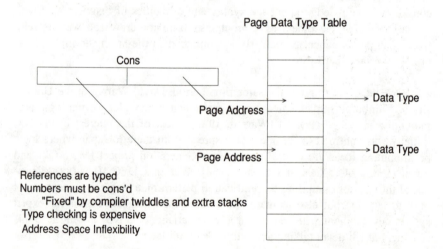

Figure 5 BIBOP data typing.

The BIBOP technique has the advantage that it needn't steal bits from the rest of a word; in particular numbers are represented to the full significance of the hardware. The DEC-10 was a 36-bit machine, and so the numbers were 36 bits long. It is also a relatively compact scheme since it only requires a table with one entry per page of virtual memory.

However this scheme also has two disadvantages. The first is that its use of storage is inefficient. Since an object can only be stored on a page reserved for objects of its particular data type, intermediate results of a numeric computation cannot be stored on the normal system stack. (Since if they were, the storage convention would force the stack to contain only numeric data.) In addition, data structures that need to contain mixtures of numeric and other data cannot store the numbers as immediate data. Instead they must store the numeric data on a page containing numbers, and use a pointer in the data structure to point to the stored number. Finally, a page which is only partially full of data of a particular type cannot be used to hold data of another type, forcing the system to have many partially filled pages.

The second disadvantage of BIBOP is that its type checking scheme is relatively expensive. To check a data type, you have to extract a page address, index into the master type table and then fetch the data type. This takes many instructions and therefore clocks several cycles. Figure 6 shows the assembly

(defun gp (a b) (+ a b))

Conventional Machine

```
      CMPI.W   #2, D6
      BEQ      L1
      MOVEA.L  (227,A4), A2
      JSR      (5,A2)
L1:   MOVEA.L  (-12,A6), A0
      MOVEA.L  (-16,A6), A1
      MOVE.L   A0, D4
      MOVE.L   A1, D5
      MOVE.W   D4, D7
      OR.W     D5, D7
      ANDI     #x3, D7
      BNE      L2
      ADD.L    D5, D4
      BVS      L3
L4:   MOVE.L   D4, (4,A6)
      MOVEA.L  (-4,A6), A5
      LEA      (-8,A6), A7
      MOVEA.L  (A7), A3
      JMP      (A3)
L3:   SUBX.L   D5, D4
L2:   MOVEA.L  (167,A4), A2
      JSR      (5,A2)
      BRA      L4
      BRA      L4
```

Symbolic Computer

```
0 ENTRY: 2 REQUIRED, 0 OPTIONAL
1 PUSH-LOCAL FP|0        ;A
2 BUILTIN +-INTERNAL STACK FP|1    ;B
3 RETURN-STACK
```

Figure 6 Conventional machine's assembly code for a generic plus operation.

code that a compiler for a M680*xx* processor has to emit to perform the type checking; clearly this is costly. Since type checking is a very frequent operation this cost is significant, slowing a program down by a factor of 2 or more.

The MACLISP implementers came up with several tricks to alleviate these problems. MACLISP uses several stacks. One of those is reserved for fixed point numbers and another is used for floating-point numbers. The compiler tries to identify those places where the code produces a temporary numeric result of a known type; when successful, it emits code that pushes the result onto the appropriate numeric stack. This requires the programmer to provide declarations to help the compiler figure out what's going on. When the compiler can't make this determination, it is forced to emit much more inefficient code which stores the temporary result in heap storage. This, of course, adds to the burden on the garbage collector.

Another trick used in MACLISP was to omit the type checking code altogether in compiled code under the assumption that the code had been debugged in the interpreter; this was probably a bad idea. Such unsafely compiled code proved very difficult to maintain and debug.

2.2.5 *Garbage Collection*

During the development of LISP systems on the DEC-10 many of our modern ideas about garbage collection were consolidated; see [Cohen, 1981] for an excellent survey of this topic. There were two main styles of garbage collector developed, both of which seize total control of the machine for a substantial period of time.

The first technique (called *Mark-Sweep*) [Schorr and Waite, 1985], builds a "free list," a list of locations in memory which are not currently being used. The algorithm has two phases. In the first, one starts at the "root nodes" (i.e., the registers of the machine as well as certain locations known to contain permanent data, such as the symbol table). These are *marked* and then anything that these locations point at is marked recursively. Of course, if you attempt to mark a location which is already marked, you simply stop that path of the recursion.

Once the mark phase completes, a linear *sweep* through the address space finds those locations which are not marked. These are linked together to form a list of free locations. These free locations are then available for new allocation.

Mark-Sweep has several problems. The first problem is where to store the mark bits; the obvious place would be in the word to be marked, but (as with data type tags) there are no free bits. So an extra table has to be allocated in memory for this purpose. Secondly, there is a significant pause during the mark and sweep process during which the machine is unavailable to the user. In the limited address space (256K words) of the DEC-10 this didn't matter very much, since the whole process takes only a few seconds. But with today's large address space machines this time grows to many minutes. Finally, Mark-Sweep does not compact the reclaimed storage. This becomes an issue when one wants to allocate contiguous structures (such as arrays) of variable size. Even though there may be more than enough words of storage on the free-list they might be so fragmented that no block is large enough for the desired structure. Pure and simple Mark-Sweep garbage collectors were, therefore, always augmented by a storage compacting facility as well. Many commercial LISP systems that are available on conventional hardware today still employ this basic strategy.

The second major style of garbage collector introduced in this period is know as *Stop-and-Copy* [Minsky, 1963; Fenichel and Yochelson, 1969]. Stop-and-Copy, like Mark-Sweep, seizes total control of the machine. However, it has the advantage that it naturally compacts the reclaimed storage. Figure 7 show the basic structure of Stop-and-Copy garbage collection in which the address space of the machine is divided into two subspaces called *old space* and *new space*. Initially, new space is empty and all of the data (both live data and garbage) reside in old space. The goal is to copy the live data from old to new space. Once this is done, old space can be "reclaimed," i.e., the entire area can be made available for new allocation. During the Stop-and-Copy process, new space is broken into three areas; two pointers are used to delineate these areas, these are called the *scavenge* pointer and the *transport* pointer. Words between the beginning of new space and the scavenge pointer are required to point only to objects in new space. Words between the scavenge pointer and the transport pointer may point either to old or new space. The area between the transport pointer and the top of new space contains free storage.

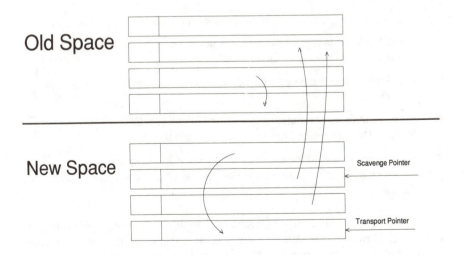

Figure 7 Stop-and-Copy garbage collecting.

Initially, the root nodes are copied to new space, the scavenge pointer points to the beginning of new space and the transport pointer points to the first word after the root nodes. Following this the garbage collector repeatedly performs the *scavenge* operation. Scavenging involves the following steps:

1. Fetch the word in the location addressed by the scavenge pointer.

2. If this word is a pointer and it points to old space, then the location in old space is *transported* to new space.

3. The word being scavenged is updated to point to the location in new space to which the word in old space has been transported.

4. If the word being scavenged is either not a pointer or doesn't point to old space, then no action is taken.

5. Finally, the scavenge pointer is advanced past the word just processed.

Scavenging involves an operation called *transporting* which involves the following steps:

1. Examine the location addressed.

2. If this location (which is in old space) is not specially marked as a *GC-forwarded* location then:

    a. Copy the word in this location to the location addressed by the transport pointer.

    b. Mark the location in old space as "GC-forwarded".

    c. Set the address part of the location in old space to the current contents of the transport pointer.

    d. Advance the transport pointer past the copy in new space (see Figure 8).

3. If the location in old space is specially marked as a GC-forwarded location then no action is required (see Figure 9).

4. Finally, return the address part of the location in old space being transported. In either case, this is the address of the new space copy of the datum.

Notice that the datum that is transported to new space may still point into old space. However, the datum itself will be located between the scavenge pointer and the transport pointer. Also notice that after we scavenge a location containing a pointer, the pointer will point to a location in new space. Therefore, everything between the start of new space and the scavenge pointer points only to new space. Finally, notice that any live datum in old space is copied to new space exactly once (because of the GC-Forwarded mark). Therefore, eventually a point is reached during the process of scavenging when all live data has been copied to new space; at this point the transport pointer will stop advancing. As we continue scavenging, however, the scavenge pointer continues to advance. Eventually it will reach the transport pointer. When this occurs, all locations in new space will be in the region below the scavenge pointer, implying that they point only to locations in new space. This means that all locations in old space are now inaccessible and can be reclaimed.

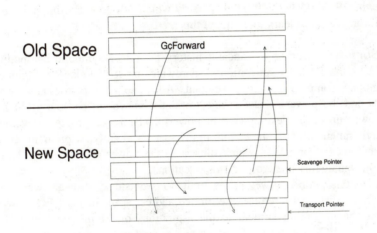

Figure 8 Scavenging and transporting.

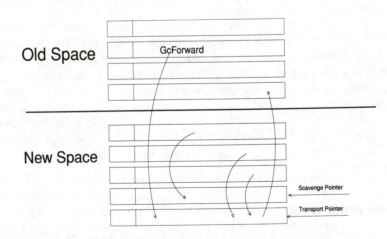

Figure 9 Scavenging an already transported location.

It is important to realize that the both types of garbage collector inherently rely on the ability to distinguish between pointer and nonpointer data types. In addition, Stop-and-Copy needs two other capabilities: it must be able to tell whether a location is in old or new space and it must be able to recognize a GC-Forwarded location. In stock hardware, these needs are met by ad hoc techniques. However, as we will soon see, the type checking capabilities of LISP Machines solve all these problems uniformly with a small addition of hardware.

Other interesting ideas about garbage collection can be found in Deutsch and Bobrow [1976], Cheney [1970], Ungar [1984] and Lieberman [Lieberman and Hewitt, 1983]. Cohen [1981] is a survey which is a good starting point for anyone who wishes to learn more about this area.

2.2.6 *Summary*

During the ancient history period of symbolic computing (typified by the DEC-10 generation of hardware) most of today's techniques for symbolic computing were developed. Adequate LISP performance was achieved and the power of LISP's object-oriented viewpoint became apparent. This showed up in the development of powerful LISP based program development environments. It also showed up in the successful early AI programs such as Shrdlu, Hacker, or Strips, which illustrated the power of LISP for building extremely complex and heterogenous applications.

During this period, however, the limitations of stock hardware were becoming clear. First and foremost, the limited address space of the DEC-10 was becoming the major impediment to the aspirations of AI programmers. The fact that the DEC-10 was timeshared among several users meant that one had to work late at night to get anything like adequate performance. Although there were graphical displays for these machines (such as the Knight TVs at MIT), they were nonstandard and were not really utilized by the LISP software. The lack of hardware support for data type checking caused serious performance bottlenecks that were only avoided by compiling code that omitted all safety checks, often leading to obscure and undebuggable software failures. Finally, the fact that the garbage collector seizes total control of the machine and causes delays during which one can't use the machine was becoming aggravating. Although these were fairly short interruptions, it was clear that this brevity was an artifact of the limited address space of the DEC-10; there just wasn't much memory to garbage collect. It was clear that if we were to progress we would need higher performance machines with special features to support the object-oriented viewpoint of LISP.

2.3 *The Recent Past*

Many of these problems began to be addressed when Xerox PARC and then the MIT AI Lab developed the first workstations. Hardware technology had developed enough by the mid-1970s that it had become possible to build a full-scale computer on a few printed circuit boards. Economically this meant that one no longer had to share the computer among a large number of researchers, but could instead dedicate a full computer to each individual. Furthermore this computer could be physically compact, fitting alongside (or underneath) the desk. Since the machine was dedicated it was also possible to use a high resolution graphical display, devoting some of the processor's power to creating a pleasant user interface.

Xerox PARC led the way with a machine called the Alto [Thacker et al., 1979]; this was the predecessor to their D-Machine series. The Alto was a microcoded machine with a large enough microstore to implement several different instruction sets; one of these was customized to supporting INTERLISP [Deutsch, 1979]. I won't spend much time talking about the Alto since it is less interesting from the point of view of symbolic computing than is the MIT CADR. However, the style of interface and the very idea of a personal computer pioneered by PARC greatly influenced the MIT efforts. The MIT machine, which we will look at in some detail, in turn greatly influenced the design of the PSI [Taki et al., 1984], the logic programming oriented machine built by ICOT, the Japanese Fifth Generation Project's research center.

2.3.1 The MIT CADR The MIT CADR [Greenblatt, 1984] was the outgrowth of a project started by Richard Greenblatt and Tom Knight at MIT in the mid-1970s. (There was an initial prototype called CONS [Knight, 1984], but the first really usable machine was substantially redesigned and so renamed CADR, which means "second" in LISP). The goal of this project was to produce a "LISP Machine," i.e., a machine that met the needs of symbolic computing. Its design directly addressed many of the shortcomings of the DEC-10 that were constraining the research community. The CADR addressed the needs of the object-oriented viewpoint by dispensing with BIBOP and instead introducing the idea that data in the machine carried their own tags.

The CADR was a 32-bit machine. It broke each word into 24 bits of data and 8 bits of tag. Six of the tag bits were used to encode data types, while the other two (called the CDR-codes) were used for representing list structures compactly. The 24-bit data field also served as an address field for pointer data. This gave a relatively large address space for its day (24 bits of word address, compared to the DEC-10's 18 bits).

The CADR introduced several major new capabilities. First, it was microcoded to check the data types on all operations. Since this was more efficient than the BIBOP scheme, the need for declarations or unsafe compiler tricks was removed. Secondly, it introduced a new "real-time" garbage collection scheme based on ideas by Henry Baker [1978] which removed the need for the garbage collector to seize total control of the machine. The Flavors [Weinreb and Moon, 1979; Moon, 1986] object-oriented programming paradigm (one of the major influences on the Common LISP Object Standard) was introduced on the CADR and special microcode was written to provide efficient support for this technique. Finally, the instruction set and data formats of the CADR were those of a stack machine, a style of architecture that seemed like a very natural way of supporting a stack-oriented language like LISP. It also introduced the idea of invisible pointers; that is specific data types which say, "Don't look here, look there." These turned out to be very important for the garbage collector (serving as the GC-Forward mark) and for logic programming (serving as logic variables). The whole operating system was written in LISP.

Figure 10 enumerates many of the hardware details of this machine. It was built in the mid to late 1970s. It had a relatively fast microcoded engine with a cycle time of 180 nanoseconds (relatively fast for this generation). The micro-engine was, by design, extremely general purpose. The purpose of this machine was to investigate structures for efficiently supporting symbolic computing and so the machine had few wired-in ideas about the nature of its instruction set or data formats. That was all implemented in the microcode. It had a large microstore, containing 16,000 words of 48 bits. The general control structure of the micro-engine was dispatching; i.e., branching to specific microcode routines based on the content of subfields of the data being processed. It had a large (1K) internal bank of fast 32-bit registers with a few special features that let these be used as a buffer for the top of the stack.

Let's look a little deeper into the way the micro-engine implemented the abstractions of symbolic computing. The basic control structure of the micro-engine, as I said, was dispatching. In fact, the micro-engine had only four types of cycles, which were: (1) Running the ALU. (2) Extracting a byte field. (3) Branching to a specific location in the microstore, and (4) Dispatching on a subfield of any datum in the processor. The subfield could be up to 7 bits long and was used as an index into a special *dispatch memory* inside the processor which contained addresses of other microcode routines to jump to.

The Cadr (son of Cons) ~ 1976
Microprogrammed, General Purpose, 32 Bit

Basic Control Structure is Dispatching

First Microcoded Lisp Engine	16K x 48 Microstore
Hardware Stack Cache	1K x 32 bits
Microcoded Data Type Checking	180 ns cycle time
Microcoded Invisibile Pointers	
Whole Operating System in Lisp	
Extremely General Instruction Set Emulator	

Figure 10 Details of the MIT CADR.

Given these capabilities, it takes the CADR 10 to 20 cycles of the micro-engine to interpret a simple instruction. The interpretation of a *plus* instruction, for example, involves the following steps:

- Extract the opcode from the word and dispatch on it (i.e., before it could do anything, it had to figure out what instruction it was to execute).
- Extract a second field from the instruction and dispatch on this to determine where to leave the result of the instruction.
- Extract another field from the instruction and dispatch on this to determine how to address the stack. In particular, it has to determine which of several internal processor registers to use as the base register for the stack address calculation.
- Extract an offset field from the instruction and add this to the base register to calculate the stack address.
- Read this location from the stack cache.
- Extract the data type field of this datum and dispatch on it to the routine appropriate for adding this kind of data.
- Run the ALU.
- Write the results back.

Each of these steps takes a few cycles since each involves a byte extraction and a dispatch cycle, at least. That's why, on average, something as simple as a *plus* instruction takes 10–20 cycles. One way of looking at this is that the CADR microcode has to perform roughly the same operations as the BIBOP scheme. The major difference is that it does not have to consult a *master type table* because the data type is stored with the datum. Secondly it performs these operations in the microcode which is faster at such tasks than a program written the instruction set of a conventional machine. Nevertheless, the CADR pays quite a performance penalty for interpreting the instruction set and data types. In addition its numeric data is nonstandard because it is only a 32-bit machine, and it uses some of those bits for data types. Fixed-point numbers are only 24 bits long and floating-point numbers don't fit into a single word and must be *cons'd*.

What is supposed to make up for this it is you have the machine all to yourself. The CADR is a machine with a faster cycle time than that of the DEC-10's which populated the labs at the time of its introduction and you didn't have share it with 20 other researchers. The assumption was that you could afford to throw away cycles. (It's an interesting side-point that the idea of a personal research machine was so powerful that at the beginning of the CADR's microcode listing was a quotation from *Tommy*, the rock opera, that said "Here comes a man to bring you a machine all of your own.")

2.3.1.1 *Incremental Garbage Collection* The CADR also introduced a further evolution of garbage collection technology which was incremental in the sense that a program could keep running while the garbage collection did its work. This technique involved a very small modification of the copying garbage collector. As you will recall, the Stop-and-Copy garbage collection works by scavenging the area of new space that contains pointers to old space; after a location is scavenged, it will necessarily point to new space. Once the scavenge pointer catches up to the transport pointer we can guarantee that there are no pointers to old space left in new space; therefore, old space can be reclaimed.

In effect, the CADR's garbage collector runs the Stop-and-Copy garbage collector in a separate process, while normal programs run in their own processes.

How can this interleaving effect the basic invariant of the Stop-and-Copy collector? There are only two ways: The first is that the processor itself might have a pointer in an internal register that points to old space. The second is that a process might allocate new storage containing a pointer to old space. In either of these cases, we would no longer be able to guarantee that no live data in new space points to old space. Both these problems can be fixed by guaranteeing that there will never be a pointer to old space inside the processor. This directly addresses the first issue and indirectly addresses the second. If the processor can never contain a pointer to old space, it can never initialize newly allocated storage to point to old space. To do so it would need to write a pointer to old space into the new storage. But to write such a pointer, it must first be in a processor register, and no processor register is allowed to point to old space.

So how do we enforce this guarantee? It's very simple. We make the processor check every datum that it reads to see whether it's a pointer that points to old space. In the CADR, this was implemented by first dispatching on the data type of the word read, to see if it is a pointer and if it is by dispatching on a field kept in the virtual memory page table which indicates whether a page is in new or old space. If both these conditions hold, the processor dispatches to the *transport* routine (which we've already seen in the Stop-and-Copy garbage collector). Since transporting always produces a pointer to new space, the processor never winds up loading a pointer to old space.

To state this more simply: The hardware was made capable of trapping on any read from memory that would have loaded a pointer to old space. The trap routine transports the data, guaranteeing that there are only new space pointers inside the processor. This small addition of hardware capability makes it possible to run a very large program in parallel with the garbage collector. The interruption of the application program is bounded by the rather small time that it takes to transport a location; therefore, the "coffee break length interruption" that used to be necessary for garbage collection is no longer necessary.

In practice, this scheme didn't work out so well. The reason is that the scavenging part of the garbage collector needs to sweep through the entire address space, touching all the pages in the virtual memory of the machine. Scavenging proceeds linearly through new space but it processes data that point to a highly random set of locations in old space, each of which needs to be transported. Transporting accesses both the page in new space with the pointer and the page in old space that it points at. Finally, it accesses the page in new space to which the datum is transported. Thus, the garbage collector can cause a large number of page faults and these are *very slow* by comparison to the speed of the processor. Therefore, while the garbage collector is running the machine thrashes. The page traffic becomes incredible, and the machine slows down unacceptably.

Nonetheless the CADR proved to be a very powerful experimental vehicle, providing the main computing platform for AI research work at MIT. After several years of use at MIT, it was time for the CADR to move into the world. Two companies spun off to commercialize the technology. LISP Machines Inc. (LMI) produced a machine with the CADR architecture called the Lambda and Symbolics Inc. as its first product repackaged the CADR as its LM-2. Texas Instruments entered into a joint technology venture with LMI which coupled the CADR's architecture to TI's NuBus (which incidentally was also designed at MIT originally). The machine is called the Explorer. TI then further developed this into a single chip implementation called the Compact LISP Machine which is the processor in the Explorer-II. Architecturally, this machine is still essentially the MIT CADR with a few new wrinkles.

2.4 *Modern Times*

Hardware advances in the late 1970s, coupled with the insights gained from the CADR experiment led to a new generation of systems that appeared in the 1980s. One major development was the creation of an entirely new LISP Machine architecture by Symbolics Inc. Symbolics was founded by many of the CADR designers who felt that enough had been learned from the CADR to design a much higher performance architecture. The resulting machine was called the 3600 [Symbolics, 1983; Moon, 1985]; it introduced special purpose hardware to perform data type checking, and a newer form of garbage collection, called *ephemeral garbage collection*, that fixed the problems uncovered in the CADR experience [Moon, 1984].

A second major set of advances that occurred during these years was the consolidation of a set of efficient technique for implementing logic programming; much of this work was done by David Warren at the University of Edinburgh and at SRI International. These techniques, known as the Warren Abstract Machine (WAM), lead to PROLOG implementations of very high-performance, opening the possibility of using logic programming techniques as part of the normal repertoire of an AI programmer. Although these techniques were developed originally in a compiler for the DEC-10, they have been adopted for a large variety of other machines. In particular, special data types were introduced in the CADR and the 3600 to support Warren's ideas and the PSI machine designed at ICOT (the Japanese Fifth Generation research center) was also influenced by these techniques.

2.4.1 *The 3600*

The first commercial 3600s were shipped to customers around the end of 1982. Like the CADR, it's a microcoded workstation; however it is a 36-bit machine, and it contains many hardware features that provide a much higher level of support for symbolic computation. In particular, many things that are implemented by dispatching in the CADR were wired directly into the hardware control structure of the 3600. Moon [1985] presents an excellent overview of this architecture.

2.4.1.1 *Trapping Control Structure*

The basic control structure of the 3600 is not dispatching but trapping. To see the difference it is useful to consider how each machine implements the *plus* instruction. As we saw before, this involves a large number of byte field extraction and dispatching steps in the CADR because neither the instruction set nor the data format is defined by the hardware. In contrast, the 3600 has a predefined instruction set format, so there are simple, direct connections that extract the opcode from an instruction and the type field from a datum. It also has much more direct support for the stack cache, including a special ALU dedicated to stack cache address calculation. The *plus* instruction takes a single cycle on the 3600; during this cycle the stack cache address is calculated, the addressed stack location (as well as the top of the stack) is read from the stack cache and driven into the ALU. In parallel with the ALU running, a special section of hardware, called the "tag processor" checks the data types of the operands; if these are not both integers, a trap signal is generated and the processor is redirected to a microcode routine that can handle the actual data types.

The strategy in the 3600 is to assume that the data types will be those which the hardware can deal with quickly; if this assumption is wrong, the machine traps to a routine that correctly handles the slower case. Now since this prediction is fairly accurate, most instructions don't need to trap. You complete most of the instructions as fast as possible, without the dispatching overhead of the CADR.

Trapping is also used in the 3600 to support the garbage collector. As you'll recall, the crucial facility needed by the CADR's garbage collector is the ability to check every datum read into the processor to see if it's a pointer to old space. In the CADR this cost several dispatching cycles. In the 3600 this facility is provided by a trap caused by the combination of the "tag processor" signalling that the datum read has a pointer data type and the "GC map" hardware signalling that the location pointed at by the datum is in old space. In the common case, when there is no trap, the check costs no time.

2.4.1.2 *Hardware Features* Let's look at some features of this machine's hardware these are shown in Figure 11. For more details see [Moon, 1984, 1985]. The 3600 has a much wider microcode word and a much more parallel micro-engine. There are about 100 bits in each microinstruction word; this wide control word controls a much larger set of facilities than that of the CADR. These include the *tag processor*, the *GC map*, the *stack cache addressing ALU*, the normal datapath's ALU, and the pipelined memory interface. The microstore contains 16K words. The machine has 36-bit words, broken into a 32-bit datum and four bits of tag (two of these bits encode the CDR code and two encode the data type). The data type tag is actually implemented in a two-level scheme. Immediate numeric data such single precision fixed and floating-point numbers are encoded by specific two bit tags. However, if the first two bits do not indicate that the data is immediate numeric data, then 4 more bits are taken from the datum part of the word. In that case, there are 6 data type bits and 28 bits of pointer address. So you have 28 bit addresses, 32 bit numbers, and enough tag to tell the difference. These data formats are known about in the hardware.

The cycle time of this machine is actually just a little slower than the CADR's (about 200 nanoseconds) but because of the greater efficiency of the micro-control system, this machine runs considerably faster than the CADR. This is because the most frequent simple instructions such as Push, Pop, Plus, etc. execute in a single cycle; additionally, function calling executes in about 20 clock cycles on the 3600 but takes close to 100 on the CADR.

Symbolics 3600 ~ 1982
Microprogrammed, Lisp Specific, 36 Bit

Basic Control Structure is Trapping

100 bit x 16K Horizontal Microcode	Concurrent Data and Control Path Execution
36-bit Data Format (Data plus Tag)	32 bit Arithmetic
Hardware Defined Data Formats	Hardware Data Type Trapping
210 ns Cycle Time	
Pipelined Memory Access	Hardware Assisted Garbage Collection

Figure 11 Details of the Symbolics 3600.

Now the overall efficiency of a computer comes from three factors. The first is the efficiency of the instruction set (i.e., how many instructions does it take to do a particular task). The second is the "architectural constant" which is the average number of clock cycles it takes to execute an instruction. The third factor is the length of a clock cycle. The last of these is obviously very much influenced by the implementation technology. The 3600 sacrificed a little on the third of these measures but improved on the first two dramatically. On balance it wound up being 3 to 5 times faster than a CADR (depending on the task).

2.4.1.3 *Memory Pipelining* The 3600 also introduced pipelining in the memory system. One of the reasons for this is that the processor runs much more quickly than its memory. This mismatch of speeds means that every access of memory causes the processor to wait for the memory to return the data. In the 3600 design, the processor is not forced to idle while waiting for the memory. Often there is some check that can be done during the idle cycles; for example, when accessing an array element, you can check that the reference is within the bounds of the array. The other thing you can do while waiting for data to return from memory is to issue another memory request; this can be done since the bus in the 3600 provides separate address and data lines and the memory is implemented as a set of separately functioning (i.e., *interleaved*) banks. When used this way, the processor can access a word from memory on every cycle, although each word comes back a few cycles after the request is issued. This type of pipelined memory accessing is used by the instruction prefetcher, by routines in the garbage collector that sequentially scan pages of memory, and by graphics routines like BITBLT.

2.4.1.4 *The Tag Processor* Structurally, the 3600 is just a conventional (stack-oriented) computer with some extra facilities added on. (It is in no sense specialized; it just has some special facilities in addition to the normal ones.) This can be seen in Figure 12 which shows the data format and the structure of the datapath of the machine. A word has a conventional 32-bit datum with an extra 4-bit tag. The 32-bit datum is processes by a normal ALU as it would be in any other computer. The tag is processed by the *tag processor*, which is the part of the machine that is unique. On each cycle, the microcode instructs the tag processor which types to check for. The ALU produces a set of signals that indicate exceptional arithmetic conditions (overflow, underflow, etc.); the tag processor produces other signals (such as whether the data is illegal, can only be handled by a trap routine, and whether its arithmetic or pointer data). The ALU (the conventional machine) and the tag processor (the symbolic computing part of the machine) run in parallel. The tag processor generates trap signals that inhibit the writing of any results into registers when the data types are illegal, just as the ALU generates traps that inhibit side effects when the results overflow the precision of the machine.

Figure 13 shows the hardware organization in a little more detail. The top of the stack is held in a bank of fast processor registers implemented as a 4K-by-36-bit internal memory. There is also a smaller scratch-pad register file, which holds a second copy of the top word of the stack as well as some other data. A typical two-input instruction takes its first operand from the top of the stack and fetches its other operand from a stack location encoded in the instruction. These two operands are processed by the ALU. In parallel, the tag processor looks at the tags of the operands and either confirms or traps the operation.

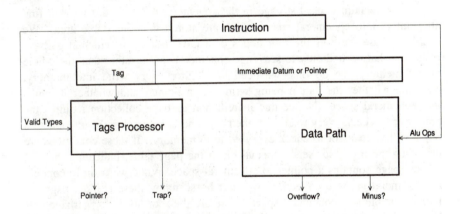

Figure 12 The datapath of the Symbolics 3600.

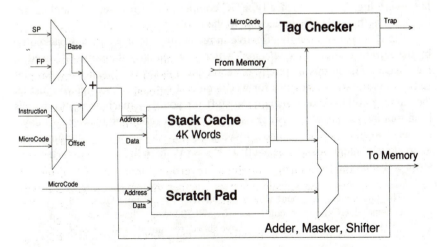

Figure 13 The stack cache and datapath of the Symbolics 3600.

2.4.1.5 *Ephemeral Garbage Collection* The 3600 introduced a third innovation in garbage collection technology, called *Ephemeral Garbage Collection* (EGC) [Moon, 1984]. This technique is aimed at overcoming the page thrashing and other large overheads associated with the CADR's incremental garbage collector. The insight behind the EGC is the observation that a small region of memory holds nearly all of the most volatile data. Typically this region (called the Ephemeral region) is where temporary results are rapidly created and equally quickly thrown away. Relative to the size of the whole address space, the Ephemeral region is tiny. Conversely, the region containing static structures (for example, knowledge bases) is huge. Clearly, we should try to concentrate our efforts on reclaiming storage from the ephemeral area since that's where we'd reclaim the most storage per unit of work done.

But to reclaim unused storage in the ephemeral region, we'd have to find all pointers into ephemeral space which are stored in more stable areas. We could then use these as the root nodes of a CADR-style incremental garbage collection that needed only to scavenge ephemeral space, rather than the whole virtual memory. To do this, we need to monitor every write into memory, checking whether the datum being written is a pointer and whether it points into ephemeral space. (Notice that incremental garbage collection requires the processor to check every read from memory, and ephemeral garbage collection requires the processor to check every write to memory.) If these conditions are met, then the processor sets a special bit in the page table, indicating that the marked page contains a pointer to ephemeral space. When we want to conduct an ephemeral garbage collection, we start by scanning these marked pages to find the pointers to ephemeral space; these are the root nodes for garbage collecting this area. From this point on, the garbage collection algorithm is identical to that used in the CADR; it's just concentrated on a very small area that has a very high payoff. Typically, EGC completes in a few seconds and causes degradation that is hardly noticeable to the user.

The EGC is exceedingly effective in reclaiming storage and it is backed up by the *Dynamic Garbage Collector* (which is essentially the same GC used in the CADR). Given this hierarchy of techniques, it's very typical that LISP Machine users run their machines for weeks on end without rebooting; you just let the garbage collector keep reclaiming stuff for you. My machine right now has been running for about four weeks straight without rebooting (4 weeks, 5 days, 3 hours, 36 minutes, 53 seconds, to be precise), supporting a continuing program development session as well as the work to edit this paper. Here are some statistics on what it's done:

> The GC generation count is 959 (1 full GC, 37 dynamic GCs, and 921 ephemeral GCs). Since cold boot 162,578,792 words have been consed, 150,960,828 words of garbage have been reclaimed, and 234,476,700

words of nongarbage have been transported. The total "scavenger work" required to accomplish this was 1,340,776,491 units.

2.4.1.6 *The Special Hardware* The 3600 contains only a few special hardware modules to support tag processing and garbage collection. I've already mentioned the existence of the tag processor, which detects and traps illegal operations, controls the dispatching for generic operations, and distinguishes pointers from immediate data for the garbage collector. Another module, called the *GC Map*, can tell us, amongst other things, whether a pointer points into ephemeral space and whether it points into old space. The special logic used by the EGC is shown in Figure 14. It forms the conjunction of two signals that these modules provide: POINTER-DATA-TYPE and POINTER-TO-EPHEMERAL; if this conjoined signal is true and there is a memory write operation being performed then the microcode turns on a bit in the page table entry for the page being written. This bit indicates that the page contains at least one pointer to ephemeral space.

These extra hardware modules are implemented by small memories inside the processor. The tag processor (see Figure 15) is an internal processor memory. It is addressed an index created by concatenating a 6-bit microcode field with the 6-bit data type field of the datum being checked. Each entry of this memory is a few bits wide and encodes a set of signals such as: "arithmetic trap," "illegal data type," "pointer data type." This memory is preprogrammed at the time you boot the machine; you can think of its contents as part of the microcode. Tag processing consists of fetching the appropriate word from this memory and driving it into the various logic modules that use these signals; in particular, the GC logic and the trapping logic.

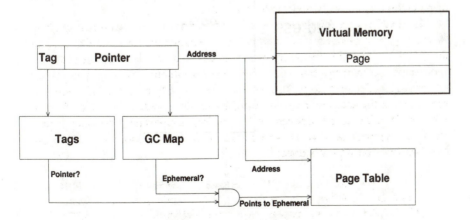

Figure 14 Hardware support for The Ephemeral Garbage Collector.

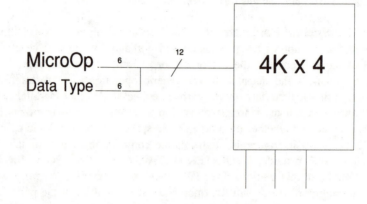

Figure 15 The tag processor of the Symbolics 3600.

The GC map (see Figure 16) is also a small memory internal to the processor, which is indexed by a subfield of a pointer's address. The contents of each word is a small number of bits that encode information such as "pointer to ephemeral space" and "pointer to old space." This memory is initialized by the virtual memory manager and the GC during the creation of a new page and the flipping of new and old space.

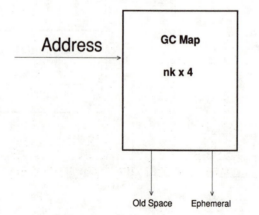

Figure 16 The Symbolics 3600 GC map.

What is the total hardware cost for providing these features? It only adds up to about 10% extra hardware, most of which is fairly cheap. What it adds up to in performance is shown in Figure 17. This shows the performance on the more interesting Gabriel benchmarks of a 3600 and a conventional 68020-based machine. Both machines are measured doing the benchmarks with full type checking enabled. The 3600 can be seen to have qualitatively better performance. It should be noted that the 68020 processor is implemented in hardware technology a generation more modern than that of the 3600, and it runs with a faster cycle time. If we were to compare systems implemented with equivalent technologies, the comparison would be even more favorable to the machine which contained special features for symbolic computing. The small addition of hardware buys a lot. Figure 18 shows why this is true. The assembly code on the left is what the 3600 would have to execute for the simple processor shown; the code on the right is what the compiler for the 68020 would have to emit. The conventional processor needs to execute roughly 10 instructions for one executed by the 3600.

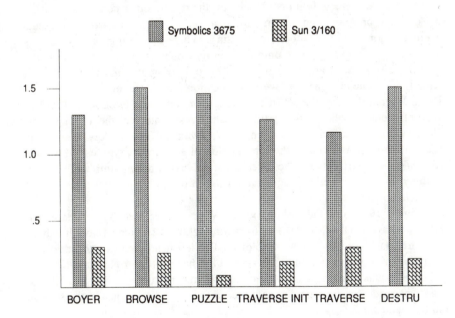

Figure 17 Comparative performance of a symbolic and a conventional processor.

Description	Conventional Machine	Symbolic Processor
Fetch Operand 1	1	
Extract Tag	1	
Fetch Operand 2	1	
Extract Tag	1	
Compare Tags	1	
Branch to Proper Add Code	1	1
Execute Add	1	
Generate Result Tag	1	
Merge Tag Into Result	1	
Store Result	1	
Total	**10**	**1**

Figure 18 Steps in a generic add operation for a symbolic and a conventional processor

2.4.2 *The Warren Abstract Machine*

While the attention of people in Cambridge was centered on LISP Machines, there were other people concentrating on logic programming and in particular, on PROLOG. This work represents another major trend in symbolic computing. Where logic programming differs most strongly from LISP programming is in its emphasis on Unification. (I suspect that people who are more involved in logic programming that I am will regard this statement as an oversimplification.) As I've mentioned earlier, David Warren developed a set of techniques for compiling PROLOG that lead to very efficient implementations; these techniques center on the efficient implementation of unification [Warren, 1977; 1980; 1983]. One key idea in the Warren Abstract Machine is the introduction of a new data type called a *logic variable*; logic variables are the objects that get bound during unification. Interestingly, in a LISP Machine, logic variables turn out to be just a special kind of invisible pointer.

Figure 19 shows the task to which Warren's techniques are addressed. Here we have a set of PROLOG clauses (or backward chaining rules, for those who are more used to this terminology). The left-hand side of each rule is a statement of a goal which might be solved by that rule; the right-hand side is a set of subgoals that must be solved for the rule to succeed. A rule with no right-hand side can be regarded as a fact; a top-level goal is just a clause with no left-hand side.

In PROLOG, when a goal is posted, the system finds rules whose left-hand sides match the goal. By matching we mean that there is an assignment of values to the logic variables (indicated by leading question marks in my notation) that makes both the goal and the head of the clause equal. Matching a variable with a constant is straightforward, this involves simply binding the variable to the constant value. However, when a variable is matched to another variable, they must be unified in such a way that if either variable is later matched against a constant, then both variables will be bound to its value.

In the example in Figure 19, we have a clause (the grandfather clause) which says that ?X is ?Y's grandfather if there is some ?Z such that ?X is ?Z's father and ?Z is ?Y's father. We start off by asking if there is someone (?WHO) that Abraham is the grandfather of. This query is matched against the head of the grandfather clause; binding ?X to Abraham and ?WHO to ?Y. The first subgoal on the right is now posted. The goal asks if there is a ?Z of which ?X is the father; but ?X is not bound to Abraham, so we really ask who is Abraham the father of. This query matches the fact the Abraham is the father of Isaac, which unifies the variable ?Z with Isaac. We then proceed to the next subgoal which asks whether ?Z is the father of ?Y. ?Z is of course now bound to Isaac and ?Y is unified with the variable ?WHO from the original query; so this query amounts to asking whose father is Isaac. This matches a fact which states that Isaac is Jacob's father. Performing this match matches ?Y with Jacob; but ?Y is unified with ?WHO from the original query so it also unifies ?WHO with Jacob. We return with these bindings in effect, learning that one possible value for ?WHO is Jacob, i.e., that Abraham is the grandfather of Jacob.

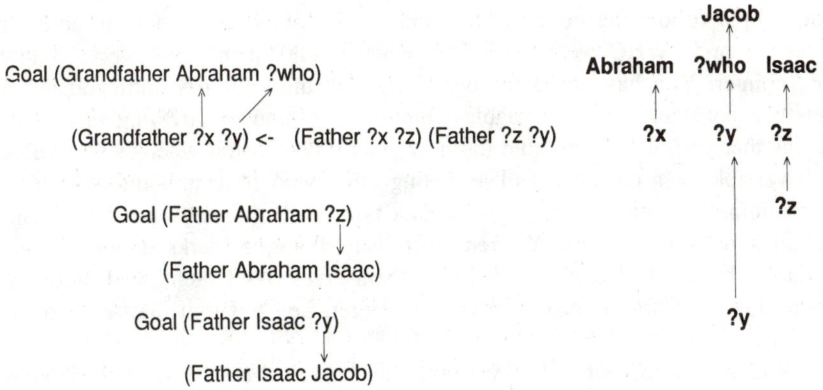

Figure 19 The reasoning task addressed by PROLOG.

If we want to get more answers (Abraham could be the grandfather of other people), we then return to the last place where a choice was made (for example, Isaac could have been the father of other children but we chose to work with Jacob first), undo the bindings created for that choice and then proceed with the next choice. This choice may create other bindings. If a particular choice doesn't work out (it leads to a subgoal which cannot be unified with the head of any clause) then we backtrack to the last choice point, undoing the bindings made at that level. A new clause for this subgoal is then chosen if there are any remaining; if not we unwind to the choice point previous to this one. So, in effect, PROLOG searches depth first and backtracks chronologically when encountering a failure. (In passing, I should mention that this same paradigm was also introduced in Carl Hewitt's Planner language somewhat earlier than the first PROLOG.)

The challenge in implementing this paradigm is to find an efficient technique for binding logic variables. In particular, it's important to notice that logic variables can get unified to other logic variables and that there is no upper bound to the number of variables that be unified into a single group. Warren's techniques are based around two insights. The first is that the depth first search technique used in PROLOG can be supported in an (extended) stack discipline. As is usual for stack-based implementations, when a clause is invoked, the variables in the clause are assigned locations in the stack frame for this invocation. Warren's second insight is that when a variable is unified, all you have to do is make it point to the thing to which it is bound (because of the stack discipline, you have to ensure that these pointers always point from more recent to older locations in the stack). To look up the value of a variable, you simple follow the pointer. Of course, if it points to another variable (as when ?Y and ?WHO were unified in our example), then you have to follow that pointer. You have to keep "dereferencing" the variables until you either get to a constant or to a variable which isn't bound to anything else. This means that you have to be able to check data types, to tell whether something is a variable or a constant, and to distinguish bound from unbound variables. Some implementations use a special data type to distinguish bound from unbound logic variables, but Warren's original technique marks unbound logic variables by the fact that they point to themselves. As I mentioned before, a bound logic variable is just an invisible pointer, i.e., a datum that says "don't look here, look there."

Warren worked out an entire instruction set based on the ideas of dereferencing and unifying logic variables [Warren, 1983]. Dereferencing involves checking the type of the datum and, if it's a bound logic variable, following it to the datum that it points to, and continuing this process until a datum is encountered which is not a bound logic variable. It turned out that our data type checking hardware was just what was needed to support dereferencing even though it had been designed for a different purpose.

Unification is the basic step of the matching process. Unification consists of first dereferencing the two items to be unified. Notice that if either of the items is a logic variable, dereferencing will produce the ultimate "home" of the datum; if the variable is bound to a constant, the home is that constant; if the variable is bound to other variables, the home is the location of the single logic variable at the end of the chain of indirect pointers. Unification then checks the data types of the two items. If both are constants, then we simply perform an equality check; if the items are equal we continue, otherwise we initiate a failure. If only one item is a logic variable, then it is bound to the other. This means that we make the location containing the home of the logic variable point to the other datum. Since a logic variable is always dereferenced before it is used, it will behave exactly as if it were the constant to which it's bound. If both items being unified are unbound logic variables, then one is made to point to the other (as I've said, the pointers are always managed so that variables more recently added to the stack point to older ones). This makes the two logic variables behave as if they were the same datum.

Of course, there needs to be some bookkeeping to keep track of choice points and the choices remaining at each one. These are kept on a special stack which is shown in Figure 20. In addition, we need to keep track of when the variables are bound so that when we fail we will know what to unbind. This information is kept on another stack called the "trail." Finally, there is another stack which hold values that cannot be kept in the main stack; the reason for needing this stack is too complex to explain here, see [Warren, 1980, 1983] for more details.

Data Areas

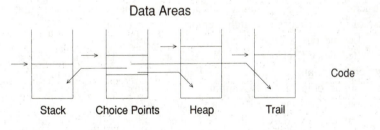

Stack   Choice Points   Heap   Trail   Code

Instruction Set:

Procedural: Proceed, Allocate, Call
Get/Put: Get-variable, Get-constant, Get-structure, Put-variable, ...
Unify: Unify-variable, unify-constant, unify-nil
Indexing: Try-me, Retry-me, Trust-me, Switch-on-term, Switch-on-constant, ...
Random Additions:

Figure 20 The Warren Abstract Machine model.

2.5 *Summary*

We have seen how, in order to present a uniform, or symmetric, view of the programming process, the object-oriented viewpoint grew up in the symbolic computing community. This viewpoint centers around the need to be able to identify the extent and type of an object just by examining it in memory. In addition, this viewpoint requires efficient support for storage management, in particular, for garbage collection.

Over the last 15 years or so, a series of very powerful techniques have been developed for supporting this viewpoint. Probably, the 3600 architecture was the first one in which there was a clear identification of what is unique and important about symbolic computing. A symbolic computer is simply a conventional computer with a small amount of extra hardware added in to check data types and support garbage collection. I think it's fair to say that the nature of the conventional processor part of the machine is not crucial as long as it provides high-performance procedure calls. It need not be a stack machine like that in the 3600; it could be a register-oriented RISC processor as well, as is being explored by the Berkeley SPUR group [Hill, 1986].

2.5.1 *The Future of Uniprocessor Symbolic Computers* I'd like to say a few things about what's coming next within the uniprocessor world. I think that the main driving force will be technology, in particular, the use of VLSI. This gives us the ability to implement a single chip microprocessor with architectural techniques that were conventionally found only in mainframes; these include pipelining, the use of "scoreboarding" techniques to execute instructions out of order safely (although no one has actually done that yet), the use of lots of caches to match memory and processor speed, and so on.

Let me talk a little bit about a LISP microprocessor I worked on; this chip is called Ivory [Baker et al., 1987; Edwards et al., 1987], and although it is not yet commercially available (as of January 1988), it has been announced. There is a single chip LISP CPU announced and shipped by TI which is called the Compact LISP Machine [Bosshart et al., 1987]. Architecturally, the CLM chip is essentially a CADR (with some further architectural tricks) implemented in a very fast VLSI technology.

The Ivory chip is much more in the 3600 tradition; it has about 3 to 5 times the performance of the 3600 measured over a typical mix of instructions. It is of the same complexity as an Intel 80386 or a Motorola 68030. Figure 21 is a photomicrograph of the chip (chip people always seem to need to show their chip pictures). The Ivory chip is more or less divided into three horizontal slices; the top is the datapath and stack cache, the middle is the control system, and the bottom is the memory interface. In the middle of the control system is a very large microstore, again comparable to what you'd see in a 80386 or a 68020 class machine.

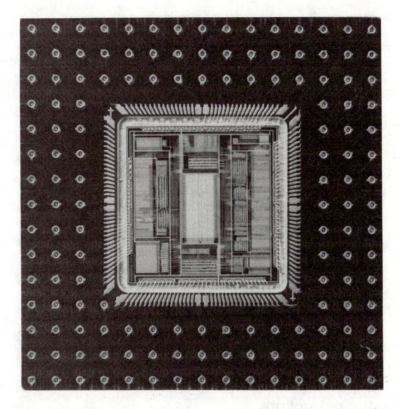

Figure 21 Photomicrograph of the Ivory processor.

Ivory is a pipelined machine. It has several separate stages, each of which is active during each cycle. An instruction flows sequentially through the pipeline stages, but you can have a different instruction in each of the stages at once. The pipeline stages are called *Instruction, Decode, Execute,* and *Confirm.* Simple instructions spend one cycle in each stage of the pipeline. Figure 22 shows a two-instruction sequence consisting of a *Pop* and an *add* instruction moving through the pipeline. In the first cycle, the Pop instruction is in the *Instruction* stage, where it is read from the on-chip instruction cache and some initial decoding is performed. The address of the next instruction to be executed is also calculated in this stage. The next stage is the *Decode* stage; this stage performs the stack cache address calculation (much as happens in the 3600) and in parallel looks up the first microinstruction to be executed for this instruction. The *Execute* stage reads the operands from the stack and runs the ALU; in parallel the tag processor performs whatever type checking is necessary. Finally, the *Confirm* stage uses the result of the type checking to determine if a

trap is necessary. If so, it backs up the pipeline (moving information from the *Confirm* stage to the *Execute* stage) and redirects the processor to the trap handling routine. Otherwise, the result of the calculation is written into the appropriate destination.

You can see from the chart in Figure 23, which is called a *Reservation Table*, that you can complete simple instructions at the rate of one per clock cycle; in addition, an instruction will inhabit each stage of the pipeline on every cycle. Because the total work is broken down into pipeline stages, the cycle rate of the clock can be made shorter than it was in the 3600. With current and near-term technology, an Ivory processor could probably be made to run with a 50-nanosecond clock. Of course, expert chip designers (like those at Motorola or Intel or TI) could make it run faster.

PROGRAM:	I	D	E	C
PUSH A				
PUSH B	**ADD**	PUSH B	PUSH A	——
ADD	POP C	**ADD**	PUSH B	PUSH A
POP C	——	POP C	**ADD**	PUSH B
	——	——	POP C	**ADD**
	——	——	——	POP C

Figure 22 Two Instructions in the Ivory Pipeline.

Sample Instructions

```
(defun bar (x y)
   (if (< 7 x 12) (foo) (+ y 2))))
```

(bar 40959 80930)

	I	D	E	C
-1	push	-	-	-
0	greaterp	push	-	-
1	**branch**	greaterp	push	-
2	lessp	**branch**	greaterp	push
3	**branch**	lessp	**branch**	greaterp
4	start-call	**branch**	lessp	**branch**
5	push	-	**branch**	lessp
6	add	push	**branch**	**branch**
7	return	add	push	**branch**

push fp|2
greaterp-no-p 7
branch-false
lessp 12
branch-false
start-call foo
finish-call return
push fp|3
add 2
return-single tos

Figure 23 A reservation chart.

Figure 24 show some statistics about Ivory. The size of the chip was about a centimeter-and-a-half on a side in the earliest version which was done using 2-micron CMOS technology. The first commercial version will be done in a 1.6 micron process and will be about a centimeter on a side, as is the TI chip. This makes it a very large, (but not impossibly large), chip to fabricate. There are about 255,000 actual transistors on the die. However, the common way of measuring chip complexity is to count the number of transistor sites; this measures the size of the internal ROMs better. Using that count, this is one of the largest chip ever done, containing nearly 400,000 transitor sites. The chip was designed very quickly (it took about 9 months from the freezing of the architecture to the first prototype chip, using a team of only 4 designers). Figure 24 also shows some numbers which tell you how much garbage collection and so on it took to do all the work needed. All the CAD tools ran on the 3600; I think these numbers show pretty clearly how important a facility the garbage collector is for large and complex problems.

In summary, an entire processor, which used to require a large box full of boards, can now be implemented in a single chip such as Ivory or the TI CLM. This means that you can now make a board which is an entire symbolic computer, including the processor, cache, main memory, and the bus interface. Such a board can be embedded inside other processors. In the near future we will certainly see LISP Machine plug-in boards for PCs, Macintoshes, Suns, MicroVAXes, etc.

Before leaving this subject, I should mention that there have been a number of interesting LISP Machine designs done outside the U.S., particularly in Japan. For example, see [Hayashi].

- CMOS - 2 Level metal
- 1.6 micron lithography
- 4.0 micron M1 Pitch
- 5.6 micron M2 Pitch
- 12.6 x 12.3 mm die size
- 156,374 N devices
- 87,438 P devices

  243,812   devices
  390K   sites
- Layout completed in 6 months

- 86,610 Electrical Nodes
- 29,025,007 bytes of CIF
  > 6000 CIF Symbols
  10,000,000 rectangles when flattened

- 17,044 Ephemeral GCs

  8,054,179,498 Words Consed
  4,090,120,205 Words Reclaimed
  6,468,520,595 Words Transported
  29,759,877,917 Units of "scavenger work"

Figure 24 Ivory statistics.

3 *Parallelism*

Now, let's turn to the future. As we've seen, one direction leads to a continued and aggressive evolution of uniprocessors leading to mainframe performance from a single processor chip. But the trend which I'd like to turn to now is parallelism. During this section of my talk, I'll describe a number of machines designed to support parallel AI programs. We'll see a lot of variation among these designs, but to state my central theme once again, symmetry and coherence are key. I'll argue that some of these machines are very much less likely to succeed than others, precisely because they fail to be symmetric or coherent. In the uniprocessor world, the need for symmetry and coherence led to a programming model, to a view of operations and data, that centered around the object-oriented viewpoint. In looking at parallel machines, this concern will persist, but the need for symmetry and coherence will show up in new ways as well.

There are a large number of dimensions along which we can characterize parallel machines (see Figure 25). One of these is grain size: Is the individual processing element a relatively large, full blown computer, say, a 16-bit or 32-bit machine, or is it small, but weak (e.g., a bit-serial processor). We'll see examples of both styles. Another dimension is the scale of the parallelism; we may divide this into three conceptual categories of small, modest, and massive. Massive parallelism involves the use of thousands to millions of processors; small scale uses 2 to 32; modest scale parallelism is the area between. Another dimension along which parallel machines differ is the style of parallel processing: Do all the processors do exactly the same thing, but on different data, (which is called SIMD, Single Instruction stream Multiple Data stream) or do they each do their own thing (which is called MIMD, Multiple Instruction, Multiple Data.) There are some combinations of these two styles, for example, an ensemble with several SIMD machines running separate SIMD programs. We'll see examples of all these.

Another dimension relates to the degree of coupling between the individual processing elements: Do the tasks they perform require very close communication and cooperation, or are they performing nearly independent and separable tasks that have low communication requirements? Need they share a common bus, memory, or address space, or do they, in fact, have separate versions of each of those? A final dimension is the style of interconnection: Are the processors laid out in a mesh where each can talk directly only to its nearest neighbors, or are they all on a single bus supporting direct connection between any pair; perhaps the processors are connected only by a local area network operating as a distributed processing system. Finally, they may be connected by a multistage switching network like an Omega network or their topology might be a higher dimensional figure such as a hypercube or a hypertorus.

Grain Size: Coarse (Microprocessor per node)
Fine (bit serial simple node)

Scale: Small (2 - 32)
Modest (Up to 1K)
Massive (Many Ks to Ms)

Processing Style: SIMD, MIMD, MultiSIMD, Cond-SIMD

Coupling: Loose, Close, Shared Memory

Interconnect: Planar Mesh
Bus
LAN
Switching Network
Hypercube
Omega

Figure 25 Dimensions of parallelism.

Since there have been many proposals, I'm forced to select a few examples that illustrate as many of these options as I can. Necessarily, I'll slight someone by omitting their ideas completely, and I'm sure that my biases will come through clearly.

3.1 *The Variable Supply Model*

The Variable Supply Model (VSM) [Singh and Genesereth, 1986] is shown in Figure 26. This is a simple idea proposed as a technique for introducing parallelism into logic programs. It is a near-term idea, implementable with current technology and minimum software complexity. This machine is a coarse-grained, small-scale, loosely connected system which uses a local area network as the interconnect. The individual processors need not share address space or memory.

The VSM is intended to support PROLOG and other paradigms that exhibit a simple structure of reducing goals to subgoals. The key idea is that anytime a goal is reduced to subgoals (or more generally, anytime a task is reduced to subtasks), the subtask can be broadcast across the network allowing another processor to work on it. Although the model doesn't assume a shared memory, it assumes that the rules are replicated in each machine (of course, if there is a shared memory, we needn't replicate the rules). In fact, not every rule need be replicated by each machine, but this assumption makes the paradigm much simpler to analyze.

Modest Scale, Coarse Grained, Loosely Coupled, LAN Connected

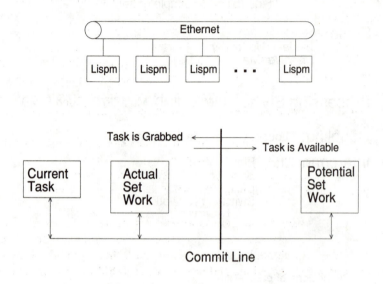

Figure 26 The Variable Supply Model.

The central problem to be confronted is that the local area network doesn't have a lot of bandwidth. There is a tradeoff between how much of the network's bandwidth you use and how much parallelism you achieve. This is easy to see by considering two extreme strategies. In the first, any new subtask is broadcast over the network, allowing any other processor to work on the task. This leads to maximum parallelism, but also uses up more network bandwidth; eventually, the performance of this approach degrades because the network is saturated and the processors wind up spending all their time trying to communicate. In the other extreme, no subtask is ever broadcast; in this case, the bandwidth of the network is not taxed at all, but you get no parallelism. For any particular problem there's a tradeoff point in the middle that successfully exploits both the processors and the network.

The VSM defines a protocol for task distribution. Each processor maintains two sets of tasks. The first set is maintained locally and includes only tasks that the processor has reserved for itself. The second set is maintained globally (it is replicated in each processor) and includes tasks that are available for any processor to work on. When a processor reduces a task to a subtask, it makes a policy choice about whether to use up network resources by broadcasting the subtask. If so, the processor broadcasts the subtask over the network and each other processor adds the new subtask to its copy of the global task pool. If the processor feels that the network is saturated or if it has no work to do, then it can decide to reserve the task for itself, simply adding it to its local task pool. When a processor runs out of private tasks, it takes a task from the global pool and broadcasts a message allocating this task to itself; all other processors must then remove the task from their copy of the global task pool. It is possible that two processors can allocate the same global task simultaneously. Each will discover this as it sees the message from the other claiming the task. One processor will relinquish the task as dictated by a tie-breaking scheme which involves the processors' ID numbers and the time at which each allocated the task.

This protocol involves relatively little overhead. For a particular problem, you can work out a policy that tends to give you good balance between parallelism and network resources. Singh and Genesereth's paper [1986] on the VSM presents an example of using the VSM in which they achieve a nearly linear speedup.

A comparison they do not make, however, is between the speed of the VSM and that of a very fast PROLOG implementation optimized for a uniprocessor. Although I do not know for sure, I suspect that a good uniprocessor implementation might exceed the performance of the VSM using many processors. One reason for my suspicion is that the VSM has a major asymmetry: Processing a subtask on a processor different from the one which processed the parent task involves broadcasting a description of the task over the network. In contrast, a subtask processed locally can use the extremely efficient techniques of the Warren Abstract Machine.

Thus, a remote processor looks very much more expensive than does the local processor. This is the sense of symmetry that will be important in discussing parallelism. If we put ourselves at one node of the multiprocessor, do all the other nodes look equally desirable to us? If not, there is an asymmetry which will tend to corrupt our programming model. The global task pool of this model also introduces a problem with coherence. In principle, every processor should have the same image of this task pool, but due to network delays this isn't true. Two processors can allocate the same task since there is a delay between the time at which each processor removes the task from its image of the global task pool and time at which the remote processor gets a notification from the network telling it that the task no longer available. There is a short time in which the two machines have an incoherent image of this shared resource. The tie breaking part of the VSM protocol is what resolves this difficulty; tie breaking in this model is not very expensive, but if it were not for the incoherent memory image, it would be unnecessary.

Singh has developed a much more complex model for parallel logic programming [Singh and Genesereth, 1987] that combines *and*-parallelism with *or*-parallelism and pipelining, but I don't have the time to describe this. In addition, I should mention that the logic programming community has proposed a large number of parallel extensions (or variations) of PROLOG [Shapiro and Takeuchi, 1983; Shapiro, 1983; 1984; Clark and Gregory, 1984].

3.2 *Production Systems*

There has also been significant interest in supporting parallel forward-chaining systems (in particular OPS-5 [Forgy, 1982]). Forward chaining is a data-driven paradigm in contrast to the goal-directed style of PROLOG. In forward-chaining systems, we have a collection of rules each of which has several trigger patterns. There is also a database of assertions, which is initially empty. As assertions are added to the database, each rule checks to see whether there is a set of assertions that match its set of trigger patterns. Each assertion from the set matches a particular pattern of the rule, binding the variables in that pattern; but it is required that a variable that occurs in more than one pattern of a rule must be bound to the same value by each of these matches. When such a set of assertions is found, the rule becomes eligible for execution; the execution of the rule can lead to new assertions being added or to old ones being removed.

In OPS-5, after all the actions of a rule are performed, the system checks to see which rules are then eligible for execution and picks a single one of these, based on a set of criteria called the "conflict resolution strategy"; the set of rules from which this selection is made is called the "conflict set." After the selected rule is executed, there will be a new conflict set (which may include many of the members of the conflict set from the previous cycle) and a new selection is made. Other forward-chaining rules do not impose this conflict resolution step, but simply allow a rule to execute whenever there is a set of assertions that consistently match its patterns.

Forgy [1982] developed an efficient algorithm for supporting this style of rule-based programming. A key component of this algorithm is a data structure called the Rete network. (*Rete*, by the way, is Latin for *spiderweb*.) The Rete network has an upper half and a lower half (see Figure 27). The upper half is a discrimination tree, which examines the incoming data (i.e., an assertion which has just been added to the database). Each node of the upper half asks a simple question about the data (such is what is the value of the next token in the assertion); based on the answer to the question, an outgoing branch that corresponds to the answer is selected and control is transferred along this branch to the next node in the network. Typically, the first several layers of the network correspond to constants that occur in a pattern of a rule. For example, if a pattern has the token FOO in the third position and the token BAR in the fifth position, then the network will have a node which asks *what is the content of the third token in the asserted data*; this node has an outgoing link corresponding to the value FOO which leads to a node that examines the fifth position; a link corresponding to the value BAR leads out from this node.

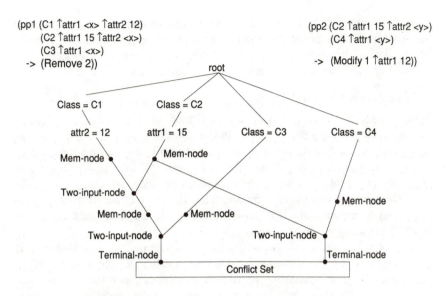

(pp1 (C1 ↑attr1 <x> ↑attr2 12)
    (C2 ↑attr1 15 ↑attr2 <x>)
    (C3 ↑attr1 <x>)
 -> (Remove 2))

(pp2 (C2 ↑attr1 15 ↑attr2 <y>)
    (C4 ↑attr1 <y>)

 -> (Modify 1 ↑attr1 12))

Figure 27 A Rete network.

Once we have passed through all the constant tests, the next node matches the variables in the pattern against the data, building a binding environment which is stored at this node. Below this node is the lower half of the network which is a merge network. The upper half finds matches to the individual patterns of a rule, but does not check whether a variable found in more than one pattern is matched consistently by the triggering assertions. The lower half of the network finds subsets of the triggering assertions that have consistent variable bindings. The structure of the lower half network consists of a series of two-input, or merge nodes. Each of these is linked to two nodes higher up in the network, for example, to two nodes which store match environments. Whenever a new environment is added to one of these upper nodes, it is compared to all the environments stored at the other of the upper nodes. If two such environments bind the variables consistently then a new environment is created and stored at the child node; this environment represents the variable bindings from both parent nodes. This child node is then paired with a node representing another pattern of the rule and the merging continues as above. Once the merging has found a set of matches for each pattern of a rule that are consistent, we get to the bottom of the network with an environment representing a rule instantiation ready for execution (i.e., it represents the rule together with the environment of its triggering matches).

3.2.1 *Dado and Non-Von*

There were two machines designed at Columbia to support this style of processing. The first of these is called *Dado* [Stolfo and Shaw, 1981, 1982, Stolfo et al., 1983] (see Figure 28). It is a massively paral-

parallel, relatively fine-grained, SIMD, tree-structured machine without shared memory. Each node of the processor tree is an 8-bit processor with a connection to two children processors and to one parent processor. Each processor has a relatively small amount of private memory (about 4K words) and they all execute a common instruction stream.

One idea for using Dado was to identify processor nodes with nodes in the Rete network (there were actually a number of different schemes for doing this, see [Gupta, 1984; Stolfo, 1984] for details). For example, it is easy to see how the upper half of the Rete network can be laid onto the tree structure of Dado. A new assertion is sent to the root processor of the tree which sends it on to one or the other of its children based on the value of some field of the data. The merging part of the Rete algorithm is also tree-like so it too is relatively easy to map onto the tree architecture of Dado. The fact that the machine is SIMD complicates this somewhat.

A second machine of this same general structure was called *Non-Von* [Shaw, 1982, 1984, 1985] (which I think of as "Dado meets the kitchen sink"), (see Figure 29). It's a massively parallel, fine-grained, tree-structured machine. However, there is also a rectilinear mesh connecting the processors at the bottom of the tree. This mesh is useful for image processing applications because you can identify the lowest level processors with individual pixels; many filtering algorithms can be performed locally, just by having each processor talk to its nearest neighbors. The tree structure can then be used to combine and process the information more globally, for example it can threshold the data.

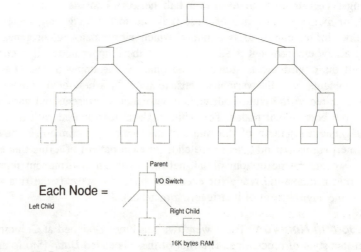

Massive, Parallel, Tree

Each Node =

Parent

I/O Switch

Left Child

Right Child

16K bytes RAM

Figure 28 Dado.

Massive, Fine-Grained, Tree and Mesh

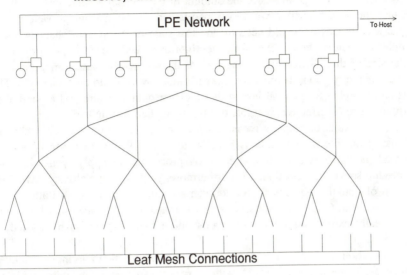

Figure 29 Non-Von.

The processors in the lower layers of Non-Von are called *small processing elements* and are 8-bit processors; those at the top are called *large processing elements*; these are Motorola 68000 processors. There is a very fast network that connects these large processing elements. The large processing elements can have disk drives with *smart read heads* for doing database applications. This is a fairly complicated machine. I don't believe that a full-blown version of the whole thing was ever built, but there were subsets constructed; typically these had 64–1000 processors.

Unfortunately both these machines speed up OPS-5 execution by a factor much smaller than the number of processors would lead you to believe. A 1000 processor system might lead to speedups of 32. The reason for this was shown in a study by Gupta [Gupta and Forgy, 1983] who simulated a variety of actual OPS-5 programs to determine how much parallelism is available in these programs. Gupta points out that almost all of what goes on in OPS-5 is matching and merging (i.e., the steps of the Rete algorithms). But the amount of parallel matching you can do is determined by how many new assertions you drop into the top of the Rete network at any one time. Typically, this number is very small—it is very often only 1. This is because the typical rule asserts or deletes a single item. When this one new assertion is added, you have to perform some tests to locate the appropriate pattern-matching nodes; once the assertion has been matched, you merely have to go through the merging process, checking what stored environments are consistent with the new assertion. Although this does lead to some parallelism, the amount of parallelism is relatively small, because the Rete algorithm was developed to reduce the amount of useless work that a uniprocessor would need to do. The state of the system changes only a little between cycles, so the work the algorithm needs to do is proportional to the size of this change, not to the size of the whole rule-base. Since the algorithm is pretty good, there really just isn't much work to do on each cycle. This is an example of a general lesson that a clever data structure and a good algorithm are more effective than lots of blindly applied parallelism.

The results of Gupta's measurements are shown in Figure 30. The parallelism available in each task is peculiar to that task but the range is not that broad. In the best case, if you have 64 processors to apply, you will get a speedup somewhat less than 15. Furthermore, you will have already passed the point of diminishing returns. As you can see, the curves have all flattened out by that point. Gupta's conclusion is that perhaps 32 processors are all that you can really exploit for OPS-5 programs; more than that would be wasted resources.

But both Von-Non and Dado involves hundreds to thousands of processors; achieving a speedup of 15 with so many resources seems particularly inefficient. The reason for this inefficiency is that the tree structure of these machines leads one to identify nodes of the Rete network with specific processors. But only a few nodes in the Rete network are active on any cycle of the algorithm, meaning that most of the processors are idle most of the time.

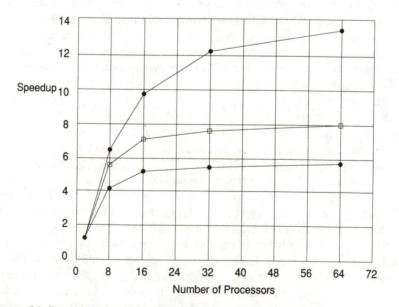

Figure 30 Production system parallelism.

We can see once again the cost of asymmetry. In these machines not all processors are equal; specific tasks can only be performed by specific processors. In addition, the time required to communicate between two processors has a delay that depends on their specific positions in the tree. Because of this, hundreds of processors are forced to do nothing even though there are tasks waiting to be performed.

3.2.2 The Production System Machine Based on these observations, Gupta and Forgy [Forgy 1982; Gupta and Forgy, 1983] proposed a radically different machine for running OPS-5 style production systems. This is a modest-scaled, course-grained, closely coupled machine in which the processors share a common bus, address space, and shared memory. Each processor would be a relatively fast 32-bit processor; the task of each processor is to execute arbitrary subtasks of the Rete algorithm that have been posted with a common hardware scheduler (see Figure 31). Each processor has a cache memory with it, which raises the issue of how these individual caches maintain a coherent memory image; there is a standard solution to this problem called *snoopy caches* developed by Goodman [1983]. The idea is that each cache watches all transactions on the shared bus. If a write transaction takes place on the bus and a cache currently has an entry for the location being written, then it replaces its current content with the new content. In addition, by watching the bus traffic, each cache can tell whether an entry is shared by other caches. The

Modest Scale, Coarse Grained, Shared Memory

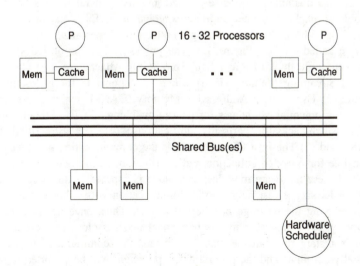

Figure 31 The proposed Production System Machine.

cache need only broadcast write transactions on the bus for those cache locations that are shared. Snoopy caches reduce the bus traffic by use of this *ownership* protocol; more importantly, they guarantee that the global image of memory is coherent.

Gupta and Forgy's simulations showed that this proposed *Production System Machine* can get the same performance as Dado and Non-Von with an investment of considerably less hardware (see also [Okuno and Gupta, 1988].

Although I agree with their conclusions in general, I would like to critique one part of their methodology. This involves the conflict resolution step in OPS-5. Conflict resolution imposes a sequential bottleneck at the end of every cycle and therefore it limits the parallelism available. We have seen results in our own simulations that suggest that there is more parallelism available if the conflict resolutions step can be omitted. However, the sequential bottleneck is also an opportunity to impose control over the production system. At the moment, our programming models are very weak, and conflict resolution is one of the few control techniques that we do have for forward-chaining systems. I find it hard to believe that conflict resolution's "carefully controlled race conditions" (to use the phrase of my colleague Steve Rowley) is really the ultimate answer to this problem, and so I think that we should interpret these results carefully.

3.2.3 *FAIM-1* I'd now like to turn to a variety of other machines. The first of these is a machine proposed at Schlumberger Palo Alto Research called FAIM-1 [Davis and Robison, 1985]. (The name stands for Fairchild AI Machine, since Fairchild was a subsidiary of Schlumberger at the time this project started.) This machine is a coarse-grained, massively parallel, loosely coupled ensemble of machines connected in a hexagonal mesh. Each machine in the ensemble is a 16-bit LISP processor with a collection of specialized little pieces of hardware added on (see Figure 32). The processor is a simplified stack machine (you might think of it as a half-sized 3600). Attached to it is: (1) The Instruction Streaming Memory (ISM) which is responsible for instruction prefetching. (2) The Context Addressable Memory (CAXM) which is responsible for fetching potential candidates for pattern matching. (3) The Stream Pipeline Unifier which actually performs unifications. (4) The Structured RAM (SRAM) and (5) The Post Office, which is the communication interface that is responsible for message collection and distribution. Each node of the network has all of these hardware modules; each node is capable of direct communication with its six nearest neighbors. Communication with other processors involves relaying the message one hop at a time. Thus, once again there is an asymmetry; each processor in this hexagonal mesh is close to six processors, but more distant from all the rest. This means that communication costs will eventually dominate and the programming paradigm will be distorted to reflect the asymmetry of the processor.

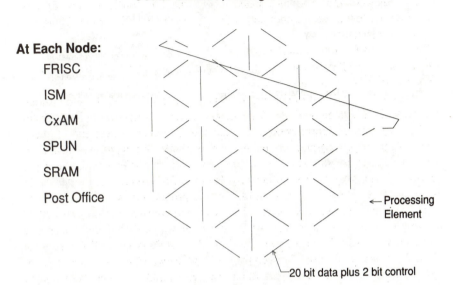

Massive, Loosely Coupled, Coase-Grained, Hexagonal Planar Grid

At Each Node:

FRISC

ISM

CxAM

SPUN

SRAM

Post Office

← Processing Element

20 bit data plus 2 bit control

Figure 32 The proposed FAIM-1 parallel processor.

FAIM-1 is a very complicated machine; unfortunately, this complexity swamped the efforts of the development team and the patience of the parent corporation. The project was cancelled before a first prototype could be fabricated.

3.2.4 *The Connection Machine* A very interesting and novel machine is the Connection Machine [Hillis 1981; Hillis and Barnes, 1987]. The initial development of this machine began at MIT under the leadership of Danny Hillis and Tom Knight; the effort then spun off into a private venture called Thinking Machines Corporation (TMC). Figure 33 shows some features of the machine, which is a massively parallel SIMD machine in which every processor executes the same instruction stream. Each processor is an extremely fine-grained bit-serial processor (i.e., it's a 1-bit processor), but there are 64,000 processors (in the initial machine—TMC aims at building larger models). Each processor has only a modest amount of local memory (4K bits) and has a router that connects it to a hypercube interconnection network (whose details I'll explain in a moment). In addition, the processors are connected in a rectilinear grid in which each processor can talk directly to its four nearest neighbors. The whole ensemble is driven by a front-end uniprocessor, typically a 3600 or a MicroVAX.

Massive SIMD, Hypercube

64K Processors
Single Bit Processor
1K bits of local memory
Router Per Processor
HyperCube Topology
Also a Grid
Controlled by Conventional Host (e.g. 3600)

Powerful Tool:
Vision
Simulation
Knowledge Representation

General Purpose Active Memory

Ultimate Associative Memory

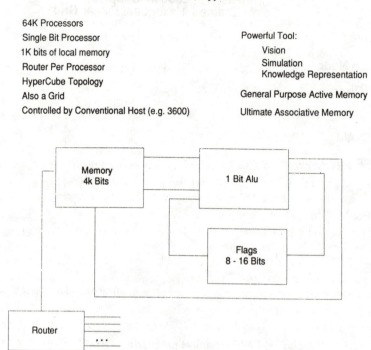

Figure 33 Features of the Connection Machine.

   The original motivation for the Connection Machine was to serve as a parallel semantic network engine (the idea grew out of Scott Fahlman's NETL proposal [Fahlman, 1979, 1980]). Roughly speaking, each processor (together with its small amount of memory) can be thought of as a node in a semantic network; the memory can contain the addresses of other nodes, in effect forming the links of the semantic network. The hypercube interconnection network can route messages between arbitrary pairs of processors in parallel with a delay that's proportional to Log_2N (where N is the number of processors). Since most semantic network operations are implemented by simple marker propagation algorithms, the Connection Machine can potentially gain significant speedups by propagating the markers in parallel. These algorithms are conducive to the SIMD style of the connection machine. A typical step in such an algorithm directs each processor to examine a particular bit in its memory and if that bit is on to send that bit to the processor whose address is stored in a particular location of its memory. The Connection Machine has been found to be useful for vision and simulation problems as well, primarily because these can take advantage of the rectilinear mesh interconnect.

The Connection Machine designers like to think of the machine as a general purpose *active memory* in which processors are intertwined with the memory. You ask the memory to do more complex things for you than you would of a normal memory, but because of the processing power attached to each memory location, it is capable of performing these operations in parallel. One such use is to employ the Connection Machine as a very sophisticated associate memory. Although it certainly isn't the ultimate associative memory, it's closer to that than anything else we happen to have in hand (on the other hand it's also a lot more expensive).

3.2.4.1 *Hardware Details*

An individual node contains 4K bits of memory, a 1-bit ALU, and a few flag bits. The basic processor cycle involves feeding three 1-bit inputs to the ALU (two from memory and one from the flags), producing two 1-bit outputs. The logic is actually just implemented by lookup tables, in effect, the opcodes are just all possible 2-output combinations of three Boolean inputs. You can program it to perform multibit addition since each step of addition takes the two obvious 1-bit inputs plus the carry-in and produces a sum and a carry-out. A sequential application of 32 such steps computes a 32-bit sum. Of course, it can be programmed to do other things as well.

As I mentioned there are two interconnection systems in the Connection Machine. The first is a rectilinear mesh connecting each node to four nearest neighbors; the second interconnect is a hypercube. The hypercube can be understood as follows: Each processor has a wire connecting it to every other processor whose address differs from its own address by exactly one bit. Figure 34 shows a three-dimensional cube in this way; the hypercube is simply the higher dimensional analog. This property makes message routing in a hypercube easy to understand. To route a message to a particular address, you simply pick some dimension (i.e., one bit of the address) for which the destination address differs from your own address. The message is sent along the wire for that dimension and the corresponding bit of the address is flipped. Notice that on each such routing step, the message is sent to a node whose address differs from that of the destination node's by one less bit. Thus, after a number of steps equal to the dimension of the hypercube the message will have to arrive at its intended destination. The delay of routing a message through a hypercube with N nodes is Log_2N; the number of wires emanating from a node is also Log_2N; the total number of wires in the hypercube is $NLog_2N$.

Each node can send out a number of messages on each cycle (and similarly it can receive a number of messages). This number is the dimension of the hypercube, because each node has that many wires connected to it. Of course, if a node has several messages bound for the same location, it can't send them all at once; therefore there needs to be a message buffer at each node. In practice there is some but not an overwhelming amount of congestion in the network.

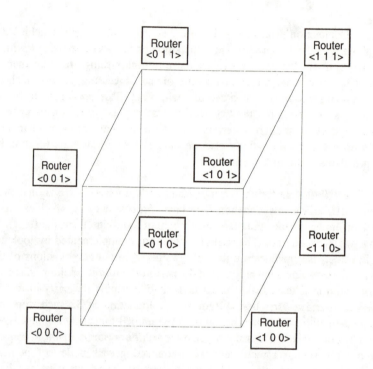

Figure 34 Hypercube interconnection.

You would like to think of each processor as being connected to every other processor by a symmetric communication system. This is partially achieved by the hypercube communication network in the Connection Machine; however, the time delay for remote communication is qualitatively higher than the time to access local memory. It is also much higher than the delay to access a processor's nearest neighbors over the rectilinear mesh. In practice, therefore, people have tried to force their computations into a pattern that emphasizes local communication; low-level vision applications are very popular for this reason; semantic network applications are harder to accommodate.

The Connection Machine is commercially available and many people are experimenting with it now. But there has been little use of it for the semantic network kinds of applications that made it seem appealing for symbolic computing to begin with. It is also an expensive machine, which limits the amount of experimentation that can happen. Finally, since it is a SIMD machine, one has to think of how to create an instruction stream that leads to a large number of processors producing useful work. This requires a programming style which isn't yet understood very well.

I think it's reasonable to say that there is some similarity between the difficulties of programming the Connection Machine and those we saw with Dado or Non-Von. The Connection Machine is more flexible (and less asymmetric), but the slowness of the hypercube routing network causes a lack of symmetry that makes one inclined not to think of the machine as a single large active memory. Again, the lack of symmetry means that for many applications the user has invested in a massive number of processors but can only use a few of them at a time. I think it's fair to say that the jury has yet to return a final verdict on the Connection Machine.

3.2.5 *The iPSC* Another hypercube machine that deserves a brief mention is the Intel iPSC. This is a hypercube connected machine with Intel $80x86$ processors at the nodes (the most recent version uses 80386 chips). Each machine has a modest amount of local memory and there is no shared address space or bus. The processors execute as a loosely coupled ensemble, passing messages through the hypercube routing network. Each processor can only execute instructions that are stored in its local memory, forcing code to be duplicated. Since there is no sharing between the nodes, the transfer of information along the links can be fairly expensive. A parallel LISP has been developed for this machine, some of whose results are shown in Figure 35. The results are fairly disappointing so far, showing the onset of the diminishing returns phenomenon at about 16 to 32 processors, and achieving a performance level that is qualitatively equal to that of the 3600. Again the lack of symmetry and coherence leads to disappointing levels of performance.

Triangle
Gabriel
Benchmark

	iPSC Single node	iPSC 16 node	iPSC 32 node	Sym-bolics 3600
T(seconds)	1,023.2	69.8	37.5	115.1
Speedup		14.8	27.6	

Figure 35 Symbolic computing benchmark. Results of the iPSC Hypercube.

3.2.6 *The BBN Butterfly* Another machine that's actually been built is the BBN *Butterfly*, which is a modest-scale, coarse-grained, tightly coupled machine. The processors are 680x0 machines (I believe the newest model uses 68020 processors) each with a modest amount of local memory; a large configuration has 256 processors (although the design accommodates more). The processors are connected to the global memory by a multistage switching network (called an Omega network). See Figure 36. A request travels through this network a stage at a time. In each stage one bit of the address is examined, a 1 routes the message downward, a 0 routes the message upward. Like the hypercube, this network requires Log_2N stages to complete the routing of a request; also like the hypercube (as long as the congestion issue is ignored) the network can transmit a request for every processor on every cycle.

The goal of the Omega network is to create the illusion of a shared global memory that is equally accessible to all processors. However, this fails in the Butterfly for two reasons: First, each processor can only execute instructions from its local memory and in any even the time to reach the global memory is qualitatively longer than the time to access local memory—the system is asymmetric. Second, there is a coherence problem. Each processor has a local cache memory but there is no general mechanism for keeping these consistent. The snoopy cache approach can't work since it relies on a shared bus that is lacking in this design. A shared bus could not provide the bandwidth needed by the large number of processors. The lack of coherence was simply accepted as a problem for the programmer to solve. Performance figures for LISP on the Butterfly have been disappointing, partly due to the lack of compiler to date and partly due to the natural consequences of the lack of symmetry and coherence.

The Butterfly and the iPSC were both originally designed with scientific computation in mind and only later investigated as symbolic computers. Both these machines have enough symmetry to support important classes of scientific calculations (such a finite element analysis computations) with high efficiency; such computations emphasize local connections along which only modest amounts of numeric data is transferred. Symbolic computation is much more irregular and involves the sharing of much more complex information. These characteristics are exactly the ones which motivated the object-oriented viewpoint that uniprocessor LISP Machines were designed to support. Unfortunately, these multiprocessors do not do a very good job of supporting this abstraction.

3.2.7 *What My Friends And I Are Doing* I'd like to briefly describe some ideas for multiprocessors that we are working on in my group at Symbolics. The common thread in each of these designs is an attempt to maintain support for the object-oriented viewpoint, for which symmetry and coherence are the *sine qua non*.

Modest Scale, Coarse Grained, Tightly Coupled, Omega Network

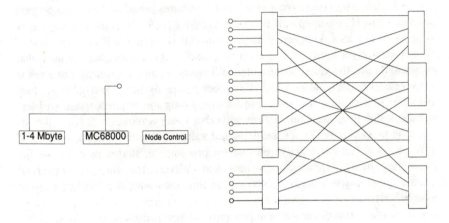

Figure 36 The BBN Butterfly Using Omega Network Interconnect.

A near-term version of this idea involves a modest-scale, shared bus, shared memory multiprocessor using Ivory chips and snoopy caches (see Figure 37). These processors are high performance and require a lot of bandwidth from the shared bus even with fairly large caches on each processor card. Because of this, the design will support only about 8 processors on the bus. This design is similar in gross detail to the Production System Machine, but the processors are intentionally full symbolic computers and the programming model is general purpose, not just production systems. The approach of using a shared bus with snoopy caches naturally produces a symmetric and coherent system and the symbolic computing features of Ivory provide high performance execution at each node.

A programming paradigm that seems very attractive for such a machine is based on the idea of *Futures* which has grown out of a long tradition in the LISP programming world; this feature has most recently appeared in a language called MultiLISP [Halstead, 1984; 1985] by Bert Halstead at MIT and in another language called QLISP [Gabriel and McCarthy, 1984] by Richard Gabriel at Stanford. A Future is an abstraction that combines a storage location with a process responsible for computing the value that should be stored in it. References to the Future are, in effect, invisible pointers (like logic variables) that say, "I'm not really the data, go look over there for the data." The Future object is treated just like any other object; a Future can be an element of a list or of any other data structure. Futures can be copied from one structure to another.

A Future only differs from other data structures when one tries to compute with its value. For example, if one tries to add a Future to some other quantity or tries to take its CAR, then something special will happen if the value of the future has not yet been computed; in this case the process requesting the value is blocked until the value is computed. When the Future is created, a process is also created to compute its value; this process runs asynchronously. In the best case, the process that is responsible for computing the Future's value will terminate and deliver the value before any other process requests it. If so, the requesting process simply uses the delivered value as if nothing had happened; if the value has not been delivered and no process has started to calculate the value, the blocked process computes and delivers the value. However, if another process has already started calculating the value, the blocked process simply waits.

From the point of view of the program, however, there is no difference between futures and other data. This leads to a data- and demand-driven form of interprocess synchronization that very naturally embeds itself into symbolic computing paradigms. A sequential LISP program can be made parallel just by wrapping a Future construct around an expression. Of course, one must be careful if there are side effects; locks must be used to guarantee the security of critical regions, and so on. So it's not a free lunch, but it is a very attractive software paradigm.

Snoopy Cache Protocol

High Bandwidth 40-bit TTL bus

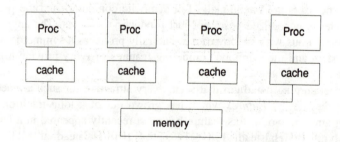

The caches watch the bus, and maintain cache coherency

Figure 37 A Snoopy cache, shared bus multiprocessor.

Futures can be supported either by mechanisms in the hardware or in the operating system (or both). Because any value might be a Future, it's much more efficient for the hardware to support Futures directly by using type-checking hardware; otherwise, the compiler must insert extra tests all over the code to check whether the data being computed with is an undelivered Future. Ivory provides hardware to treat Futures as a special kind of invisible pointer, making the system support for Futures simpler and much more efficient. We see the power of both forms of symmetry that we've talked about; the data type checking hardware that was created for uniprocessor symbolic computing makes Futures seem to be the same as any other object. The symmetric and coherent shared memory multiprocessor architecture allows each processor to execute any task as efficiently as any other processor. Together these features provide a powerful base for experimenting with high-performance parallel symbolic computations.

A second machine that is being investigated in our group is *Aurora*, a massively parallel machine, proposed by Tom Knight. The prototype version of this is intended to be a 64-way multiprocessor, but the goal is to support a thousand or more processors. The interconnect is a multistage switching network, similar to that in the BBN Butterfly, but with much higher performance.

O(64) 2000X multiprocessor

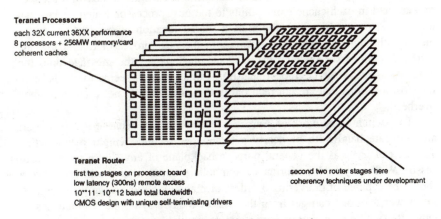

Teranet Processors
each 32X current 36XX performance
8 processors + 256MW memory/card
coherent caches

Teranet Router
first two stages on processor board
low latency (300ns) remote access
10**11 - 10**12 baud total bandwidth
CMOS design with unique self-terminating drivers

second two router stages here
coherency techniques under development

Support for most parallel programming models:
    shared memory, futures, virtual processors, actors, data-level parallelism

Concept can be scaled to ~1000 processor range

Figure 38 Tom Knight's proposed Aurora machine.

This is shown in Figure 38. This design uses a packaging trick used in the Butterfly; half of the boards are vertically aligned while the other half are horizontal. The first few stages of switching takes place on the vertical boards and then the remaining stages are on the horizontal boards. So to create a connection between any two processors, you route vertically on the first processor's board to the correct vertical level; you then connect through the backplane to a horizontal board at that height; then you switch horizontally to the correct horizontal position. The signal then returns through the backplane where it is connected directly to the second processor.

The exciting feature of this network is that Knight is designing it to have very low latency; it will take about 300 nanoseconds to route a request between any two processors. Each processor has associated with it a cache and a bank of memory. The memory is not thought of as a private resource of that processor. In general, a processor fetches instructions and data from its cache, not the local memory; when a processor takes a cache miss, the cache controller will get the appropriate word from main memory. This usually requires it to make a request through the network, but if the location is located in the local memory, it need not use the routing network. The difference in access times between these two cases is designed to be fairly small. So the need for symmetry is satisfied.

The other main goal of the design is to maintain cache consistency; as we saw in the Butterfly, this is difficult when there is no shared bus. This is solved in Knight's design by adding complexity to the caches; when a memory location is cached by several processors, the cache entries are linked into a list; a special field in each cache entry points to the next processor which caches that location. A processor which modifies a shared location is required to send a message through the switching network to the next processor that shares the value; this processor updates its state and then passes the message onto the next processor. If the degree of sharing is small (which seems to be the case for most locations that are not read-only), this process does not cause too much overhead.

The switching network of Aurora is called *Teranet* because it can support an aggregate bandwidth of nearly a terabit per second. Knight believes that Teranet can serve as the general purpose backplane of any future parallel processor. With very high-performance symbolic processors at the nodes, Aurora should be capable of delivering 3 orders of magnitude more aggregate computing power than one can get from the best of today's symbolic computing systems. Its symmetry makes it very good at simulating any of the parallel programming paradigms that I've discussed in the context of symbolic computing; in addition, it appears to be a very good match to many numeric parallel processing problems as well. Finally as we look ahead in the next section to more speculative paradigms, we will see that Aurora might be a nearly perfect engine for these approaches as well.

4 *Beyond the Fringe*

I'd now like to turn to some very adventurous ideas that may or may not pan out. The first of these is a very clever idea of Knight's, called LIQUID that may be a very important technique for supporting general purpose parallel computing. The other two ideas are motivated by biological metaphors and fall within the general area of "connectionism."

4.1 *LIQUID*

LIQUID [Knight, 1986] (which I'm told stands for **LI**sp **QUI**ck **D**amn-it) is a technique for automatically extracting parallelism from a program even in the presence of side-effects. It's a clever idea with a great deal of similarity to a technique from the database literature called *optimistic concurrency*. The goal of LIQUID is to achieve parallelism without having to modify the program. The technique depends both on a novel compiler and a novel cache structure.

I'll try to explain the LIQUID idea in stages. To start, let's assume that the program is completely side-effect free. In such cases, the amount of parallelism is limited only by the data dependencies. That is, no operation can be executed until its inputs are computed. A dataflow network (or the right set of Futures) will give you as much parallelism as is available.

Of course, most programs aren't side-effect free, and this is often for good reason. So our goal is to get parallelism even in the case when there are side-effects. The basic insight is shown in Figure 39. The compiler breaks the program up into little blocks each of which begins with a prologue that loads operands into the processor; the main section of the block then computes results; finally the epilogue writes the results back into memory. There is a natural sequence to these blocks which is their relative position in the original program; the blocks are forced to finish execution according to this ordering. However, we will let a block start executing as soon as possible in an attempt to keep all the processors busy.

Since we are allowing the blocks to execute out of order, it's possible that a block will load a value from a particular location before the block that should produce its value completes its execution and writes its output. Knight's optimistic concurrency trick is to ignore this problem and solve it dynamically during execution using special cache hardware. Each processor has two caches: The first, called the dependency cache, contains an image of any location from which the processor has loaded a value; the second caches all locations into which the processor has written a value. The cache locations in this second cache are not written out until the block finishes. At that point, the processor attempts to "confirm" the block; but it must wait until all preceding blocks have been confirmed. A block is confirmed simply by writing back all the modified cache locations.

A program consists of a sequence of blocks:

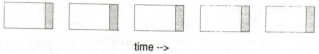

time -->

Assign each block to one processor:

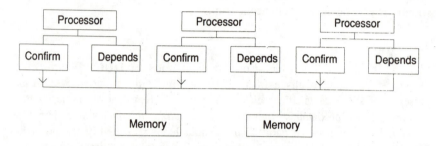

Optimistic Concurrency (Kung & Robinson)

Assume transactions are non-conflicting
Perform them in parallel
Check the validity of the assumption
Restart if the prediction was wrong

Figure 39 Knight's proposed LIQUID architecture.

As a block is confirmed, all other processors "snoop" at the bus, trying to determine if a location in their dependency cache is being written. If so, and if the value written is different from that in the cache, then the processor must abort the execution of its current block and restart. This is because the computation has been performed with an incorrect input value.

The reason this technique is called "optimistic concurrency" is that we try to maximize parallelism by being optimistic about conflicts. We start computations off by assuming that a conflict won't occur; if our optimism pays off, we win big. If not, we simply back up and do the work we would have had to do anyhow. (Notice the similarity between this idea and the trapping control structure of the 3600 that is used for data type checking). In the best case, LIQUID confirms one side-effect per clock cycle and this is the only limit on its performance.

4.2 Connectionist Machines

The next two proposals that I will discuss hark back to cybernetic ideas that were popular in the late 1950s and early 1960s just before there was a field called Artificial Intelligence. These machines try to mimic the behavior of neurons, using a large number of processors (large enough to correspond to the millions of neurons in biological systems) and a communication network that can connect them. The goal is to be able to simulate the complicated interactions between neurons. The connectionist model is a graph structure in which the nodes are processors and the links are labelled with a weight indicating the strength of the connection. Some of the processors have a connection to a value that represents a sensory input.

4.2.1 *The Boltzmann Machine*

The Boltzmann Machine is described in [Hinton et al., 1984; Fahlman and Hinton, 1983]. This design was influenced by the optimization technique known as "simulated annealing" [Kirkpatrick, 1983]. Simulated annealing is a hill-climbing technique in which the search program tries to take the path of steepest descent; however, if the search space isn't strictly monotonic, this strategy can get stuck at local minima that are not globally optimum (the search is seen as going downhill). Simulated annealing fixes this problem by allowing the search to proceed against the gradient under the guidance of a probability function. There is a free parameter in this probability function called the *temperature* which initially allows the search to go uphill rather frequently. As time progresses, the temperature is decreased, limiting the ability to move against the gradient. The general effect is that in the initial phases the process jumps around the space conducting a global search, but as time goes on it focuses. The jumping around tends to keep the system from getting stuck at a local minimum.

The Boltzmann Machine is a system that does this type of search. In particular, it conducts a search for the settings of the state of its nodes that leads to a minimum value for a synthetic quantity called the "Energy" of the system which is shown in Figure 40. This is a function of the weights (W_{ij}) on the links, the state (S_i) of each node, and the difference between the input (IN_i) applied to each node and a threshold value (Θ_i) for that node. In the Boltzmann Machine, the state of a node is Boolean; the node is either on or off, which makes the quantities shown very easy to compute.

Each node can determine the state it should assume using only local information (i.e., the value of its input, its own state, and that of its neighbors in the network plus the weight on its connections). The effect that a particular node can have on the total energy is the quantity ΔE in Figure 40. This is the difference in total system energy that would result if this node should flip from the false state to the true state. Each node chooses to flip its state based on this quantity; however, it does this probabilistically. If flipping would minimize the energy, the node always flips; however, it will also flip sometimes even if this would increase the energy. It makes this choice will probability P_k which depends on the ΔE_k and the free parameter T.

Massive, Fine grained, Boolean State, Probabilistic

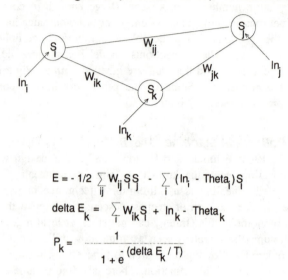

$$E = -\,1/2 \sum_{ij} W_{ij} S_i S_j \; - \; \sum_i (In_i - Theta_i\,) S_i$$

$$delta\,E_k = \sum_i W_{ik} S_i + In_k - Theta_k$$

$$P_k = \frac{1}{1 + e^{-\,(delta\,E_k\,/\,T)}}$$

Figure 40 The Boltzmann Machine.

We can think of the link weights and the threshold values as representing the content of the network and the inputs as representing a *sensory image*. By minimizing the energy, the system tries to find that state which most closely "matches" the input. This structure leads to many interesting properties that seem to mimic biological systems. It is *distributed*, in the sense that an individual node represents something only through its connections to its neighbors. It is *robust* in that the malfunction or total loss of a single node usually has little effect on the overall behavior. It is *associative* in that it is capable of finding the nearest match to input, and it is *massively parallel*.

4.2.2 *Neural Networks* Hopfield [Hopfield, 1982; Hopfield and Tank, 1986] and many others, have taken the biological analogy further. In their model the individual nodes are analog, not digital systems. There is, however, a very similar set of equations that describe such systems, as long as the nodes exhibit a nonlinear, amplifying response curve such as that shown in Figure 41. These systems too have a notion of a global energy, and they also tend to find the optimum value of this quantity. Hopfield's interest seems to be in using such systems to solve classic optimization problems, such as the travelling salesman class of problems. Physically constructing a system with nonlinear analog elements is very difficult; in any event, virtually any interesting property of such a system can be simulated by a digital system.

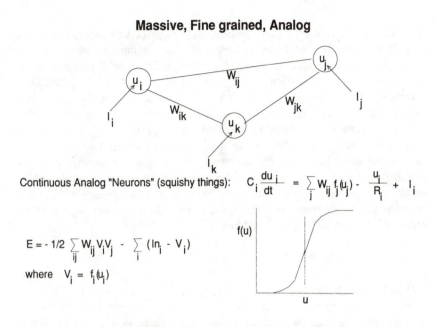

Massive, Fine grained, Analog

Continuous Analog "Neurons" (squishy things): $C_i \dfrac{du_i}{dt} = \sum_j W_{ij}\, f_j(u_j) - \dfrac{u_i}{R_i} + I_i$

$$E = -1/2 \sum_{ij} W_{ij} V_i V_j - \sum_i (In_i - V_i)$$

where $V_i = f_i(u_i)$

$f(u)$

u

Figure 41 A neural network using nonlinear elements.

4.2.3 *Connectionism and Learning*   There is another reason for the inter-est in connectionist systems. In certain classes of connectionist networks, the settings of the weights and threshold values (which represent what the network "knows") can be inferred automatically from a sequence of "training ex-amples" [Hinton et al., 1984] which means that one never needs to program the machine. This removes the greatest objection to the architecture which is the extreme tedium that would be involved in setting the thresholds and weights by hand. However, it remains to be seen whether such connectionist systems can learn interesting behavior from relatively short training sequences. The pro-spect of investing the same number of years in training a neural network as we do in training a child is not very exciting. The data available so far is very pre-liminary; there is, however, an enormous outburst of interest in connectionist systems.

What are the architectural implications of these systems? I guess I should say that I'm still fairly skeptical about current connectionist models, although I do think that something more or less like connectionism will play an important role in AI eventually. I'm also convinced that connectionism will never be the only important technique in AI; symbolic processes are clearly part of cogni-tion and will be as much a part of the ultimate AI architecture as will con-nectionist processes.

I don't believe that the machines that support connectionist ideas need to bear a very direct relationship to the topological structure of the connectionist networks, nor do I believe that connectionism requires special purpose hardware. We've already seen many examples of how a symmetric hardware system can be the most effective simulator of an algorithmic paradigm, even when the topology of the hardware is not identical to that of the data structures manipulated by the algorithm. In particular, it seems to me that the Aurora machine could simulate connectionist systems as effectively as any special purpose architecture which maps the network topology directly into hardware. Such an approach would allow us to integrate connectionist ideas with more classical AI ideas in a general framework of symbolic computing; the connectionist part of the system would play a crucial but specialized role. There would be a symmetry between these two styles of processing; each would have access to the capabilities that the other can provide it and neither would be fenced off in a special purpose machine.

5 *Conclusions*

In summary, what can I say about what's going to happen in the future? It seems pretty clear to me that uniprocessors aren't dead yet. It is in this domain that we best know how to structure problems and architectures to achieve the desirable properties of symmetry and coherence. Without the structuring power of these abstractions, we programmers run into complexity barriers that we cannot surmount. In fact, I think that sequential programming will continue to be the dominant computing paradigm for a long, long time. There is still a lot more performance we can get out of uniprocessors; the technology revolution that drives this may be starting to slow down, but it's still progressing rapidly.

But it's equally clear that parallelism will assume increasing importance. My best guess is that those forms of parallelism which look the most like uniprocessors, in the sense of being symmetric and coherent, will be the ones that programmers will find the most convenient.

Many of the ideas I've covered in this talk are unlikely to withstand the test of time and will disappear. Indeed, several of the parallel processing proposals have already died (Non-Von, FAIM-1). But some of the ideas we looked at are too powerful to be entirely wrong. Data type checking and garbage collection seem too valuable to throw away, particularly now that we understand them so well.

One thing is certain: We will continue to get higher and higher levels of performance. Lots of companies talk about boosting performance by a factor of 2 every year. Obviously that won't go on forever, but it will go on for a while. The other thing that's certain is that the computer architects who think up and build these machines will probably get pretty worn out. But we have a good time doing it.

References

Ackley, D. H., Hinton, G. E. and Sejnowski, T. J., 1985. A learning algorithm for Boltzmann machines. *Cognitive Science* **9**:147–169.

Allen, D., Steinberg, S. and Stabile, L., 1987. Recent developments in Butterfly LISP. In *Proceedings of the Sixth National Conference on Artificial Intelligence*, Seattle, Washington, pp. 2–6. Morgan Kaufmann Publishers, San Mateo, California.

Baker, H. G., 1978. List processing in real time on a serial computer. *Communications of ACM* **21**(4):280–294.

Baker, C., Chan, D., Cherry, J., Corry, A., Efland, G., Edwards, B., Matson, M., Minsky, H., Nestler, E., Reti, K., Sarrazin, D., Sommer, C., Tan, D. and Weste, N., 1987. The Symbolics Ivory processor: A 40-bit tagged architecture LISP microprocessor. In *Proceedings of the IEEE International Conference on Computer Design*, Rye Brook, New York.

Bates, R., Dyer, D., Koomen, H., 1982. Implementation of Interlisp on a VAX. In *Proceedings of the 1982 Symposium on LISP and Functional Programming*. ACM, New York.

Billstrom, D. Brandenburg, J., and Teeter, J., 1979. CCLISP on the iPSC concurrent computer. In *Proceedings of the Sixth National Conference on Artificial Intelligence*, Seattle, Washington, pp. 7–12. Morgan Kaufmann Publishers, San Mateo, California.

Bobrow, D. G., Darley, L. D., Murphy, D. L., Solomon, C. and Teitelman, W., 1966. The BBN LISP System. AFCRL-66-180, Bolt Beranek and Newman, Cambridge, Massachusetts.

Bobrow, D. G. and Clark, D., 1979. Compact encodings of list structure. *ACM TOPLAS* **1**(2):266.

Bosshart, P. W., Hewes, C. R., et al., 1987. A 553K-transistor LISP processor chip. *IEEE International Solid State Circuits Conference Digest of Technical Papers*, pp. 202–203.

Burton, R. R. et al., 1981. Interlisp-D overview. In Papers on Interlisp-D, Xerox PARC, CIS-5 (SSL-80-4).

Cheney, C. J., 1970. A nonrecursive list compacting algorithm. *Communications of ACM* **13**(11):677–678.

Clark, Keith and Gregory, Steve, 1984. Notes on systems programming in parlog. In *Proceedings of the International Conference on Fifth Generation Computer Systems*. ICOT.

Cohen, J., 1981. Garbage collection of linked data structures. *ACM Computing Surveys* **13**(3).

Davis, A. and Robison, S., 1985. The architecture of the FAIM-1 symbolic multiprocessing system. In *Proceedings of the Ninth International Joint Conference on Artificial Intelligence*, Los Angeles, pp. 32–38. Morgan Kaufmann, San Mateo, California.

Deutsch, L. P and Berkeley, E. C. The LISP implementation for the PDP-1 computer. *The Programming Language Lisp: Its Operation and Applications,* E. C. Berkeley and Daniel G. Bobrow, ed.

Deutsch, L. P., and Bobrow, D. G., 1976. An efficient, incremental, automatic garbage collector. *Communications of ACM* **19**(9):522–526.

Deutsch, L. P and Lampson, B. W. *Reference Manual, 930 LISP.* University of California at Berkeley.

Deutsch, L. P., 1979. Experience with a microprogrammed Interlisp system. *IEEE Transactions on Computers* **TSC-28**(10).

Digital Equipment Corporation, 1982. *VAX-11 Architecture Reference Manual.*

Drumheller, M., 1986. Connection machine stereomatching. In *Proceedings of the Fifth National Conference on Artificial Intelligence,* Philadelphia, Pennsylvania, pp. 748–753. Morgan Kaufmann Publishers, San Mateo, California.

Eastlake, D. E., 1972. ITS status report. AI Memo 238, MIT Artificial Intelligence Laboratory.

Edwards, B., Efland, G. and Weste, N., 1987. The Symbolics I-Machine architecture: A symbolic processor architecture for VLSI implementation. In *Proceedings of the IEEE International Conference on Computer Design,* Rye Brook, New York.

Fahlman, S. E., 1979. *NETL: A System for Representing and Using Real-World Knowledge.* MIT Press, Cambridge, Massachusetts.

Fahlman, S. E., 1980. Preliminary design for a million-element NETL machine. Technical Report, Department of Computer Science, Carnegie-Mellon University.

Fahlman, Scott E. and Hinton, Geoffrey E., 1983. Massively parallel architectures for AI: NETL, THISTLE and Boltzmann machines. In *Proceedings of the Third National Conference on Artificial Intelligence,* Washington, D.C., pp. 109–113. Morgan Kaufmann Publishers, San Mateo, California.

Feldman, J. A., Ballard, D. H., 1982. Connectionist models and their properties. *Cognitive Science* **6**:205–254.

Fenichel, R. R. and Yochelson, J. C., 1969. A LISP garbage-collector for virtual memory computer systems. *Communications of ACM* **12**(11):611–612.

Forgy, C., Gupta, A, Newell, A. and Wedig, R., 1984. Initial assesment of architectures for production systems. In *Proceedings of the Fourth National Conference on Artificial Intelligence,* Austin, Texas, pp. 116–120. Morgan Kaufmann Publishers, San Mateo, California.

Forgy, C. L., 1982. Rete: A fast algorithm for the many pattern/many object pattern matching problem. *Artificial Intelligence.*

Gabriel, R. P. and McCarthy, J., 1984. Queue-based multiprocessing LISP. *Symposium on LISP and Functional Programming.*

Gabriel, Richard P., 1985. *Performance and Evaluation of LISP Systems.* MIT Press, Cambridge, Massachusetts.

Goodman, J. R., 1983. Using cache memory to reduce processor memory traffic. In *Proceedings of the 10th Annual International Symposium on Computer Architecture*.

Greenblatt, R. D. et al., 1984. The LISP Machine. *Interactive Programming Environments*, D. R. Barstow, H. E. Shrobe, E. Sandewall, eds. McGraw-Hill, New York.

Gupta, A. and Forgy C. L., 1983. Measurements on production systems. Carnegie Mellon University.

Gupta, A., 1984. Implementing OPS-5 production systems on DADO. *International Conference on Parallel Processing*.

Halstead, R., 1984. Implementation of MultiLISP: LISP on a multiprocessor. In *Proceedings of the 1984 Symposium on LISP and Fuctional Programming*, Austin, Texas. ACM.

Halstead, R., 1985. MultiLISP: A language for concurrent symbolic computation. *ACM TOPLAS*.

Hayashi, H., Hattori, A., and Akimoto, H. ALPHA: High-performance LISP Machine equipped with a new stack structure and real time garbage collection system. Fujitsu Laboratories, Ltd. draft report.

Hill, M. et al., 1986. Design decisions in SPUR. *IEEE Computer* **19**(1):8–22.

Hillis, W. D., 1981. The Connection Machine. Technical Report 646, MIT Artificial Intelligence Laboratory, Cambridge Massachusetts.

Hillis, W. D. and Barnes, J., 1987. Programming a highly parallel computer. *Nature* **326**(6108):27–30.

Hillyer and Shaw, D., 1986. Execution of OPS-5 programs on a massively parallel machine. *Journal of Parallel and Distributed Computing* **3**(2):236–268.

Hinton, G. E., 1981. Implementing semantic networks in parallel hardware. *Parallel Models of Associative Memory*, G. E. Hinton and J. A. Anderson, ed. Erlbaum, Hillsdale, N.J.

Hinton, G. E. and Sejnowski, T. J., 1983. Analyzing cooperative computation. In *Proceedings of the Fifth Annual Conference of the Cognitive Science Society*, Rochester, N.Y.

Hinton, G. E., Sejnowski, T. and Ackley, D., 1984. Boltzmann machines: Constraint satisfaction machines that learn. CMU-CS-84-119, Carnegie Mellon University.

Hopfield, J. J., 1982. Neural networks and physical systems with emergent collective computational abilities. In *Proceedings of the National Academy of Sciences USA*, 79, pp. 2554–2558.

Hopfield, J. J. and Tank, D. W., 1986. Computing with neural circuits: A model. *Science* **233**(4764):625–632.

Ishida, T. and Stolfo, S., 1984. Simultaneous firing of production rules on tree-structured machines. Technical Report, Department of Computer Science, Columbia University, New York.

Kirkpatrick, S., Gelatt, C. D. and Vecci, M. P., 1983. Optimization by simulated annealing. *Science* **220**:671–680.

Knight, Thomas, 1984. The CONS microprocessor. Working Paper 80, MIT Artificial Intelligence Laboratory, Cambridge Massachusetts.

Knuth, D. E., 1968. *The Art of Computer Programming, Volume 3*. Addison-Wesley, Reading, Massachusetts, pp. 417–419.

Lieberman, H., and Hewitt, C., 1983. A real-time garbage collector based on the lifetimes of objects. *Communications of ACM* **26**(6):419–429.

Massinter, L. and Deutsch, L. P., 1981. Local optimization for a compiler for stack-based LISP machines. In Papers on InterLISP-D, Xerox PARC CIS-5 (SSL-80-4).

Massinter, L., 1981. InterLISP-VAX: A report. Department of Computer Science, Stanford University, Stanford, California. STAN-CS-81-879.

McCarthy, John, Brayton, R., Edwards, D., Fox, P. A., Hodes, L., Luckham, D., Maling K., Park, D., and Russell, S., 1960. LISP 1 programmer's manual. Artificial Intelligence Group, Computation Center and Research Laboratory of Electronics, Cambridge, Massachusetts.

McCarthy, John, P. W. Abrahams, D. J. Edwards, T. P. Hart, and M. I. Levin, 1962. *LISP 1.5 Programmer's Manual*. The MIT Press, Cambridge, Massachusetts.

McCarthy, John, 1978. History of LISP. *ACM Sigplan Notices* **13**(8):217–223.

McClelland, J. L. and Rumelhard, D. E., ed., 1986. *Parallel Distributed Processing: Explorations in the Microstructure of Cognition*. MIT Press, Cambridge, Massachusetts.

Minsky, Marvin, 1963. A LISP garbage collector using serial secondary storage. Memo #58, MIT AI Lab. Cambridge Massachusetts.

Moon, David, 1974. The Maclisp reference manual version 0. LCS, MIT.

Moore, J Strother. The Interlisp virtual machine specification. CSL-76-6, Xerox PARC.

Moon, David, 1976. Architecture of the Symbolics 3600. *12th IEEE International Symposium on Computer Architecture* .

Moon, David, 1984. Garbage collection in a large LISP system. In *Proceedings of the 1984 Symposium on LISP and Functional Programming*, pp. 235–246. ACM.

Moon, David, 1986. Object-oriented programming with Flavors. In *Proceedings of OOPSLA*, pp. 1–8.

Moto-Oka, T. and Fuchi, K., 1983. The architectures in the Fifth Generation computers. *Information Processing* **83**, R.E.A. Mason, ed.

Moto-Oka, T. and Stone, H. S., 1984. Fifth Generation computer systems: A Japanese project. *Computer* (March):6–13.

Newell, Allen, 1961. *Information Processing Language V Manual*. Prentice-Hall, Englewood Cliffs, New Jersey

Okuno, H. G. and Gupta, A., 1988. High-level language approach to parallel execution of OPS-5. *Fourth IEEE Conference on Artificial Intelligence Applications,* San Diego.

Rumelhard, D. E., Hinton, G. E. and Williams, R. J., 1986. Learning internal representations by error propagation. *Parallel Distributed Processing: Explorations in the Microstructure of Cognition,* J. L. McClelland and D. E. Rumelhard, ed. MIT Press, Cambridge, Massachusetts.

Samson, Peter, 1966. PDP-6 LISP. Memo # 98, AI Group, Computation Center and RLE, MIT, Cambridge, Massachusetts.

Sandewall, Erik, 1978. Programming in the interactive environment: The LISP experience. *ACM Computing Surveys* **10**(1):35–72.

Schorr, H. and Waite, W. M., 1985. An efficient machine independent procedure for garbage collection in various list structures. *Communications of ACM* **10**(8):501–506.

Shapiro, E. Y., 1983. A subset of concurrent PROLOG and its interpreter. Technical Report TR-003, ICOT, Tokyo.

Shapiro, E. Y. and Takeuchi, A., 1983. Object-oriented programming in concurrent PROLOG. *New Generation Computing 1,* pp. 25–48. Ohmsha, Ltd and Springer-Verlag.

Shapiro, E. Y., 1984. Systems programming in concurrent PROLOG. In *Proceedings of the Eleventh Symposium on Principles of Programming Languages.* ACM.

Shaw, D. E., 1982. The Non-Von supercomputer. Technical Report. Department of Computer Science, Columbia University, New York.

Shaw, D. E., 1984. SIMD and MSIMD variants of the Non-Von supercomputer. In *Proceedings of the Spring 1984 Compcon,* San Francisco.

Shaw, D. E., 1985. Non-Von's applicability to three AI task areas. In *Proceedings of the Ninth International Joint Conference on Artificial Intelligence,* Los Angeles, pp. 61–71. Morgan Kaufmann Publishers, San Mateo, California.

Singh, Vineet and Genesereth, Michael R., 1986. PM: A parallel execution model for backward-chaining deductions. Stanford Knowledge Systems Lab Report No. KSL-85-18, Stanford, California.

Singh, Vineet and Genesereth, Michael R., 1987. A variable supply model for distributing deductions. In *Proceedings of the Ninth International Joint Conference on Artificial Intelligence,* Los Angeles, pp. 39–45. Morgan Kaufmann Publishers, San Mateo, California.

Stallman, R., 1981, 1984. EMACS: The extensible, customizable display editor. Memo 519a 1981, MIT Artificial Intelligence Laboratory. Also in *Interactive Programming Environments,* Barstow, Shrobe and Sandewell, ed. McGraw-Hill, New York.

Steele, G. L., 1977a. Fast arithmetic in MACLISP. In *Proceedings of the 1977 MACSYMA Users' Conference*, NASA Scientific and Technical Information Office, Washington D.C.

Steele, G. L., 1977b. Data representation in PDP-10 MacLISP. In *Proceedings of the 1977 MACSYMA Users' Conference*, NASA Scientific and Technical Information Office, Washington D.C.

Steele,G. L., 1984. *Common LISP: The Language*. Digital Press.

Steinberg, S., Allen, D. Bagnall, L., Scott, C., 1986. The Butterfly LISP system. In *Proceedings of the Fifth National Conference on Artificial Intelligence*, Philadelphia, Pennsylvania, pp. 730–734. Morgan Kaufmann Publishers, San Mateo, California.

Stolfo, S. and Shaw, D., 1981. Specialized hardware for production systems. Technical Report, Department of Computer Science, Columbia University, New York.

Stolfo, S. and Shaw, D., 1982. DADO: A tree-structured machine architecture for production systems. In *Proceedings of the Second National Conference on Artificial Intelligence*, Pittsburg, Pennsylvania, pp. 242–246. Morgan Kaufmann Publishers, San Mateo, California.

Stolfo, S. Miranker, D. and Shaw, D., 1983. Architecture and applications of DADO: A large-scale parallel computer for AI. In *Proceedings of the Eighth International Joint Conference on Artificial Intelligence*, Karlsruhe, West Germany, pp. 850–854. Morgan Kaufmann Publishers, San Mateo, California.

Stolfo, S., 1984. Five algorithms for production system execution on the DADO machine. In *Proceedings of the Fourth National Conference on Artificial Intelligence*, Austin, Texas. Morgan Kaufmann Publishers, San Mateo, California.

Symbolics Inc, 1983. 3600 technical summary.

Taki, K., Yokota, M., Yamamoto, A., Nishikawa, H., Uchida, S., Nakashima, H. and Mitsuishi, A., 1984. Personal Sequential Inference Machine (PSI). In *Proceedings of the International Conference on Fifth Generation Computer Systems*, pp. 398–409

Teitelman, Warren, 1978. INTERLISP reference manual. Xerox PARC and BBN.

Thacker, C. P., McCreight, E. M., Lampson, B. W., Sproull, R. B. and Boggs, D. R., 1979. ALTO: A personal computer. CSL-79-11 Xerox PARC.

Tick, E. and Warren, D. H. D., 1984. Towards a pipelined PROLOG processor. *New Generation Computing* 2:323–345.

Touretsky, D. S., 1985. Symbols among the neurons: Details of a connectionist inference architecture. In *Proceedings of the Ninth International Joint Conference on Artificial Intelligence*, Los Angeles, pp. 238–243. Morgan Kaufmann Publishers, San Mateo, California.

Ungar, D., 1984. Generation scavenging: A non-disruptive high performance storage reclamation algorithm. In *Proceedings of the SIGSOFT/SIGPLAN Practical Programming Environments Conference*, pp. 157–167. ACM.

Warren, D. H. D., 1977. *Applied Logic: Its Use and Implementation as a Programming Tool*. PhD. dissertation, University of Edinburgh, 1977. Also available as Technical Note 290, Artificial Intelligence Center, SRI International.

Warren, D. H. D., 1980. An improved PROLOG implementation which optimises tail recursion. Research Paper 156, Department of Artificial Intelligence, University of Edinburgh, Scotland.

Warren, D. H. D., 1983. An abstract PROLOG instruction set. Technical Report No. 309. Artificial Intelligence Center, SRI International.

Weinreb, D. L., 1979. *A Real-Time Display-oriented Editor for the LISP Machine*. S.B. Thesis, Department of Electrical Engineering and Computer Science, MIT.

Weinreb, D. L. and Moon, D., 1979. LISP Machine manual. MIT Artificial Intelligence Laboratory.

Weinreb, D. and Moon, D., 1980. Flavors: Message passing in the LISP Machine. MIT AI Laboratory, Memo # 602.

White, John L., 1967. PDP-6 LISP (LISP 1.6) revised. Memo #116a, MIT Artificial Intelligence Laboratory.

15

The Common LISP Object System:
An Example of Integrating Programming Paradigms[1]

Daniel G. Bobrow

Xerox Palo Alto Research Center

Palo Alto, California

Overview

A programming paradigm is a supported style of programming with significant advantages for a domain of problems. Many programming paradigms have been added on top of LISP, but few have been tightly integrated. Common LISP Object System (CLOS) is a model of a good integration. CLOS blends the object-oriented programming paradigm smoothly and tightly with the usual procedure-oriented paradigm of LISP. Functions and methods are combined in a more general abstraction. Message passing is invoked via normal LISP function call, and methods are viewed as partial descriptions of procedures. LISP data types are integrated with object classes. With these integrations, it is easy to incrementally move a program between the procedure and object-oriented styles.

---

1 This paper is based on a talk given at AAAI-86. At that time, CommonLoops was the example used of tight integration of paradigms. Since that time, the Common LISP Object System has emerged as a better example (see the Acknowledgments section of this survey).

1 *Introduction*

Choosing the right tool for a task is an important step toward rapid and successful completion of that job. In programming, what corresponds to a tool is often a style of programming that fits the task at hand. To be useful, this style must not only have available the appropriate semantic primitives—it must also be supported by the language and system in which it is embedded. We call such a style a paradigm after Kuhn's use of the term because a supported style can reflect and demand a particular worldview. Kuhn talks about shifts of paradigms in science, and conflicts between competing paradigms. One often sees such shifts and conflicts in the programming world. Adherents of styles such as LISP's procedural symbolic programming, Smalltalk-80's object-oriented programming, or PROLOG's logic programming, argue that all problems are best solved in a system supporting just *their* worldview.

The argument for having a single paradigm is that it provides a simple, uniform base. One learns a small collection of tools and somehow feels equipped to tackle any problem. However, when another style can make a task easier, adherents of any of the "one true ways" usually try to provide a complex cliché in their language to aid in doing the task. On the other hand, there have been people who have claimed that all one needs is a tool kit of several well supported styles of doing business within a single system. It is harder, perhaps, to learn this larger collection of tools, but having them available allows a program to be written in the style best suited to the problem it is solving. The forms of expression are important because programs are used for communication not only to machines but to programmers. A good form not only highlights what is important but suppresses distracting details. A good form supports invariants over program change. Procedural abstraction is a simple example. It suppresses the detail involved with storing return addresses, etc., and allows the implementation of a procedure to be changed without requiring changes in the caller.

As another example, consider programming based on production systems such as OPS-5 [Forgy, 1982]. Each rule has a set of conditions on elements that must exist in a workspace to allow that rule to fire. Firing a rule can make changes in the elements of the workspace. Since adding or changing a single element in the workspace may enable more than one rule to fire, and since only one is allowed to fire, a separate conflict resolution mechanism is necessary to choose the rule that fires. Thus this paradigm supports separation of concerns of rule applicability from selection of the rule to be fired. It is easier to specify behavior contingent on data being examined in a rule-based system than in a procedure based system where a procedure must specify an order in which data elements are examined. On the other hand, production systems must use special clichés to ensure a specified ordering for firing rules.

Production systems have been built in LISP, and most such systems allow easy calls back and forth between LISP and the production system. But there isn't a simple abstraction that covers both styles of programming, and that allows smooth and incremental transition between these styles.

Over the last decade many systems have been written that add objects to LISP (e.g., Flavors, Loops, Object LISP.) Each of these has attracted a group of users who recognize the benefits of message sending and specialization and have endorsed an object-oriented style. LISP provides an important approach for factoring programs that is different from common practice in object-oriented programming. The object languages in these systems have been embedded in LISP with different degrees of integration. We argue that in the Common LISP Object System (CLOS) we have done more than merge these two paradigms. We claim to have developed abstractions that unify the two. In this survey we present the linguistic mechanisms that we have developed for integrating these styles. We argue that the unification results in something greater than the sum of the parts, that is, that the mechanisms needed for integrating object-oriented and procedure-oriented approaches give CLOS surprising strength.

This smooth integration of ideas can work efficiently in LISP systems implemented on a wide variety of machines. PCL, a portable implementation of CLOS is available and is being used in many Common LISP implementations. We chose Common LISP as the base because it is a de facto LISP standard, supported on almost all commercial LISP workstations. As part of the Common LISP standards effort, the X3J13 subcommittee [Bobrow, DeMichiel, Gabriel, Keene, Kiczales, and Moon, 1987, 1988]. has been developing a detailed specification for this object-oriented extension.

2 *Methods and Functions*

In LISP, functions are applied to arguments. The code that is run is determined only by the name of the function. The LISP form

```
(foo a b)
```

can be interpreted in terms of a function-calling primitive, `funcall` as

```
(funcall(function-specified-by 'foo) a b).
```

In object-oriented systems one "sends messages" to objects. The code that is run is determined by both the name of the message and the type (class) of the object. Methods defined for a particular selector are associated with a class.

In the next section we will indicate how we merge the ideas of LISP data types and object classes. The following message using selector `sel`,

```
(send a 'sel b)
```

can be interpreted as the function call

```
(funcall (method-specified-by 'sel (type-of a)) a b)
```

The collection of all methods defined for `sel` defines the "generic" function for that selector. Which method is run when a generic function is invoked is determined by the type of the first argument. Thus a method is a partial description of a generic function restricted to objects of a particular type. With this understanding of method invocation, we can reinterpret all standard LISP calls `(foo a b)` as meaning

```
(funcall(method-specified-by 'foo(type-of a))a b)
```

if there is a method defined for `foo` and `(type-of a)`. We use the term "generic function" to refer to a function defined using a set of methods.

A method for `move` applicable only when the first argument is of type `block` is defined in CLOS as follows:

```
(defmethod move((obj block)x y)
;for moving a block.
```

The code for this method is added to the generic function for `move`, and is invoked for objects of type `block`, or any subtype. If there was an existing method for the same selector and type, `defmethod` replaces that method. To invoke this method, one simply writes:

```
(move block1 x-pos y-pos)
```

Given that `block1` is of type `block`, the code above will be invoked. Other methods for `move` could be defined for the first argument being a `window`, a `sketch`, and so on. If more than one method is applicable (because of subclassing), the most specific method is used.

2.1 *Default Methods*

One can use the `defmethod` form without specifying any types for the arguments:

```
(defmethod move(thing x y)...)
```

This method is run when no more specific method of the generic function for `move` is applicable. When only such a default method is supplied, it is like defining an ordinary LISP function. There is no speed penalty for using such default methods instead of functions.

The difference between defining a default method and defining an ordinary LISP function is that the latter is not allowed to be augmented by specialized method definitions. This protects users from inadvertently overriding or specializing predefined functions where perhaps special compilation optimizations have been used. For example, in most LISP implementations, calls to the primitives `car`, `cdr`, and `cons` are compiled specially for efficiency. Specializing these functions could have disastrous effect on system efficiency and/or no effect on previously compiled code.

Where it is possible and useful to be able to define methods, CLOS supports defining a generic function and making the existing function its default method. Additional methods can then be added to that generic function.

2.2 *Multi-Methods*

CLOS extends LISP's function call even further. It allows a method to be specified in terms of the types of any number of arguments to the form. It interprets the form `(foo a b)` as

```
(funcall(method-specified-by 'foo(type-of a)(type-of b))a b)
```

Thus, unlike most other object-oriented schemes, CLOS allows method-lookup to be based on more than the class of the first argument. For example,

```
(defmethod insidep((w window)(x integer)(y integer)) ...)
```

defines the method for `insidep` when the first argument is a window and the second and third arguments are integers.

For any set of arguments, there may be several methods whose type specifications match. The most specific applicable method is called. Method specificity is determined by the specificity of the leftmost type specifiers which differ. However, as discussed below, other regimes can be implemented using the meta-objects facility.

2.3 *Individual Methods*

Another extension in CLOS is definition of methods that are specialized to individuals. By this we mean that some methods are applicable only if called with a specific object as argument. We interpret the function call of `(foo a b)` as follows:

```
(funcall(method-specified-by 'foo a b)a b).
```

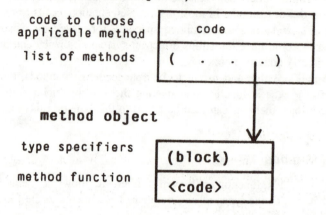

Figure 1 These objects are used for interpretation of a call. The generic function contains both the code that selects the method to be calleed and the list of methods that comprise it. It uses the information in the method object; the method object is also used in the compilation of the code for the specific method.

For example, this would allow a special-case for a connection to a particular host on a network for some period of time when special rerouting needs to be done, or to define a method for moving a particular window.

```
(defmethod move ((w(eql *prompt-window*))(x integer)(y integer))
...)
```

This is a method applicable to an individual more specific than any method just specified on types.

2.4 *Method and Generic Function Objects*

In CLOS all the data structures used to implement the system are objects. In particular, defining a method uses both a method and a generic function object.

The method object represents the method being defined. The method object contains the type-specifiers and the code for the method. The generic function object contains a list of all the methods defined on a particular selector. Hence, it describes the generic function. Together, the generic function and all of its methods produce the LISP code that is called when the selector is invoked to determine which method to call. Thus the generic function is both an *object with state*, and a *funcallable object* (in that sense, it is like a *closure* in Common LISP). Because the method-lookup and calling mechanisms are under control of the generic function and method objects, specialized method-lookup and method-combination mechanisms can be implemented by defining new classes of generic functions and methods that specialize parts of the method-lookup protocol.

2.5 *Method Combination*

Frequently, when one specializes behavior for a given class of object, the desire is to add only a little behavior to the methods of the superclasses.

CLOS provides a procedural mechanism combining a more specific method with one that is shadowed. The CLOS function `call-next-method` is defined to run the next most specific method matching the arguments of the current method. If there is no such method an error is signaled.

For example,

```
(defmethod move((w bounded-window)(x integer)(y integer))
(cond   ((in-bounds-p w x y)(call-next-method))
        (t ... ;; set x y to closest point inside
         (call-next-method w x y))))
```

defines a method that specializes the move method on window so that it always moves in-bounds.

The `call-next-method` is essentially the mechanism of method combination found in Smalltalk-80, Loops, Director, and Object LISP. In Smalltalk-80 and Loops, it was called sending a message to `super` as opposed to `self`. This mechanism is both powerful and simple. It allows arbitrary combination of inherited code with current code using LISP as the combination language.

CLOS also supports a declarative means of specifying method combination, adapted from the New Flavors mechanism. Parts of methods that play different roles can be defined separately and combined in an effective method. For example, `:before` and `:after` parts can be specified for any method, and these will be run before and after any primary method, without requiring any knowledge in the primary method. Before and after parts can be attached any place in the inheritance chain. In CLOS, this feature is specified using a special method-combination object that helps in the selection of the appropriate code for building a method combination. CLOS also provides an interface for users to define their own new method combinations, based on that designed for New Flavors.

Method and generic function objects are used to implement both `call-next-method` and the user-defined method combination mechanism. This provides the flexibility of choosing a mixture of procedural or declarative method combination. In addition, the existence of these meta-objects allows experimentation with other kinds of combination and invocation. A possible user extension that has been explored by some users is the integration of logic programming into the CLOS framework. Logic programming requires specialized method and generic function objects to combine method clauses using backtracking search.

2.6 *Processing of Method Code*

The code that implements a method is interpreted and compiled in a context in which the method object is available. The method can use information from the type-specifiers to optimize parts of the method body, or to provide special syntax within the body of the method to access the slots of arguments to the method. Because this processing is done using a defined protocol of messages to the method object, it can be extended by users.

3 *Defining Classes*

CLOS uses `defclass` to define its classes, similar to the `defstruct` construct found in Common LISP for defining composite structures.

```
(def class position ()
((x-coord :initform 0 :accessor position-x-coord)
(y-coord :initform 0 :accessor position-y-coord)))
```

defines a class named `position`, and specifies that instances of that class should have two slots, `x-coord` and `y-coord`, each initialized to 0. As a side effect of defining this class, using the `:accessor` option, `defclass` defines methods on the generic function `position-x-coord` and `position-y-coord` to access the slots of an instance. An updating form using `setf` on these generic functions can be used to change the values in the slots, e.g.,

```
(setf(position-x-coord i-1)13)
```

An extension of a previously defined class can be defined using `def-class`.

```
(defclass 3d-position(position)((z-coord 0)))
```

The new class is a subclass of the old, and includes all of its slots and may add slots of its own. Thus `3d-position` has slots `x-coord`, `y-coord`, and `z-coord`, and inherits all methods defined on `position`.

3.1 *Metaclasses*

In CLOS, classes are themselves instances of other classes. These special classes are known as metaclasses. Figure 2 indicates the relationships of the classes defined above, and their metaclass `structure-class`.

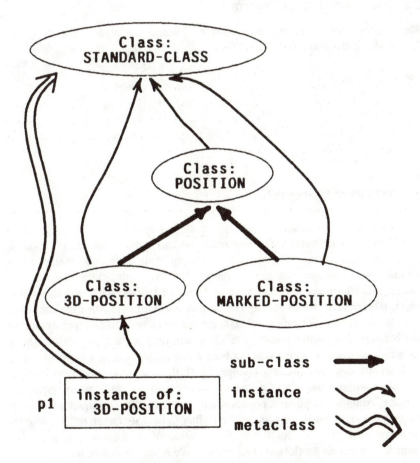

Figure 2 Three different relations are illustrated in this diagram. `3d-position` and `marked-position` are both subclasses of `position`, and inherit its structure and behavior. `p1` is an instance of `3d-position`. The three `position` classes are instances of `structure-class`. We call `structure-class` the "metaclass" of `p1`, since it is the class of its class.

Metaclasses control the behavior of the class as a whole, and the class-related behavior of the instances such as initialization, as do Smalltalk-80 metaclasses. In Flavors, the Flavors themselves are not instances of any Flavor, and hence their behavior is uniform.

In CLOS, metaclasses have important additional roles. A metaclass controls the representation of instances of the class; it specifies the order of inheritance for classes; finally, it controls allocation and access to instance slots.

3.2 *Representation of Objects*

Metaclasses control the representation of instances. Consider the following definitions of the class `position`:

```
(defclass position()
(   (x-coord :initform 0)
    (y-coord :initform 0))
(:metaclass structure-class))
```

```
(defclass position()
(   (x-coord :initform 0)
    (y-coord :initform 0))
(:metaclass standard-class))
```

In the first definition, the `structure-class` metaclass is specified. In some implementations, this can cause a significant difference in the representation. An instance of `position` created with metaclass `structure-class` could be represented as a linear block of storage with two data items, which is very efficient in space. The second definition specifies the metaclass `standard-class`. For this metaclass, the instances need to be represented in a flexible way that allows updating of the structure. For example, this might be done using a level of indirection between a header and the storage for the data. Such an instance can track any changes in its class (adding or deleting instance variables) without users of the instance needing to do anything to update the instance. Automatic updating occurs when access to slots is requested. The instance can even change its class and invisibly update its structure. Because the metaclass is responsible for the implementation of the instance, it is also responsible for access to slots of the instance. We return to this below.

3.3 *Multiple Inheritance*

Many metaclasses allow multiple inheritance. For example,

```
(defclass titled-window(window titled-thing)())
```

defines a new class, `titled-window`, that includes both `window` and `titled-thing` as superclasses. Under control of the metaclass, the new class will inherit slots from all the superclasses. Although the usual inheritance for slots is to take the union of those specified in the superclasses, some metaclasses could signal an error if there were an overlap in names.

The class being defined is the root of a directed graph from which descriptions are inherited. The specified order of the included classes determines a local precedence among the classes. Subclass–superclass relationships also specify a precedence order. This precedence relation is used to compute a non-duplicating linear order used for inheritance. This class precedence list is determines inheritance of the class.

The metaclass determines the algorithm for computing the class precedence list from the local precedences. The algorithm used by the metaclass `standard-class` is a topological sort using the precedence relationship specified by the local order and the subclass–superclass relationship. Ambiguities in the topological sort are resolved by trying to keep all superclasses of any given subclass together. In almost all simple cases, this algorithm produces the same linearization as the Loops rule *left to right, depth first, up to joins*, but the algorithm produces more intuitive results for the rare (in programming) complicated cases.

The precedence relationships may be inconsistent; for example, a local precedence list might specify that `C1` comes before `C2`, and `C1` is somehow a super of `C2`. In this case, CLOS signals an error.

3.4 *Initial Classes in* CLOS

CLOS uses the flexibility provided by metaclasses to define classes that correspond to the primitive LISP types. These classes are part of the same class lattice as all other CLOS classes. Thus the LISP data-type space is included in the CLOS class lattice. This means that methods can be defined on the LISP built-in classes as well as on types defined by `defstruct`. This is a significant difference from New Flavors.

As shown in Figure 3, CLOS provides several pre-defined metaclasses that provide functionality for structures of Common LISP, the built-in types, and the metaclass `standard-class` designed to facilitate exploratory programming [Sheil, 1984]. The user can define a new metaclass to provide other functionality for a different object system. For example, with Gary Drescher, we have looked at defining a metaclass that supports Object LISP [Drescher, 1986] inheritance and behavior.

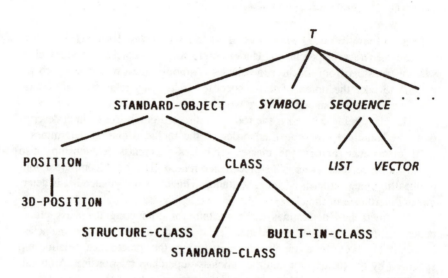

Figure 3 Classes in italics are instances of `built-in-class`, all others are instances of `standard-class`. T is the superclass of everything in CLOS. It corresponds to the Common LISP type specifier of the same name. `class` is a primitive class used to implement metaclasses. All metaclasses have `class` as a superclass.

3.5 *Slot Options in Class*

The representation of instances used by class allows allocation strategies for slots in addition to the usual direct allocation of storage in the instance. A `:class` allocation specifies that the slot is stored only in the class; no storage is allocated for it in the instances. The slot is then shared by all instances of the class. Updating the value in one instance is seen by all. This option provides functionality similar to class variables in Smalltalk-80 and Loops, except that CLOS class variables share the same name space with instance variables. Changing the `:allocation` option of a slot does not require the user of the class to change the source code that accesses that slot.

An extension that has been considered, and has been incorporated using the metaclass mechanism is a `:dynamic` allocation that specifies storage for this slot should be allocated in the instance, but only when the slot is first used. If the first access is a `fetch`, then storage is allocated, the `:initform` is evaluated, and the value is stored in the slot and returned. If the first access is a `setf`, the storage is allocated, the value is stored in the slot, and returned. This allows infrequently used slots to have initialization declarations, but take storage only if needed.

Another extension allows objects to have slots that do not appear in the `defclass` declaration. This gives objects their own property lists: This is analogous to Flavor's `plist-mixin` flavor. It differs from a `plist-mixin` in that there is uniform access to slots independent of whether they were declared.

4 CLOS Implementation

CLOS can be implemented efficiently, even on conventional machines. The most important cases for time-critical applications are well understood and have been implemented in several object-oriented systems.

4.1 Method Lookup

Implementation of method lookup can be specialized with respect to four cases: where there is only one method defined for a particular selector, where the only method has no type specification, where all the methods have specifiers only on their first argument, and the general case.

4.1.1 Single Method In this case there is only one nondefault method defined on the selector. A static analysis of Loops and Flavors code shows that approximately 50% of the selectors fall in this category. In this case the generic function can compile into appropriate type checks and an open call to the method. Thus the method-lookup time adds only the time required to check the types of the arguments, a necessary overhead.

4.1.2 Default Method Only This case is similar to the single method case except that the method has no type specifiers at all, so it is always applicable. In this case no type checks are required. The generic function runs as if it were defined as an ordinary function.

4.1.3 Classical Methods Only When there are multiple methods, all of which only have type specifiers on their first argument, the situation is the same as in Smalltalk-80 and Flavors. We call this "classical" to stress its equivalence to classical object programming systems. On stock hardware this can be implemented using any of the proven method-lookup caching schemes. The cache can either be a global cache, a selector-specific cache, a callee cache, or a caller cache. Variations have been used in Smalltalk-80 systems [Krasner, 1983], Loops, and Flavors. On specialized hardware this can be implemented using the same mechanisms as in Flavors. A default method can easily be combined with a set of classical methods, calling it instead of a standard error.

4.1.4 *General Case*

In the remaining case, a selector has more than one method, and at least one of them has a type specifier on other than the first argument. A standard case might have type specifiers for the first two arguments, e.g., where the types for show could be:

```
(square, display-stream)
(square, print-stream)
(circle, display-stream)
...
```

In our current implementation of multi-method invocation, we have built a straightforward extension of the caching techniques used for classical method lookup. We do not have enough experience with multi-methods to know what other common patterns should be optimized.

In classical object-oriented programming, this example could be handled by introducing a second level of message sending. Instead of having separate multi-methods for each case, one could (by convention) write two methods for each case [Ingalls, 1986]. Thus, the show message for square would send a second message to the stream (show-square-on) that would embed the type information about square implicitly in the selector.

Multi-method lookup in CLOS is faster than multiple sequential method lookups. The overhead for doing lookup is the time of an extra function call (a call to the generic function, which then calls the chosen method) plus the time of a type check for each specialized argument.

4.2 *Slot Access and Metaclasses*

Slot access can be implemented in a variety of ways. The metaclass standard-class uses a caching technique similar to that used in Smalltalk-80. The metaclass structure-class, because it does not allow multiple inheritance, can compile out the slot lookups in the standard way. The metaclass standard-class uses the mapping-table technique used in Flavors.

We have also looked at extensions to CLOS that compile out the cost of method lookup and slot lookup entirely. Having metaclasses and generic function objects should allow the specification of special ways of optimizing a call to a generic function when the types of some of the arguments are known at compile time. In certain cases the appropriate method can be determined at compile time so that no method lookup need occur at run time. The body of the method might even be compiled in-line.

Compilation of calls to accessor functions is a common case where in-line expansion works well. The resulting code can access the slot directly. Meta-classes which do this kind of optimization are useful in production versions of applications where the time to change a program vs. program execution speed tradeoffs is heavily biased toward execution speed.

Flexibility to use different slot access or method-lookup schemes based on the metaclass is an important feature of CLOS. Efficiency is a matter of tradeoffs. Object systems without metaclasses must choose one set of tradeoffs and implement it as well as possible. Users have to live with the tradeoffs chosen by the implementers. In CLOS, different sets of tradeoffs can be imple-mented, allowing users to choose which set of tradeoffs is appropriate for a given situation.

5 *CLOS and other Systems*

In this section we consider several important object-oriented languages. All of these languages have been influential in the design of CLOS, and we try to note similarities and differences. A general overview of features of object languages and multi-paradigm systems can be found in [Stefik and Bobrow, 1986].

5.1 *Loops*

Loops [Bobrow and Stefik, 1983] is a multi-paradigm system for knowledge programming implemented in Interlisp-D. It is integrated into the interactive environment provided by Interlisp-D. It also provides special environmental capabilities, such as class browsers and object inspectors. The design of CLOS draws on our experience with Loops, but is a major departure from it.

CLOS provides new functionality but also introduces many minor incom-patibilities and lacks some functionality of Loops as discussed below. Features of Loops such as composite objects that are appropriately implemented in terms of the CLOS kernel are not discussed. Modifying Loops to run on top of CLOS will require a substantial programming effort.

5.1.1 *Class Variables* Loops supports the notion of class variables that are accessed via special functions. CLOS provides :class variables which provide nearly equivalent functionality. There are not, however, different name spaces for instance variables and class variables as there are in Loops. We now believe that the advantages for modifiability of a program outweigh the advan-tages of multiple name spaces.

5.1.2 *Default Values* Loops supports the notion of a default value which at slot access time finds the default value in the class or the superclasses of the class. CLOS provides `initforms` in slot descriptions that specify how to compute the default value at creation time. The essential difference is that in Loops an instance tracks the slot description until given a local value while CLOS always gives a local value at creation time. The Loops behavior can be implemented in CLOS using annotated values as described in the section on open design questions. In our experience, initial values are satisfactory for most of the applications of default values.

5.1.3 *Slot Properties* In Loops a slot can have named properties in addition to a value. This provides a convenient way to store more information about a value without interfering with access of the value. This can be supported using annotated values.

5.1.4 *Active Values* In Loops a value can be active, so that specified functions can be run when a slot containing an active value is accessed. CLOS can be extended to provide comparable capabilities.

5.2 *Smalltalk-80 System*

The Smalltalk-80 system [Goldberg and Robson, 1983] is both an object-oriented programming language and a vertically integrated programming environment that is uniformly object structured. The strength and importance of the Smalltalk-80 system rests not only with its object-oriented programming style, but also in the careful engineering of the set of kernel classes and their behavior that define the Smalltalk-80 image.

In terms of its provisions for class definition, name lookup, method discrimination, and method combination, CLOS can be viewed as a superset of Smalltalk-80, with some notable exceptions.

The Smalltalk-80 virtual machine directly supports only single superclass inheritance. Nevertheless, additional inheritance schemes can be implemented (by changing the manner in which new classes are defined), and multiple superclass inheritance is included as part of the standard Smalltalk-80 environment. It operates substantially the same as in CLOS, except that multiply inherited methods for the same selector must be redefined at the common subclass, or else an error will result when the method is invoked. This Smalltalk-80 feature is inconvenient for mixin classes that specialize standard methods as used in Flavors and Loops.

The Smalltalk-80 multiple inheritance scheme provides an explicit scheme for method combination: Objects can send messages to themselves in a way that specifies from which superclass method lookup is to proceed. This is done by composing the name of the superclass with the selector; e.g., an instance of

`ReadWriteStream` may send itself the message `ReadStream next` to indicate that the `ReadStream` superclass is to supply the method. This explicitness can cause problems because methods build in as constants information about the class hierarchy, which may change.

Classes and metaclasses bear the same relationship to each other and there is some overlap of function in both systems. However, there are some significant differences in functionality. Instances of all Smalltalk-80 classes (except for the compiled-method class) are realized in terms of just three basic implementations: *pointer objects*, *word objects*, and *byte objects*. The class definition directly determines which implementation is to be used. By convention in Smalltalk-80 each class has a unique metaclass.

In many Smalltalk-80 implementations, enumerating the instances of a class is intended to be computationally bearable (just how bearable depends on implementation dependent factors, e.g., whether and how virtual memory is implemented). As a result, Smalltalk-80 classes can broadcast to their instances. This makes them extensional, as well as intensional, characterizations of sets of objects. Since even integers have a class in CLOS, it is not generally useful to enumerate all instances of every class. It is straightforward in CLOS to implement a metaclass that allows a class to keep a list of instances it has created.

Similarly, in some Smalltalk-80 systems, one can find all references to a particular object. It is even possible to interchange all the references to one object with all the references to some other object, regardless of their respective classes. In effect, the two objects exchange identities. This operation is inexpensive if references to objects are made indirectly through an object table, which is the standard practice. This capability enables, among other things, cheap resizing of instances of variable-length classes. In CLOS, instances of classes created by the metaclass `standard-class` can easily modify their contents and class pointers to achieve the same functionality.

Smalltalk-80 provides class variables, which are shared by all the instances of a class and its subclasses, and pool variables, which are shared by all instances of some set of classes and their subclasses. The effect of class variables is directly achieved in CLOS through the `:allocation` class slot option. The effect of Smalltalk-80's pool variables can be achieved through the expedient of defining a common superclass among the classes to be "pooled" that contributes nothing but a shared slot.

Smalltalk-80 differs more fundamentally from CLOS in that Smalltalk-80 objects are encapsulated, and control primitives are based upon message passing. In Smalltalk-80, unlike CLOS, only methods of an object can access and update the state directly (this is not strictly true, but the operations provided for breaking encapsulation are viewed as just that, and are used primarily for building debuggers, viewers, and so on). All other methods must send messages.

Conditionals, iteration, and the like in Smalltalk-80 are done via message passing, and contexts (stack frames) are first class objects. CLOS relies upon the Common LISP control constructs that in general are special forms and cannot be specialized.

5.3 *New Flavors*

CLOS is practically a superset of New Flavors. CLOS and New Flavors share the notion of generic function. In developing CLOS we have included the New Flavors mechanism for user-defined method combination.

The important difference between CLOS and New Flavors is the existence of *meta-objects* in CLOS. Meta-objects make CLOS much more extensible. Meta-objects allow experimentation with other kinds of object systems. They allow CLOS to treat primitive LISP types as classes. Methods can be defined on those types, and the standard CLOS mechanisms for accessing the slots of a structure can be used to access the fields of primitive LISP objects.

5.4 *Other Object Languages*

Object LISP [Drescher, 1986] also integrates objects and LISP. Unlike CLOS, Object LISP distinguishes fundamentally between LISP types and Object LISP objects. This means that one cannot define methods on existing types. Another difference is that Object LISP supports only classical methods.

T shares with CLOS the common syntax for message sending and function call. Like Object LISP, T supports only classical methods and there is no integration of LISP types with objects [Rees and Adams, 1982].

5.5 *Adding Access-Oriented Programming to CLOS*

Access-oriented programming is one of the popular features of Loops and several frame languages such as KEE, UNITS, and STROBE. The merits of this feature are often confounded with the merits of its various implementations. In this section, we try to separate these issues, and indicate alternative implementations available in CLOS.

In access-oriented programming, fetching from or storing in an object can cause user-defined operations to be invoked. Procedural annotations (or active values) associate objects with slots so that methods are invoked when values are fetched and stored. It is also useful to associate other information with a slot in addition to its value. Structural (or property) annotations associate arbitrary extendible property lists with a value in an object. Collectively these kinds of annotations are called annotated values. These annotations can be installed on slots and can be nested recursively.

Annotated values reify the notion of storage cell and are a valuable abstraction for organizing programs. Structural annotations can be used for incore documentation. They are also used for attaching records for different purposes. For example, such annotations can record histories of changes, dependencies on other slots, or degrees of belief. Procedural annotations can be used as interfaces between programs that compute and programs that monitor those computations. For example, they can represent probes that connect slots in a simulation program to viewers and gauges in a display program.

Annotated values are conveniently represented as objects, and must satisfy a number of criteria for efficiency of operation and noninterference [Stefik et al., 1986]. When multiple annotations are installed on the same value, the access operations must compose in the same order as the nesting. Annotated values can be implemented in different ways that optimize performance depending on the expected patterns of common use.

One implementation of annotated values in CLOS would require the slot access primitives of the metaclass check whether the value is an active value object. The active value check can be made fast if the active value objects are wrapped in a unique data type. This technique for implementing active values has been used successfully in Loops. Hardware or microcode support of this fast check would allow the use of annotated values in ordinary LISP structures (e.g., in cons-cells), greatly extending the utility of this abstraction.

Alternatively, a procedural implementation of annotated values could be built upon the ability in CLOS to specialize methods with respect to individuals. For those slots for which a special action is desired upon access, one can define methods for those accessors and objects that do the special action.

CLOS is capable of supporting either implementation. In addition, we believe that it is appropriate in CLOS to provide metaclasses that can support annotated values according to the needs of optimization. If active values are to be attached and detached frequently, checking dynamically for annotated values may be preferable to changing the generic function frequently. If probes are usually installed only once, then one may prefer the lower overhead of the procedural implementation. If access to properties is relatively rare compared with the access to values, then differentiating property access at compile time might be preferred.

It is useful to be able to view a program that uses annotations in terms of that abstraction, rather than in implementation terms. The issue of supporting views of programs is discussed more generally in the next section.

5.6 *Programming Environment Support*

Programming environments must provide computational support for particular views (or perspectives) of programs [Stefik and Bobrow, 1986]. A view is said to support a particular programming abstraction when the elements of the view are in the terminology of the abstraction, and the operations possible within that viewer are those appropriate for the abstraction.

For example, a viewer that supports the view of a program in terms of annotated values would show annotated values, not methods or wrappers that make up their implementation. The installation and nesting of annotated values are the appropriate actions available in the viewer.

Another important and popular view of object-oriented programs is that classes are defined by their slots and methods. While program listings often show structure and methods separated, it is useful to view such programs as organized in terms of classes with access to slot and method descriptions. CLOS viewers can also provide access to any multi-method from all of its associated classes. CLOS supports both the classical view of object-oriented programming, with appropriate extensions.

Views of classes can be organized around semantic categories, as in the standard Smalltalk-80 browser, or around a graph of the class inheritance lattice of some portion of the system, as in Loops and CommonLoops. In the latter case, certain operations become natural to perform directly through the lattice browser—for example, promoting methods or slots to more general classes, or changing the inheritance structure. Changing the name of a slot or selector through a browser can invoke analysis routines that can find and change all occurrences of the name in code.

Viewers on CLOS can also support a procedural abstraction. They can provide static browsers of program-calling structure, where each generic function is considered as a single function. Through such browsers, one can get access to individual method definitions from the corresponding generic function.

To provide viable support for programming with an abstraction, the viewers must be integrated with the debugging system. For example, to support a view of program in terms of methods, it should not be necessary to understand how methods are implemented or to refer to methods created automatically by the system. Rather, debugging should use the same terms that the programmer uses in writing the program.

6 Summary and Conclusions

Over the last ten years many systems have been written that add object-oriented programming to LISP (e.g., Flavors, Loops, Object LISP). Each of these has attracted a group of users who recognize the benefits of message sending and specialization and have endorsed the object-oriented style. The object-languages in these systems have been embedded in LISP with different degrees of integration.

Interest in object-oriented programming has also been spurred by work in expert systems. Several knowledge-programming systems (ART, KEE, Strobe,

UNITS, etc.) have emerged. These systems have included variations and extensions on object-oriented programming, and tools for creating knowledge bases in terms of objects. As research continues, additional knowledge programming systems will emerge. Each of these will have their advocates and perhaps their niche in the range of applications and computer architectures. All of these systems can benefit from an object-oriented base that is efficient and extensible.

The creation of a good base involves both theoretical language design and engineering concerns. CLOS has attempted to respond to several kinds of pressure on the design of such a system.

The applications community wants to use a system for its work. The language must be suitable for state-of-the-art applications and systems that they build on top of it. The language must have an efficient implementation. It must be a graceful extension of Common LISP because existing code and existing programming skills need to be preserved.

Vendors share these interests. They want their systems to provide a suitable base for a large fraction of the applications. They want the kernel of the language to be lean, easy to maintain, and efficient; they want the kernel to be principled and free of idiosyncratic features with no enduring value beyond their history. Vendors don't want to implement multiple versions of object languages, gratuitously different and incompatible.

The research community has somewhat different interests. Like the application community, it needs to be able to share code, but it is concerned with being able to try out other ways of doing things. New ideas for languages come out of the experience of the research community. To build higher-level languages, the base must provide mechanisms for open-ended experimentation.

CLOS has responded to these pressures by providing a base for experimentation through the use of meta-objects, while capturing in its kernel the ability to implement the features of current object-oriented systems. By integrating classes with the LISP type system, and using a syntax for method invocation that is identical to the LISP function call, CLOS makes possible a smooth and incremental transition from using only the functional paradigm for user code to using the object paradigm. As a portable system implemented in a widely available base, it allows users the choice of hardware and environments. It allows them a road to the future.

Acknowledgments

This paper is based on a talk given at the 1986 National Conference on Artificial Intelligence. At that time, CommonLoops was the example used of tight integration of paradigms. Since that time, the Common LISP Object System has emerged as a better example. It incorporates good ideas from CommonLoops, New Flavors, and from the X3J13 Common LISP Object System Specification subcommittee consisting of Daniel G. Bobrow, Linda G. DeMichiel, Patrick Dussud, Richard P. Gabriel, Sonya E. Keene, Jim Kempf Gregor Kiczales, and David A. Moon. Their contributions to the design have helped make this a better paper. I also want to thank my coauthors of an earlier paper on Common-Loops that I have adapted for this article [Bobrow et al., 1986]; they are Ken Kahn, Gregor Kiczales, Larry Masinter, Mark Stefik, and Frank Zdybel. Any mistakes that remain are solely the responsibility of the author.

References

Bobrow, D. G, L. G. DeMichiel, R. P. Gabriel, S. E. Keene, G. Kiczales, and D. A. Moon, 1987–88. X3J13 standards committee documents 88-002 and 88-003.

Bobrow, D. G., Kahn, K., Kiczales, G., Masinter, L., Stefik, M., and Zdybel, F., 1986. CommonLoops, merging Common Lisp and object-oriented programming. In *Proceedings of the ACM OOPSLA '86 Conference.*

Bobrow, Daniel G. and Stefik, Mark, 1983. *The Loops Manual.* Intelligent Systems Laboratory, Xerox Corporation.

Bobrow, Daniel G. and Stefik, Mark, 1986. Perspectives on artificial intelligence programming. *Science* **231**(4741):951.

Dresher, Gary, 1986. *Object LISP User Manual.* LMI, 1000 Massachusetts Avenue, Cambridge, MA.

Forgy, C. L., 1982. Rete: A fast algorithm for the many pattern/many object pattern match problem. *Artificial Intelligence* **19**(1).

Goldberg, A. and D. Robson, 1983. *Smalltalk-80: The Language and its Implementation.* Addison-Wesley, Reading, MA.

Ingalls, D. H., 1986. A simple technique for handling multiple polymorphism In *Proceedings of ACM OOPSLA '86 Conference.*

Moon, D., 1986. New Flavors. In *Proceedings of the ACM OOPSLA Conference.*

Krasner, Glenn, ed., 1983. *Smalltalk-80: Bits of History, Words of Advice.* Addison-Wesley, Reading, MA.

Rees, J. A. and Adams, N. I., 1982. T: A dialect of Lisp or, Lamda: The ultimate software tool. In *ACM Symposium on Lisp and Functional Programming.*

Sheil, B., 1984. Power tools for programmers. *Interactive Programming Environments*, Barstow, D. et al., ed. McGraw Hill, New York.

Steele, G. L., 1984. *Common Lisp: The Language.* Digital Press.

Stefik, M. and Bobrow, D. G., 1986. Object-oriented programming: Themes and variations. *AI Magazine* **6**(4).

Stefik, M., Bobrow, D. G., and Kahn, K., 1986. Integrating access-oriented programming into a multi-paradigm environment. *IEEE Software.*

16

Artificial Intelligence and Software Engineering

David Barstow
Schlumberger-Doll Research
Ridgefield, Connecticut

Introduction

This paper is based on a talk titled "Artificial Intelligence and Software Engineering." That's actually a bit broader than I'm going to be. In particular, I'm only going to look at attempts to apply AI techniques to software engineering problems. So I will specifically not discuss indirect contributions from AI to software engineering, of which there are many. I also won't discuss the application of software engineering techniques when you're building AI systems, of which there is a great need.

There are three parts to this paper. First, I'm going to give an overview of software engineering, because it's important to understand what software engineering is, and I think many of us have been remarkably ignorant about it. Then I'll look at the state of the art in research on the application of AI to software engineering. Finally, I'll look at what the impact of all this might be on the practice of software engineering.

Part I

It's conventional to divide software engineering activities into two categories, usually referred to as programming-in-the-small and programming-in-the-large [DeRemer and Kron, 1976]. Programming-in-the-small is typically done by individuals or very small groups. A typical project might be a few thousand lines long, and it's typically not more than a few months of effort. Programming-in-the-large is done by very large groups of people, and programs have several hundred thousand or millions of lines, with very long intended lifetimes. Now these are obviously ends of a spectrum, but the issues involved in these two different categories are really quite different. So it's a useful distinction to try to make. Let me illustrate both of these by considering two problems that you, as a software engineer, might get involved with.

1.1 *Programming-in-the-Small*

The first example is related to Schlumberger's activities in oil well logging (Figure 1a). Basically, our service involves lowering an instrument down an oil well, pulling it back out, making measurements along the way, and then interpreting those measurements in terms of the things that our clients, oil companies, are interested in. For example, where is the oil? So, imagine that a tool designer has just built a new tool and you've been asked to write the software for it. Let's think about what you would do.

The first thing you do is try to write a specification for that software, some kind of complete and precise description of what the software is supposed to do (Figure 1b). As suggested by the bubbles in the figure, while you're doing this, you need to know something about the tool and about the physics upon which the tool's sensors are based.

Now, the next thing you do is realize that it will be a moderately big program, so you want to reduce it into more manageable pieces, as shown in Figure 1c. While you're doing this, you obviously need to know about the specification. You also need to know about the architecture of the machine you're going to run the software on, and you need to know the programming techniques that you learned when you were in school. You also find that you have to talk to the tool designer because, despite everybody's best attempts, the specification is neither complete nor precise.

Once you've got the little pieces, you try to implement them (Figure 1d). This again requires knowledge of the architecture of the target machine and programming techniques. And once again, you need to talk to the tool designer. Then comes testing (Figure 1e).

The goal here is to ensure that the source code actually implements what the specification says it ought to implement. This involves taking some data,

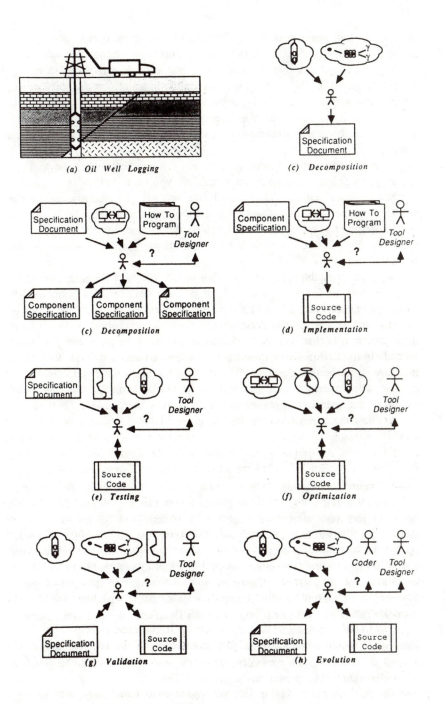

(a) Oil Well Logging

(c) Decomposition

(c) Decomposition

(d) Implementation

(e) Testing

(f) Optimization

(g) Validation

(h) Evolution

Figure 1 Programming-in-the-small.

studying the tool again, and talking with the tool designer to make sure you've covered all the cases. And in the process, of course, you change the code.

Next you find out that the code isn't fast enough and needs to be optimized (Figure 1f). There are some very tight constraints on the software for logging, and you find out that the software doesn't meet those. So you get out your stopwatch, study the architecture of the target machine, study the tool again, talk to the tool designer again, and finally try to get the code to be fast enough.

Then you ask yourself whether this really implements what the tool designer wants (Figure 1g). As you recall, all you've tested so far is that it matches the specification. Validation is the process of making sure that the specification specifies the software that the tool designer wants, that it satisfies the tool designer's real needs. In order to do this, you obviously need to make measurements, you need to study the tool and the physics, and you need to talk to the tool designer.

Now, you may think you're done, but in fact you're not, because someone has been busy designing a new tool, or perhaps developing a better understanding of the physics. So you have to rewrite the code to satisfy the needs of the new tool or the new understanding of physics (Figure 1h). One of the things you find is that you're not the same person you were when you wrote the code in the first place. So you have to talk to the coder who did it the first time as well as the tool designer. When you talk to the coder, you need to understand what decisions were made when he or she wrote the software. And not only what decisions were made, but why they were made. That is, you need to know the rationale for the decisions.

1.2 *Programming-in-the-Large*

For an example of programming-in-the-large, imagine you work for the Internal Revenue Service, and Congress passes a new tax law (Figure 2a). You've been told you have to write the software to process the tax returns. I don't know about you, but first I would panic. But once that panic is over, you realize that the first thing to do is figure out what's going on in the tax law. That is, you have to do requirements analysis (Figure 2b). Now, let's suppose there are 1800 pages of "legalese." There are no doubt numerous ambiguities, probably intentional, adding to what is already a rather difficult problem for you, so you talk to a tax expert to help you figure it all out, and you also hire a number of people to work with you.

Now, once you think you understand the tax law, the next thing you have to do is break the system down into components that can be considered or attacked as problems of programming-in-the-small (Figure 2c). That's usually called "design." In order to do this, it turns out you need to know some software engineering techniques, and you find again that you're talking to a tax expert.

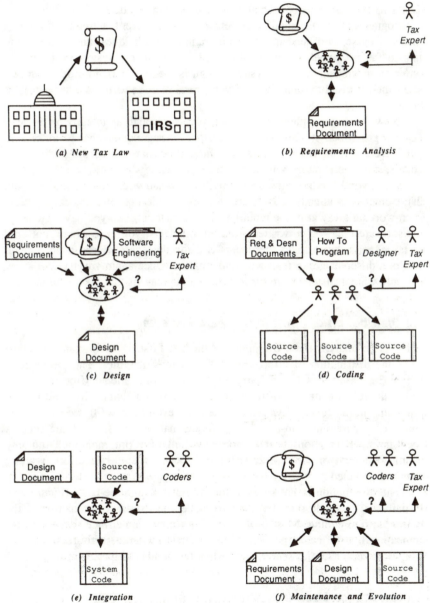

(a) New Tax Law

(b) Requirements Analysis

(c) Design

(d) Coding

(e) Integration

(f) Maintenance and Evolution

Figure 2

Now, having done the design, you go through the coding process (Figure 2d). This typically involves smaller groups of people, and it can be thought of as programming-in-the-small, for relatively independent activities. In doing this, of course, you need to know programming techniques, and you need to talk to the tax expert, but you also need to talk to the system designers, in order to understand why the system design is the way it is, in order to understand the nature of the interfaces of your piece of code with the other pieces of code.

Now, having completed the coding, you go through an integration process, again a group activity (Figure 2e). You get everything together to make sure you have the right large system. The integrators may not be the same as the coders, so the integrators have to talk to the coders.

Now, you have the same case here that you had with tool software (Figure 2f). Congress is already talking about changing the tax law. So while you've been working away at it, the requirements are changing. So you have to change the software that you've written. And in doing this, you have to talk not only to tax experts, but also to the coders and the designers. Because once again you're a different group than when you started. Once again you have to know not only what decisions were made, but also the reasons that they were made.

1.3 *Distribution of Effort in Software Projects*

Let's try to analyze these examples a little bit. First, it's important to understand the distribution of effort among the various activities. The pie chart in Figure 3a, based loosely on Barry Boehm's Cocomo model [Boehm, 1981], shows the relative amount of time spent in different activities involved in programming-in-the-small. (I've actually left off evolution; we'll see that in the chart for programming-in-the-large.) Notice that only a fifth of the time is spent in implementation, what we normally think of as programming. And only a little over half of the time is spent with code. Overall, the effort is pretty evenly distributed.

The distribution is not so even for programming-in-the-large (Figure 3b). In particular, according to the Cocomo model, an extremely small part of the time goes into coding. Most of the time goes into maintenance and evolution, something like 60 or 70 percent of the effort on a large software system. In fact, more recent studies seem to show that the number is increasing.

1.4 *Knowledge Used in Software Activities*

The next thing to look at is the knowledge used during these activities. We can see five general categories. Three obvious categories are software engineering methodologies, programming techniques, and the architecture of the target

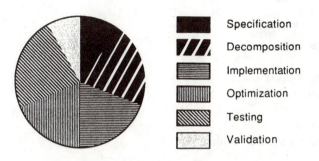

(a)   *Programming-in-the-Small*

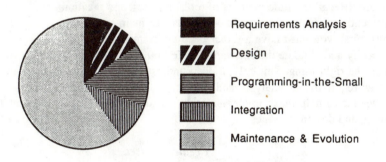

(b)   *Programming-in-the-Large*

Figure 3 Distribution of effort in software projects.

machine. The other two are, I think, more interesting. One is the amount that you have to know about the application domain; the other is the history of the target software. Let's consider these in a little more detail.

	Used
Programming-in-the-Small	
Specification	✔
Decomposition	
Implementation	✔
Testing	✔
Validation	✔
Programming-in-the-Large	
Requirements Analysis	✔
Design	✔
Integration	
Maintenance and Evolution	✔

Figure 4 Knowledge of the application domain.

Figure 4 shows the various software activities, with check marks indicating activities which require a substantial amount of knowledge about the application domain. (Recall the little pictures of tools, physics, and taxation and the figures representing tool designers and tax experts.) Domain knowledge is used in two ways. First, you must have a rather deep understanding of the domain in order to specify and validate the software, where you want to make sure that you are doing the right thing. Similarly, a deep understanding of the domain is needed during requirements analysis and evolution. Second, you must use domain knowledge to help make implementation decisions during the implementation, testing, and design activities.

	Created	Used
Programming-in-the-Small		
Specification	✔	
Decomposition	✔	
Implementation	✔	
Testing		✔
Optimization	✔	✔
Validation		✔
Programming-in-the-Large		
Requirements Analysis	✔	
Design	✔	
Integration	✔	✔
Maintenance and Evolution	✔	✔

Figure 5 Knowledge of the target software.

Now, let's look at knowledge of the target software, that is, knowledge of what decisions were made earlier in the development process. It is interesting that, whereas knowledge of the domain exists *a priori*, knowledge of the target software is created during the process of writing the software. Figure 5 has check marks indicating where a significant number of decisions are made, and those are the places where that knowledge comes into existence. The second set of check marks indicates where that knowledge is used. Perhaps the most important mark is the one next to maintenance and evolution, because knowledge created throughout the earlier phases is relied on to a very great degree during maintenance and evolution.

1.5 *Techniques for Knowledge Management*

In fact, I would make the following assertion: *The high cost of software development and evolution is primarily due to the ineffectiveness of current techniques for managing knowledge about the application domain and about the implementation history.*

Let's look at what those current techniques are. They're listed in Figure 6, roughly in increasing order of frequency of use. Sometimes we have requirements documents, more frequently we have design or specification documents, and people usually put some comments in the code. But most of the time we rely on human memory and the wastebasket. That is, we think we will remember the decisions we made when we look at the code later, and we may just throw away any thoughts that we had about it, believing that they won't matter.

The weaknesses of these techniques are obvious. First, most of the information is not recorded. And in fact, that's one of the reasons for the great cost of the later phases of software engineering activities. Second, complex interactions are not made explicit. That is, you may make a design decision early on in the software development process that has ramifications throughout the code. And if all you have are the comments to look at, then you're not going to understand the nature of those interactions. And finally, of course, the information is difficult to access. If it was thrown away or put in somebody's memory, it's obviously very difficult to retrieve.

- Requirements Documents
- Design Documents
- Specification Documents
- Comments in Code
- Human Memory
- Wastebasket

Figure 6 Current techniques for knowledge management.

In other words, software engineering is fraught with uncertainty: A major source of problems during software development is uncertainty about requirements; a major source of problems during software evolution is uncertainty about design and implementation decisions made during development.

1.6 *The Need for AI Techniques*

So these are, to my mind, the fundamental problems faced by software engineering, and obviously, I believe that AI techniques ought to be able to come to the rescue here. A straightforward argument says that: (a) Effective knowledge management requires computer support and (b) Computer support for knowledge management requires AI techniques. Now, when I say the same kinds of things to software engineering audiences, this is the basic argument that I feel like I have to make. I would hope that I don't have to make this argument here, but in case *you* have to make it some time, that's the argument.

Now, it's certainly not the case that only AI is necessary, and we can mention many other computer technologies that are absolutely required to solve the software engineering problem, including at least data bases, communication systems, and user interfaces. But I think the argument for the necessity of AI is quite strong.

1.7 *Review*

Let's review what we've established so far. Software engineering activities are knowledge intensive, especially requiring knowledge of the application domain and of the target software. Many software engineering costs are due to the ineffectiveness of current techniques for managing the knowledge. And AI techniques ought to be able to help manage the knowledge more effectively.

Part II

Let's see what's been done in trying to apply AI techniques to software engineering activities. In doing this, I will look at several different paradigms, the results of the work to date, and the directions that I think we ought to be pursuing.

2.1 *Deductive Synthesis*

The first paradigm is usually referred to as deductive synthesis, and essentially it relies on an analogy between programming and theorem proving. In particular, there's an analogy between a specification and a theorem, and an analogy between a program and the proof of the corresponding theorem. So the idea is that, in a mechanical way, you can go from a specification to a theorem, then you run your theorem prover forward to get a proof, and from the structure of the proof you go back to the program.

Let me just summarize what some of the basic techniques are. Typically, a specification will consist of two parts, a pre-condition and a post-condition. A pre-condition is usually a predicate on the input variables, say $P(X)$. A post-condition is a predicate on the input and output variables, say $Q(X, Y)$. The essence is that the software writer can assume that $P(X)$ holds of the inputs and must write software that guarantees that $Q(X, Y)$ is satisfied after the program halts. This specification corresponds to the theorem $\forall X \, \exists \, Y \, P(X) \Rightarrow Q(X, Y)$, and if we have a proof of this theorem, we can take the structure of the proof and map it into a program. For example, a constructive proof typically corresponds to an assignment statement, a case analysis corresponds to a conditional, and induction corresponds to recursion. There is, of course, a lot of detail in these techniques; I'm just trying to summarize them here.

The history of the technique goes back to two Ph.D. theses [Green, 1969; Waldinger, 1969]. Both came up with essentially the same observation, the correspondence between programs and proofs. Around 1980, Manna and Waldinger developed a new formulation [Manna and Waldinger, 1980]. It's fundamentally the same technique, but it's a new formulation that makes it a little bit easier to work with. They call it the tableau method. An interesting recent development is some work by Smith, looking at decomposition strategies and derived pre-conditions, with the goal of getting to some relatively more complicated kinds of algorithms, such as divide-and-conquer algorithms [Smith, 1985]. The state of the art is that there have been some demonstrations for some very simple programs, things like sorting, greatest common divisor, and binary search [Manna and Waldinger, 1985]. Those are really pretty simple programs.

So what are the major issues? One issue relates to size and complexity: How do you write larger and more complex programs? The work of Smith, for example, is aimed in that direction, but has not gotten very far. A second issue relates to the efficiency of the resulting program. And to understand this issue, you have to go back to the basic technique, where you're doing all of the work in the theorem-proving domain. So if you want an optimal program, then you have to make sure that you find the proof that corresponds to that optimal program. Typically, optimal programs are longer than the average program that someone will write. And so typically, the proof will be longer than the proof for the average program that you want to write. And therefore, you're trying to guide the theorem prover to find a long proof instead of a short proof, and most theorem provers are not oriented in that direction. So this is, I think, a fundamental weakness for this paradigm.

2.2 *Program Verification*

The second paradigm, program verification, is also based on theorem-proving techniques. The essence of it is that, from a specification and from a program, you can derive in a mechanical way some things called verification conditions. Now, if you can show that those verification conditions hold, that is, if you can run your theorem prover and find a proof, then that guarantees that the program satisfies the specification.

Let me illustrate the technique with an example. Suppose the specification's pre-condition is $P(X)$ and the post-condition is $Q(X, Y)$, and the program is:

```
if R(X) then Y ← F(X) else Y ← G(X)
```

Then the verification condition is

$$P(X) \Rightarrow (R(X) \Rightarrow Q(X, F(X))) \land (\neg R(X) \Rightarrow Q(X, G(X)))$$

You can see the correspondences among the parts of the pre-condition, post-condition, program, and verification condition. Of course, verification conditions for larger programs are much larger than this simple example.

This all goes back fundamentally to work in the 1960s on the semantics of programming languages by people like Floyd, Hoare, and Dijkstra [Floyd, 1967; Hoare, 1969; Dijkstra, 1976]. The first program verifier that I know about was by King [1971]. In the 1970s, there were a very large number of rather substantial verification projects, at places like Stanford, SRI and ISI. In the 1980s, we've had some successful demonstrations on small but nonetheless real-life programs, for example, encryption algorithms and certain kinds of secure operating systems. So the state of the art here is that we've had demonstrations for non-trivial algorithms, certainly more complicated algorithms than was the case in deductive synthesis, and also some other kinds of small programs and work on abstract data types. All of these have required a substantial amount of effort, both by the user and by the theorem prover. So it's certainly not a straightforward task to force one of these proofs to go through. But people have succeeded in doing it.

One major issue with program verification is size: The larger the program, the larger the verification condition, hence the more difficult it is to find the proof. Another issue is that writing specifications, even after you have the code, can turn out to be a rather difficult problem.

2.3 *Transformational Implementation*

Now, the third paradigm is one that is usually referred to as transformational implementation. The basic idea here is that you start with the specification and transform it through a potentially very large number of very little steps, the end result of which is the program that satisfies the specifications. Now, with this paradigm, the techniques are not as clearly understood as they are in the case of verification and deductive synthesis. But we can identify certain categories of things that you have to do if you want to build a system like this.

One such thing to have is a wide-spectrum language, a term coined by Bauer [Bauer et al., 1978]. The basic idea here is that you need some coherent framework for representing the program during the entire process of going from a specification down to the code at the bottom. And since there are different concepts that appear in the specifications than appear in the code, you need to span a range of concepts, and that's why it's called a wide-spectrum language. Some of the concepts that you need to span here include abstract and concrete data types and operators, and different kinds of computational paradigms.

You also need a library of transformations. This is, after all, the mechanism to get from one step to the next in the transformation process. Some of the kinds of transformations that have been worked on include data type and operator refinement and global reformulations. A typical library may have many hundreds of transformations, so building the library is, itself, a major piece of work.

The other problem that can happen here is that, as you're going through the transformational process, there may be several different transformations that can be applied at the same time. So in fact, you have a search tree. Each of the different paths down the tree leads to a different program, and choosing one path over another amounts to making an implementation decision. The potential for explosive growth in that tree is very clear, and the trees can get extremely large, especially when you have thousands of steps. So search control is clearly important. People have looked at several techniques. One involves efficiency analysis—analyzing an intermediate-level program and guessing what the efficiency is going to be like. Heuristic techniques can be used to simplify or eliminate the need for analysis. However, user interaction is the most common technique to date; that is, the user decides which transformation to apply at any given point. One interesting technique is the idea of replay. That is, once you've gone through a sequence of transformations and you know which transformations were applied to which parts of the program, if you change the specification a little bit, you can replay the same sequence of transformations, or something close to it, and thereby save a lot of the work of thinking about which transformations to apply to those steps.

The history of the technique goes back to the early 1970s, when there were a number of transformation projects at places like Munich [Bauer et al., 1982], Stanford [Green, 1976], ISI [Balzer, 1981], Harvard [Cheatham et al., 1979], and elsewhere [Partsch and Steinbruggen, 1983]. In 1978, I used transformations as a way of representing programming knowledge, a way of encoding knowledge about programming techniques [Barstow, 1979]. At about the same time, Kant did some work on using efficiency considerations to guide the search [Kant, 1983; Kant and Barstow, 1981]. Both of these were done as part of the PSI project at Stanford. Around 1982 or so, a couple of results came out of the Information Sciences Institute work that I think are worth noting. One is due to Fickas who attempted to use heuristics to guide the search [Fickas, 1985a]; another involved some work by Wile on describing transformation histories, essentially laying the basis for the replay idea [Wile, 1983].

So what's the state of the art? There's routine use of such systems in research settings, such as ISI [Balzer, 1985] and the Kestrel Institute [Smith et al., 1985]. And there are some attempts to demonstrate practical value for the transformational technology, including some commercial ventures that have every incentive to make the technology work. So I think one of the nice results that we can expect soon is a demonstration of practical value.

Now, what are the major issues? First, how do you want to specify things? All the projects use different techniques for specification, so I don't think there's any general agreement on that [Balzer et al., 1983; Balzer et al., 1978; Smith et al., 1985]. Second, search control: As I mentioned, there are a variety of approaches, and it does seem to be an issue that we have to address, and we really don't know how yet. And third, the implementation history: You need to record that implementation history somehow, and we only are beginning to understand ways to do that.

2.4 Programmer's Assistant

The fourth paradigm is usually called the programmer's assistant. The underlying idea comes from the observation that a human programmer has a great deal of knowledge about programming techniques. If you could build a system that shared that kind of knowledge, then the system ought to be able to help the programmer in the process of developing a program.

One of the basic techniques involves representing programs. You want to represent what you know about programs, not at the level of syntax of the target language, but rather at a somewhat more abstract level. Some of the techniques that have been developed include data flow, control flow, and hierarchical decomposition. Just as with transformations, you need a library of these things, usually called plans, and it's very similar to having a library of transformations. You also need a mechanism to do some kind of analysis. The basic idea here is that you do a data and control flow analysis on the program and then try to match that against what you have in the library. And the problem is that it won't always match, but it'll be close, so you have to transform things, either the plan or the program you're looking at, in order to find the right kind of match.

The history of this basically goes back to the Programmer's Apprentice project begun at MIT in the 1970s and described in a paper by Rich and Shrobe which is still worth reading [Rich and Shrobe, 1978]. Rich's thesis described the first plan representation system [Rich, 1981]. Waters, in the same project, did some work on integrating a conventional EMACS editor with a library of plans for doing some synthesis and analysis [Waters, 1985]. In a related effort, Johnson built a program that used similar techniques to analyze student programs to make suggestions to help the students learn about programming [Johnson and Soloway, 1985]. Now, the state of the art is that we've had some demonstrations of the use of plans for analysis and synthesis. To my knowledge, the size of the programs that have been analyzed are typically a few lines, perhaps a page or two. Some of the ones that have been synthesized using plans may go up to half-a-dozen pages.

So what are the major issues? I think it has turned out that analysis is much more difficult than had been hoped originally when Rich and Shrobe made their first proposal. And I think this difficulty is a very major issue, and it may turn out to be the stopper for this. Recognition is part of analysis, and some good matching techniques have been developed, but it's not clear whether that can carry us far enough to do analysis. And then, as with all the other paradigms, there's the question of large programs. All these systems work to one degree or another on programs that range from a few lines to a few pages. So the question here, as with the others, is what happens when you look at larger programs.

2.5. Other Work

Now, I want to cite several other pieces of work. I don't have time to go into them in detail, but there have been a variety of efforts in other ways of applying AI techniques to software engineering. These include alternative specification techniques, such as natural language [Heidorn, 1976] and examples [Smith, 1984]. Some work has been done at ISI on monitoring change and evolution in software [Balzer, 1987]. Swartout did some work on explaining software [Swartout, 1983]. Kant and Steier did some work on analyzing protocols for designing algorithms [Kant, 1985; Steier and Kant, 1985]. Greenspan and Fickas have both done some work on trying to use knowledge representation techniques in requirements analysis for programming-in-the-large. [Borgida et al., 1985; Fickas, 1985b]. And there has also been some work on data structure selection [Katz and Zimmerman, 1981]. There are other projects that I've left out, I just wanted to suggest some of the things that have been done. The reason I've picked four paradigms to describe in a little more detail is that I think they're the ones that have had the most attention. Because of that, we can say there really are a paradigms that have been explored.

2.6 *Practical Utility*

Now, one of the things that I'm afraid we have not seen is a demonstration of the utility of AI techniques to support software engineering in practical situations. I wish I were wrong in saying this, but I don't believe I am. The closest I think we have come are those few programs that have been verified with very great effort, and there are suggestions that some of the commercial work may be panning out. But I don't think we've yet had any really solid demonstrations of the practicality of all this. Now, I'd like to see if we can explore why: If there have been 20 years or so of work on this, why haven't we demonstrated anything practical?

I think one of the reasons is that it really is a hard problem. To see that, let's try to compare software engineering with medicine, an area in which AI seems to have had more success. Now, I'm *not* trying to compare software engineers and doctors in terms of their intelligence or skills. Rather, I want to look at the characteristics of the tasks that these people are performing, and Figure 7 shows five dimensions for comparison. The check marks indicate that the particular domain seems to have a greater amount or a greater diversity of knowledge.

In the first dimension, accumulated expertise, there have been something like two orders of magnitude more time spent on medicine than on software engineering, something like 2,000 years to 20 years. So there's certainly a greater amount of accumulated expertise in medicine. But that may not make it a harder task, because one result of that accumulated expertise is a set of useful abstractions. Doctors have nice short words that they can use to refer to things, and I think that we in software engineering haven't really developed those necessary abstractions yet. So although the check says that medicine ought to be harder, it is kind of double-edged.

The second dimension is complexity of subject, and it certainly seems to me that people are more complicated than any of the software systems that anybody's been able to build so far. I think medicine has a clear edge there.

On the other hand, we can look at the third dimension, variation of subjects. Depending on how you count, there are one or two varieties of people. However, if you look at software systems, there is enormous diversity. There are real-time systems, data base systems, communication systems, data analysis systems, and so on. So this great diversity means that you can't just teach a person all about software engineering and expect it to apply in all situations. So diversity is a major problem for software engineering.

The fourth dimension is the run-time environment. Your doctor may ask you whether people smoke where you work, but he's not likely to ask you much more about the environment in which you "run." And yet, when we build software systems, those systems have to interact with the world, and we have to study that interaction very, very carefully, or else the software isn't going to

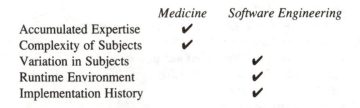

	Medicine	*Software Engineering*
Accumulated Expertise	✔	
Complexity of Subjects	✔	
Variation in Subjects		✔
Runtime Environment		✔
Implementation History		✔

Figure 7 Amount and diversity of knowledge.

be correct. So a great deal more attention has to be paid to the run time environment in the case of software.

The final dimension is the implementation history. It's really not necessary for doctors to know why we have two hands or why we've evolved the way we have. But in the case of software, especially for maintenance, it's very important to know what decisions were made and why they were made. So that is another area in which software engineering at least appears to be somewhat more complicated than medicine.

So the amount and diversity of knowledge is one reason that I think that Software Engineering really is a very hard problem. So maybe it's not so bad that we haven't demonstrated practical successes yet.

But I think there's another reason, one for which we may bear more responsibility. And that's that most of the research on AI applied to software engineering has been relatively narrowly focused, missing what I think are many issues of practical importance. The focus, if you add up everything that's been done, has largely been on algorithm design, and a little more on data structure selection. But it turns out that if you look at how various kinds of effort are distributed, algorithm design and data structure selection are really only a small part of programming. And programming in fact is only a small part of software engineering. So it's as if we're solving a very small part of a very small part of the problem. The end result is that, if we successfully automated away algorithm design and data structure selection, there would be only a minimal impact on software engineering. To see this, let's look back at our two example software projects.

Figure 8a shows various activities involved in producing. software for logging tools. The dots indicate major time-consuming activities and the checks indicate activities which make significant use of algorithms and data structures. You spend most of your time studying the tool and the physics, testing and validating the functionality, measuring performance, and looking at existing programs that you've written or that other people have written. Algorithm design will help you in writing signal processing algorithms and in writing code for computations and input and output. Notice the mismatch—most of the effort in AI applied to software engineering has been aimed at helping in ways that are relatively inconsequential in this particular category of software.

- Studying tool and physics
  Studying target machine and communication system
✔ Writing signal processing algorithms
✔ Writing code for computations and input/output
- Testing and validating functionality
- Measuring performance
- Studying existing algorithms

8a Logging tool software.

- Studying tax law
  Designing overall system structure
✔ Designing data base and communications systems
✔ Writing code for calculations and input/output
- Testing components and complete system
- Studying existing programs
- Communicating with colleagues

8b Tax Return software.

Figure 8 Importance of algorithms and data structures. The dots indicate major time-consuming activities and the checks indicate activities which make significant use of algorithms and data structures.

We can say the same thing about writing tax software (Figure 8b). A very large part of your time is spent studying the tax law, communicating with your colleagues, looking at other programs, and testing the various components of the complete system. Algorithm design and data structure selection are going to help a bit in designing data bases and communication systems, and in writing code for calculations and input and output. So once again, we see that the bulk of the effort has gone into activities that are relatively inconsequential.

2.7 *Major Research Issues*

So, if that's the case, what *are* the consequential research issues? For programming-in-the-small, I'd like to suggest three. One is the representation of domain knowledge. You remember the number of times, in Figures 1 and 2, that there was a little bubble that showed something about the domain in those various activities. I think the best plan of attack is to build several systems that are domain specific and that actually work in practical situations, and then to get down to the fundamental issue here, which is, how do you represent domain knowledge, for use by a programming or software engineering system, in a way that's domain independent? The second issue relates to techniques for controlling search, especially in the transformational paradigm. We have had a little bit of progress on those, but the space is so huge here that it's a very critical issue. The third issue involves representing the implementation history. How do you represent, in some kind of useful way, the design decisions, the implementation decisions that have led from a specification down to a program? Now, the early transformational systems represented that as a sequence of transformations. But a sequence of a thousand transformations is not a very useful way to represent that information. There has to be more structure to it. So the question is, what kind of structure can we impose on that kind of representation? Now, I was being critical a few minutes ago about the application of AI to software engineering. In fact, all these issues are being addressed in one way or another, so the situation isn't quite as bad as completely ignoring the major issues.

On the other hand, it unfortunately is the case that the research issues related to *programming-in-the-large* have been almost totally ignored. So here are some issues that are ripe for working on and you don't have to worry about someone having solved them already. First, the representation of domain knowledge: Again, just as in the case of programming-in-the-small, it's a major issue. Here the question is, can you develop techniques to represent what you know about a domain as a result of doing a requirements analysis? There's been a little work on some relatively small examples, but it's certainly a major issue that we ought to be able to resolve, or that we ought to at least attack. Second, what are good techniques for describing large systems? At present we have a few techniques, such as the plan representation, for describing small programs. Can we find reasonable techniques for representing large systems and the interactions among the various components, in some kind of manageable way?

A third and related issue is, can we represent, again in a manageable way, the design history of large systems? This is to me the single most important problem. So if you want to hit something, if you want to solve a problem with high impact, this is the one I would suggest you look at. How do you represent the design history of very large systems? And I have no idea, no clue at all, about how to go about it. I hope one of you can come up with a clue. Finally, there are models of collaborative work. Especially in programming-in-the-large, you spend a lot of your time just talking with people. So, to the degree that we can develop models of collaborative work, that ought to help in the area of programming-in-the-large, but I don't see it as being substantially different from models of collaborative work in other areas [Association for Computing Machinery, 1986; Stefik et al., 1987].

2.8 *Practical Experimentation*

In order to achieve practical results, one guideline in addressing these issues is to build experimental systems in practical situations. If there was a failing in the first decade of work on AI applied to software engineering, it was that we weren't following this guideline. We thought programming was writing little algorithms, like they taught us in school. That's not what programming and software engineering are all about. So we really have to look at realistic, practical situations, in order to make sure that we're addressing the right sorts of issues. So here are a few suggestions about the kinds of systems that I think are ripe for attacking. Domain specific automatic programming systems: I'll give you an example of one of those in a minute. Very high level language compilers: The REFINE[1] system being marketed by Reasoning Systems is an example based on the transformational implementation paradigm [*REFINE Users Guide*, 1985]. Program library manager: Software reuse is a hot topic these days in discussions of software productivity. One of the problems in reuse is, if you have a large library, how do you find the piece that you want to reuse? So, a manager that would help you find your way through that library would certainly be a valuable thing. Data structure selection advisor: A couple of data structure selectors have been built, but they haven't really been tested in practical situations, so I think that's ripe for doing. Project management advisor: There is certainly a lot of expertise that project managers have, and that ought to be able to be captured. Finally, a maintenance advisor for a specific system: It's important to notice that qualification for a specific system. I've heard people suggest that you ought to be able to build a maintenance advisor. After all, if maintenance and evolution is a major cost area, and you have people who do maintenance and evolution, then you ought to be able to build an advisor, using standard rule-based expert systems techniques. I think that's folly, at least to think that you could build one to work in general. Because in fact, a lot of the knowledge that the good maintainers and evolvers have is knowledge about the details of the specific system that they are maintaining and evolving. But that suggests that perhaps you could build one for a very specific system. So find a system that you think is going to have a long lifetime, a system that comes with some people who are good at maintaining and evolving it, and try to codify their expertise.

2.9 ΦNIX

Now, just to illustrate one of these, I want to describe a project that we're working on at Schlumberger-Doll Research. It's a project we call ΦNIX, a domain-specific automatic programming system for software that controls and records data from oil well logging tools [Barstow, 1985a, 1985b]. In fact, that's the very first example I showed you earlier. There are two basic goals. One is to enable a user, and you can think of a tool designer here, to describe a

---

1 REFINE is a trademark of Reasoning Systems, Inc., Palo Alto, California.

problem in terms that are natural to him or her. The other goal is automatically to write software that is robust and efficient enough for routine use, because we want to put the software out on a truck and log a well with it. And that, I think, is a very valuable attribute of our efforts, because it gives us a kind of reality check.

Now, it turns out that logging software is rather interesting computationally. It's a mixture of value- and behavior-oriented computations. There are real-time constraints, due both to the communications systems and the physics. These are non-terminating programs. Most of the formal definitions of automatic programming say that the specifications are going to be satisfied when the program halts. If the program halts in our case, the specifications are without doubt not satisfied. There are concurrent constructs in our target architecture, so we get a chance to look at a bit of parallelism. And it's clearly a case of programming-in-the-small. This, at least, gives us a little bit of hope that we might be able to have some success, I think. And one of the other things that I like about logging software is that it's a special case of a more general class of software, namely device-control software.

There are five basic features to our approach. First, we're separating the total process into a formalization process and an implementation process, a rather standard type of separation. The formalization process we're imagining to be interactive, with the system possessing a significant amount of knowledge about the domain, in particular, knowledge about the tool in the form of a model of the device.

We specify software by what we call *stream expressions*. We model the interaction of the software with its external environment in terms of temporal sequences of values called *streams*, and a specification is a statement of constraints on the input and output streams. We're using a transformational approach with search control based on a certain kind of performance measure. In our case, it's not a measure of the absolute cost of something, because these programs are supposed to run forever, so their absolute cost ought to be infinite. Rather, we're looking at a measure of the load that they put on the processor as the guideline for search control.

That's about all I'm going to say about ΦNIX here. We haven't logged a well yet, so we certainly haven't demonstrated practicality, but I'm hoping that some time in the not-too-distant future, we will be able to do that.

2.10 *Review*

Let's see what ground we've covered in Part II. I think the important thing here is to see that research on AI applied to software engineering has had virtually no demonstrations of practical value. And it's important for us to understand why. In part it's because software engineering is a harder problem, I think, than others that have been addressed somewhat more successfully with

AI techniques, and in part because the research has been narrowly focused. I think that is changing. We're beginning to understand what we have to look at in order to have a practical impact on software engineering. I'm optimistic that we'll have more results in the future.

Part III

Now let's go on to Part III, where I'd like to look at what the impact of all this might be on software engineering. But first let's think about what the prospects are for practical results. I'd like to do this by analogy. If you look back at the history of rule-based systems, the first ones were built around 1970, for example, Mycin [Shortliffe, 1976]. The first, what I would call solid, practical use of the technology was around 1980 with XCON (then called R1) [McDermott, 1981], and depending on whose publicity you look at, it seems they're in widespread use, and have been for a couple of years. So let's say that there's something like a 15-year gap between experimental systems and widespread use.

Now, in the application of AI techniques to software engineering, if we could have started spanning that 15-year gap last year, we ought to have widespread use in 2001. For programming-in-the-small, I'm actually a little bit more optimistic than that. I think we are close to having some experimental systems, things like ΦNIX that we're working on, or the REFINE system, or work at ISI [Balzer, 1985], AT&T [Kelley, 1987], Mitre [Brown, 1985], and several other places [Prywes et al., 1979]. Any one of these may turn out to be a good experimental system in a practical situation. I think there's good hope of having some actual use in practical situations sometime in the 1990s. If so, maybe before the next century we will have relatively widespread use of programming support systems based on AI for programming-in-the-small.

I'm considerably more pessimistic about programming-in-the-large. I think the earliest that we can hope for any kind of experimental system in practical situations is the 1990s, and I hope I'm not being too optimistic in saying that. I think the issues are just extremely difficult, and that's why I want to stress again that there is a single issue on which, if we could marshal a whole lot of work on it, we might make some progress; that is, how do you capture the design of a large system? And it's that issue that I think is either going to make or break the work in this area. But I certainly don't expect to see practical systems by earlier than sometime in the next century.

But let's assume success and see what the impact might be. In terms of the direct impact on software engineering, I think we're likely to gain a factor of two or three in productivity, a few hundred percent, based on some simple back-of-the-envelope calculations. Figure 9a shows what the impact of having an automatic programming system might be on programming-in-the-small. On

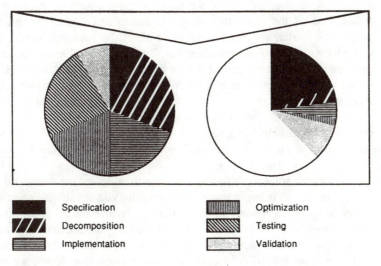

Specification   **Optimization**

Decomposition   **Testing**

Implementation   **Validation**

(a) Automatic Programming on Programming-in-the-Small

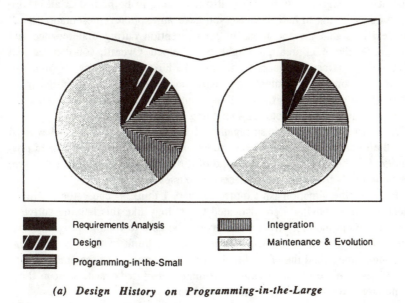

Requirements Analysis   **Integration**

Design   **Maintenance & Evolution**

Programming-in-the-Small

(a) Design History on Programming-in-the-Large

Figure 9 Direct impact of artificial intelligence on software engineering activities.

the left is the same pie chart I showed you earlier. On the right is what I think
the effort might be if you had one of these hypothetical automatic programming systems. One of the interesting things to see is that the specification
would probably be harder, and would take more effort, because you wouldn't
be able to get by with inadequate specifications. You'd be forced to make sure
they're adequate. So that would probably take more work. On the other hand,
decomposition and implementation and optimization ought to be substantially
helped. Testing really ought to go away—if there's one thing we ought to buy
out of this, it's to get away from the need for testing. But validation, that is,
making sure you have the right program and the specifications are right, is not
likely to be affected at all. So we can see here a factor of two or three or so
overall.

Now, let's suppose someone's figured out how to represent the design history of a large system, what might that do? Here again, you see the pie chart I
showed earlier. Requirements analysis is not likely to be affected at all. Design
might actually be speeded up, because a lot of design is a collaborative effort,
and if you have a formal representation of the thing you're designing, that
ought to help the communication process. So we can guess that design might
be a little bit easier. The programming-in-the-small part is not going to be
helped at all. Integration is probably also not going to be helped at all. Maintenance might be cut in half, because you have an explicit representation of all
those decisions that are the focus of your attention during maintenance and
evolution. So that's an area that ought to be helped. Overall, you can see that
you've gained a factor of about one-and-a-half on productivity. If you also
throw in an automatic programming system, then the programming-in-the-small
piece ought to go down a bit, as well as maintenance and evolution. So you'll
find again, that you get a factor of something like two or three.

Now, when I first put these together, I was rather disappointed. I wanted
to be able to say that you could get orders of magnitude improvement in productivity. And based simply on this kind of direct effect, I think that's not true.
If we think that's true, then we're deceiving ourselves.

However, the situation isn't quite that bad, I think, because there will be
indirect effects of having a sophisticated technology like this helping software
engineering. One indirect effect is that you'll be able to look at programs that
are now in the programming-in-the-large area, but think of them as programming-in-the-small. And the effort involved in programming-in-the-small is substantially less, so we ought to gain something there just because we can think
of some large problems as being small problems.

But more interestingly, I think the successful application of AI techniques
to software engineering activities will enable the use of profoundly different
software development paradigms. And this is where I think the real gain in all
of this is going to be.

Let's look at a couple of examples. Let's think about what automatic programming would do for rapid prototyping. There's a lot of emphasis now on building rapid prototypes of software systems in order to understand the requirements, to understand what it is that you want the system to do. Not how to build it, but what it is you want it to do. Now, if we have automatic programming systems, we ought to be able to build those prototypes much more rapidly, and therefore do the requirements analysis much more rapidly; and in addition, we ought to be able to convert to a final product more easily because we have a formal representation of the specifications. We don't just have the prototype, we also have the specifications for the prototype. And this in fact is one of the effects that people using REFINE have noted. So there is some indication that the indirect impact may actually be happening.

As another example, think of what a design history would do for software reuse. I mentioned before that one problem in software reuse is finding the thing you want to reuse. The other problem is that it isn't quite what you want. It may be very close, but not quite. And what not quite means is that some implementation decisions were not made correctly, at least from your point of view. There may have been hundreds or thousands of decisions made along the way, but some of them, a few of them, are not the ones that you would have made if you were writing the software in the first place. Now, normally that means that you can't reuse the software, or you have to go through a great deal of evolution on that software. But if we had a representation of the design history that allowed us to replay most of the development of that software automatically, then all we would have to worry about are those few decisions that were made in the wrong way. And therefore, it ought to be much easier to reuse software that is similar, but not identical, to what is required.

3.1 *Review*

So let's review Part III. I think that practical results for programming-in-the-small ought to be achievable in the 1990s, and there's a lot of work now that ought to get us there. But for programming-in-the-large, I think the practical results are really very, very far away, not before the turn of the century. Finally, the real impact of AI will not be directly on software engineering in terms of automating or supporting specific individual activities, but rather, indirectly, by letting us use profoundly different paradigms.

4 *Conclusion*

Now let me pop up one more level and summarize what I've tried to say. First, software engineering activities are knowledge intensive. They require substantial knowledge of the application domain and the target software itself, and AI techniques ought to be able to help manage that knowledge effectively. But unfortunately, past research has not demonstrated practical success in this area, in part because of the amount and diversity of the knowledge, and in part because the efforts have been relatively narrowly focused. For programming-in-the-small, I think the time is right for substantial experiments in practical situations. For programming-in-the-large, I think there are several major research issues, most importantly, how to represent the design of large systems, that have to be addressed before there will be any practical demonstrations. And finally, the real long-term impact of AI will not be on the individual activities, but rather on the software development paradigms that it will let us use.

Note

For other discussions of the relationship between AI and SE, see Simon's presentation at the Seventh International Conference on Software Engineering [Simon, 1986], Brooks's presentation at the 1986 International Federation of Information Processing Conference [Brooks, 1987], the special issue of *IEEE Transactions on Software Engineering* [Mostow, 1985], the report on the Knowledge-Based Software Assistant [Green et al., 1983], and several collections of papers [Barstow et al., 1984; Biermann et al., 1984; Rich and Waters, 1986].

Acknowledgments

This paper is an edited transcript of a presentation at the Sixth National Conference on Artificial Intelligence, Seattle, Washington, July 17, 1987; based in part on presentations at the IBM Thomas J. Watson Research Center, Yorktown Heights, New York, October 30, 1986, and at the Ninth International Conference on Software Engineering, Monterey, California, April 1, 1987. The presentation and paper have benefited substantially from suggestions from Bob Balzer, Paul Barth, Barry Boehm, Steve Fickas, Cordell Green, Sol Greenspan, Elaine Kant, and Stan Vestal.

References

Association for Computing Machinery, 1986. *Proceedings of the Conference on Computer-Supported Cooperative Work*, Austin, Texas.

Balzer, R., N. Goldman, and D. Wile, 1978. Informality in program specifications. *IEEE Transactions on Software Engineering* 4(1):94–103. Reprinted in Rich and Waters, 1986.

Balzer, R., 1981. Transformational programming: An example. *IEEE Transactions on Software Engineering* 7(1):3–14.

Balzer, R., D. Cohen, M. Feather, N. Goldman, W. Swartout, and D. Wile, 1983. Operational specification as the basis for specification validation. *Theory and Practice of Software Technology*, Ferrari, Bolognani, and Goguen, ed. North Holland, Amsterdam.

Balzer, R., 1985. A 15 year perspective on automatic programming. *IEEE Transactions on Software Engineering* 11(11):1257–1268.

Balzer, R., 1987. Living in the next-generation operating system. *IEEE Software* 4(6):77–85.

Barstow, D., 1979. An experiment in knowledge-based automatic programming. *Artificial Intelligencene* 12(2):73–119. Reprint Rich and Waters, 1986.

Barstow, D., 1982. The roles of knowledge and deduction in algorithm design. *Machine Intelligence 10*, J. Hayes, D. Michie, and Y.-H. Pao, ed. Ellis Horwood and Wiley, New York. Reprinted in Biermann et al., 1984.

Barstow, D., 1984. A perspective on automatic programming. *AI Magazine* 5(1):5–27.

Barstow, D., H. Shrobe, and E. Sandewall, ed., 1984. *Interactive Programming Environments*. McGraw-Hill, New York.

Barstow, D., 1985a. Automatic programming for streams. In *Proceedings of the Ninth International Joint Conference on Artificial Intelligence*, Los Angeles, CA, pp. 232–237. Morgan Kaufmann, San Mateo, California.

Barstow, D., 1985b. Domain-specific automatic programming. *IEEE Transactions on Software Engineering* 11(11):1321–1336.

Bauer, F., M. Broy, W. Dosch, R. Gnatz, B. Krieg-Brückner, A. Laut, M. Luckmann, T. Matzner, B. Möller, H. Partsch, P. Pepper, K. Samelson, R. Steinbrüggen, M. Wirsing, and H. Wössner, 1978. Programming in a wide spectrum language: A collection of examples. *Science of Computer Programming* 1:73–114.

Bauer, F., M. Broy, W. Dosch, F. Geiselbrechtinger, W. Hesse, R. Gnatz, B. Krieg-Brückner, A. Laut, T. Matzner, B. Möller, F. Nickl, H. Partsch, P. Pepper, K. Samelson, M. Wirsing, and H. Wössner, 1982. *Algorithmic Language and Program Development*. Springer-Verlag, New York.

Biermann, A., G. Guiho, and Y. Kodratoff, ed., 1984. *Automatic Program Construction Techniques*. Macmillan, New York.

Boehm, B., 1981. *Software Engineering Economics*. Prentice-Hall, Englewood Cliffs, New Jersey.

Borgida, A., S. Greenspan, and J. Mylopoulos, 1985. Knowledge representation as the basis for requirements specifications. *IEEE Computer* 18(4):82–91. Reprinted in Rich and Waters, 1986.

Brooks, F. P., 1987. No silver bullet: Essence and accidents of software engineering. *IEEE Computer* **20**(4):10–19.

Brown, R., 1985. Automation of programming: The ISFI experiments. Technical Report M85-21, MITRE, Bedford, Massachusetts.

Burstall, R. and J. Darlington, 1977. A transformation system for developing recursive programs. *Journal of the ACM* **24**(1):44–67.

Cheatham, T., J. Townley, and G. Holloway, 1979. A system for program refinement. In *Fourth International Conference on Software Engineering*, Munich, Germany, pp. 53–62. Reprinted in Barstow et al., 1984.

DeRemer, F. and H. Kron, 1976. Programming in the large versus programming in the small. *IEEE Transactions on Software Engineering* **2**(2):80–86.

Dijkstra, E. W., 1976. *A Discipline of Programming*. Prentice-Hall, Englewood Cliffs, New Jersey.

Fickas, S., 1985a. Automating the transformational development of software. *IEEE Transactions on Software Engineering* **11**(11):1268–1277.

Fickas, S., 1985b. A knowledge-based approach to specification acquisition and construction. Technical Report CIT-TR 85-13, Department of Computer Science, University of Oregon.

Floyd, R., 1967. Assigning meaning to programs. *Mathematical Aspects of Computer Science*, J. Schwartz, ed., pp. 19–32. American Mathematical Society.

Green, C., 1969. Application of theorem proving to problem solving. In *Proceedings of the First International Joint Conference on Artificial Intelligence*, Washington, D.C., pp. 219–239. Morgan Kaufmann, San Mateo, California.

Green, C., 1976. The design of the program synthesis system. In *Second International Conference on Software Engineering*, San Francisco, pp. 4–18.

Green, C., D. Luckham, R. Balzer, T. Cheatham, and C. Rich, 1983. Report on a knowledge-based software assistant. Technical Report, Kestrel Institute. Reprinted in Rich and Waters, 1986.

Heidorn, G., 1976. Automatic programming through natural language dialogue: A survey. *IBM Journal of Research and Development* **20**(4):302–313. Reprinted in Rich and Waters, 1986.

Hoare, C. A. R., 1969. An axiomatic basis for computer programming. *Communications of the ACM* **12**(10):576–583.

Johnson, W. and E. Soloway, 1985. PROUST: Knowledge-based program understanding. *IEEE Transactions on Software Engineering* **11**(3):267–275. Reprinted in Rich and Waters, 1986.

Kant, E. and D. Barstow, 1981. The refinement paradigm: The interaction of coding and efficiency knowledge in program synthesis. *IEEE Transactions on Software Engineering* **7**(5):458–471. Reprinted in Barstow et al., 1984.

Kant, E., 1983. On the efficient synthesis of efficient programs. *Artificial Intelligence Journal* **20**(3):253–306. Reprinted in Rich and Waters, 1986.

Kant, E., 1985. Understanding and automating algorithm design. *IEEE Transactions on Software Engineering* **11**(11):1361–1374.

Katz, S. and R. Zimmerman, 1981. An advisory system for developing data representations. In *Proceedings of the Seventh International Joint Conference on Artificial Intelligence*, Vancouver, British Columbia, Canada, pp. 1030–1036. Morgan Kaufmann, San Mateo, California.

Kelley, V. E., 1987. Inferring formal software specifications from episodic descriptions. In *Proceedings of the Sixth National Conference on Artificial Intelligence*, Seattle, Washington, 127–132. Morgan Kaufmann, San Mateo.

King, J. C., 1971. Proving programs to be correct. *IEEE Transactions on Computers* **20**(11).

Manna, Z. and R. Waldinger, 1980. A deductive approach to program synthesis. *ACM Transactions on Programming Languages and Systems* **2**(1):90–121. Reprinted in Rich and Waters, 1986.

Manna, Z. and R. Waldinger, 1985. The origin of the binary-search paradigm. In *Proceedings of the Ninth International Joint Conference on Artificial Intelligence*, Los Angeles, CA, pp. 222–224. Morgan Kaufmann, San Mateo, California.

McDermott, J., 1981. R1: The formative years. *AI Magazine* **2**(2):21–29.

Mostow, J., ed., 1985. Special issue on artificial intelligence and software engineering. *IEEE Transactions on Software Engineering* **11**(11).

Partsch, H. and R. Steinbrüggen, 1983. Program transformation systems. *Computing Surveys* **15**(3):199–236.

Prywes, N., A. Pnuelli, and S. Shastry, 1979. Use of a nonprocedural specification language and associated program generator in software development. *ACM Transactions on Programming Languages and Systems* **1**(2):196–217.

REFINE Users Guide, 1985. Reasoning Systems, Inc., Palo Alto, California.

Rich, C. and H. Shrobe, 1978. Initial report on a Lisp programmer's apprentice. *IEEE Transactions on Software Engineering* **4**(6):456–467. Reprinted in Barstow et al., 1984.

Rich, C., 1981. A formal representation for plans in the programmer's apprentice. In *Proceedings of the Seventh International Joint Conference on Artificial Intelligence*, Vancouver, British Columbia, Canada, pp. 1044–1052. Morgan Kaufmann, San Mateo, California.

Rich, C. and R. Waters, ed., 1986. *Readings in Artificial Intelligence and Software Engineering*. Morgan Kaufmann, San Mateo, California.

Shortliffe, E. H., 1976. *Computer-Based Medical Consultations: MYCIN*. Elsevier-North Holland, New York.

Simon, H., 1986. Whether software engineering needs to be artificially intelligent. *IEEE Transactions on Software Engineering* **12**(7):726–732.

Smith, D., 1984. The synthesis of Lisp programs from examples: A survey. *Automatic Program Construction Techniques*, A. Biermann, G. Guiho, and Y. Kodratoff, ed., pp. 307–324. Macmillan, New York.

Smith, D., 1985. Top-down synthesis of divide-and-conquer algorithms. *Artificial Intelligence Journal* **27**(1):43–96. Reprinted in Rich and Waters, 1986.

Smith, D., G. Kotik, and S. Westfold, 1985. Research on knowledge-based software environments at Kestrel Institute. *IEEE Transactions on Software Engineering* **11**(11):1278–1295.

Stefik, M., G. Foster, D. Bobrow, K. Kahn, S. Lanning, and L. Suchman, 1987. Beyond the chalkboard: Computer support for collaboration and problem solving in meetings. *Communications of the ACM* **30**(1):32–47.

Steier, D. and E. Kant, 1985. The roles of execution and analysis in algorithm design. *IEEE Transactions on Software Engineering* **11**(11):1374–1386.

Swartout, W., 1983. Xplain: A system for creating and explaining expert consulting systems. *Artificial Intelligence Journal* **21**(3):285–325.

Waldinger, R., 1969. PROW: A step toward automatic program writing. In *Proceedings of the First International Joint Conference on Artificial Intelligence*, Washington, D.C., pp. 241–252. Morgan Kaufmann, San Mateo, California.

Waters, R., 1985. The programmer's apprentice: A session with KBEmacs. *IEEE Transactions on Software Engineering* **11**(11):1296–1320. Reprinted in Rich and Waters, 1986.

Wile, D., 1983. Program developments: Formal explanations of implementations. *Communications of the ACM* **26**(11):902–911. Reprinted in Rich and Waters, 1986.

Acknowledgments
and Figure Credits

Chapter 1

Fig. 1: B.S. Bloom "Advantages of One-to-One Tutoring," *Educational Researcher*, vol. 13, pp. 4–16. © 1984 with American Educational Researcher, Washington D.C.; reprinted with permission. Figs. 6 and 7: J. Roschelle, "The Envisioning Machine," J. Roschelle, *Mental Models Qualitative Physics, and Computer Simulations*, unpublished; reprinted with permission. Fig. 8: J. Smith, "Alternative Reality Kit," ARK, unpublished; reprinted with permission. Figs. 9 and 10: J.S. Brown and R.R. Burton,"*SOPHIE*," unpublished; reprinted with permission. Fig. 19: W. Clancy "Conversation with MYCIN," *Transfer of Rule-Based Expertise Through Tutorial Dialogue*. © 1979 Ph.D. Dissertation, Department of Computer Science, Stanford University; reprinted with permission. Fig. 20: W. Clancy "The Doctor as Teacher," Case Management for Rule-based Tutorials, in *Proceedings of the International Joint Conference on Artificial Intelligence*, © 1979; reprinted with permission. Figs. 21 and 22: "Rephrased Conversation With Guidon," adapted from M. Richer and Clancy, W., *IEEE Computer Graphics and Applications*, vol. 5, pp. 51–64,. © 1985 by IEEE; reprinted with permission. Fig. 23: J. Anderson, Boyle, C., and Yost, G. "Geometry Tutor," © 1985, *Proceedings of the International Joint Conference on Artificial Intelligence*, Los Angeles, CA; reprinted with permission. Fig. 24: J. Anderson and Reiser, B., "The Lisp Tutor," *BYTE* vol. 10, pp. 159–175. © 1986, BYTE Magazine, Petersborough, NJ; reprinted with permission. Fig. 25:

C. Foss "Algebraland," *3rd International Conference on Artificial Intelligence and Education* p. 27. © 1987, Learning Research and Development Center, University of Pittsburgh; reprinted with permission. Figs. 26 and 27: J. Hollan, E. Hutchins, and L. Weitzman, "STEAMER Icons" *AI Magazine*, Summer. © 1984, published by the American Association of Artificial Intelligence; reprinted with permission. Figs. 28 and 29: D. Towne, A. Munroe, Q. Pizzini, and D. Surmon, "IMTS Icons," *Abstracts of the Third International Conference on Artificial Intelligence* p. 54. © 1987 by the Learning Research and Development Center, University of Pittsburgh; reprinted with permission. Figs. 30–32: J. Bonar, R. Cunningham, and J., Schultz "Economics Tutor," "OPTICS Tutor," "Electronics Tutor," *Proceedings of the Eighth Annual Conference of the Cognitive Science Society.* © 1986 by the Cognitive Science Society; reprinted with permission.

Chapter 3

Fig. 3: Alker, H.R., Jr., Lehnert, W.G., and Schneider, D.K. "The New Testament in a Plot Unit Graph" in Graziella Tonfoni, (ed.), *Artificial Intelligence and Text Understanding: Plot Units and Summarization Procedures*, Quaderni di Ricerca Linguistica; permission pending. Fig. 4: Dyer, M. "Knowledge Dependency Graph," *Encyclopedia of Artificial Intelligence.* © 1987 by John Wiley and Sons, Inc; reprinted with permission. Fig. 16: Lehnert, W.G. "Semantic Memory vs. Episodic Memory," from a special issue on *Meaning and Mental Representations*, edited by Umberto Eco, Marco Santambrogio, and Patrizia Violi. VS 44/45, pp. 155–179. © 1987 by Indiana University Press; reprinted with permission. Fig. 17: Reisbeck, C. and Martin, C. "Direct Memory Access Parsing," in Riesbeck and Kolodner (eds.), *Experience, Memory and Reasoning*, Hillsdale, NJ: © 1986 by Lawrence Erlbaum Publishers; reprinted with permission.

Index